VISTAS

INTRODUCCIÓN A LA LENGUA ESPAÑOLA

Volume 2
Lessons 6–12

FOURTH EDITION

José A. Blanco

Philip Redwine Donley, Late
Austin Community College

VISTA HIGHER LEARNING
Boston, Massachusetts

The **VISTAS, Fourth Edition** cover features the work of award winning photographer, Jean-Dominique Dallet. Famous for its beloved literary hero, Don Quijote, the landscape depicted here from the **Castilla La Mancha** region of Spain, is one of the many locations in the Spanish-speaking world that you will learn about in **VISTAS**.

Publisher: José A. Blanco
Executive Editor: Sarah Kenney
Managing Editors: Deborah Coffey (Print), Paola Ríos Schaaf (Technology)
Senior Project Manager (Print): Gabriela Ferland
Editors: Christian Biagetti (Technology), John DeCarli (Technology), Darío González (Technology), Mónica M. González Peña, Lauren Krolick, Paula A. Orrego, Carolina Zapata
Production and Design Director: Marta Kimball
Design Manager: Susan Prentiss
Design and Production Team: Manuela Arango, María Eugenia Castaño, Oscar Díez, Paula Díez, Mauricio Henao, Jhoany Jiménez, Erik Restrepo, Sónia Teixeira, Andrés F. Vanegas García, Nick Ventullo

Library of Congress Control Number: 2010934550

1 2 3 4 5 6 7 8 9 RJ 16 15 14 13 12 11

TO THE STUDENT

To Vista Higher Learning's great pride, **VISTAS** became the best-selling new introductory college Spanish program in more than a decade in its first edition, and its success has only grown over time. It is now our pleasure to welcome you to **VISTAS**, **Fourth Edition**, your gateway to the Spanish language and to the vibrant cultures of the Spanish-speaking world.

A direct result of extensive reviews and ongoing input from students and instructors, **VISTAS 4/e** includes both the highly successful, ground-breaking features of the original program, plus many exciting new elements designed to keep **VISTAS** the most student-friendly program available. Here are just some of the features you will encounter:

Original, hallmark features

- A unique, easy-to-navigate design built around color-coded sections that appear either completely on one page or on spreads of two facing pages
- Integration of an appealing video, up-front in each lesson of the student text
- Practical, high-frequency vocabulary in meaningful contexts
- Clear, comprehensive grammar explanations with high-impact graphics and other special features that make structures easier to learn and use
- Ample guided practice to make you comfortable with the vocabulary and grammar you are learning and to give you a solid foundation for communication
- An emphasis on communicative interactions with a classmate, small groups, the full class, and your instructor
- A process approach to the development of reading, writing, and listening skills
- Coverage of the entire Spanish-speaking world and integration of everyday culture
- Unprecedented learning support through on-the-spot student sidebars and on-page correlations to the print and technology ancillaries for each lesson section
- A complete set of print and technology ancillaries to help you learn Spanish

NEW! to the Fourth Edition

- A dynamic new **Fotonovela** video that presents language and culture in an engaging context
- In-text integration of the enormously successful **Flash cultura**
- An improved **En pantalla** section, featuring new TV clips as well as authentic short films
- **VText**, an online virtual interactive student edition
- New content and features on the **VISTAS** Supersite, including flashcards with audio, more grammar diagnostics, audio record-submit activities, a powerful bilingual dictionary, and much more, all designed to help you learn

VISTAS 4/e has eighteen lessons, each of which is organized exactly the same way. To familiarize yourself with the organization of the text, as well as its original and new features, turn to page xiv and take the **at-a-glance** tour.

table of contents

table of contents

cultura	estructura	adelante

table of contents

	contextos	fotonovela
Lección 9 **Las fiestas**  Volume 2	Parties and celebrations . . . . . 300 Personal relationships. . . . . . . 301 Stages of life 302	**El Día de Muertos** . . . . 304 **Pronunciación** The letters **h, j,** and **g** 307
Lección 10 **En el consultorio** 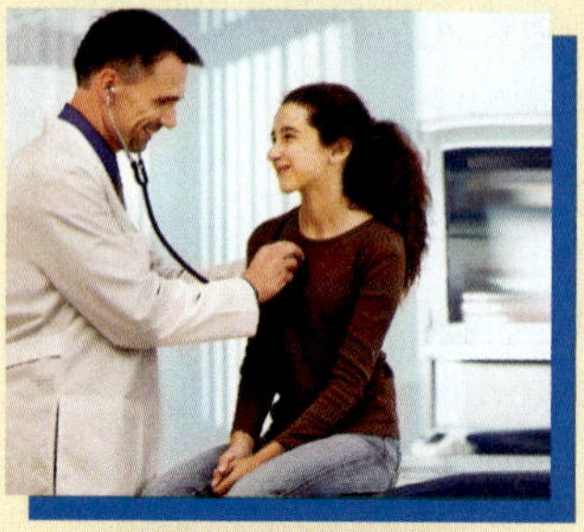 Volume 2	Health and medical terms . . . 332 Parts of the body . . . . 332 Symptoms and medical conditions . . . . 332 Health professions. 332	**¡Qué dolor!** . . . . 336 **Ortografía** El acento y las sílabas fuertes 339
Lección 11 **La tecnología**  Volume 2	Home electronics . . . . 368 Computers and the Internet . . 368 The car and its accessories . . 370	**En el taller** . . . . 372 **Ortografía** La acentuación de palabras similares 375
Lección 12 **La vivienda**  Volumes 2 & 3	Parts of a house . . . . 404 Household chores . . . . 404 Table settings. 406	**Los quehaceres** . . . . 408 **Ortografía** Mayúsculas y minúsculas . . 411

table of contents

cultura	estructura	adelante

	contextos	fotonovela

Lección 17

Un festival de arte

Volume 3

Lección 18

Las actualidades

Volume 3

Consulta (*Reference*)

Volumes 1–3

Lesson Openers
outline the content and features of each lesson.

La familia

3

Communicative Goals

You will learn how to:

- Talk about your family and friends
- Describe people and things
- Express possession

contextos

pages 78–81
- The family
- Identifying people
- Professions and occupations

fotonovela

pages 82–85

The Díaz family spends Sunday afternoon in Xochimilco. Marissa meets the extended family and answers questions about her own family. The group has a picnic and takes a boat ride through the canals.

cultura

pages 86–87
- Surnames and families in the Spanish-speaking world
- Spain's Royal Family

estructura

pages 88–105
- Descriptive adjectives
- Possessive adjectives
- Present tense of **-er** and **-ir** verbs
- Present tense of **tener** and **venir**
- **Recapitulación**

adelante

pages 106–113

Lectura: A brief article about families
Escritura: A letter to a friend
Escuchar: A conversation between friends
En pantalla
Flash cultura
Panorama: Ecuador

A PRIMERA VISTA
- ¿Cuántos chicos hay en la foto?
- ¿Hay una mujer a la izquierda? ¿Y a la derecha?
- ¿Hay una cosa en la mano de la mujer?
- ¿Conversan ellos? ¿Trabajan? ¿Viajan?
- ¿Están lejos de su casa?

A primera vista activities jump-start the lessons, allowing you to use the Spanish you know to talk about the photos.

Communicative goals highlight the real-life tasks you will be able to carry out in Spanish by the end of each lesson.

Contextos

presents vocabulary in meaningful contexts.

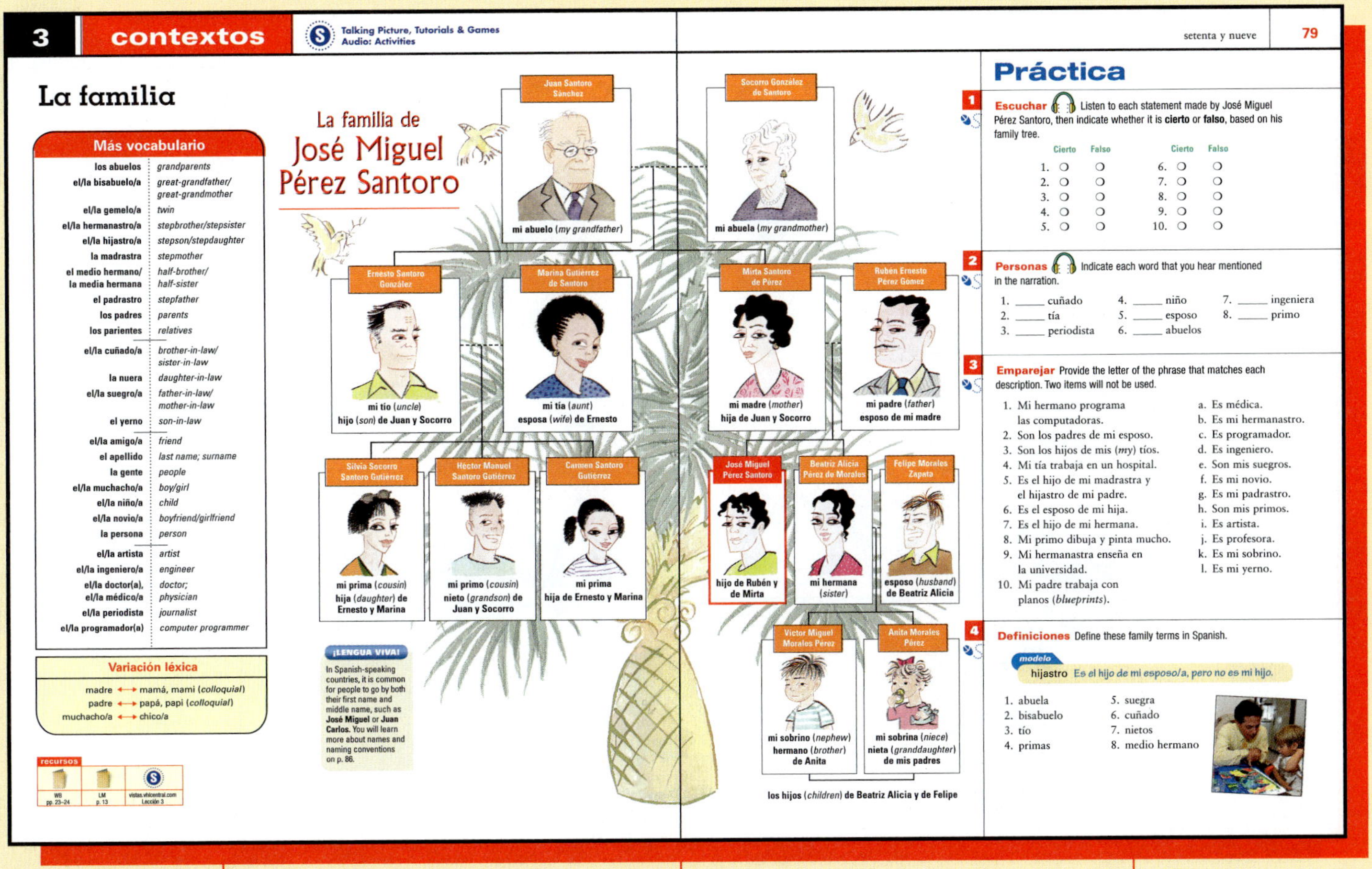

3 contextos

Talking Picture, Tutorials & Games
Audio: Activities

setenta y nueve 79

La familia

Más vocabulario

los abuelos	grandparents
el/la bisabuelo/a	great-grandfather/ great-grandmother
el/la gemelo/a	twin
el/la hermanastro/a	stepbrother/stepsister
el/la hijastro/a	stepson/stepdaughter
la madrastra	stepmother
el medio hermano/ la media hermana	half-brother/ half-sister
el padrastro	stepfather
los padres	parents
los parientes	relatives
el/la cuñado/a	brother-in-law/ sister-in-law
la nuera	daughter-in-law
el/la suegro/a	father-in-law/ mother-in-law
el yerno	son-in-law
el/la amigo/a	friend
el apellido	last name; surname
la gente	people
el/la muchacho/a	boy/girl
el/la niño/a	child
el/la novio/a	boyfriend/girlfriend
la persona	person
el/la artista	artist
el/la ingeniero/a	engineer
el/la doctor(a), el/la médico/a	doctor; physician
el/la periodista	journalist
el/la programador(a)	computer programmer

Variación léxica

madre ←→ mamá, mami (*colloquial*)
padre ←→ papá, papi (*colloquial*)
muchacho/a ←→ chico/a

recursos: WB pp. 23–24; LM p. 13; vistas.vhlcentral.com Lección 3

¡LENGUA VIVA!
In Spanish-speaking countries, it is common for people to go by both their first name and middle name, such as **José Miguel** or **Juan Carlos**. You will learn more about names and naming conventions on p. 86.

Práctica

1 Escuchar Listen to each statement made by José Miguel Pérez Santoro, then indicate whether it is **cierto** or **falso**, based on his family tree.

	Cierto	Falso		Cierto	Falso
1.	❍	❍	6.	❍	❍
2.	❍	❍	7.	❍	❍
3.	❍	❍	8.	❍	❍
4.	❍	❍	9.	❍	❍
5.	❍	❍	10.	❍	❍

2 Personas Indicate each word that you hear mentioned in the narration.

1. _____ cuñado
2. _____ tía
3. _____ periodista
4. _____ niño
5. _____ esposo
6. _____ abuelos
7. _____ ingeniera
8. _____ primo

3 Emparejar Provide the letter of the phrase that matches each description. Two items will not be used.

1. Mi hermano programa las computadoras.
2. Son los padres de mi esposo.
3. Son los hijos de mis (*my*) tíos.
4. Mi tía trabaja en un hospital.
5. Es el hijo de mi madrastra y el hijastro de mi padre.
6. Es el esposo de mi hija.
7. Es el hijo de mi hermana.
8. Mi primo dibuja y pinta mucho.
9. Mi hermanastra enseña en la universidad.
10. Mi padre trabaja con planos (*blueprints*).

a. Es médica.
b. Es mi hermanastro.
c. Es programador.
d. Es ingeniero.
e. Son mis suegros.
f. Es mi novio.
g. Es mi padrastro.
h. Son mis primos.
i. Es artista.
j. Es profesora.
k. Es mi sobrino.
l. Es mi yerno.

4 Definiciones Define these family terms in Spanish.

modelo
hijastro *Es el hijo de mi esposo/a, pero no es mi hijo.*

1. abuela
2. bisabuelo
3. tío
4. primas
5. suegra
6. cuñado
7. nietos
8. medio hermano

Más vocabulario boxes call out other important theme-related vocabulary in easy-to-reference Spanish-English lists.

Illustrations High-frequency vocabulary is introduced through expansive, full-color illustrations.

Práctica This section always begins with two listening exercises and continues with activities that practice the new vocabulary in meaningful contexts.

Variación léxica presents alternate words and expressions used throughout the Spanish-speaking world.

Recursos The icons in the **Recursos** boxes let you know exactly which print and technology ancillaries you can use to reinforce and expand on every section of every lesson.

Comunicación activities allow you to use the vocabulary creatively in interactions with a partner, a small group, or the entire class.

Fotonovela

follows the adventures of a group of students living and traveling in Mexico.

Personajes The photo-based conversations take place among a cast of recurring characters—a Mexican family with two college-age children, and their group of friends.

Fotonovela Video Updated for the Fourth Edition, the **NEW!** video episodes that correspond to this section are available for viewing online. For more information on the **Fotonovela** Video, turn to page xxviii.

Conversations Taken from the **NEW!** **Fotonovela** Video, the conversations reinforce vocabulary from **Contextos**. They also preview structures from the upcoming **Estructura** section in context *and* in a comprehensible way.

Icons signal activities by type (pair, group, audio, info gap) and let you know which activities can be completed online. For a legend explaining all icons used in the student text, see page xxxi.

Expresiones útiles These expressions organize new, active structures by language function so you can focus on using them for real-life, practical purposes.

Pronunciación & Ortografía

present the rules of Spanish pronunciation and spelling.

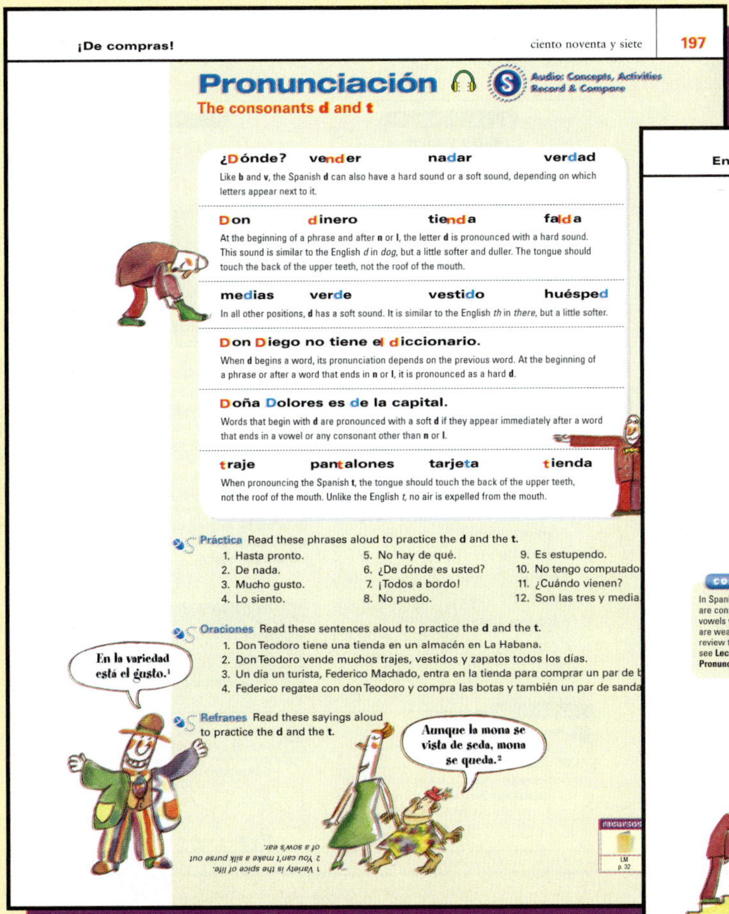

¡De compras! ciento noventa y siete 197

Pronunciación Audio: Concepts, Activities Record & Compare

The consonants **d** and **t**

¿Dónde? vender nadar verdad

Like **b** and **v**, the Spanish **d** can also have a hard sound or a soft sound, depending on which letters appear next to it.

Don dinero tienda falda

At the beginning of a phrase and after **n** or **l**, the letter **d** is pronounced with a hard sound. This sound is similar to the English *d* in *dog*, but a little softer and duller. The tongue should touch the back of the upper teeth, not the roof of the mouth.

medias verde vestido huésped

In all other positions, **d** has a soft sound. It is similar to the English *th* in *there*, but a little softer.

Don Diego no tiene el diccionario.

When **d** begins a word, its pronunciation depends on the previous word. At the beginning of a phrase or after a word that ends in **n** or **l**, it is pronounced as a hard **d**.

Doña Dolores es de la capital.

Words that begin with **d** are pronounced with a soft **d** if they appear immediately after a word that ends in a vowel or any consonant other than **n** or **l**.

traje pantalones tarjeta tienda

When pronouncing the Spanish **t**, the tongue should touch the back of the upper teeth, not the roof of the mouth. Unlike the English *t*, no air is expelled from the mouth.

Práctica Read these phrases aloud to practice the **d** and the **t**.

1. Hasta pronto.
2. De nada.
3. Mucho gusto.
4. Lo siento.
5. No hay de qué.
6. ¿De dónde es usted?
7. ¡Todos a bordo!
8. No puedo.
9. Es estupendo.
10. No tengo computado
11. ¿Cuándo vienen?
12. Son las tres y media

Oraciones Read these sentences aloud to practice the **d** and the **t**.

1. Don Teodoro tiene una tienda en un almacén en La Habana.
2. Don Teodoro vende muchos trajes, vestidos y zapatos todos los días.
3. Un día un turista, Federico Machado, entra en la tienda para comprar un par de b
4. Federico regatea con don Teodoro y compra las botas y también un par de sanda

Refranes Read these sayings aloud to practice the **d** and the **t**.

En la variedad está el gusto.[1]

Aunque la mona se vista de seda, mona se queda.[2]

1 Variety is the spice of life.
2 You can't make a silk purse out of a sow's ear.

recursos LM p. 32

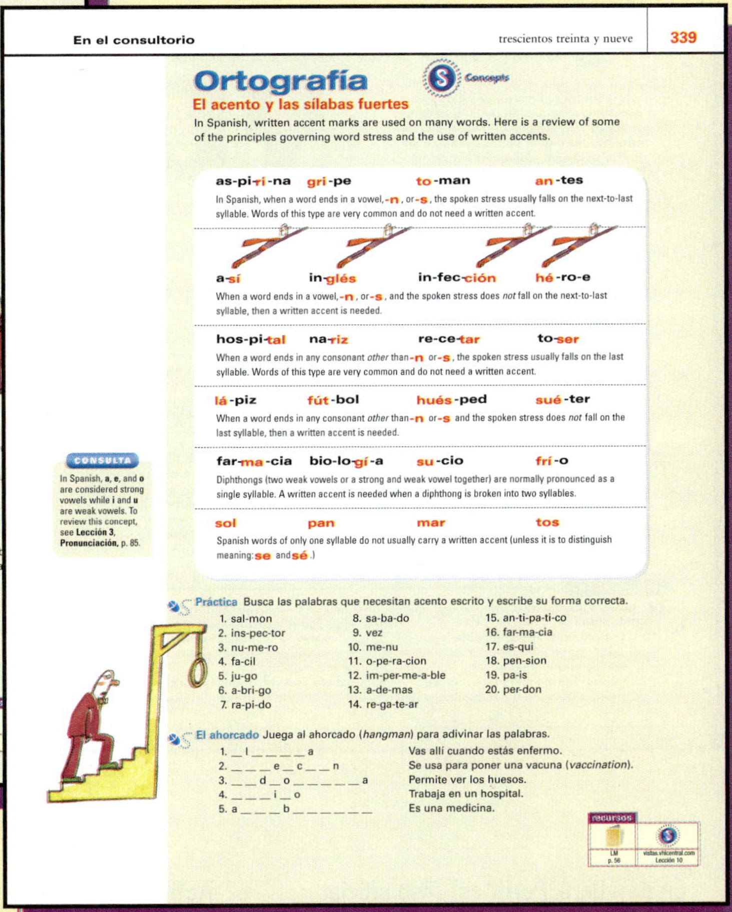

En el consultorio trescientos treinta y nueve 339

Ortografía Concepts

El acento y las sílabas fuertes

In Spanish, written accent marks are used on many words. Here is a review of some of the principles governing word stress and the use of written accents.

as-pi-ri-na gri-pe to-man an-tes

In Spanish, when a word ends in a vowel, **-n**, or **-s**, the spoken stress usually falls on the next-to-last syllable. Words of this type are very common and do not need a written accent.

a-sí in-glés in-fec-ción hé-ro-e

When a word ends in a vowel, **-n**, or **-s**, and the spoken stress does *not* fall on the next-to-last syllable, then a written accent is needed.

hos-pi-tal na-riz re-ce-tar to-ser

When a word ends in any consonant *other* than **-n** or **-s**, the spoken stress usually falls on the last syllable. Words of this type are very common and do not need a written accent.

lá-piz fút-bol hués-ped sué-ter

When a word ends in any consonant *other* than **-n** or **-s** and the spoken stress does *not* fall on the last syllable, then a written accent is needed.

far-ma-cia bio-lo-gí-a su-cio frí-o

Diphthongs (two weak vowels or a strong and weak vowel together) are normally pronounced as a single syllable. A written accent is needed when a diphthong is broken into two syllables.

sol pan mar tos

Spanish words of only one syllable do not usually carry a written accent (unless it is to distinguish meaning: **se** and **sé**.)

CONSULTA

In Spanish, **a**, **e**, and **o** are considered strong vowels while **i** and **u** are weak vowels. To review this concept, see **Lección 3, Pronunciación**, p. 85.

Práctica Busca las palabras que necesitan acento escrito y escribe su forma correcta.

1. sal-mon
2. ins-pec-tor
3. nu-me-ro
4. fa-cil
5. ju-go
6. a-bri-go
7. ra-pi-do
8. sa-ba-do
9. vez
10. me-nu
11. o-pe-ra-cion
12. im-per-me-a-ble
13. a-de-mas
14. re-ga-te-ar
15. an-ti-pa-ti-co
16. far-ma-cia
17. es-qui
18. pen-sion
19. pa-is
20. per-don

El ahorcado Juega al ahorcado (*hangman*) para adivinar las palabras.

1. _ l _ _ _ _ a — Vas allí cuando estás enfermo.
2. _ _ _ e _ c _ _ n — Se usa para poner una vacuna (*vaccination*).
3. _ _ d _ o _ _ _ _ _ a — Permite ver los huesos.
4. _ _ _ i _ o — Trabaja en un hospital.
5. a _ _ _ b _ _ _ _ _ _ — Es una medicina.

recursos LM p. 56 vistas.vhlcentral.com Lección 10

Pronunciación explains the sounds and pronunciation of Spanish in Lessons 1–9.

Supersite icon An icon indicates which additional resources are available on the **VISTAS** Supersite (vistas.vhlcentral.com). For more information, see page xxvii.

Ortografía focuses on topics related to Spanish spelling in Lessons 10–18.

Cultura

exposes you to different aspects of Hispanic culture tied to the lesson theme.

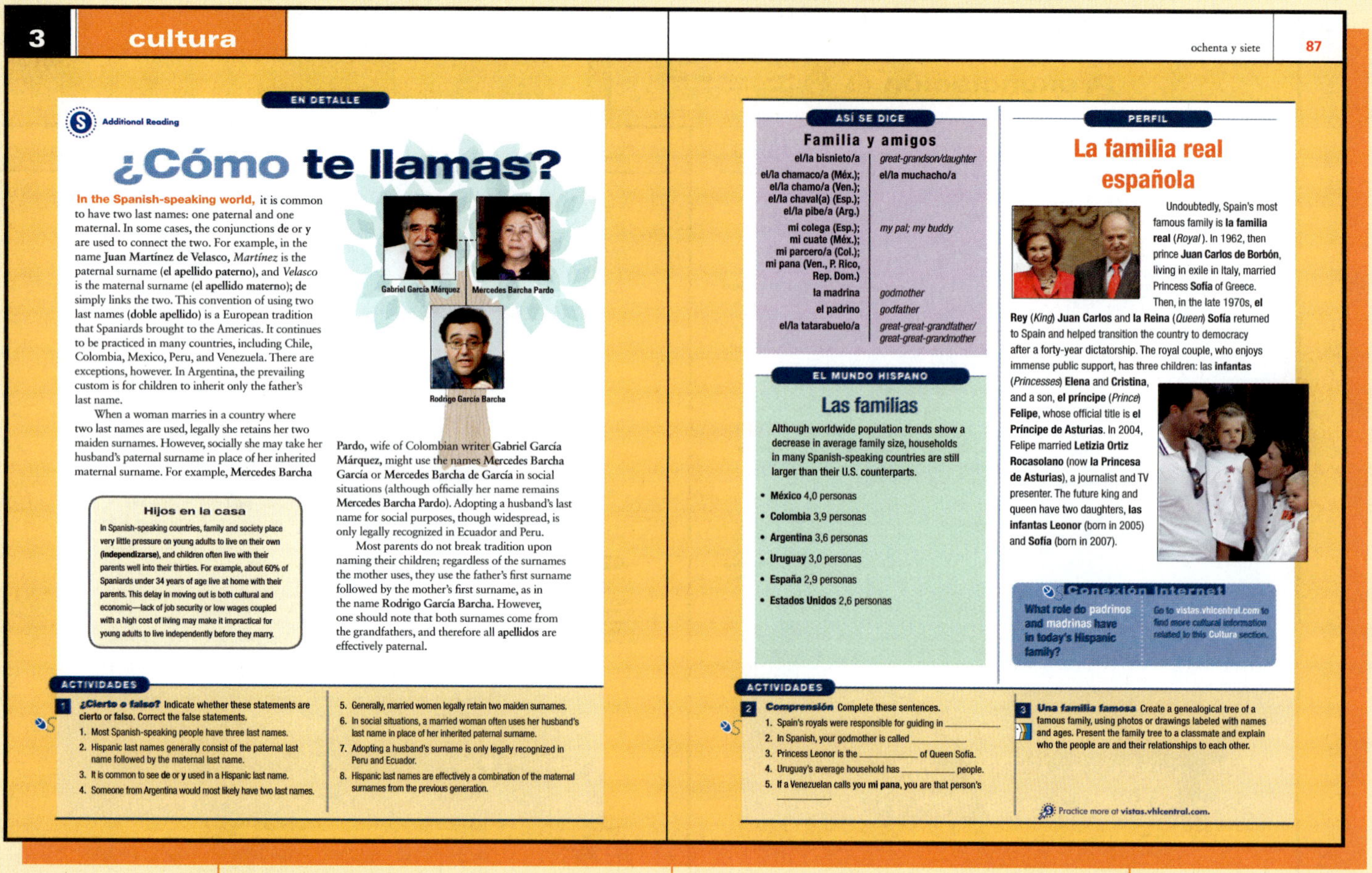

3 cultura

EN DETALLE

Additional Reading

¿Cómo te llamas?

In the Spanish-speaking world, it is common to have two last names: one paternal and one maternal. In some cases, the conjunctions **de** or **y** are used to connect the two. For example, in the name **Juan Martínez de Velasco,** *Martínez* is the paternal surname (**el apellido paterno**), and *Velasco* is the maternal surname (**el apellido materno**); **de** simply links the two. This convention of using two last names (**doble apellido**) is a European tradition that Spaniards brought to the Americas. It continues to be practiced in many countries, including Chile, Colombia, Mexico, Peru, and Venezuela. There are exceptions, however. In Argentina, the prevailing custom is for children to inherit only the father's last name.

When a woman marries in a country where two last names are used, legally she retains her two maiden surnames. However, socially she may take her husband's paternal surname in place of her inherited maternal surname. For example, **Mercedes Barcha Pardo,** wife of Colombian writer **Gabriel García Márquez,** might use the names **Mercedes Barcha García** or **Mercedes Barcha de García** in social situations (although officially her name remains **Mercedes Barcha Pardo**). Adopting a husband's last name for social purposes, though widespread, is only legally recognized in Ecuador and Peru.

Most parents do not break tradition upon naming their children; regardless of the surnames the mother uses, they use the father's first surname followed by the mother's first surname, as in the name **Rodrigo García Barcha.** However, one should note that both surnames come from the grandfathers, and therefore all **apellidos** are effectively paternal.

Gabriel García Márquez

Mercedes Barcha Pardo

Rodrigo García Barcha

Hijos en la casa

In Spanish-speaking countries, family and society place very little pressure on young adults to live on their own (**independizarse**), and children often live with their parents well into their thirties. For example, about 60% of Spaniards under 34 years of age live at home with their parents. This delay in moving out is both cultural and economic—lack of job security or low wages coupled with a high cost of living may make it impractical for young adults to live independently before they marry.

ACTIVIDADES

1 **¿Cierto o falso?** Indicate whether these statements are **cierto** or **falso**. Correct the false statements.

1. Most Spanish-speaking people have three last names.
2. Hispanic last names generally consist of the paternal last name followed by the maternal last name.
3. It is common to see **de** or **y** used in a Hispanic last name.
4. Someone from Argentina would most likely have two last names.
5. Generally, married women legally retain two maiden surnames.
6. In social situations, a married woman often uses her husband's last name in place of her inherited paternal surname.
7. Adopting a husband's surname is only legally recognized in Peru and Ecuador.
8. Hispanic last names are effectively a combination of the maternal surnames from the previous generation.

ochenta y siete 87

ASÍ SE DICE

Familia y amigos

el/la bisnieto/a	*great-grandson/daughter*
el/la chamaco/a (Méx.); el/la chamo/a (Ven.); el/la chaval(a) (Esp.); el/la pibe/a (Arg.)	**el/la muchacho/a**
mi colega (Esp.); mi cuate (Méx.); mi parcero/a (Col.); mi pana (Ven., P. Rico, Rep. Dom.)	*my pal; my buddy*
la madrina	*godmother*
el padrino	*godfather*
el/la tatarabuelo/a	*great-great-grandfather/ great-great-grandmother*

EL MUNDO HISPANO

Las familias

Although worldwide population trends show a decrease in average family size, households in many Spanish-speaking countries are still larger than their U.S. counterparts.

- **México** 4,0 personas
- **Colombia** 3,9 personas
- **Argentina** 3,6 personas
- **Uruguay** 3,0 personas
- **España** 2,9 personas
- **Estados Unidos** 2,6 personas

PERFIL

La familia real española

Undoubtedly, Spain's most famous family is **la familia real** (*Royal*). In 1962, then prince **Juan Carlos de Borbón,** living in exile in Italy, married Princess **Sofía** of Greece. Then, in the late 1970s, **el Rey** (*King*) **Juan Carlos** and **la Reina** (*Queen*) **Sofía** returned to Spain and helped transition the country to democracy after a forty-year dictatorship. The royal couple, who enjoys immense public support, has three children: las **infantas** (*Princesses*) **Elena** and **Cristina,** and a son, **el príncipe** (*Prince*) **Felipe,** whose official title is **el Príncipe de Asturias.** In 2004, Felipe married **Letizia Ortiz Rocasolano** (now **la Princesa de Asturias**), a journalist and TV presenter. The future king and queen have two daughters, **las infantas Leonor** (born in 2005) and **Sofía** (born in 2007).

Conexión Internet

What role do padrinos and madrinas have in today's Hispanic family?

Go to vistas.vhlcentral.com to find more cultural information related to this Cultura section.

ACTIVIDADES

2 **Comprensión** Complete these sentences.

1. Spain's royals were responsible for guiding in ________.
2. In Spanish, your godmother is called ________.
3. Princess Leonor is the ________ of Queen Sofía.
4. Uruguay's average household has ________ people.
5. If a Venezuelan calls you **mi pana**, you are that person's ________.

3 **Una familia famosa** Create a genealogical tree of a famous family, using photos or drawings labeled with names and ages. Present the family tree to a classmate and explain who the people are and their relationships to each other.

Practice more at **vistas.vhlcentral.com.**

En detalle & Perfil(es) Two articles on the lesson theme focus on a specific place, custom, person, group, or tradition in the Spanish-speaking world. In Spanish starting in Lesson 7, these features also provide reading practice.

Activities check your understanding of the material and lead you to further exploration. A mouse icon indicates that activities are available on the **VISTAS** Supersite (**vistas.vhlcentral.com**).

Así se dice & El mundo hispano Lexical and comparative features expand cultural coverage to people, traditions, customs, trends, and vocabulary throughout the Spanish-speaking world.

Coverage While the **Panorama** section takes a regional approach to cultural coverage, **Cultura** is theme-driven, covering several Spanish-speaking regions in every lesson.

Conexión Internet A mouse icon leads you to research a topic related to the lesson theme on the **VISTAS** Supersite (**vistas.vhlcentral.com**).

Estructura
presents Spanish grammar in a graphic-intensive format.

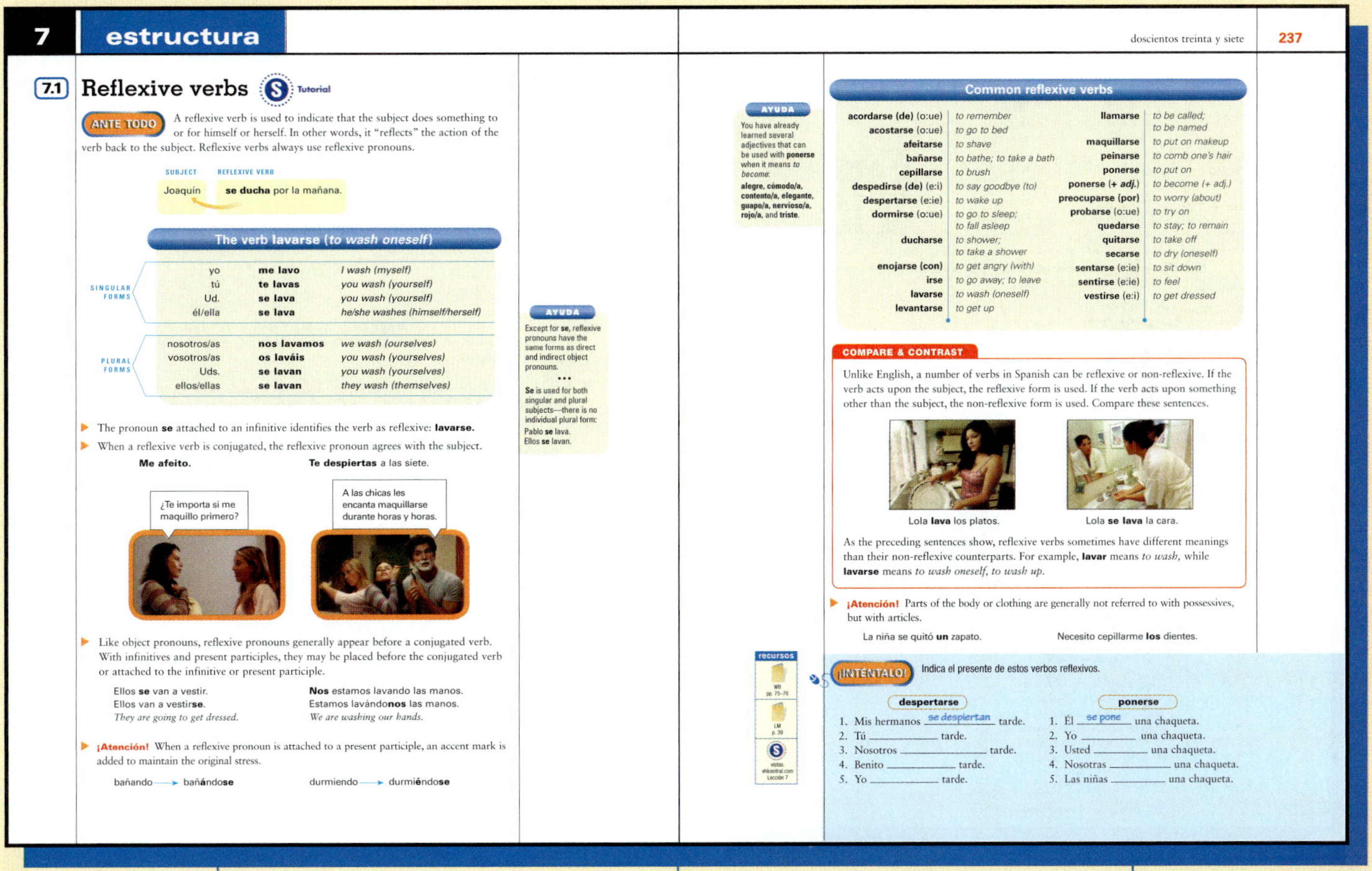
7 estructura

doscientos treinta y siete 237

7.1 Reflexive verbs

Tutorial

ANTE TODO A reflexive verb is used to indicate that the subject does something to or for himself or herself. In other words, it "reflects" the action of the verb back to the subject. Reflexive verbs always use reflexive pronouns.

SUBJECT	REFLEXIVE VERB
Joaquín	**se ducha** por la mañana.

The verb lavarse (*to wash oneself*)

SINGULAR FORMS	yo	**me lavo**	*I wash (myself)*
	tú	**te lavas**	*you wash (yourself)*
	Ud.	**se lava**	*you wash (yourself)*
	él/ella	**se lava**	*he/she washes (himself/herself)*
PLURAL FORMS	nosotros/as	**nos lavamos**	*we wash (ourselves)*
	vosotros/as	**os laváis**	*you wash (yourselves)*
	Uds.	**se lavan**	*you wash (yourselves)*
	ellos/ellas	**se lavan**	*they wash (themselves)*

- The pronoun **se** attached to an infinitive identifies the verb as reflexive: **lavarse.**
- When a reflexive verb is conjugated, the reflexive pronoun agrees with the subject.

Me afeito. **Te despiertas** a las siete.

¿Te importa si me maquillo primero?

A las chicas les encanta maquillarse durante horas y horas.

- Like object pronouns, reflexive pronouns generally appear before a conjugated verb. With infinitives and present participles, they may be placed before the conjugated verb or attached to the infinitive or present participle.

Ellos **se** van a vestir.
Ellos van a vestir**se**.
They are going to get dressed.

Nos estamos lavando las manos.
Estamos lavándo**nos** las manos.
We are washing our hands.

- **¡Atención!** When a reflexive pronoun is attached to a present participle, an accent mark is added to maintain the original stress.

bañando → bañándo**se** durmiendo → durmiéndo**se**

AYUDA
Except for **se**, reflexive pronouns have the same forms as direct and indirect object pronouns.
Se is used for both singular and plural subjects—there is no individual plural form:
Pablo **se** lava.
Ellos **se** lavan.

AYUDA
You have already learned several adjectives that can be used with **ponerse** when it means *to become*:
alegre, cómodo/a, contento/a, elegante, guapo/a, nervioso/a, rojo/a, and **triste**.

Common reflexive verbs

acordarse (de) (o:ue)	*to remember*	**llamarse**	*to be called; to be named*
acostarse (o:ue)	*to go to bed*	**maquillarse**	*to put on makeup*
afeitarse	*to shave*	**peinarse**	*to comb one's hair*
bañarse	*to bathe; to take a bath*	**ponerse**	*to put on*
cepillarse	*to brush*	**ponerse** (+ *adj.*)	*to become (+ adj.)*
despedirse (de) (e:i)	*to say goodbye (to)*	**preocuparse (por)**	*to worry (about)*
despertarse (e:ie)	*to wake up*	**probarse** (o:ue)	*to try on*
dormirse (o:ue)	*to go to sleep; to fall asleep*	**quedarse**	*to stay; to remain*
ducharse	*to shower; to take a shower*	**quitarse**	*to take off*
enojarse (con)	*to get angry (with)*	**secarse**	*to dry (oneself)*
irse	*to go away; to leave*	**sentarse** (e:ie)	*to sit down*
lavarse	*to wash (oneself)*	**sentirse** (e:ie)	*to feel*
levantarse	*to get up*	**vestirse** (e:i)	*to get dressed*

COMPARE & CONTRAST

Unlike English, a number of verbs in Spanish can be reflexive or non-reflexive. If the verb acts upon the subject, the reflexive form is used. If the verb acts upon something other than the subject, the non-reflexive form is used. Compare these sentences.

Lola **lava** los platos. Lola **se lava** la cara.

As the preceding sentences show, reflexive verbs sometimes have different meanings than their non-reflexive counterparts. For example, **lavar** means *to wash,* while **lavarse** means *to wash oneself, to wash up.*

- **¡Atención!** Parts of the body or clothing are generally not referred to with possessives, but with articles.

La niña se quitó **un** zapato. Necesito cepillarme **los** dientes.

recursos
WB pp. 75–76
LM p. 39
vistas.vhlcentral.com Lección 7

¡INTÉNTALO! Indica el presente de estos verbos reflexivos.

despertarse
1. Mis hermanos se despiertan tarde.
2. Tú ________ tarde.
3. Nosotros ________ tarde.
4. Benito ________ tarde.
5. Yo ________ tarde.

ponerse
1. Él se pone una chaqueta.
2. Yo ________ una chaqueta.
3. Usted ________ una chaqueta.
4. Nosotras ________ una chaqueta.
5. Las niñas ________ una chaqueta.

Ante todo This introduction eases you into the grammar with definitions of grammatical terms, reminders about what you already know of English grammar, and Spanish grammar you have learned in earlier lessons.

Compare & Contrast This feature focuses on aspects of grammar that native speakers of English may find difficult, clarifying similarities and differences between Spanish and English.

Diagrams To clarify concepts, clear and easy-to-grasp grammar explanations are reinforced by diagrams that colorfully present sample words, phrases, and sentences.

Charts To help you learn, colorful, easy-to-use charts call out key grammatical structures and forms, as well as important related vocabulary.

Student sidebars provide you with on-the-spot linguistic, cultural, or language-learning information directly related to the materials in front of you.

¡Inténtalo! offers an easy first step into each grammar point. A mouse icon indicates these activities are available with auto-grading on the **VISTAS** Supersite (**vistas.vhlcentral.com**).

Estructura

provides directed and communicative practice.

Práctica

1 **Emparejar** Find the words in column B that are the opposite of the words in column A. One word in B will not be used.

A	B
1. guapo	a. delgado
2. moreno	b. pequeño
3. alto	c. malo
4. gordo	d. feo
5. joven	e. viejo
6. grande	f. rubio
7. simpático	g. antipático
	h. bajo

2 **Completar** Indicate the nationalities of these people by selecting the correct adjectives and changing their forms when necessary.

1. Penélope Cruz es ________.
2. Carlos Fuentes es un gran escritor (*writer*) de México; es ________.
3. Ellen Page y Avril Lavigne son ________.
4. Giorgio Armani es un diseñador de modas (*fashion designer*) ________.
5. Daisy Fuentes es de La Habana, Cuba; ella es ________.
6. Emma Watson y Daniel Radcliffe son actores ________.
7. Heidi Klum y Boris Becker son ________.
8. Apolo Anton Ohno y Shaun White son ________.

NOTA CULTURAL
Carlos Fuentes (1928–) is one of Mexico's best-known writers. His novel, ***La muerte*** (*death*) ***de Artemio Cruz***, explores the psyche of a Mexican revolutionary.

3 **Describir** Look at the drawing and describe each family member using as many adjectives as possible.

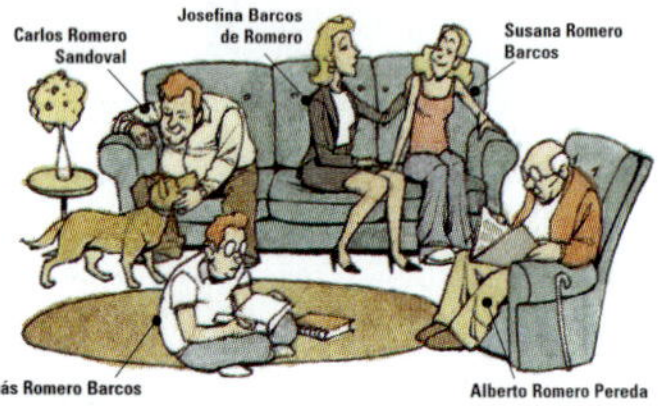

1. Susana Romero Barcos es ________.
2. Tomás Romero Barcos es ________.
3. Los dos hermanos son ________.
4. Josefina Barcos de Romero es ________.
5. Carlos Romero Sandoval es ________.
6. Alberto Romero Pereda es ________.
7. Tomás y su (*his*) padre son ________.
8. Susana y su (*her*) madre son ________.

Practice more at **vistas.vhlcentral.com.**

Comunicación

4 **Entrevista** In pairs, use these questions to interview each other. Be prepared to report the results of your interviews to the class.

1. ¿Dónde comes al mediodía? ¿Comes mucho?
2. ¿Cuándo asistes a tus clases?
3. ¿Cuál es tu clase favorita? ¿Por qué?
4. ¿Dónde vives?
5. ¿Con quién vives?
6. ¿Qué cursos debes tomar el próximo (*next*) semestre?
7. ¿Lees el periódico (*newspaper*)? ¿Qué periódico lees y cuándo?
8. ¿Recibes muchos mensajes de texto (*text messages*)? ¿De quién(es)?
9. ¿Escribes poemas?
10. ¿Crees en fantasmas (*ghosts*)?

5 **¿Acción o descripción?** In small groups, take turns choosing a verb from the list. Then choose to act out the verb or give a description. The other members of the group will say what you are doing. Be creative!

abrir (un libro, una puerta, una mochila)
aprender (a bailar, a hablar francés, a dibujar)
asistir (a una clase de yoga, a un concierto de rock, a una clase interesante)
beber (agua, Coca-Cola)
comer (pasta, un sándwich, pizza)
compartir (un libro, un sándwich)
correr (en el parque, en un maratón)
escribir (una composición, un mensaje de texto [*text message*], con lápiz)
leer (una carta [*letter*] de amor, un mensaje electrónico [*e-mail message*], un periódico [*newspaper*])
recibir un regalo (*gift*)
¿?

modelo
Estudiante 1: (*pantomimes typing a keyboard*)
Estudiante 2: ¿Escribes un mensaje electrónico?
Estudiante 1: Sí.

modelo
Estudiante 1: Soy estudiante y tomo muchas clases. Vivo en Roma.
Estudiante 2: ¿Comes pasta?
Estudiante 1: No, no como pasta.
Estudiante 3: ¿Aprendes a hablar italiano?
Estudiante 1: ¡Sí!

Síntesis

6 **Horario** Your instructor will give you and a partner incomplete versions of Alicia's schedule. Fill in the missing information on the schedule by talking to your partner. Be prepared to reconstruct Alicia's complete schedule with the class.

Práctica A wide range of guided, yet meaningful exercises weave current and previously learned vocabulary together with the current grammar point.

Comunicación Opportunities for creative expression use the lesson's grammar and vocabulary. These activities take place with a partner, in small groups, or with the whole class.

Síntesis activities integrate the current grammar point with previously learned points, providing built-in, consistent review and recycling as you progress through the text.

Information Gap activities engage you and a partner in problem-solving and other situations based on handouts your instructor gives you. However, you and your partner each have only half of the information you need, so you must work together to accomplish the task at hand.

Sidebars The **Notas culturales** expand coverage of the cultures of Spanish-speaking peoples and countries, while **Ayuda** sidebars provide on-the-spot language support.

NEW! Additional activities New to the Fourth Edition, the Activity Pack provides additional communicative and discrete practice for every grammar point. Your instructor will distribute these handouts for review and extra practice.

Estructura

Recapitulación reviews the grammar of each lesson and provides a short quiz, available with auto-grading on the Supersite.

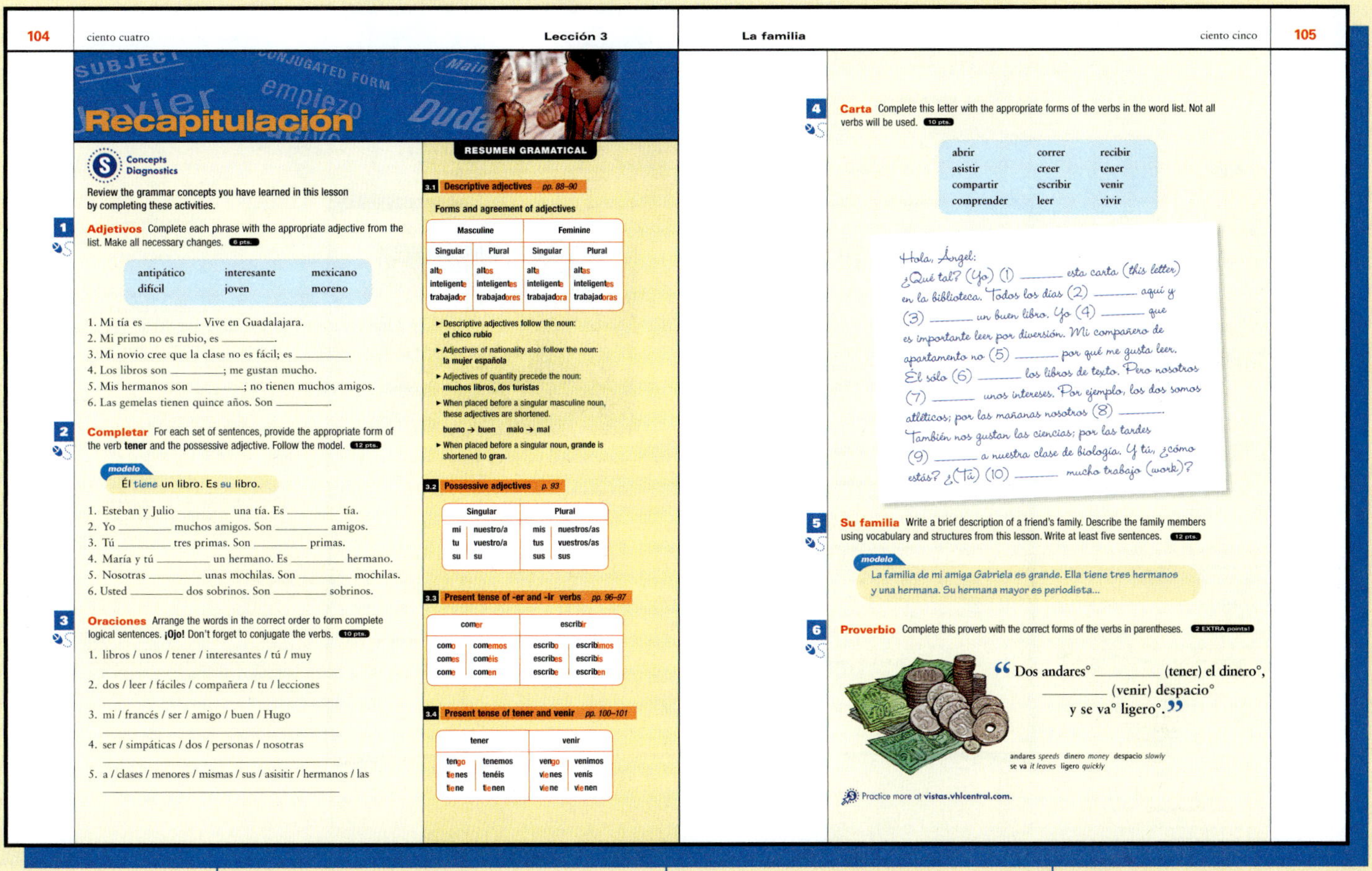

104 ciento cuatro Lección 3

Recapitulación

Concepts Diagnostics

Review the grammar concepts you have learned in this lesson by completing these activities.

1 **Adjetivos** Complete each phrase with the appropriate adjective from the list. Make all necessary changes. 6 pts.

antipático, interesante, mexicano, difícil, joven, moreno

1. Mi tía es ________. Vive en Guadalajara.
2. Mi primo no es rubio, es ________.
3. Mi novio cree que la clase no es fácil; es ________.
4. Los libros son ________; me gustan mucho.
5. Mis hermanos son ________; no tienen muchos amigos.
6. Las gemelas tienen quince años. Son ________.

2 **Completar** For each set of sentences, provide the appropriate form of the verb **tener** and the possessive adjective. Follow the model. 12 pts.

modelo

Él tiene un libro. Es su libro.

1. Esteban y Julio ________ una tía. Es ________ tía.
2. Yo ________ muchos amigos. Son ________ amigos.
3. Tú ________ tres primas. Son ________ primas.
4. María y tú ________ un hermano. Es ________ hermano.
5. Nosotras ________ unas mochilas. Son ________ mochilas.
6. Usted ________ dos sobrinos. Son ________ sobrinos.

3 **Oraciones** Arrange the words in the correct order to form complete logical sentences. ¡Ojo! Don't forget to conjugate the verbs. 10 pts.

1. libros / unos / tener / interesantes / tú / muy
2. dos / leer / fáciles / compañera / tu / lecciones
3. mi / francés / ser / amigo / buen / Hugo
4. ser / simpáticas / dos / personas / nosotras
5. a / clases / menores / mismas / sus / asisitir / hermanos / las

RESUMEN GRAMATICAL

3.1 Descriptive adjectives pp. 88–90

Forms and agreement of adjectives

Masculine		Feminine	
Singular	Plural	Singular	Plural
alto	altos	alta	altas
inteligente	inteligentes	inteligente	inteligentes
trabajador	trabajadores	trabajadora	trabajadoras

- Descriptive adjectives follow the noun: el chico rubio
- Adjectives of nationality also follow the noun: la mujer española
- Adjectives of quantity precede the noun: muchos libros, dos turistas
- When placed before a singular masculine noun, these adjectives are shortened.

bueno → buen malo → mal

- When placed before a singular noun, grande is shortened to gran.

3.2 Possessive adjectives p. 93

Singular		Plural	
mi	nuestro/a	mis	nuestros/as
tu	vuestro/a	tus	vuestros/as
su	su	sus	sus

3.3 Present tense of -er and -ir verbs pp. 96–97

comer		escribir	
como	comemos	escribo	escribimos
comes	coméis	escribes	escribís
come	comen	escribe	escriben

3.4 Present tense of tener and venir pp. 100–101

tener		venir	
tengo	tenemos	vengo	venimos
tienes	tenéis	vienes	venís
tiene	tienen	viene	vienen

La familia ciento cinco 105

4 **Carta** Complete this letter with the appropriate forms of the verbs in the word list. Not all verbs will be used. 10 pts.

abrir, asistir, compartir, comprender, correr, creer, escribir, leer, recibir, tener, venir, vivir

Hola, Ángel:

¿Qué tal? (Yo) (1) ________ esta carta (this letter) en la biblioteca. Todos los días (2) ________ aquí y (3) ________ un buen libro. Yo (4) ________ que es importante leer por diversión. Mi compañero de apartamento no (5) ________ por qué me gusta leer. Él sólo (6) ________ los libros de texto. Pero nosotros (7) ________ unos intereses. Por ejemplo, los dos somos atléticos; por las mañanas nosotros (8) ________. También nos gustan las ciencias; por las tardes (9) ________ a nuestra clase de biología. Y tú, ¿cómo estás? ¿(Tú) (10) ________ mucho trabajo (work)?

5 **Su familia** Write a brief description of a friend's family. Describe the family members using vocabulary and structures from this lesson. Write at least five sentences. 12 pts.

modelo

La familia de mi amiga Gabriela es grande. Ella tiene tres hermanos y una hermana. Su hermana mayor es periodista...

6 **Proverbio** Complete this proverb with the correct forms of the verbs in parentheses. 2 EXTRA points!

“Dos andares° ________ (tener) el dinero°, ________ (venir) despacio° y se va° ligero°.”

andares speeds dinero money despacio slowly se va it leaves ligero quickly

Practice more at vistas.vhlcentral.com.

Resumen gramatical This review panel provides you with an easy-to-study summary of the basic concepts of the lesson's grammar, with page references to the full explanations.

Activities A series of activities, moving from directed to open-ended, systematically test your mastery of the lesson's grammar. The section ends with a riddle or puzzle using the grammar from the lesson.

Points Each activity is assigned a point value to help you track your progress. All **Recapitulación** sections add up to fifty points, plus two additional points for successfully completing the bonus activity.

Supersite icon An icon lets you know that **Recapitulación** can be completed online with diagnostics to help you identify where you are strong or where you might need review.

NEW! Extra practice An icon indicates when there is extra practice available online. In this case, after you finish **Recapitulación**, you can complete a set of follow-up activities to compare your results!

Adelante

Lectura develops reading skills in the context of the lesson theme.

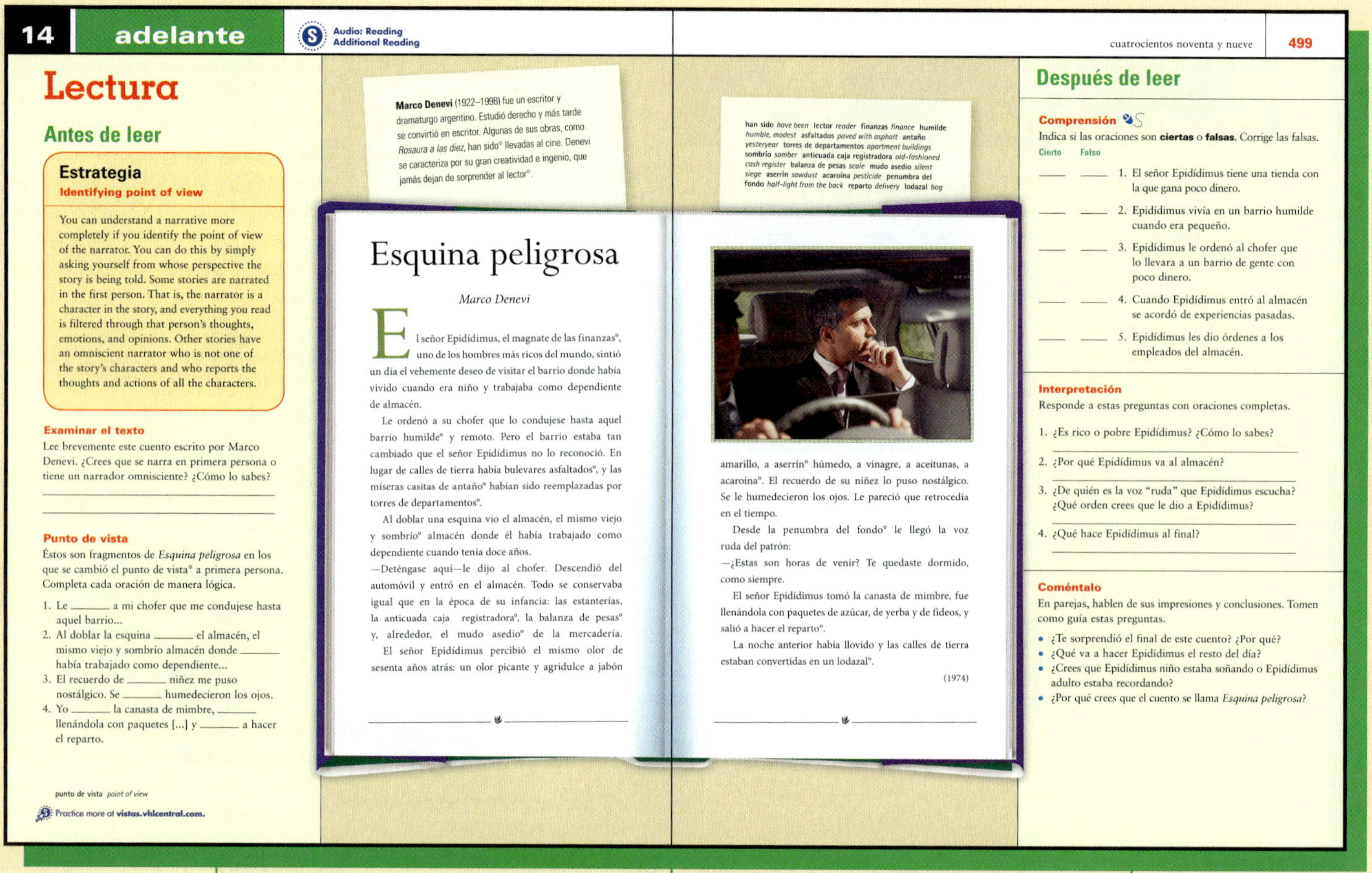

14 adelante

Audio: Reading
Additional Reading

Lectura

Antes de leer

Estrategia
Identifying point of view

You can understand a narrative more completely if you identify the point of view of the narrator. You can do this by simply asking yourself from whose perspective the story is being told. Some stories are narrated in the first person. That is, the narrator is a character in the story, and everything you read is filtered through that person's thoughts, emotions, and opinions. Other stories have an omniscient narrator who is not one of the story's characters and who reports the thoughts and actions of all the characters.

Examinar el texto

Lee brevemente este cuento escrito por Marco Denevi. ¿Crees que se narra en primera persona o tiene un narrador omnisciente? ¿Cómo lo sabes?

____

____

Punto de vista

Éstos son fragmentos de *Esquina peligrosa* en los que se cambió el punto de vista° a primera persona. Completa cada oración de manera lógica.

1. Le ______ a mi chofer que me condujese hasta aquel barrio...
2. Al doblar la esquina ______ el almacén, el mismo viejo y sombrío almacén donde ______ había trabajado como dependiente...
3. El recuerdo de ______ niñez me puso nostálgico. Se ______ humedecieron los ojos.
4. Yo ______ la canasta de mimbre, ______ llenándola con paquetes [...] y ______ a hacer el reparto.

punto de vista *point of view*

Practice more at **vistas.vhlcentral.com.**

Marco Denevi (1922–1998) fue un escritor y dramaturgo argentino. Estudió derecho y más tarde se convirtió en escritor. Algunas de sus obras, como *Rosaura a las diez*, han sido° llevadas al cine. Denevi se caracteriza por su gran creatividad e ingenio, que jamás dejan de sorprender al lector°.

Esquina peligrosa

Marco Denevi

El señor Epidídimus, el magnate de las finanzas°, uno de los hombres más ricos del mundo, sintió un día el vehemente deseo de visitar el barrio donde había vivido cuando era niño y trabajaba como dependiente de almacén.

Le ordenó a su chofer que lo condujese hasta aquel barrio humilde° y remoto. Pero el barrio estaba tan cambiado que el señor Epidídimus no lo reconoció. En lugar de calles de tierra había bulevares asfaltados°, y las míseras casitas de antaño° habían sido reemplazadas por torres de departamentos°.

Al doblar una esquina vio el almacén, el mismo viejo y sombrío° almacén donde él había trabajado como dependiente cuando tenía doce años.

—Deténgase aquí—le dijo al chofer. Descendió del automóvil y entró en el almacén. Todo se conservaba igual que en la época de su infancia: las estanterías, la anticuada caja registradora°, la balanza de pesas° y, alrededor, el mudo asedio° de la mercadería.

El señor Epidídimus percibió el mismo olor de sesenta años atrás: un olor picante y agridulce a jabón amarillo, a aserrín° húmedo, a vinagre, a aceitunas, a acaroína°. El recuerdo de su niñez lo puso nostálgico. Se le humedecieron los ojos. Le pareció que retrocedía en el tiempo.

Desde la penumbra del fondo° le llegó la voz ruda del patrón:

—¿Estas son horas de venir? Te quedaste dormido, como siempre.

El señor Epidídimus tomó la canasta de mimbre, fue llenándola con paquetes de azúcar, de yerba y de fideos, y salió a hacer el reparto°.

La noche anterior había llovido y las calles de tierra estaban convertidas en un lodazal°.

(1974)

han sido *have been* **lector** *reader* **finanzas** *finance* **humilde** *humble, modest* **asfaltados** *paved with asphalt* **antaño** *yesteryear* **torres de departamentos** *apartment buildings* **sombrío** *somber* **anticuada caja registradora** *old-fashioned cash register* **balanza de pesas** *scale* **mudo asedio** *silent siege* **aserrín** *sawdust* **acaroína** *pesticide* **penumbra del fondo** *half-light from the back* **reparto** *delivery* **lodazal** *bog*

cuatrocientos noventa y nueve 499

Después de leer

Comprensión

Indica si las oraciones son **ciertas** o **falsas**. Corrige las falsas.

Cierto	Falso	
____	____	1. El señor Epidídimus tiene una tienda con la que gana poco dinero.
____	____	2. Epidídimus vivía en un barrio humilde cuando era pequeño.
____	____	3. Epidídimus le ordenó al chofer que lo llevara a un barrio de gente con poco dinero.
____	____	4. Cuando Epidídimus entró al almacén se acordó de experiencias pasadas.
____	____	5. Epidídimus les dio órdenes a los empleados del almacén.

Interpretación

Responde a estas preguntas con oraciones completas.

1. ¿Es rico o pobre Epidídimus? ¿Cómo lo sabes?
2. ¿Por qué Epidídimus va al almacén?
3. ¿De quién es la voz "ruda" que Epidídimus escucha? ¿Qué orden crees que le dio a Epidídimus?
4. ¿Qué hace Epidídimus al final?

Coméntalo

En parejas, hablen de sus impresiones y conclusiones. Tomen como guía estas preguntas.

- ¿Te sorprendió el final de este cuento? ¿Por qué?
- ¿Qué va a hacer Epidídimus el resto del día?
- ¿Crees que Epidídimus niño estaba soñando o Epidídimus adulto estaba recordando?
- ¿Por qué crees que el cuento se llama *Esquina peligrosa*?

Antes de leer Valuable reading strategies and pre-reading activities strengthen your reading abilities in Spanish.

Readings Selections related to the lesson theme recycle vocabulary and grammar you have learned. The selections in Lessons 1–12 are cultural texts, while those in Lessons 13–18 are literary pieces.

Después de leer Activities include post-reading exercises that review and check your comprehension of the reading as well as expansion activities.

NEW! Selections Three readings are new to this edition. Lessons 1 and 11 now offer authentic comics by Quino and Tute, while lesson 14 now has a short story by Marco Denevi.

Adelante

Escritura develops writing skills while *Escuchar* practices listening skills in the context of the lesson theme.

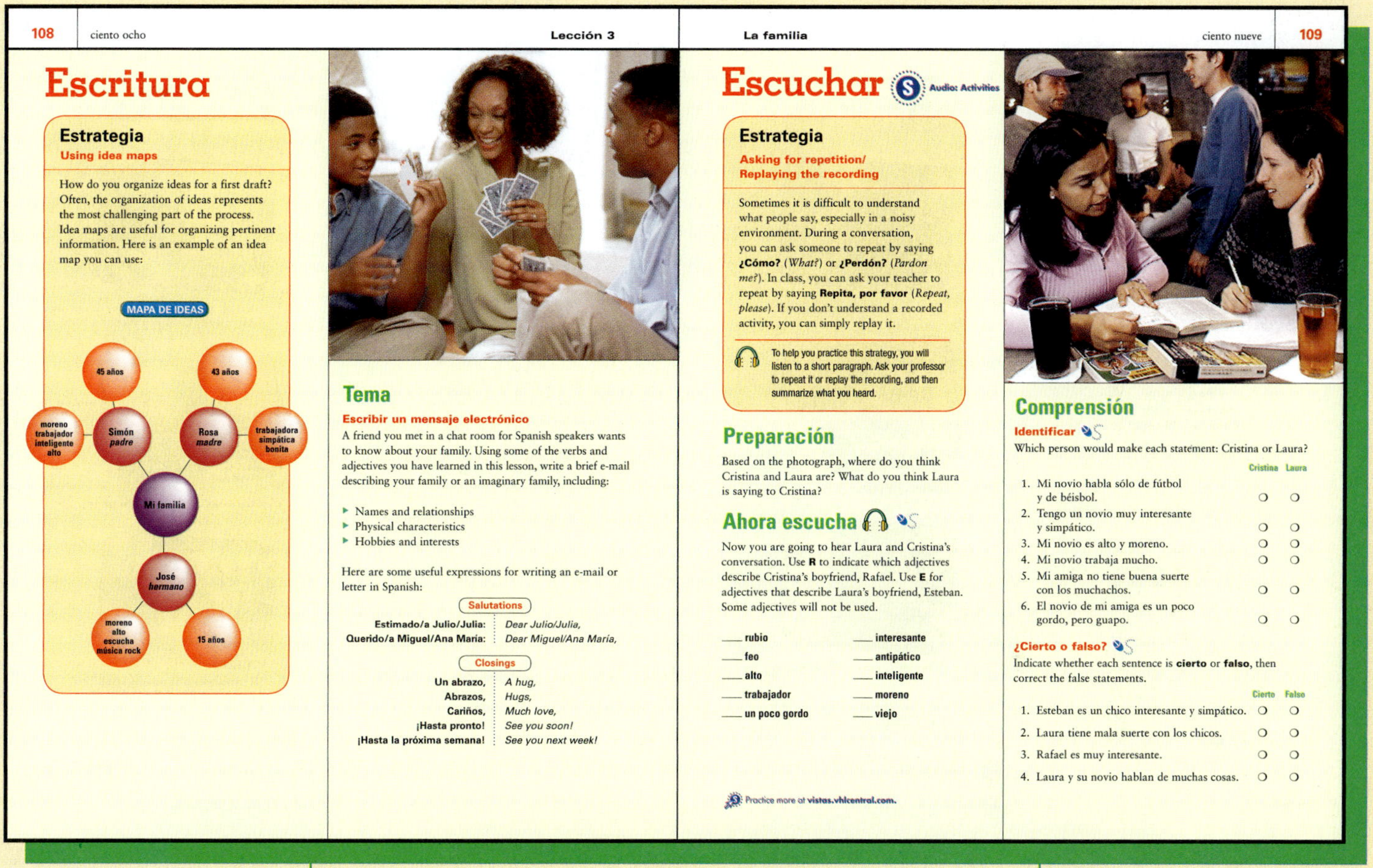

108 ciento ocho **Lección 3**

Escritura

Estrategia

Using idea maps

How do you organize ideas for a first draft? Often, the organization of ideas represents the most challenging part of the process. Idea maps are useful for organizing pertinent information. Here is an example of an idea map you can use:

Tema

Escribir un mensaje electrónico

A friend you met in a chat room for Spanish speakers wants to know about your family. Using some of the verbs and adjectives you have learned in this lesson, write a brief e-mail describing your family or an imaginary family, including:

- Names and relationships
- Physical characteristics
- Hobbies and interests

Here are some useful expressions for writing an e-mail or letter in Spanish:

Salutations

Estimado/a Julio/Julia:	*Dear Julio/Julia,*
Querido/a Miguel/Ana María:	*Dear Miguel/Ana María,*

Closings

Un abrazo,	*A hug,*
Abrazos,	*Hugs,*
Cariños,	*Much love,*
¡Hasta pronto!	*See you soon!*
¡Hasta la próxima semana!	*See you next week!*

La familia ciento nueve 109

Escuchar

Audio: Activities

Estrategia

Asking for repetition/ Replaying the recording

Sometimes it is difficult to understand what people say, especially in a noisy environment. During a conversation, you can ask someone to repeat by saying **¿Cómo?** (*What?*) or **¿Perdón?** (*Pardon me?*). In class, you can ask your teacher to repeat by saying **Repita, por favor** (*Repeat, please*). If you don't understand a recorded activity, you can simply replay it.

To help you practice this strategy, you will listen to a short paragraph. Ask your professor to repeat it or replay the recording, and then summarize what you heard.

Preparación

Based on the photograph, where do you think Cristina and Laura are? What do you think Laura is saying to Cristina?

Ahora escucha

Now you are going to hear Laura and Cristina's conversation. Use **R** to indicate which adjectives describe Cristina's boyfriend, Rafael. Use **E** for adjectives that describe Laura's boyfriend, Esteban. Some adjectives will not be used.

___ rubio	___ interesante
___ feo	___ antipático
___ alto	___ inteligente
___ trabajador	___ moreno
___ un poco gordo	___ viejo

Practice more at **vistas.vhlcentral.com.**

Comprensión

Identificar

Which person would make each statement: Cristina or Laura?

	Cristina	Laura
1. Mi novio habla sólo de fútbol y de béisbol.	○	○
2. Tengo un novio muy interesante y simpático.	○	○
3. Mi novio es alto y moreno.	○	○
4. Mi novio trabaja mucho.	○	○
5. Mi amiga no tiene buena suerte con los muchachos.	○	○
6. El novio de mi amiga es un poco gordo, pero guapo.	○	○

¿Cierto o falso?

Indicate whether each sentence is **cierto** or **falso**, then correct the false statements.

	Cierto	Falso
1. Esteban es un chico interesante y simpático.	○	○
2. Laura tiene mala suerte con los chicos.	○	○
3. Rafael es muy interesante.	○	○
4. Laura y su novio hablan de muchas cosas.	○	○

Estrategia Strategies help you prepare for the writing and listening tasks to come.

Escritura The **Tema** describes the writing topic and includes suggestions for approaching it.

Escuchar A recorded conversation or narration develops your listening skills in Spanish. **Preparación** prepares you for listening to the recorded passage.

Ahora escucha walks you through the passage, and **Comprensión** checks your listening comprehension.

Adelante

En pantalla and *Flash cultura* present additional video tied to the lesson theme.

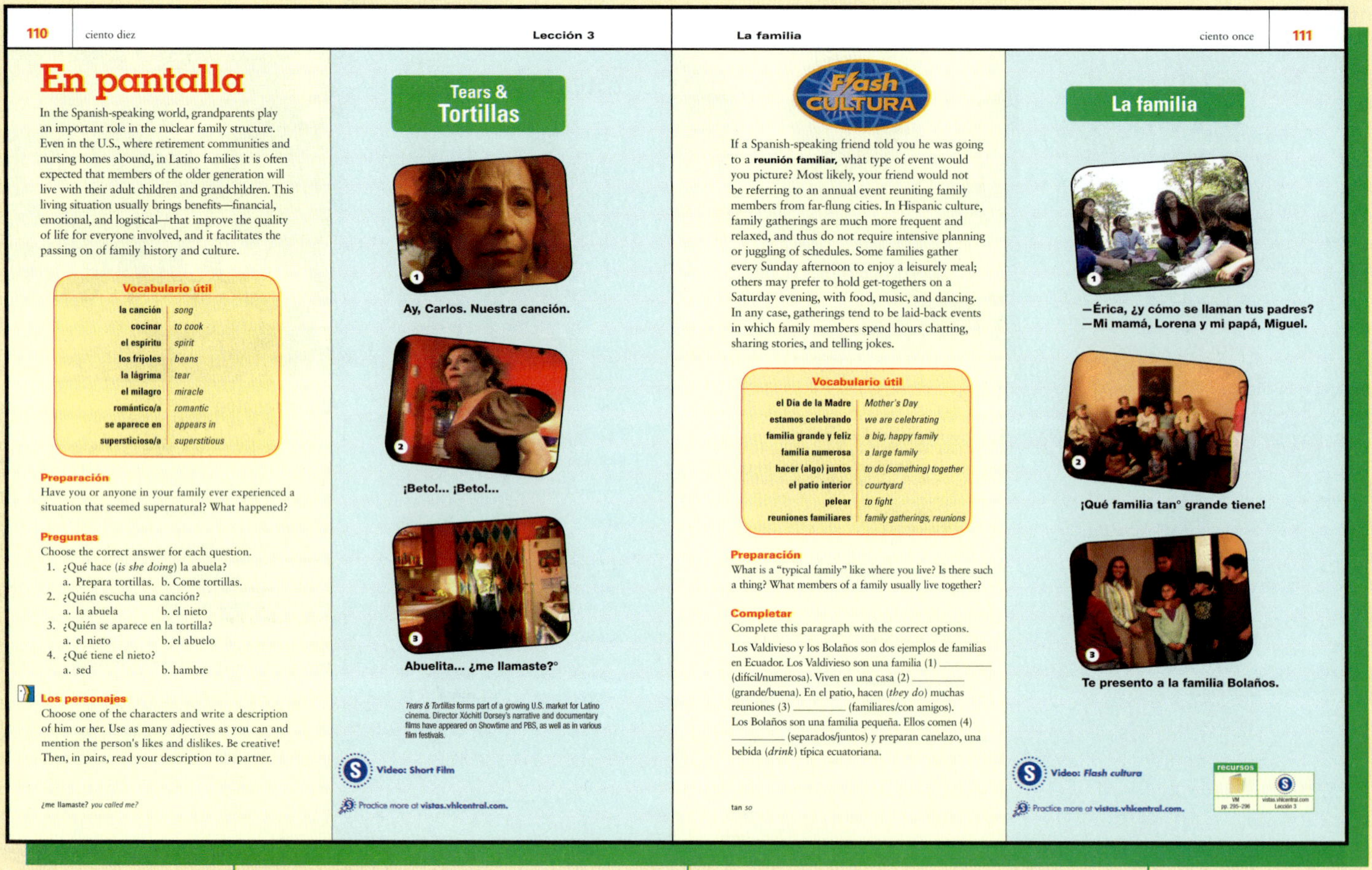

En pantalla TV clips, many **NEW!** to this edition, give you additional exposure to authentic language. The clips include commercials, newscasts, short films, and TV shows that feature the language, vocabulary, and theme of the lesson.

Presentation Cultural notes, video stills with captions, and vocabulary support all prepare you to view the clips. Activities check your comprehension and expand on the ideas presented.

NEW! Cortometraje The **En pantalla** sections for lessons 3, 15, and 16 now feature authentic short films from the U.S., Mexico, and Spain. Pre-and post-viewing support is increased in lessons 15 and 16.

Supersite icon Icons lead you to the Supersite (**vistas.vhlcentral.com**), where you can view the videos and get further practice.

Flash cultura An icon lets you know that the enormously successful **Flash cultura** Video offers specially-shot content tied to the lesson theme.

NEW! Activities Due to the overwhelming popularity of the **Flash cultura** Video, previewing support and comprehension activities are now integrated into the student text. To learn more about the video, turn to page xxx.

Panorama
presents the nations of the Spanish-speaking world.

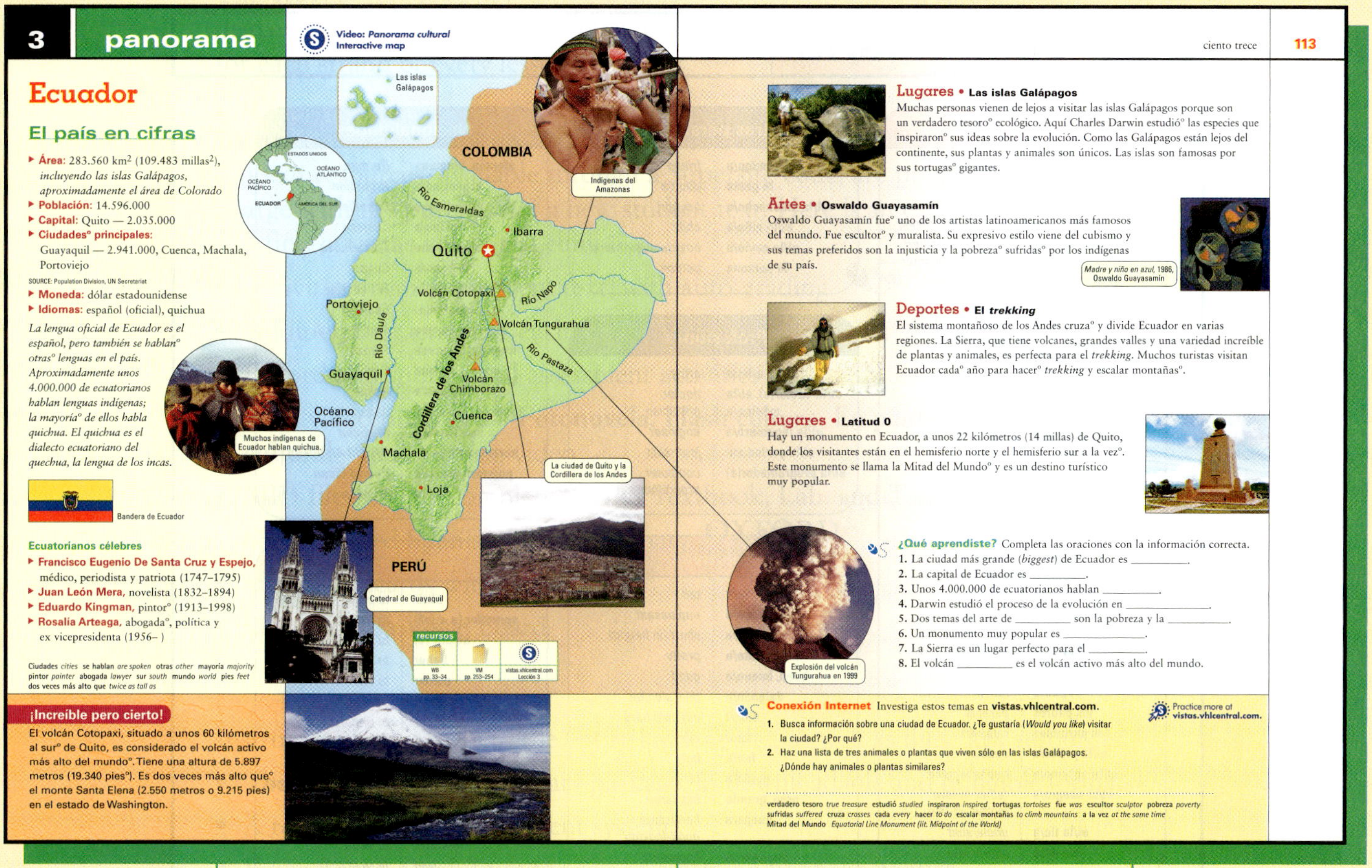

3 panorama

Video: *Panorama cultural*
Interactive map

Ecuador

El país en cifras

- **Área:** 283.560 km² (109.483 millas²), *incluyendo las islas Galápagos, aproximadamente el área de Colorado*
- **Población:** 14.596.000
- **Capital:** Quito — 2.035.000
- **Ciudades° principales:** Guayaquil — 2.941.000, Cuenca, Machala, Portoviejo

SOURCE: Population Division, UN Secretariat

- **Moneda:** dólar estadounidense
- **Idiomas:** español (oficial), quichua

La lengua oficial de Ecuador es el español, pero también se hablan° otras° lenguas en el país. Aproximadamente unos 4.000.000 de ecuatorianos hablan lenguas indígenas; la mayoría° de ellos habla quichua. El quichua es el dialecto ecuatoriano del quechua, la lengua de los incas.

Muchos indígenas de Ecuador hablan quichua.

Bandera de Ecuador

Ecuatorianos célebres

- **Francisco Eugenio De Santa Cruz y Espejo,** médico, periodista y patriota (1747–1795)
- **Juan León Mera,** novelista (1832–1894)
- **Eduardo Kingman,** pintor° (1913–1998)
- **Rosalía Arteaga,** abogada°, política y ex vicepresidenta (1956–)

Ciudades *cities* se hablan *are spoken* otras *other* mayoría *majority* pintor *painter* abogada *lawyer* sur *south* mundo *world* pies *feet* dos veces más alto que *twice as tall as*

¡Increíble pero cierto!
El volcán Cotopaxi, situado a unos 60 kilómetros al sur° de Quito, es considerado el volcán activo más alto del mundo°. Tiene una altura de 5.897 metros (19.340 pies°). Es dos veces más alto que° el monte Santa Elena (2.550 metros o 9.215 pies) en el estado de Washington.

ciento trece 113

Lugares • Las islas Galápagos
Muchas personas vienen de lejos a visitar las islas Galápagos porque son un verdadero tesoro° ecológico. Aquí Charles Darwin estudió° las especies que inspiraron° sus ideas sobre la evolución. Como las Galápagos están lejos del continente, sus plantas y animales son únicos. Las islas son famosas por sus tortugas° gigantes.

Artes • Oswaldo Guayasamín
Oswaldo Guayasamín fue° uno de los artistas latinoamericanos más famosos del mundo. Fue escultor° y muralista. Su expresivo estilo viene del cubismo y sus temas preferidos son la injusticia y la pobreza° sufridas° por los indígenas de su país.

Madre y niño en azul, 1986, Oswaldo Guayasamín

Deportes • El *trekking*
El sistema montañoso de los Andes cruza° y divide Ecuador en varias regiones. La Sierra, que tiene volcanes, grandes valles y una variedad increíble de plantas y animales, es perfecta para el *trekking*. Muchos turistas visitan Ecuador cada° año para hacer° *trekking* y escalar montañas°.

Lugares • Latitud 0
Hay un monumento en Ecuador, a unos 22 kilómetros (14 millas) de Quito, donde los visitantes están en el hemisferio norte y el hemisferio sur a la vez°. Este monumento se llama la Mitad del Mundo° y es un destino turístico muy popular.

Explosión del volcán Tungurahua en 1999

¿Qué aprendiste? Completa las oraciones con la información correcta.
1. La ciudad más grande (*biggest*) de Ecuador es ________.
2. La capital de Ecuador es ________.
3. Unos 4.000.000 de ecuatorianos hablan ________.
4. Darwin estudió el proceso de la evolución en ____________.
5. Dos temas del arte de ________ son la pobreza y la ________.
6. Un monumento muy popular es ____________.
7. La Sierra es un lugar perfecto para el ________.
8. El volcán ________ es el volcán activo más alto del mundo.

Conexión Internet Investiga estos temas en **vistas.vhlcentral.com**.
1. Busca información sobre una ciudad de Ecuador. ¿Te gustaría (*Would you like*) visitar la ciudad? ¿Por qué?
2. Haz una lista de tres animales o plantas que viven sólo en las islas Galápagos. ¿Dónde hay animales o plantas similares?

Practice more at vistas.vhlcentral.com.

verdadero tesoro *true treasure* estudió *studied* inspiraron *inspired* tortugas *tortoises* fue *was* escultor *sculptor* pobreza *poverty* sufridas *suffered* cruza *crosses* cada *every* hacer *to do* escalar montañas *to climb mountains* a la vez *at the same time* Mitad del Mundo *Equatorial Line Monument (lit. Midpoint of the World)*

El país en cifras presents interesting key facts about the featured country.

Maps point out major cities, rivers, and geographical features and situate the country in the context of its immediate surroundings and the world.

Readings A series of brief paragraphs explores facets of the country's culture such as history, places, fine arts, literature, and aspects of everyday life.

¡Increíble pero cierto! highlights an intriguing fact about the country or its people.

Conexión Internet offers Internet activities on the **VISTAS** Supersite (**vistas.vhlcentral.com**) for additional avenues of discovery.

***Panorama cultural* Video** This video's authentic footage takes you to the featured Spanish-speaking country, letting you experience the sights and sounds of an aspect of its culture. To learn more about the video, turn to page xxx.

FOTONOVELA VIDEO PROGRAM

The cast NEW!

Here are the main characters you will meet in the **Fotonovela** Video:

From Mexico,
Jimena Díaz Velázquez

From Argentina,
Juan Carlos Rossi

From Mexico,
Felipe Díaz Velázquez

From the U.S.,
Marissa Wagner

From Mexico,
María Eugenia (Maru) Castaño Ricaurte

From Spain,
Miguel Ángel Lagasca Martínez

Brand-new and fully integrated with your text, the **VISTAS 4/e Fotonovela** Video is a dynamic and contemporary window into the Spanish language. The new video centers around the Díaz family, whose household includes two college-aged children and a visiting student from the U.S. Over the course of an academic year, Jimena, Felipe, Marissa, and their friends explore **el D.F.** and other parts of Mexico as they make plans for their futures. Their adventures take them through some of the greatest natural and cultural treasures of the Spanish-speaking world, as well as the highs and lows of everyday life.

The **Fotonovela** section in each textbook lesson is actually an abbreviated version of the dramatic episode featured in the video. Therefore, each **Fotonovela** section can be done before you see the corresponding video episode, after it, or as a section that stands alone.

In each dramatic segment, the characters interact using the vocabulary and grammar you are studying. As the storyline unfolds, the episodes combine new vocabulary and grammar with previously taught language, exposing you to a variety of authentic accents along the way. At the end of each episode, the **Resumen** section highlights the grammar and vocabulary you are studying.

We hope you find the new **Fotonovela** Video to be an engaging and useful tool for learning Spanish!

EN PANTALLA VIDEO PROGRAM

The **VISTAS** Supersite features an authentic video clip for each lesson. Clip formats include commercials, news stories, and even short films. These clips, many **NEW!** to the Fourth Edition, have been carefully chosen to be comprehensible for students learning Spanish, and are accompanied by activities and vocabulary lists to facilitate understanding. More importantly, though, these clips are a fun and motivating way to improve your Spanish!

Here are the countries represented in each lesson in **En pantalla:**

Lesson 1 U.S.	Lesson 7 Argentina	Lesson 13 Argentina
Lesson 2 Chile	Lesson 8 Peru	Lesson 14 Argentina
Lesson 3 U.S.	Lesson 9 Chile	Lesson 15 Mexico
Lesson 4 Peru	Lesson 10 Argentina	Lesson 16 Spain
Lesson 5 Mexico	Lesson 11 Colombia	Lesson 17 Mexico
Lesson 6 Mexico	Lesson 12 Argentina	Lesson 18 Mexico

FLASH CULTURA VIDEO PROGRAM

In the dynamic **Flash cultura** Video, young people from all over the Spanish-speaking world share aspects of life in their countries with you. The similarities and differences among Spanish-speaking countries that come up through their adventures will challenge you to think about your own cultural practices and values. The segments provide valuable cultural insights as well as linguistic input; the episodes will introduce you to a variety of accents and vocabulary as they gradually move into Spanish.

PANORAMA CULTURAL VIDEO PROGRAM

The **Panorama cultural** Video is integrated with the **Panorama** section in each lesson. Each segment is 2–3 minutes long and consists of documentary footage from each of the countries featured. The images were specially chosen for interest level and visual appeal, while the all-Spanish narrations were carefully written to reflect the vocabulary and grammar covered in the textbook.

ICONS AND *RECURSOS* BOXES

Icons

Familiarize yourself with these icons that appear throughout **VISTAS, Fourth Edition**.

Icons legend

Listening activity/section	Hoja de actividades
Pair activity	Textbook activity available online
Group activity	Content on the Supersite available for this section
Information Gap activity	

- The Information Gap activities and those involving **Hojas de actividades** (*activity sheets*) require handouts that your instructor will give you.
- You will see the listening icon in each lesson's **Contextos**, **Pronunciación**, **Escuchar,** and **Vocabulario** sections.
- A note next to the Supersite icon will let you know exactly what type of content is available online. See p. xxvii for a list of available resources.
- Additional practice on the Supersite, not included in the textbook, is indicated with this icon:

Practice more at **vistas.vhlcentral.com.**

Recursos

Recursos boxes let you know exactly what print and technology ancillaries you can use to reinforce and expand on every section of the lessons in your textbook. They even include page numbers when applicable. See the next page for a description of the ancillaries.

Recursos boxes legend

WB pp. 37–38 — Workbook	VM pp. 219–220 — Video Manual
LM p. 19 — Lab Manual	VISTAS Supersite

STUDENT ANCILLARIES

▶ **Supersite**
Student access to the Supersite (**vhlcentral.com**) is free with the purchase of a new student text. The Student Supersite provides:
- Textbook and extra-practice activities
- All **VISTAS 4/e** video programs
- Textbook Audio Program MP3s (audio recordings for the listening based textbook activities and recordings of the active vocabulary for each lesson of the student text)
- Lab Audio Program MP3s
- Study resources (online dictionary, tutorials, flashcards)

See page xxvii for a complete list of resources.

▶ **Supersite Plus**
The Student Supersite Plus provides:
- The **VISTAS 4/e** Supersite.
- **WebSAM**, the entire Workbook, Video Manual, and Lab Manual online, as well as a robust learning management system that completely integrates with the **VISTAS 4/e** Supersite.
- Instructor-enabled Wimba Pronto.

▶ NEW! **VText**
The online virtual interactive student edition provides students with:
- Note-taking and highlighting capabilities
- Easy browsing via table of contents or page number
- Links to textbook mouse-icon activities
- Assignments and grades on the **VText** page
- Direct access to all Supersite resources

▶ **Workbook/Video Manual**
The Workbook/Video Manual contains the workbook activities for each textbook lesson, activities for the **Fotonovela** Video, and pre-, while-, and post-viewing activities for the **Flash cultura** and **Panorama cultural** Videos.

▶ **Lab Manual**
The Lab Manual contains lab activities for each textbook lesson for use with the Lab Audio Program.

***Fotonovela* Video DVD**
The **Fotonovela** DVD provides the complete **Fotonovela** Video Program with subtitles in English and Spanish.

En línea 3.0
The ground-breaking online version of **VISTAS 4/e, En línea 3.0** allows students to interact with the textbook, do practice activities, complete tests, and communicate with their instructors and e-partners online. For instructors, it also has complete classroom management tools.

INSTRUCTOR ANCILLARIES

▶ **Instructor's Annotated Edition (IAE)**
The IAE contains a wealth of teaching information. The expanded trim size and enhanced design of **VISTAS 4/e** make the annotations and facsimile student pages easy to read and reference in the classroom.

▶ NEW! **Activity Pack**
The **VISTAS** Activity Pack offers discrete and communicative practice for individuals, pairs, and groups. Formats include surveys, multiple choice questions, information gap activities, role-plays, board games, and more.

▶ **Supersite**
The password-protected Instructor Supersite allows instructors to assign and track student progress through its course management system. Instructors have full access to the Student Supersite, and seamless integration with the **VISTAS 4/e WebSAM** and **VText**. Instructor Resources for easy access and download include:
- Classroom handouts for the textbook
- Answers to directed activities in the textbook
- Audioscripts
- Video program transcripts and translations
- Workbook/Lab Manual/Video Manual Answer Keys
- Overhead Transparencies
- Grammar *PowerPoints*

▶ **Supersite Plus**
Supersite Plus offers:
- The complete **VISTAS 4/e** Supersite
- The **WebSAM** online Workbook/Lab Manual/Video Manual, with auto-graded and instructor-graded activities, and oral record-submit activities
- NEW! **Wimba Pronto**, with instant messaging, video calling, whiteboard for online collaboration and demonstration, application sharing, and online office hours

▶ **Instructor's DVD Set**
Three video DVDs (**Fotonovela, Flash cultura,** and **Panorama cultural**) available with subtitles in English and Spanish.

Testing Program
The Testing Program is provided in three formats: within a powerful Test Generator, in customizable .rtf files, and as PDFs.

NEW! Volume I of the Testing Program contains quizzes for each **Contextos** presentation and each **Estructura** grammar point. There are two versions of each quiz.

NEW! Volume II of the Testing Program contains two additional versions (**Prueba E** and **Prueba F**) of the tests for each textbook lesson.

In addition to the six versions of tests for each textbook lesson, Volume II also contains quarter exams, semester exams, listening scripts, answer keys for the tests, and optional test items for culture, video, and reading sections.

acknowledgments

On behalf of its authors and editors, Vista Higher Learning expresses its sincere appreciation to the many instructors and college professors across the U.S. and Canada who contributed their ideas and suggestions. Their insights and detailed comments were invaluable to us as we created the Fourth Edition.

VISTAS, Fourth Edition, is the direct result of extensive reviews and ongoing input from both students and instructors using the Third Edition. Accordingly, we gratefully acknowledge those who shared their suggestions, recommendations, and ideas as we prepared this Fourth Edition.

We express our sincere appreciation to over 150 instructors using the Third Edition who completed our online review. Their comments and suggestions were instrumental in shaping the entire **VISTAS 4/e** program.

Finally, we thank those instructors who also served as editors and writers, including Martín Gaspar of Harvard University, Ronna Feit of Nassau Community College, and Mercedes Hussey Pailos of Brevard Community College.

Reviewers

Joseph Alonso
The Evergreen State College, WA

Aleta Anderson
Grand Rapids Community College, MI

Blanca Anderson
Loyola University, LA

Patricia Antunez
Choate Rosemary Hall, CT

Damian Bacich
San Jose State University, CA

Vicki Baggia
Phillips Exeter Academy, NH

Christine Bain
Drake University, IA

Catherine R. Baranello
SUNY Cortland, NY

Cindy Barnett
Murray State University, KY

Kevin Beard
Richland College, TX

Leon Bensadon
University of Washington, WA

Leela Bingham
San Diego Mesa College, CA

Joelle Bonamy
Nicholls State University, LA

Josephine Books
Inver Hills Community College, MN

Genevieve Breedon
Darton College, GA

Amy Brevik
Concordia College, MN

Carol Brinks
Interlochen Arts Academy, MI

Froylan Cabuto
Cerritos College, CA

Ramiro F. Canto-Lugo
Yuba College, CA

Ezequiel Cardenas
Cuyamaca College, CA

Beth Cardon
Georgia Perimeter College, GA

Monica Casco
Queens College, NY

Kirby Chadwick
Scottsdale Community College, AZ

Donald R. Clymer
Eastern Mennonite University, VA

Vilma Concha-Chiaraviglio
Meredith College, NC

Mary Condon
Park Center International Baccalaureate School, MN

Lisa Contreras
Transylvania University, KY

Raymond D. Cornelius III
Daytona State College/DeLand Campus, FL

Dominic Corraro
Notre Dame High School, CT

Antonio Crespo
Grossmont College, CA

Miryam Criado
Hanover College, IN

José Cruz
Fayetteville Technical Community College, NC

William R. Cummins
Ashland University, OH

Debra Currere
Rock Valley College, IL

Deborah Cutler
Pima Community College, AZ

Patricia S. Davis
Darton College, GA

Callie K. DeBellis
Meredith College, NC

Alberto Descalzo de Blas
Franciscan University of Steubenville, OH

Rejane Dias
Lake Land College, IL

Lucia Dzikowski
Seminole Community College, FL

Teresa Dombrowski
John Tyler Community College, VA

Hayden D. Duncan
Gustavus Adolphus College, MN

Deborah Edson
Tidewater Community College, VA

Steven Egland
Husson University, ME

Kristen Elley
Kennesaw State University, GA

Carol Faber
Grand Valley State University, MI

Joseph Fallis
John Tyler Community College, VA

Mary Farsaci
North Yarmouth Academy, ME

Linda Fix
Minnesota School of Business, MN

Ruston Ford
Indian Hills Community College, IA

Flor Frau
Knox College, IL

Sarah Fritz
Madison Area Technical College, WI

Dianne Fruit
Cascadia Community College, WA

Prospero N. Garcia
University of Massachusetts, Amherst, MA

LeeAnn Gilroy
Solon High School, IA

Guillermo Giron
San Joaquin Delta College, CA

Angela M. Gonzales
University of Kentucky, KY

Lucila Gonzalez-Cirre
Cerro Coso Community College, CA

Kate Grovergrys
Madison Area Technical College, WI

Marta C. Gumpert
Southeastern Louisiana University, LA

John Hall
Minnesota State University, Moorhead, MN

Richard Heath
Kirkwood Community College, IA

Claudio Hidalgo
Kirkwood Community College, IA

Carmen M. Hernández
Grossmont College, CA

Karla Hernández
Cuyamaca College, CA

Maria Eugenia Hernandez-Hall
Scottsdale College, AZ

Nan Hussey
Houghton College, NY

Stewart James-Lejarcegui
Iowa Wesleyan College, IA

Hilda M. Kachmar
College of St. Catherine, MN

Richard Keenan
Corpus Christi College, BC

Ruthanne Keenan Orihuela
University of Idaho, ID

Darcie Khanukayev
Cerro Coso Community College, CA

Telma Koch
Oakwood Friends, NY

Ruth F. Konopka
Grossmont College, CA

Marcela Labounty
College of Southern Nevada, NV

Stephanie Langston
Georgia Perimeter College, GA

Louis Lanni
Edison State College, Collier Campus, FL

Jean LeLoup
SUNY Cortland, NY

Raul de Leon
San Diego Mesa College, CA

Patricia M. Lestrade
Mississippi State University, MS

Carla Ligo
Grove City College, PA

Pamela Llorens
Miami Dade College, FL

Debora Maldonado-DeOliveira
Meredith College, NC

Jodie Marion
Mt. Hood Community College, WA

Nereyda Maroot
Fresno City College, CA

Patricia Martin
Calvary Christian School, KY

Laura Martinez
Centralia College, WA

María Inés Martínez
University of Manitoba, Canada

Fernando Mayoral
Edison State College, FL

Leticia McGrath
Georgia Southern University, GA

Michael McGrath
Georgia Southern University, GA

MaryYetta McKelva
Grayson County College, TX

Albert Meggers
Cosby High School, VA

Luis Millan
Minnesota School of Business, MN

David Miller
St. Andrew's School of Delaware, DE

acknowledgments

Jerome Miner
Knox College, IL

Deborah Mistron
Middle Tennessee State University, TN

Clayton Mitchell
Drake University, IA

Laura Lee Moore
Pearl River Community College, MS

Iani Moreno
Suffolk University, MA

Gabriel Mucino
Concordia University, WI

Jose A. Narbona
Rice University, TX

Kelly Negaard
Minnesota School of Business, MN

Sherry Pachman
St. Michael's College, VT

Joseph Palumbo
College of Southern Nevada, NV

Elizabeth Parr
Darton College, GA

Maria C. Perez
Iowa Western Community College, IA

Maria Elena Perez
Lubbock Christian University, TX

Martha Perez-Bendorf
Kirkwood Commuity College, IA

Jennifer Perry
East Carolina University, NC

Melissa Pilkington
Georgia Institute of Technology, GA

Lori Piotrowski
College of Southern Nevada, NV

Thomas R. Porter
Southern Virginia University, VA

Antonio Prado
Knox College, IL

Kay Queen
Lon Morris College, TX

Robin Ragan
Knox College, IL

Aida Ramos-Sellman
Goucher College, MD

Jacqueline M. Ramsey
Concordia University Wisconsin, WI

Kenneth Randall
Cincinnati Country Day School, OH

Caterina Reitano
University of Manitoba, Canada

Jose Manuel Reyes
Hanover College, KY

Nelly Rios-Freund
University of Saint Thomas, MN

Monica Rivas
Mission College, FL

Wallace J. Robertson
Ivy Tech Community College, IN

Patricia Robitaille
Cincinnati Country Day School, OH

Monica Rodriguez
Lyon College, AR

Amie Russell
Mississippi State University, MS

Virginia Sánchez-Bernardy
San Diego Mesa College, CA

Eduardo Santa Cruz
Hanover College, IN

Jeffrey Schmidt
Crafton Hill College, CA

Dora Schoenbrun-Fernandez
San Diego Mesa College, CA

Elizabeth Schwartz
San Joaquin Delta College, CA

Amber Schwegman
Northwest Nazarene University, ID

Linda Q. Sites
Piedmont Virginia Community College, VA

Anita Smith
Pitt Community College, NC

Nancy Smith
Allegheny College, PA

Kathleen Spinnenweber
Franciscan University, OH

Carol Stuardo
Cuyamaca College, CA

Cristina Szterensus
Rock Valley College, IL

Roy Tanner
Truman State University, MO

Ron Tapia
Ivy Tech Community College, IN

Alison Tatum-Davis
Goucher College, MD

John Nicholas Tavernakis
College of San Mateo, CA

Robert Taylor
Grand Rapids Community College, MI

Rachel Tease
National-Louis University, WI

Daniel G. Tight
University of St. Thomas, MN

Linda Tracy
Santa Rosa Junior College, CA

Jorge Trinchet
Murray State University, KY

James R. Wilson
Madison Area Technical College, WI

Wendy Valenteen
Mercersburg Academy, PA

María Villagomez
Napa Valley College, CA

María Villalobos-Buehner
Grand Valley State University, MI

Hilde Votaw
University of Oklahoma, OK

Virginia Young
Grossmont College, CA

¡De compras!

6

Communicative Goals

You will learn how to:

- Talk about and describe clothing
- Express preferences in a store
- Negotiate and pay for items you buy

A PRIMERA VISTA

- ¿Está comprando algo la chica?
- ¿Crees que busca una maleta o una blusa?
- ¿Está contenta o enojada?
- ¿Cómo es la chica?

En el mercado

Los chicos van de compras al mercado. ¿Quién hizo la mejor compra?

PERSONAJES

FELIPE

JUAN CARLOS

Video: *Fotonovela*
Record and Compare

MARISSA Oigan, vamos al mercado.

JUAN CARLOS ¡Sí! Los chicos en un equipo y las chicas en otro.

FELIPE Tenemos dos horas para ir de compras.

MARU Y don Guillermo decide quién gana.

1

JIMENA Esta falda azul es muy elegante.

MARISSA ¡Sí! Además, este color está de moda.

MARU Éste rojo es de algodón.

2

MARISSA ¿Me das aquella blusa rosada? Me parece que hace juego con esta falda, ¿no? ¿No tienen otras tallas?

JIMENA Sí, aquí. ¿Qué talla usas?

MARISSA Uso talla 4.

JIMENA La encontré. ¡Qué ropa más bonita!

3

(*En otra parte del mercado*)

FELIPE Juan Carlos compró una camisa de muy buena calidad.

MIGUEL (*a la vendedora*) ¿Puedo ver ésos, por favor?

VENDEDORA Sí, señor. Le doy un muy buen precio.

4

(*Las chicas encuentran unas bolsas.*)

VENDEDOR Ésta de rayas cuesta 190 pesos, ésta 120 pesos y ésta 220 pesos.

5

6

VENDEDOR Son 530 por las tres bolsas. Pero como ustedes son tan bonitas, son 500 pesos.

MARU Señor, no somos turistas ricas. Somos estudiantes pobres.

VENDEDOR Bueno, son 480 pesos.

MARISSA **JIMENA** **MARU** **MIGUEL** **DON GUILLERMO** **VENDEDORA** **VENDEDOR**

7

JUAN CARLOS Miren, mi nueva camisa. Elegante, ¿verdad?

FELIPE A ver, Juan Carlos... te queda bien.

8

MARU ¿Qué compraste?

MIGUEL Sólo esto.

MARU ¡Qué bonitos aretes! Gracias, mi amor.

9

JUAN CARLOS Y ustedes, ¿qué compraron?

JIMENA Bolsas.

MARU Acabamos de comprar tres bolsas por sólo 480 pesos. ¡Una ganga!

10

FELIPE Don Guillermo, usted tiene que decidir quién gana. ¿Los chicos o las chicas?

DON GUILLERMO El ganador es... Miguel. ¡Porque no compró nada para él, sino para su novia!

Expresiones útiles

Talking about clothing

¡Qué ropa más bonita!
What nice clothing!
Esta falda azul es muy elegante.
This blue skirt is very elegant.
Está de moda.
It's in style.
Éste rojo es de algodón/lana.
This red one is cotton/wool.
Ésta de rayas/lunares/cuadros es de seda.
This striped / polka-dotted / plaid one is silk.
Es de muy buena calidad.
It's very good quality.
¿Qué talla usas/llevas?
What size do you wear?
Uso/Llevo talla 4.
I wear a size 4.
¿Qué número calza?
What size shoe do you wear?
Yo calzo siete.
I wear a size seven.

Negotiating a price

¿Cuánto cuesta?
How much does it cost?
Demasiado caro/a.
Too expensive.
Es una ganga.
It's a bargain.

Saying what you bought

¿Qué compraste?/¿Qué compró usted?
What did you buy?
Sólo compré esto.
I only bought this.
¡Qué bonitos aretes!
What beautiful earrings!
Y ustedes, ¿qué compraron?
And you guys, what did you buy?

Additional vocabulary

híjole *wow*

recursos

VM pp. 223–224	vistas.vhlcentral.com Lección 6

¿Qué pasó?

1 **¿Cierto o falso?** Indicate whether each sentence is **cierto** or **falso**. Correct the false statements.

	Cierto	Falso
1. Jimena dice que la falda azul no es elegante.	❍	❍
2. Juan Carlos compra una camisa.	❍	❍
3. Marissa dice que el azul es un color que está de moda.	❍	❍
4. Miguel compra unas sandalias para Maru.	❍	❍

NOTA CULTURAL

Las guayaberas are a popular men's shirt worn in hot climates. They are usually made of cotton, linen, or silk and decorated with pleats, pockets and sometimes embroidery. They can be worn instead of a jacket to formal occasions or as everyday clothing.

2 **Identificar** Provide the first initial of the person who would make each statement.

___ 1. ¿Te gusta cómo se me ven mis nuevos aretes?
___ 2. Juan Carlos compró una camisa de muy buena calidad.
___ 3. No podemos pagar 500, señor, eso es muy caro.
___ 4. Aquí tienen ropa de muchas tallas.
___ 5. Esta falda me gusta mucho, el color azul es muy elegante.
___ 6. Hay que darnos prisa, sólo tenemos dos horas para ir de compras.

MARU

FELIPE

JIMENA

3 **Completar** Answer the questions using the information in the **Fotonovela**.

1. ¿Qué talla es Marissa?
2. ¿Cuánto les pide el vendedor por las tres bolsas?
3. ¿Cuál es el precio que pagan las tres amigas por las bolsas?
4. ¿Qué dice Juan Carlos sobre su nueva camisa?
5. ¿Quién ganó al hacer las compras? ¿Por qué?

AYUDA

When discussing prices, it's important to keep in mind singular and plural forms of verbs.

La **camisa cuesta** diez dólares.

Las **botas cuestan** sesenta dólares.

El **precio** de las botas **es** sesenta dólares.

Los **precios** de la ropa **son** altos.

4 **Conversar** With a partner, role-play a conversation between a customer and a salesperson in an open-air market. Use these expressions and also look at **Expresiones útiles** on the previous page.

¿Qué desea?	Estoy buscando...	Prefiero el/la rojo/a.
What would you like?	*I'm looking for...*	*I prefer the red one.*

Cliente/a	Vendedor(a)
Say good afternoon.	→ Greet the customer and ask what he/she would like.
Explain that you are looking for a particular item of clothing.	→ Show him/her some items and ask what he/she prefers.
Discuss colors and sizes.	→ Discuss colors and sizes.
Ask for the price and begin bargaining.	→ Tell him/her a price. Negotiate a price.
Settle on a price and purchase the item.	→ Accept a price and say thank you.

Practice more at **vistas.vhlcentral.com.**

Pronunciación

Audio: Concepts, Activities
Record & Compare

The consonants d and t

¿Dónde? vender nadar verdad

Like **b** and **v**, the Spanish **d** can also have a hard sound or a soft sound, depending on which letters appear next to it.

Don dinero tienda falda

At the beginning of a phrase and after **n** or **l**, the letter **d** is pronounced with a hard sound. This sound is similar to the English *d* in *dog*, but a little softer and duller. The tongue should touch the back of the upper teeth, not the roof of the mouth.

medias verde vestido huésped

In all other positions, **d** has a soft sound. It is similar to the English *th* in *there*, but a little softer.

Don Diego no tiene el diccionario.

When **d** begins a word, its pronunciation depends on the previous word. At the beginning of a phrase or after a word that ends in **n** or **l**, it is pronounced as a hard **d**.

Doña Dolores es de la capital.

Words that begin with **d** are pronounced with a soft **d** if they appear immediately after a word that ends in a vowel or any consonant other than **n** or **l**.

traje pantalones tarjeta tienda

When pronouncing the Spanish **t**, the tongue should touch the back of the upper teeth, not the roof of the mouth. Unlike the English *t*, no air is expelled from the mouth.

Práctica Read these phrases aloud to practice the **d** and the **t**.

1. Hasta pronto.
2. De nada.
3. Mucho gusto.
4. Lo siento.
5. No hay de qué.
6. ¿De dónde es usted?
7. ¡Todos a bordo!
8. No puedo.
9. Es estupendo.
10. No tengo computadora.
11. ¿Cuándo vienen?
12. Son las tres y media.

Oraciones Read these sentences aloud to practice the **d** and the **t**.

1. Don Teodoro tiene una tienda en un almacén en La Habana.
2. Don Teodoro vende muchos trajes, vestidos y zapatos todos los días.
3. Un día un turista, Federico Machado, entra en la tienda para comprar un par de botas.
4. Federico regatea con don Teodoro y compra las botas y también un par de sandalias.

Refranes Read these sayings aloud to practice the **d** and the **t**.

1 Variety is the spice of life.
2 You can't make a silk purse out of a sow's ear.

recursos
LM p. 32
vistas.vhlcentral.com Lección 6

EN DETALLE

Additional Reading

Los mercados al aire libre

Mercados al aire libre are an integral part of commerce and culture in the Spanish-speaking world. Whether they take place daily or weekly, these markets are an important forum where tourists, locals, and vendors interact. People come to the marketplace to shop, socialize, taste local foods, and watch street performers. Wandering from one **puesto** (*stand*) to the next, one can browse fresh fruits and vegetables, clothing, CDs and DVDs, and **artesanías** (*crafts*). Some markets offer a mix of products, while others specialize in food, fashion, or used merchandise, such as antiques and books.

When shoppers see an item they like, they can bargain with the vendor. Friendly bargaining is an expected ritual and may result in a significantly lower price. When selling food, vendors may give the customer a little extra of what they purchase; this free addition is known as **la ñapa**.

Many open-air markets are also tourist attractions. The market in Otavalo, Ecuador, is world-famous and has taken place every Saturday since pre-Incan times. This market is well-known for the colorful textiles woven by the **otavaleños**, the indigenous people of the area. One can also find leather goods and wood carvings from nearby towns. Another popular market is **El Rastro**, held every Sunday in Madrid, Spain. Sellers set up **puestos** along the streets to display their wares, which range from local artwork and antiques to inexpensive clothing and electronics.

Mercado de Otavalo

Otros mercados famosos

Mercado	Lugar	Productos
Feria Artesanal de Recoleta	Buenos Aires, Argentina	artesanías
Mercado Central	Santiago, Chile	mariscos°, pescado°, frutas, verduras°
Tianguis Cultural del Chopo	Ciudad de México, México	ropa, música, revistas, libros, arte, artesanías
El mercado de Chichicastenango	Chichicastenango, Guatemala	frutas y verduras, flores°, cerámica, textiles

mariscos *seafood* pescado *fish* verduras *vegetables* flores *flowers*

ACTIVIDADES

1 **¿Cierto o falso?** Indicate whether these statements are **cierto** or **falso**. Correct the false statements.

1. Generally, open-air markets specialize in one type of goods.
2. Bargaining is commonplace at outdoor markets.
3. Only new goods can be found at open-air markets.
4. A Spaniard in search of antiques could search at **El Rastro**.
5. If you are in Guatemala and want to buy ceramics, you can go to Chichicastenango.
6. A **ñapa** is a tax on open-air market goods.
7. The **otavaleños** weave colorful textiles to sell on Saturdays.
8. Santiago's **Mercado Central** is known for books and music.

ASÍ SE DICE

La ropa

la chamarra (Méx.)	**la chaqueta**
de manga corta/larga	*short/long-sleeved*
los mahones (P. Rico); el pantalón de mezclilla (Méx.); los tejanos (Esp.); los vaqueros (Arg., Cuba, Esp., Uru.)	**los bluejeans**
la marca	*brand*
la playera (Méx.); la remera (Arg.)	**la camiseta**

EL MUNDO HISPANO

Diseñadores de moda

- **Adolfo Domínguez** (España) Su ropa tiene un estilo minimalista y práctico. Usa telas° naturales y cómodas en sus diseños.
- **Silvia Tcherassi** (Colombia) Los colores vivos y las líneas asimétricas de sus vestidos y trajes muestran influencias tropicales.

- **Óscar de la Renta** (República Dominicana) Diseña ropa opulenta para la mujer clásica.
- **Narciso Rodríguez** (EE.UU.) En sus diseños delicados y finos predominan los colores blanco y negro. Hizo° el vestido de boda° de Carolyn Bessette Kennedy.

telas *fabrics* **Hizo** *He made* **de boda** *wedding*

PERFIL

Carolina Herrera

In 1980, at the urging of some friends, **Carolina Herrera** created a fashion collection as a "test." The Venezuelan designer received such a favorable response that within one year she moved her family from Caracas to New York City and created her own label, Carolina Herrera, Ltd.

"I love elegance and intricacy, but whether it is in a piece of clothing or a fragrance, the intricacy must appear as simplicity," Herrera once stated. She quickly found that many sophisticated women agreed; from the start, her sleek and glamorous designs have been in constant demand. Over the years, Herrera has grown her brand into a veritable fashion empire that encompasses her fashion and bridal collections, cosmetics, perfume, and accessories that are sold around the globe.

Conexión Internet

¿Qué marcas de ropa son populares en el mundo hispano?

Go to **vistas.vhlcentral.com** to find more cultural information related to this **Cultura** section.

ACTIVIDADES

2 Comprensión Complete these sentences.

1. Adolfo Domínguez usa telas ______ y ______ en su ropa.
2. Si hace fresco en el D.F., puedes llevar una ______.
3. La diseñadora ______ hace ropa, perfumes y más.
4. La ropa de ______ muestra influencias tropicales.
5. Los ______ son una ropa casual en Puerto Rico.

3 Mi ropa favorita Write a brief description of your favorite article of clothing. Mention what store it is from, the brand, colors, fabric, style, and any other information. Then get together with a small group, collect the descriptions, and take turns reading them aloud at random. Can the rest of the group guess whose favorite piece of clothing is being described?

Practice more at **vistas.vhlcentral.com.**

6.1 Saber and conocer

S Tutorial

ANTE TODO Spanish has two verbs that mean *to know*: **saber** and **conocer**. They cannot be used interchangeably. Note the irregular **yo** forms.

The verbs saber and conocer

		saber *(to know)*	**conocer** *(to know)*
SINGULAR FORMS	yo	**sé**	**conozco**
	tú	**sabes**	**conoces**
	Ud./él/ella	**sabe**	**conoce**
PLURAL FORMS	nosotros/as	**sabemos**	**conocemos**
	vosotros/as	**sabéis**	**conocéis**
	Uds./ellos/ellas	**saben**	**conocen**

- **Saber** means *to know a fact or piece(s) of information* or *to know how to do something.*

No **sé** tu número de teléfono.
I don't know your telephone number.

Mi hermana **sabe** hablar francés.
My sister knows how to speak French.

- **Conocer** means *to know* or *be familiar/acquainted* with a person, place, or thing.

¿**Conoces** la ciudad de Nueva York?
Do you know New York City?

No **conozco** a tu amigo Esteban.
I don't know your friend Esteban.

- When the direct object of **conocer** is a person or pet, the personal **a** is used.

¿Conoces La Habana? *but* ¿Conoces **a** Celia Cruz?
Do you know Havana? — *Do you know Celia Cruz?*

- **¡Atención!** **Parecer** (*to seem*) and **ofrecer** (*to offer*) are conjugated like **conocer**.

- **¡Atención!** **Conducir** (*to drive*) and **traducir** (*to translate*) also have an irregular **yo** form, but since they are **-ir** verbs, they are conjugated differently from **conocer**.

conducir	**conduzco, conduces, conduce, conducimos, conducís, conducen**
traducir	**traduzco, traduces, traduce, traducimos, traducís, traducen**

NOTA CULTURAL

Cuban singer **Celia Cruz** (1924–2003), known as the "Queen of Salsa," recorded many albums over her long career. Adored by her fans, she was famous for her colorful and lively on-stage performances.

¡INTÉNTALO! Provide the appropriate forms of these verbs.

saber

1. José no ___sabe___ la hora.
2. Sara y yo ________ jugar al tenis.
3. ¿Por qué no ________ tú estos verbos?
4. Mis padres ________ hablar japonés.
5. Yo ________ a qué hora es la clase.
6. Usted no ________ dónde vivo.
7. Mi hermano no ________ nadar.
8. Nosotros ________ muchas cosas.

conocer

1. Usted y yo ___conocemos___ bien Miami.
2. ¿Tú ________ a mi amigo Manuel?
3. Sergio y Taydé ________ mi pueblo.
4. Emiliano ________ a mis padres.
5. Yo ________ muy bien el centro.
6. ¿Ustedes ________ la tienda Gigante?
7. Nosotras ________ una playa hermosa.
8. ¿Usted ________ a mi profesora?

recursos

WB p. 61
LM p. 33
vistas.vhlcentral.com Lección 6

Práctica y Comunicación

1

Completar Indicate the correct verb for each sentence.

1. Mis hermanos (conocen/saben) conducir, pero yo no (sé/conozco).
2. —¿(Conocen/Saben) ustedes dónde está el estadio? —No, no lo (conocemos/sabemos).
3. —¿(Conoces/Sabes) a Lady Gaga? —Bueno, (sé/conozco) quién es, pero no la (conozco/sé).
4. Mi profesora (sabe/conoce) Cuba y también (conoce/sabe) bailar salsa.

2

Combinar Combine elements from each column to create sentences.

A	B	C
Shakira	(no) conocer	Conan O'Brien
los Yankees	(no) saber	cantar y bailar
el primer ministro de Canadá		La Habana Vieja
mis amigos y yo		muchas personas importantes
tú		hablar dos lenguas extranjeras
		jugar al béisbol

3

Preguntas In pairs, ask each other these questions. Answer with complete sentences.

1. ¿Conoces a un(a) cantante famoso/a? ¿Te gusta cómo canta?
2. En tu familia, ¿quién sabe cantar bien? ¿Tu opinión es objetiva?
3. Y tú, ¿conduces bien o mal? ¿Y tus amigos?
4. Si un(a) amigo/a no conduce muy bien, ¿le ofreces crítica constructiva?
5. ¿Cómo parece estar el/la profesor(a) hoy? ¿Y tus compañeros de clase?

4

Entrevista Jot down three things you know how to do, three people you know, and three places you are familiar with. Then, in a small group, find out what you have in common.

modelo

Estudiante 1: *¿Conocen ustedes a David Lomas?*
Estudiante 2: *Sí, conozco a David. Vivimos en la misma residencia estudiantil.*
Estudiante 3: *No, no lo conozco. ¿Cómo es?*

5

Anuncio In groups, read the ad and answer these questions.

1. Busquen ejemplos de los verbos **saber** y **conocer**.
2. ¿Qué saben del Centro Comercial Oviedo?
3. ¿Qué pueden hacer en el Centro Comercial Oviedo?
4. ¿Conocen otros centros comerciales similares? ¿Cómo se llaman? ¿Dónde están?
5. ¿Conocen un centro comercial en otro país? ¿Cómo es?...

Practice more at **vistas.vhlcentral.com.**

6.2 Indirect object pronouns

Tutorial

ANTE TODO In **Lección 5**, you learned that a direct object receives the action of the verb directly. In contrast, an indirect object receives the action of the verb indirectly.

SUBJECT	I.O. PRONOUN	VERB	DIRECT OBJECT	INDIRECT OBJECT
Roberto	**le**	presta	cien pesos	**a Luisa**.
Roberto		*lends*	*100 pesos*	*to Luisa.*

An indirect object is a noun or pronoun that answers the question *to whom* or *for whom* an action is done. In the preceding example, the indirect object answers this question: **¿A quién le presta Roberto cien pesos?** *To whom does Roberto lend 100 pesos?*

Indirect object pronouns

Singular forms		Plural forms	
me	(to, for) *me*	**nos**	(to, for) *us*
te	(to, for) *you* (fam.)	**os**	(to, for) *you* (fam.)
le	(to, for) *you* (form.) (to, for) *him; her*	**les**	(to, for) *you* (form.) (to, for) *them*

- **¡Atención!** The forms of indirect object pronouns for the first and second persons (**me**, **te**, **nos**, **os**) are the same as the direct object pronouns. Indirect object pronouns agree in number with the corresponding nouns, but not in gender.

Using indirect object pronouns

- Spanish speakers commonly use both an indirect object pronoun and the noun to which it refers in the same sentence. This is done to emphasize and clarify to whom the pronoun refers.

I.O. PRONOUN	INDIRECT OBJECT	I.O. PRONOUN	INDIRECT OBJECT
Ella **le** vende la ropa **a Elena**.		**Les** prestamos el dinero **a Inés y a Álex**.	

- Indirect object pronouns are also used without the indirect object noun when the person for whom the action is being done is known.

Ana **le** presta la falda **a Elena**.
Ana lends her skirt to Elena.

También **le** presta unos jeans.
She also lends her a pair of jeans.

CONSULTA

For more information on accents, see **Lección 4, Pronunciación**, p. 123, **Lección 10, Ortografía**, p. 339, and **Lección 11, Ortografía**, p. 375.

- Indirect object pronouns are usually placed before the conjugated form of the verb. In negative sentences the pronoun is placed between **no** and the conjugated verb.

Martín **me** compra un regalo.
Martín is buying me a gift.

Eva **no me** escribe cartas.
Eva doesn't write me letters.

- When a conjugated verb is followed by an infinitive or the present progressive, the indirect object pronoun may be placed before the conjugated verb or attached to the infinitive or present participle. **¡Atención!** When an indirect object pronoun is attached to a present participle, an accent mark is added to maintain the proper stress.

Él no quiere **pagarte**./
Él no **te** quiere pagar.
He does not want to pay you.

Él está **escribiéndole** una postal a ella./
Él **le** está escribiendo una postal a ella.
He is writing a postcard to her.

- Because the indirect object pronouns **le** and **les** have multiple meanings, Spanish speakers often clarify to whom the pronouns refer with the preposition **a** + [*pronoun*] or **a** + [*noun*].

UNCLARIFIED STATEMENTS	CLARIFIED STATEMENTS
Yo **le** compro un abrigo.	Yo **le** compro un abrigo **a usted/él/ella**.
Ella **le** describe un libro.	Ella **le** describe un libro **a Juan**.

UNCLARIFIED STATEMENTS	CLARIFIED STATEMENTS
Él **les** vende unos sombreros.	Él **les** vende unos sombreros **a ustedes/ellos/ellas**.
Ellos **les** hablan muy claro.	Ellos **les** hablan muy claro **a los clientes**.

- The irregular verbs **dar** (*to give*) and **decir** (*to say; to tell*) are often used with indirect object pronouns.

The verbs dar and decir

	Singular forms			Plural forms	
	dar	**decir**		**dar**	**decir**
yo	**doy**	**digo**	nosotros/as	**damos**	**decimos**
tú	**das**	**dices**	vosotros/as	**dais**	**decís**
Ud./él/ella	**da**	**dice**	Uds./ellos/ellas	**dan**	**dicen**

Me dan una fiesta cada año.
They give (throw) me a party every year.

Te digo la verdad.
I'm telling you the truth.

Voy a **darle** consejos.
I'm going to give her advice.

No **les digo** mentiras a mis padres.
I don't tell lies to my parents.

recursos

WB pp. 62–63

LM p. 34

vistas.vhlcentral.com Lección 6

¡INTÉNTALO! Use the cues in parentheses to provide the correct indirect object pronoun for each sentence.

1. Juan __le__ quiere dar un regalo. (*to Elena*)
2. María ______ prepara un café. (*for us*)
3. Beatriz y Felipe ______ escriben desde (*from*) Cuba. (*to me*)
4. Marta y yo ______ compramos unos guantes. (*for them*)
5. Los vendedores ______ venden ropa. (*to you, fam. sing.*)
6. La dependienta ______ muestra los guantes. (*to us*)

Práctica

1 **Completar** Fill in the blanks with the correct pronouns to complete Mónica's description of her family's holiday shopping.

1. Juan y yo ________ damos una blusa a nuestra hermana Gisela.
2. Mi tía ________ da a nosotros una mesa para la casa.
3. Gisela ________ da dos corbatas a su novio.
4. A mi mamá yo ________ doy un par de guantes negros.
5. A mi profesora ________ doy dos libros de José Martí.
6. Juan ________ da un regalo a mis padres.
7. Mis padres ________ dan un traje nuevo a mí.
8. Y a ti, yo ________ doy un regalo también. ¿Quieres verlo?

NOTA CULTURAL

Cuban writer and patriot **José Martí** (1853–1895) was born in **La Habana Vieja**, the old colonial center of Havana. Founded by Spanish explorers in the early 1500s, Havana, along with San Juan, Puerto Rico, served as a major stopping point for Spaniards traveling to Mexico and South America.

2 **En La Habana** Describe what happens on Pascual's trip to Cuba based on the cues provided.

1. ellos / cantar / canción / (mí)

2. él / comprar / libros / (sus hijos) / Plaza de Armas

3. yo / preparar el almuerzo (*lunch*) / (ti)

4. él / explicar cómo llegar / (conductor)

5. mi novia / sacar / foto / (nosotros)

6. el guía (*guide*) / mostrar / catedral de San Cristóbal / (ustedes)

NOTA CULTURAL

La Habana Vieja, Cuba, is the site of another well-known outdoor market. Located in the **Plaza de la Catedral**, it is a place where Cuban painters, artists, and sculptors sell their work, and other vendors offer handmade crafts and clothing.

3 **Combinar** Use an item from each column and an indirect object pronoun to create logical sentences.

modelo

Mis padres les dan regalos a mis primos.

A	B	C	D
yo	comprar	mensajes electrónicos	mí
el dependiente	dar	corbata	ustedes
el profesor Arce	decir	dinero en efectivo	clienta
la vendedora	escribir	tarea	novia
mis padres	explicar	problemas	primos
tú	pagar	regalos	ti
nosotros/as	prestar	ropa	nosotros
¿?	vender	¿?	¿?

Practice more at **vistas.vhlcentral.com.**

Comunicación

4

Entrevista In pairs, take turns asking and answering for whom you do these activities. Use the model as a guide.

cantar canciones de amor (*love songs*)	escribir mensajes electrónicos
comprar ropa	mostrar fotos de un viaje
dar una fiesta	pedir dinero
decir mentiras	preparar comida (*food*) mexicana

modelo

escribir mensajes electrónicos
Estudiante 1: *¿A quién le escribes mensajes electrónicos?*
Estudiante 2: *Le escribo mensajes electrónicos a mi hermano.*

5

¡Somos ricos! You and your classmates chipped in on a lottery ticket and you won! Now you want to spend money on your loved ones. In groups of three, discuss what each person is buying for family and friends.

modelo

Estudiante 1: *Quiero comprarle un vestido de Carolina Herrera a mi madre.*
Estudiante 2: *Y yo voy a darles un automóvil nuevo a mis padres.*
Estudiante 3: *Voy a comprarles una casa a mis padres, pero a mis amigos no les voy a dar nada.*

6

Entrevista Use these questions to interview a classmate.

1. ¿Qué tiendas, almacenes o centros comerciales prefieres?
2. ¿A quién le compras regalos cuando hay rebajas?
3. ¿A quién le prestas dinero cuando lo necesita?
4. Quiero ir de compras. ¿Cuánto dinero me puedes prestar?
5. ¿Te dan tus padres su tarjeta de crédito cuando vas de compras?

Síntesis

7

Minidrama In groups of three, take turns playing the roles of two shoppers and a clerk in a clothing store. The shoppers should talk about the articles of clothing they are looking for and for whom they are buying the clothes. The clerk should recommend several items based on the shoppers' descriptions. Use these expressions and also look at **Expresiones útiles** on page 195.

Me queda grande/pequeño. *It's big/small on me.*	**¿Está en rebaja?** *Is it on sale?*
¿Tiene otro color? *Do you have another color?*	**También estoy buscando...** *I'm also looking for...*

ite tense of regular verbs

Tutorial

In order to talk about events in the past, Spanish uses two simple tenses: the preterite and the imperfect. In this lesson, you will learn how to form the preterite tense, which is used to express actions or states completed in the past.

Preterite of regular -ar, -er, and -ir verbs

		-ar verbs **comprar**	-er verbs **vender**	-ir verbs **escribir**
SINGULAR FORMS	yo	compr**é** *I bought*	vend**í** *I sold*	escrib**í** *I wrote*
	tú	compr**aste**	vend**iste**	escrib**iste**
	Ud./él/ella	compr**ó**	vend**ió**	escrib**ió**
PLURAL FORMS	nosotros/as	compr**amos**	vend**imos**	escrib**imos**
	vosotros/as	compr**asteis**	vend**isteis**	escrib**isteis**
	Uds./ellos/ellas	compr**aron**	vend**ieron**	escrib**ieron**

- **¡Atención!** The **yo** and **Ud./él/ella** forms of all three conjugations have written accents on the last syllable to show that it is stressed.
- As the chart shows, the endings for regular **-er** and **-ir** verbs are identical in the preterite.

- Note that the **nosotros/as** forms of regular **-ar** and **-ir** verbs in the preterite are identical to the present tense forms. Context will help you determine which tense is being used.

En invierno **compramos** ropa.	Anoche **compramos** unos zapatos.
In the winter, we buy clothing.	*Last night we bought some shoes.*

- **-Ar** and **-er** verbs that have a stem change in the present tense are regular in the preterite. They do *not* have a stem change.

	PRESENT	PRETERITE
cerrar (e:ie)	La tienda **cierra** a las seis.	La tienda **cerró** a las seis.
volver (o:ue)	Carlitos **vuelve** tarde.	Carlitos **volvió** tarde.
jugar (u:ue)	Él **juega** al fútbol.	Él **jugó** al fútbol.

- **¡Atención! -Ir** verbs that have a stem change in the present tense also have a stem change in the preterite.

CONSULTA

There are a few high-frequency irregular verbs in the preterite. You will learn more about them in **Estructura 9.1**, p. 310.

CONSULTA

You will learn about stem-changing verbs in **Estructura 8.1**, p. 274.

- Verbs that end in **-car**, **-gar**, and **-zar** have a spelling change in the first person singular (**yo** form) in the preterite.

bus**car**	bus**c-**	**qu-**	yo bus**qu**é
lle**gar**	lle**g-**	**gu-**	yo lle**gu**é
empe**zar**	empe**z-**	**c-**	yo empe**c**é

- Except for the **yo** form, all other forms of **-car**, **-gar**, and **-zar** verbs are regular in the preterite.

- Three other verbs—**creer**, **leer**, and **oír**—have spelling changes in the preterite. The **i** of the verb endings of **creer**, **leer**, and **oír** carries an accent in the **yo**, **tú**, **nosotros/as**, and **vosotros/as** forms, and changes to **y** in the **Ud./él/ella** and **Uds./ellos/ellas** forms.

creer	cre-	cre**í**, cre**í**ste, cre**y**ó, cre**í**mos, cre**í**steis, cre**y**eron
leer	le-	le**í**, le**í**ste, le**y**ó, le**í**mos, le**í**steis, le**y**eron
oír	o-	o**í**, o**í**ste, o**y**ó, o**í**mos, o**í**steis, o**y**eron

- **Ver** is regular in the preterite, but none of its forms has an accent.

ver → vi, viste, vio, vimos, visteis, vieron

Words commonly used with the preterite

anoche	*last night*	**pasado/a (*adj.*)**	*last; past*
anteayer	*the day before yesterday*	**el año pasado**	*last year*
		la semana pasada	*last week*
ayer	*yesterday*	**una vez**	*once; one time*
de repente	*suddenly*	**dos veces**	*twice; two times*
desde... hasta...	*from... until...*	**ya**	*already*

Ayer llegué a Santiago de Cuba.
Yesterday I arrived in Santiago de Cuba.

Anoche oí un ruido extraño.
Last night I heard a strange noise.

- **Acabar de** + [*infinitive*] is used to say that something has just occurred. Note that **acabar** is in the present tense in this construction.

Acabo de comprar una falda.
I just bought a skirt.

Acabas de ir de compras.
You just went shopping.

recursos
WB pp. 65–66
LM p. 35
vistas.vhlcentral.com Lección 6

¡INTÉNTALO! Provide the appropriate preterite forms of the verbs.

	comer	salir	comenzar	leer
1. ellas	comieron	salieron	comenzaron	leyeron
2. tú	______	______	______	______
3. usted	______	______	______	______
4. nosotros	______	______	______	______
5. yo	______	______	______	______

Práctica

1

Completar Andrea is talking about what happened last weekend. Complete each sentence by choosing the correct verb and putting it in the preterite.

1. El viernes a las cuatro de la tarde, la profesora Mora __________ (asistir, costar, usar) a una reunión (*meeting*) de profesores.
2. A la una, yo __________ (llegar, bucear, llevar) a la tienda con mis amigos.
3. Mis amigos y yo __________ (comprar, regatear, gastar) dos o tres cosas.
4. Yo __________ (costar, comprar, escribir) unos pantalones negros y mi amigo Mateo __________ (gastar, pasear, comprar) una camisa azul.
5. Después, nosotros __________ (llevar, vivir, comer) cerca de un mercado.
6. A las tres, Pepe __________ (hablar, pasear, nadar) con su novia por teléfono.
7. El sábado por la tarde, mi mamá __________ (escribir, beber, vivir) una carta.
8. El domingo mi tía __________ (decidir, salir, escribir) comprarme un traje.
9. A las cuatro de la tarde, mi tía __________ (beber, salir, encontrar) el traje y después nosotras __________ (acabar, ver, salir) una película.

2

Preguntas Imagine that you have a pesky friend who keeps asking you questions. Respond that you already did or have just done what he/she asks. Make sure you and your partner take turns playing the role of the pesky friend and responding to his/her questions.

modelo

leer la lección
Estudiante 1: *¿Leíste la lección?*
Estudiante 2: *Sí, ya la leí./Sí, acabo de leerla.*

1. escribir el mensaje electrónico
2. lavar (*to wash*) la ropa
3. oír las noticias (*news*)
4. comprar pantalones cortos
5. practicar los verbos
6. pagar la cuenta (*bill*)
7. empezar la composición
8. ver la película *Diarios de motocicleta*

NOTA CULTURAL

Based on Ernesto "Che" Guevara's diaries, ***Diarios de motocicleta*** (2004) traces the road trip of Che (played by Gael García Bernal) with his friend Alberto Granado (played by Rodrigo de la Serna) through Argentina, Chile, Peru, Colombia, and Venezuela.

3

¿Cuándo? Use the time expressions from the word bank to talk about when you and others did the activities listed.

anoche	anteayer	el mes pasado	una vez
ayer	la semana pasada	el año pasado	dos veces

1. mi compañero/a de cuarto: llegar tarde a clase
2. mi mejor (*best*) amigo/a: salir con un(a) chico/a guapo/a
3. mis padres: ver una película
4. yo: llevar un traje/vestido
5. el presidente/primer ministro de mi país: asistir a una conferencia internacional
6. mis amigos y yo: comer en un restaurante
7. ¿?: comprar algo (*something*) bueno, bonito y barato

Practice more at **vistas.vhlcentral.com.**

Comunicación

4 **Ayer** Jot down at what time you did these activities yesterday. Then get together with a classmate and find out at what time he or she did these activities. Be prepared to share your findings with the class.

1. desayunar
2. empezar la primera clase
3. almorzar
4. ver a un(a) amigo/a
5. salir de clase
6. volver a la residencia/casa

5 **Las vacaciones** Imagine that you took these photos on a vacation with friends. Get together with a partner and use the pictures to tell him or her about your trip.

6 **El fin de semana** Your instructor will give you and your partner different incomplete charts about what four employees at **Almacén Gigante** did last weekend. After you fill out the chart based on each other's information, you will fill out the final column about your partner.

Síntesis

7 **Conversación** Get together with a partner and have a conversation about what you did last week using verbs from the word bank. Don't forget to include school activities, shopping, and pastimes.

acampar	comer	gastar	tomar
asistir	comprar	hablar	trabajar
bailar	correr	jugar	vender
beber	escribir	leer	ver
buscar	estudiar	oír	viajar

6.4 Demonstrative adjectives and pronouns

Demonstrative adjectives

Tutorial

ANTE TODO In Spanish, as in English, demonstrative adjectives are words that "demonstrate" or "point out" nouns. Demonstrative adjectives precede the nouns they modify and, like other Spanish adjectives you have studied, agree with them in gender and number. Observe these examples and then study the chart below.

esta camisa	**ese** vendedor	**aquellos** zapatos
this shirt	*that salesman*	*those shoes (over there)*

Demonstrative adjectives

Singular		Plural		
MASCULINE	FEMININE	MASCULINE	FEMININE	
este	**esta**	**estos**	**estas**	*this; these*
ese	**esa**	**esos**	**esas**	*that; those*
aquel	**aquella**	**aquellos**	**aquellas**	*that; those (over there)*

- There are three sets of demonstrative adjectives. To determine which one to use, you must establish the relationship between the speaker and the noun(s) being pointed out.
- The demonstrative adjectives **este**, **esta**, **estos**, and **estas** are used to point out nouns that are close to the speaker and the listener.

- The demonstrative adjectives **ese**, **esa**, **esos**, and **esas** are used to point out nouns that are not close in space and time to the speaker. They may, however, be close to the listener.

- The demonstrative adjectives **aquel**, **aquella**, **aquellos**, and **aquellas** are used to point out nouns that are far away from the speaker and the listener.

Demonstrative pronouns

- Demonstrative pronouns are identical to their corresponding demonstrative adjectives, with the exception that they traditionally carry an accent mark on the stressed vowel. The **Real Academia** now requires this accent only for clarification but it is still commonly used.

Demonstrative pronouns

Singular		Plural	
MASCULINE	FEMININE	MASCULINE	FEMININE
éste	**ésta**	**éstos**	**éstas**
ése	**ésa**	**ésos**	**ésas**
aquél	**aquélla**	**aquéllos**	**aquéllas**

—¿Quieres comprar **este suéter**?
Do you want to buy this sweater?

—No, no quiero **éste**. Quiero **ése**.
No, I don't want this one. I want that one.

—¿Vas a leer **estas revistas**?
Are you going to read these magazines?

—Sí, voy a leer **éstas**. También voy a leer **aquéllas**.
Yes, I'm going to read these. I'll also read those (over there).

- **¡Atención!** Like demonstrative adjectives, demonstrative pronouns agree in gender and number with the corresponding noun.

Este libro es de Pablito. **Éstos** son de Juana.

- There are three neuter demonstrative pronouns: **esto**, **eso**, and **aquello**. These forms refer to unidentified or unspecified nouns, situations, ideas, and concepts. They do not change in gender or number and never carry an accent mark.

—¿Qué es **esto**?
What's this?

—**Eso** es interesante.
That's interesting.

—**Aquello** es bonito.
That's pretty.

recursos
WB pp. 67–68
LM p. 36
vistas.vhlcentral.com Lección 6

¡INTÉNTALO! Provide the correct form of the demonstrative adjective for these nouns.

1. la falda / este ___esta falda___
2. los estudiantes / este ______
3. los países / aquel ______
4. la ventana / ese ______
5. los periodistas / ese ______
6. el chico / aquel ______
7. las sandalias / este ______
8. las chicas / aquel ______

Práctica

1 **Cambiar** Make the singular sentences plural and the plural sentences singular.

modelo
Estas camisas son blancas.
Esta camisa es blanca.

1. Aquellos sombreros son muy elegantes.
2. Ese abrigo es muy caro.
3. Estos cinturones son hermosos.
4. Esos precios son muy buenos.
5. Estas faldas son muy cortas.
6. ¿Quieres ir a aquel almacén?
7. Esas blusas son baratas.
8. Esta corbata hace juego con mi traje.

2 **Completar** Here are some things people might say while shopping. Complete the sentences with the correct demonstrative pronouns.

1. No me gustan esos zapatos. Voy a comprar ________. (*these*)
2. ¿Vas a comprar ese traje o ________? (*this one*)
3. Esta guayabera es bonita, pero prefiero ________. (*that one*)
4. Estas corbatas rojas son muy bonitas, pero ________ son fabulosas. (*those*)
5. Estos cinturones cuestan demasiado. Prefiero ________. (*those over there*)
6. ¿Te gustan esas botas o ________? (*these*)
7. Esa bolsa roja es bonita, pero prefiero ________. (*that one over there*)
8. No voy a comprar estas botas; voy a comprar ________. (*those over there*)
9. ¿Prefieres estos pantalones o ________? (*those*)
10. Me gusta este vestido, pero voy a comprar ________. (*that one*)
11. Me gusta ese almacén, pero ________ es mejor (*better*). (*that one over there*)
12. Esa blusa es bonita, pero cuesta demasiado. Voy a comprar ________. (*this one*)

3 **Describir** With your partner, look for two items in the classroom that are one of these colors: **amarillo, azul, blanco, marrón, negro, verde, rojo.** Take turns pointing them out to each other, first using demonstrative adjectives, and then demonstrative pronouns.

modelo
azul
Estudiante 1: *Esta silla es azul. Aquella mochila es azul.*
Estudiante 2: *Ésta es azul. Aquélla es azul.*

Now use demonstrative adjectives and pronouns to discuss the colors of your classmates' clothing. One of you can ask a question about an article of clothing, using the wrong color. Your partner will correct you and point out that color somewhere else in the room.

modelo
Estudiante 1: *¿Esa camisa es negra?*
Estudiante 2: *No, ésa es azul. Aquélla es negra.*

Practice more at **vistas.vhlcentral.com.**

Comunicación

4

Conversación With a classmate, use demonstrative adjectives and pronouns to ask each other questions about the people around you. Use expressions from the word bank and/or your own ideas.

¿A qué hora...?	¿Cuántos años tiene(n)...?
¿Cómo es/son...?	¿De dónde es/son...?
¿Cómo se llama...?	¿De quién es/son...?
¿Cuándo...?	¿Qué clases toma(n)...?

modelo

Estudiante 1: *¿Cómo se llama esa chica?*
Estudiante 2: *Se llama Rebeca.*
Estudiante 1: *¿A qué hora llegó aquel chico a la clase?*
Estudiante 2: *A las nueve.*

5

En una tienda Imagine that you and a classmate are in Madrid shopping at Zara. Study the floor plan, then have a conversation about your surroundings. Use demonstrative adjectives and pronouns.

NOTA CULTURAL

Zara is an international clothing company based in Spain. Its innovative processes take a product from the design room to the manufacturing shelves in less than a month. This means that the merchandise is constantly changing to keep up with the most current trends.

modelo

Estudiante 1: *Me gusta este suéter azul.*
Estudiante 2: *Yo prefiero aquella chaqueta.*

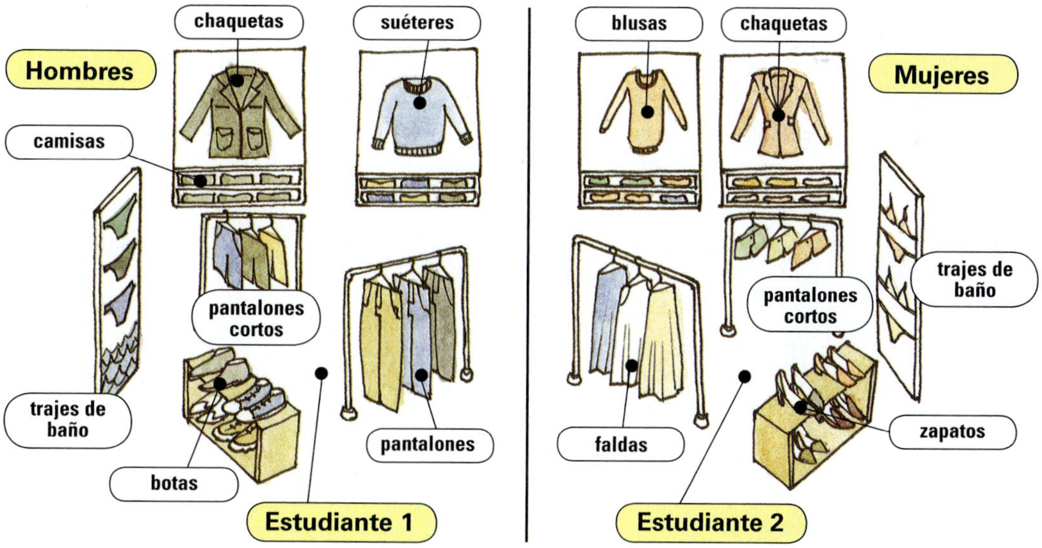

Síntesis

6

Diferencias Your instructor will give you and a partner each a drawing of a store. They are almost identical, but not quite. Use demonstrative adjectives and pronouns to find seven differences.

modelo

Estudiante 1: *Aquellas gafas de sol son feas, ¿verdad?*
Estudiante 2: *No. Aquellas gafas de sol son hermosas.*

Recapitulación

Concepts Diagnostics

Review the grammar concepts you have learned in this lesson by completing these activities.

1 **Completar** Complete the chart with the correct preterite or infinitive form of the verbs. 15 pts.

Infinitive	yo	ella	ellos
			tomaron
		abrió	
comprender			
	leí		
pagar			

2 **En la tienda** Look at the drawing and complete the conversation with demonstrative adjectives and pronouns. 7 pts.

CLIENTE Buenos días, señorita. Deseo comprar (1) __________ corbata.

VENDEDORA Muy bien, señor. ¿No le interesa mirar (2) __________ trajes que están allá? Hay unos que hacen juego con la corbata.

CLIENTE (3) __________ de allá son de lana, ¿no? Prefiero ver (4) __________ traje marrón que está detrás de usted.

VENDEDORA Estupendo. Como puede ver, es de seda. Cuesta seiscientos cincuenta dólares.

CLIENTE Ah... eh... no, creo que sólo voy a comprar la corbata, gracias.

VENDEDORA Bueno... si busca algo más económico, hay rebaja en (5) __________ sombreros. Cuestan sólo treinta dólares.

CLIENTE ¡Magnífico! Me gusta (6) __________, el blanco que está hasta arriba (*at the top*). Y quiero pagar todo con (7) __________ tarjeta.

VENDEDORA Sí, señor. Ahora mismo le traigo el sombrero.

RESUMEN GRAMATICAL

6.1 Saber and conocer *p. 200*

saber	conocer
sé	conozco
sabes	conoces
sabe	conoce
sabemos	conocemos
sabéis	conocéis
saben	conocen

- **saber** = to know facts/how to do something
- **conocer** = to know a person, place, or thing

6.2 Indirect object pronouns *pp. 202–203*

Indirect object pronouns

Singular	Plural
me	nos
te	os
le	les

- **dar** = doy, das, da, damos, dais, dan
- **decir (e:i)** = digo, dices, dice, decimos, decís, dicen

6.3 Preterite tense of regular verbs *pp. 206–207*

comprar	vender	escribir
compré	vendí	escribí
compraste	vendiste	escribiste
compró	vendió	escribió
compramos	vendimos	escribimos
comprasteis	vendisteis	escribisteis
compraron	vendieron	escribieron

Verbs with spelling changes in the preterite

- **-car:** buscar → yo busqué
- **-gar:** llegar → yo llegué
- **-zar:** empezar → yo empecé
- **creer:** creí, creíste, creyó, creímos, creísteis, creyeron
- **leer:** leí, leíste, leyó, leímos, leísteis, leyeron
- **oír:** oí, oíste, oyó, oímos, oísteis, oyeron
- **ver:** vi, viste, vio, vimos, visteis, vieron

6.4 Demonstrative adjectives and pronouns pp. 210–211

Demonstrative adjectives

Singular		Plural	
Masc.	Fem.	Masc.	Fem.
este	esta	estos	estas
ese	esa	esos	esas
aquel	aquella	aquellos	aquellas

Demonstrative pronouns

Singular		Plural	
Masc.	Fem.	Masc.	Fem.
éste	ésta	éstos	éstas
ése	ésa	ésos	ésas
aquél	aquélla	aquéllos	aquéllas

3 **¿Saber o conocer?** Complete each dialogue with the correct form of **saber** or **conocer**. 10 pts.

1. —¿Qué ________ hacer tú?
   —(Yo) ________ jugar al fútbol.
2. —¿________ tú esta tienda de ropa?
   —No, (yo) no la ________. ¿Es buena?
3. —¿Tus padres no ________ a tu novio?
   —No, ¡ellos no ________ que tengo novio!
4. —Mi compañero de cuarto todavía no me ________ bien.
   —Y tú, ¿lo quieres ________ a él?
5. —¿________ ustedes dónde está el mercado?
   —No, nosotros no ________ bien esta ciudad.

4 **Oraciones** Form complete sentences using the information provided. Use indirect object pronouns and the present tense of the verbs. 10 pts.

1. Javier / prestar / el abrigo / a Maripili
   ____
2. nosotros / vender / ropa / a los clientes
   ____
3. el vendedor / traer / las camisetas / a mis amigos y a mí
   ____
4. yo / querer dar / consejos / a ti
   ____
5. ¿tú / ir a comprar / un regalo / a mí?
   ____

5 **Mi última compra** Write a short paragraph describing the last time you went shopping. Use at least four verbs in the preterite tense. 8 pts.

modelo
El viernes pasado, busqué unos zapatos en el centro comercial...

6 **Poema** Write the missing words to complete the excerpt from the poem *Romance sonámbulo* by Federico García Lorca. 2 EXTRA points!

“Verde que ______ quiero verde.
Verde viento. Verdes ramas°.
El barco sobre la mar
y el caballo en la montaña, [...]
Verde que te quiero ______ (*green*).”

ramas *branches*

Practice more at **vistas.vhlcentral.com.**

Audio: Reading
Additional Reading

Lectura

Antes de leer

Estrategia
Skimming

Skimming involves quickly reading through a document to absorb its general meaning. This allows you to understand the main ideas without having to read word for word. When you skim a text, you might want to look at its title and subtitles. You might also want to read the first sentence of each paragraph.

Examinar el texto

Look at the format of the reading selection. How is it organized? What does the organization of the document tell you about its content?

Buscar cognados

Scan the reading selection to locate at least five cognates. Based on the cognates, what do you think the reading selection is about?

1. ____________ 4. ____________
2. ____________ 5. ____________
3. ____________

The reading selection is about ____________.

Impresiones generales

Now skim the reading selection to understand its general meaning. Jot down your impressions. What new information did you learn about the document by skimming it? Based on all the information you now have, answer these questions in Spanish.

1. Who created this document?
2. What is its purpose?
3. Who is its intended audience?

Corona

¡Corona tiene las ofertas más locas del verano!

La tienda más elegante de la ciudad con precios increíbles

Carteras
ELEGANCIA
Colores anaranjado, blanco, rosado y amarillo
Ahora: 15.000 pesos
50% de rebaja

Sandalias de playa
GINO
Números del 35 al 38
A sólo 12.000 pesos
50% de descuento

Faldas largas
ROPA BONITA
Algodón. De distintos colores
Talla mediana
Precio especial: 8.000 pesos

Blusas de seda
BAMBÚ
De cuadros y de lunares
Ahora: 21.000 pesos
40% de rebaja

Vestido de algodón
PANAMÁ
Colores blanco, azul y verde
Ahora: 18.000 pesos
30% de rebaja

Accesorios
BELLEZA
Cinturones, gafas de sol, sombreros, medias
Diversos estilos
Todos con un 40% de rebaja

Lunes a sábado de 9 a 21 horas.
Domingo de 10 a 14 horas.

¡Grandes rebajas!

Real° Liquidación°

¡La rebaja está de moda en Corona!

y con la tarjeta de crédito más conveniente del mercado.

Chaquetas
CASINO
Microfibra. Colores negro, café y gris
Tallas: P, M, G, XG
Ahora: 22.500 pesos

Zapatos
COLOR
Italianos y franceses
Números del 40 al 45
A sólo 20.000 pesos

Pantalones
OCÉANO
Colores negro, gris y café
Ahora: 11.500 pesos
30% de rebaja

Ropa interior
ATLÁNTICO
Tallas: P, M, G
Colores blanco, negro y gris
40% de rebaja

Traje inglés
GALES
Modelos originales
Ahora: 105.000 pesos
30% de rebaja

Accesorios
GUAPO
Gafas de sol, corbatas, cinturones, calcetines
Diversos estilos
Todos con un 40% de rebaja

Real *Royal* **Liquidación** *Clearance sale* **caballeros** *gentlemen*

Por la compra de 40.000 pesos, puede llevar un regalo gratis.

- Un hermoso cinturón de señora
- Un par de calcetines
- Una corbata de seda
- Una bolsa para la playa
- Una mochila
- Unas medias

Después de leer

Completar

Complete this paragraph about the reading selection with the correct forms of the words from the word bank.

almacén	hacer juego	tarjeta de crédito
caro	increíble	tienda
dinero	pantalones	verano
falda	rebaja	zapato

En este anuncio de periódico, el ______________ Corona anuncia la liquidación de ______________ con grandes ______________. Con muy poco ______________ usted puede conseguir ropa fina y elegante. Si no tiene dinero en efectivo, puede utilizar su ______________ y pagar luego. Para el caballero con gustos refinados, hay ______________ importados de París y Roma. La señora elegante puede encontrar blusas de seda que ______________ con todo tipo de ______________ o ______________. Los precios de esta liquidación son realmente ______________.

¿Cierto o falso?

Indicate whether each statement is **cierto** or **falso**. Correct the false statements.

1. Hay sandalias de playa.
2. Las corbatas tienen una rebaja del 30%.
3. El almacén Corona tiene un departamento de zapatos.
4. Normalmente las sandalias cuestan 22.000 pesos.
5. Cuando gastas 30.000 pesos en la tienda, llevas un regalo gratis.
6. Tienen carteras amarillas.

Preguntas

In pairs, take turns asking and answering these questions.

1. Imagina que vas a ir a la tienda Corona. ¿Qué departamentos vas a visitar? ¿El departamento de ropa para señoras, el departamento de ropa para caballeros...?
2. ¿Qué vas a buscar en Corona?
3. ¿Hay tiendas similares a la tienda Corona en tu pueblo o ciudad? ¿Cómo se llaman? ¿Tienen muchas gangas?

Escritura

Estrategia

How to report an interview

There are several ways to prepare a written report about an interview. For example, you can transcribe the interview verbatim, you can simply summarize it, or you can summarize it but quote the speakers occasionally. In any event, the report should begin with an interesting title and a brief introduction, which may include the five Ws (*what, where, when, who, why*) and the H (*how*) of the interview. The report should end with an interesting conclusion. Note that when you transcribe dialogue in Spanish, you should pay careful attention to format and punctuation.

Writing dialogue in Spanish

- If you need to transcribe an interview verbatim, you can use speakers' names to indicate a change of speaker.

CARMELA ¿Qué compraste? ¿Encontraste muchas gangas?

ROBERTO Sí, muchas. Compré un suéter, una camisa y dos corbatas. Y tú, ¿qué compraste?

CARMELA Una blusa y una falda muy bonitas. ¿Cuánto costó tu camisa?

ROBERTO Sólo diez dólares. ¿Cuánto costó tu blusa?

CARMELA Veinte dólares.

- You can also use a dash (*raya*) to mark the beginning of each speaker's words.

—¿Qué compraste?
—Un suéter y una camisa muy bonitos. Y tú, ¿encontraste muchas gangas?
—Sí... compré dos blusas, tres camisetas y un par de zapatos.
—¡A ver!

Tema

Escribe un informe

Write a report for the school newspaper about an interview you conducted with a student about his or her shopping habits and clothing preferences. First, brainstorm a list of interview questions. Then conduct the interview using the questions below as a guide, but feel free to ask other questions as they occur to you.

Examples of questions:

- ¿Cuándo vas de compras?
- ¿Adónde vas de compras?
- ¿Con quién vas de compras?
- ¿Qué tiendas, almacenes o centros comerciales prefieres?
- ¿Compras ropa de catálogos o por Internet?
- ¿Prefieres comprar ropa cara o barata? ¿Por qué? ¿Te gusta buscar gangas?
- ¿Qué ropa llevas cuando vas a clase?
- ¿Qué ropa llevas cuando sales a bailar?
- ¿Qué ropa llevas cuando practicas un deporte?
- ¿Cuáles son tus colores favoritos? ¿Compras mucha ropa de esos colores?
- ¿Les das ropa a tu familia o a tus amigos/as?

Escuchar

Audio: Activities

Estrategia

Listening for linguistic cues

You can enhance your listening comprehension by listening for specific linguistic cues. For example, if you listen for the endings of conjugated verbs, or for familiar constructions, such as **acabar de** + [*infinitive*] or **ir a** + [*infinitive*], you can find out whether an event already took place, is taking place now, or will take place in the future. Verb endings also give clues about who is participating in the action.

To practice listening for linguistic cues, you will now listen to four sentences. As you listen, note whether each sentence refers to a past, present, or future action. Also jot down the subject of each sentence.

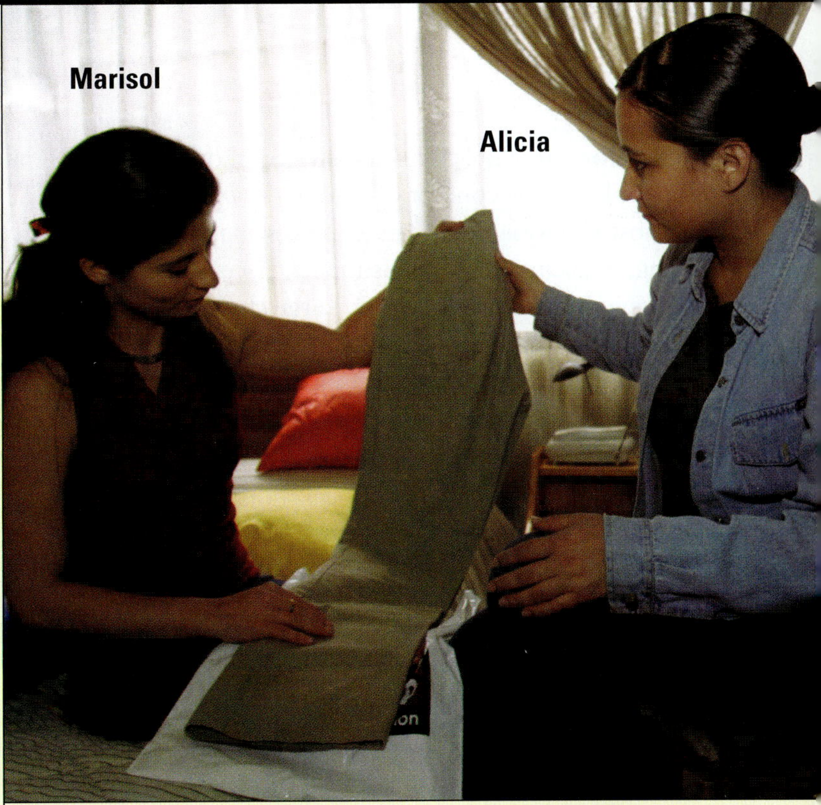

Preparación

Based on the photograph, what do you think Marisol has recently done? What do you think Marisol and Alicia are talking about? What else can you guess about their conversation from the visual clues in the photograph?

Ahora escucha

Now you are going to hear Marisol and Alicia's conversation. Make a list of the clothing items that each person mentions. Then put a check mark after the item if the person actually purchased it.

Marisol	Alicia
1. ________	1. ________
2. ________	2. ________
3. ________	3. ________
4. ________	4. ________

Comprensión

¿Cierto o falso?

Indicate whether each statement is **cierto** or **falso**. Then correct the false statements.

1. Marisol y Alicia acaban de ir de compras juntas (*together*).
2. Marisol va a comprar unos pantalones y una blusa mañana.
3. Marisol compró una blusa de cuadros.
4. Alicia compró unos zapatos nuevos hoy.
5. Alicia y Marisol van a ir al café.
6. Marisol gastó todo el dinero de la semana en ropa nueva.

Preguntas

Discuss the following questions with a classmate. Be sure to explain your answers.

1. ¿Crees que Alicia y Marisol son buenas amigas? ¿Por qué?
2. ¿Cuál de las dos estudiantes es más ahorradora (*frugal*)? ¿Por qué?
3. ¿Crees que a Alicia le gusta la ropa que Marisol compró?
4. ¿Crees que la moda es importante para Alicia? ¿Para Marisol? ¿Por qué?
5. ¿Es importante para ti estar a la moda? ¿Por qué?

En pantalla

Grocery stores in Mexico make one-stop shopping easy! Similar to the concept of a *Super-Walmart* in the U.S., most **supermercados**° in Mexico sell appliances, clothing, medicine, gardening supplies, electronics, and toys in addition to groceries. Large chains, like **Comercial Mexicana**, and smaller grocery stores alike typically sell a variety of products, allowing customers to satisfy all of their routine weekly shopping needs in one trip. Watch the **En pantalla** videoclip to see how one customer takes advantage of one-stop shopping at his local supermarket.

Vocabulario útil

con lo que ahorré	*with what I saved*
corazón	*sweetheart*
de peluche	*stuffed (toy)*
dragón	*dragon*
¿Me lo compras?	*Would you buy it for me?*

Comprensión

Indicate whether each statement is **cierto** or **falso**.

	Cierto	Falso
1. El niño quiere un elefante de peluche.	❍	❍
2. La señora usa un vestido rojo.	❍	❍
3. El niño sigue a la señora hasta la caja.	❍	❍
4. La señora no es la mamá del niño.	❍	❍

Conversar

With a partner, use these cues to create a conversation in Spanish between two friends at a clothing store.

Estudiante 1: Would you buy me a(n)...?
Estudiante 2: No, because it costs...
Estudiante 1: Please! I always (**siempre**) buy you...
Estudiante 2: OK, I will buy you this... How much does it cost?
Estudiante 1: It's on sale! It only costs....

supermercados *supermarkets*

Anuncio de Comercial Mexicana

1 **¿Me lo compras?**

2 **No, corazón.**

3 **¿Me lo compras, me lo compras, me lo compras?**

Video: TV Clip

Practice more at **vistas.vhlcentral.com.**

Flash CULTURA

In the Spanish-speaking world, most city dwellers shop at large supermarkets and little stores that specialize in just one item, such as a butcher shop (**carnicería**), vegetable market (**verdulería**), perfume shop (**perfumería**), or hat shop (**sombrerería**). In small towns where supermarkets are less common, many people rely exclusively on specialty shops. This requires shopping more frequently—often every day or every other day for perishable items—but also means that the foods they consume are fresher and the goods are usually locally produced. Each neighborhood generally has its own shops, so people don't have to walk far to find fresh bread (at a **panadería**) for the midday meal.

Vocabulario útil

colones (pl.)	*currency from Costa Rica*
¿Cuánto vale?	*¿Cuánto cuesta?*
descuento	*discount*
disculpe	*excuse me*
¿Dónde queda...?	*Where is... located?*
los helados	*ice cream*
el regateo	*bargaining*

Preparación

Have you ever been to an open-air market? What did you buy? Have you ever negotiated a price? What did you say?

Comprensión

Select the option that best summarizes this episode.

a. Randy Cruz va al mercado al aire libre para comprar papayas. Luego va al Mercado Central. Él les pregunta a varios clientes qué compran, prueba (*tastes*) platos típicos y busca la heladería.

b. Randy Cruz va al mercado al aire libre para comprar papayas y pedir un descuento. Luego va al Mercado Central para preguntarles a los clientes qué compran en los mercados.

Comprar en los mercados

1 **Trescientos colones.**

2 **... pero me hace un buen descuento.**

3 **¿Qué compran en el Mercado Central?**

Video: *Flash cultura*

Practice more at **vistas.vhlcentral.com.**

recursos	
VM pp. 301–302	vistas.vhlcentral.com Lección 6

Video: *Panorama cultural*
Interactive map

Cuba

El país en cifras

- **Área:** 110.860 km^2 (42.803 $millas^2$), *aproximadamente el área de Pensilvania*
- **Población:** 11.213.000
- **Capital:** La Habana—2.100.000

La Habana Vieja fue declarada° Patrimonio° Cultural de la Humanidad por la UNESCO en 1982. Este distrito es uno de los lugares más fascinantes de Cuba. En La Plaza de Armas, se puede visitar el majestuoso Palacio de Capitanes Generales, que ahora es un museo. En la calle° Obispo, frecuentada por el autor Ernest Hemingway, hay hermosos cafés, clubes nocturnos y tiendas elegantes.

- **Ciudades principales:** Santiago de Cuba; Camagüey; Holguín; Guantánamo

SOURCE: Population Division, UN Secretariat

- **Moneda:** peso cubano
- **Idiomas:** español (oficial)

Bandera de Cuba

Cubanos célebres

- **Carlos Finlay,** doctor y científico (1833–1915)
- **José Martí,** político y poeta (1853–1895)
- **Fidel Castro,** ex primer ministro, ex comandante en jefe° de las fuerzas armadas (1926–)
- **Zoé Valdés,** escritora (1959–)
- **Ibrahim Ferrer,** músico (1927–2005)

fue declarada *was declared* Patrimonio *Heritage* calle *street* comandante en jefe *commander in chief* liviano *light* colibrí abeja *bee hummingbird* ave *bird* mundo *world* miden *measure* pesan *weigh*

Gran Teatro de La Habana

Plaza del Capitolio

Los coco taxis son un medio de transporte cubano muy popular.

La música es parte esencial de la vida en Cuba.

recursos		
WB pp. 69–70	VM pp. 259–260	vistas.vhlcentral.com Lección 6

¡Increíble pero cierto!

Pequeño y liviano°, el colibrí abeja° de Cuba es una de las más de 320 especies de colibrí y es también el ave° más pequeña del mundo°. Menores que muchos insectos, estas aves minúsculas miden° 5 centímetros y pesan° sólo 1,95 gramos.

Baile • **Ballet Nacional de Cuba**

La bailarina Alicia Alonso fundó el Ballet Nacional de Cuba en 1948, después de° convertirse en una estrella° internacional en el Ballet de Nueva York y en Broadway. El Ballet Nacional de Cuba es famoso en todo el mundo por su creatividad y perfección técnica.

Economía • **La caña de azúcar y el tabaco**

La caña de azúcar° es el producto agrícola° que más se cultiva en la isla y su exportación es muy importante para la economía del país. El tabaco, que se usa para fabricar los famosos puros° cubanos, es otro cultivo° de mucha importancia.

Gente • **Población**

La población cubana tiene raíces° muy heterogéneas. La inmigración a la isla fue determinante° desde la colonia hasta mediados° del siglo° XX. Los cubanos de hoy son descendientes de africanos, europeos, chinos y antillanos, entre otros.

Música • **Buena Vista Social Club**

En 1997 nace° el fenómeno musical conocido como *Buena Vista Social Club*. Este proyecto reúne° a un grupo de importantes músicos de Cuba, la mayoría ya mayores, con una larga trayectoria interpretando canciones clásicas del son° cubano. Ese mismo año ganaron un *Grammy*. Hoy en día estos músicos son conocidos en todo el mundo, y personas de todas las edades bailan al ritmo° de su música.

¿Qué aprendiste? Responde a las preguntas con una oración completa.

1. ¿Qué autor está asociado con la Habana Vieja?
2. ¿Por qué es famoso el Ballet Nacional de Cuba?
3. ¿Cuáles son los dos cultivos más importantes para la economía cubana?
4. ¿Qué fabrican los cubanos con la planta del tabaco?
5. ¿De dónde son muchos de los inmigrantes que llegaron a Cuba?
6. ¿En qué año ganó un *Grammy* el disco *Buena Vista Social Club*?

Conexión Internet Investiga estos temas en **vistas.vhlcentral.com.**

Practice more at **vistas.vhlcentral.com.**

1. Busca información sobre un(a) cubano/a célebre. ¿Por qué es célebre? ¿Qué hace? ¿Todavía vive en Cuba?
2. Busca información sobre una de las ciudades principales de Cuba. ¿Qué atracciones hay en esta ciudad?

después de *after* **estrella** *star* **caña de azúcar** *sugar cane* **agrícola** *farming* **puros** *cigars* **cultivo** *crop* **raíces** *roots* **determinante** *deciding* **mediados** *halfway through* **siglo** *century* **nace** *is born* **reúne** *gets together* **son** *Cuban musical genre* **ritmo** *rhythm*

La ropa

el abrigo	*coat*
los (blue)jeans	*jeans*
la blusa	*blouse*
la bolsa	*purse; bag*
la bota	*boot*
los calcetines (el calcetín)	*sock(s)*
la camisa	*shirt*
la camiseta	*t-shirt*
la cartera	*wallet*
la chaqueta	*jacket*
el cinturón	*belt*
la corbata	*tie*
la falda	*skirt*
las gafas (de sol)	*(sun)glasses*
los guantes	*gloves*
el impermeable	*raincoat*
las medias	*pantyhose; stockings*
los pantalones	*pants*
los pantalones cortos	*shorts*
la ropa	*clothing; clothes*
la ropa interior	*underwear*
las sandalias	*sandals*
el sombrero	*hat*
el suéter	*sweater*
el traje	*suit*
el traje de baño	*bathing suit*
el vestido	*dress*
los zapatos de tenis	*sneakers*

Verbos

conducir	*to drive*
conocer	*to know; to be acquainted with*
ofrecer	*to offer*
parecer	*to seem*
saber	*to know; to know how*
traducir	*to translate*

Ir de compras

el almacén	*department store*
la caja	*cash register*
el centro comercial	*shopping mall*
el/la cliente/a	*customer*
el/la dependiente/a	*clerk*
el dinero	*money*
(en) efectivo	*cash*
el mercado (al aire libre)	*(open-air) market*
un par (de zapatos)	*a pair (of shoes)*
el precio (fijo)	*(fixed; set) price*
la rebaja	*sale*
el regalo	*gift*
la tarjeta de crédito	*credit card*
la tienda	*shop; store*
el/la vendedor(a)	*salesperson*
costar (o:ue)	*to cost*
gastar	*to spend (money)*
hacer juego (con)	*to match (with)*
llevar	*to wear; to take*
pagar	*to pay*
regatear	*to bargain*
usar	*to wear; to use*
vender	*to sell*

Adjetivos

barato/a	*cheap*
bueno/a	*good*
cada	*each*
caro/a	*expensive*
corto/a	*short (in length)*
elegante	*elegant*
hermoso/a	*beautiful*
largo/a	*long*
loco/a	*crazy*
nuevo/a	*new*
otro/a	*other; another*
pobre	*poor*
rico/a	*rich*

Los colores

el color	*color*
amarillo/a	*yellow*
anaranjado/a	*orange*
azul	*blue*
blanco/a	*white*
gris	*gray*
marrón, café	*brown*
morado/a	*purple*
negro/a	*black*
rojo/a	*red*
rosado/a	*pink*
verde	*green*

Palabras adicionales

acabar de (+ *inf.*)	*to have just done something*
anoche	*last night*
anteayer	*the day before yesterday*
ayer	*yesterday*
de repente	*suddenly*
desde	*from*
dos veces	*twice; two times*
hasta	*until*
pasado/a (*adj.*)	*last; past*
el año pasado	*last year*
la semana pasada	*last week*
prestar	*to lend; to loan*
una vez	*once; one time*
ya	*already*

Indirect object pronouns	*See page 202.*
Demonstrative adjectives and pronouns	*See page 210.*
Expresiones útiles	*See page 195.*

recursos

LM p. 36 | vistas.vhlcentral.com Lección 6

Audio: Vocabulary

La rutina diaria

7

Communicative Goals

You will learn how to:

- **Describe your daily routine**
- **Talk about personal hygiene**
- **Reassure someone**

A PRIMERA VISTA

- **¿Está él en casa o en una tienda?**
- **¿Está contento o enojado?**
- **¿Cómo es él?**
- **¿Qué colores hay en la foto?**

¿Qué pasó?

1

¿Cierto o falso? Indica si lo que dicen estas oraciones es **cierto** o **falso.** Corrige las oraciones falsas.

1. Marissa va a ver una película de Pedro Almodóvar con unas amigas.
2. Jimena se va a encontrar con Elena en dos horas.
3. Felipe se siente muy feo después de afeitarse.
4. Jimena quiere maquillarse.
5. Marissa quiere ir al café para molestar a Juan Carlos.

2

Identificar Identifica quién puede decir estas oraciones. Puedes usar cada nombre más de una vez.

1. No puedo usar el baño porque siempre están aquí, o bañándose o maquillándose. ________________
2. Quiero arreglarme el pelo porque voy al cine esta noche. ________________
3. Hoy voy a ir a la biblioteca. ________________
4. ¡Necesito arreglarme! ________________
5. Te gusta Juan Carlos. ________________
6. ¿Por qué quieres afeitarte cuando estamos en el baño? ________________

MARISSA

FELIPE

JIMENA

3

Ordenar Ordena correctamente los planes que tiene Marissa.

____ a. Voy al café.
____ b. Me arreglo el pelo.
____ c. Molesto a Felipe.
____ d. Me encuentro con unas amigas.
____ e. Entro al baño.
____ f. Voy al cine.

4

En el baño Trabajen en parejas para representar los papeles de dos compañeros/as de cuarto que deben usar el baño al mismo tiempo para hacer su rutina diaria. Usen las instrucciones como guía.

Estudiante 1	Estudiante 2
Di (*Say*) que quieres arreglarte porque vas a ir al cine.	→ Di (*Say*) que necesitas arreglarte porque te vas a encontrar con tus amigos/as.
Pregunta si puedes secarte el pelo.	→ Responde que no porque necesitas lavarte la cara.
Di que puede lavarse la cara, pero que después necesitas secarte el pelo.	→ Di que puede secarse el pelo, pero que después necesitas peinarte.

Practice more at **vistas.vhlcentral.com.**

Pronunciación

Audio: Concepts, Activities
Record & Compare

The consonant r

ropa **r**utina **r**ico **R**amón

In Spanish, **r** has a strong trilled sound at the beginning of a word. No English words have a trill, but English speakers often produce a trill when they imitate the sound of a motor.

gusta**r** du**r**ante p**r**ime**r**o c**r**ema

In any other position, **r** has a weak sound similar to the English *tt* in *better* or the English *dd* in *ladder*. In contrast to English, the tongue touches the roof of the mouth behind the teeth.

piza**rr**a co**rr**o ma**rr**ón abu**rr**ido

The letter combination **rr**, which only appears between vowels, always has a strong trilled sound.

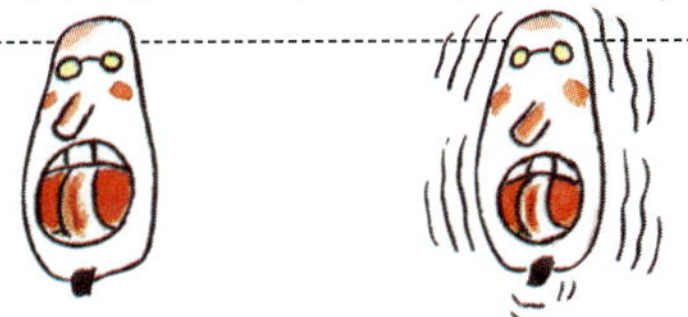

ca**r**o ca**rr**o pe**r**o pe**rr**o

Between vowels, the difference between the strong trilled **rr** and the weak **r** is very important, as a mispronunciation could lead to confusion between two different words.

Práctica Lee las palabras en voz alta, prestando (*paying*) atención a la pronunciación de la **r** y la **rr**.

1. Perú
2. Rosa
3. borrador
4. madre
5. comprar
6. favor
7. rubio
8. reloj
9. Arequipa
10. tarde
11. cerrar
12. despertador

Oraciones Lee las oraciones en voz alta, prestando atención a la pronunciación de la **r** y la **rr**.

1. Ramón Robles Ruiz es programador. Su esposa Rosaura es artista.
2. A Rosaura Robles le encanta regatear en el mercado.
3. Ramón nunca regatea... le aburre regatear.
4. Rosaura siempre compra cosas baratas.
5. Ramón no es rico, pero prefiere comprar cosas muy caras.
6. ¡El martes Ramón compró un carro nuevo!

Refranes Lee en voz alta los refranes, prestando atención a la **r** y a la **rr**.

recursos
LM p. 38
vistas.vhlcentral.com Lección 7

1 A dog's bark is worse than its bite.
2 Rome wasn't built in a day.

EN DETALLE

Additional Reading

La siesta

¿Sientes cansancio° después de comer?

¿Te cuesta° volver al trabajo° o a clase después del almuerzo? Estas sensaciones son normales. A muchas personas les gusta relajarse° después de almorzar. Este momento de descanso es **la siesta**. La siesta es popular en los países hispanos y viene de una antigua costumbre° del área del Mediterráneo. La palabra *siesta* viene del latín, es una forma corta de decir "sexta hora". La sexta hora del día es después del mediodía, el momento de más calor. Debido al° calor y al cansancio, los habitantes de España, Italia, Grecia y Portugal tienen la costumbre de dormir la siesta desde hace° más de° dos mil años. Los españoles y los portugueses llevaron la costumbre a los países americanos.

Aunque hoy día esta costumbre está desapareciendo en las grandes ciudades, la siesta todavía es importante en la cultura hispana. En pueblos pequeños, por ejemplo, muchas oficinas° y tiendas tienen la costumbre de cerrar por dos o tres horas después del mediodía. Los empleados van a su casa, almuerzan con sus familias, duermen la siesta o hacen actividades, como ir al gimnasio, y luego regresan al trabajo entre las 2:30 y las 4:30 de la tarde.

Los estudios científicos explican que una siesta corta después de almorzar ayuda° a trabajar más y mejor° durante la tarde. Pero ¡cuidado! Esta siesta debe durar° sólo entre veinte y cuarenta minutos. Si dormimos más, entramos en la fase de sueño profundo y es difícil despertarse.

Hoy, algunas empresas° de los EE.UU., Canadá, Japón, Inglaterra y Alemania tienen salas° especiales donde los empleados pueden dormir la siesta.

¿Dónde duermen la siesta?

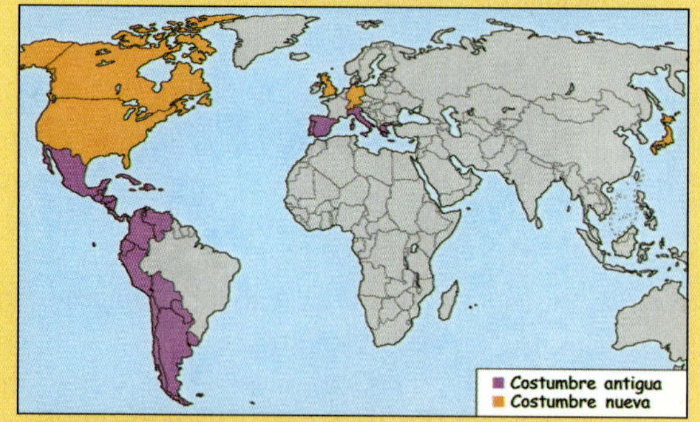

En los lugares donde la siesta es una costumbre antigua, las personas la duermen en su casa. En los países donde la siesta es una costumbre nueva, la gente duerme en sus lugares de trabajo o en centros de siesta.

Sientes cansancio *Do you feel tired* **Te cuesta** *Is it hard for you* **trabajo** *work* **relajarse** *to relax* **antigua costumbre** *old custom* **Debido al** *Because (of)* **desde hace** *for* **más de** *more than* **aunque** *although* **está desapareciendo** *is disappearing* **oficinas** *offices* **ayuda** *helps* **mejor** *better* **durar** *last* **algunas empresas** *some businesses* **salas** *rooms*

ACTIVIDADES

1 **¿Cierto o falso?** Indica si lo que dicen las oraciones es **cierto** o **falso**. Corrige la información falsa.

1. La costumbre de la siesta empezó en Asia.
2. La palabra *siesta* está relacionada con la sexta hora del día.
3. Los españoles y los portugueses llevaron la costumbre de la siesta a Latinoamérica.
4. La siesta ayuda a trabajar más y mejor durante la tarde.
5. Los horarios de trabajo de las grandes ciudades hispanas son los mismos que los pueblos pequeños.
6. Una siesta larga siempre es mejor que una siesta corta.
7. En los Estados Unidos, los empleados de algunas empresas pueden dormir la siesta en el trabajo.
8. Es fácil despertar de un sueño profundo.

ASÍ SE DICE

El cuidado personal

el aseo; el excusado; el servicio; el váter (Esp.)	el baño
el cortaúñas	*nail clippers*
el desodorante	*deodorant*
el enjuague bucal	*mouthwash*
el hilo dental/ la seda dental	*dental floss*
la máquina de afeitar/ de rasurar (Méx.)	*electric razor*

EL MUNDO HISPANO

Costumbres especiales

- **México y El Salvador** Los vendedores pasan por las calles anunciando a gritos° su mercancía°: tanques de gas y flores° en México; pan y tortillas en El Salvador.
- **Costa Rica** Para encontrar las direcciones°, los costarricenses usan referencias a anécdotas, lugares o características geográficas. Por ejemplo: *200 metros norte de la iglesia Católica, frente al°supermercado Mi Mega.*
- **Argentina** En Tigre, una ciudad junto al Río° de la Plata, la gente usa barcos particulares°, barcos colectivos° y barcos-taxi para ir de una isla a otra. Todas las mañanas, un barco colectivo recoge° a los niños y los lleva a la escuela.

gritos *shouts* mercancía *merchandise* flores *flowers* direcciones *addresses* frente al *opposite* río *river* particulares *private* barcos colectivos *collective boats* recoge *picks up*

PERFIL

El mate

El mate es una parte muy importante de la rutina diaria en muchos países. Es una bebida° muy similar al té que se consume en Argentina, Uruguay y Paraguay. Tradicionalmente se bebe caliente° con una *bombilla*° y en un recipiente° que también se llama *mate*. Por ser amarga, algunos le agregan° azúcar para suavizar su sabor°. El mate se puede tomar a cualquier° hora y en cualquier lugar, aunque en Argentina las personas prefieren sentarse en círculo e ir pasando el mate de mano en mano mientras° conversan. Los uruguayos, por otra parte, acostumbran llevar el agua° caliente para el mate en un termo° bajo el brazo° y lo beben mientras caminan. Si ves a una persona con un termo bajo el brazo y un mate en la mano, ¡es casi seguro que es de Uruguay!

bebida *drink* caliente *hot* bombilla *straw (in Argentina)* recipiente *container* amarga *bitter* le agregan *add* suavizar su sabor *soften its flavor* cualquier *any* mientras *while* agua *water* termo *thermos* bajo el brazo *under their arm*

Conexión Internet

¿Qué costumbres son populares en los países hispanos?

Go to **vistas.vhlcentral.com** to find more cultural information related to this **Cultura** section.

ACTIVIDADES

2 **Comprensión** Completa las oraciones.

1. Uso ______________ para limpiar (*to clean*) entre los dientes.
2. En ________ las personas compran pan y tortillas a los vendedores que pasan por la calle.
3. El ________ es una bebida similar al té.
4. Los uruguayos beben mate mientras ________.

3 **¿Qué costumbres tienes?** Escribe cuatro oraciones sobre una costumbre que compartes con tus amigos o con tu familia (por ejemplo: ir al cine, ir a eventos deportivos, leer, comer juntos, etc.). Explica qué haces, cuándo lo haces y con quién.

Practice more at **vistas.vhlcentral.com.**

7.1 Reflexive verbs

Tutorial

ANTE TODO A reflexive verb is used to indicate that the subject does something to or for himself or herself. In other words, it "reflects" the action of the verb back to the subject. Reflexive verbs always use reflexive pronouns.

SUBJECT	REFLEXIVE VERB
Joaquín	**se ducha** por la mañana.

The verb lavarse (*to wash oneself*)

SINGULAR FORMS	yo	**me lavo**	*I wash (myself)*
	tú	**te lavas**	*you wash (yourself)*
	Ud.	**se lava**	*you wash (yourself)*
	él/ella	**se lava**	*he/she washes (himself/herself)*
PLURAL FORMS	nosotros/as	**nos lavamos**	*we wash (ourselves)*
	vosotros/as	**os laváis**	*you wash (yourselves)*
	Uds.	**se lavan**	*you wash (yourselves)*
	ellos/ellas	**se lavan**	*they wash (themselves)*

AYUDA

Except for **se**, reflexive pronouns have the same forms as direct and indirect object pronouns.

•••

Se is used for both singular and plural subjects—there is no individual plural form:

Pablo **se** lava.
Ellos **se** lavan.

- The pronoun **se** attached to an infinitive identifies the verb as reflexive: **lavarse.**
- When a reflexive verb is conjugated, the reflexive pronoun agrees with the subject.

Me afeito. **Te despiertas** a las siete.

- Like object pronouns, reflexive pronouns generally appear before a conjugated verb. With infinitives and present participles, they may be placed before the conjugated verb or attached to the infinitive or present participle.

Ellos **se** van a vestir.
Ellos van a vestir**se**.
They are going to get dressed.

Nos estamos lavando las manos.
Estamos lavándo**nos** las manos.
We are washing our hands.

- **¡Atención!** When a reflexive pronoun is attached to a present participle, an accent mark is added to maintain the original stress.

bañando ⟶ bañ**á**ndo**se** durmiendo ⟶ durmi**é**ndo**se**

AYUDA

You have already learned several adjectives that can be used with **ponerse** when it means *to become*:

alegre, cómodo/a, contento/a, elegante, guapo/a, nervioso/a, rojo/a, and **triste**.

Common reflexive verbs

acordarse (de) (o:ue)	*to remember*
acostarse (o:ue)	*to go to bed*
afeitarse	*to shave*
bañarse	*to bathe; to take a bath*
cepillarse	*to brush*
despedirse (de) (e:i)	*to say goodbye (to)*
despertarse (e:ie)	*to wake up*
dormirse (o:ue)	*to go to sleep; to fall asleep*
ducharse	*to shower; to take a shower*
enojarse (con)	*to get angry (with)*
irse	*to go away; to leave*
lavarse	*to wash (oneself)*
levantarse	*to get up*
llamarse	*to be called; to be named*
maquillarse	*to put on makeup*
peinarse	*to comb one's hair*
ponerse	*to put on*
ponerse (+ ***adj.***)	*to become (+ adj.)*
preocuparse (por)	*to worry (about)*
probarse (o:ue)	*to try on*
quedarse	*to stay; to remain*
quitarse	*to take off*
secarse	*to dry (oneself)*
sentarse (e:ie)	*to sit down*
sentirse (e:ie)	*to feel*
vestirse (e:i)	*to get dressed*

COMPARE & CONTRAST

Unlike English, a number of verbs in Spanish can be reflexive or non-reflexive. If the verb acts upon the subject, the reflexive form is used. If the verb acts upon something other than the subject, the non-reflexive form is used. Compare these sentences.

Lola **lava** los platos.

Lola **se lava** la cara.

As the preceding sentences show, reflexive verbs sometimes have different meanings than their non-reflexive counterparts. For example, **lavar** means *to wash,* while **lavarse** means *to wash oneself, to wash up.*

▶ **¡Atención!** Parts of the body or clothing are generally not referred to with possessives, but with articles.

La niña se quitó **un** zapato.

Necesito cepillarme **los** dientes.

recursos

WB pp. 75–76

LM p. 39

vistas.vhlcentral.com Lección 7

¡INTÉNTALO!

Indica el presente de estos verbos reflexivos.

despertarse

1. Mis hermanos __se despiertan__ tarde.
2. Tú ____________ tarde.
3. Nosotros ____________ tarde.
4. Benito ____________ tarde.
5. Yo ____________ tarde.

ponerse

1. Él __se pone__ una chaqueta.
2. Yo ____________ una chaqueta.
3. Usted ____________ una chaqueta.
4. Nosotras ____________ una chaqueta.
5. Las niñas ____________ una chaqueta.

Práctica

1

Nuestra rutina La familia de Blanca sigue la misma rutina todos los días. Según Blanca, ¿qué hacen ellos?

modelo

mamá / despertarse a las 5:00

Mamá se despierta a las cinco.

1. Roberto y yo / levantarse a las 7:00
2. papá / ducharse primero y / luego afeitarse
3. yo / lavarse la cara y / vestirse antes de tomar café
4. mamá / peinarse y / luego maquillarse
5. todos (nosotros) / sentarse a la mesa para comer
6. Roberto / cepillarse los dientes después de comer
7. yo / ponerse el abrigo antes de salir
8. nosotros / despedirse de mamá

NOTA CULTURAL

Como en los EE.UU., **tomar café** en el desayuno es muy común en los países hispanos.

En muchas familias, incluso los niños toman café con leche (*milk*) en el desayuno antes de ir a la escuela.

El café en los países hispanos generalmente es más fuerte que en los EE.UU., y el descafeinado no es muy popular.

2

La fiesta elegante Selecciona el verbo apropiado y completa las oraciones con la forma correcta.

1. Tú __________ (lavar / lavarse) el auto antes de ir a la fiesta.
2. Nosotros no __________ (acordar / acordarse) de comprar los regalos.
3. Para llegar a tiempo, Raúl y Marta __________ (acostar / acostarse) a los niños antes de salir.
4. Yo __________ (sentir / sentirse) cómoda en mi vestido nuevo.
5. Mis amigos siempre __________ (vestir / vestirse) con ropa muy elegante.
6. Los cocineros __________ (probar / probarse) la comida antes de servirla.
7. Usted __________ (preocupar / preocuparse) mucho por llegar antes que (*before*) los demás invitados, ¿no?
8. En general, __________ (afeitar / afeitarse) yo mismo, pero hoy es un día especial y el barbero (*barber*) me __________ (afeitar / afeitarse). ¡Será una fiesta inolvidable!

¡LENGUA VIVA!

In Spain a car is called **un coche**, while in many parts of Latin America it is known as **un carro**. Although you'll be understood using either of these terms, using **auto (automóvil)** will surely get you where you want to go.

3

Describir Mira los dibujos y describe lo que estas personas hacen.

1. el joven

2. Carmen

3. Juan

4. ellos

5. Estrella

6. Toni

Comunicación

4

Preguntas personales En parejas, túrnense para hacerse estas preguntas.

1. ¿A qué hora te levantas durante la semana?
2. ¿A qué hora te levantas los fines de semana?
3. ¿Prefieres levantarte tarde o temprano? ¿Por qué?
4. ¿Te enojas frecuentemente con tus amigos?
5. ¿Te preocupas fácilmente? ¿Qué te preocupa?
6. ¿Qué te pone contento/a?
7. ¿Qué haces cuando te sientes triste?
8. ¿Y cuando te sientes alegre?
9. ¿Te acuestas tarde o temprano durante la semana?
10. ¿A qué hora te acuestas los fines de semana?

5

Charadas En grupos, jueguen a las charadas. Cada persona debe pensar en dos oraciones con verbos reflexivos. La primera persona que adivina la charada dramatiza la siguiente.

6

Debate En grupos, discutan este tema: ¿Quiénes necesitan más tiempo para arreglarse (*to get ready*) antes de salir, los hombres o las mujeres? Hagan una lista de las razones (*reasons*) que tienen para defender sus ideas e informen a la clase.

7

La coartada Hoy se cometió un crimen entre las 7 y las 11 de la mañana. En parejas, imaginen que uno de ustedes es un sospechoso y el otro un policía investigador. El policía le pregunta al sospechoso qué hace habitualmente a esas horas y el sospechoso responde. Luego, el policía presenta las respuestas del sospechoso ante el jurado (la clase) y entre todos deciden si es culpable o no.

Síntesis

8

La familia ocupada Tú y tu compañero/a asisten a un programa de verano en Lima, Perú. Viven con la familia Ramos. Tu profesor(a) te va a dar la rutina incompleta que la familia sigue en las mañanas. Trabaja con tu compañero/a para completarla.

modelo

Estudiante 1: ¿Qué hace el señor Ramos a las seis y cuarto?
Estudiante 2: El señor Ramos se levanta.

Practice more at **vistas.vhlcentral.com.**

7.2 Indefinite and negative words

Tutorial

ANTE TODO Indefinite words refer to people and things that are not specific, for example, *someone* or *something*. Negative words deny the existence of people and things or contradict statements, for instance, *no one* or *nothing*. Spanish indefinite words have corresponding negative words, which are opposite in meaning.

Indefinite and negative words

Indefinite words		Negative words	
algo	*something; anything*	**nada**	*nothing; not anything*
alguien	*someone; somebody; anyone*	**nadie**	*no one; nobody; not anyone*
alguno/a(s), algún	*some; any*	**ninguno/a, ningún**	*no; none; not any*
o... o	*either... or*	**ni... ni**	*neither... nor*
siempre	*always*	**nunca, jamás**	*never, not ever*
también	*also; too*	**tampoco**	*neither; not either*

- There are two ways to form negative sentences in Spanish. You can place the negative word before the verb, or you can place **no** before the verb and the negative word after.

Nadie se levanta temprano.
No one gets up early.

No se levanta nadie temprano.
No one gets up early.

Ellos **nunca gritan**.
They never shout.

Ellos **no gritan nunca**.
They never shout.

- Because they refer to people, **alguien** and **nadie** are often used with the personal **a**. The personal **a** is also used before **alguno/a, algunos/as,** and **ninguno/a** when these words refer to people and they are the direct object of the verb.

—Perdón, señor, ¿busca usted **a alguien**?
—No, gracias, señorita, no busco **a nadie**.

—Tomás, ¿buscas **a alguno** de tus hermanos?
—No, mamá, no busco **a ninguno**.

- **¡Atención!** Before a masculine, singular noun, **alguno** and **ninguno** are shortened to **algún** and **ningún**.

—¿Tienen ustedes **algún** amigo peruano?

—No, no tenemos **ningún** amigo peruano.

AYUDA

Alguno/a, algunos/as are not always used in the same way English uses *some* or *any*. Often, **algún** is used where *a* would be used in English.

¿Tienes algún libro que hable de los incas?
Do you have ***a*** *book that talks about the Incas?*

Note that **ninguno/a** is rarely used in the plural.

—¿Visitaste algunos museos?
—No, no visité ninguno.

COMPARE & CONTRAST

In English, it is incorrect to use more than one negative word in a sentence. In Spanish, however, sentences frequently contain two or more negative words. Compare these Spanish and English sentences.

Nunca le escribo a **nadie**.
I never write to anyone.

No me preocupo por **nada nunca**.
I do not ever worry about anything.

As the preceding sentences show, once an English sentence contains one negative word (for example, *not* or *never*), no other negative word may be used. Instead, indefinite (or affirmative) words are used. In Spanish, however, once a sentence is negative, no other affirmative (that is, indefinite) word may be used. Instead, all indefinite ideas must be expressed in the negative.

- **Pero** is used to mean *but*. The meaning of **sino** is *but rather* or *on the contrary*. It is used when the first part of the sentence is negative and the second part contradicts it.

Los estudiantes no se acuestan temprano **sino** tarde.
The students don't go to bed early, but rather late.

María no habla francés **sino** español.
María doesn't speak French, but rather Spanish.

Esas gafas son caras, **pero** bonitas.
Those glasses are expensive, but pretty.

José es inteligente, **pero** no saca buenas notas.
José is intelligent but doesn't get good grades.

¡INTÉNTALO!

Cambia las oraciones para que sean negativas.

1. Siempre se viste bien.
   Nunca se viste bien.
   No se viste bien nunca.
2. Alguien se ducha.
   _____ se ducha.
   _____ se ducha _____.
3. Ellas van también.
   Ellas _____ van.
   Ellas _____ van _____.
4. Alguien se pone nervioso.
   _____ se pone nervioso.
   _____ se pone nervioso _____.
5. Tú siempre te lavas las manos.
   Tú _____ te lavas las manos.
   Tú _____ te lavas las manos _____.
6. Voy a traer algo.
   _____ voy a traer _____.
7. Juan se afeita también.
   Juan _____ se afeita.
   Juan _____ se afeita _____.
8. Mis amigos viven en una residencia o en casa.
   Mis amigos _____ viven _____ en una residencia _____ en casa.
9. La profesora hace algo en su escritorio.
   La profesora _____ hace _____ en su escritorio.
10. Tú y yo vamos al mercado.
    _____ tú _____ yo vamos al mercado.
11. Tienen un espejo en su casa.
    _____ tienen _____ espejo en su casa.
12. Algunos niños se ponen sus abrigos.
    _____ niño se pone su abrigo.

recursos
WB pp. 77–78
LM p. 40
vistas.vhlcentral.com Lección 7

Práctica

1

¿Pero o sino? Forma oraciones sobre estas personas usando **pero** o **sino**.

modelo

muchos estudiantes viven en residencias estudiantiles / muchos de ellos quieren vivir fuera del *(off)* campus

Muchos estudiantes viven en residencias estudiantiles, pero muchos de ellos quieren vivir fuera del campus.

1. Marcos nunca se despierta temprano / siempre llega puntual a clase
2. Lisa y Katarina no se acuestan temprano / muy tarde
3. Alfonso es inteligente / algunas veces es antipático
4. los directores de la residencia no son ecuatorianos / peruanos
5. no nos acordamos de comprar champú / compramos jabón
6. Emilia no es estudiante / profesora
7. no quiero levantarme / tengo que ir a clase
8. Miguel no se afeita por la mañana / por la noche

2

Completar Completa esta conversación. Usa expresiones negativas en tus respuestas. Luego, dramatiza la conversación con un(a) compañero/a.

AURELIO Ana María, ¿encontraste algún regalo para Eliana?
ANA MARÍA (1)________________________
AURELIO ¿Viste a alguna amiga en el centro comercial?
ANA MARÍA (2)________________________
AURELIO ¿Me llamó alguien?
ANA MARÍA (3)________________________
AURELIO ¿Quieres ir al teatro o al cine esta noche?
ANA MARÍA (4)________________________
AURELIO ¿No quieres salir a comer?
ANA MARÍA (5)________________________
AURELIO ¿Hay algo interesante en la televisión esta noche?
ANA MARÍA (6)________________________
AURELIO ¿Tienes algún problema?
ANA MARÍA (7)________________________

Practice more at **vistas.vhlcentral.com.**

Comunicación

3

Opiniones Completa estas oraciones de una manera lógica. Luego, compara tus respuestas con las de un(a) compañero/a.

1. Mi habitación es __________, pero __________.
2. Por la noche me gusta __________, pero __________.
3. Un(a) profesor(a) ideal no es __________, sino __________.
4. Mis amigos son __________, pero __________.

4

En el campus En parejas, háganse preguntas sobre qué hay en su universidad: residencias bonitas, departamento de ingeniería, cines, librerías baratas, estudiantes guapos/as, equipo de fútbol, playa, clases fáciles, museo, profesores/as estrictos/as. Sigan el modelo.

modelo

Estudiante 1: *¿Hay algunas residencias bonitas?*
Estudiante 2: *Sí, hay una/algunas. Está(n) detrás del estadio.*
Estudiante 1: *¿Hay algún museo?*
Estudiante 2: *No, no hay ninguno.*

5

Quejas En parejas, hagan una lista de cinco quejas (*complaints*) comunes que tienen los estudiantes. Usen expresiones negativas.

modelo

Nadie me entiende.

Ahora hagan una lista de cinco quejas que los padres tienen de sus hijos.

modelo

Nunca limpian sus habitaciones.

6

Anuncios En parejas, lean el anuncio y contesten las preguntas.

1. ¿Es el anuncio positivo o negativo? ¿Por qué?
2. ¿Qué palabras indefinidas hay?
3. Escriban el texto del anuncio cambiando todo por expresiones negativas.

Ahora preparen su propio (*own*) anuncio usando expresiones afirmativas y negativas.

Síntesis

7

Encuesta Tu profesor(a) te va a dar una hoja de actividades para hacer una encuesta. Circula por la clase y pídeles a tus compañeros que comparen las actividades que hacen durante la semana con las que hacen durante los fines de semana. Escribe las respuestas.

7.3 Preterite of ser and ir

Tutorial

ANTE TODO In **Lección 6**, you learned how to form the preterite tense of regular **-ar**, **-er**, and **-ir** verbs. The following chart contains the preterite forms of **ser** (*to be*) and **ir** (*to go*). Since these forms are irregular, you will need to memorize them.

Preterite of ser and ir

		ser *(to be)*	ir *(to go)*
SINGULAR FORMS	yo	**fui**	**fui**
	tú	**fuiste**	**fuiste**
	Ud./él/ella	**fue**	**fue**
PLURAL FORMS	nosotros/as	**fuimos**	**fuimos**
	vosotros/as	**fuisteis**	**fuisteis**
	Uds./ellos/ellas	**fueron**	**fueron**

AYUDA

Note that, whereas regular **-er** and **-ir** verbs have accent marks in the **yo** and **Ud./él/ella** forms of the preterite, **ser** and **ir** do not.

- Since the preterite forms of **ser** and **ir** are identical, context clarifies which of the two verbs is being used.

Él **fue** a comprar champú y jabón.
He went to buy shampoo and soap.

¿Cómo **fue** la película anoche?
How was the movie last night?

¡INTÉNTALO! Completa las oraciones usando el pretérito de **ser** e **ir**.

ir

1. Los viajeros ___fueron___ a Perú.
2. Patricia ________ a Cuzco.
3. Tú ________ a Iquitos.
4. Gregorio y yo ________ a Lima.
5. Yo ________ a Trujillo.
6. Ustedes ________ a Arequipa.
7. Mi padre ________ a Lima.
8. Nosotras ________ a Cuzco.
9. Él ________ a Machu Picchu.
10. Usted ________ a Nazca.

ser

1. Usted ___fue___ muy amable.
2. Yo ________ muy cordial.
3. Ellos ________ simpáticos.
4. Nosotros ________ muy tontos.
5. Ella ________ antipática.
6. Tú ________ muy generoso.
7. Ustedes ________ cordiales.
8. La gente ________ amable.
9. Tomás y yo ________ muy felices.
10. Los profesores ________ buenos.

recursos

WB p. 79

LM p. 41

vistas.vhlcentral.com Lección 7

Práctica y Comunicación

1

Completar Completa estas conversaciones con la forma correcta del pretérito de **ser** o **ir**. Indica el infinitivo de cada forma verbal.

Conversación 1

		ser	ir
RAÚL	¿Adónde (1)__________ ustedes de vacaciones?	❍	❍
PILAR	(2)__________ a Perú.	❍	❍
RAÚL	¿Cómo (3)__________ el viaje?	❍	❍
▶ PILAR	¡(4)__________ estupendo! Machu Picchu y El Callao son increíbles.	❍	❍
RAÚL	¿(5)__________ caro el viaje?	❍	❍
PILAR	No, el precio (6)__________ muy bajo. Sólo costó tres mil dólares.	❍	❍

Conversación 2

		ser	ir
ISABEL	Tina y Vicente (7)__________ novios, ¿no?	❍	❍
LUCÍA	Sí, pero ahora no. Anoche Tina (8)__________ a comer con Gregorio	❍	❍
	y la semana pasada ellos (9)__________ al partido de fútbol.	❍	❍
ISABEL	¿Ah sí? Javier y yo (10)__________ al partido y no los vimos.	❍	❍

NOTA CULTURAL

La ciudad peruana de **El Callao**, fundada en 1537, fue por muchos años el puerto (*port*) más activo de la costa del Pacífico en Suramérica. En el siglo XVIII, se construyó (*was built*) una fortaleza allí para proteger (*protect*) la ciudad de los ataques de piratas y bucaneros.

2

Descripciones Forma oraciones con estos elementos. Usa el pretérito.

A	B	C	D
yo	(no) ir	a un restaurante	ayer
tú	(no) ser	en autobús	anoche
mi compañero/a		estudiante	anteayer
nosotros		muy simpático/a	la semana pasada
mis amigos		a la playa	el año pasado
ustedes		dependiente/a en una tienda	

3

Preguntas En parejas, túrnense para hacerse estas preguntas.

1. ¿Cuándo fuiste al cine por última vez? ¿Con quién fuiste?
2. ¿Fuiste en auto, en autobús o en metro? ¿Cómo fue el viaje?
3. ¿Cómo fue la película?
4. ¿Fue una película de terror, de acción o un drama?
5. ¿Fue una de las mejores películas que viste? ¿Por qué?
6. ¿Fueron buenos los actores o no? ¿Cuál fue el mejor?
7. ¿Adónde fuiste/fueron después?
8. ¿Fue una buena idea ir al cine?
9. ¿Fuiste feliz ese día?

4

El viaje En parejas, escriban un diálogo de un(a) viajero/a hablando con el/la agente de viajes sobre un viaje que hizo recientemente. Usen el pretérito de **ser** e **ir**.

modelo

Agente: ¿Cómo fue el viaje?
Viajero: El viaje fue maravilloso/horrible...

Practice more at **vistas.vhlcentral.com.**

7.4 Verbs like gustar

Tutorial

ANTE TODO In **Lección 2**, you learned how to express preferences with **gustar**. You will now learn more about the verb **gustar** and other similar verbs. Observe these examples.

Me gusta ese champú.

ENGLISH EQUIVALENT
I like that shampoo.
LITERAL MEANING
That shampoo is pleasing to me.

¿**Te gustaron** las clases?

ENGLISH EQUIVALENT
Did you like the classes?
LITERAL MEANING
Were the classes pleasing to you?

- As the examples show, constructions with **gustar** do not have a direct equivalent in English. The literal meaning of this construction is *to be pleasing to (someone)*, and it requires the use of an indirect object pronoun.

INDIRECT OBJECT PRONOUN	VERB	SUBJECT	SUBJECT	VERB	DIRECT OBJECT
Me	**gusta**	ese champú.	*I*	*like*	*that shampoo.*

- In the diagram above, observe how in the Spanish sentence the object being liked **(ese champú)** is really the subject of the sentence. The person who likes the object, in turn, is an indirect object because it answers the question: *To whom is the shampoo pleasing?*

- Other verbs in Spanish are used in the same way as **gustar**. Here is a list of the most common ones.

Verbs like gustar

aburrir	*to bore*	**importar**	*to be important to; to matter*
encantar	*to like very much; to love* (inanimate objects)	**interesar**	*to be interesting to; to interest*
faltar	*to lack; to need*	**molestar**	*to bother; to annoy*
fascinar	*to fascinate; to like very much*	**quedar**	*to be left over; to fit* (clothing)

¡ATENCIÓN!

Faltar expresses what is lacking or missing.
Me falta una página. *I'm missing one page.*

Quedar expresses how much of something is left.
Nos quedan tres pesos. *We have three pesos left.*

• • •

Quedar also means *to fit*. It can be used to tell how something looks (on someone).
Estos zapatos me quedan bien. *These shoes fit me well.*
Esa camisa te queda muy bien. *That shirt looks good on you.*

- The most commonly used verb forms of **gustar** and similar verbs are the third person (singular and plural). When the object or person being liked is singular, the singular form (**gusta**) is used. When two or more objects or persons are being liked, the plural form (**gustan**) is used. Observe the following diagram:

me, te, le, nos, os, les	SINGULAR	encanta interesó	la película el concierto
	PLURAL	importan fascinaron	las vacaciones los museos de Lima

- To express what someone likes or does not like to do, use an appropriate verb followed by an infinitive. The singular form is used even if there is more than one infinitive.

Nos molesta comer a las nueve.
It bothers us to eat at nine o'clock.

Les encanta bailar y **cantar** en las fiestas.
They love to dance and sing at parties.

AYUDA

Note that the **a** must be repeated if there is more than one person.
A Armando y **a Carmen** les molesta levantarse temprano.

- As you learned in **Lección 2**, the construction **a** + [*pronoun*] (**a mí, a ti, a usted, a él,** etc.) is used to clarify or to emphasize who is pleased, bored, etc. The construction **a** + [*noun*] can also be used before the indirect object pronoun to clarify or to emphasize who is pleased.

A los turistas les gustó mucho Machu Picchu.
The tourists liked Machu Picchu a lot.

A ti te gusta cenar en casa, pero **a mí** me aburre.
You like eating dinner at home, but I get bored.

- **¡Atención! Mí** (*me*) has an accent mark to distinguish it from the possessive adjective **mi** (*my*).

¡INTÉNTALO! Indica el pronombre de objeto indirecto y la forma del tiempo presente adecuados en cada oración.

fascinar

1. A él __le fascina__ viajar.
2. A mí ______ bailar.
3. A nosotras ______ cantar.
4. A ustedes ______ leer.
5. A ti ______ correr y patinar.
6. A ellos ______ los aviones.
7. A mis padres ______ caminar.
8. A usted ______ jugar al tenis.
9. A mi esposo y a mí ______ dormir.
10. A Alberto ______ dibujar y pintar.
11. A todos ______ opinar.
12. A Pili ______ los sombreros.

aburrir

1. A ellos __les aburren__ los deportes.
2. A ti ______ las películas.
3. A usted ______ los viajes.
4. A mí ______ las revistas.
5. A Jorge y a Luis ______ los perros.
6. A nosotros ______ las vacaciones.
7. A ustedes ______ el béisbol.
8. A Marcela ______ los libros.
9. A mis amigos ______ los museos.
10. A ella ______ el ciclismo.
11. A Omar ______ ir de compras.
12. A ti y a mí ______ el baile.

recursos
WB pp. 80–82
LM p. 42
vistas.vhlcentral.com Lección 7

Práctica

1

Completar
Completa las oraciones con todos los elementos necesarios.

1. ________ Adela ________ (encantar) la música de Tito "El Bambino".
2. A ________ me ________ (interesar) la música de otros países.
3. A mis amigos ________ (encantar) las canciones (*songs*) de Calle 13.
4. A Juan y ________ Rafael no les ________ (molestar) la música alta (*loud*).
5. ________ nosotros ________ (fascinar) los grupos de pop latino.
6. ________ señor Ruiz ________ (interesar) más la música clásica.
7. A ________ me ________ (aburrir) la música clásica.
8. ¿A ________ te ________ (faltar) dinero para el concierto de Carlos Santana?
9. No. Ya compré el boleto y ________ (quedar) cinco dólares.
10. ¿Cuánto dinero te ________ (quedar) a ________?

NOTA CULTURAL

Hoy día, la música latina es popular en los EE.UU. gracias a artistas como **Shakira**, de nacionalidad colombiana, y **Tito "El Bambino"**, puertorriqueño. Otros artistas, como **Carlos Santana** y **Gloria Estefan**, difundieron (*spread*) la música latina en los años 60, 70, 80 y 90.

2

Describir
Mira los dibujos y describe lo que está pasando. Usa los verbos de la lista.

aburrir	faltar	molestar
encantar	interesar	quedar

1. a Ramón

2. a nosotros

3. a ti

4. a Sara

3

Gustos
Forma oraciones con los elementos de las columnas.

modelo

A ti te interesan las ruinas de Machu Picchu.

A	B	C
yo	aburrir	despertarse temprano
tú	encantar	mirarse en el espejo
mi mejor amigo/a	faltar	la música rock
mis amigos y yo	fascinar	las pantuflas rosadas
Bart y Homero Simpson	interesar	la pasta de dientes con menta (*mint*)
Shakira	molestar	las ruinas de Machu Picchu
Antonio Banderas		los zapatos caros

Comunicación

4

Preguntas En parejas, túrnense para hacer y contestar estas preguntas.

1. ¿Te gusta levantarte temprano o tarde? ¿Por qué? ¿Y a tu compañero/a de cuarto?
2. ¿Te gusta acostarte temprano o tarde? ¿Y a tu compañero/a de cuarto?
3. ¿Te gusta dormir la siesta?
4. ¿Te encanta acampar o prefieres quedarte en un hotel cuando estás de vacaciones?
5. ¿Qué te gusta hacer en el verano?
6. ¿Qué te fascina de esta universidad? ¿Qué te molesta?
7. ¿Te interesan más las ciencias o las humanidades? ¿Por qué?
8. ¿Qué cosas te aburren?

5

Completar Trabajen en parejas. Túrnense para completar estas frases de una manera lógica.

1. A mi novio/a le fascina(n)...
2. A mi mejor (*best*) amigo/a no le interesa(n)...
3. A mis padres les importa(n)...
4. A nosotros nos molesta(n)...
5. A mis hermanos les aburre(n)...
6. A mi compañero/a de cuarto le aburre(n)...
7. A los turistas les interesa(n)...
8. A los jugadores profesionales les encanta(n)...
9. A nuestro/a profesor(a) le molesta(n)...
10. A mí me importa(n)...

6

La residencia Tú y tu compañero/a de clase son los directores de una residencia estudiantil en Perú. Su profesor(a) les va a dar a cada uno de ustedes las descripciones de cinco estudiantes. Con la información tienen que escoger quiénes van a ser compañeros de cuarto. Después, completen la lista.

Síntesis

7

Situación Trabajen en parejas para representar los papeles de un(a) cliente/a y un(a) dependiente/a en una tienda de ropa. Usen las instrucciones como guía.

Dependiente/a	Cliente/a
Saluda al/a la cliente/a y pregúntale en qué le puedes servir.	→ Saluda al/a la dependiente/a y dile (*tell him/her*) qué quieres comprar y qué colores prefieres.
Pregúntale si le interesan los estilos modernos y empieza a mostrarle la ropa.	→ Explícale que los estilos modernos te interesan. Escoge las cosas que te interesan.
Habla de los gustos del/de la cliente/a.	→ Habla de la ropa (me queda(n) bien/mal, me encanta(n)...).
Da opiniones favorables al/a la cliente/a (las botas te quedan fantásticas...).	→ Decide cuáles son las cosas que te gustan y qué vas a comprar.

Recapitulación

Concepts Diagnostics

Completa estas actividades para repasar los conceptos de gramática que aprendiste en esta lección.

1 **Completar** Completa la tabla con la forma correcta de los verbos. 6 pts.

yo	tú	nosotros	ellas
me levanto			
	te afeitas		
		nos vestimos	
			se secan

2 **Hoy y ayer** Cambia los verbos del presente al pretérito. 5 pts.

1. Vamos de compras hoy. ________ de compras hoy.
2. Por último, voy a poner el despertador. Por último, ________ a poner el despertador.
3. Lalo es el primero en levantarse. Lalo ________ el primero en levantarse.
4. ¿Vas a tu habitación? ¿________ a tu habitación?
5. Ustedes son profesores. Ustedes ________ profesores.

3 **Reflexivos** Completa cada conversación con la forma correcta de los verbos reflexivos. 11 pts.

TOMÁS Yo siempre (1) ________ (bañarse) antes de (2) ________ (acostarse). Esto me relaja porque no (3) ________ (dormirse) fácilmente. Y así puedo (4) ________ (levantarse) más tarde. Y tú, ¿cuándo (5) ________ (ducharse)?

LETI Pues por la mañana, para poder (6) ________ (despertarse).

DAVID ¿Cómo (7) ________ (sentirse) Pepa hoy?

MARÍA Todavía está enojada.

DAVID ¿De verdad? Ella nunca (8) ________ (enojarse) con nadie.

BETO ¿(Nosotros) (9) ________ (Irse) de esta tienda? Estoy cansado.

SARA Pero antes vamos a (10) ________ (probarse) estos sombreros. Si quieres, después (nosotros) (11) ________ (sentarse) un rato.

RESUMEN GRAMATICAL

7.1 Reflexive verbs *pp. 236–237*

lavarse	
me lavo	nos lavamos
te lavas	os laváis
se lava	se lavan

7.2 Indefinite and negative words *pp. 240–241*

Indefinite words	Negative words
algo	nada
alguien	nadie
alguno/a(s), algún	ninguno/a, ningún
o... o	ni... ni
siempre	nunca, jamás
también	tampoco

7.3 Preterite of ser and ir *p. 244*

► The preterite of **ser** and **ir** are identical. Context will determine the meaning.

ser and ir	
fui	fuimos
fuiste	fuisteis
fue	fueron

7.4 Verbs like gustar *pp. 246–247*

aburrir	importar
encantar	interesar
faltar	molestar
fascinar	quedar

me, te, le, nos, os, les →
SINGULAR: encanta / interesó → la película / el concierto
PLURAL: importan / fascinaron → las vacaciones / los museos

► Use the construction a + [*noun/pronoun*] to clarify the person in question.

A mí me encanta ver películas, ¿y **a ti**?

4 **Conversaciones** Completa cada conversación de manera lógica con palabras de la lista. No tienes que usar todas las palabras. 8 pts.

algo	nada	ningún	siempre
alguien	nadie	nunca	también
algún	ni... ni	o... o	tampoco

1. —¿Tienes ______ plan para esta noche?
   —No, prefiero quedarme en casa. Hoy no quiero ver a ______.
   —Yo ______ me quedo. Estoy muy cansado.
2. —¿Puedo entrar? ¿Hay ______ en el cuarto de baño?
   —Sí. ¡Un momento! Ahora mismo salgo.
3. —¿Puedes prestarme ______ para peinarme? No encuentro ______ mi cepillo ______ mi peine.
   —Lo siento, yo ______ encuentro los míos (*mine*).
4. —¿Me prestas tu maquillaje?
   —Lo siento, no tengo. ______ me maquillo.

5 **Oraciones** Forma oraciones completas con los elementos dados (*given*). Usa el presente de los verbos. 8 pts.

1. David y Juan / molestar / levantarse temprano
2. Lucía / encantar / las películas de terror
3. todos (nosotros) / importar / la educación
4. tú / aburrir / ver / la televisión

6 **Rutinas** Escribe seis oraciones que describan las rutinas de dos personas que conoces. 12 pts.

modelo

Mi tía se despierta temprano, pero mi primo...

7 **Adivinanza** Completa la adivinanza con las palabras que faltan y adivina la respuesta. ¡2 puntos EXTRA!

"Cuanto más° ______ (*it dries you*), más se moja°."
¿Qué es? ______

Cuanto más *The more* se moja *it gets wet*

Practice more at **vistas.vhlcentral.com.**

Escritura

Estrategia

Sequencing events

Paying strict attention to sequencing in a narrative will ensure that your writing flows logically from one part to the next.

Every composition should have an introduction, a body, and a conclusion. The introduction presents the subject, the setting, the situation, and the people involved. The main part, or the body, describes the events and people's reactions to these events. The conclusion brings the narrative to a close.

Adverbs and adverbial phrases are sometimes used as transitions between the introduction, the body, and the conclusion. Here is a list of commonly used adverbs in Spanish:

Adverbios

además; también	*in addition; also*
al principio; en un principio	*at first*
antes (de)	*before*
después	*then*
después (de)	*after*
entonces; luego	*then*
más tarde	*later*
primero	*first*
pronto	*soon*
por fin; finalmente	*finally*
al final	*finally*

Tema

Escribe tu rutina

Imagina tu rutina diaria en uno de estos lugares:

- una isla desierta
- el Polo Norte
- un crucero° transatlántico
- un desierto

Escribe una composición en la que describes tu rutina diaria en uno de estos lugares o en algún otro lugar interesante que imagines°. Mientras planeas tu composición, considera cómo cambian algunos de los elementos más básicos de tu rutina diaria en el lugar que escogiste°. Por ejemplo, ¿dónde te acuestas en el Polo Norte? ¿Cómo te duchas en el desierto?

Usa el presente de los verbos reflexivos que conoces e incluye algunos de los adverbios de esta página para organizar la secuencia de tus actividades. Piensa también en la información que debes incluir en cada sección de la narración. Por ejemplo, en la introducción puedes hacer una descripción del lugar y de las personas que están allí, y en la conclusión puedes dar tus opiniones acerca del° lugar y de tu vida diaria allí.

crucero *cruise ship* **que imagines** *that you dream up* **escogiste** *you chose* **acerca del** *about the*

Escuchar

Audio: Activities

Estrategia

Using background information

Once you discern the topic of a conversation, take a minute to think about what you already know about the subject. Using this background information will help you guess the meaning of unknown words or linguistic structures.

To help you practice this strategy, you will now listen to a short paragraph. Jot down the subject of the paragraph, and then use your knowledge of the subject to listen for and write down the paragraph's main points.

Preparación

Según la foto, ¿dónde están Carolina y Julián? Piensa en lo que sabes de este tipo de situación. ¿De qué van a hablar?

Ahora escucha

Ahora escucha la entrevista entre Carolina y Julián, teniendo en cuenta (*taking into account*) lo que sabes sobre este tipo de situación. Elige la información que completa correctamente cada oración.

1. Julián es ____.
   a. político
   b. deportista profesional
   c. artista de cine
2. El público de Julián quiere saber de ____.
   a. sus películas
   b. su vida
   c. su novia
3. Julián habla de ____.
   a. sus viajes y sus rutinas
   b. sus parientes y amigos
   c. sus comidas favoritas
4. Julián ____.
   a. se levanta y se acuesta a diferentes horas todos los días
   b. tiene una rutina diaria
   c. no quiere hablar de su vida

Comprensión

¿Cierto o falso?

Indica si las oraciones son **ciertas** o **falsas** según la información que Julián da en la entrevista.

1. Es difícil despertarme; generalmente duermo hasta las diez.
2. Pienso que mi vida no es más interesante que las vidas de ustedes.
3. Me gusta tener tiempo para pensar y meditar.
4. Nunca hago mucho ejercicio; no soy una persona activa.
5. Me fascinan las actividades tranquilas, como escribir y escuchar música clásica.
6. Los viajes me parecen aburridos.

Preguntas

1. ¿Qué tiene Julián en común con otras personas de su misma profesión?
2. ¿Te parece que Julián siempre fue rico? ¿Por qué?
3. ¿Qué piensas de Julián como persona?

Practice more at **vistas.vhlcentral.com.**

En pantalla

En la mayor parte de Argentina, Uruguay y Paraguay, y en algunas partes de Chile, Colombia y Centroamérica, las personas tienen la costumbre° de usar **vos** en lugar de **tú** al hablar o escribir. Este uso es conocido como **el voseo** y se refleja también en la manera de conjugar los verbos. El uso de **vos** como tratamiento de respeto pasó a ser° de uso coloquial a partir del° siglo° XVI.

Vocabulario útil

rehacé	*redo* (en el voseo)
volvete	*become* (en el voseo)

Opciones

Escoge la opción correcta para cada oración.

1. El plomero (*plumber*) va a romper el ___ del chico.
   a. cepillo b. lavabo c. espejo
2. El chico y la chica ___ la primera vez que se ven (*they see each other*).
   a. bailan b. gritan c. se peinan
3. Al chico ___ conocer a la chica.
   a. le interesa b. le molesta c. le aburre
4. Al final ___ rompe el espejo.
   a. la chica b. el chico c. el plomero

La cita

En parejas, imaginen que los chicos del anuncio tienen una primera cita (*date*). Escriban una conversación entre ellos donde hablen sobre lo que les encanta y lo que les molesta. Después dramatícenla para la clase y decidan entre todos si los chicos son compatibles o no.

Anuncio de champú Sedal

Acá hay que romper°.

—Soledad.
—Mariano.

—¿Salís°?
—Sí, ¿por°?

Video: TV Clip

costumbre *custom* pasó a ser *became* a partir del *starting in the* siglo *century*
Acá hay... *We need to break it here.* ¿Salís? ¿Sales? (en el voseo) ¿por? *why?*

Practice more at **vistas.vhlcentral.com.**

Flash cultura

En este episodio de *Flash cultura* vas a conocer unos entremeses° españoles llamados **tapas.** Hay varias teorías sobre el origen de su nombre. Una dice que viene de la costumbre antigua° de **tapar**° los vasos de vino para evitar° que insectos o polvo entren en° ellos. Otra teoría cuenta que el rey Alfonso X debía° beber un poco de vino por indicación médica y decidió acompañarlo° con algunos bocados° para tapar los efectos del alcohol. Cuando estuvo° mejor, ordenó que siempre en Castilla se sirviera° algo de comer con las bebidas° alcohólicas.

Vocabulario útil

económicas	*inexpensive*
montaditos	*bread slices with assorted toppings*
pagar propinas	*to tip*
tapar el hambre	*to take the edge off (lit. putting the lid on one's hunger)*

Preparación

En el área donde vives, ¿qué hacen las personas normalmente después del trabajo (*work*)? ¿Van a sus casas? ¿Salen con amigos? ¿Comen?

Ordenar

Ordena estos sucesos de manera lógica.

____ a. El empleado cuenta los palillos (*counts the toothpicks*) de los montaditos que Mari Carmen comió.
____ b. Mari Carmen va al barrio de la Ribera.
____ c. Un hombre en un bar explica cuándo sale a tomar tapas.
____ d. Un hombre explica la tradición de los montaditos o pinchos.
____ e. Carmen le pregunta a la chica si los montaditos son buenos para la salud.

entremeses *hors d'oeuvres* **antigua** *ancient* **tapar** *cover* **evitar** *avoid* **entren en** *would get in* **debía** *should* **acompañarlo** *accompany it* **bocados** *snacks* **estuvo** *he was* **se sirviera** *they should serve* **bebidas** *drinks* **sueles** *do you tend*

Tapas para todos los días

Estamos en la Plaza Cataluña, el puro centro de Barcelona.

—¿Cuándo sueles° venir a tomar tapas?
—Generalmente después del trabajo.

Estos son los montaditos, o también llamados pinchos. ¿Te gustan?

Video: *Flash cultura*

Practice more at **vistas.vhlcentral.com.**

recursos

VM pp. 303–304 | vistas.vhlcentral.com Lección 7

Video: *Panorama cultural*
Interactive map

Perú

El país en cifras

- **Área:** 1.285.220 km² (496.224 millas²), *un poco menos que el área de Alaska*
- **Población:** 31.197.000
- **Capital:** Lima —9.659.000
- **Ciudades principales:** Arequipa —848.000, Trujillo, Chiclayo, Callao, Iquitos

SOURCE: Population Division, UN Secretariat

Iquitos es un puerto muy importante en el río Amazonas. Desde Iquitos se envían° muchos productos a otros lugares, incluyendo goma°, nueces°, madera°, arroz°, café y tabaco. Iquitos es también un destino popular para los ecoturistas que visitan la selva°.

- **Moneda:** nuevo sol
- **Idiomas:** español (oficial); quechua, aimara y otras lenguas indígenas (oficiales en los territorios donde se usan)

Bandera de Perú

Peruanos célebres

- **Clorinda Matto de Turner,** escritora (1854–1909)
- **César Vallejo,** poeta (1892–1938)
- **Javier Pérez de Cuéllar,** diplomático (1920–)
- **Mario Vargas Llosa,** escritor (1936–)

Mario Vargas Llosa, Premio Nobel de Literatura 2010

se envían *are shipped* goma *rubber* nueces *nuts* madera *timber* arroz *rice* selva *jungle* Hace más de *More than... ago* grabó *engraved* tamaño *size*

Bailando marinera norteña en Trujillo

Calle en la ciudad de Iquitos

Pasaje Santa Rosa de Lima

Mercado indígena en Cuzco

recursos		
WB pp. 83–84	VM pp. 261–262	vistas.vhlcentral.com Lección 7

¡Increíble pero cierto!

Hace más de° dos mil años la civilización nazca de Perú grabó° más de dos mil kilómetros de líneas en el desierto. Los dibujos sólo son descifrables desde el aire. Uno de ellos es un cóndor del tamaño° de un estadio. Las Líneas de Nazca son uno de los grandes misterios de la humanidad.

Lugares • Lima

Lima es una ciudad moderna y antigua° a la vez°. La Iglesia de San Francisco es notable por su arquitectura barroca colonial. También son fascinantes las exhibiciones sobre los incas en el Museo Oro del Perú y en el Museo Nacional de Antropología y Arqueología. Barranco, el barrio° bohemio de la ciudad, es famoso por su ambiente cultural y sus bares y restaurantes.

BRASIL

Historia • Machu Picchu

A 80 kilómetros al noroeste de Cuzco está Machu Picchu, una ciudad antigua del Imperio inca. Está a una altitud de 2.350 metros (7.710 pies), entre dos cimas° de los Andes. Cuando los españoles llegaron a Perú y recorrieron la región, nunca encontraron Machu Picchu. En 1911, el arqueólogo estadounidense Hiram Bingham la descubrió. Todavía no se sabe ni cómo se construyó° una ciudad a esa altura, ni por qué los incas la abandonaron. Sin embargo°, esta ciudad situada en desniveles° naturales es el ejemplo más conocido de la arquitectura inca.

Artes • La música andina

Machu Picchu aún no existía° cuando se originó la música cautivadora° de las culturas indígenas de los Andes. Los ritmos actuales de la música andina tienen influencias españolas y africanas. Varios tipos de flauta°, entre ellos la quena y la zampoña, caracterizan esta música. En las décadas de los sesenta y los setenta se popularizó un movimiento para preservar la música andina, y hasta° Simon y Garfunkel incorporaron a su repertorio la canción *El cóndor pasa*.

Economía • Llamas y alpacas

Perú se conoce por sus llamas, alpacas, guanacos y vicuñas, todos ellos animales mamíferos° parientes del camello. Estos animales todavía tienen una enorme importancia en la economía del país. Dan lana para exportar a otros países y para hacer ropa, mantas°, bolsas y otros artículos artesanales. La llama se usa también para la carga y el transporte.

BOLIVIA

¿Qué aprendiste? Responde a las preguntas con una oración completa.

1. ¿Qué productos envía Iquitos a otros lugares?
2. ¿Cuáles son las lenguas oficiales de Perú?
3. ¿Por qué es notable la Iglesia de San Francisco en Lima?
4. ¿Qué información sobre Machu Picchu no se sabe todavía?
5. ¿Qué son la quena y la zampoña?
6. ¿Qué hacen los peruanos con la lana de sus llamas y alpacas?

Conexión Internet Investiga estos temas en **vistas.vhlcentral.com**.

1. Investiga la cultura incaica. ¿Cuáles son algunos de los aspectos interesantes de su cultura?
2. Busca información sobre dos artistas, escritores o músicos peruanos y presenta un breve informe a tu clase.

Practice more at **vistas.vhlcentral.com.**

antigua *old* **a la vez** *at the same time* **barrio** *neighborhood* **cimas** *summits* **se construyó** *was built* **Sin embargo** *However* **desniveles** *uneven pieces of land* **aún no existía** *didn't exist yet* **cautivadora** *captivating* **flauta** *flute* **hasta** *even* **mamíferos** *mammalian* **mantas** *blankets*

Los verbos reflexivos

acordarse (de) (o:ue)	*to remember*
acostarse (o:ue)	*to go to bed*
afeitarse	*to shave*
bañarse	*to bathe; to take a bath*
cepillarse el pelo	*to brush one's hair*
cepillarse los dientes	*to brush one's teeth*
despedirse (de) (e:i)	*to say goodbye (to)*
despertarse (e:ie)	*to wake up*
dormirse (o:ue)	*to go to sleep; to fall asleep*
ducharse	*to shower; to take a shower*
enojarse (con)	*to get angry (with)*
irse	*to go away; to leave*
lavarse la cara	*to wash one's face*
lavarse las manos	*to wash one's hands*
levantarse	*to get up*
llamarse	*to be called; to be named*
maquillarse	*to put on makeup*
peinarse	*to comb one's hair*
ponerse	*to put on*
ponerse (+ *adj.*)	*to become (+ adj.)*
preocuparse (por)	*to worry (about)*
probarse (o:ue)	*to try on*
quedarse	*to stay; to remain*
quitarse	*to take off*
secarse	*to dry oneself*
sentarse (e:ie)	*to sit down*
sentirse (e:ie)	*to feel*
vestirse (e:i)	*to get dressed*

Palabras de secuencia

antes (de)	*before*
después	*afterwards; then*
después (de)	*after*
durante	*during*
entonces	*then*
luego	*then*
más tarde	*later (on)*
por último	*finally*

Palabras afirmativas y negativas

algo	*something; anything*
alguien	*someone; somebody; anyone*
alguno/a(s), algún	*some; any*
jamás	*never; not ever*
nada	*nothing; not anything*
nadie	*no one; nobody; not anyone*
ni... ni	*neither... nor*
ninguno/a, ningún	*no; none; not any*
nunca	*never; not ever*
o... o	*either... or*
siempre	*always*
también	*also; too*
tampoco	*neither; not either*

En el baño

el baño, el cuarto de baño	*bathroom*
el champú	*shampoo*
la crema de afeitar	*shaving cream*
la ducha	*shower*
el espejo	*mirror*
el inodoro	*toilet*
el jabón	*soap*
el lavabo	*sink*
el maquillaje	*makeup*
la pasta de dientes	*toothpaste*
la toalla	*towel*

Verbos similares a gustar

aburrir	*to bore*
encantar	*to like very much; to love (inanimate objects)*
faltar	*to lack; to need*
fascinar	*to fascinate; to like very much*
importar	*to be important to; to matter*
interesar	*to be interesting to; to interest*
molestar	*to bother; to annoy*
quedar	*to be left over; to fit (clothing)*

Palabras adicionales

el despertador	*alarm clock*
las pantuflas	*slippers*
la rutina diaria	*daily routine*
por la mañana	*in the morning*
por la noche	*at night*
por la tarde	*in the afternoon; in the evening*

Expresiones útiles	*See page 231.*

recursos

LM p. 42

vistas.vhlcentral.com Lección 7

Audio: Vocabulary

La comida

8

Communicative Goals

You will learn how to:

- Order food in a restaurant
- Talk about and describe food

A PRIMERA VISTA

- ¿Dónde está ella?
- ¿Qué hace?
- ¿Es parte de su rutina diaria?
- ¿Qué colores hay en la foto?

EN DETALLE

Additional Reading

Frutas y verduras de América

Imagínate una pizza sin salsa° de tomate o una hamburguesa sin papas fritas. Ahora piensa que quieres ver una película, pero las palomitas de maíz° y el chocolate no existen. ¡Qué mundo° tan insípido°! Muchas de las comidas más populares del mundo tienen ingredientes esenciales que son originarios del continente llamado Nuevo Mundo. Estas frutas y verduras no fueron introducidas en Europa sino hasta° el siglo° XVI.

El tomate, por ejemplo, era° usado como planta ornamental cuando llegó por primera vez a Europa porque pensaron que era venenoso°. El maíz, por su parte, era ya la base de la comida de muchos países latinoamericanos muchos siglos antes de la llegada de los españoles.

La papa fue un alimento° básico para los incas. Incluso consiguieron deshidratarla para almacenarla° por largos períodos de tiempo. El cacao (planta con la que se hace el chocolate) fue muy importante para los aztecas y los mayas. Ellos usaban sus semillas° como moneda° y como ingrediente de diversas salsas. También las molían° para preparar una bebida, mezclándolas° con agua ¡y con chile!

El aguacate°, la guayaba°, la papaya, la piña y el maracuyá (o fruta de la pasión) son otros ejemplos de frutas originarias de América que son hoy día conocidas en todo el mundo.

Mole

¿En qué alimentos encontramos estas frutas y verduras?

Tomate: pizza, ketchup, salsa de tomate, sopa de tomate

Maíz: palomitas de maíz, tamales, tortillas, arepas (Colombia y Venezuela), pan

Papa: papas fritas, frituras de papa°, puré de papas°, sopa de papas, tortilla de patatas (España)

Cacao: mole (México), chocolatinas°, cereales, helados°, tartas°

Aguacate: guacamole (México), coctel de camarones, sopa de aguacate, nachos, enchiladas hondureñas

salsa *sauce* palomitas de maíz *popcorn* mundo *world* insípido *flavorless* hasta *until* siglo *century* era *was* venenoso *poisonous* alimento *food* almacenarla *to store it* semillas *seeds* moneda *currency* las molían *they used to grind them* mezclándolas *mixing them* aguacate *avocado* guayaba *guava* frituras de papa *chips* puré de papas *mashed potatoes* chocolatinas *chocolate bars* helados *ice cream* tartas *cakes*

ACTIVIDADES

1 **¿Cierto o falso?** Indica si lo que dicen las oraciones es cierto o falso. Corrige la información falsa.

1. El tomate se introdujo a Europa como planta ornamental.
2. Los incas sólo consiguieron almacenar las papas por poco tiempo.
3. Los aztecas y los mayas usaron las papas como moneda.
4. El maíz era una comida poco popular en Latinoamérica.
5. El aguacate era el alimento básico de los incas.
6. En México se hace una salsa con chocolate.
7. El aguacate, la guayaba, la papaya, la piña y el maracuyá son originarios de América.
8. Las arepas se hacen con cacao.
9. El aguacate es un ingrediente del cóctel de camarones.
10. En España hacen una tortilla con papas.

ASÍ SE DICE

La comida

el banano (Col.), el cambur (Ven.), el guineo (Nic.), el plátano (Amér. L., Esp.)	la banana
el choclo (Amér. S.), el elote (Méx.), el jojoto (Ven.), la mazorca (Esp.)	*corncob*
las caraotas (Ven.), los porotos (Amér. S.), las habichuelas (P. R.)	los frijoles
el durazno (Méx.)	el melocotón
el jitomate (Méx.)	el tomate

EL MUNDO HISPANO

Algunos platos típicos

- **Ceviche peruano:** Es un plato de pescado crudo° que se marina° en jugo de limón, con sal, pimienta, cebolla y ají°. Se sirve con lechuga, maíz, camote° y papa amarilla.
- **Gazpacho andaluz:** Es una sopa fría típica del sur de España. Se hace con verduras crudas y molidas°: tomate, ají, pepino° y ajo. También lleva pan, sal, aceite y vinagre.
- **Sancocho colombiano:** Es una sopa de pollo, pescado o carne con plátano, maíz, zanahoria, yuca, papas, cebolla, cilantro y ajo. Se sirve con arroz blanco.

crudo *raw* se marina *gets marinated* ají *pepper* camote *sweet potato* molidas *mashed* pepino *cucumber*

PERFIL

Ferran Adrià: arte en la cocina°

¿Qué haces si un amigo te invita a comer croquetas líquidas o paella de *Kellogg's*? ¿Piensas que es una broma°? ¡Cuidado! Puedes estar perdiendo la oportunidad de probar los platos de uno de los chefs más innovadores del mundo°: **Ferran Adrià**.

Aire de zanahorias

Este artista de la cocina basa su éxito° en la creatividad y en la química. Adrià modifica combinaciones de ingredientes y juega con contrastes de gustos y sensaciones: frío-caliente, crudo-cocido°, dulce°-salado°... A partir de nuevas técnicas, altera° la textura° de los alimentos sin alterar su sabor°. Sus platos sorprendentes° y divertidos atraen a muchos nuevos chefs a su academia de cocina experimental. Quizás un día compraremos° en el supermercado té esférico°, carne líquida y espuma° de tomate.

cocina *kitchen* broma *joke* mundo *world* éxito *success* cocido *cooked* dulce *sweet* salado *savory* sabor *taste* sorprendentes *surprising* compraremos *we will buy* esférico *spheric* espuma *foam*

Conexión Internet

¿Qué platos comen los hispanos en los Estados Unidos?

Go to **vistas.vhlcentral.com** to find more cultural information related to this **Cultura** section.

ACTIVIDADES

2 Comprensión Empareja cada palabra con su definición.

1. fruta amarilla
2. sopa típica de Colombia
3. ingrediente del ceviche
4. chef español

a. gazpacho
b. Ferran Adrià
c. sancocho
d. guineo
e. pescado

3 ¿Qué plato especial hay en tu región? Escribe cuatro oraciones sobre un plato típico de tu región. Explica los ingredientes que contiene y cómo se sirve.

Practice more at **vistas.vhlcentral.com.**

Comparisons of equality

- This construction is used to make comparisons of equality.

tan + [*adjective* / *adverb*] + **como** **tanto/a(s)** + [*singular noun* / *plural noun*] + **como**

- **¡Atención!** Note that unlike **tan**, **tanto** acts as an adjective and therefore agrees in number and gender with the noun it modifies.

Estas uvas son **tan ricas como** aquéllas.
These grapes are as tasty as those ones (are).

Yo probé **tantos platos como** él.
I tried as many dishes as he did.

- **Tan** and **tanto** can also be used for emphasis, rather than to compare, with these meanings: **tan** *so*, **tanto** *so much*, **tantos/as** *so many*.

¡Tu almuerzo es **tan** grande!
Your lunch is so big!

¡Comes **tanto**!
You eat so much!

¡Comes **tantas** manzanas!
You eat so many apples!

¡Preparan **tantos** platos!
They prepare so many dishes!

- Comparisons of equality with verbs are formed by placing **tanto como** after the verb. Note that in this construction **tanto** does not change in number or gender.

[*verb*] + **tanto como**

Tú viajas **tanto como** mi tía.
You travel as much as my aunt (does).

Ellos hablan **tanto como** mis hermanas.
They talk as much as my sisters.

Sabemos **tanto como** ustedes.
We know as much as you (do).

No estudio **tanto como** Felipe.
I don't study as much as Felipe (does).

Irregular comparisons

▶ Some adjectives have irregular comparative forms.

Irregular comparative forms

Adjective		Comparative form	
bueno/a	*good*	**mejor**	*better*
malo/a	*bad*	**peor**	*worse*
grande	*big*	**mayor**	*bigger*
pequeño/a	*small*	**menor**	*smaller*
joven	*young*	**menor**	*younger*
viejo/a	*old*	**mayor**	*older*

CONSULTA

To review how descriptive adjectives like **bueno**, **malo**, and **grande** shorten before nouns, see **Estructura 3.1**, p. 90.

▶ When **grande** and **pequeño/a** refer to age, the irregular comparative forms, **mayor** and **menor**, are used. However, when these adjectives refer to size, the regular forms, **más grande** and **más pequeño/a**, are used.

Yo soy **menor** que tú.
I'm younger than you.

Pedí un plato **más pequeño**.
I ordered a smaller dish.

Nuestro hijo es **mayor** que el hijo de los Andrade.
Our son is older than the Andrades' son.

La ensalada de Isabel es **más grande** que ésa.
Isabel's salad is bigger than that one.

▶ The adverbs **bien** and **mal** have the same irregular comparative forms as the adjectives **bueno/a** and **malo/a**.

Julio nada **mejor** que los otros chicos.
Julio swims better than the other boys.

Ellas cantan **peor** que las otras chicas.
They sing worse than the other girls.

recursos

WB pp. 91–92

LM p. 47

vistas.vhlcentral.com Lección 8

¡INTÉNTALO! Escribe el equivalente de las palabras en inglés.

1. Ernesto mira más televisión que (*than*) Alberto.
2. Tú eres ________ (*less*) simpático que Federico.
3. La camarera sirve ________ (*as much*) carne como pescado.
4. Recibo ________ (*more*) propinas que tú.
5. No estudio ________ (*as much as*) tú.
6. ¿Sabes jugar al tenis tan bien ________ (*as*) tu hermana?
7. ¿Puedes beber ________ (*as many*) refrescos como yo?
8. Mis amigos parecen ________ (*as*) simpáticos como ustedes.

Práctica

1 **Escoger** Escoge la palabra correcta para comparar a dos hermanas muy diferentes. Haz los cambios necesarios.

1. Lucila es más alta y más bonita ________ Tita. (de, más, menos, que)
2. Tita es más delgada porque come ________ verduras que su hermana. (de, más, menos, que)
3. Lucila es más ________ que Tita porque es alegre. (listo, simpático, bajo)
4. A Tita le gusta comer en casa. Va a ________ restaurantes que su hermana. (más, menos, que) Es tímida, pero activa. Hace ________ ejercicio (*exercise*) que su hermana. (más, tanto, menos) Todos los días toma más ________ cinco vasos (*glasses*) de agua mineral. (que, tan, de)
5. Lucila come muchas papas fritas y se preocupa ________ que Tita por comer frutas. (de, más, menos) ¡Son ________ diferentes! Pero se llevan (*they get along*) muy bien. (como, tan, tanto)

2 **Emparejar** Compara a Mario y a Luis, los novios de Lucila y Tita, completando las oraciones de la columna A con las palabras o frases de la columna B.

A

1. Mario es ________ como Luis.
2. Mario viaja tanto ________ Luis.
3. Luis toma ________ clases de cocina (*cooking*) como Mario.
4. Luis habla ________ tan bien como Mario.
5. Mario tiene tantos ________ como Luis.
6. ¡Qué casualidad (*coincidence*)! Mario y Luis también son hermanos, pero no hay tanta ________ entre ellos como entre Lucila y Tita.

B

tantas
diferencia
tan interesante
amigos extranjeros
como
francés

3 **Oraciones** Combina elementos de las columnas A, B y C para hacer comparaciones. Escribe oraciones completas.

modelo

Arnold Schwarzenegger tiene tantos autos como Jennifer Aniston.
Jennifer Aniston es menos musculosa que Arnold Schwarzenegger.

A	B	C
la comida japonesa	costar	la gente de Montreal
el fútbol	saber	la música *country*
Arnold Schwarzenegger	ser	el brócoli
el pollo	tener	el presidente de los EE.UU.
la gente de Vancouver	¿?	la comida italiana
la primera dama (*lady*) de los EE.UU.		el hockey
las universidades privadas		Jennifer Aniston
las espinacas		las universidades públicas
la música rap		la carne de res

Practice more at **vistas.vhlcentral.com.**

Comunicación

4

Intercambiar En parejas, hagan comparaciones sobre diferentes cosas. Pueden usar las sugerencias de la lista u otras ideas.

AYUDA

You can use these adjectives in your comparisons:
bonito/a
caro/a
elegante
interesante
inteligente

modelo

Estudiante 1: Los pollos de *Pollitos del Corral* son muy ricos.
Estudiante 2: Pues yo creo que los pollos de *Rostipollos* son tan buenos como los pollos de *Pollitos del Corral.*
Estudiante 1: Ummm... no tienen tanta mantequilla como los pollos de *Pollitos del Corral.* Tienes razón. Son muy sabrosos.

restaurantes en tu ciudad/pueblo
cafés en tu comunidad
tiendas en tu ciudad/pueblo

periódicos en tu ciudad/pueblo
revistas favoritas
libros favoritos

comidas favoritas
los profesores
los cursos que toman

5

Conversar En grupos, túrnense para hacer comparaciones entre ustedes mismos (*yourselves*) y una persona de cada categoría de la lista.

- una persona de tu familia
- un(a) amigo/a especial
- una persona famosa

Síntesis

6

La familia López En grupos, túrnense para hablar de Sara, Sabrina, Cristina, Ricardo y David y hacer comparaciones entre ellos.

modelo

Estudiante 1: Sara es tan alta como Sabrina.
Estudiante 2: Sí, pero David es más alto que ellas.
Estudiante 3: En mi opinión, él es guapo también.

8.4 Superlatives

Tutorial

ANTE TODO Both English and Spanish use superlatives to express the highest or lowest degree of a quality.

el/la mejor	**el/la peor**	**el/la más alto/a**
the best	*the worst*	*the tallest*

- This construction is used to form superlatives. Note that the noun is always preceded by a definite article and that **de** is equivalent to the English *in* or *of*.

el/la/los/las + [*noun*] + **más/menos** + [*adjective*] + **de**

- The noun can be omitted if the person, place, or thing referred to is clear.

¿El restaurante Las Delicias?
Es **el más elegante** de la ciudad.
The restaurant Las Delicias?
It's the most elegant (one) in the city.

Recomiendo el pollo asado.
Es **el más sabroso** del menú.
I recommend the roast chicken.
It's the most delicious on the menu.

- Here are some irregular superlative forms.

Irregular superlatives

Adjective		Superlative form	
bueno/a	*good*	**el/la mejor**	*(the) best*
malo/a	*bad*	**el/la peor**	*(the) worst*
grande	*big*	**el/la mayor**	*(the) biggest*
pequeño/a	*small*	**el/la menor**	*(the) smallest*
joven	*young*	**el/la menor**	*(the) youngest*
viejo/a	*old*	**el/la mayor**	*(the) eldest*

- The absolute superlative is equivalent to *extremely, super,* or *very*. To form the absolute superlative of most adjectives and adverbs, drop the final vowel, if there is one, and add **-ísimo/a(s).**

malo → **mal-** → **malísimo**
¡El bistec está **malísimo**!

mucho → **much-** → **muchísimo**
Comes **muchísimo**.

- Note these spelling changes.

rico → **riquísimo** **largo** → **larguísimo** **feliz** → **felicísimo**
fácil → **facilísimo** **joven** → **jovencísimo** **trabajador** → **trabajadorcísimo**

¡ATENCIÓN!

While **más** alone means *more*, after **el, la, los** or **las**, it means *most*. Likewise, **menos** can mean *less* or *least*.

Es **el café más rico del** país.
It's the most delicious coffee in the country.

Es **el menú menos caro de** todos éstos.
It is the least expensive menu of all of these.

CONSULTA

The rule you learned in **Estructura 8.3** (p. 283) regarding the use of **mayor/menor** with age, but not with size, is also true with superlative forms.

¡INTÉNTALO! Escribe el equivalente de las palabras en inglés.

1. Marisa es la más inteligente (*the most intelligent*) de todas.
2. Ricardo y Tomás son ______________ (*the least boring*) de la fiesta.
3. Miguel y Antonio son ______________ (*the worst*) estudiantes de la clase.
4. Mi profesor de biología es ______________ (*the oldest*) de la universidad.

recursos
WB pp. 93–94
LM p. 48
vistas.vhlcentral.com Lección 8

Práctica y Comunicación

1

El más... Responde a las preguntas afirmativamente. Usa las palabras entre paréntesis.

modelo
El cuarto está sucísimo, ¿no? (residencia)
Sí, es el más sucio de la residencia.

1. El almacén Velasco es buenísimo, ¿no? (centro comercial)
2. La silla de tu madre es comodísima, ¿no? (casa)
3. Ángela y Julia están nerviosísimas por el examen, ¿no? (clase)
4. Jorge es jovencísimo, ¿no? (mis amigos)

2

Completar Tu profesor(a) te va a dar una hoja de actividades con descripciones de José Valenzuela Carranza y Ana Orozco Hoffman. Completa las oraciones con las palabras de la lista.

altísima	del	mayor	peor
atlética	guapísimo	mejor	periodista
bajo	la	menor	trabajadorcísimo
de	más	Orozco	Valenzuela

1. José tiene 22 años; es el ____________ y el más ____________ de su familia. Es ____________ y ____________. Es el mejor ____________ de la ciudad y el ____________ jugador de baloncesto.
2. Ana es la más ____________ y ____________ mejor jugadora de baloncesto del estado. Es la ____________ de sus hermanos (tiene 28 años) y es ____________. Estudió la profesión ____________ difícil ____________ todas: medicina.
3. Jorge es el ____________ jugador de videojuegos de su familia.
4. Mauricio es el menor de la familia ____________.
5. El abuelo es el ____________ de todos los miembros de la familia Valenzuela.
6. Fifí es la perra más antipática ____________ mundo.

3

Superlativos Trabajen en parejas para hacer comparaciones. Usen los superlativos.

modelo
Angelina Jolie, Bill Gates, Jimmy Carter
Estudiante 1: *Bill Gates es el más rico de los tres.*
Estudiante 2: *Sí, ¡es riquísimo! Y Jimmy Carter es el mayor de los tres.*

1. Guatemala, Argentina, España
2. Jaguar, Prius, Smart
3. la comida mexicana, la comida francesa, la comida árabe
4. Paris Hilton, Meryl Streep, Katie Holmes
5. Ciudad de México, Buenos Aires, Nueva York
6. *Don Quijote de la Mancha, Cien años de soledad, Como agua para chocolate*
7. el fútbol americano, el golf, el béisbol
8. las películas románticas, las películas de acción, las películas cómicas

Recapitulación

Concepts Diagnostics

Completa estas actividades para repasar los conceptos de gramática que aprendiste en esta lección.

1 **Completar** Completa la tabla con la forma correcta del pretérito. 9 pts.

Infinitive	yo	usted	ellos
dormir			
servir			
vestirse			

2 **La cena** Completa la conversación con el pretérito de los verbos. 7 pts.

PAULA ¡Hola, Daniel! ¿Qué tal el fin de semana?

DANIEL Muy bien. Marta y yo (1) __________ (conseguir) hacer muchas cosas, pero lo mejor fue la cena del sábado.

PAULA Ah, ¿sí? ¿Adónde fueron?

DANIEL Al restaurante Vistahermosa. Es elegante, así que (nosotros) (2) __________ (vestirse) bien.

PAULA Y, ¿qué platos (3) __________ (pedir, ustedes)?

DANIEL Yo (4) __________ (pedir) camarones y Marta (5) __________ (preferir) el pollo. Y al final, el camarero nos (6) __________ (servir) flan.

PAULA ¡Qué rico!

DANIEL Sí. Pero después de la cena Marta no (7) __________ (sentirse) bien.

3 **Camareros** Genaro y Úrsula son camareros en un restaurante. Completa la conversación que tienen con su jefe usando pronombres. 8 pts.

JEFE Úrsula, ¿le ofreciste agua fría al cliente de la mesa 22?

ÚRSULA Sí, (1) ____________________ de inmediato.

JEFE Genaro, ¿los clientes de la mesa 5 te pidieron ensaladas?

GENARO Sí, (2) ____________________.

ÚRSULA Genaro, ¿recuerdas si ya me mostraste los vinos nuevos?

GENARO Sí, ya (3) ____________________.

JEFE Genaro, ¿van a pagarte la cuenta los clientes de la mesa 5?

GENARO Sí, (4) ____________________ ahora mismo.

RESUMEN GRAMATICAL

8.1 Preterite of stem-changing verbs p. 274

servir	dormir
serví	dormí
serviste	dormiste
sirvió	durmió
servimos	dormimos
servisteis	dormisteis
sirvieron	durmieron

8.2 Double object pronouns pp. 277–278

Indirect Object Pronouns: **me, te, le (se), nos, os, les (se)**

Direct Object Pronouns: **lo, la, los, las**

Le escribí la carta. → Se la escribí.

Nos van a servir los platos. → Nos los van a servir./ Van a servírnoslos.

8.3 Comparisons pp. 281–283

Comparisons of inequality

más/menos +	*adj., adv., n.*	+ **que**
verb + **más/menos** + **que**		

Comparisons of equality

tan +	*adj., adv.*	+ **como**
tanto/a(s) +	*noun*	+ **como**
verb + **tanto como**		

Irregular comparative forms

bueno/a	mejor
malo/a	peor
grande	mayor
pequeño/a	menor
joven	menor
viejo/a	mayor

8.4 Superlatives *p. 286*

el/la/ los/las +	*noun*	+ más/ menos +	*adjective*	+ de

► Irregular superlatives follow the same pattern as irregular comparatives.

4 **El menú** Observa el menú y sus características. Completa las oraciones basándote en los elementos dados. Usa comparativos y superlativos. 14 pts.

Ensaladas	*Precio*	*Calorías*
Ensalada de tomates	$9.00	170
Ensalada de mariscos	$12.99	325
Ensalada de zanahorias	$9.00	200
Platos principales		
Pollo con champiñones	$13.00	495
Cerdo con papas	$10.50	725
Atún con espárragos	$18.95	495

1. ensalada de mariscos / otras ensaladas / costar
   La ensalada de mariscos ______________ las otras ensaladas.
2. pollo con champiñones / cerdo con papas / calorías
   El pollo con champiñones tiene ______________ el cerdo con papas.
3. atún con espárragos / pollo con champiñones / calorías
   El atún con espárragos tiene ______________ el pollo con champiñones.
4. ensalada de tomates / ensalada de zanahorias / caro
   La ensalada de tomates es ______________ la ensalada de zanahorias.
5. cerdo con papas / platos principales / caro
   El cerdo con papas es ______________ los platos principales.
6. ensalada de zanahorias / ensalada de tomates / costar
   La ensalada de zanahorias ______________ la ensalada de tomates.
7. ensalada de mariscos / ensaladas / caro
   La ensalada de mariscos es ______________ las ensaladas.

5 **Dos restaurantes** ¿Cuál es el mejor restaurante que conoces? ¿Y el peor? Escribe un párrafo de por lo menos (*at least*) seis oraciones donde expliques por qué piensas así. Puedes hablar de la calidad de la comida, el ambiente, los precios, el servicio, etc. 12 pts.

6 **Adivinanza** Completa la adivinanza y adivina la respuesta. ¡2 puntos EXTRA!

"En el campo yo nací°,
mis hermanos son
los ________ (*garlic, pl.*),
y aquél que llora° por mí
me está partiendo°
en pedazos°."
¿Quién soy? ________

nací *was born* **llora** *cries* **partiendo** *cutting* **pedazos** *pieces*

Practice more at **vistas.vhlcentral.com.**

Audio: Reading
Additional Reading

Lectura

Antes de leer

Estrategia

Reading for the main idea

As you know, you can learn a great deal about a reading selection by looking at the format and looking for cognates, titles, and subtitles. You can skim to get the gist of the reading selection and scan it for specific information. Reading for the main idea is another useful strategy; it involves locating the topic sentences of each paragraph to determine the author's purpose for writing a particular piece. Topic sentences can provide clues about the content of each paragraph, as well as the general organization of the reading. Your choice of which reading strategies to use will depend on the style and format of each reading selection.

Examinar el texto

En esta sección tenemos dos textos diferentes. ¿Qué estrategias puedes usar para leer la crítica culinaria°? ¿Cuáles son las apropiadas para familiarizarte con el menú? Utiliza las estrategias más eficaces° para cada texto. ¿Qué tienen en común? ¿Qué tipo de comida sirven en el restaurante?

Identificar la idea principal

Lee la primera frase de cada párrafo de la crítica culinaria del restaurante **La feria del maíz.** Apunta° el tema principal de cada párrafo. Luego lee todo el primer párrafo. ¿Crees que el restaurante le gustó al autor de la crítica culinaria? ¿Por qué? Ahora lee la crítica entera. En tu opinión, ¿cuál es la idea principal de la crítica? ¿Por qué la escribió el autor? Compara tus opiniones con las de un(a) compañero/a.

crítica culinaria *restaurant review* eficaces *efficient*
Apunta *Jot down*

Practice more at **vistas.vhlcentral.com.**

M E N Ú

Entremeses

Tortilla servida con
- Ajiaceite (chile, aceite)
- Ajicomino (chile, comino)

Pan tostado servido con
- Queso frito a la pimienta
- Salsa de ajo y mayonesa

Sopas

- Tomate
- Cebolla
- Verduras
- Pollo y huevo
- Carne de res
- Mariscos

Entradas

Tomaticán
(tomate, papas, maíz, chile, arvejas y zanahorias)

Tamales
(maíz, azúcar, ajo, cebolla)

Frijoles enchilados
(frijoles negros, carne de cerdo o de res, arroz, chile)

Chilaquil
(tortilla de maíz, queso, hierbas y chile)

Tacos
(tortillas, pollo, verduras y salsa)

Cóctel de mariscos
(camarones, langosta, vinagre, sal, pimienta, aceite)

Postres°

- Plátanos caribeños
- Cóctel de frutas al ron°
- Uvate (uvas, azúcar de caña y ron)
- Flan napolitano
- Helado° de piña y naranja
- Pastel° de yogur

Después de leer

Preguntas

En parejas, contesten estas preguntas sobre la crítica culinaria de **La feria del maíz.**

1. ¿Quién es el dueño y chef de **La feria del maíz**?
2. ¿Qué tipo de comida se sirve en el restaurante?
3. ¿Cuál es el problema con el servicio?
4. ¿Cómo es el ambiente del restaurante?
5. ¿Qué comidas probó el autor?
6. ¿Quieren ir ustedes al restaurante **La feria del maíz**? ¿Por qué?

23F

Gastronomía

Por Eduardo Fernández

La feria del maíz

Sobresaliente°. En el nuevo restaurante **La feria del maíz** va a encontrar la perfecta combinación entre la comida tradicional y el encanto° de la vieja ciudad de Antigua. Ernesto Sandoval, antiguo jefe de cocina° del famoso restaurante **El fogón**, está teniendo mucho éxito° en su nueva aventura culinaria.

La feria del maíz
13 calle 4-41 Zona 1
La Antigua, Guatemala
2329912

lunes a sábado
10:30am-11:30pm
domingo 10:00am-10:00pm

Comida
Servicio
Ambiente
Precio

El gerente°, el experimentado José Sierra, controla a la perfección la calidad del servicio. El camarero que me atendió esa noche fue muy amable en todo momento. Sólo hay que comentar que, debido al éxito inmediato de **La feria del maíz**, se necesitan más camareros para atender a los clientes de una forma más eficaz. En esta ocasión, el mesero se tomó unos veinte minutos en traerme la bebida.

Afortunadamente, no me importó mucho la espera entre plato y plato, pues el ambiente es tan agradable que me sentí como en casa. El restaurante mantiene el estilo colonial de Antigua. Por dentro°, es elegante y rústico a la vez. Cuando el tiempo lo permite, se puede comer también en el patio, donde hay muchas flores.

El servicio de camareros y el ambiente agradable del local pasan a un segundo plano cuando llega la comida, de una calidad extraordinaria. Las tortillas de casa se sirven con un ajiaceite delicioso. La sopa de mariscos es excelente y los tamales, pues, tengo que confesar que son mejores que los de mi abuelita. También recomiendo los tacos de pollo, servidos con un mole buenísimo. De postre, don Ernesto me preparó su especialidad, unos plátanos caribeños sabrosísimos.

Los precios pueden parecer altos° para una comida tradicional, pero la calidad de los productos con que se cocinan los platos y el exquisito ambiente de **La feria del maíz** garantizan° una experiencia inolvidable°.

Bebidas

- Cerveza negra
- Chilate (bebida de maíz, chile y cacao)
- Jugos de fruta
- Agua mineral
- Té helado
- Vino tinto/blanco
- Ron

Postres *Desserts* ron *rum* Helado *Ice cream* Pastel *Cake* Sobresaliente *Outstanding* encanto *charm* jefe de cocina *head chef* éxito *success* gerente *manager* Por dentro *Inside* altos *high* garantizan *guarantee* inolvidable *unforgettable*

Un(a) guía turístico/a

Tú eres un(a) guía turístico/a en Guatemala. Estás en el restaurante **La feria del maíz** con un grupo de turistas norteamericanos. Ellos no hablan español y quieren pedir de comer, pero necesitan tu ayuda. Lee nuevamente el menú e indica qué error comete cada turista.

1. La señora Johnson es diabética y no puede comer azúcar. Pide sopa de verduras y tamales. No pide nada de postre.
2. Los señores Petit son vegeterianos y piden sopa de tomate, frijoles enchilados y plátanos caribeños.
3. El señor Smith, que es alérgico al chocolate, pide tortilla servida con ajiaceite, chilaquil y chilate para beber.
4. La adorable hija del señor Smith tiene sólo cuatro años y le gustan mucho las verduras y las frutas naturales. Su papá le pide tomaticán y un cóctel de frutas.
5. La señorita Jackson está a dieta y pide uvate, flan napolitano y helado.

Escritura

Estrategia

Expressing and supporting opinions

Written reviews are just one of the many kinds of writing which require you to state your opinions. In order to convince your reader to take your opinions seriously, it is important to support them as thoroughly as possible. Details, facts, examples, and other forms of evidence are necessary. In a restaurant review, for example, it is not enough just to rate the food, service, and atmosphere. Readers will want details about the dishes you ordered, the kind of service you received, and the type of atmosphere you encountered. If you were writing a concert or album review, what kinds of details might your readers expect to find?

It is easier to include details that support your opinions if you plan ahead. Before going to a place or event that you are planning to review, write a list of questions that your readers might ask. Decide which aspects of the experience you are going to rate and list the details that will help you decide upon a rating. You can then organize these lists into a questionnaire and a rating sheet. Bring these forms with you to help you make your opinions and to remind you of the kinds of information you need to gather in order to support those opinions. Later, these forms will help you organize your review into logical categories. They can also provide the details and other evidence you need to convince your readers of your opinions.

Tema

Escribir una crítica

Escribe una crítica culinaria° sobre un restaurante local para el periódico de la universidad. Clasifica el restaurante dándole de una a cinco estrellas° y anota tus recomendaciones para futuros clientes del restaurante. Incluye tus opiniones acerca de°:

- La comida
  ¿Qué tipo de comida es? ¿Qué tipo de ingredientes usan? ¿Es de buena calidad? ¿Cuál es el mejor plato? ¿Y el peor? ¿Quién es el/la chef?
- El servicio
  ¿Es necesario esperar mucho para conseguir una mesa? ¿Tienen los camareros un buen conocimiento del menú? ¿Atienden a los clientes con rapidez° y cortesía?
- El ambiente
  ¿Cómo es la decoración del restaurante? ¿Es el ambiente informal o elegante? ¿Hay música o algún tipo de entretenimiento°? ¿Hay un bar? ¿Un patio?
- Información práctica
  ¿Cómo son los precios? ¿Se aceptan tarjetas de crédito? ¿Cuál es la dirección° y el número de teléfono? ¿Quién es el/la dueño/a? ¿El/La gerente?

crítica culinaria *restaurant review* **estrellas** *stars* **acerca de** *about* **rapidez** *speed* **entretenimiento** *entertainment* **dirección** *address*

Escuchar

Audio: Activities

Estrategia

Jotting down notes as you listen

Jotting down notes while you listen to a conversation in Spanish can help you keep track of the important points or details. It will help you to focus actively on comprehension rather than on remembering what you have heard.

To practice this strategy, you will now listen to a paragraph. Jot down the main points you hear.

Preparación

Mira la foto. ¿Dónde están estas personas y qué hacen? ¿Sobre qué crees que están hablando?

Ahora escucha

Rosa y Roberto están en un restaurante. Escucha la conversación entre ellos y la camarera y toma nota de cuáles son los especiales del día, qué pidieron y qué bebidas se mencionan.

Especiales del día

Entremeses

____

Plato principal

____

____

____

¿Qué pidieron?

Roberto

____

Rosa

____

Bebidas

____

____

Comprensión

Seleccionar

Usa tus notas para seleccionar la opción correcta para completar cada oración.

1. Dos de los mejores platos del restaurante son ______.
   a. los entremeses del día y el cerdo
   b. el salmón y el arroz con pollo
   c. la carne y el arroz con pollo
2. La camarera ______.
   a. los lleva a su mesa, les muestra el menú y les sirve el postre
   b. les habla de los especiales del día, les recomienda unos platos y ellos deciden qué van a comer
   c. les lleva unas bebidas, les recomienda unos platos y les sirve pan
3. Roberto va a comer ______ Rosa.
   a. tantos platos como
   b. más platos que
   c. menos platos que

Preguntas

En grupos de tres o cuatro, respondan a las preguntas: ¿Conocen los platos que Rosa y Roberto pidieron? ¿Conocen platos con los mismos ingredientes? ¿En qué son diferentes o similares? ¿Cuál les gusta más? ¿Por qué?

En pantalla

Los niños en los países hispanos suelen° comer algunos platos que no son muy comunes en los hogares° estadounidenses. Por ejemplo, muchos de los dulces° tradicionales de Colombia se hacen con frutas naturales. En algunas familias mexicanas se sirven pepinos° y jícamas° con limón y chile en polvo° como merienda a media tarde. Y para la comida, en muchos países, les sirven hígado o morcilla° a los niños porque son muy nutritivos. En este anuncio, vas a conocer a un niño peruano al que no le gusta el hígado.

Vocabulario útil

el cuco	*bogeyman*
fascículos	*parts*
el hígado	*liver*
nutritivo	*nutritious*
recetas	*recipes*
se los lleva...	*are taken away by...*
te dijo	*told you*

Ordenar

Pon en orden lo que ves en el anuncio de televisión. No vas a usar dos elementos.

_____ a. pescado
_____ b. periódicos
_____ c. sal y pimienta
_____ d. mamá
_____ e. cuco
_____ f. langosta
_____ g. niño
_____ h. recetas

Test

Responde a las preguntas. Después comparte tus respuestas con dos o tres compañeros/as para saber quién es el/la más osado/a (*daring*).

1. ¿Cuál es tu plato favorito?
2. ¿Cuál es el plato más exótico que has probado (*that you have tried*)? ¿Te gustó o no?
3. ¿Qué plato exótico te gustaría (*would you like*) probar?
4. ¿Qué plato no quieres probar nunca? ¿Por qué?

Anuncio de El Comercio

¡Grrrrrrr!

Y tú, ¿quién eres?

El cuco...

Video: TV Clip

Practice more at **vistas.vhlcentral.com.**

suelen *are in the habit of* **hogares** *homes* **dulces** *candy* **pepino** *cucumber* **jícama** *yam bean* **polvo** *powder* **morcilla** *blood sausage*

Flash Cultura

España y la mayoría de los países de Latinoamérica tienen una producción muy abundante de frutas y verduras. Es por esto que en los hogares° hispanos se acostumbra° cocinar° con productos frescos° más que con alimentos° que vienen en latas° o frascos°. Las salsas mexicanas, el gazpacho español y el sancocho colombiano, por ejemplo, deben prepararse con ingredientes frescos para que mantengan° su sabor° auténtico. Actualmente, en los Estados Unidos está creciendo el interés en cocinar con productos frescos y orgánicos. Cada vez hay más mercados° donde los agricultores° pueden vender sus frutas y verduras directamente° al público. Además, las personas prefieren consumir productos locales de temporada°. En este episodio de *Flash cultura* vas a ver algunas de las frutas y verduras típicas de la comida hispana.

Vocabulario útil

blanda	*soft*
cocinar	*to cook*
dura	*hard*
¿Está lista para ordenar?	*Are you ready to order?*
el plato	*dish (in a meal)*
pruébala	*try it, taste it*
las ventas	*sales*

Preparación

¿Probaste alguna vez comida latina? ¿La compraste en un supermercado o fuiste a un restaurante? ¿Qué plato(s) probaste? ¿Te gustó?

¿Cierto o falso?

Indica si cada oración es **cierta** o **falsa**.

1. En Los Ángeles hay comida de países latinoamericanos y de España.
2. Leticia explica que la tortilla del taco americano es blanda y la del taco mexicano es dura.
3. Las ventas de salsa son bajas en los Estados Unidos.
4. Leticia fue a un restaurante ecuatoriano.
5. Leticia probó Inca Kola en un supermercado.

hogares *homes* **se acostumbra** *they are used* **cocinar** *to cook* **frescos** *fresh* **alimentos** *foods* **latas** *cans* **frascos** *jars* **para que mantengan** *so that they keep* **sabor** *flavor* **mercados** *markets* **agricultores** *farmers* **directamente** *directly* **de temporada** *seasonal* **mostrará** *will show*

La comida latina

1 **La mejor comida latina no sólo se encuentra en los grandes restaurantes.**

2 **Marta nos mostrará° algunos de los platos de la comida mexicana.**

3 **... hay más lugares donde podemos comprar productos hispanos.**

Video: *Flash cultura*

Practice more at **vistas.vhlcentral.com.**

recursos

VM pp. 305–306	vistas.vhlcentral.com Lección 8

Video: *Panorama cultural*
Interactive map

Guatemala

El país en cifras

- **Área:** 108.890 km^2 (42.042 millas^2), *un poco más pequeño que Tennessee*
- **Población:** 16.227.000
- **Capital:** Ciudad de Guatemala—1.281.000
- **Ciudades principales:** Quetzaltenango, Escuintla, Mazatenango, Puerto Barrios

SOURCE: Population Division, UN Secretariat

- **Moneda:** quetzal
- **Idiomas:** español (oficial), lenguas mayas, xinca, garífuna

El español es la lengua de un 60 por ciento° de la población; el otro 40 por ciento tiene como lengua materna el xinca, el garífuna o, en su mayoría°, una de las lenguas mayas (cakchiquel, quiché y kekchícomo, entre otras). Una palabra que las lenguas mayas tienen en común es ixim*, que significa 'maíz', un cultivo° de mucha importancia en estas culturas.*

Palacio Nacional de la Cultura en la Ciudad de Guatemala

Mujeres indígenas limpiando cebollas

Bandera de Guatemala

Iglesia de la Merced en Antigua Guatemala

recursos

WB	VM	vistas.vhlcentral.com
pp. 95–96	pp. 263–264	Lección 8

Guatemaltecos célebres

- **Carlos Mérida,** pintor (1891–1984)
- **Miguel Ángel Asturias,** escritor (1899–1974)
- **Margarita Carrera,** poeta y ensayista (1929–)
- **Rigoberta Menchú Tum,** activista (1959–), premio Nobel de la Paz° en 1992

por ciento *percent* **en su mayoría** *most of them* **cultivo** *crop* **Paz** *Peace* **telas** *fabrics* **tinte** *dye* **aplastados** *crushed* **hace... destiñan** *keeps the colors from running*

¡Increíble pero cierto!

¿Qué "ingrediente" secreto se encuentra en las telas° tradicionales de Guatemala? ¡El mosquito! El excepcional tinte° de estas telas es producto de una combinación de flores y de mosquitos aplastados°. El insecto hace que los colores no se destiñan°. Quizás es por esto que los artesanos representan la figura del mosquito en muchas de sus telas.

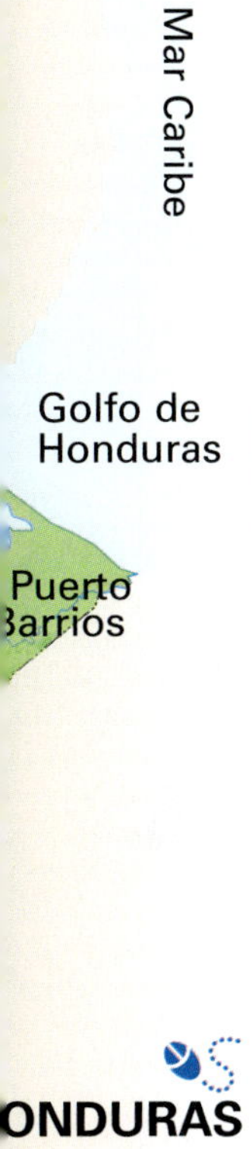

Ciudades • Antigua Guatemala

Antigua Guatemala fue fundada en 1543. Fue una capital de gran importancia hasta 1773, cuando un terremoto° la destruyó. Sin embargo, conserva el carácter original de su arquitectura y hoy es uno de los centros turísticos del país. Su celebración de la Semana Santa° es, para muchas personas, la más importante del hemisferio.

Naturaleza • El quetzal

El quetzal simbolizó la libertad para los antiguos° mayas porque creían° que este pájaro° no podía° vivir en cautiverio°. Hoy el quetzal es el símbolo nacional. El pájaro da su nombre a la moneda nacional y aparece también en los billetes° del país. Desafortunadamente, está en peligro° de extinción. Para su protección, el gobierno mantiene una reserva ecológica especial.

Historia • Los mayas

Desde 1500 a.C. hasta 900 d.C., los mayas habitaron gran parte de lo que ahora es Guatemala. Su civilización fue muy avanzada. Los mayas fueron arquitectos y constructores de pirámides, templos y observatorios. También descubrieron° y usaron el cero antes que los europeos, e inventaron un calendario complejo° y preciso.

Artesanía • La ropa tradicional

La ropa tradicional de los guatemaltecos se llama *huipil* y muestra el amor° de la cultura maya por la naturaleza. Ellos se inspiran en las flores°, plantas y animales para crear sus diseños° de colores vivos° y formas geométricas. El diseño y los colores de cada *huipil* indican el pueblo de origen y a veces también el sexo y la edad° de la persona que lo lleva.

¿Qué aprendiste? Responde a cada pregunta con una oración completa.

1. ¿Qué significa la palabra *ixim*?
2. ¿Quién es Rigoberta Menchú?
3. ¿Qué pájaro representa a Guatemala?
4. ¿Qué simbolizó el quetzal para los mayas?
5. ¿Cuál es la moneda nacional de Guatemala?
6. ¿De qué fueron arquitectos los mayas?
7. ¿Qué celebración de la Antigua Guatemala es la más importante del hemisferio para muchas personas?
8. ¿Qué descubrieron los mayas antes que los europeos?
9. ¿Qué muestra la ropa tradicional de los guatemaltecos?
10. ¿Qué indica un *huipil* con su diseño y sus colores?

Conexión Internet Investiga estos temas en **vistas.vhlcentral.com.**

1. Busca información sobre Rigoberta Menchú. ¿De dónde es? ¿Qué libros publicó? ¿Por qué es famosa?
2. Estudia un sitio arqueológico de Guatemala para aprender más sobre los mayas y prepara un breve informe para tu clase.

Practice more at **vistas.vhlcentral.com.**

terremoto *earthquake* **Semana Santa** *Holy Week* **antiguos** *ancient* **creían** *they believed* **pájaro** *bird* **no podía** *couldn't* **cautiverio** *captivity* **los billetes** *bills* **peligro** *danger* **descubrieron** *they discovered* **complejo** *complex* **amor** *love* **flores** *flowers* **diseños** *designs* **vivos** *bright* **edad** *age*

Las comidas

el/la camarero/a	*waiter/waitress*
la comida	*food; meal*
la cuenta	*bill*
el/la dueño/a	*owner; landlord*
el menú	*menu*
la propina	*tip*
la sección de (no) fumar	*(non) smoking section*
el almuerzo	*lunch*
la cena	*dinner*
el desayuno	*breakfast*
los entremeses	*hors d'oeuvres; appetizers*
el plato (principal)	*(main) dish*
delicioso/a	*delicious*
rico/a	*tasty; delicious*
sabroso/a	*tasty; delicious*

Las frutas

la banana	*banana*
las frutas	*fruits*
el limón	*lemon*
la manzana	*apple*
el melocotón	*peach*
la naranja	*orange*
la pera	*pear*
la uva	*grape*

Las verduras

las arvejas	*peas*
la cebolla	*onion*
el champiñón	*mushroom*
la ensalada	*salad*
los espárragos	*asparagus*
los frijoles	*beans*
la lechuga	*lettuce*
el maíz	*corn*
las papas/patatas (fritas)	*(fried) potatoes; French fries*
el tomate	*tomato*
las verduras	*vegetables*
la zanahoria	*carrot*

La carne y el pescado

el atún	*tuna*
el bistec	*steak*
los camarones	*shrimp*
la carne	*meat*
la carne de res	*beef*
la chuleta (de cerdo)	*(pork) chop*
la hamburguesa	*hamburger*
el jamón	*ham*
la langosta	*lobster*
los mariscos	*shellfish*
el pavo	*turkey*
el pescado	*fish*
el pollo (asado)	*(roast) chicken*
la salchicha	*sausage*
el salmón	*salmon*

Otras comidas

el aceite	*oil*
el ajo	*garlic*
el arroz	*rice*
el azúcar	*sugar*
los cereales	*cereal; grains*
el huevo	*egg*
la mantequilla	*butter*
la margarina	*margarine*
la mayonesa	*mayonnaise*
el pan (tostado)	*(toasted) bread*
la pimienta	*black pepper*
el queso	*cheese*
la sal	*salt*
el sándwich	*sandwich*
la sopa	*soup*
el vinagre	*vinegar*
el yogur	*yogurt*

Las bebidas

el agua (mineral)	*(mineral) water*
la bebida	*drink*
el café	*coffee*
la cerveza	*beer*
el jugo (de fruta)	*(fruit) juice*
la leche	*milk*
el refresco	*soft drink; soda*
el té (helado)	*(iced) tea*
el vino (blanco/tinto)	*(white/red) wine*

Verbos

escoger	*to choose*
merendar (e:ie)	*to snack*
morir (o:ue)	*to die*
pedir (e:i)	*to order (food)*
probar (o:ue)	*to taste; to try*
recomendar (e:ie)	*to recommend*
saber	*to taste; to know*
saber a	*to taste like*
servir (e:i)	*to serve*

Las comparaciones

como	*like; as*
más de (+ *number*)	*more than*
más... que	*more... than*
menos de (+ *number*)	*fewer than*
menos... que	*less... than*
tan... como	*as... as*
tantos/as... como	*as many... as*
tanto... como	*as much... as*
el/la mayor	*the eldest*
el/la mejor	*the best*
el/la menor	*the youngest*
el/la peor	*the worst*
mejor	*better*
peor	*worse*

Expresiones útiles	*See page 269.*

recursos

LM p. 48 | vistas.vhlcentral.com Lección 8

Audio: Vocabulary

Las fiestas

9

Communicative Goals

You will learn how to:

- **Express congratulations**
- **Express gratitude**
- **Ask for and pay the bill at a restaurant**

A PRIMERA VISTA

- **¿Se conocen ellos?**
- **¿Cómo se sienten, alegres o tristes?**
- **¿Está el hombre más contento que la mujer?**
- **¿De qué color es su ropa?**

Las etapas de la vida de Sergio

el nacimiento

la niñez

la adolescencia

la juventud

la madurez

la vejez

Más vocabulario

la edad	*age*
el estado civil	*marital status*
las etapas de la vida	*the stages of life*
la muerte	*death*
casado/a	*married*
divorciado/a	*divorced*
separado/a	*separated*
soltero/a	*single*
viudo/a	*widower/widow*

5 **Las etapas de la vida** Identifica las etapas de la vida que se describen en estas oraciones.

1. Mi abuela se jubiló y se mudó (*moved*) a Viña del Mar.
2. Mi padre trabaja para una compañía grande en Santiago.
3. ¿Viste a mi nuevo sobrino en el hospital? Es precioso y ¡tan pequeño!
4. Mi abuelo murió este año.
5. Mi hermana celebró su fiesta de quince años.
6. Mi hermana pequeña juega con muñecas (*dolls*).

NOTA CULTURAL

Viña del Mar es una ciudad en la costa de Chile, situada al oeste de Santiago. Tiene playas hermosas, excelentes hoteles, casinos y buenos restaurantes. El poeta Pablo Neruda pasó muchos años allí.

¡LENGUA VIVA!

The term **quinceañera** refers to a girl who is celebrating her 15th birthday. The party is called **la fiesta de quince años**.

6 **Cambiar** En parejas, imaginen que son dos hermanos/as de diferentes edades. Cada vez que el/la hermano/a menor dice algo, se equivoca. El/La hermano/a mayor lo/la corrige (*corrects him/her*), cambiando las expresiones subrayadas (*underlined*). Túrnense para ser mayor y menor, decir algo equivocado y corregir.

modelo

Estudiante 1: La <u>niñez</u> es cuando trabajamos mucho.
Estudiante 2: No, te equivocas (*you're wrong*). La madurez es cuando trabajamos mucho.

1. <u>El nacimiento</u> es el fin de la vida.
2. <u>La juventud</u> es la etapa cuando nos jubilamos.
3. A los sesenta y cinco años, muchas personas <u>comienzan a trabajar</u>.
4. Julián y nuestra prima <u>se divorcian</u> mañana.
5. Mamá <u>odia</u> a su hermana.
6. El abuelo murió, por eso la abuela es <u>separada</u>.
7. Cuando te gradúas de la universidad, estás en la etapa de <u>la adolescencia</u>.
8. Mi tío nunca se casó; es <u>viudo</u>.

AYUDA

Other ways to contradict someone:
No es verdad. *It's not true.*
Creo que no. *I don't think so.*
¡Claro que no! *Of course not!*
¡Qué va! *No way!*

Practice more at **vistas.vhlcentral.com.**

Comunicación

7

Una fiesta Trabaja con dos compañeros/as para planear una fiesta. Recuerda incluir la siguiente información.

1. ¿Qué tipo de fiesta es? ¿Dónde va a ser? ¿Cuándo va a ser?
2. ¿A quiénes van a invitar?
3. ¿Qué van a comer? ¿Quiénes van a llevar o a preparar la comida?
4. ¿Qué van a beber? ¿Quiénes van a traer las bebidas?
5. ¿Cómo planean entretener a los invitados? ¿Van a bailar o a jugar algún juego?
6. Después de la fiesta, ¿quiénes van a limpiar (*to clean*)?

8

Encuesta Tu profesor(a) va a darte una hoja de actividades. Haz las preguntas de la hoja a dos o tres compañeros/as de clase para saber qué actitudes tienen en sus relaciones personales. Luego comparte los resultados de la encuesta con la clase y comenta tus conclusiones.

Preguntas	Nombres	Actitudes
1. ¿Te importa la amistad? ¿Por qué?		
2. ¿Es mejor tener un(a) buen(a) amigo/a o muchos/as amigos/as?		
3. ¿Cuáles son las características que buscas en tus amigos/as?		
4. ¿Tienes novio/a? ¿A qué edad es posible enamorarse?		
5. ¿Deben las parejas hacer todo juntos? ¿Deben tener las mismas opiniones? ¿Por qué?		

¡LENGUA VIVA!

While a **buen(a) amigo/a** is a *good friend*, the term **amigo/a íntimo/a** refers to a *close friend*, or a very good friend, without any romantic overtones.

9

Minidrama En parejas, consulten la ilustración de la página 302 y luego, usando las palabras de la lista, preparen un minidrama para representar las etapas de la vida de Sergio. Pueden inventar más información sobre su vida.

amor	celebrar	enamorarse	romper
boda	comprometerse	graduarse	salir
cambiar	cumpleaños	jubilarse	separarse
casarse	divorciarse	nacer	tener una cita

El Día de Muertos

La familia Díaz conmemora el Día de Muertos.

PERSONAJES: MARISSA · JIMENA · FELIPE · JUAN CARLOS

Video: *Fotonovela*
Record and Compare

MAITE FUENTES El Día de Muertos se celebra en México el primero y el segundo de noviembre. Como pueden ver, hay calaveras de azúcar, flores, música y comida por todas partes. Ésta es una fiesta única que todos deben ver por lo menos una vez en la vida.

MARISSA *Holy moley!* ¡Está delicioso!

TÍA ANA MARÍA Mi mamá me enseñó a prepararlo. El mole siempre fue el plato favorito de mi papá. Mi hijo Eduardo nació el día de su cumpleaños. Por eso le pusimos su nombre.

TÍO RAMÓN ¿Dónde están mis hermanos?

JIMENA Mi papá y Felipe están en el otro cuarto. Esos dos antipáticos no quieren decirnos qué están haciendo. Y la tía Ana María...

TÍO RAMÓN ... está en la cocina.

TÍA ANA MARÍA Marissa, ¿le puedes llevar esa foto que está ahí a Carolina? La necesita para el altar.

MARISSA Sí. ¿Son sus padres?

TÍA ANA MARÍA Sí, el día de su boda.

MARISSA ¿Cómo se conocieron?

TÍA ANA MARÍA En la fiesta de un amigo. Fue amor a primera vista.

MARISSA (*Señala la foto.*) La voy a llevar al altar.

TÍA ANA MARÍA Ramón, ¿cómo estás?

TÍO RAMÓN Bien, gracias. ¿Y Mateo? ¿No vino contigo?

TÍA ANA MARÍA No. Ya sabes que me casé con un doctor y, pues, trabaja muchísimo.

SRA. DÍAZ · SR. DÍAZ · TÍA ANA MARÍA · TÍO RAMÓN · TÍA NAYELI · DON DIEGO · MARTA · VALENTINA · MAITE FUENTES

7

SR. DÍAZ Familia Díaz, deben prepararse...

FELIPE ... ¡para la sorpresa de sus vidas!

8

JUAN CARLOS Gracias por invitarme.

SR. DÍAZ Juan Carlos, como eres nuestro amigo, ya eres parte de la familia.

9

(En el cementerio)

JIMENA Yo hice las galletas y el pastel. ¿Dónde los puse?

MARTA Postres... ¿Cuál prefiero? ¿Galletas? ¿Pastel? ¡Dulces!

VALENTINA Me gustan las galletas.

10

SR. DÍAZ Brindamos por ustedes, mamá y papá.

TÍO RAMÓN Todas las otras noches estamos separados. Pero esta noche estamos juntos.

TÍA ANA MARÍA Con gratitud y amor.

Expresiones útiles

Discussing family history

El mole siempre fue el plato favorito de mi papá.
Mole *was always my dad's favorite dish.*
Mi hijo Eduardo nació el día de su cumpleaños.
My son Eduardo was born on his birthday.
Por eso le pusimos su nombre.
That's why we named him after him (after my father).
¿Cómo se conocieron sus padres?
How did your parents meet?
En la fiesta de un amigo. Fue amor a primera vista.
At a friend's party. It was love at first sight.

Talking about a party/celebration

Ésta es una fiesta única que todos deben ver por lo menos una vez.
This is a unique celebration that everyone should see at least once.
Gracias por invitarme.
Thanks for inviting me.
Brindamos por ustedes.
A toast to you.

Additional vocabulary

alma *soul*
altar *altar*
ángel *angel*
calavera de azúcar *skull made out of sugar*
cementerio *cemetery*
cocina *kitchen*
disfraz *costume*

recursos

VM pp. 229–230	vistas.vhlcentral.com Lección 9

¿Qué pasó?

1 **Completar** Completa las oraciones con la información correcta, según la **Fotonovela**.

1. El Día de Muertos es una ________________ única que todos deben ver.
2. La tía Ana María preparó ________________ para celebrar.
3. Marissa lleva la ________________ al altar.
4. Jimena hizo las ________________ y el ________________.
5. Marta no sabe qué ________________ prefiere.

2 **Identificar** Identifica quién puede decir estas oraciones. Vas a usar un nombre dos veces.

1. Mis padres se conocieron en la fiesta de un amigo.
2. El Día de Muertos se celebra con flores, calaveras de azúcar, música y comida.
3. Gracias por invitarme a celebrar este Día de Muertos.
4. Los de la foto son mis padres el día de su boda.
5. A mí me gustan mucho las galletas.
6. ¡Qué bueno que estás aquí, Juan Carlos! Eres uno más de la familia.

SR. DÍAZ

MAITE FUENTES

JUAN CARLOS

VALENTINA

TÍA ANA MARÍA

3 **Seleccionar** Selecciona algunas de las opciones de la lista para completar las oraciones.

amor	días de fiesta	pasarlo bien	salieron
el champán	divorciarse	postres	se enamoraron
cumpleaños	flan	la quinceañera	una sorpresa

1. El Sr. Díaz y Felipe prepararon ________________ para la familia.
2. Los ________________, como el Día de Muertos, se celebran con la familia.
3. Eduardo, el hijo de Ana María, nació el día del ________________ de su abuelo.
4. La tía Ana María siente gratitud y ________________ hacia (*toward*) sus padres.
5. Los días de fiesta también son para ________________ con los amigos.
6. El Día de Muertos se hacen muchos ________________.
7. Los padres de la tía Ana María ________________ a primera vista.

4 **Una cena** Trabajen en grupos para representar una conversación en una cena de Año Nuevo.

- Una persona brinda por el año que está por comenzar y por estar con su familia y amigos.
- Cada persona del grupo habla de cuál es su comida favorita en año nuevo.
- Después de la cena, una persona del grupo dice que es hora de (*it's time to*) comer las uvas.
- Cada persona del grupo dice qué desea para el año que empieza.
- Después, cada persona del grupo debe desear Feliz Año Nuevo a las demás.

NOTA CULTURAL

Comer doce uvas a las doce de la noche del 31 de diciembre de cada año es una costumbre que nació en España y que también se observa en varios países de Latinoamérica. Se debe comer una uva por cada una de las 12 campanadas (*strokes*) del reloj y se cree que (*it's believed that*) quien lo hace va a tener un año próspero.

Practice more at **vistas.vhlcentral.com.**

Pronunciación

Audio: Concepts, Activities
Record & Compare

The letters h, j, and g

helado **hombre** **hola** **hermosa**

The Spanish **h** is always silent.

José **jubilarse** **dejar** **pareja**

The letter **j** is pronounced much like the English *h* in *his*.

agencia **general** **Gil** **Gisela**

The letter **g** can be pronounced three different ways. Before **e** or **i**, the letter **g** is pronounced much like the English *h*.

Gustavo, gracias por llamar el domingo.

At the beginning of a phrase or after the letter **n**, the Spanish **g** is pronounced like the English *g* in *girl*.

Me gradué en agosto.

In any other position, the Spanish **g** has a somewhat softer sound.

Guerra **conseguir** **guantes** **agua**

In the combinations **gue** and **gui**, the **g** has a hard sound and the **u** is silent. In the combination **gua**, the **g** has a hard sound and the **u** is pronounced like the English *w*.

Práctica Lee las palabras en voz alta, prestando atención a la **h,** la **j** y la **g.**

1. hamburguesa
2. jugar
3. oreja
4. guapa
5. geografía
6. magnífico
7. espejo
8. hago
9. seguir
10. gracias
11. hijo
12. galleta
13. Jorge
14. tengo
15. ahora
16. guantes

Oraciones Lee las oraciones en voz alta, prestando atención a la **h,** la **j** y la **g.**

1. Hola. Me llamo Gustavo Hinojosa Lugones y vivo en Santiago de Chile.
2. Tengo una familia grande; somos tres hermanos y tres hermanas.
3. Voy a graduarme en mayo.
4. Para celebrar mi graduación, mis padres van a regalarme un viaje a Egipto.
5. ¡Qué generosos son!

Refranes Lee los refranes en voz alta, prestando atención a la **h,** la **j** y la **g.**

1 Too much of a good thing.
2 The clothes don't make the man.

recursos

LM p. 50	vistas.vhlcentral.com Lección 9

EN DETALLE

Additional Reading

Semana Santa: vacaciones y tradición

¿Te imaginas pasar veinticuatro horas tocando un tambor° entre miles de personas? Así es como mucha gente celebra el Viernes Santo° en el pequeño pueblo de **Calanda,** España.

De todas las celebraciones hispanas, la Semana Santa° es una de las más espectaculares y únicas.

Procesión en Sevilla, España

Semana Santa es la semana antes de Pascua°, una celebración religiosa que conmemora la Pasión de Jesucristo. Generalmente, la gente tiene unos días de vacaciones en esta semana. Algunas personas aprovechan° estos días para viajar, pero otras prefieren participar en las tradicionales celebraciones religiosas en las calles. En **Antigua,** Guatemala, hacen alfombras° de flores° y altares; también organizan Vía Crucis° y danzas. En las famosas procesiones y desfiles° religiosos de **Sevilla,** España, los fieles° sacan a las calles imágenes religiosas. Las imágenes van encima de plataformas ricamente decoradas con abundantes flores y velas°. En la procesión, los penitentes llevan túnicas y unos sombreros cónicos que les cubren° la cara°. En sus manos llevan faroles° o velas encendidas.

Alfombra de flores en Antigua, Guatemala

Si visitas algún país hispano durante la Semana Santa, debes asistir a un desfile. Las playas y las discotecas pueden esperar hasta la semana siguiente.

Otras celebraciones famosas

Ayacucho, Perú: Además de alfombras de flores y procesiones, aquí hay una antigua tradición llamada "quema de la chamiza"°.

Iztapalapa, Ciudad de México: Es famoso el Vía Crucis del cerro° de la Estrella. Es una representación del recorrido° de Jesucristo con la cruz°.

Popayán, Colombia: En las procesiones "chiquitas" los niños llevan imágenes que son copias pequeñas de las que llevan los mayores.

tocando un tambor *playing a drum* **Viernes Santo** *Good Friday* **Semana Santa** *Holy Week* **Pascua** *Easter Sunday* **aprovechan** *take advantage of* **alfombras** *carpets* **flores** *flowers* **Vía Crucis** *Stations of the Cross* **desfiles** *parades* **fieles** *faithful* **velas** *candles* **cubren** *cover* **cara** *face* **faroles** *lamps* **quema de la chamiza** *burning of brushwood* **cerro** *hill* **recorrido** *route* **cruz** *cross*

ACTIVIDADES

1 ¿Cierto o falso? Indica si lo que dicen las oraciones sobre Semana Santa en países hispanos es **cierto** o **falso.** Corrige las falsas.

1. La Semana Santa se celebra después de Pascua.
2. Las personas tienen días libres durante la Semana Santa.
3. Todas las personas asisten a las celebraciones religiosas.
4. En los países hispanos, las celebraciones se hacen en las calles.
5. En Antigua y en Ayacucho es típico hacer alfombras de flores.
6. En Sevilla, sacan imágenes religiosas a las calles.
7. En Sevilla, las túnicas cubren la cara.
8. En la procesión en Sevilla algunas personas llevan flores en sus manos.
9. El Vía Crucis de Iztapalapa es en el interior de una iglesia.
10. Las procesiones "chiquitas" son famosas en Sevilla, España.

ASÍ SE DICE

Fiestas y celebraciones

la despedida de soltero/a	*bachelor(ette) party*
el día feriado/festivo	el día de fiesta
disfrutar	*to enjoy*
festejar	celebrar
los fuegos artificiales	*fireworks*
pasarlo en grande	divertirse mucho
la vela	*candle*

EL MUNDO HISPANO

Celebraciones latinoamericanas

- **Oruro, Bolivia** Durante el carnaval de Oruro se realiza la famosa Diablada, una antigua danza° que muestra la lucha° entre el Bien y el Mal: ángeles contra° demonios.
- **Panchimalco, El Salvador** La primera semana de mayo, Panchimalco se cubre de flores y de color. También hacen el Desfile de las palmas° y bailan danzas antiguas.
- **Quito, Ecuador** El mes de agosto es el Mes de las Artes. Danza, teatro, música, cine, artesanías° y otros eventos culturales inundan la ciudad.
- **San Pedro Sula, Honduras** En junio se celebra la Feria Juniana. Hay comida típica, bailes, desfiles, conciertos, rodeos, exposiciones ganaderas° y eventos deportivos y culturales.

danza *dance* lucha *fight* contra *versus* palmas *palm leaves* artesanías *handcrafts* exposiciones ganaderas *cattle shows*

PERFIL

Festival de Viña del Mar

En 1959 unos estudiantes de **Viña del Mar**, Chile, celebraron una fiesta en una casa de campo conocida como la Quinta Vergara donde hubo° un espectáculo° musical. En 1960 repitieron el evento. Asistió tanta gente que muchos vieron el espectáculo parados° o sentados en el suelo°. Algunos se subieron a los árboles°.

Años después, se convirtió en el **Festival Internacional de la Canción**. Este evento se celebra en febrero, en el mismo lugar donde empezó. ¡Pero ahora nadie necesita subirse a un árbol para verlo! Hay un anfiteatro con capacidad para quince mil personas.

En el festival hay concursos° musicales y conciertos de artistas famosos como Calle 13 y Nelly Furtado.

Nelly Furtado

hubo *there was* espectáculo *show* parados *standing* suelo *floor* se subieron a los árboles *climbed trees* concursos *competitions*

Conexión Internet

¿Qué celebraciones hispanas hay en los Estados Unidos y Canadá?

Go to **vistas.vhlcentral.com** to find more cultural information related to this **Cultura** section.

ACTIVIDADES

2 Comprensión Responde a las preguntas.

1. ¿Cuántas personas por día pueden asistir al Festival de Viña del Mar?
2. ¿Qué es la Diablada?
3. ¿Qué celebran en Quito en agosto?
4. Nombra dos atracciones en la Feria Juniana de San Pedro Sula.
5. ¿Qué es la Quinta Vergara?

3 ¿Cuál es tu celebración favorita? Escribe un pequeño párrafo sobre la celebración que más te gusta de tu comunidad. Explica cómo se llama, cuándo ocurre y cómo es.

Practice more at **vistas.vhlcentral.com.**

9.1 Irregular preterites

S Tutorial

ANTE TODO You already know that the verbs **ir** and **ser** are irregular in the preterite. You will now learn other verbs whose preterite forms are also irregular.

Preterite of tener, venir, and decir

		tener (**u**-stem)	**venir** (**i**-stem)	**decir** (**j**-stem)
SINGULAR FORMS	yo	tuv**e**	vin**e**	dij**e**
	tú	tuv**iste**	vin**iste**	dij**iste**
	Ud./él/ella	tuv**o**	vin**o**	dij**o**
PLURAL FORMS	nosotros/as	tuv**imos**	vin**imos**	dij**imos**
	vosotros/as	tuv**isteis**	vin**isteis**	dij**isteis**
	Uds./ellos/ellas	tuv**ieron**	vin**ieron**	dij**eron**

- **¡Atención!** The endings of these verbs are the regular preterite endings of **-er/-ir** verbs, except for the **yo** and **usted/él/ella** forms. Note that these two endings are unaccented.

- These verbs observe similar stem changes to **tener, venir,** and **decir**.

INFINITIVE	U-STEM	PRETERITE FORMS
poder	pud-	pude, pudiste, pudo, pudimos, pudisteis, pudieron
poner	pus-	puse, pusiste, puso, pusimos, pusisteis, pusieron
saber	sup-	supe, supiste, supo, supimos, supisteis, supieron
estar	estuv-	estuve, estuviste, estuvo, estuvimos, estuvisteis, estuvieron

INFINITIVE	I-STEM	PRETERITE FORMS
querer	quis-	quise, quisiste, quiso, quisimos, quisisteis, quisieron
hacer	hic-	hice, hiciste, hizo, hicimos, hicisteis, hicieron

INFINITIVE	J-STEM	PRETERITE FORMS
traer	traj-	traje, trajiste, trajo, trajimos, trajisteis, trajeron
conducir	conduj-	conduje, condujiste, condujo, condujimos, condujisteis, condujeron
traducir	traduj-	traduje, tradujiste, tradujo, tradujimos, tradujisteis, tradujeron

- **¡Atención!** Most verbs that end in **-cir** are **j**-stem verbs in the preterite. For example, **producir** → **produje, produjiste,** etc.

  Produjimos un documental sobre los accidentes en la casa.
  We produced a documentary about accidents in the home.

- Notice that the preterites with **j**-stems omit the letter **i** in the **ustedes/ellos/ellas** form.

  Mis amigos **trajeron** comida a la fiesta.
  My friends brought food to the party.

  Ellos **dijeron** la verdad.
  They told the truth.

The preterite of dar

SINGULAR FORMS		PLURAL FORMS	
yo	d**i**	nosotros/as	d**imos**
tú	d**iste**	vosotros/as	d**isteis**
Ud./él/ella	d**io**	Uds./ellos/ellas	d**ieron**

- The endings for **dar** are the same as the regular preterite endings for **-er** and **-ir** verbs, except that there are no accent marks.

La camarera me **dio** el menú.
The waitress gave me the menu.

Los invitados le **dieron** un regalo.
The guests gave him/her a gift.

Le **di** a Juan algunos consejos.
I gave Juan some advice.

Nosotros **dimos** una gran fiesta.
We gave a great party.

- The preterite of **hay** (*inf.* **haber**) is **hubo** (*there was; there were*).

CONSULTA
Note that there are other ways to say *there was* or *there were* in Spanish. See **Estructura 10.1**, p. 342.

Marissa le dio la foto a la Sra. Díaz.

Hubo una celebración en casa de los Díaz.

¡INTÉNTALO! Escribe la forma correcta del pretérito de cada verbo que está entre paréntesis.

1. (querer) tú quisiste
2. (decir) usted ________
3. (hacer) nosotras ________
4. (traer) yo ________
5. (conducir) ellas ________
6. (estar) ella ________
7. (tener) tú ________
8. (dar) ella y yo ________
9. (traducir) yo ________
10. (haber) ayer ________
11. (saber) usted ________
12. (poner) ellos ________
13. (venir) yo ________
14. (poder) tú ________
15. (querer) ustedes ________
16. (estar) nosotros ________
17. (decir) tú ________
18. (saber) ellos ________
19. (hacer) él ________
20. (poner) yo ________
21. (traer) nosotras ________
22. (tener) yo ________
23. (dar) tú ________
24. (poder) ustedes ________

recursos
WB pp. 99–100
LM p. 51
vistas.vhlcentral.com Lección 9

Práctica

1

Completar Completa estas oraciones con el pretérito de los verbos entre paréntesis.

1. El sábado __________ (haber) una fiesta sorpresa para Elsa en mi casa.
2. Sofía _______ (hacer) un pastel para la fiesta y Miguel ________ (traer) un flan.
3. Los amigos y parientes de Elsa __________ (venir) y __________ (traer) regalos.
4. El hermano de Elsa no ________ (venir) porque _________ (tener) que trabajar.
5. Su tía María Dolores tampoco __________ (poder) venir.
6. Cuando Elsa abrió la puerta, todos gritaron: "¡Feliz cumpleaños!" y su esposo le __________ (dar) un beso.
7. Elsa no __________ (saber) cómo reaccionar (*react*). __________ (Estar) un poco nerviosa al principio, pero pronto sus amigos __________ (poner) música y ella __________ (poder) relajarse bailando con su esposo.
8. Al final de la noche, todos __________ (decir) que se divirtieron mucho.

NOTA CULTURAL

El **flan** es un postre muy popular en los países de habla hispana. Se prepara con huevos, leche y azúcar y se sirve con salsa de caramelo. Existen variedades deliciosas como el flan de chocolate o el flan de coco.

2

Describir En parejas, usen verbos de la lista para describir lo que estas personas hicieron. Deben dar por lo menos dos oraciones por cada dibujo.

dar	hacer	tener	traer
estar	poner	traducir	venir

1. el señor López

2. Norma

3. anoche nosotros

4. Roberto y Elena

Practice more at **vistas.vhlcentral.com.**

Comunicación

3

Preguntas En parejas, túrnense para hacerse y responder a estas preguntas.

1. ¿Fuiste a una fiesta de cumpleaños el año pasado? ¿De quién?
2. ¿Quiénes fueron a la fiesta?
3. ¿Quién condujo el auto?
4. ¿Cómo estuvo el ambiente de la fiesta?
5. ¿Quién llevó regalos, bebidas o comida? ¿Llevaste algo especial?
6. ¿Hubo comida? ¿Quién la hizo? ¿Hubo champán?
7. ¿Qué regalo hiciste tú? ¿Qué otros regalos trajeron los invitados?
8. ¿Cuántos invitados hubo en la fiesta?
9. ¿Qué tipo de música hubo?
10. ¿Qué te dijeron algunos invitados de la fiesta?

4

Encuesta Tu profesor(a) va a darte una hoja de actividades. Para cada una de las actividades de la lista, encuentra a alguien que hizo esa actividad en el tiempo indicado.

modelo

traer dulces a clase
Estudiante 1: ¿Trajiste dulces a clase?
Estudiante 2: Sí, traje galletas y helado a la fiesta del fin del semestre.

Actividades	Nombres
1. ponerse un disfraz (*costume*) de Halloween	
2. traer dulces a clase	
3. conducir su auto a clase	
4. estar en la biblioteca ayer	
5. dar un regalo a alguien ayer	
6. poder levantarse temprano esta mañana	
7. hacer un viaje a un país hispano en el verano	
8. tener una cita anoche	
9. ir a una fiesta el fin de semana pasado	
10. tener que trabajar el sábado pasado	

Síntesis

5

Conversación En parejas, preparen una conversación en la que uno/a de ustedes va a visitar a su hermano/a para explicarle por qué no fue a su fiesta de graduación y para saber cómo estuvo la fiesta. Incluyan esta información en la conversación:

- cuál fue el menú
- quiénes vinieron a la fiesta y quiénes no pudieron venir
- quiénes prepararon la comida o trajeron algo
- si él/ella tuvo que preparar algo
- lo que la gente hizo antes y después de comer
- cómo lo pasaron, bien o mal

9.2 Verbs that change meaning in the preterite

Tutorial

ANTE TODO The verbs **conocer, saber, poder,** and **querer** change meanings when used in the preterite. Because of this, each of them corresponds to more than one verb in English, depending on its tense.

Verbs that change meaning in the preterite

	Present	Preterite
conocer	*to know; to be acquainted with* **Conozco** a esa pareja. *I know that couple.*	*to meet* **Conocí** a esa pareja ayer. *I met that couple yesterday.*
saber	*to know information; to know how to do something* **Sabemos** la verdad. *We know the truth.*	*to find out; to learn* **Supimos** la verdad anoche. *We found out (learned) the truth last night.*
poder	*to be able; can* **Podemos** hacerlo. *We can do it.*	*to manage; to succeed (could and did)* **Pudimos** hacerlo ayer. *We managed to do it yesterday.*
querer	*to want; to love* **Quiero** ir, pero tengo que trabajar. *I want to go but I have to work.*	*to try* **Quise** evitarlo, pero fue imposible. *I tried to avoid it, but it was impossible.*

¡ATENCIÓN!

In the preterite, the verbs **poder** and **querer** have different meanings, depending on whether they are used in affirmative or negative sentences.

pude *I succeeded*
no pude *I failed (to)*
quise *I tried (to)*
no quise *I refused (to)*

¡INTÉNTALO! Elige la respuesta más lógica.

1. Yo no hice lo que me pidieron mis padres. ¡Tengo mis principios!
   a. No quise hacerlo. b. No supe hacerlo.
2. Hablamos por primera vez con Nuria y Ana en la boda.
   a. Las conocimos en la boda. b. Les dijimos en la boda.
3. Por fin hablé con mi hermano después de llamarlo siete veces.
   a. No quise hablar con él. b. Pude hablar con él.
4. Josefina se acostó para relajarse. Se durmió inmediatamente.
   a. Pudo relajarse. b. No pudo relajarse.
5. Después de mucho buscar, encontraste la definición en el diccionario.
   a. No supiste la respuesta. b. Supiste la respuesta.
6. Las chicas fueron a la fiesta. Cantaron y bailaron mucho.
   a. Ellas pudieron divertirse. b. Ellas no supieron divertirse.

recursos
WB p. 101
LM p. 52
vistas.vhlcentral.com Lección 9

Práctica y Comunicación

1

Carlos y Eva Forma oraciones con los siguientes elementos. Usa el pretérito y haz todos los cambios necesarios. Al final, inventa la razón del divorcio de Carlos y Eva.

1. anoche / mi esposa y yo / saber / que / Carlos y Eva / divorciarse
2. los / conocer / viaje / isla de Pascua
3. no / poder / hablar / mucho / con / ellos / ese día
4. pero / ellos / ser / simpático / y / nosotros / hacer planes / vernos / con más / frecuencia
5. yo / poder / encontrar / su / número / teléfono / páginas / amarillo
6. (yo) querer / llamar / los / ese día / pero / no / tener / tiempo
7. cuando / los / llamar / nosotros / poder / hablar / Eva
8. nosotros / saber / razón / divorcio / después / hablar / ella
9. ______________________________

NOTA CULTURAL

La isla de Pascua es un remoto territorio chileno situado en el océano Pacífico Sur. Sus inmensas estatuas son uno de los mayores misterios del mundo: nadie sabe cómo o por qué se crearon. Para más información, véase **Panorama**, p. 329.

2

Completar Completa estas frases de una manera lógica.

1. Ayer mi compañero/a de cuarto supo...
2. Esta mañana no pude...
3. Conocí a mi mejor amigo/a en...
4. Mis padres no quisieron...
5. Mi mejor amigo/a no pudo...
6. Mi novio/a y yo nos conocimos en...
7. La semana pasada supe...
8. Ayer mis amigos quisieron...

3

Telenovela En parejas, escriban el diálogo para una escena de una telenovela (*soap opera*). La escena trata de una situación amorosa entre tres personas: Mirta, Daniel y Raúl. Usen el pretérito de **conocer, poder, querer** y **saber** en su diálogo.

Síntesis

4

Conversación En una hoja de papel, escribe dos listas: las cosas que hiciste durante el fin de semana y las cosas que quisiste hacer, pero no pudiste. Luego, compara tu lista con la de un(a) compañero/a, y expliquen ambos por qué no pudieron hacer esas cosas.

9.3 ¿Qué? and ¿cuál?

Tutorial

ANTE TODO You've already learned how to use interrogative words and phrases. As you know, **¿qué?** and **¿cuál?** or **¿cuáles?** mean *what?* or *which?* However, they are not interchangeable.

- **¿Qué?** is used to ask for a definition or an explanation.

¿**Qué** es el flan?
What is flan?

¿**Qué** estudias?
What do you study?

- **¿Cuál(es)?** is used when there is more than one possibility to choose from.

¿**Cuál** de los dos prefieres, el vino o el champán?
Which of these (two) do you prefer, wine or champagne?

¿**Cuáles** son tus medias, las negras o las blancas?
Which ones are your socks, the black ones or the white ones?

- **¿Cuál?** cannot be used before a noun; in this case, **¿qué?** is used.

¿**Qué** sorpresa te dieron tus amigos?
What surprise did your friends give you?

¿**Qué** colores te gustan?
What colors do you like?

- **¿Qué?** used before a noun has the same meaning as **¿cuál?**

¿**Qué regalo** te gusta?
What (Which) gift do you like?

¿**Qué dulces** quieren ustedes?
What (Which) sweets do you want?

Review of interrogative words and phrases

¿a qué hora?	*at what time?*	**¿cuántos/as?**	*how many?*
¿adónde?	*(to) where?*	**¿de dónde?**	*from where?*
¿cómo?	*how?*	**¿dónde?**	*where?*
¿cuál(es)?	*what?; which?*	**¿por qué?**	*why?*
¿cuándo?	*when?*	**¿qué?**	*what?; which?*
¿cuánto/a?	*how much?*	**¿quién(es)?**	*who?*

¡INTÉNTALO! Completa las preguntas con **¿qué?** o **¿cuál(es)?**, según el contexto.

1. ¿ Cuál de los dos te gusta más?
2. ¿ ________ es tu teléfono?
3. ¿ ________ tipo de pastel pediste?
4. ¿ ________ es una galleta?
5. ¿ ________ haces ahora?
6. ¿ ________ son tus platos favoritos?
7. ¿ ________ bebidas te gustan más?
8. ¿ ________ es esto?
9. ¿ ________ es el mejor?
10. ¿ ________ es tu opinión?
11. ¿ ________ fiestas celebras tú?
12. ¿ ________ botella de vino prefieres?
13. ¿ ________ es tu helado favorito?
14. ¿ ________ pones en la mesa?
15. ¿ ________ restaurante prefieres?
16. ¿ ________ estudiantes estudian más?
17. ¿ ________ quieres comer esta noche?
18. ¿ ________ es la sorpresa mañana?
19. ¿ ________ postre prefieres?
20. ¿ ________ opinas?

recursos
WB p. 102
LM p. 53
vistas.vhlcentral.com Lección 9

Práctica y Comunicación

1 **Completar** Tu clase de español va a crear un sitio web. Completa estas preguntas con alguna(s) palabra(s) interrogativa(s). Luego, con un(a) compañero/a, hagan y contesten las preguntas para obtener la información para el sitio web.

1. ¿__________ es la fecha de tu cumpleaños?
2. ¿__________________ naciste?
3. ¿__________ es tu estado civil?
4. ¿_______________ te relajas?
5. ¿__________ es tu mejor amigo/a?
6. ¿__________ cosas te hacen reír?
7. ¿__________ postres te gustan? ¿__________ te gusta más?
8. ¿__________ problemas tuviste en la primera cita con alguien?

2 **Una invitación** En parejas, lean esta invitación. Luego, túrnense para hacer y contestar preguntas con **qué** y **cuál** basadas en la información de la invitación.

modelo

Estudiante 1: ¿Cuál es el nombre del padre de la novia?
Estudiante 2: Su nombre es Fernando Sandoval Valera.

Fernando Sandoval Valera
Isabel Arzipe de Sandoval

Lorenzo Vásquez Amaral
Elena Soto de Vásquez

tienen el agrado de invitarlos
a la boda de sus hijos

María Luisa y José Antonio

La ceremonia religiosa tendrá lugar
el sábado 10 de junio a las dos de la tarde
en el Templo de Santo Domingo
(Calle Santo Domingo, 961).

Después de la ceremonia, sírvanse pasar a la recepción en el salón de baile del Hotel Metrópoli (Sotero del Río, 465).

¡LENGUA VIVA!

The word **invitar** is not always used exactly like *invite*. Sometimes, if you say **Te invito un café,** it means that you are offering to buy that person a coffee.

3 **Quinceañera** Trabaja con un(a) compañero/a. Uno/a de ustedes es el/la director(a) del salón de fiestas "Renacimiento". La otra persona es el padre/la madre de Sandra, quien quiere hacer la fiesta de quince años de su hija gastando menos de $25 por invitado. Su profesor(a) va a darles la información necesaria para confirmar la reservación.

modelo

Estudiante 1: ¿Cuánto cuestan los entremeses?
Estudiante 2: Depende. Puede escoger champiñones por 50 centavos o camarones por dos dólares.
Estudiante 1: ¡Uf! A mi hija le gustan los camarones, pero son muy caros.
Estudiante 2: Bueno, también puede escoger quesos por un dólar por invitado.

Practice more at **vistas.vhlcentral.com.**

9.4 Pronouns after prepositions

Tutorial

ANTE TODO In Spanish, as in English, the object of a preposition is the noun or pronoun that follows a preposition. Observe the following diagram.

PREPOSITION	NOUN	PREPOSITION	PRONOUN
La sopa es para	Alicia	y para	él.

Prepositional pronouns

	Singular		Plural	
preposition +	**mí**	*me*	**nosotros/as**	*us*
	ti	*you (fam.)*	**vosotros/as**	*you (fam.)*
	Ud.	*you (form.)*	**Uds.**	*you (form.)*
	él	*him*	**ellos**	*them (m.)*
	ella	*her*	**ellas**	*them (f.)*

- Note that, except for **mí** and **ti,** these pronouns are the same as the subject pronouns. **¡Atención! Mí** (*me*) has an accent mark to distinguish it from the possessive adjective **mi** (*my*).

- The preposition **con** combines with **mí** and **ti** to form **conmigo** and **contigo,** respectively.

  —¿Quieres venir **conmigo** a Concepción?
  Do you want to come with me to Concepción?

  —Sí, gracias, me gustaría ir **contigo.**
  Yes, thanks, I would like to go with you.

- The preposition **entre** is followed by **tú** and **yo** instead of **ti** and **mí.**

  Papá va a sentarse **entre tú y yo**.
  Dad is going to sit between you and me.

CONSULTA
For more prepositions, refer to **Estructura 2.3,** p. 60.

¡INTÉNTALO! Completa estas oraciones con las preposiciones y los pronombres apropiados.

1. *(with him)* No quiero ir con él.
2. *(for her)* Las galletas son ________.
3. *(for me)* Los mariscos son ________.
4. *(with you,* pl. form.*)* Preferimos estar ________.
5. *(with you,* sing. fam.*)* Me gusta salir ________.
6. *(with me)* ¿Por qué no quieres tener una cita ________?
7. *(for her)* La cuenta es ________.
8. *(for them,* m.*)* La habitación es muy pequeña ________.
9. *(with them,* f.*)* Anoche celebré la Navidad ________.
10. *(for you,* sing. fam.*)* Este beso es ________.
11. *(with you,* sing. fam.*)* Nunca me aburro ________.
12. *(with you,* pl. form.*)* ¡Qué bien que vamos ________!
13. *(for you,* sing. fam.*)* ________ la vida es muy fácil.
14. *(for them,* f.*)* ________ no hay sorpresas.

recursos
WB pp. 103–104
LM p. 54
vistas.vhlcentral.com Lección 9

Práctica y Comunicación

1

Completar David sale con sus amigos a comer. Para saber quién come qué, lee el mensaje electrónico que David le envió (*sent*) a Cecilia dos días después y completa el diálogo en el restaurante con los pronombres apropiados.

modelo

Camarero: Los camarones en salsa verde, ¿para quién son?
David: Son para ___ella___.

Para: Cecilia | Asunto: El menú

Hola, Cecilia:
¿Recuerdas la comida del viernes? Quiero repetir el menú en mi casa el miércoles. Ahora voy a escribir lo que comimos, luego me dices si falta algún plato. Yo pedí el filete de pescado y Maribel camarones en salsa verde. Tatiana pidió un plato grandísimo de machas a la parmesana. Diana y Silvia pidieron langostas, ¿te acuerdas? Y tú, ¿qué pediste? Ah, sí, un bistec grande con papas. Héctor también pidió un bistec, pero más pequeño. Miguel pidió pollo y vino tinto para todos. Y la profesora comió ensalada verde porque está a dieta. ¿Falta algo? Espero tu mensaje. Hasta pronto. David.

NOTA CULTURAL

Las **machas a la parmesana** son un plato muy típico de Chile. Se prepara con machas, un tipo de almeja (*clam*) que se encuentra en Suramérica. Las machas a la parmesana se hacen con queso parmesano, limón, sal, pimienta y mantequilla, y luego se ponen en el horno (*oven*).

CAMARERO El filete de pescado, ¿para quién es?
DAVID Es para (1)__________.
CAMARERO Aquí está. ¿Y las machas a la parmesana y las langostas?
DAVID Las machas son para (2)__________.
SILVIA Y DIANA Las langostas son para (3)__________.
CAMARERO Tengo un bistec grande...
DAVID Cecilia, es para (4)__________, ¿no es cierto? Y el bistec más pequeño es para (5)__________.
CAMARERO ¿Y la botella de vino?
MIGUEL Es para todos (6)__________, y el pollo es para (7)__________.
CAMARERO (*a la profesora*) Entonces la ensalada verde es para (8)__________.

2

Compartir Tu profesor(a) va a darte una hoja de actividades en la que hay un dibujo. En parejas, hagan preguntas para saber dónde está cada una de las personas en el dibujo. Ustedes tienen dos versiones diferentes de la ilustración. Al final deben saber dónde está cada persona.

modelo

Estudiante 1: ¿Quién está al lado de Óscar?
Estudiante 2: Alfredo está al lado de él.

Alfredo	Dolores	Graciela	Raúl
Sra. Blanco	Enrique	Leonor	Rubén
Carlos	Sra. Gómez	Óscar	Yolanda

AYUDA

Here are some other useful prepositions: **al lado de, debajo de, a la derecha de, a la izquierda de, cerca de, lejos de, delante de, detrás de, entre.**

Practice more at **vistas.vhlcentral.com.**

Recapitulación

S Concepts Diagnostics

Completa estas actividades para repasar los conceptos de gramática que aprendiste en esta lección.

1 **Completar** Completa la tabla con el pretérito de los verbos. 9 pts.

Infinitive	yo	ella	nosotros
conducir			
hacer			
saber			

2 **Mi fiesta** Completa este mensaje electrónico con el pretérito de los verbos de la lista. Vas a usar cada verbo sólo una vez. 10 pts.

dar	haber	tener
decir	hacer	traer
estar	poder	venir
	poner	

Hola, Omar:

Como tú no (1) ________ venir a mi fiesta de cumpleaños, quiero contarte cómo fue. El día de mi cumpleaños, muy temprano por la mañana, mis hermanos me (2) ________ una gran sorpresa: ellos (3) ________ un regalo delante de la puerta de mi habitación: ¡una bicicleta roja preciosa! Mi madre nos preparó un desayuno riquísimo. Después de desayunar, mis hermanos y yo (4) ________ que limpiar toda la casa, así que (*therefore*) no (5) ________ más celebración hasta la tarde. A las seis y media (nosotros) (6) ________ una barbacoa en el patio de la casa. Todos los invitados (7) ________ bebidas y regalos. (8) ________ todos mis amigos, excepto tú, ¡qué pena! :-(La fiesta (9) ________ muy animada hasta las diez de la noche, cuando mis padres (10) ________ que los vecinos (*neighbors*) iban a (*were going to*) protestar y entonces todos se fueron a sus casas.

RESUMEN GRAMATICAL

9.1 Irregular preterites *pp. 310–311*

u-stem	estar poder poner saber tener	estuv- pud- pus- sup- tuv-	-e, -iste, -o, -imos, -isteis, -(i)eron
i-stem	hacer querer venir	hic- quis- vin-	
j-stem	conducir decir traducir traer	conduj- dij- traduj- traj-	

- Preterite of **dar**: **di, diste, dio, dimos, disteis, dieron**
- Preterite of **hay** (*inf.* **haber**): **hubo**

9.2 Verbs that change meaning in the preterite *p. 314*

Present	Preterite
conocer	
to know; to be acquainted with	*to meet*
saber	
to know info.; to know how to do something	*to find out; to learn*
poder	
to be able; can	*to manage; to succeed*
querer	
to want; to love	*to try*

9.3 ¿Qué? and ¿cuál? *p. 316*

- Use **¿qué?** to ask for a definition or an explanation.
- Use **¿cuál(es)?** when there is more than one possibility to choose from.
- **¿Cuál?** cannot be used before a noun; use **¿qué?** instead.
- **¿Qué?** used before a noun has the same meaning as **¿cuál?**

9.4 Pronouns after prepositions *p. 318*

Prepositional pronouns

	Singular	Plural
Preposition +	mí ti Ud. él ella	nosotros/as vosotros/as Uds. ellos ellas

▸ Exceptions: **conmigo, contigo, entre tú y yo**

3 **¿Presente o pretérito?** Escoge la forma correcta de los verbos en paréntesis. 6 pts.

1. Después de muchos intentos (*tries*), (podemos/pudimos) hacer una piñata.
2. —¿Conoces a Pepe?
   —Sí, lo (conozco/conocí) en tu fiesta.
3. Como no es de aquí, Cristina no (sabe/supo) mucho de las celebraciones locales.
4. Yo no (quiero/quise) ir a un restaurante grande, pero tú decides.
5. Ellos (quieren/quisieron) darme una sorpresa, pero Nina me lo dijo todo.
6. Mañana se terminan las vacaciones; por fin (podemos/pudimos) volver a la escuela.

4 **Preguntas** Escribe una pregunta para cada respuesta con los elementos dados. Empieza con **qué**, **cuál** o **cuáles** de acuerdo con el contexto y haz los cambios necesarios. 8 pts.

1. —¿? / pastel / querer —Quiero el pastel de chocolate.
2. —¿? / ser / sangría —La sangría es una bebida típica española.
3. —¿? / ser / restaurante favorito —Mis restaurantes favoritos son Dalí y Jaleo.
4. —¿? / ser / dirección electrónica —Mi dirección electrónica es paco@email.com.

5 **¿Dónde me siento?** Completa la conversación con los pronombres apropiados. 7 pts.

JUAN A ver, te voy a decir dónde te vas a sentar. Manuel, ¿ves esa silla? Es para ________. Y esa otra silla es para tu novia, que todavía no está aquí.

MANUEL Muy bien, yo la reservo para ________.

HUGO ¿Y esta silla es para ________ (*me*)?

JUAN No, Hugo. No es para ________. Es para Carmina, que viene con Julio.

HUGO No, Carmina y Julio no pueden venir. Hablé con ________ y me avisaron.

JUAN Pues ellos se lo pierden (*it's their loss*). ¡Más comida para ________ (*us*)!

CAMARERO Aquí tienen el menú. Les doy un minuto y enseguida estoy con ________.

6 **Cumpleaños feliz** Escribe cinco oraciones que describan cómo celebraste tu último cumpleaños. Usa el pretérito y los pronombres que aprendiste en esta lección. 10 pts.

7 **Poema** Completa este fragmento del poema *Elegía nocturna* de Carlos Pellicer con el pretérito de los verbos entre paréntesis. ¡2 puntos EXTRA!

“Ay de mi corazón° que nadie ________ (querer)
tomar de entre mis manos desoladas.
Tú ________ (venir) a mirar sus llamaradas°
y le miraste arder° claro° y sereno.”

corazón *heart* llamaradas *flames* arder *to burn* claro *clear*

Practice more at **vistas.vhlcentral.com.**

Audio: Reading
Additional Reading

Lectura

Antes de leer

Estrategia

Recognizing word families

Recognizing root words can help you guess the meaning of words in context, ensuring better comprehension of a reading selection. Using this strategy will enrich your Spanish vocabulary as you will see below.

Examinar el texto

Familiarízate con el texto usando las estrategias de lectura más efectivas para ti. ¿Qué tipo de documento es? ¿De qué tratan° las cuatro secciones del documento? Explica tus respuestas.

Raíces°

Completa el siguiente cuadro° para ampliar tu vocabulario. Usa palabras de la lectura de esta lección y vocabulario de las lecciones anteriores. ¿Qué significan las palabras que escribiste en el cuadro?

Verbos	Sustantivos	Otras formas
1. agradecer *to thank, to be grateful for*	*agradecimiento/gracias* *gratitude/thanks*	*agradecido* *grateful, thankful*
2. estudiar	________	________
3. ________	________	celebrado
4. ________	baile	________
5. bautizar	________	________

¿De qué tratan...? *What are... about?* Raíces *Roots* cuadro *chart*

Practice more at **vistas.vhlcentral.com.**

Vida social

Matrimonio Espinoza Álvarez-Reyes Salazar

El día sábado 17 de junio a las 19 horas, se celebró el matrimonio de Silvia Reyes y Carlos Espinoza en la catedral de Santiago. La ceremonia fue oficiada por el pastor Federico Salas y participaron los padres de los novios, el señor Jorge Espinoza y señora y el señor José Alfredo Reyes y señora. Después de la ceremonia, los padres de los recién casados ofrecieron una fiesta bailable en el restaurante La Misión.

Bautismo

José María recibió el bautismo el 26 de junio.

Sus padres, don Roberto Lagos Moreno y doña María Angélica Sánchez, compartieron la alegría de la fiesta con todos sus parientes y amigos. La ceremonia religiosa tuvo lugar° en la catedral de Aguas Blancas. Después de la ceremonia, padres, parientes y amigos celebraron una fiesta en la residencia de la familia Lagos.

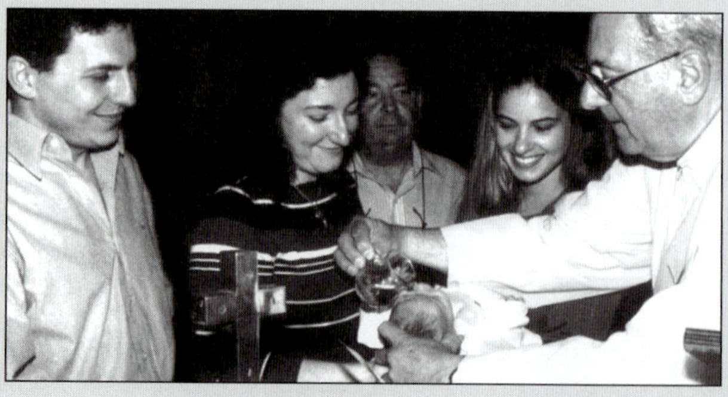

32B

Fiesta de quince años

El doctor don Amador Larenas Fernández y la señora Felisa Vera de Larenas celebraron los quince años de su hija Ana Ester junto a sus parientes y amigos. La quinceañera reside en la ciudad de Valparaíso y es estudiante del Colegio Francés. La fiesta de presentación en sociedad de la señorita Ana Ester fue el día viernes 2 de mayo a las 19 horas en el Club Español. Entre los invitados especiales asistieron el alcalde° de la ciudad, don Pedro Castedo, y su esposa. La música estuvo a cargo de la Orquesta Americana. ¡Feliz cumpleaños, le deseamos a la señorita Ana Ester en su fiesta bailable!

Expresión de gracias

Carmen Godoy Tapia

Agradecemos° sinceramente a todas las personas que nos acompañaron en el último adiós a nuestra apreciada esposa, madre, abuela y tía, la señora Carmen Godoy Tapia. El funeral tuvo lugar el día 28 de junio en la ciudad de Viña del Mar. La vida de Carmen Godoy fue un ejemplo de trabajo, amistad, alegría y amor para todos nosotros. Su esposo, hijos y familia agradecen de todo corazón° su asistencia° al funeral a todos los parientes y amigos.

tuvo lugar *took place* **alcalde** *mayor* **Agradecemos** *We thank* **de todo corazón** *sincerely* **asistencia** *attendance*

Después de leer

Corregir

Escribe estos comentarios otra vez para corregir la información errónea.

1. El alcalde y su esposa asistieron a la boda de Silvia y Carlos.
2. Todos los anuncios (*announcements*) describen eventos felices.
3. Felisa Vera de Larenas cumple quince años.
4. Roberto Lagos y María Angélica Sánchez son hermanos.
5. Carmen Godoy Tapia les dio las gracias a las personas que asistieron al funeral.

Identificar

Escribe el nombre de la(s) persona(s) descrita(s) (*described*).

1. Dejó viudo a su esposo el 28 de junio.
2. Sus padres y todos los invitados brindaron por él, pero él no entendió por qué.
3. El Club Español les presentó una cuenta considerable.
4. Unió a los novios en santo matrimonio.
5. Su fiesta de cumpleaños se celebró en Valparaíso.

Un anuncio

Trabajen en grupos pequeños para inventar un anuncio breve sobre una celebración importante. Puede ser una graduación, un matrimonio o una gran fiesta en la que ustedes participan. Incluyan la siguiente información.

1. nombres de los participantes
2. la fecha, la hora y el lugar
3. qué se celebra
4. otros detalles de interés

Escritura

Estrategia

Planning and writing a comparative analysis

Writing any kind of comparative analysis requires careful planning. Venn diagrams are useful for organizing your ideas visually before comparing and contrasting people, places, objects, events, or issues. To create a Venn diagram, draw two circles that overlap one another and label the top of each circle. List the differences between the two elements in the outer rings of the two circles, then list their similarities where the two circles overlap. Review the following example.

Diferencias y similitudes

La lista de palabras y expresiones a la derecha puede ayudarte a escribir este tipo de ensayo (*essay*).

Tema

Escribir una composición

Compara una celebración familiar (como una boda, una fiesta de cumpleaños o una graduación) a la que tú asististe recientemente con otro tipo de celebración. Utiliza palabras y expresiones de esta lista.

Para expresar similitudes

además; también	*in addition; also*
al igual que	*the same as*
como	*as; like*
de la misma manera	*in the same manner (way)*
del mismo modo	*in the same manner (way)*
tan + [*adjetivo*] + como	*as* + [adjective] + *as*
tanto/a(s) + [*sustantivo*] + como	*as many/much* + [noun] + *as*

Para expresar diferencias

a diferencia de	*unlike*
a pesar de	*in spite of*
aunque	*although*
en cambio	*on the other hand*
más/menos... que	*more/less . . . than*
no obstante	*nevertheless; however*
por el contrario	*on the contrary*
por otro lado	*on the other hand*
sin embargo	*nevertheless; however*

Escuchar

Audio: Activities

Estrategia

Guessing the meaning of words through context

When you hear an unfamiliar word, you can often guess its meaning by listening to the words and phrases around it.

To practice this strategy, you will now listen to a paragraph. Jot down the unfamiliar words that you hear. Then listen to the paragraph again and jot down the word or words that give the most useful clues to the meaning of each unfamiliar word.

Preparación

Lee la invitación. ¿De qué crees que van a hablar Rosa y Josefina?

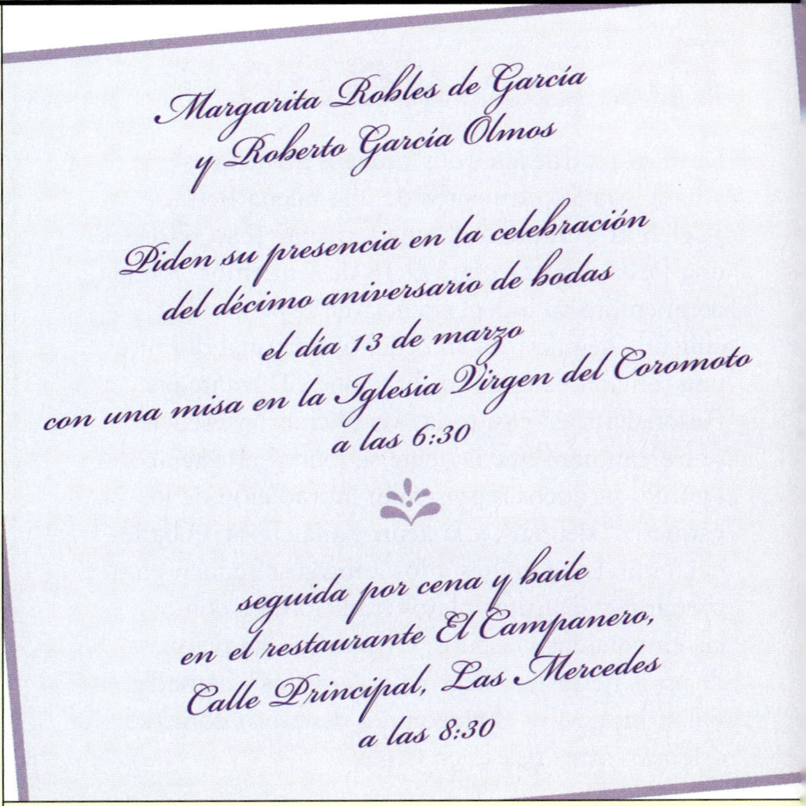

Margarita Robles de García
y Roberto García Olmos

Piden su presencia en la celebración
del décimo aniversario de bodas
el día 13 de marzo
con una misa en la Iglesia Virgen del Coromoto
a las 6:30

seguida por cena y baile
en el restaurante El Campanero,
Calle Principal, Las Mercedes
a las 8:30

Ahora escucha

Ahora escucha la conversación entre Josefina y Rosa. Cuando oigas una de las palabras de la columna A, usa el contexto para identificar el sinónimo o la definición en la columna B.

A	B
___ 1. festejar	a. conmemoración religiosa de una muerte
___ 2. dicha	b. tolera
___ 3. bien parecido	c. suerte
___ 4. finge (fingir)	d. celebrar
___ 5. soporta (soportar)	e. me divertí
___ 6. yo lo disfruté (disfrutar)	f. horror
	g. crea una ficción
	h. guapo

Practice more at **vistas.vhlcentral.com.**

Comprensión

¿Cierto o falso?

Lee cada oración e indica si lo que dice es **cierto** o **falso.** Corrige las oraciones falsas.

1. No invitaron a mucha gente a la fiesta de Margarita y Roberto porque ellos no conocen a muchas personas.
2. Algunos fueron a la fiesta con pareja y otros fueron sin compañero/a.
3. Margarita y Roberto decidieron celebrar el décimo aniversario porque no hicieron una fiesta el día de su boda.
4. Rafael les parece interesante a Rosa y a Josefina.
5. Josefina se divirtió mucho en la fiesta porque bailó toda la noche con Rafael.

Preguntas

Responde a estas preguntas con oraciones completas.

1. ¿Son solteras Rosa y Josefina? ¿Cómo lo sabes?
2. ¿Tienen las chicas una amistad de mucho tiempo con la pareja que celebra su aniversario? ¿Cómo lo sabes?

En pantalla

Desfiles°, música, asados°, fuegos artificiales° y baile son los elementos de una buena fiesta. ¿Celebrar durante toda una semana? ¡Eso sí que es una fiesta espectacular! El 18 de septiembre Chile conmemora su independencia de España y los chilenos demuestran su orgullo° nacional durante una semana llena de celebraciones. Durante las Fiestas Patrias° casi todas las oficinas° y escuelas se cierran para que la gente se reúna° a festejar. Desfiles y rodeos representan la tradición de los vaqueros° del país, y la gente baila cueca, el baile nacional. Las familias y los amigos se reúnen para preparar y disfrutar platos tradicionales como las empanadas y asados. Otra de las tradiciones de estas fiestas es hacer volar cometas°, llamadas volantines. Mira el video para descubrir cómo se celebran otras fiestas en Chile.

Vocabulario útil

conejo	*bunny*
disfraces	*costumes*
mariscal	*traditional Chilean soup with raw seafood*
sustos	*frights*
vieja (Chi.)	*mother*

Seleccionar

Selecciona la palabra que no está relacionada con cada grupo.

1. disfraces • noviembre • arbolito • sustos
2. volantines • arbolito • regalos • diciembre
3. conejo • enero • huevitos • chocolates
4. septiembre • volantines • disfraces • asado

Fiesta

Trabajen en grupos de tres. Imaginen que van a organizar una fiesta para celebrar el 4 de julio. Escriban una invitación electrónica para invitar a sus parientes y amigos a la fiesta. Describan los planes que tienen para la fiesta y díganles a sus amigos qué tiene que traer cada uno.

Desfiles/Paradas *Parades* **asados** *barbecues* **fuegos artificiales** *fireworks* **orgullo** *pride* **Fiestas Patrias** *Independence Day celebrations* **oficinas** *offices* **se reúna** *would get together* **vaqueros** *cowboys* **cometas/volantines** *kites*

Fiestas patrias: Chilevisión

Noviembre: disfraces°, dulces...

Mayo: besito, tarjeta, tecito con la mamá...

Septiembre... Septiembre: familia, parada militar...

Video: TV Clip

Practice more at **vistas.vhlcentral.com.**

Flash cultura

El Día de los Reyes Magos* es una celebración muy popular en muchos países hispanos. No sólo es el día en que los reyes les traen regalos a los niños, también es una fiesta llena° de tradiciones. La tarde del 5 de enero, en muchas ciudades como Barcelona, España, se hace un desfile° en que los reyes regalan dulces a los niños y reciben sus cartas° con peticiones. Esa noche, antes de irse a dormir, los niños deben dejar un zapato junto a la ventana° y un bocado° para los reyes. En Puerto Rico, por ejemplo, los niños ponen una caja con hierba° bajo su cama para alimentar a los camellos° de los reyes.

Vocabulario útil	
los cabezudos	*carnival figures with large heads*
los carteles	*posters*
fiesta de pueblo	*popular celebration*
santos de palo	*wooden saints*

Preparación

¿Se celebra la Navidad en tu país? ¿Qué otras fiestas importantes se celebran? En cada caso, ¿cuántos días dura la fiesta? ¿Cuáles son las tradiciones y actividades típicas? ¿Hay alguna comida típica en esa celebración?

Elegir

Indica cuál de las dos opciones resume mejor este episodio.

a. Las Navidades puertorriqueñas son las más largas y terminan después de las fiestas de la calle San Sebastián. Esta fiesta de pueblo se celebra con baile, música y distintas expresiones artísticas típicas.

b. En la celebración de las Navidades puertorriqueñas, los cabezudos son una tradición de España y son el elemento más importante de la fiesta. A la gente le gusta bailar y hacer procesiones por la noche.

** According to the Christian tradition, the Three Wise Men were the three kings that traveled to Bethlehem after the birth of Baby Jesus, carrying with them gifts of gold, frankincense and myrrh to pay him homage.*

llena *full* desfile *parade* cartas *letters* ventana *window* bocado *snack* hierba *grass* alimentar los camellos *feed the camels*

Las fiestas

1
Los cabezudos son una tradición [...] de España.

2
Hay mucha gente y mucho arte.

3
Es una fiesta de pueblo... una tradición. Vengo todos los años.

Video: *Flash cultura*

Practice more at **vistas.vhlcentral.com.**

recursos
VM pp. 307–308
vistas.vhlcentral.com Lección 9

Video: *Panorama cultural*
Interactive map

Chile

El país en cifras

- **Área:** 756.950 km^2 (292.259 $millas^2$), *dos veces el área de Montana*
- **Población:** 17.926.000 *Aproximadamente el 80 por ciento de la población del país es urbana.*
- **Capital:** Santiago de Chile—6.237.000
- **Ciudades principales:** Valparaíso—911.000, Concepción, Viña del Mar, Temuco

SOURCE: Population Division, UN Secretariat

- **Moneda:** peso chileno
- **Idiomas:** español (oficial), mapuche

El puerto de Valparaíso

La costa de Viña del Mar

Edificio antiguo en Santiago

Una celebración en Temuco

Torres del Paine

recursos

WB	VM	vistas.vhlcentral.com
pp. 105–106	pp. 265–266	Lección 9

Bandera de Chile

Chilenos célebres

- **Bernardo O'Higgins,** militar° y héroe nacional (1778–1842)
- **Gabriela Mistral,** Premio Nobel de Literatura, 1945; poeta y diplomática (1889–1957)
- **Pablo Neruda,** Premio Nobel de Literatura, 1971; poeta (1904–1973)
- **Isabel Allende,** novelista (1942–)

Pablo Neruda

militar *soldier* terremoto *earthquake* heridas *wounded* hogar *home* desierto *desert* el más seco *the driest* mundo *world* han tenido *have had* ha sido usado *has been used* Marte *Mars*

¡Increíble pero cierto!

El desierto° de Atacama, en el norte de Chile, es el más seco° del mundo°. Con más de cien mil km^2 de superficie, algunas zonas de este desierto nunca han tenido° lluvia. Atacama ha sido usado° como escenario para representar a Marte° en películas y series de televisión.

Lugares • La isla de Pascua

La isla de Pascua° recibió ese nombre porque los exploradores holandeses° llegaron a la isla por primera vez el día de Pascua de 1722. Ahora es parte del territorio de Chile. La isla de Pascua es famosa por los *moái*, estatuas enormes que representan personas con rasgos° muy exagerados. Estas estatuas las construyeron los *rapa nui*, los antiguos habitantes de la zona. Todavía no se sabe mucho sobre los *rapa nui*, ni tampoco se sabe por qué decidieron abandonar la isla.

Deportes • Los deportes de invierno

Hay muchos lugares para practicar deportes de invierno en Chile porque las montañas nevadas de los Andes ocupan gran parte del país. El Parque Nacional Villarrica, por ejemplo, situado al pie de un volcán y junto a° un lago, es un sitio popular para el esquí y el *snowboard*. Para los que prefieren deportes más extremos, el centro de esquí Valle Nevado organiza excursiones para practicar heliesquí.

Ciencias • Astronomía

Los observatorios chilenos, situados en los Andes, son lugares excelentes para las observaciones astronómicas. Científicos° de todo el mundo van a Chile para estudiar las estrellas° y otros cuerpos celestes. Hoy día Chile está construyendo nuevos observatorios y telescopios para mejorar las imágenes del universo.

Economía • El vino

La producción de vino comenzó en Chile en el siglo° XVI. Ahora la industria del vino constituye una parte importante de la actividad agrícola del país y la exportación de sus productos está aumentando° cada vez más. Los vinos chilenos son muy apreciados internacionalmente por su gran variedad, sus ricos y complejos sabores° y su precio moderado. Los más conocidos son los vinos de Aconcagua y del valle del Maipo.

¿Qué aprendiste? Responde a cada pregunta con una oración completa.

1. ¿Qué porcentaje (*percentage*) de la población chilena es urbana?
2. ¿Qué son los *moái*? ¿Dónde están?
3. ¿Qué deporte extremo ofrece el centro de esquí Valle Nevado?
4. ¿Por qué van a Chile científicos de todo el mundo?
5. ¿Cuándo comenzó la producción de vino en Chile?
6. ¿Por qué son apreciados internacionalmente los vinos chilenos?

Conexión Internet Investiga estos temas en **vistas.vhlcentral.com.**

1. Busca información sobre Pablo Neruda e Isabel Allende. ¿Dónde y cuándo nacieron? ¿Cuáles son algunas de sus obras (*works*)? ¿Cuáles son algunos de los temas de sus obras?
2. Busca información sobre sitios donde los chilenos y los turistas practican deportes de invierno en Chile. Selecciona un sitio y descríbeselo a tu clase.

Practice more at **vistas.vhlcentral.com.**

La isla de Pascua *Easter Island* holandeses *Dutch* rasgos *features* junto a *beside* Científicos *Scientists* estrellas *stars* siglo *century* aumentando *increasing* complejos sabores *complex flavors*

Las celebraciones

el aniversario (de bodas)	*(wedding) anniversary*
la boda	*wedding*
el cumpleaños	*birthday*
el día de fiesta	*holiday*
la fiesta	*party*
el/la invitado/a	*guest*
la Navidad	*Christmas*
la quinceañera	*young woman celebrating her fifteenth birthday*
la sorpresa	*surprise*
brindar	*to toast* (drink)
celebrar	*to celebrate*
divertirse (e:ie)	*to have fun*
invitar	*to invite*
pasarlo bien/mal	*to have a good/bad time*
regalar	*to give* (a gift)
reírse (e:i)	*to laugh*
relajarse	*to relax*
sonreír (e:i)	*to smile*
sorprender	*to surprise*

Los postres y otras comidas

la botella (de vino)	*bottle (of wine)*
el champán	*champagne*
los dulces	*sweets; candy*
el flan (de caramelo)	*baked (caramel) custard*
la galleta	*cookie*
el helado	*ice cream*
el pastel (de chocolate)	*(chocolate) cake; pie*
el postre	*dessert*

Las relaciones personales

la amistad	*friendship*
el amor	*love*
el divorcio	*divorce*
el estado civil	*marital status*
el matrimonio	*marriage*
la pareja	*(married) couple; partner*
el/la recién casado/a	*newlywed*
casarse (con)	*to get married (to)*
comprometerse (con)	*to get engaged (to)*
divorciarse (de)	*to get divorced (from)*
enamorarse (de)	*to fall in love (with)*
llevarse bien/mal (con)	*to get along well/ badly (with)*
odiar	*to hate*
romper (con)	*to break up (with)*
salir (con)	*to go out (with); to date*
separarse (de)	*to separate (from)*
tener una cita	*to have a date; to have an appointment*
casado/a	*married*
divorciado/a	*divorced*
juntos/as	*together*
separado/a	*separated*
soltero/a	*single*
viudo/a	*widower/widow*

Las etapas de la vida

la adolescencia	*adolescence*
la edad	*age*
el estado civil	*marital status*
las etapas de la vida	*the stages of life*
la juventud	*youth*
la madurez	*maturity; middle age*
la muerte	*death*
el nacimiento	*birth*
la niñez	*childhood*
la vejez	*old age*
cambiar (de)	*to change*
graduarse (de/en)	*to graduate (from/in)*
jubilarse	*to retire (from work)*
nacer	*to be born*

Palabras adicionales

la alegría	*happiness*
el beso	*kiss*
conmigo	*with me*
contigo	*with you*
¡Felicidades!/ ¡Felicitaciones!	*Congratulations!*
¡Feliz cumpleaños!	*Happy birthday!*

Expresiones útiles	*See page 305.*

En el consultorio 10

Communicative Goals

You will learn how to:

- **Describe how you feel physically**
- **Talk about health and medical conditions**

A PRIMERA VISTA

- ¿Están en una farmacia o en un hospital?
- ¿El hombre es médico o dentista?
- ¿Qué hace él, una operación o un examen médico?
- ¿Crees que la paciente está nerviosa?

Talking Picture, Tutorials & Games
Audio: Activities

En el consultorio

Más vocabulario

la clínica	*clinic*
el consultorio	*doctor's office*
el/la dentista	*dentist*
el examen médico	*physical exam*
la farmacia	*pharmacy*
el hospital	*hospital*
la operación	*operation*
la sala de emergencia(s)	*emergency room*
el cuerpo	*body*
el oído	*(sense of) hearing; inner ear*
el accidente	*accident*
la salud	*health*
el síntoma	*symptom*
caerse	*to fall (down)*
darse con	*to bump into; to run into*
doler (o:ue)	*to hurt*
enfermarse	*to get sick*
estar enfermo/a	*to be sick*
poner una inyección	*to give an injection*
recetar	*to prescribe*
romperse (la pierna)	*to break (one's leg)*
sacar(se) un diente	*to have a tooth removed*
sufrir una enfermedad	*to suffer an illness*
torcerse (o:ue) (el tobillo)	*to sprain (one's ankle)*
toser	*to cough*

Variación léxica

gripe ⟷ gripa (*Col., Gua., Méx.*)
resfriado ⟷ catarro (*Cuba, Esp., Gua.*)
sala de emergencia(s) ⟷ sala de urgencias (*Arg., Col., Esp., Méx.*)
romperse ⟷ quebrarse (*Arg., Gua.*)

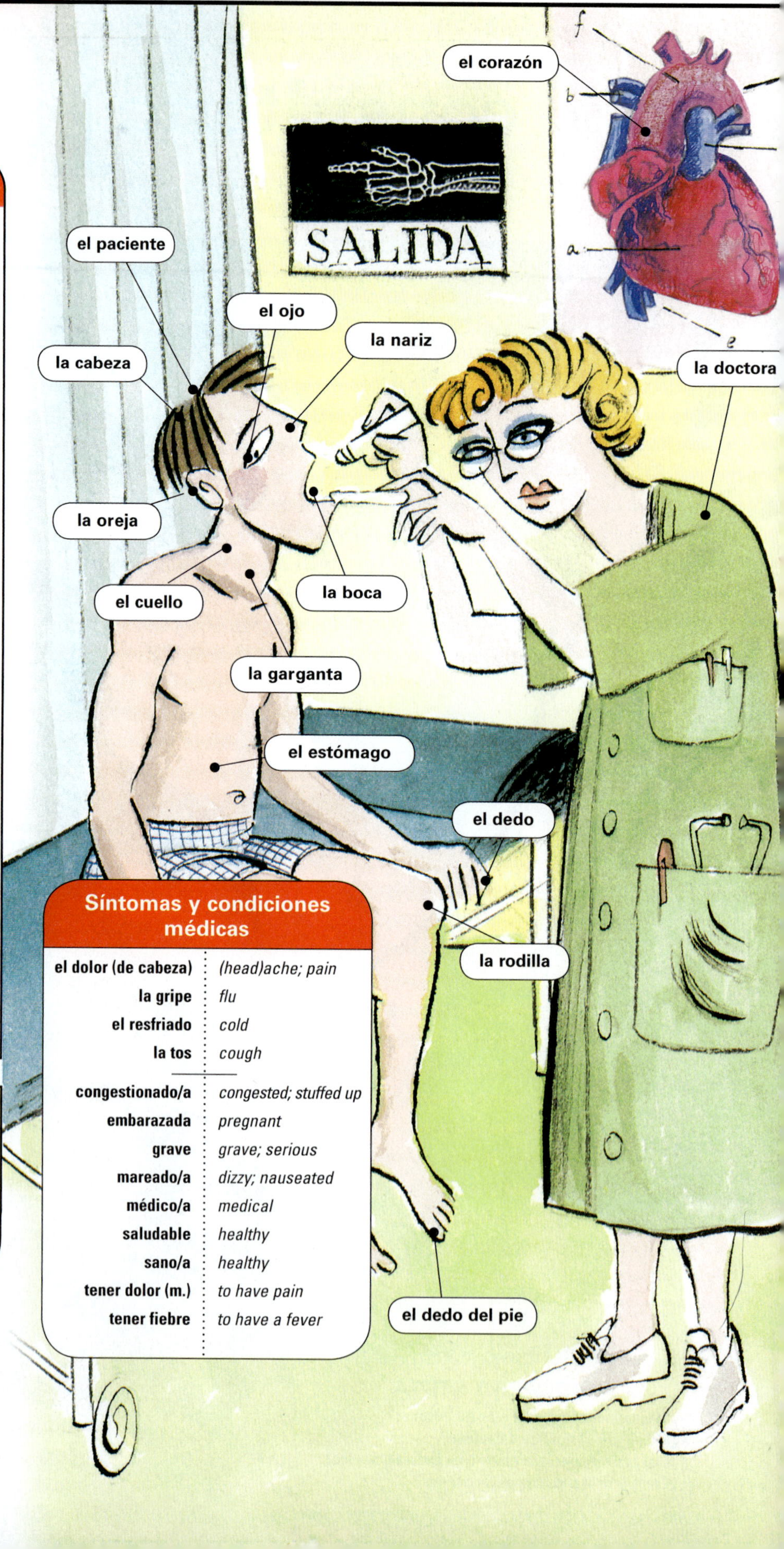

Síntomas y condiciones médicas

el dolor (de cabeza)	*(head)ache; pain*
la gripe	*flu*
el resfriado	*cold*
la tos	*cough*
congestionado/a	*congested; stuffed up*
embarazada	*pregnant*
grave	*grave; serious*
mareado/a	*dizzy; nauseated*
médico/a	*medical*
saludable	*healthy*
sano/a	*healthy*
tener dolor (m.)	*to have pain*
tener fiebre	*to have a fever*

recursos

WB	LM	vistas.vhlcentral.com
pp. 109–110	p. 55	Lección 10

La medicina

el antibiótico	*antibiotic*
la aspirina	*aspirin*
la pastilla	*pill; tablet*
la receta	*prescription*

Práctica

1 Escuchar Escucha las preguntas y selecciona la respuesta más adecuada.

a. Tengo dolor de cabeza y fiebre.
b. No fui a la clase porque estaba (*I was*) enfermo.
c. Me caí la semana pasada jugando al tenis.
d. Debes ir a la farmacia.
e. Porque tengo gripe.
f. Sí, tengo mucha tos por las noches.
g. Lo llevaron directamente a la sala de emergencia.
h. No sé. Todavía tienen que tomarme la temperatura.

1. ______ 3. ______ 5. ______ 7. ______
2. ______ 4. ______ 6. ______ 8. ______

2 Seleccionar Escucha la conversación entre Daniel y su doctor y selecciona la respuesta que mejor complete cada oración.

1. Daniel cree que tiene ____.
   a. gripe b. un resfriado c. la temperatura alta
2. A Daniel le duele la cabeza, estornuda, tose y ____.
   a. se cae b. tiene fiebre c. está congestionado
3. El doctor le ____.
   a. pone una inyección b. toma la temperatura
   c. mira el oído
4. A Daniel no le gustan ____.
   a. las inyecciones b. los antibióticos c. las visitas al doctor
5. El doctor dice que Daniel tiene ____.
   a. gripe b. un resfriado c. fiebre
6. Después de la consulta Daniel va a ____.
   a. la sala de emergencia b. la clínica c. la farmacia

3 Completar Completa las oraciones con una palabra de la misma familia de la palabra subrayada. Usa la forma correcta de cada palabra.

1. Cuando <u>oyes</u> algo, usas el ________.
2. Cuando te <u>enfermas</u>, te sientes ________ y necesitas ir al consultorio para ver a la ________.
3. ¿Alguien ________? Creo que oí un <u>estornudo</u> (*sneeze*).
4. No puedo <u>arrodillarme</u> (*kneel down*) porque me lastimé la ________ en un accidente de coche.
5. ¿Vas al ________ para <u>consultar</u> al médico?
6. Si te rompes un <u>diente</u>, vas al ________.

4 Contestar Mira el dibujo y contesta las preguntas.

1. ¿Qué hace la doctora?
2. ¿Qué hay en la pared (*wall*)?
3. ¿Qué hace la enfermera?
4. ¿Qué hace el paciente?
5. ¿A quién le duele la garganta?
6. ¿Qué tiene la paciente?

5

Asociaciones Trabajen en parejas para identificar las partes del cuerpo que ustedes asocian con estas actividades. Sigan el modelo.

modelo

nadar
Estudiante 1: Usamos los brazos para nadar.
Estudiante 2: Usamos las piernas también.

1. hablar por teléfono
2. tocar el piano
3. correr en el parque
4. escuchar música
5. ver una película
6. toser
7. llevar zapatos
8. comprar perfume
9. estudiar biología
10. comer pollo asado

AYUDA

Remember that in Spanish, parts of the body are usually referred to with an article and not a possessive adjective: **Me duelen los pies.** The indirect object pronoun **me** is used to express the concept of *my*.

6

Cuestionario Contesta el cuestionario seleccionando las respuestas que reflejen mejor tus experiencias. Suma (*Add*) los puntos de cada respuesta y anota el resultado. Después, con el resto de la clase, compara y analiza los resultados del cuestionario y comenta lo que dicen de la salud y de los hábitos de todo el grupo.

¿Tienes buena salud?

27–30 puntos	Salud y hábitos excelentes
23–26 puntos	Salud y hábitos buenos
22 puntos o menos	Salud y hábitos problemáticos

1. ¿Con qué frecuencia te enfermas? (resfriados, gripe, etc.)
Cuatro veces por año o más. (1 punto)
Dos o tres veces por año. (2 puntos)
Casi nunca. (3 puntos)

2. ¿Con qué frecuencia tienes dolores de estómago o problemas digestivos?
Con mucha frecuencia. (1 punto)
A veces. (2 puntos)
Casi nunca. (3 puntos)

3. ¿Con qué frecuencia sufres de dolores de cabeza?
Frecuentemente. (1 punto)
A veces. (2 puntos)
Casi nunca. (3 puntos)

4. ¿Comes verduras y frutas?
No, casi nunca como verduras ni frutas. (1 punto)
Sí, a veces. (2 puntos)
Sí, todos los días. (3 puntos)

5. ¿Eres alérgico/a a algo?
Sí, a muchas cosas. (1 punto)
Sí, a algunas cosas. (2 puntos)
No. (3 puntos)

6. ¿Haces ejercicios aeróbicos?
No, casi nunca hago ejercicios aeróbicos. (1 punto)
Sí, a veces. (2 puntos)
Sí, con frecuencia. (3 puntos)

7. ¿Con qué frecuencia te haces un examen médico?
Nunca o casi nunca. (1 punto)
Cada dos años. (2 puntos)
Cada año y/o antes de empezar a practicar un deporte. (3 puntos)

8. ¿Con qué frecuencia vas al dentista?
Nunca voy al dentista. (1 punto)
Sólo cuando me duele un diente. (2 puntos)
Por lo menos una vez por año. (3 puntos)

9. ¿Qué comes normalmente por la mañana?
No como nada por la mañana. (1 punto)
Tomo una bebida dietética. (2 puntos)
Como cereal y fruta. (3 puntos)

10. ¿Con qué frecuencia te sientes mareado/a?
Frecuentemente. (1 punto)
A veces. (2 puntos)
Casi nunca. (3 puntos)

Practice more at **vistas.vhlcentral.com.**

Comunicación

7

¿Qué les pasó? Trabajen en un grupo de dos o tres personas. Hablen de lo que les pasó y de cómo se sienten las personas que aparecen en los dibujos.

1. Adela

2. Francisco

3. Pilar

4. Pedro

5. Cristina

6. Félix

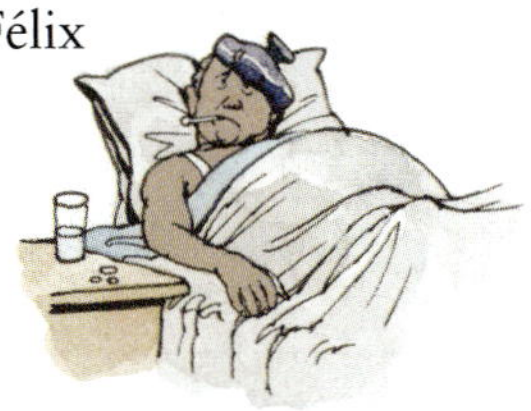

8

Un accidente Cuéntale a la clase de un accidente o una enfermedad que tuviste. Incluye información que conteste estas preguntas.

- ✓ ¿Qué ocurrió?
- ✓ ¿Dónde ocurrió?
- ✓ ¿Cuándo ocurrió?
- ✓ ¿Cómo ocurrió?
- ✓ ¿Quién te ayudó y cómo?
- ✓ ¿Tuviste algún problema después del accidente o después de la enfermedad?
- ✓ ¿Cuánto tiempo tuviste el problema?

9

Crucigrama Tu profesor(a) les va a dar a ti y a un(a) compañero/a un crucigrama *(crossword)* incompleto. Tú tienes las palabras que necesita tu compañero/a y él/ella tiene las palabras que tú necesitas. Tienen que darse pistas para completarlo. No pueden decir la palabra necesaria; deben utilizar definiciones, ejemplos y frases.

modelo

10 horizontal: La usamos para hablar.
14 vertical: Es el médico que examina los dientes.

¡Qué dolor!

Jimena no se siente bien y tiene que ir al doctor.

PERSONAJES

ELENA

JIMENA

Video: *Fotonovela*
Record and Compare

1

ELENA ¿Cómo te sientes?

JIMENA Me duele un poco la garganta. Pero no tengo fiebre.

ELENA Creo que tienes un resfriado. Te voy a llevar a casa.

2

ELENA ¿Don Diego ya fue a la farmacia? ¿Cuánto tiempo hace que lo llamaste?

JIMENA Hace media hora. Ay, qué cosas, de niña apenas me enfermaba. No perdí ni un solo día de clases.

ELENA Yo tampoco.

3

ELENA Nunca tenía resfriados, pero me rompí el brazo dos veces. Mi hermana y yo estábamos paseando en bicicleta y casi me di con un señor que caminaba por la calle. Me caí y me rompí el brazo.

4

JIMENA ¿Qué es esto?

ELENA Es té de jengibre. Cuando me dolía el estómago, mi mamá siempre me hacía tomarlo. Se dice que es bueno para el dolor de estómago.

JIMENA Pero no me duele el estómago.

5

JIMENA Hola, don Diego. Gracias por venir.

DON DIEGO Fui a la farmacia. Aquí están las pastillas para el resfriado. Se debe tomar una cada seis horas con las comidas. Y no se deben tomar más de seis pastillas al día.

6

(*La Sra. Díaz llama a Jimena.*)

JIMENA Hola, mamá. Don Diego me trajo los medicamentos... ¿Al doctor? ¿Estás segura? Allá nos vemos. (*A Elena*) Mi mamá ya hizo una cita para mí con el Dr. Meléndez.

DON DIEGO

SRA. DÍAZ

DR. MELÉNDEZ

7

SRA. DÍAZ ¿Te pusiste un suéter anoche?

JIMENA No, mamá. Se me olvidó.

SRA. DÍAZ Doctor, esta jovencita salió anoche, se le olvidó ponerse un suéter y parece que le dio un resfriado.

8

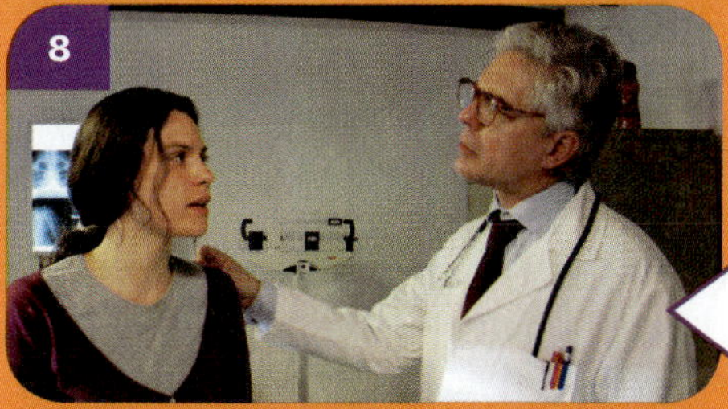

DR. MELÉNDEZ Jimena, ¿cuáles son tus síntomas?

JIMENA Toso con frecuencia y me duele la garganta.

DR. MELÉNDEZ ¿Cuánto tiempo hace que tienes estos síntomas?

JIMENA Hace dos días que me duele la garganta.

9

DR. MELÉNDEZ Muy bien. Aquí no tienes infección. No tienes fiebre. Te voy a mandar algo para la garganta. Puedes ir por los medicamentos inmediatamente a la farmacia.

10

SRA. DÍAZ Doctor, ¿cómo está? ¿Es grave?

DR. MELÉNDEZ No, no es nada grave. Jimena, la próxima vez, escucha a tu mamá. ¡Tienes que usar suéter!

Expresiones útiles

Discussing medical conditions

¿Cómo te sientes?
How do you feel?
Me duele un poco la garganta.
My throat hurts a little.
No me duele el estómago.
My stomach doesn't hurt.
De niño/a apenas me enfermaba.
As a child, I rarely got sick.
¡Soy alérgico/a a chile!
I'm allergic to chili powder!

Discussing remedies

Se dice que el té de jengibre es bueno para el dolor de estómago.
They say ginger tea is good for stomach aches.
Aquí están las pastillas para el resfriado.
Here are the pills for your cold.
Se debe tomar una cada seis horas.
You should take one every six hours.

Expressions with hacer

Hace + [*period of time*] **que** + [*present /preterite*]
¿Cuánto tiempo hace que tienes estos síntomas?
How long have you had these symptoms?
Hace dos días que me duele la garganta.
My throat has been hurting for two days.
¿Cuánto tiempo hace que lo llamaste?
How long has it been since you called him?
Hace media hora.
It's been a half hour (since I called).

Additional vocabulary

canela *cinnamon*
miel *honey*
terco *stubborn*

recursos
VM pp. 231–232
vistas.vhlcentral.com Lección 10

¿Qué pasó?

1

¿Cierto o falso? Decide si lo que dicen estas oraciones sobre Jimena es **cierto** o **falso**. Corrige las oraciones falsas.

	Cierto	Falso
1. Dice que de niña apenas se enfermaba.	❍	❍
2. Tiene dolor de garganta y fiebre.	❍	❍
3. Olvidó ponerse un suéter anoche.	❍	❍
4. Hace tres días que le duele la garganta.	❍	❍
5. El doctor le dice que tiene una infección.	❍	❍

2

Identificar Identifica quién puede decir estas oraciones.

1. Como dice tu mamá, tienes que usar suéter.
2. Por pasear en bicicleta me rompí el brazo dos veces.
3. ¿Cuánto tiempo hace que toses y te duele la garganta?
4. Tengo cita con el Dr. Meléndez.
5. Dicen que el té de jengibre es muy bueno para los dolores de estómago.
6. Nunca perdí un día de clases porque apenas me enfermaba.

DR. MELÉNDEZ

ELENA

JIMENA

3

Ordenar Pon estos sucesos en el orden correcto.

a. Jimena va a ver al doctor. ______
b. El doctor le dice a la Sra. Díaz que no es nada serio. ______
c. Elena le habla a Jimena de cuando se rompió el brazo. ______
d. El doctor le receta medicamentos. ______
e. Jimena le dice a Elena que le duele la garganta. ______
f. Don Diego le trae a Jimena las pastillas para el resfriado. ______

4

En el consultorio Trabajen en parejas para representar los papeles de un(a) médico/a y su paciente. Usen las instrucciones como guía.

El/La médico/a	El/La paciente
Pregúntale al / a la paciente qué le pasó.	→ Dile que te caíste en casa. Describe tu dolor.
Pregúntale cuánto tiempo hace que se cayó.	→ Describe la situación. Piensas que te rompiste el dedo.
Mira el dedo. Debes recomendar un tratamiento (*treatment*) al / a la paciente.	→ Debes hacer preguntas al / a la médico/a sobre el tratamiento (*treatment*).

AYUDA

Here are some useful expressions:

¿Cómo se lastimó...?
¿Qué le pasó?
¿Cuánto tiempo hace que...?
Tengo...
Estoy...
¿Es usted alérgico/a a algún medicamento?
Usted debe...

Ortografía

Concepts

El acento y las sílabas fuertes

In Spanish, written accent marks are used on many words. Here is a review of some of the principles governing word stress and the use of written accents.

as-pi-ri-na **gri-pe** **to-man** **an-tes**

In Spanish, when a word ends in a vowel, **-n**, or **-s**, the spoken stress usually falls on the next-to-last syllable. Words of this type are very common and do not need a written accent.

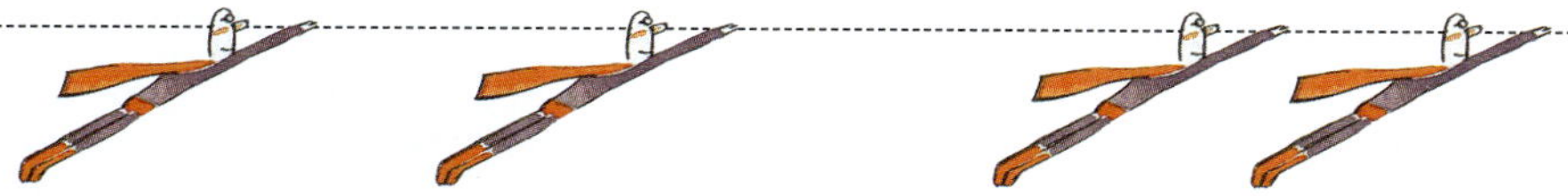

a-sí **in-glés** **in-fec-ción** **hé-ro-e**

When a word ends in a vowel, **-n**, or **-s**, and the spoken stress does *not* fall on the next-to-last syllable, then a written accent is needed.

hos-pi-tal **na-riz** **re-ce-tar** **to-ser**

When a word ends in any consonant *other* than **-n** or **-s**, the spoken stress usually falls on the last syllable. Words of this type are very common and do not need a written accent.

lá-piz **fút-bol** **hués-ped** **sué-ter**

When a word ends in any consonant *other* than **-n** or **-s** and the spoken stress does *not* fall on the last syllable, then a written accent is needed.

far-ma-cia **bio-lo-gí-a** **su-cio** **frí-o**

Diphthongs (two weak vowels or a strong and weak vowel together) are normally pronounced as a single syllable. A written accent is needed when a diphthong is broken into two syllables.

sol **pan** **mar** **tos**

Spanish words of only one syllable do not usually carry a written accent (unless it is to distinguish meaning: **se** and **sé**.)

CONSULTA

In Spanish, **a**, **e**, and **o** are considered strong vowels while **i** and **u** are weak vowels. To review this concept, see **Lección 3**, **Pronunciación**, p. 85.

Práctica Busca las palabras que necesitan acento escrito y escribe su forma correcta.

1. sal-mon
2. ins-pec-tor
3. nu-me-ro
4. fa-cil
5. ju-go
6. a-bri-go
7. ra-pi-do
8. sa-ba-do
9. vez
10. me-nu
11. o-pe-ra-cion
12. im-per-me-a-ble
13. a-de-mas
14. re-ga-te-ar
15. an-ti-pa-ti-co
16. far-ma-cia
17. es-qui
18. pen-sion
19. pa-is
20. per-don

El ahorcado Juega al ahorcado (*hangman*) para adivinar las palabras.

1. _ l _ _ _ _ a — Vas allí cuando estás enfermo.
2. _ _ _ e _ c _ _ n — Se usa para poner una vacuna (*vaccination*).
3. _ _ d _ o _ _ _ _ _ a — Permite ver los huesos.
4. _ _ _ i _ o — Trabaja en un hospital.
5. a _ _ _ b _ _ _ _ _ _ — Es una medicina.

recursos

LM p. 56 | vistas.vhlcentral.com Lección 10

EN DETALLE

Additional Reading

Servicios de salud

¿Sabías que en los países hispanos no necesitas pagar por los servicios de salud? Ésta es una de las diferencias que hay entre países como los Estados Unidos y los países hispanos.

En la mayor parte de estos países, el gobierno ofrece servicios médicos muy baratos o gratuitos° a sus ciudadanos°. Los turistas y extranjeros también pueden tener acceso a los servicios médicos a bajo° costo. La Seguridad Social y organizaciones similares son las responsables de gestionar° estos servicios.

Naturalmente, esto no funciona igual° en todos los países. En Ecuador, México y Perú, la situación varía según las regiones. Los habitantes de las ciudades y pueblos grandes tienen acceso a más servicios médicos, mientras que quienes viven en pueblos remotos sólo cuentan con° pequeñas clínicas.

Por su parte, Costa Rica, Colombia, Cuba y España tienen sistemas de salud muy desarrollados°.

Cruz verde de farmacia en Madrid, España

En España, por ejemplo, todas las personas tienen acceso a ellos y en muchos casos son completamente gratuitos. Según un informe de la Organización Mundial de la Salud, el sistema de salud español ocupa el séptimo° lugar del mundo. Esto se debe no sólo al buen funcionamiento° del sistema, sino también al nivel de salud general de la población. Impresionante, ¿no?

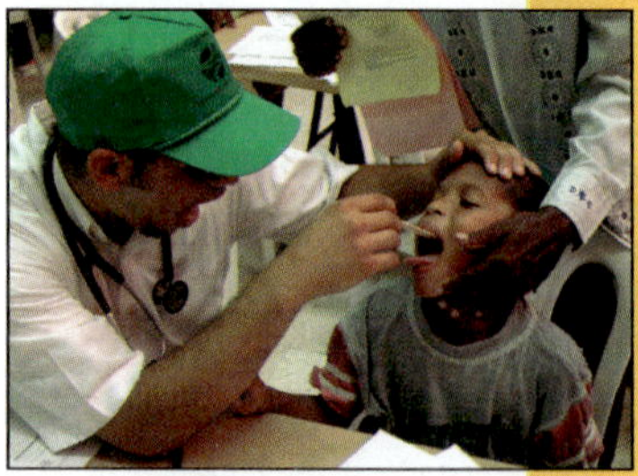

Consulta médica en la República Dominicana

Las farmacias

Farmacia de guardia: Las farmacias generalmente tienen un horario comercial. Sin embargo°, en cada barrio° hay una farmacia de guardia que abre las veinticuatro horas del día.

Productos farmacéuticos: Todavía hay muchas farmacias tradicionales que están más especializadas en medicinas y productos farmacéuticos. No venden una gran variedad de productos.

Recetas: Muchos medicamentos se venden sin receta médica. Los farmacéuticos aconsejan° a las personas sobre problemas de salud y les dan las medicinas.

Cruz° verde: En muchos países, las farmacias tienen como símbolo una cruz verde. Cuando la cruz verde está encendida°, la farmacia está abierta.

gratuitos *free (of charge)* ciudadanos *citizens* bajo *low* gestionar *to manage* igual *in the same way* cuentan con *have* desarrollados *developed* séptimo *seventh* funcionamiento *operation* Sin embargo *However* barrio *neighborhood* aconsejan *advise* Cruz *Cross* encendida *lit (up)*

ACTIVIDADES

1 **¿Cierto o falso?** Indica si lo que dicen las oraciones es **cierto** o **falso**. Corrige la información falsa.

1. En los países hispanos los gobiernos ofrecen servicios de salud accesibles a sus ciudadanos.
2. En los países hispanos los extranjeros tienen que pagar mucho dinero por los servicios médicos.
3. El sistema de salud español es uno de los mejores del mundo.
4. Las farmacias de guardia abren sólo los sábados y domingos.
5. En los países hispanos las farmacias venden una gran variedad de productos.
6. Los farmaceúticos de los países hispanos aconsejan a los enfermos y venden algunas medicinas sin necesidad de receta.
7. En México y otros países, los pueblos remotos cuentan con grandes centros médicos.
8. Muchas farmacias usan una cruz verde como símbolo.

ASÍ SE DICE

La salud

el chequeo (Esp., Méx.)	el examen médico
la droguería (Col.)	la farmacia
la herida	*injury; wound*
la píldora	la pastilla
los primeros auxilios	*first aid*
la sangre	*blood*

EL MUNDO HISPANO

Remedios caseros° y plantas medicinales

- **Achiote°** En Suramérica se usa para curar inflamaciones de garganta. Las hojas° de achiote se cuecen° en agua, se cuelan° y se hacen gárgaras° con esa agua.
- **Ají** En Perú se usan cataplasmas° de las semillas° de ají para aliviar los dolores reumáticos y la tortícolis°.
- **Azúcar** En Nicaragua y otros países centroamericanos se usa el azúcar para detener° la sangre en pequeñas heridas.
- **Sábila (aloe vera)** En Latinoamérica, el jugo de las hojas de sábila se usa para reducir cicatrices°. Se recomienda aplicarlo sobre la cicatriz dos veces al día, durante varios meses.

Remedios caseros *Home remedies* Achiote *Annatto* hojas *leaves* se cuecen *are cooked* se cuelan *they are drained* gárgaras *gargles* cataplasmas *pastes* semillas *seeds* tortícolis *stiff neck* detener *to stop* cicatrices *scars*

PERFILES

Curanderos° y chamanes

Códice Florentino, México, siglo XVI

¿Quieres ser doctor(a), juez(a)°, político/a o psicólogo/a? En algunas sociedades de las Américas **los curanderos** y **los chamanes** no tienen que escoger entre estas profesiones porque ellos son mediadores de conflictos y dan consejos a la comunidad. Su opinión es muy respetada.

Desde las culturas antiguas° de las Américas muchas personas piensan que la salud del cuerpo y de la mente sólo puede existir si hay un equilibrio entre el ser humano y la naturaleza. Los curanderos y los chamanes son quienes cuidan este equilibrio.

Los curanderos se especializan más en enfermedades físicas, mientras que los chamanes están más relacionados con los males° de la mente y el alma°. Ambos° usan plantas, masajes y rituales y sus conocimientos se basan en la tradición, la experiencia, la observación y la intuición.

Cuzco, Perú

Curanderos *Healers* juez(a) *judge* antiguas *ancient* males *illnesses* alma *soul* Ambos *Both*

Conexión Internet

¿Cuáles son algunos hospitales importantes del mundo hispano?

Go to **vistas.vhlcentral.com** to find more cultural information related to this **Cultura** section.

ACTIVIDADES

2 Comprensión Responde a las preguntas.

1. ¿Cómo se les llama a las farmacias en Colombia?
2. ¿Qué parte del achiote se usa para curar la garganta?
3. ¿Cómo se aplica la sábila para reducir cicatrices?
4. En algunas partes de las Américas, ¿quiénes mantienen el equilibrio entre el ser humano y la naturaleza?
5. ¿Qué usan los curanderos y chamanes para curar?

3 ¿Qué haces cuando tienes gripe? Escribe cuatro oraciones sobre las cosas que haces cuando tienes gripe. Explica si vas al médico, si tomas medicamentos o si sigues alguna dieta especial. Después, comparte tu texto con un(a) compañero/a.

Practice more at **vistas.vhlcentral.com.**

10.1 The imperfect tense

Tutorial

ANTE TODO In **Lecciones 6–9,** you learned the preterite tense. You will now learn the imperfect, which describes past activities in a different way.

The imperfect of regular verbs

		cantar	beber	escribir
SINGULAR FORMS	yo	cant**aba**	beb**ía**	escrib**ía**
	tú	cant**abas**	beb**ías**	escrib**ías**
	Ud./él/ella	cant**aba**	beb**ía**	escrib**ía**
PLURAL FORMS	nosotros/as	cant**ábamos**	beb**íamos**	escrib**íamos**
	vosotros/as	cant**abais**	beb**íais**	escrib**íais**
	Uds./ellos/ellas	cant**aban**	beb**ían**	escrib**ían**

¡ATENCIÓN!
Note that the imperfect endings of **-er** and **-ir** verbs are the same. Also note that the **nosotros** form of **-ar** verbs always carries an accent mark on the first **a** of the ending. All forms of **-er** and **-ir** verbs in the imperfect carry an accent on the first **i** of the ending.

De niña apenas me enfermaba.

Cuando me dolía el estómago, mi mamá me daba té de jengibre.

- There are no stem changes in the imperfect.

entender (e:ie)	**Entendíamos** japonés. *We used to understand Japanese.*
servir (e:i)	El camarero les **servía** el café. *The waiter was serving them coffee.*
doler (o:ue)	A Javier le **dolía** el tobillo. *Javier's ankle was hurting.*

- The imperfect form of **hay** is **había** *(there was; there were; there used to be).*

AYUDA
Like **hay, había** can be followed by a singular or plural noun.
Había un solo médico en la sala.
Había dos pacientes allí.

- **¡Atención! Ir, ser,** and **ver** are the only verbs that are irregular in the imperfect.

The imperfect of irregular verbs

		ir	ser	ver
SINGULAR FORMS	yo	ib**a**	er**a**	ve**ía**
	tú	ib**as**	er**as**	ve**ías**
	Ud./él/ella	ib**a**	er**a**	ve**ía**
PLURAL FORMS	nosotros/as	íb**amos**	ér**amos**	ve**íamos**
	vosotros/as	ib**ais**	er**ais**	ve**íais**
	Uds./ellos/ellas	ib**an**	er**an**	ve**ían**

CONSULTA

You will learn more about the contrast between the preterite and the imperfect in **Estructura 10.2**, pp. 346–347.

Uses of the imperfect

- As a general rule, the imperfect is used to describe actions which are seen by the speaker as incomplete or "continuing," while the preterite is used to describe actions which have been completed. The imperfect expresses what was happening at a certain time or how things used to be. The preterite, in contrast, expresses a completed action.

—¿Qué te **pasó**?
What happened to you?

—Me **torcí** el tobillo.
I sprained my ankle.

—¿Dónde **vivías** de niño?
Where did you live as a child?

—**Vivía** en San José.
I lived in San José.

- These expressions are often used with the imperfect because they express habitual or repeated actions: **de niño/a** (*as a child*), **todos los días** (*every day*), **mientras** (*while*).

Uses of the imperfect

1. Habitual or repeated actions	**Íbamos** al parque los domingos. *We used to go to the park on Sundays.*
2. Events or actions that were in progress	Yo **leía** mientras él **estudiaba**. *I was reading while he was studying.*
3. Physical characteristics	**Era** alto y guapo. *He was tall and handsome.*
4. Mental or emotional states	**Quería** mucho a su familia. *He loved his family very much.*
5. Telling time	**Eran** las tres y media. *It was 3:30.*
6. Age	Los niños **tenían** seis años. *The children were six years old.*

¡INTÉNTALO! Indica la forma correcta de cada verbo en el imperfecto.

1. Mis hermanos ___veían___ (ver) televisión todas las tardes.
2. Yo ______________ (viajar) en el tren de las 3:30.
3. ¿Dónde ______________ (vivir) Samuel de niño?
4. Tú ______________ (hablar) con Javier.
5. Leonardo y yo ______________ (correr) por el parque.
6. Ustedes ______________ (ir) a la clínica.
7. Nadia ______________ (bailar) merengue.
8. ¿Cuándo ______________ (asistir) tú a clase de español?
9. Yo ______________ (ser) muy feliz.
10. Nosotras ______________ (comprender) las preguntas.

recursos

WB pp. 111–112

LM p. 57

vistas.vhlcentral.com Lección 10

Práctica

1 **Completar** Primero, completa las oraciones con el imperfecto de los verbos. Luego, pon las oraciones en orden lógico y compáralas con las de un(a) compañero/a.

a. El doctor dijo que no __________ (ser) nada grave. ______
b. El doctor __________ (querer) ver la nariz del niño. ______
c. Su mamá __________ (estar) dibujando cuando Miguelito entró llorando. ______
d. Miguelito __________ (tener) la nariz hinchada (*swollen*). Fueron al hospital. ______
e. Miguelito no __________ (ir) a jugar más. Ahora quería ir a casa a descansar. ______
f. Miguelito y sus amigos __________ (jugar) al béisbol en el patio. ______
g. __________ (Ser) las dos de la tarde. ______
h. Miguelito le dijo a la enfermera que __________ (dolerle) la nariz. ______

2 **Transformar** Forma oraciones completas para describir lo que hacían Julieta y César. Usa las formas correctas del imperfecto y añade todas las palabras necesarias.

1. Julieta y César / ser / paramédicos
2. trabajar / juntos y / llevarse / muy bien
3. cuando / haber / accidente, / siempre / analizar / situación / con cuidado
4. preocuparse / mucho / por / pacientes
5. si / paciente / tener / mucho / dolor, / ponerle / inyección

3 **En la escuela de medicina** Usa los verbos de la lista para completar las oraciones con las formas correctas del imperfecto. Algunos verbos se usan más de una vez.

caerse	enfermarse	ir	querer	tener
comprender	estornudar	pensar	sentirse	tomar
doler	hacer	poder	ser	toser

1. Cuando Javier y Victoria __________ estudiantes de medicina, siempre __________ que ir al médico.
2. Cada vez que él __________ un examen, a Javier le __________ mucho la cabeza.
3. Cuando Victoria __________ ejercicios aeróbicos, siempre __________ mareada.
4. Todas las primaveras, Javier ______________ mucho porque es alérgico al polen.
5. Victoria también __________ de su bicicleta camino a la escuela.
6. Después de comer en la cafetería, a Victoria siempre le __________ el estómago.
7. Javier ____________ ser médico para ayudar a los demás.
8. Pero no ____________ por qué él ____________ con tanta frecuencia.
9. Cuando Victoria __________ fiebre, no __________ ni leer el termómetro.
10. A Javier __________ los dientes, pero nunca __________ ir al dentista.
11. Victoria ________________ mucho cuando __________ congestionada.
12. Javier y Victoria __________ que nunca __________ a graduarse.

Practice more at **vistas.vhlcentral.com.**

Comunicación

4

Entrevista Trabajen en parejas. Un(a) estudiante usa estas preguntas para entrevistar a su compañero/a. Luego compartan los resultados de la entrevista con la clase.

1. Cuando eras estudiante de primaria, ¿te gustaban tus profesores/as?
2. ¿Veías mucha televisión cuando eras niño/a?
3. Cuando tenías diez años, ¿cuál era tu programa de televisión favorito?
4. Cuando eras niño/a, ¿qué hacía tu familia durante las vacaciones?
5. ¿Cuántos años tenías en 2005?
6. Cuando estabas en el quinto año escolar, ¿qué hacías con tus amigos/as?
7. Cuando tenías once años, ¿cuál era tu grupo musical favorito?
8. Antes de tomar esta clase, ¿sabías hablar español?

5

Describir En parejas, túrnense para describir cómo eran sus vidas cuando eran niños. Pueden usar las sugerencias de la lista u otras ideas. Luego informen a la clase sobre la vida de su compañero/a.

NOTA CULTURAL

El Parque Nacional Tortuguero está en la costa del Caribe, al norte de la ciudad de Limón, en Costa Rica. Varias especies de tortuga (*turtle*) van a las playas del parque para poner (*lay*) sus huevos. Esto ocurre de noche, y hay guías que llevan pequeños grupos de turistas a observar este fenómeno biológico.

modelo

De niña, mi familia y yo siempre íbamos a Tortuguero. Tomábamos un barco desde Limón, y por las noches mirábamos las tortugas (*turtles*) en la playa. Algunas veces teníamos suerte, porque las tortugas venían a poner (*lay*) huevos. Otras veces, volvíamos al hotel sin ver ninguna tortuga.

- las vacaciones
- ocasiones especiales
- qué hacías durante el verano
- celebraciones con tus amigos/as
- celebraciones con tu familia
- cómo era tu escuela
- cómo eran tus amigos/as
- los viajes que hacías
- a qué jugabas
- qué hacías cuando te sentías enfermo/a

Síntesis

6

En el consultorio Tu profesor(a) te va a dar una lista incompleta con los pacientes que fueron al consultorio del doctor Donoso ayer. En parejas, conversen para completar sus listas y saber a qué hora llegaron las personas al consultorio y cuáles eran sus problemas.

10.2 The preterite and the imperfect

Tutorial

ANTE TODO Now that you have learned the forms of the preterite and the imperfect, you will learn more about how they are used. The preterite and the imperfect are not interchangeable. In Spanish, the choice between these two tenses depends on the context and on the point of view of the speaker.

COMPARE & CONTRAST

Use the preterite to...

1. Express actions that are viewed by the speaker as completed

Sandra **se rompió** la pierna.
Sandra broke her leg.

Fueron a Buenos Aires ayer.
They went to Buenos Aires yesterday.

2. Express the beginning or end of a past action

La película **empezó** a las nueve.
The movie began at nine o'clock.

Ayer **terminé** el proyecto para la clase de química.
Yesterday I finished the project for chemistry class.

3. Narrate a series of past actions or events

La doctora me **miró** los oídos, me **hizo** unas preguntas y **escribió** la receta.
The doctor looked in my ears, asked me some questions, and wrote the prescription.

Me di con la mesa, **me caí** y **me lastimé** el pie.
I bumped into the table, I fell, and I injured my foot.

Use the imperfect to...

1. Describe an ongoing past action with no reference to its beginning or end

Sandra **esperaba** al doctor.
Sandra was waiting for the doctor.

El médico **se preocupaba** por sus pacientes.
The doctor worried about his patients.

2. Express habitual past actions and events

Cuando **era** joven, **jugaba** al tenis.
When I was young, I used to play tennis.

De niño, Eduardo **se enfermaba** con mucha frecuencia.
As a child, Eduardo used to get sick very frequently.

3. Describe physical and emotional states or characteristics

La chica **quería** descansar. **Se sentía** mal y **tenía** dolor de cabeza.
The girl wanted to rest. She felt ill and had a headache.

Ellos **eran** altos y **tenían** ojos verdes.
They were tall and had green eyes.

Estábamos felices de ver a la familia.
We were happy to see our family.

AYUDA

These words and expressions, as well as similar ones, commonly occur with the preterite: **ayer, anteayer, una vez, dos veces, tres veces, el año pasado, de repente.**

They usually imply that an action has happened at a specific point in time. For a review, see **Estructura 6.3**, p. 207.

AYUDA

These words and expressions, as well as similar ones, commonly occur with the imperfect: **de niño/a, todos los días, mientras, siempre, con frecuencia, todas las semanas.** They usually express habitual or repeated actions in the past.

- The preterite and the imperfect often appear in the same sentence. In such cases, the imperfect describes what *was happening*, while the preterite describes the action that "interrupted" the ongoing activity.

Miraba la tele cuando **sonó** el teléfono.
I was watching TV when the phone rang.

Felicia **leía** el periódico cuando **llegó** Ramiro.
Felicia was reading the newspaper when Ramiro arrived.

- You will also see the preterite and the imperfect together in narratives such as fiction, news, and the retelling of events. The imperfect provides background information, such as time, weather, and location, while the preterite indicates the specific events that occurred.

Eran las dos de la mañana y el detective ya no **podía** mantenerse despierto. **Se bajó** lentamente del coche, **estiró** las piernas y **levantó** los brazos hacia el cielo oscuro.
It was two in the morning, and the detective could no longer stay awake. He slowly stepped out of the car, stretched his legs, and raised his arms toward the dark sky.

La luna **estaba** llena y no **había** en el cielo ni una sola nube. De repente, el detective **escuchó** un grito espeluznante proveniente del parque.
The moon was full and there wasn't a single cloud in the sky. Suddenly, the detective heard a piercing scream coming from the park.

Un médico colombiano desarrolló una vacuna contra la malaria

En 1986, el doctor colombiano Manuel Elkin Patarroyo creó la primera vacuna sintética para combatir la malaria. Esta enfermedad parecía haberse erradicado hacía décadas en muchas partes del mundo. Sin embargo, justo cuando Patarroyo terminó de elaborar la inmunización, los casos de malaria empezaban a aumentar de nuevo. En mayo de 1993, el doctor colombiano cedió la patente de la vacuna a la Organización Mundial de la Salud en nombre de Colombia. Los grandes laboratorios farmacéuticos presionaron a la OMS porque querían la vacuna. Las presiones no tuvieron éxito y, en 1995, el doctor Patarroyo y la OMS pactaron continuar con el acuerdo incial: la vacuna seguía siendo propiedad de la OMS.

¡INTÉNTALO! Elige el pretérito o el imperfecto para completar la historia. Explica por qué se usa ese tiempo verbal en cada ocasión.

1. ___Eran___ (Fueron/Eran) las doce.
2. __________ (Hubo/Había) mucha gente en la calle.
3. A las doce y media, Tomás y yo __________ (entramos/entrábamos) en el restaurante Tárcoles.
4. Todos los días yo __________ (almorcé/almorzaba) con Tomás al mediodía.
5. El camarero __________ (llegó/llegaba) inmediatamente con el menú.
6. Nosotros __________ (empezamos/empezábamos) a leerlo.
7. Yo __________ (pedí/pedía) el pescado.
8. De repente, el camarero __________ (volvió/volvía) a nuestra mesa.
9. Y nos __________ (dio/daba) una mala noticia.
10. Desafortunadamente, no __________ (tuvieron/tenían) más pescado.
11. Por eso Tomás y yo __________ (decidimos/decidíamos) comer en otro lugar.
12. __________ (Llovió/Llovía) mucho cuando __________ (salimos/salíamos) del restaurante.
13. Así que __________ (regresamos/regresábamos) al restaurante Tárcoles.
14. Esta vez, __________ (pedí/pedía) arroz con pollo.

recursos
WB pp. 113–116
LM p. 58
vistas.vhlcentral.com Lección 10

Práctica

1 **En el periódico** Completa esta noticia con las formas correctas del pretérito o el imperfecto.

Un accidente trágico

Ayer temprano por la mañana (1)________ (haber) un trágico accidente en el centro de San José cuando el conductor de un autobús no (2)________ (ver) venir un carro. La mujer que (3)________ (manejar) el carro (4)________ (morir) al instante y los paramédicos (5)________ (tener) que llevar al pasajero al hospital porque (6)________ (sufrir) varias fracturas. El conductor del autobús (7)________ (decir) que no (8)________ (ver) el carro hasta el último momento porque (9)________ (estar) muy nublado y (10)________ (llover). Él (11)________ (intentar) (*to attempt*) dar un viraje brusco (*to swerve*), pero (12)________ (perder) el control del autobús y no (13)________ (poder) evitar (*to avoid*) el accidente. Según nos informaron, no (14)________ (lastimarse) ningún pasajero del autobús.

AYUDA

Reading Spanish-language newspapers is a good way to practice verb tenses. You will find that both the imperfect and the preterite occur with great regularity. Many newsstands carry international papers, and many Spanish-language newspapers (such as Spain's ***El País***, Mexico's ***Reforma***, and Argentina's ***Clarín***) are on the Web.

2 **Seleccionar** Utiliza el tiempo verbal adecuado, según el contexto.

1. La semana pasada, Manolo y Aurora ________ (querer) dar una fiesta. ________ (Decidir) invitar a seis amigos y servirles mucha comida.
2. Manolo y Aurora ________ (estar) preparando la comida cuando Elena ________ (llamar). Como siempre, ________ (tener) que estudiar para un examen.
3. A las seis, ________ (volver) a sonar el teléfono. Su amigo Francisco tampoco ________ (poder) ir a la fiesta, porque ________ (tener) fiebre. Manolo y Aurora ________ (sentirse) muy tristes, pero ________ (tener) que preparar la comida.
4. Después de otros quince minutos, ________ (sonar) el teléfono. Sus amigos, los señores Vega, ________ (estar) en camino (*en route*) al hospital: a su hijo le ________ (doler) mucho el estómago. Sólo dos de los amigos ________ (poder) ir a la cena.
5. Por supuesto, ________ (ir) a tener demasiada comida. Finalmente, cinco minutos antes de las ocho, ________ (llamar) Ramón y Javier. Ellos ________ (pensar) que la fiesta ________ (ser) la próxima semana.
6. Tristes, Manolo y Aurora ________ (sentarse) a comer solos. Mientras ________ (comer), pronto ________ (llegar) a la conclusión de que ________ (ser) mejor estar solos: ¡La comida ________ (estar) malísima!

3 **Completar** Completa las frases de una manera lógica. Usa el pretérito o el imperfecto. En parejas, comparen sus respuestas.

1. De niño/a, yo...
2. Yo conducía el auto mientras...
3. Anoche mi novio/a...
4. Ayer el/la profesor(a)...
5. La semana pasada un(a) amigo/a...
6. Con frecuencia mis padres...
7. Esta mañana en la cafetería...
8. Hablábamos con el doctor cuando...

Practice more at **vistas.vhlcentral.com.**

Comunicación

4 **Entrevista** Usa estas preguntas para entrevistar a un(a) compañero/a acerca de su primer(a) novio/a. Si quieres, puedes añadir otras preguntas.

1. ¿Quién fue tu primer(a) novio/a?
2. ¿Cuántos años tenías cuando lo/la conociste?
3. ¿Cómo era él/ella?
4. ¿Qué le gustaba hacer? ¿Tenían ustedes los mismos pasatiempos?
5. ¿Por cuánto tiempo salieron ustedes?
6. ¿Adónde iban cuando salían?
7. ¿Pensaban casarse?
8. ¿Cuándo y por qué rompieron?

5 **La sala de emergencias** En parejas, miren la lista e inventen qué les pasó a estas personas que están en la sala de emergencias.

modelo

Eran las tres de la tarde. Como todos los días, Pablo jugaba al fútbol con sus amigos. Estaba muy contento. De repente, se cayó y se rompió el brazo. Entonces fue a la sala de emergencias.

Paciente	Edad	Hora	Estado
1. Pablo Romero	9 años	15:20	hueso roto (el brazo)
2. Estela Rodríguez	45 años	15:25	tobillo torcido
3. Lupe Quintana	29 años	15:37	embarazada, dolores
4. Manuel López	52 años	15:45	infección de garganta
5. Marta Díaz	3 años	16:00	congestión, fiebre
6. Roberto Salazar	32 años	16:06	dolor de oído
7. Marco Brito	18 años	16:18	daño en el cuello, posible fractura
8. Ana María Ortiz	66 años	16:29	reacción alérgica a un medicamento

6 **Situación** Anoche alguien robó (*stole*) el examen de la **Lección 10** de la oficina de tu profesor(a) y tú tienes que averiguar quién lo hizo. Pregúntales a tres compañeros dónde estaban, con quién estaban y qué hicieron entre las ocho y las doce de la noche.

Síntesis

7 **La primera vez** En grupos, cuéntense cómo fue la primera vez que les pusieron una inyección, se rompieron un hueso, pasaron la noche en un hospital, estuvieron mareados/as, etc. Incluyan estos datos en su conversación: una descripción del tiempo que hacía, sus edades, qué pasó y cómo se sentían.

10.3

Constructions with se

Tutorial

ANTE TODO In **Lección 7,** you learned how to use **se** as the third person reflexive pronoun (**Él se despierta. Ellos se visten. Ella se baña.**). **Se** can also be used to form constructions in which the person performing the action is not expressed or is de-emphasized.

Impersonal constructions with se

- In Spanish, verbs that are not reflexive can be used with **se** to form impersonal constructions. These are statements in which the person performing the action is not defined.

Se habla español en Costa Rica.
Spanish is spoken in Costa Rica.

Se puede leer en la sala de espera.
You can read in the waiting room.

Se hacen operaciones aquí.
They perform operations here.

Se necesitan medicinas enseguida.
They need medicine right away.

AYUDA

In English, the passive voice or indefinite subjects (*you, they, one*) are used where Spanish uses impersonal constructions with **se**.

- **¡Atención!** Note that the third person singular verb form is used with singular nouns and the third person plural form is used with plural nouns.

Se vende ropa. **Se venden** camisas.

- You often see the impersonal **se** in signs, advertisements, and directions.

Se for unplanned events

- **Se** also describes accidental or unplanned events. In this construction, the person who performs the action is de-emphasized, implying that the accident or unplanned event is not his or her direct responsibility. Note this construction.

se + [INDIRECT OBJECT PRONOUN] + [VERB] + [SUBJECT]

Se me cayó la pluma.

▶ In this type of construction, what would normally be the direct object of the sentence becomes the subject, and it agrees with the verb, not with the indirect object pronoun.

	I.O. PRONOUN	VERB		SUBJECT
Se	me, te, le, nos, os, les	quedó cayó dañó	SINGULAR	la receta. la taza. el radio.
		rompieron olvidaron perdieron	PLURAL	las botellas. las pastillas. las llaves.

▶ These verbs are the ones most frequently used with **se** to describe unplanned events.

Verbs commonly used with se

caer	*to fall; to drop*	**perder (e:ie)**	*to lose*
dañar	*to damage; to break down*	**quedar**	*to be left behind*
olvidar	*to forget*	**romper**	*to break*

Se me perdió el teléfono de la farmacia.
I lost the pharmacy's phone number.

Se nos olvidaron los pasajes.
We forgot the tickets.

▶ **¡Atención!** While Spanish has a verb for *to fall* (**caer**), there is no direct translation for *to drop*. **Dejar caer** (*To let fall*) or a **se** construction is often used to mean *to drop*.

El médico **dejó caer** la aspirina.
The doctor dropped the aspirin.

A mí **se me cayeron** los cuadernos.
I dropped the notebooks.

▶ To clarify or emphasize who the person involved in the action is, this construction commonly begins with the preposition **a** + [*noun*] or **a** + [*prepositional pronoun*].

Al paciente se le perdió la receta.
The patient lost his prescription.

A ustedes se les quedaron los libros en casa.
You left the books at home.

CONSULTA
For an explanation of prepositional pronouns, refer to **Estructura 9.4,** p. 318.

¡INTÉNTALO! Completa las oraciones con **se** impersonal y los verbos en presente.

A

1. Se enseñan (enseñar) cinco lenguas en esta universidad.
2. ________________ (comer) muy bien en Las Delicias.
3. ________________ (vender) muchas camisetas allí.
4. ________________ (servir) platos exquisitos cada noche.

Completa las oraciones con **se** y los verbos en pretérito.

B

1. Se me rompieron (*I broke*) las gafas.
2. ________________ (*You* (fam., sing.) *dropped*) las pastillas.
3. ________________ (*They lost*) la receta.
4. ________________ (*You* (form., sing.) *left*) aquí la radiografía.

recursos
WB pp. 117–118
LM p. 59
vistas.vhlcentral.com Lección 10

Práctica

1 **¿Cierto o falso?** Lee estas oraciones sobre la vida en 1901. Indica si lo que dice cada oración es **cierto** o **falso**. Luego corrige las oraciones falsas.

1. Se veía mucha televisión.
2. Se escribían muchos libros.
3. Se viajaba mucho en tren.
4. Se montaba a caballo.
5. Se mandaba correo electrónico.
6. Se preparaban comidas en casa.
7. Se llevaban minifaldas.
8. Se pasaba mucho tiempo con la familia.

2 **Traducir** Traduce estos letreros (*signs*) y anuncios al español.

1. Nurses needed
2. Eating and drinking prohibited
3. Programmers sought
4. English is spoken
5. Computers sold
6. No talking
7. Teacher needed
8. Books sold
9. Do not enter
10. Spanish is spoken

3 **¿Qué pasó?** Mira los dibujos e indica lo que pasó en cada uno.

1. camarero / pastel

2. Sr. Álvarez / espejo

3. Arturo / tarea

4. Sra. Domínguez / llaves

5. Carla y Lupe / botellas de vino

6. Juana / platos

Comunicación

4 **¿Distraído/a yo?** Trabajen en parejas y usen estas preguntas para averiguar cuál de los/las dos es más distraído/a (*absentminded*).

¿Alguna vez...

1. se te olvidó invitar a alguien a una fiesta o comida? ¿A quién?
2. se te quedó algo importante en la casa? ¿Qué?
3. se te perdió algo importante durante un viaje? ¿Qué?
4. se te rompió algo muy caro? ¿Qué?

¿Sabes...

5. si se permite el ingreso (*admission*) de perros al parque cercano a la universidad?
6. si en el supermercado se aceptan cheques?
7. dónde se arreglan zapatos y botas?
8. qué se sirve en la cafetería de la universidad los lunes?

5 **Opiniones** En parejas, terminen cada oración con ideas originales. Después, comparen los resultados con la clase para ver qué pareja tuvo las mejores ideas.

1. No se tiene que dejar propina cuando...
2. Antes de viajar, se debe...
3. Si se come bien, ...
4. Para tener una vida sana, se debe...
5. Se sirve la mejor comida en...
6. Se hablan muchas lenguas en...

Síntesis

6 **Anuncios** En grupos, preparen dos anuncios de televisión para presentar a la clase. Usen el imperfecto y por lo menos dos construcciones con **se** en cada uno.

modelo

Se me cayeron unos libros en el pie y me dolía mucho. Pero ahora no, gracias a SuperAspirina 500. ¡Dos pastillas y se me fue el dolor! Se puede comprar SuperAspirina 500 en todas las farmacias Recetamax.

10.4 Adverbs

Tutorial

ANTE TODO Adverbs are words that describe how, when, and where actions take place. They can modify verbs, adjectives, and even other adverbs. In previous lessons, you have already learned many Spanish adverbs, such as the ones below.

aquí	hoy	nunca
ayer	mal	siempre
bien	muy	temprano

- The most common adverbs end in **-mente**, equivalent to the English ending *-ly*.

  verdaderamente *truly, really* **generalmente** *generally* **simplemente** *simply*

- To form these adverbs, add **-mente** to the feminine form of the adjective. If the adjective does not have a special feminine form, just add **-mente** to the standard form. **¡Atención!** Adjectives do not lose their accents when adding **-mente**.

ADJECTIVE	FEMININE FORM	SUFFIX	ADVERB
seguro	segura	-mente	seguramente
fabuloso	fabulosa	-mente	fabulosamente
enorme		-mente	enormemente
fácil		-mente	fácilmente

- Adverbs that end in **-mente** generally follow the verb, while adverbs that modify an adjective or another adverb precede the word they modify.

  Maira dibuja **maravillosamente**.
  Maira draws wonderfully.

  Sergio está **casi siempre** ocupado.
  Sergio is almost always busy.

Common adverbs and adverbial expressions

a menudo	*often*	**así**	*like this; so*	**menos**	*less*
a tiempo	*on time*	**bastante**	*enough; rather*	**muchas veces**	*a lot; many times*
a veces	*sometimes*	**casi**	*almost*	**poco**	*little*
además (de)	*furthermore; besides*	**con frecuencia**	*frequently*	**por lo menos**	*at least*
apenas	*hardly; scarcely*	**de vez en cuando**	*from time to time*	**pronto**	*soon*
		despacio	*slowly*	**rápido**	*quickly*

¡ATENCIÓN!

When a sentence contains two or more adverbs in sequence, the suffix **-mente** is dropped from all but the last adverb.

Ex: **El médico nos habló simple y abiertamente.** *The doctor spoke to us simply and openly.*

¡ATENCIÓN!

Rápido functions as an adjective (**Ella tiene una computadora rápida.**) as well as an adverb (**Ellas corren rápido.**). Note that as an adverb, **rápido** does not need to agree with any other word in the sentence. You can also use the adverb **rápidamente (Ella corre rápidamente.)**.

recursos

WB pp. 119–120

LM p. 60

vistas.vhlcentral.com Lección 10

¡INTÉNTALO! Transforma los adjetivos en adverbios.

1. alegre alegremente
2. constante ___________
3. gradual ___________
4. perfecto ___________
5. real ___________
6. frecuente ___________
7. tranquilo ___________
8. regular ___________
9. maravilloso ___________
10. normal ___________
11. básico ___________
12. afortunado ___________

Práctica

1

Escoger Completa la historia con los adverbios adecuados.

1. La cita era a las dos, pero llegamos ______________. (mientras, nunca, tarde)
2. El problema fue que ______________ se nos dañó el despertador. (aquí, ayer, despacio)
3. La recepcionista no se enojó porque sabe que normalmente llego ______________. (a veces, a tiempo, poco)
4. ______________ el doctor estaba listo. (Por lo menos, Muchas veces, Casi)
5. ______________ tuvimos que esperar cinco minutos. (Así, Además, Apenas)
6. El doctor dijo que nuestra hija Irene necesitaba cambiar su rutina diaria ______________. (temprano, menos, inmediatamente)
7. El doctor nos explicó ______________ las recomendaciones del Cirujano General (*Surgeon General*) sobre la salud de los jóvenes. (de vez en cuando, bien, apenas)
8. ______________ nos dijo que Irene estaba bien, pero tenía que hacer más ejercicio y comer mejor. (Bastante, Afortunadamente, A menudo)

NOTA CULTURAL

La doctora Antonia Novello, de Puerto Rico, fue la primera mujer y la primera hispana en tomar el cargo de **Cirujana General** de los Estados Unidos (1990–1993).

Comunicación

2

Aspirina Lee el anuncio y responde a las preguntas con un(a) compañero/a.

1. ¿Cuáles son los adverbios que aparecen en el anuncio?
2. Según el anuncio, ¿cuáles son las ventajas (*advantages*) de este tipo de aspirina?
3. ¿Tienen ustedes dolores de cabeza? ¿Qué toman para curarlos?
4. ¿Qué medicamentos ven con frecuencia en los anuncios de televisión? Escriban descripciones de varios de estos anuncios. Usen adverbios en sus descripciones.

Practice more at **vistas.vhlcentral.com.**

Recapitulación

Concepts Diagnostics

Completa estas actividades para repasar los conceptos de gramática que aprendiste en esta lección.

1 **Completar** Completa el cuadro con la forma correcta del imperfecto. 12 pts.

yo/Ud./él/ella	tú	nosotros	Uds./ellos/ellas
era			
	cantabas		
		veníamos	
			querían

2 **Adverbios** Escoge el adverbio correcto de la lista para completar estas oraciones. Lee con cuidado las oraciones; los adverbios sólo se usan una vez. No vas a usar uno de los adverbios. 8 pts.

a menudo	apenas	fácilmente
a tiempo	casi	maravillosamente
además	despacio	por lo menos

1. Pablito se cae ________; un promedio (*average*) de cuatro veces por semana.
2. No me duele nada y no sufro de ninguna enfermedad; me siento ____________ bien.
3. —Doctor, ¿cómo supo que tuve una operación de garganta? —Muy ________, lo leí en su historial médico.
4. ¿Le duele mucho la espalda (*back*)? Entonces tiene que levantarse ________.
5. Ya te sientes mucho mejor, ¿verdad? Mañana puedes volver al trabajo; tu temperatura es ________ normal.
6. Es importante hacer ejercicio con regularidad, ________ tres veces a la semana.
7. El examen médico no comenzó ni tarde ni temprano. Comenzó ________, a las tres de la tarde.
8. Parece que ya te estás curando del resfriado. ________ estás congestionada.

RESUMEN GRAMATICAL

10.1 The imperfect tense pp. 342–343

The imperfect of regular verbs

cantar	beber	escribir
cantaba	bebía	escribía
cantabas	bebías	escribías
cantaba	bebía	escribía
cantábamos	bebíamos	escribíamos
cantabais	bebíais	escribíais
cantaban	bebían	escribían

- There are no stem changes in the imperfect: **entender (e:ie) → entendía; servir (e:i) → servía; doler (o:ue) → dolía**
- The imperfect of **hay** is **había**.
- Only three verbs are irregular in the imperfect.
  ir: **iba, ibas, iba, íbamos, ibais, iban**
  ser: **era, eras, era, éramos, erais, eran**
  ver: **veía, veías, veía, veíamos, veíais, veían**

10.2 The preterite and the imperfect pp. 346–347

Preterite	Imperfect
1. Completed actions **Fueron a Buenos Aires ayer.**	1. Ongoing past action **De niño, usted jugaba al fútbol.**
2. Beginning or end of past action **La película empezó a las nueve.**	2. Habitual past actions **Todos los domingos yo visitaba a mi abuela.**
3. Series of past actions or events **Me caí y me lastimé el pie.**	3. Description of states or characteristics **Ella era alta. Quería descansar.**

10.3 Constructions with se pp. 350–351

Impersonal constructions with se

Se	prohíbe fumar.
	habla español.
	hablan varios idiomas.

Se for unplanned events		
Se	me, te, le, nos, os, les	cayó la taza.
		dañó el radio.
		rompieron las botellas.
		olvidaron las llaves.

10.4 Adverbs *p. 354*

Formation of adverbs		
fácil	→	fácilmente
seguro	→	seguramente
verdadero	→	verdaderamente

3 **Un accidente** Escoge el imperfecto o el pretérito según el contexto para completar esta conversación. 10 pts.

NURIA Hola, Felipe. ¿Estás bien? ¿Qué es eso? ¿(1) (Te lastimaste/Te lastimabas) el pie?

FELIPE Ayer (2) (tuve/tenía) un pequeño accidente.

NURIA Cuéntame. ¿Cómo (3) (pasó/pasaba)?

FELIPE Bueno, (4) (fueron/eran) las cinco de la tarde y (5) (llovió/llovía) mucho cuando (6) (salí/salía) de la casa en mi bicicleta. No (7) (vi/veía) a una chica que (8) (caminó/caminaba) en mi dirección, y los dos (9) (nos caímos/nos caíamos) al suelo (*ground*).

NURIA Y la chica, ¿está bien ella?

FELIPE Sí. Cuando llegamos al hospital, ella sólo (10) (tuvo/tenía) dolor de cabeza.

4 **Oraciones** Escribe oraciones con **se** a partir de los elementos dados (*given*). Usa el tiempo especificado entre paréntesis y añade pronombres cuando sea necesario. 10 pts.

modelo

Carlos / quedar / la tarea en casa (pretérito)
A Carlos se le quedó la tarea en casa.

1. en la farmacia / vender / medicamentos (presente)
2. ¿(tú) / olvidar / las llaves / otra vez? (pretérito)
3. (yo) / dañar / la computadora (pretérito)
4. en esta clase / prohibir / hablar inglés (presente)
5. ellos / romper / las gafas / en el accidente (pretérito)

5 **En la consulta** Escribe al menos cinco oraciones sobre tu última visita al médico. Incluye cinco verbos en pretérito y cinco en imperfecto. Habla de qué te pasó, cómo te sentías, cómo era el/la doctor(a), qué te dijo, etc. Usa tu imaginación. 10 pts.

6 **Refrán** Completa el refrán con las palabras que faltan. ¡2 puntos EXTRA!

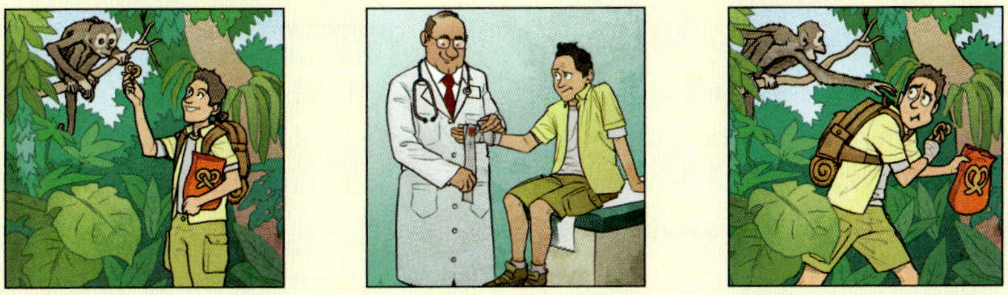

"Lo que ________ (*well*) se aprende, nunca ________ pierde."

Practice more at **vistas.vhlcentral.com.**

Audio: Reading
Additional Reading

Lectura

Antes de leer

Estrategia
Activating background knowledge

Using what you already know about a particular subject will often help you better understand a reading selection. For example, if you read an article about a recent medical discovery, you might think about what you already know about health in order to understand unfamiliar words or concepts.

Examinar el texto

Utiliza las estrategias de lectura que tú consideras más efectivas para hacer algunas observaciones preliminares acerca del texto. Después trabajen en parejas para comparar sus observaciones acerca del texto. Luego contesten estas preguntas:

- Analicen el formato del texto: ¿Qué tipo de texto es? ¿Dónde creen que se publicó este artículo?
- ¿Quiénes son Carla Baron y Tomás Monterrey?
- Miren la foto del libro. ¿Qué sugiere el título del libro sobre su contenido?

Conocimiento previo

Ahora piensen en su conocimiento previo° sobre el cuidado de la salud en los viajes. Consideren estas preguntas:

- ¿Viajaron alguna vez a otro estado o a otro país?
- ¿Tuvieron problemas durante sus viajes con el agua, la comida o el clima del lugar?
- ¿Olvidaron poner en su maleta algún medicamento que después necesitaron?
- Imaginen que su compañero/a se va de viaje. Díganle por lo menos cinco cosas que debe hacer para prevenir cualquier problema de salud.

conocimiento previo *background knowledge*

Practice more at **vistas.vhlcentral.com.**

Libro de la semana

Después de leer

Correspondencias

Busca las correspondencias entre los problemas y las recomendaciones.

Problemas

1. el agua _____
2. el sol _____
3. la comida _____
4. la identificación _____
5. el clima _____

Recomendaciones

a. Hay que adaptarse a los ingredientes desconocidos (*unknown*).
b. Toma sólo productos purificados (*purified*).
c. Es importante llevar ropa adecuada cuando viajas.
d. Lleva loción o crema con alta protección solar.
e. Lleva tu pasaporte.

Entrevista a Carla Baron

por Tomás Monterrey

Tomás: ¿Por qué escribió su libro *Cómo hacer un viaje saludable y feliz*?

Carla: Me encanta viajar, conocer otras culturas y escribir. Mi primer viaje lo hice cuando era estudiante universitaria. Todavía recuerdo el día en que llegamos a San Juan, Puerto Rico. Era el panorama ideal para unas vacaciones maravillosas, pero al llegar a la habitación del hotel, bebí mucha agua de la llave° y luego pedí un jugo de frutas con mucho hielo°. El clima en San Juan es tropical y yo tenía mucha sed y calor. Los síntomas llegaron en menos de media hora: pasé dos días con dolor de estómago y corriendo al cuarto de baño cada diez minutos. Desde entonces, siempre que viajo sólo bebo agua mineral y llevo un pequeño bolso con medicinas necesarias, como pastillas para el dolor y también bloqueador solar, una crema repelente de mosquitos y un desinfectante.

Tomás: ¿Son reales° las situaciones que se narran en su libro?

Carla: Sí, son reales y son mis propias° historias°. A menudo los autores crean caricaturas divertidas de un turista en dificultades. ¡En mi libro la turista en dificultades soy yo!

Tomás: ¿Qué recomendaciones puede encontrar el lector en su libro?

Carla: Bueno, mi libro es anecdótico y humorístico, pero el tema de la salud se trata° de manera seria. En general, se dan recomendaciones sobre ropa adecuada para cada sitio, consejos para protegerse del sol, y comidas y bebidas adecuadas para el turista que viaja al Caribe o Suramérica.

Tomás: ¿Tiene algún consejo para las personas que se enferman cuando viajan?

Carla: Muchas veces los turistas toman el avión sin saber nada acerca del país que van a visitar. Ponen toda su ropa en la maleta, toman el pasaporte, la cámara fotográfica y ¡a volar°! Es necesario tomar precauciones porque nuestro cuerpo necesita adaptarse al clima, al sol, a la humedad, al agua y a la comida. Se trata de° viajar, admirar las maravillas del mundo y regresar a casa con hermosos recuerdos. En resumen, el secreto es "prevenir en vez de° curar".

llave *faucet* hielo *ice* reales *true* propias *own* historias *stories* se trata *is treated* ¡a volar! *Off they go!* Se trata de *It's a question of* en vez de *instead of*

Seleccionar

Selecciona la respuesta correcta.

1. El tema principal de este libro es ____.
   a. Puerto Rico b. la salud y el agua c. otras culturas
   d. el cuidado de la salud en los viajes
2. Las situaciones narradas en el libro son ____.
   a. autobiográficas b. inventadas c. ficticias
   d. imaginarias
3. ¿Qué recomendaciones no vas a encontrar en este libro? ____
   a. cómo vestirse adecuadamente
   b. cómo prevenir las quemaduras solares
   c. consejos sobre la comida y la bebida
   d. cómo dar propina en los países del Caribe o de Suramérica
4. En opinión de la señorita Baron, ____.
   a. es bueno tomar agua de la llave y beber jugo de frutas con mucho hielo
   b. es mejor tomar solamente agua embotellada (*bottled*)
   c. los minerales son buenos para el dolor abdominal
   d. es importante visitar el cuarto de baño cada diez minutos
5. ¿Cuál de estos productos no lleva la autora cuando viaja a otros países? ____
   a. desinfectante
   b. crema repelente
   c. detergente
   d. pastillas medicinales

Escritura

Estrategia

Mastering the simple past tenses

In Spanish, when you write about events that occurred in the past you will need to know when to use the preterite and when to use the imperfect tense. A good understanding of the uses of each tense will make it much easier to determine which one to use as you write.

Look at the summary of the uses of the preterite and the imperfect and write your own example sentence for each of the rules described.

Preterite vs. imperfect

Preterite

1. Completed actions
____
____
2. Beginning or end of past actions
____
____
3. Series of past actions
____
____

Imperfect

1. Ongoing past actions
____
____
2. Habitual past actions
____
____
3. Mental, physical, and emotional states and characteristics in the past
____
____

Get together with a few classmates to compare your example sentences. Then use these sentences and the chart as a guide to help you decide which tense to use as you are writing a story or other type of narration about the past.

Tema

Escribir una historia

Escribe una historia acerca de una experiencia tuya° (o de otra persona) con una enfermedad, accidente o problema médico. Tu historia puede ser real o imaginaria y puede tratarse de un incidente divertido, humorístico o desastroso. Incluye todos los detalles relevantes. Consulta la lista de sugerencias° con detalles que puedes incluir.

- Descripción del/de la paciente
  nombre y apellidos
  edad
  características físicas
  historial médico°
- Descripción de los síntomas
  enfermedades
  accidente
  problemas médicos
- Descripción del tratamiento°
  tratamientos
  recetas
  operaciones

tuya *of yours* **sugerencias** *suggestions* **historial médico** *medical history* **tratamiento** *treatment*

Escuchar

Audio: Activities

Estrategia

Listening for specific information

You can listen for specific information effectively once you identify the subject of a conversation and use your background knowledge to predict what kinds of information you might hear.

To practice this strategy, you will listen to a paragraph from a letter Marta wrote to a friend about her fifteenth birthday celebration. Before you listen to the paragraph, use what you know about this type of party to predict the content of the letter. What kinds of details might Marta include in her description of the celebration? Now listen to the paragraph and jot down the specific information Marta relates. Then compare these details to the predictions you made about the letter.

Preparación

Mira la foto. ¿Con quién crees que está conversando Carlos Peña? ¿De qué están hablando?

Ahora escucha

Ahora escucha la conversación de la señorita Méndez y Carlos Peña. Marca las frases donde se mencionan los síntomas de Carlos.

1. ____ Tiene infección en los ojos.
2. ____ Se lastimó el dedo.
3. ____ No puede dormir.
4. ____ Siente dolor en los huesos.
5. ____ Está mareado.
6. ____ Está congestionado.
7. ____ Le duele el estómago.
8. ____ Le duele la cabeza.
9. ____ Es alérgico a la aspirina.
10. ____ Tiene tos.
11. ____ Le duele la garganta.
12. ____ Se rompió la pierna.
13. ____ Tiene dolor de oído.
14. ____ Tiene frío.

Comprensión

Preguntas

1. ¿Tiene fiebre Carlos?
2. ¿Cuánto tiempo hace que le duele la garganta a Carlos?
3. ¿Qué tiene que hacer el médico antes de recetarle algo a Carlos?
4. ¿A qué hora es su cita con el médico?
5. Después de darle una cita con el médico, ¿qué otra información le pide a Carlos la señorita del consultorio?
6. En tu opinión, ¿qué tiene Carlos? ¿Gripe? ¿Un resfriado? ¿Alergias? Explica tu opinión.

Diálogo

Con un(a) compañero/a, escribe el diálogo entre el Dr. Aguilar y Carlos Peña en el consultorio del médico. Usa la información del diálogo telefónico para pensar en lo que dice el médico mientras examina a Carlos. Imagina cómo responde Carlos y qué preguntas le hace al médico. ¿Cuál es el diagnóstico del médico?

Practice more at **vistas.vhlcentral.com.**

En pantalla

Si tienes dolor de estómago, un calambre° u otra dolencia° simple y no quieres ir al médico, puedes ir a la farmacia. En muchos países hispanos, no necesitas una receta para comprar algunas medicinas y, además, los farmacéuticos están capacitados° para recetar medicamentos en casos de enfermedades leves°. Mucha gente los visita pidiendo consejos para aliviar sus males°. Antes, los boticarios° eran una especie de artesanos° de las medicinas que ejercían bajo la tutela° de los médicos. Ahora, su profesión tiene un carácter más científico e incluso forma parte de la oferta educativa de muchas universidades.

Vocabulario útil

el bondi	*bus (Arg.)*
la cancha	*stadium (Arg.)*
los hinchas	*sports fans (usually soccer; Arg.)*
se hace el duro	*acts tough*
tirarse	*to jump, to dive*
trepar	*to climb*

Preparación

¿Conoces alguna persona temeraria (*reckless*) a quien le gusten las situaciones de riesgo (*risky*)? Comparte alguna de sus anécdotas con la clase.

¿Cierto o falso?

Indica si lo que dice cada oración es **cierto** o **falso**. Corrige las oraciones falsas.

1. Bailaba en la bañadera y se cayó.
2. Se cayó del techo (*roof*) cuando quiso arreglar una ventana.
3. Se bajó del (*got off of*) tren en movimiento.
4. Saltó del escenario temerariamente.

Un chico travieso

Sin duda, Miguel era un niño muy travieso (*mischievous*). En parejas, imaginen cómo fue su niñez: describan lo que hacía en su casa, en la escuela y con sus amigos. Usen el imperfecto.

calambre *cramp* **dolencia** *ailment* **capacitados** *qualified* **leves** *mild* **males** *illnesses* **boticarios** *pharmacists* **artesanos** *craftsmen* **ejercían...** *practiced under the guidance*

Anuncio de Anaflex

1

—Voy a treparme a arreglar la antena.
—¡Sí, Miguel!

2

... bailo en la cancha la *Macarena*...

3

Cualquiera se hace el duro cuando tiene con qué.

Video: TV Clip

Practice more at **vistas.vhlcentral.com.**

Flash CULTURA

Argentina tiene una gran tradición médica influenciada desde el siglo XIX por la medicina francesa. Tres de los cinco premios Nobel de esta nación están relacionados con investigaciones médicas que han hecho° grandes aportes° al avance de las ciencias de la salud. Además, existen otros adelantos° de médicos argentinos que han hecho historia. Entre ellos se cuentan el *bypass* coronario, desarrollado° por el cirujano° René Favaloro en 1967, y la técnica de cirugía cardiovascular sin circulación extracorpórea° desarrollada en 1978 por Federico Benetti, quien es considerado uno de los padres de la cirugía cardíaca moderna.

Vocabulario útil

la cita previa	*previous appointment*
la guardia	*emergency room*
Me di un golpe.	*I got hit.*
la práctica	*rotation (hands-on medical experience)*

Preparación

¿Qué haces si tienes un pequeño accidente o quieres hacer una consulta? ¿Visitas a tu médico general o vas al hospital? ¿Debes pedir un turno (*appointment*)?

¿Cierto o falso?

Indica si las oraciones son **ciertas** o **falsas**.

1. Silvina tuvo un accidente en su automóvil.
2. Silvina fue a la guardia del hospital.
3. La guardia del hospital está abierta sólo durante el día y es necesario tener cita previa.
4. Los entrevistados (*interviewees*) tienen enfermedades graves.
5. En Argentina, los médicos reciben la certificación cuando terminan la práctica.

amplia *ample* **han hecho** *have done* **aportes** *contributions* **adelantos** *advances* **desarrollado** *developed* **cirujano** *surgeon* **extracorpórea** *out-of-body* **podría** *could*

La salud

1 **¿Le podría° pedir que me explique qué es la guardia?**

2 **Nuestro hospital público es gratuito para todas las personas.**

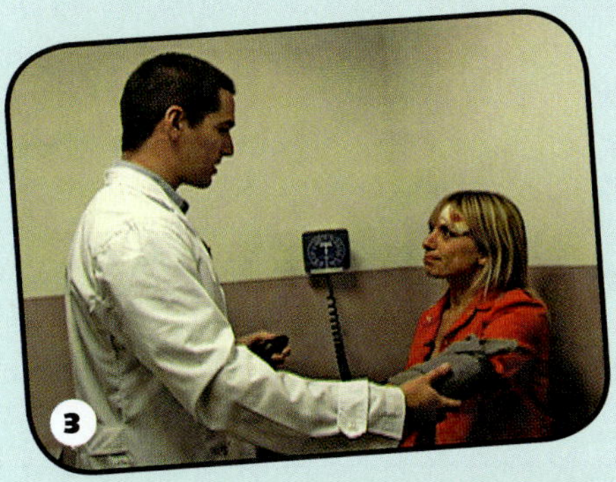

3 **... la carrera de medicina comienza con el primer año de la universidad.**

Video: *Flash cultura*

Practice more at **vistas.vhlcentral.com.**

recursos

VM pp. 309–310	vistas.vhlcentral.com Lección 10

Video: *Panorama cultural*
Interactive map

Costa Rica

El país en cifras

- **Área:** 51.100 km^2 (19.730 $millas^2$), *aproximadamente el área de Virginia Occidental°*
- **Población:** 4.957.000

Costa Rica es el país de Centroamérica con la población más homogénea. El 94% de sus habitantes es blanco y mestizo°. Más del 50% de la población es de ascendencia° española y un alto porcentaje tiene sus orígenes en otros países europeos.

- **Capital:** San José —1.655.000
- **Ciudades principales:** Alajuela, Cartago, Puntarenas, Heredia

SOURCE: Population Division, UN Secretariat

- **Moneda:** colón costarricense
- **Idioma:** español (oficial)

Bandera de Costa Rica

Costarricenses célebres

- **Carmen Lyra,** escritora (1888–1949)
- **Chavela Vargas,** cantante (1919–)
- **Óscar Arias Sánchez,** ex presidente de Costa Rica (1941–)
- **Claudia Poll,** nadadora° olímpica (1941–)

Óscar Arias recibió el Premio Nobel de la Paz en 1987.

Virginia Occidental *West Virginia* **mestizo** *of indigenous and white parentage* **ascendencia** *descent* **nadadora** *swimmer* **ejército** *army* **gastos** *expenditures* **invertir** *to invest* **cuartel** *barracks*

Mercado Central en San José

Vista del volcán Arenal

Edificio Metálico en San José

Basílica de Nuestra Señora de los Ángeles en Cartago

recursos		
WB pp. 121–122	VM pp. 267–268	vistas.vhlcentral.com Lección 10

¡Increíble pero cierto!

Costa Rica es el único país latinoamericano que no tiene ejército°. Sin gastos° militares, el gobierno puede invertir° más dinero en la educación y las artes. En la foto aparece el Museo Nacional de Costa Rica, antiguo cuartel° del ejército.

Lugares • Los parques nacionales

El sistema de parques nacionales de Costa Rica ocupa aproximadamente el 12% de su territorio y fue establecido° para la protección de su biodiversidad. En los parques, los ecoturistas pueden admirar montañas, cataratas° y una gran variedad de plantas exóticas. Algunos ofrecen también la oportunidad de ver quetzales°, monos°, jaguares, armadillos y mariposas° en su hábitat natural.

Economía • Las plantaciones de café

Costa Rica fue el primer país centroamericano en desarrollar° la industria del café. En el siglo° XIX, los costarricenses empezaron a exportar esta semilla a Inglaterra°, lo que significó una contribución importante a la economía de la nación. Actualmente, más de 50.000 costarricenses trabajan en el cultivo del café. Este producto representa cerca del 15% de sus exportaciones anuales.

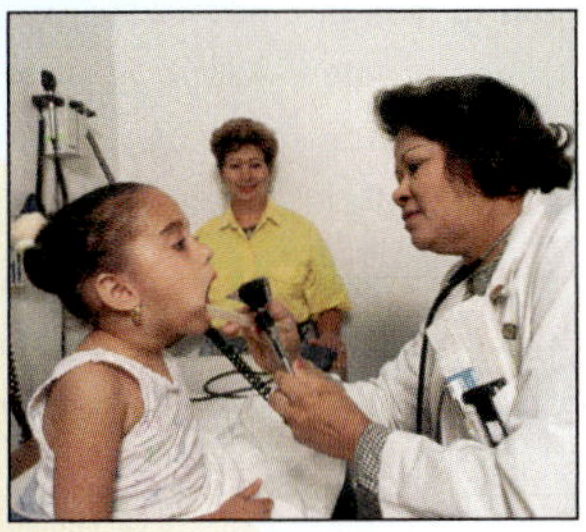

Sociedad • Una nación progresista

Costa Rica es un país progresista. Tiene un nivel de alfabetización° del 96%, uno de los más altos de Latinoamérica. En 1870, esta nación centroamericana abolió la pena de muerte° y en 1948 eliminó el ejército e hizo obligatoria y gratuita° la educación para todos sus ciudadanos.

Parque Morazán en San José

¿Qué aprendiste? Responde a las preguntas con oraciones completas.

1. ¿Cómo se llama la capital de Costa Rica?
2. ¿Quién es Claudia Poll?
3. ¿Qué porcentaje del territorio de Costa Rica ocupan los parques nacionales?
4. ¿Para qué se establecieron los parques nacionales?
5. ¿Qué pueden ver los turistas en los parques nacionales?
6. ¿Cuántos costarricenses trabajan en las plantaciones de café hoy día?
7. ¿Cuándo eliminó Costa Rica la pena de muerte?

Conexión Internet Investiga estos temas en **vistas.vhlcentral.com**.

Practice more at **vistas.vhlcentral.com.**

1. Busca información sobre Óscar Arias Sánchez. ¿Quién es? ¿Por qué se le considera (*is he considered*) un costarricense célebre?
2. Busca información sobre los artistas de Costa Rica. ¿Qué artista, escritor o cantante te interesa más? ¿Por qué?

establecido *established* **cataratas** *waterfalls* **quetzales** *type of tropical bird* **monos** *monkeys* **mariposas** *butterflies* **en desarrollar** *to develop* **siglo** *century* **Inglaterra** *England* **nivel de alfabetización** *literacy rate* **pena de muerte** *death penalty* **gratuita** *free*

El cuerpo

la boca	*mouth*
el brazo	*arm*
la cabeza	*head*
el corazón	*heart*
el cuello	*neck*
el cuerpo	*body*
el dedo	*finger*
el dedo del pie	*toe*
el estómago	*stomach*
la garganta	*throat*
el hueso	*bone*
la nariz	*nose*
el oído	*(sense of) hearing; inner ear*
el ojo	*eye*
la oreja	*(outer) ear*
el pie	*foot*
la pierna	*leg*
la rodilla	*knee*
el tobillo	*ankle*

La salud

el accidente	*accident*
el antibiótico	*antibiotic*
la aspirina	*aspirin*
la clínica	*clinic*
el consultorio	*doctor's office*
el/la dentista	*dentist*
el/la doctor(a)	*doctor*
el dolor (de cabeza)	*(head)ache; pain*
el/la enfermero/a	*nurse*
el examen médico	*physical exam*
la farmacia	*pharmacy*
la gripe	*flu*
el hospital	*hospital*
la infección	*infection*
el medicamento	*medication*
la medicina	*medicine*
la operación	*operation*
el/la paciente	*patient*
la pastilla	*pill; tablet*
la radiografía	*X-ray*
la receta	*prescription*
el resfriado	*cold (illness)*
la sala de emergencia(s)	*emergency room*
la salud	*health*
el síntoma	*symptom*
la tos	*cough*

Verbos

caerse	*to fall (down)*
dañar	*to damage; to break down*
darse con	*to bump into; to run into*
doler (o:ue)	*to hurt*
enfermarse	*to get sick*
estar enfermo/a	*to be sick*
estornudar	*to sneeze*
lastimarse (el pie)	*to injure (one's foot)*
olvidar	*to forget*
poner una inyección	*to give an injection*
prohibir	*to prohibit*
recetar	*to prescribe*
romper	*to break*
romperse (la pierna)	*to break (one's leg)*
sacar(se) un diente	*to have a tooth removed*
ser alérgico/a (a)	*to be allergic (to)*
sufrir una enfermedad	*to suffer an illness*
tener dolor *(m.)*	*to have a pain*
tener fiebre	*to have a fever*
tomar la temperatura	*to take someone's temperature*
torcerse (o:ue) (el tobillo)	*to sprain (one's ankle)*
toser	*to cough*

Adjetivos

congestionado/a	*congested; stuffed-up*
embarazada	*pregnant*
grave	*grave; serious*
mareado/a	*dizzy; nauseated*
médico/a	*medical*
saludable	*healthy*
sano/a	*healthy*

Adverbios

a menudo	*often*
a tiempo	*on time*
a veces	*sometimes*
además (de)	*furthermore; besides*
apenas	*hardly; scarcely*
así	*like this; so*
bastante	*enough; rather*
casi	*almost*
con frecuencia	*frequently*
de niño/a	*as a child*
de vez en cuando	*from time to time*
despacio	*slowly*
menos	*less*
mientras	*while*
muchas veces	*a lot; many times*
poco	*little*
por lo menos	*at least*
pronto	*soon*
rápido	*quickly*
todos los días	*every day*

Expresiones útiles *See page 337.*

Audio: Vocabulary

recursos

LM p. 60

vistas.vhlcentral.com Lección 10

La tecnología 11

Communicative Goals

You will learn how to:

- Talk about using technology and electronics
- Use common expressions on the telephone
- Talk about car trouble

A PRIMERA VISTA

- ¿Qué hace la chica?
- ¿Crees que usa su computadora con frecuencia?
- ¿Es una chica saludable?
- ¿Qué partes del cuerpo se ven en la foto?

Talking Picture, Tutorials & Games
Audio: Activities

La tecnología

Más vocabulario

la cámara digital/de video	*digital/video camera*
el canal	*(TV) channel*
el correo de voz	*voice mail*
el estéreo	*stereo*
el *fax*	*fax (machine)*
la pantalla táctil	*touch screen*
el reproductor de CD	*CD player*
la televisión por cable	*cable television*
el video	*video*
el archivo	*file*
arroba	*@ symbol*
el blog	*blog*
la conexión inalámbrica	*wireless connection*
la dirección electrónica	*e-mail address*
Internet	*Internet*
el mensaje de texto	*text message*
la página principal	*home page*
el programa de computación	*software*
la red	*network; Web*
el sitio web	*website*
apagar	*to turn off*
borrar	*to erase*
descargar	*to download*
escanear	*to scan*
funcionar	*to work*
grabar	*to record*
guardar	*to save*
imprimir	*to print*
llamar	*to call*
navegar (en Internet)	*to surf (the Internet)*
poner, prender	*to turn on*
sonar (o:ue)	*to ring*
descompuesto/a	*not working; out of order*
lento/a	*slow*
lleno/a	*full*

Variación léxica

computadora ⟷ ordenador (*Esp.*), computador (*Col.*)
descargar ⟷ bajar (*Arg., Col., Esp., Ven.*)

recursos
WB pp. 123–124
LM p. 61
vistas.vhlcentral.com Lección 11

Práctica

1 Escuchar Escucha la conversación entre dos amigas. Después completa las oraciones.

1. María y Ana están en ______.
   a. una tienda b. un cibercafé c. un restaurante
2. A María le encantan ______.
   a. los celulares b. las cámaras digitales c. los cibercafés
3. Ana prefiere guardar las fotos en ______.
   a. la pantalla b. un archivo c. un cederrón
4. María quiere tomar un café y ______.
   a. poner la computadora b. sacar fotos digitales
   c. navegar en Internet
5. Ana paga por el café y ______.
   a. el uso de Internet b. la impresora c. el cederrón

2 ¿Cierto o falso? Escucha las oraciones e indica si lo que dice cada una es **cierto** o **falso**, según el dibujo.

1. ______	5. ______
2. ______	6. ______
3. ______	7. ______
4. ______	8. ______

3 Oraciones Escribe oraciones usando estos elementos. Usa el pretérito y añade las palabras necesarias.

1. yo / descargar / fotos / Internet
2. tú / apagar / televisor / diez / noche
3. Daniel y su esposa / comprar / computadora portátil / ayer
4. Sara y yo / ir / cibercafé / para / navegar en Internet
5. Jaime / decidir / comprar / reproductor de MP3
6. teléfono celular / sonar / pero / yo / no contestar

4 Preguntas Mira el dibujo y contesta las preguntas.

1. ¿Qué tipo de café es?
2. ¿Cuántas impresoras hay? ¿Cuántos ratones?
3. ¿Por qué vinieron estas personas al café?
4. ¿Qué hace el camarero?
5. ¿Qué hace la mujer en la computadora? ¿Y el hombre?
6. ¿Qué máquinas están cerca del televisor?
7. ¿Dónde hay un cibercafé en tu comunidad?
8. ¿Por qué puedes tú necesitar un cibercafé?

En la gasolinera

Más vocabulario

la autopista, la carretera	*highway*
la calle	*street*
la circulación, el tráfico	*traffic*
el garaje, el taller (mecánico)	*(mechanic's) garage; repair shop*
la licencia de conducir	*driver's license*
el/la mecánico/a	*mechanic*
la policía	*police (force)*
la velocidad máxima	*speed limit*
arrancar	*to start*
arreglar	*to fix; to arrange*
bajar(se) de	*to get off of/out of (a vehicle)*
conducir, manejar	*to drive*
estacionar	*to park*
parar	*to stop*
subir(se) a	*to get on/into (a vehicle)*

5 **Completar** Completa estas oraciones con las palabras correctas.

1. Para poder conducir legalmente, necesitas...
2. Puedes poner las maletas en...
3. Si tu carro no funciona, debes llevarlo a...
4. Para llenar el tanque de tu coche, necesitas ir a...
5. Antes de un viaje largo, es importante revisar...
6. Otra palabra para autopista es...
7. Mientras hablas por teléfono celular, no es buena idea...
8. Otra palabra para coche es...

¡LENGUA VIVA!

Aunque **carro** es el término que se usa en la mayoría de países hispanos, no es el único. En España, por ejemplo, se dice **coche**, y en Argentina, Chile y Uruguay se dice **auto**.

6 **Conversación** Completa la conversación con las palabras de la lista.

el aceite	la gasolina	llenar	el parabrisas	el taller
el baúl	las llantas	manejar	revisar	el volante

EMPLEADO Bienvenido al (1)__________ mecánico *Óscar*. ¿En qué le puedo servir?

JUAN Buenos días. Quiero (2)__________ el tanque y revisar (3)__________, por favor.

EMPLEADO Con mucho gusto. Si quiere, también le limpio (4)__________.

JUAN Sí, gracias. Está un poquito sucio. La próxima semana tengo que (5)__________ hasta Buenos Aires. ¿Puede cambiar (6)__________? Están gastadas (*worn*).

EMPLEADO Claro que sí, pero voy a tardar (*it will take me*) un par de horas.

JUAN Mejor regreso mañana. Ahora no tengo tiempo. ¿Cuánto le debo por (7)__________?

EMPLEADO Sesenta pesos. Y veinticinco por (8)__________ y cambiar el aceite.

CONSULTA

For more information about **Buenos Aires**, see **Panorama**, p. 400.

Comunicación

7

Preguntas Trabajen en grupos y túrnense para contestar estas preguntas. Después compartan sus respuestas con la clase.

1. a. ¿Tienes un teléfono celular? ¿Para qué lo usas?
   b. ¿Qué utilizas más: el teléfono o el correo electrónico? ¿Por qué?
   c. En tu opinión, ¿cuáles son las ventajas (*advantages*) y desventajas de los diferentes modos de comunicación?
2. a. ¿Con qué frecuencia usas la computadora?
   b. ¿Para qué usas Internet?
   c. ¿Tienes tu propio blog? ¿Cómo es?
3. a. ¿Miras la televisión con frecuencia? ¿Qué programas ves?
   b. ¿Dónde miras tus programas favoritos, en la tele o en la computadora?
   c. ¿Ves películas en la computadora? ¿Cuál es tu película favorita de todos los tiempos (*of all time*)?
   d. ¿A través de (*By*) qué medio escuchas música? ¿Radio, estéreo, reproductor de MP3 o computadora?
4. a. ¿Tienes licencia de conducir?
   b. ¿Cuánto tiempo hace que la conseguiste?
   c. ¿Tienes carro? Descríbelo.
   d. ¿Llevas tu carro al taller? ¿Para qué?

NOTA CULTURAL

Algunos sitios web utilizan códigos para identificar su país de origen. Éstos son los códigos para algunos países hispanohablantes:

Argentina	.ar
Colombia	.co
España	.es
México	.mx
Venezuela	.ve

CONSULTA

To review expressions like **hace... que**, see **Lección 10, Expresiones útiles**, p. 337.

8

Postal En parejas, lean la tarjeta postal. Después contesten las preguntas.

19 julio de 1979

Hola, Paco:

¡Saludos! Estamos de viaje por unas semanas. La Costa del Sol es muy bonita. No hemos encontrado (*we haven't found*) a tus amigos porque nunca están en casa cuando llamamos. El teléfono suena y suena y nadie contesta. Vamos a seguir llamando.

Sacamos muchas fotos muy divertidas. Cuando regresemos y las revelemos (*get them developed*), te las voy a enseñar. Las playas son preciosas. Hasta ahora el único problema fue que la oficina en la cual reservamos un carro perdió nuestros papeles y tuvimos que esperar mucho tiempo.

También tuvimos un pequeño problema con el hotel. La agencia de viajes nos reservó una habitación en un hotel que está muy lejos de todo. No podemos cambiarla, pero no me importa mucho. A pesar de eso, estamos contentos.

Tu hermana, Gabriela

Francisco Jiménez
San Lorenzo 3250
Rosario, Argentina 2000

1. ¿Cuáles son los problemas que ocurren en el viaje de Gabriela?
2. Con la tecnología de hoy, ¿existen los mismos problemas cuando se viaja? ¿Por qué?
3. Hagan una comparación entre la tecnología de los años 70 y 80 y la de hoy.
4. Imaginen que la hija de Gabriela escribe un correo electrónico sobre el mismo tema con fecha de hoy. Escriban ese correo, incorporando la tecnología actual (teléfonos celulares, Internet, cámaras digitales, etc.). Inventen nuevos problemas.

En el taller

El coche de Miguel está descompuesto y Maru tiene problemas con su computadora.

PERSONAJES

MIGUEL

JORGE

Video: *Fotonovela*
Record and Compare

1

MIGUEL ¿Cómo lo ves?

JORGE Creo que puedo arreglarlo. ¿Me pasas la llave?

2

JORGE ¿Y dónde está Maru?

MIGUEL Acaba de enviarme un mensaje de texto: "Última noticia sobre la computadora portátil: todavía está descompuesta. Moni intenta arreglarla. Voy para allá".

3

JORGE ¿Está descompuesta tu computadora?

MIGUEL No, la mía no, la suya. Una amiga la está ayudando.

JORGE Un mal día para la tecnología, ¿no?

4

MIGUEL Ella está preparando un proyecto para ver si puede hacer sus prácticas profesionales en el Museo de Antropología.

JORGE ¿Y todo está en la computadora?

MIGUEL Y claro.

5

MARU Buenos días, Jorge.

JORGE ¡Qué gusto verte, Maru! ¿Cómo está la computadora?

MARU Mi amiga Mónica recuperó muchos archivos, pero muchos otros se borraron.

6

MARU Estamos en una triste situación. Yo necesito una computadora nueva, y Miguel necesita otro coche.

JORGE Y un televisor nuevo para mí, por favor.

MARU

7

MARU ¿Qué vamos a hacer, Miguel?

MIGUEL Tranquila, cariño. Por eso tenemos amigos como Jorge y Mónica. Nos ayudamos los unos a los otros.

8

JORGE ¿No te sientes afortunada, Maru? No te preocupes. Sube.

MIGUEL ¡Por fin!

MARU Gracias, Jorge. Eres el mejor mecánico de la ciudad.

9

MIGUEL ¿Cuánto te debo por el trabajo?

JORGE Hombre, no es nada. Guárdalo para el coche nuevo. Eso sí, recomiéndame con tus amigos.

MIGUEL Gracias, Jorge.

10

JORGE No manejes en carretera. Revisa el aceite cada 1.500 kilómetros y asegúrate de llenarle el tanque... No manejes con el cofre abierto. Nos vemos.

Expresiones útiles

Giving instructions to a friend

¿Me pasas la llave?
Can you pass me the wrench?
No lo manejes en carretera.
Don't drive it on the highway.
Revisa el aceite cada 1.500 kilómetros.
Check the oil every 1,500 kilometers.
Asegúrate de llenar el tanque.
Make sure to fill up the tank.
No manejes con el cofre abierto.
Don't drive with the hood open.
Recomiéndame con tus amigos.
Recommend me to your friends.

Taking a phone call

Aló./Bueno./Diga.
Hello.
¿Quién habla?/ ¿De parte de quién?
Who is speaking/calling?
Con él/ella habla.
Speaking.
¿Puedo dejar un recado?
May I leave a message?

Reassuring someone

Tranquilo/a, cariño.
Relax, sweetie.
Nos ayudamos los unos a los otros.
We help each other out.
No te preocupes.
Don't worry.

Additional vocabulary

entregar *to hand in*
el intento *attempt*
la noticia *news*
el proyecto *project*
recuperar *to recover*

recursos

VM pp. 233–234	vistas.vhlcentral.com Lección 11

¿Qué pasó?

1

Seleccionar Selecciona las respuestas que completan correctamente estas oraciones.

1. Jorge intenta arreglar ____.
   a. la computadora de Maru b. el coche de Miguel c. el teléfono celular de Felipe
2. Maru dice que se borraron muchos ____ de su computadora.
   a. archivos b. sitios web c. mensajes de texto
3. Jorge dice que necesita un ____.
   a. navegador GPS b. reproductor de DVD c. televisor
4. Maru dice que Jorge es el mejor ____.
   a. mecánico de la ciudad b. amigo del mundo c. compañero de la clase
5. Jorge le dice a Miguel que no maneje su coche en ____.
   a. el tráfico b. el centro de la ciudad c. la carretera

2

Identificar Identifica quién puede decir estas oraciones.

1. Cómprate un coche nuevo y recomiéndame con tus amigos.
2. El mensaje de texto de Maru dice que su computadora todavía está descompuesta.
3. Mi amiga Mónica me ayudó a recuperar muchos archivos, pero necesito una computadora nueva.
4. No conduzcas con el cofre abierto y recuerda que el tanque debe estar lleno.
5. Muchos de los archivos de mi computadora se borraron.

MARU

MIGUEL

JORGE

3

Problema mecánico Trabajen en parejas para representar los papeles de un(a) mecánico/a y un(a) cliente/a que está llamando al taller porque su carro está descompuesto. Usen las instrucciones como guía.

Mecánico/a		Cliente/a
Contesta el teléfono con un saludo y el nombre del taller.	→	Saluda y explica que tu carro está descompuesto.
Pregunta qué tipo de problema tiene exactamente.	→	Explica que tu carro no arranca cuando hace frío.
Di que debe traer el carro al taller.	→	Pregunta cuándo puedes llevarlo.
Ofrece una hora para revisar el carro.	→	Acepta la hora que ofrece el/la mecánico/a.
Da las gracias y despídete.	→	Despídete y cuelga (*hang up*) el teléfono.

Ahora cambien los papeles y representen otra conversación. Ustedes son un(a) técnico/a y un(a) cliente/a. Usen estas ideas:

el celular no guarda mensajes
la computadora no descarga fotos
la impresora imprime muy lentamente
el reproductor de DVD está descompuesto

Practice more at **vistas.vhlcentral.com.**

Ortografía

Concepts

La acentuación de palabras similares

Although accent marks usually indicate which syllable in a word is stressed, they are also used to distinguish between words that have the same or similar spellings.

Él maneja el coche. **Sí, voy si quieres.**

Although one-syllable words do not usually carry written accents, some *do* have accent marks to distinguish them from words that have the same spelling but different meanings.

Sé cocinar. **Se baña.** **¿Tomas té?** **Te duermes.**

Sé (*I know*) and **té** (*tea*) have accent marks to distinguish them from the pronouns **se** and **te**.

para mí **mi cámara** **Tú lees.** **tu estéreo**

Mí (*Me*) and **tú** (*you*) have accent marks to distinguish them from the possessive adjectives **mi** and **tu**.

¿Por qué vas? **Voy porque quiero.**

Several words of more than one syllable also have accent marks to distinguish them from words that have the same or similar spellings.

Éste es rápido. **Este tren es rápido.**

Demonstrative pronouns have accent marks to distinguish them from demonstrative adjectives.

¿Cuándo fuiste? **Fui cuando me llamó.**
¿Dónde trabajas? **Voy al taller donde trabajo.**

Adverbs have accent marks when they are used to convey a question.

Práctica Marca los acentos en las palabras que los necesitan.

ANA Alo, soy Ana. ¿Que tal?
JUAN Hola, pero... ¿por que me llamas tan tarde?
ANA Porque mañana tienes que llevarme a la universidad. Mi auto esta dañado.
JUAN ¿Como se daño?
ANA Se daño el sabado. Un vecino (*neighbor*) choco con (*crashed into*) el.

Crucigrama Utiliza las siguientes pistas (*clues*) para completar el crucigrama. ¡Ojo con los acentos!

Horizontales

1. Él _________ levanta.
4. No voy _________ no puedo.
7. Tú _________ acuestas.
9. ¿_________ es el examen?
10. Quiero este video y _________.

Verticales

2. ¿Cómo _________ usted?
3. Eres _________ mi hermano.
5. ¿_________ tal?
6. Me gusta _________ suéter.
8. Navego _________ la red.

	1	2			3				
				4			5		6
		7	8						
9							10		

recursos

LM p. 62

vistas.vhlcentral.com Lección 11

EN DETALLE

Additional Reading

El teléfono celular

¿Cómo te comunicas con tus amigos y familia? En algunos países hispanos, el servicio de teléfono común° es bastante caro, por lo que el teléfono celular, más accesible y barato, es el favorito de mucha gente.

El servicio más popular entre los jóvenes es el sistema de tarjetas prepagadas°, porque no requiere de un contrato ni de cuotas° extras. En muchos países, puedes encontrar estas tarjetas en cualquier° tienda o recargar el saldo° de tu celular por Internet.

Los celulares de los años 80, grandes e incómodos, eran un símbolo de estatus y estaban limitados al uso de la voz°. Las funciones que entonces° sólo existían en la ciencia ficción, ahora son una realidad. Los celulares de hoy tienen muchas funciones: cámara de fotos o de video, agenda electrónica°, navegador GPS, juegos, conexión a Internet, reproductor de MP3… Con los teléfonos actuales se puede interactuar en las redes sociales° de Internet y, gracias a la tecnología táctil, acceder a sus aplicaciones de forma diferente y rápida.

Con la evolución de los celulares, muchas personas han dejado de usar ciertos aparatos°: ¿para qué una cámara, un reproductor de música y un celular separados si puedes tener todo en uno°?

El uso de los celulares

- En el mundo se intercambian cerca de 500 mil millones de mensajes de texto al año.
- En los EE.UU., el 53% de los hispanos con celular lo usan para conectarse a Internet y el 84% de los hispanos menores de 30 años tiene un celular.
- América Latina tiene 179 millones de usuarios de teléfonos celulares. De ellos, el 73% utiliza programas de mensajería instantánea, el 82% navega por Internet y el 55% transfiere datos como videos y fotos.

común *ordinary* prepagadas *prepaid* cuotas *fees* cualquier *any* recargar el saldo *to buy more minutes* voz *voice* en ese entonces *back then* agenda electrónica *PDA* redes sociales *social Networks* aparatos *appliances* todo en uno *all in one*

ACTIVIDADES

1 **¿Cierto o falso?** Indica si lo que dicen estas oraciones es **cierto** o **falso**. Corrige la información falsa.

1. El teléfono común es un servicio caro en algunos países.
2. Muchas personas usan más el teléfono celular que el teléfono común.
3. Es difícil encontrar tarjetas prepagadas en los países hispanos.
4. En los años 80 los celulares eran un símbolo de estatus.
5. Los primeros teléfonos celulares eran muy cómodos y pequeños.
6. Hoy en día muy pocas personas usan el celular para sacar fotos y oír música.
7. En los EE.UU., el 12% de los hispanos usa el celular para conectarse a Internet.

ASÍ SE DICE

La tecnología

los audífonos (Méx., Col.), los auriculares (Arg.), los cascos (Esp.)	*headset; earphones*
el móvil (Esp.)	el celular
el manos libres (Amér. S.)	*hands-free system*
la memoria	*memory*
mensajear (Méx.)	enviar y recibir mensajes de texto

EL MUNDO HISPANO

Las bicimotos

- **Argentina** El *ciclomotor* se usa mayormente° para repartir a domicilio° comidas y medicinas.
- **Perú** La *motito* se usa mucho para el reparto a domicilio de pan fresco todos los días.
- **México** La *Vespa* se usa para evitar° el tráfico en grandes ciudades.
- **España** La población usa el *Vespino* para ir y volver al trabajo cada día.
- **Puerto Rico** Una *scooter* es el medio de transporte favorito en las zonas rurales.
- **República Dominicana** Las *moto-taxis* son el medio de transporte más económico, ¡pero no olvides el casco°!

mayormente *mainly* repartir a domicilio *home delivery of* evitar *to avoid* casco *helmet*

PERFIL

Los mensajes de texto

¿Qué tienen en común un **mensaje de texto** y un telegrama?: la necesidad de decir lo máximo en el menor espacio posible —y rápidamente—. Así como los abuelos se las arreglaron° para hacer más baratos sus telegramas, que se cobraban° por número de palabras, ahora los jóvenes buscan ahorrar° espacio, tiempo y dinero, en sus mensajes de texto. Esta economía del lenguaje dio origen al **lenguaje chat**, una forma de escritura muy creativa y compacta. Olvídate de la gramática, la puntuación y la ortografía: es tan flexible que evoluciona° todos los días con el uso que cada quien° le da, aunque° hay muchas palabras y expresiones ya establecidas°. Fácilmente encontrarás° abreviaturas (**xq?**, "¿Por qué?"; **tkm**, "Te quiero mucho."), sustitución de sonidos por números (**a2**, "Adiós."; **5mntrios**, "Sin comentarios."), símbolos (**ad+**, "además") y omisión de vocales y acentos (**tb**, "también"; **k tl?**, "¿Qué tal?"). Ahora que lo sabes, si un amigo te envía: **cont xfa, m dbs $!**°, puedes responderle: **ntp, ns vms + trd**°.

se las arreglaron *they managed to* se cobraban *were charged* ahorrar *to save* evoluciona *evolves* cada quien *each person* aunque *although* establecidas *fixed* encontrarás *you will find* cont xfa, m dbs $! Contesta, por favor, ¡me debes dinero! ntp, ns vms +trd No te preocupes, nos vemos más tarde.

Conexión Internet

¿Qué sitios web son populares entre los jóvenes hispanos?

Go to **vistas.vhlcentral.com** to find more cultural information related to this **Cultura** section.

ACTIVIDADES

2 Comprensión Responde a las preguntas.

1. ¿Cuáles son tres formas de decir *headset*?
2. ¿Para qué se usan las bicimotos en Argentina?
3. ¿Qué dio origen al "lenguaje chat"?
4. ¿Es importante escribir los acentos en los mensajes de texto?

3 ¿Cómo te comunicas? Escribe un párrafo breve en donde expliques qué utilizas para comunicarte con tus amigos/as (correo electrónico, redes sociales, teléfono, etc.) y de qué hablan cuando se llaman por teléfono.

Practice more at **vistas.vhlcentral.com.**

11.1 Familiar commands

Tutorial

ANTE TODO In Spanish, the command forms are used to give orders or advice. You use **tú** commands (**mandatos familiares**) when you want to give an order or advice to someone you normally address with the familiar **tú**.

Affirmative tú commands

Infinitive	Present tense él/ella form	Affirmative tú command
hablar	habla	**habla** (tú)
guardar	guarda	**guarda** (tú)
prender	prende	**prende** (tú)
volver	vuelve	**vuelve** (tú)
pedir	pide	**pide** (tú)
imprimir	imprime	**imprime** (tú)

- Affirmative **tú** commands usually have the same form as the **él/ella** form of the present indicative.

Guarda el documento antes de cerrarlo.
Save the document before closing it.

Imprime tu tarea para la clase de inglés.
Print your homework for English class.

- There are eight irregular affirmative **tú** commands.

Irregular affirmative tú commands

decir	**di**	salir	**sal**
hacer	**haz**	ser	**sé**
ir	**ve**	tener	**ten**
poner	**pon**	venir	**ven**

¡**Sal** ahora mismo!
Leave at once!

Haz los ejercicios.
Do the exercises.

- Since **ir** and **ver** have the same **tú** command (**ve**), context will determine the meaning.

Ve al cibercafé con Yolanda.
Go to the cybercafé with Yolanda.

Ve ese programa... es muy interesante.
See that program... it's very interesting.

- The negative **tú** commands are formed by dropping the final -**o** of the **yo** form of the present tense. For -**ar** verbs, add -**es**. For -**er** and -**ir** verbs, add -**as**.

Negative tú commands

Infinitive	Present tense yo form	Negative tú command
hablar	hablo	**no hables** (tú)
guardar	guardo	**no guardes** (tú)
prender	prendo	**no prendas** (tú)
volver	vuelvo	**no vuelvas** (tú)
pedir	pido	**no pidas** (tú)

Héctor, **no pares** el carro aquí.
Héctor, don't stop the car here.

No prendas la computadora todavía.
Don't turn on the computer yet.

¡ATENCIÓN!

In affirmative commands, reflexive, indirect, and direct object pronouns are always attached to the end of the verb. In negative commands, these pronouns always precede the verb.

Bórralos./No los borres.

Escríbeles un correo electrónico./**No les escribas** un correo electrónico.

• • •

When a pronoun is attached to an affirmative command that has two or more syllables, an accent mark is added to maintain the original stress:

borra → **bórralos**
prende → **préndela**
imprime → **imprímelo**

- Verbs with irregular **yo** forms maintain the same irregularity in their negative **tú** commands. These verbs include **conducir, conocer, decir, hacer, ofrecer, oír, poner, salir, tener, traducir, traer, venir,** and **ver**.

No pongas el cederrón en la computadora.
Don't put the CD-ROM in the computer.

No conduzcas tan rápido.
Don't drive so fast.

- Note also that stem-changing verbs keep their stem changes in negative **tú** commands.

No p**ie**rdas tu celular.
Don't lose your cell phone.

No v**ue**lvas a esa gasolinera.
Don't go back to that gas station.

No rep**i**tas las instrucciones.
Don't repeat the instructions.

- Verbs ending in -**car**, -**gar**, and -**zar** have a spelling change in the negative **tú** commands.

sa**car**	**c** → **qu**	no sa**qu**es
apa**gar**	**g** → **gu**	no apa**gu**es
almor**zar**	**z** → **c**	no almuer**c**es

- The following verbs have irregular negative **tú** commands.

Irregular negative tú commands

dar	**no des**
estar	**no estés**
ir	**no vayas**
saber	**no sepas**
ser	**no seas**

recursos
WB pp. 125–126
LM p. 63
vistas.vhlcentral.com Lección 11

¡INTÉNTALO! Indica los mandatos familiares afirmativos y negativos de estos verbos.

1. correr ___Corre___ más rápido. No ___corras___ más rápido.
2. llenar ________ el tanque. No ________ el tanque.
3. salir ________ ahora. No ________ ahora.
4. descargar ________ ese documento. No ________ ese documento.
5. levantarse ________ temprano. No ________ temprano.
6. hacerlo ________ ya. No ________ ahora.

Práctica

1

Completar Tu mejor amigo no entiende nada de tecnología y te pide ayuda. Completa los comentarios de tu amigo con el mandato de cada verbo.

1. No __________ en una hora. __________ ahora mismo. (venir)
2. __________ tu tarea después. No la __________ ahora. (hacer)
3. No __________ a la tienda a comprar papel para la impresora. __________ a la cafetería a comprarme algo de comer. (ir)
4. No __________ que no puedes abrir un archivo. __________ que el programa de computación funciona sin problemas. (decirme)
5. __________ generoso con tu tiempo y no __________ antipático si no entiendo fácilmente. (ser)
6. __________ mucha paciencia y no __________ prisa. (tener)
7. __________ tu teléfono celular, pero no __________ la computadora. (apagar)

2

Cambiar Pedro y Marina no pueden ponerse de acuerdo (*agree*) cuando viajan en su carro. Cuando Pedro dice que algo es necesario, Marina expresa una opinión diferente. Usa la información entre paréntesis para formar las órdenes que Marina le da a Pedro.

modelo

Pedro: Necesito revisar el aceite del carro. (seguir hasta el próximo pueblo)
Marina: *No revises el aceite del carro. Sigue hasta el próximo pueblo.*

1. Necesito conducir más rápido. (parar el carro)
2. Necesito poner el radio. (hablarme)
3. Necesito almorzar ahora. (comer más tarde)
4. Necesito sacar los discos compactos. (manejar con cuidado)
5. Necesito estacionar el carro en esta calle. (pensar en otra opción)
6. Necesito volver a esa gasolinera. (arreglar el carro en un taller)
7. Necesito leer el mapa. (pedirle ayuda a aquella señora)
8. Necesito dormir en el carro. (acostarse en una cama)

3

Problemas Tú y tu compañero/a trabajan en el centro de computadoras de la universidad. Muchos estudiantes están llamando con problemas. Denles órdenes para ayudarlos a resolverlos.

modelo

Problema: *No veo nada en la pantalla.*
Tu respuesta: *Prende la pantalla de tu computadora.*

apagar...	descargar...	grabar...	imprimir...	prender...
borrar...	funcionar...	guardar...	navegar...	volver...

1. No me gusta este programa de computación.
2. Tengo miedo de perder mi documento.
3. Prefiero leer este sitio web en papel.
4. Mi correo electrónico funciona muy lentamente.
5. Busco información sobre los gauchos de Argentina.
6. Tengo demasiados archivos en mi computadora.
7. Mi computadora se congeló (*froze*).
8. Quiero ver las fotos del cumpleaños de mi hermana.

NOTA CULTURAL

Los gauchos (*nomadic cowboys*), conocidos por su habilidad (*skill*) para montar a caballo y utilizar el lazo, viven en la Región Pampeana, una llanura muy extensa ubicada en el centro de Argentina y dedicada a la agricultura (*agriculture*).

Comunicación

4

Órdenes Circula por la clase e intercambia mandatos negativos y afirmativos con tus compañeros/as. Debes seguir las órdenes que ellos te dan o reaccionar apropiadamente.

modelo

Estudiante 1: *Dame todo tu dinero.*
Estudiante 2: *No, no quiero dártelo. Muéstrame tu cuaderno.*
Estudiante 1: *Aquí está.*
Estudiante 3: *Ve a la pizarra y escribe tu nombre.*
Estudiante 4: *No quiero. Hazlo tú.*

5

Anuncios Miren este anuncio. Luego, en grupos pequeños, preparen tres anuncios adicionales para tres escuelas que compiten (*compete*) con ésta.

Síntesis

6

¡Tanto que hacer! Tu profesor(a) te va a dar una lista de diligencias (*errands*). Algunas las hiciste tú y algunas las hizo tu compañero/a. Las diligencias que ya hicieron tienen esta marca ✔. Pero quedan cuatro diligencias por hacer. Dale órdenes a tu compañero/a y él/ella responde para confirmar si hay que hacerla o si ya la hizo.

modelo

Estudiante 1: *Llena el tanque.*
Estudiante 2: *Ya llené el tanque. / ¡Ay, no! Tenemos que llenar el tanque.*

11.2 Por and para

Tutorial

ANTE TODO Unlike English, Spanish has two words that mean *for*: **por** and **para.** These two prepositions are not interchangeable. Study the following charts to see how they are used.

- **Por** and **para** are most commonly used to describe aspects of movement, time, and action, but in different circumstances.

Por	Para
Movement	
Through or by a place La excursión nos llevó **por** el centro. *The tour took us through downtown.*	**Towards a destination** Mis amigos van **para** el estadio. *My friends are going to the stadium.*
Time	
Duration of an event Ana navegó la red **por** dos horas. *Ana surfed the net for two hours.*	**Action deadline** Tengo que escribir un ensayo **para** mañana. *I have to write an essay by tomorrow.*
Action	
Reason or motive for an action or circumstance Llegué a casa tarde **por** el tráfico. *I got home late because of the traffic.*	**Indication of for whom something is intended or done** Estoy preparando una sorpresa **para** Eduardo. *I'm preparing a sorprise for Eduardo.*

- Here is a complete list of all of the uses of **por** and **para**.

Por is used to indicate...

1. **Movement: Motion or a general location** . . *(around, through, along, by)*	Pasamos **por** el parque y **por** el río. *We passed by the park and along the river.*
2. **Time: Duration of an action** . . . . *(for, during, in)*	Estuve en la Patagonia **por** un mes. *I was in Patagonia for a month.*
3. **Action: Reason or motive for an action** . . *(because of, on account of, on behalf of)*	Lo hizo **por** su familia. *She did it on behalf of her family.*
4. **Object of a search** . . . . *(for, in search of)*	Vengo **por** ti a las ocho. *I'm coming for you at eight.* Manuel fue **por** su cámara digital. *Manuel went in search of his digital camera.*
5. **Means by which something is done** . . . *(by, by way of, by means of)*	Ellos viajan **por** la autopista. *They travel by (by way of) the highway.*
6. **Exchange or substitution** . . . . *(for, in exchange for)*	Le di dinero **por** el reproductor de MP3. *I gave him money for the MP3 player.*
7. **Unit of measure** . . . . *(per, by)*	José manejaba a 120 kilómetros **por** hora. *José was driving 120 kilometers per hour.*

¡ATENCIÓN!

Por is also used in several idiomatic expressions, including:

por aquí *around here*
por ejemplo *for example*
por eso *that's why; therefore*
por fin *finally*

AYUDA

Remember that when giving an exact time, **de** is used instead of **por** before **la mañana, la tarde,** or **la noche**.

La clase empieza a las nueve **de** la mañana.

•••

In addition to **por**, **durante** is also commonly used to mean *for* when referring to time.

Esperé al mecánico **durante** cincuenta minutos.

Para is used to indicate...

1. **Movement: Destination** . . . . (*toward, in the direction of*)	Salimos **para** Córdoba el sábado. *We are leaving for Córdoba on Saturday.*
2. **Time: Deadline or a specific time in the future** . . . . (*by, for*)	Él va a arreglar el carro **para** el viernes. *He will fix the car by Friday.*
3. **Action: Purpose or goal** + [*infinitive*]. . . . (*in order to*)	Juan estudia **para** (ser) mecánico. *Juan is studying to be a mechanic.*
4. **Purpose** + [*noun*] . . . . (*for, used for*)	Es una llanta **para** el carro. *It's a tire for the car.*
5. **The recipient of something** . . . . (*for*)	Compré una impresora **para** mi hijo. *I bought a printer for my son.*
6. **Comparison with others or an opinion**. . (*for, considering*)	**Para** un joven, es demasiado serio. *For a young person, he is too serious.* **Para** mí, esta lección no es difícil. *For me, this lesson isn't difficult.*
7. **In the employment of** . . . . (*for*)	Sara trabaja **para** Telecom Argentina. *Sara works for Telecom Argentina.*

- In many cases it is grammatically correct to use either **por** or **para** in a sentence. The meaning of the sentence is different, however, depending on which preposition is used.

Caminé **por** el parque. *I walked through the park.*	Caminé **para** el parque. *I walked to (toward) the park.*
Trabajó **por** su padre. *He worked for (in place of) his father.*	Trabajó **para** su padre. *He worked for his father('s company).*

¡INTÉNTALO! Completa estas oraciones con las preposiciones **por** o **para**.

1. Fuimos al cibercafé ___por___ la tarde.
2. Necesitas un navegador GPS ______ encontrar la casa de Luis.
3. Entraron ______ la puerta.
4. Quiero un pasaje ______ Buenos Aires.
5. ______ arrancar el carro, necesito la llave.
6. Arreglé el televisor ______ mi amigo.
7. Estuvieron nerviosos ______ el examen.
8. ¿No hay una gasolinera ______ aquí?
9. El reproductor de MP3 es ______ usted.
10. Juan está enfermo. Tengo que trabajar ______ él.
11. Estuvimos en Canadá ______ dos meses.
12. ______ mí, el español es fácil.
13. Tengo que estudiar la lección ______ el lunes.
14. Voy a ir ______ la carretera.
15. Compré dulces ______ mi novia.
16. Compramos el auto ______ un buen precio.

recursos
WB pp. 127–128
LM p. 64
vistas.vhlcentral.com Lección 11

Práctica

1 **Completar** Completa este párrafo con las preposiciones **por** o **para.**

El mes pasado mi esposo y yo hicimos un viaje a Buenos Aires y sólo pagamos dos mil dólares (1)_______ los pasajes. Estuvimos en Buenos Aires (2)_______ una semana y paseamos por toda la ciudad. Durante el día caminamos (3)_______ la plaza San Martín, el microcentro y el barrio de La Boca, donde viven muchos artistas. (4)_______ la noche fuimos a una tanguería, que es una especie de teatro, (5)_______ mirar a la gente bailar tango. Dos días después decidimos hacer una excursión (6)_______ las pampas (7)_______ ver el paisaje y un rodeo con gauchos. Alquilamos (*We rented*) un carro y manejamos (8)_______ todas partes y pasamos unos días muy agradables. El último día que estuvimos en Buenos Aires fuimos a Galerías Pacífico (9)_______ comprar recuerdos (*souvenirs*) (10)_______ nuestros hijos y nietos. Compramos tantos regalos que tuvimos que pagar impuestos (*duties*) en la aduana al regresar.

2 **Oraciones** Crea oraciones originales con los elementos de las columnas. Une los elementos usando **por** o **para.**

modelo

Fuimos a Mar del Plata por razones de salud para visitar a un especialista.

(no) fue al mercado	por/para	comprar frutas	por/para	¿?
(no) fuimos a las montañas	por/para	tres días	por/para	¿?
(no) fuiste a Mar del Plata	por/para	razones de salud	por/para	¿?
(no) fueron a Buenos Aires	por/para	tomar el sol	por/para	¿?

NOTA CULTURAL

Mar del Plata es un centro turístico en la costa de Argentina. La ciudad es conocida como "la perla del Atlántico" y todos los años muchos turistas visitan sus playas y casinos.

3 **Describir** Usa **por** o **para** y el tiempo presente para describir estos dibujos.

1. _______________

2. _______________

3. _______________

4. _______________

5. _______________

6. _______________

Comunicación

4

Descripciones Usa **por** o **para** y completa estas frases de manera lógica. Luego, compara tus respuestas con las de un(a) compañero/a.

1. En casa, hablo con mis amigos...
2. Mi padre/madre trabaja...
3. Ayer fui al taller...
4. Los miércoles tengo clases...
5. A veces voy a la biblioteca...
6. Esta noche tengo que estudiar...
7. Necesito... dólares...
8. Compré un regalo...
9. Mi mejor amigo/a estudia...
10. Necesito hacer la tarea...

5

Situación En parejas, dramaticen esta situación. Utilicen muchos ejemplos de **por** y **para.**

Hijo/a	Padre/Madre
Pídele dinero a tu padre/madre.	Pregúntale a tu hijo/a para qué lo necesita.
Dile que quieres comprar un carro.	Pregúntale por qué necesita un carro.
Explica tres razones por las que necesitas un carro.	Explica por qué sus razones son buenas o malas.
Dile que por no tener un carro tu vida es muy difícil.	Decide si vas a darle el dinero y explica por qué.

Síntesis

6

Una subasta (*auction*) Cada estudiante debe traer a la clase un objeto o una foto del objeto para vender. En grupos, túrnense para ser el/la vendedor(a) y los postores (*bidders*). Para empezar, el/la vendedor(a) describe el objeto y explica para qué se usa y por qué alguien debe comprarlo.

modelo

Vendedora: *Aquí tengo un reproductor de CD. Pueden usarlo para disfrutar su música favorita o para escuchar canciones en español. Sólo hace un año que lo compré y todavía funciona perfectamente. ¿Quién ofrece $ 1.500 para empezar?*

Postor(a) 1: *Pero los reproductores de CD son anticuados. Te doy $ 20.*

Vendedora: *Ah, pero éste es muy especial porque viene con el CD que grabé cuando quería ser cantante de ópera.*

Postor(a) 2: *Ah, ¡entonces te doy $ 100!*

11.3 Reciprocal reflexives

Tutorial

ANTE TODO In **Lección 7**, you learned that reflexive verbs indicate that the subject of a sentence does the action to itself. Reciprocal reflexives, on the other hand, express a shared or reciprocal action between two or more people or things. In this context, the pronoun means *(to) each other* or *(to) one another.*

Luis y Marta **se** miran en el espejo.
Luis and Marta look at themselves in the mirror.

Luis y Marta **se** miran.
Luis and Marta look at each other.

- Only the plural forms of the reflexive pronouns (**nos**, **os**, **se**) are used to express reciprocal actions because the action must involve more than one person or thing.

Cuando **nos vimos** en la calle, **nos abrazamos**.
When we saw each other on the street, we hugged (one another).

Ustedes **se** van a **encontrar** en el cibercafé, ¿no?
You are meeting (each other) at the cybercafé, right?

Nos ayudamos cuando usamos la computadora.
We help each other when we use the computer.

Las amigas **se saludaron** y **se besaron**.
The friends greeted each other and kissed (one another).

¡ATENCIÓN!

Here is a list of common verbs that can express reciprocal actions:

abrazar(se) *to hug; to embrace (each other)*
ayudar(se) *to help (each other)*
besar(se) *to kiss (each other)*
encontrar(se) *to meet (each other); to run into (each other)*
saludar(se) *to greet (each other)*

¡INTÉNTALO! Indica el reflexivo recíproco adecuado de estos verbos en el presente o el pretérito.

presente

1. (escribir) Los novios se escriben.
   Nosotros ________.
   Ana y Ernesto ________.
2. (escuchar) Mis tíos ________.
   Nosotros ________.
   Ellos ________.
3. (ver) Nosotros ________.
   Fernando y Tomás ________.
   Ustedes ________.
4. (llamar) Ellas ________.
   Mis hermanos ________.
   Pepa y yo ________.

pretérito

1. (saludar) Nicolás y tú se saludaron.
   Nuestros vecinos ________.
   Nosotros ________.
2. (hablar) Los amigos ________.
   Elena y yo ________.
   Ustedes ________.
3. (conocer) Alberto y yo ________.
   Ustedes ________.
   Ellos ________.
4. (encontrar) Ana y Javier ________.
   Los primos ________.
   Mi hermana y yo ________.

recursos

WB pp. 129–130
LM p. 65
vistas.vhlcentral.com Lección 11

Práctica y Comunicación

1 **Un amor recíproco** Describe a Laura y a Elián usando los verbos recíprocos.

modelo

Laura veía a Elián todos los días. Elián veía a Laura todos los días.
Laura y Elián se veían todos los días.

1. Laura conocía bien a Elián. Elián conocía bien a Laura.
2. Laura miraba a Elián con amor. Elián la miraba con amor también.
3. Laura entendía bien a Elián. Elián entendía bien a Laura.
4. Laura hablaba con Elián todas las noches por teléfono. Elián hablaba con Laura todas las noches por teléfono.
5. Laura ayudaba a Elián con sus problemas. Elián la ayudaba también con sus problemas.

2 **Describir** Mira los dibujos y describe lo que estas personas hicieron.

1. Las hermanas __________.

2. Ellos __________.

3. Gilberto y Mercedes __________ / __________ / __________.

4. Tú y yo __________ / __________.

3 **Preguntas** En parejas, túrnense para hacerse estas preguntas.

1. ¿Se vieron tú y tu mejor amigo/a ayer? ¿Cuándo se ven ustedes normalmente?
2. ¿Dónde se encuentran tú y tus amigos?
3. ¿Se ayudan tú y tu mejor amigo/a con sus problemas?
4. ¿Se entienden bien tus compañeros de clase?
5. ¿Dónde se conocieron tú y tu mejor amigo/a? ¿Cuánto tiempo hace que se conocen ustedes?
6. ¿Cuándo se dan regalos tú y tu novio/a?
7. ¿Se escriben tú y tus amigos mensajes de texto o prefieren llamarse por teléfono?
8. ¿Siempre se llevan bien tú y tu compañero/a de cuarto? Explica.

Practice more at **vistas.vhlcentral.com.**

11.4 Stressed possessive adjectives and pronouns

Tutorial

ANTE TODO Spanish has two types of possessive adjectives: the unstressed (or short) forms you learned in **Lección 3** and the stressed (or long) forms. The stressed forms are used for emphasis or to express *of mine, of yours,* and so on.

Stressed possessive adjectives

Masculine singular	Feminine singular	Masculine plural	Feminine plural	
mío	**mía**	**míos**	**mías**	*my; (of) mine*
tuyo	**tuya**	**tuyos**	**tuyas**	*your; (of) yours* (fam.)
suyo	**suya**	**suyos**	**suyas**	*your; (of) yours* (form.); *his; (of) his; her; (of) hers; its*
nuestro	**nuestra**	**nuestros**	**nuestras**	*our; (of) ours*
vuestro	**vuestra**	**vuestros**	**vuestras**	*your; (of) yours* (fam.)
suyo	**suya**	**suyos**	**suyas**	*your; (of) yours* (form.); *their; (of) theirs*

- **¡Atención!** Used with **un/una**, these possessives are similar in meaning to the English expression *of mine/yours/*etc.

  Juancho es **un** amigo **mío.**
  Juancho is a friend of mine.

  Ella es **una** compañera **nuestra**.
  She is a classmate of ours.

- Stressed possessive adjectives agree in gender and number with the nouns they modify. While unstressed possessive adjectives are placed before the noun, stressed possessive adjectives are placed after the noun they modify.

  su impresora → la impresora **suya**
  her printer → *her printer*

  nuestros televisores → los televisores **nuestros**
  our television sets → *our television sets*

- A definite article, an indefinite article, or a demonstrative adjective usually precedes a noun modified by a stressed possessive adjective.

  Me encantan
  unos discos compactos **tuyos**. *I love some of your CDs.*
  los discos compactos **tuyos**. *I love your CDs.*
  estos discos compactos **tuyos**. *I love these CDs of yours.*

- Since **suyo, suya, suyos,** and **suyas** have more than one meaning, you can avoid confusion by using the construction: [*article*] + [*noun*] + **de** + [*subject pronoun*].

  el teclado **suyo** →
  el teclado **de él/ella/usted** *his/her keyboard*
  el teclado **de ustedes/ellos/ellas** *your keyboard*

CONSULTA

This is the same construction you learned in **Lección 3** for clarifying **su** and **sus**. To review unstressed possessive adjectives, see **Estructura 3.2**, p. 93.

Possessive pronouns

- Possessive pronouns are used to replace a noun + [*possessive adjective*]. In Spanish, the possessive pronouns have the same forms as the stressed possessive adjectives, but they are preceded by a definite article.

la cámara **nuestra**	▶	**la nuestra**
el navegador GPS **tuyo**	▶	**el tuyo**
los archivos **suyos**	▶	**los suyos**

- A possessive pronoun agrees in number and gender with the noun it replaces.

—Aquí está **mi coche**. ¿Dónde está **el tuyo**?
Here's my car. Where is yours?

—**El mío** está en el taller de mi hermano.
Mine is at my brother's garage.

—¿Tienes **las revistas** de Carlos?
Do you have Carlos' magazines?

—No, pero tengo **las nuestras.**
No, but I have ours.

¡INTÉNTALO! Indica las formas tónicas (*stressed*) de estos adjetivos posesivos y los pronombres posesivos correspondientes.

	adjetivos	pronombres
1. su cámara digital	la cámara digital suya	la suya
2. mi televisor		
3. nuestros discos compactos		
4. tus calculadoras		
5. su monitor		
6. mis videos		
7. nuestra impresora		
8. tu estéreo		
9. nuestro cederrón		
10. mi computadora		

recursos

WB pp. 131–132

LM p. 66

vistas.vhlcentral.com Lección 11

Práctica

1 **Oraciones** Forma oraciones con estas palabras. Usa el presente y haz los cambios necesarios.

1. un / amiga / suyo / vivir / Mendoza
2. ¿me / prestar / calculadora / tuyo?
3. el / coche / suyo / nunca / funcionar / bien
4. no / nos / interesar / problemas / suyo
5. yo / querer / cámara digital / mío / ahora mismo
6. un / amigos / nuestro / manejar / como / loco

2 **¿Es suyo?** Un policía ha capturado (*has captured*) al hombre que robó (*robbed*) en tu casa. Ahora quiere saber qué cosas son tuyas. Túrnate con un(a) compañero/a para hacer el papel del policía y usa las pistas (*clues*) para contestar las preguntas.

modelo

no/viejo

Policía: Esta impresora, ¿es suya?

Estudiante: No, no es mía. La mía era más vieja.

1. sí

2. no/pequeño

3. sí

4. sí

5. no/grande

6. no/caro

3 **Conversaciones** Completa estas conversaciones con las formas adecuadas de los pronombres posesivos.

1. —La casa de ellos estaba en la Avenida Alvear. ¿Dónde estaba la casa de ustedes?
   —____________ estaba en la calle Bolívar.
2. —A Carmen le encanta su monitor nuevo.
   —¿Sí? A José no le gusta ____________.
3. —Puse mis discos aquí. ¿Dónde pusiste ____________, Alfonso?
   —Puse ____________ en el escritorio.
4. —Se me olvidó traer mis llaves. ¿Trajeron ustedes ____________?
   —No, dejamos ____________ en casa.
5. —Yo compré mi computadora en una tienda y Marta compró ____________ en Internet. Y ____________, ¿dónde la compraste?
   —____________ es de Cíbermax.

Comunicación

4 **Vendedores competitivos** Trabajen en grupos de tres. Uno/a de ustedes va a una tienda a comprar un aparato tecnológico (reproductor de MP3, computadora portátil, monitor, etc.). Los/as otros/as dos son empleados/as de dos marcas rivales y compiten para convencer al/a la cliente/a de que compre su producto. Usen los adjetivos posesivos y túrnense para comprar y vender. ¿Quién es el/la mejor vendedor/a?

modelo

Estudiante 1: Buenos días, quiero comprar un reproductor de MP3.
Estudiante 2: Tengo lo que necesita. El mío, tiene capacidad para 500 canciones.
Estudiante 3: El tuyo es muy viejo, con el mío también puedes ver videos…

5 **Comparar** Trabajen en parejas. Intenta (*Try to*) convencer a tu compañero/a de que algo que tú tienes es mejor que lo que él/ella tiene. Pueden hablar de sus carros, reproductores de MP3, teléfonos celulares, clases, horarios o trabajos.

modelo

Estudiante 1: Mi computadora tiene una pantalla de quince pulgadas (*inches*). ¿Y la tuya?
Estudiante 2: La mía es mejor porque tiene una pantalla de diecisiete pulgadas.
Estudiante 1: Pues la mía…

Síntesis

6 **Inventos locos** En grupos pequeños, imaginen que construyeron un aparato tecnológico revolucionario. Dibujen su invento y descríbanlo contestando estas preguntas. Incluyan todos los detalles que crean (*that you believe*) necesarios. Luego, compártanlo con la clase. Utilicen los posesivos, **por** y **para** y el vocabulario de **Contextos**.

modelo

Nuestro aparato se usa para cocinar huevos y funciona de una manera muy fácil…

- ¿Para qué se usa?
- ¿Cómo es?
- ¿Cuánto cuesta?
- ¿Qué personas van a comprar este aparato?

Recapitulación

Concepts Diagnostics

Completa estas actividades para repasar los conceptos de gramática que aprendiste en esta lección.

1 **Completar** Completa la tabla con las formas de los mandatos familiares. 8 pts.

Infinitivo	Mandato	
	Afirmativo	Negativo
comer	come	no comas
hacer		
sacar		
venir		
ir		

2 **Por y para** Completa el diálogo con **por** o **para**. 10 pts.

MARIO Hola, yo trabajo (1) ________ el periódico de la universidad. ¿Puedo hacerte unas preguntas?

INÉS Sí, claro.

MARIO ¿Navegas mucho (2) ________ la red?

INÉS Sí, todos los días me conecto a Internet (3) ________ leer mi correo y navego (4) ________ una hora. También me gusta hablar (5) ________ *Skype* con mis amigos. Es muy bueno y, (6) ________ mí, es divertido.

MARIO ¿Y qué piensas sobre hacer la tarea en la computadora?

INÉS En general, me parece bien, pero (7) ________ ejemplo, anoche hice unos ejercicios (8) ________ la clase de álgebra y al final me dolieron los ojos. (9) ________ eso a veces prefiero hacer la tarea a mano.

MARIO Muy bien. Muchas gracias (10) ________ tu tiempo.

3 **Posesivos** Completa las oraciones y confirma de quién son las cosas. 6 pts.

1. —¿Éste es mi bolígrafo? —Sí, es el ________ (*fam.*).
2. —¿Ésta es la cámara de tu papá? —Sí, es la ________.
3. —¿Ese teléfono es de Pilar? —Sí, es el ________.
4. —¿Éstos son los cederrones de ustedes? —No, no son ________.
5. —¿Ésta es tu computadora portátil? —No, no es ________.
6. —¿Ésas son mis fotos? —Sí, son las ________ (*form.*).

RESUMEN GRAMATICAL

11.1 Familiar commands *pp. 378–379*

tú commands		
Infinitive	Affirmative	Negative
guardar	**guarda**	**no guardes**
volver	**vuelve**	**no vuelvas**
imprimir	**imprime**	**no imprimas**

► Irregular **tú** command forms

dar → **no des**
decir → **di**
estar → **no estés**
hacer → **haz**
ir → **ve, no vayas**
poner → **pon**
saber → **no sepas**
salir → **sal**
ser → **sé, no seas**
tener → **ten**
venir → **ven**

► Verbs ending in **-car**, **-gar**, **-zar** have a spelling change in the negative **tú** commands:

sacar → no sa**qu**es
apagar → no apa**gu**es
almorzar → no almuer**c**es

11.2 Por and para *pp. 382–383*

► Uses of **por**:

motion or general location; duration; reason or motive; object of a search; means by which something is done; exchange or substitution; unit of measure

► Uses of **para**:

destination; deadline; purpose or goal; recipient of something; comparison or opinion; in the employment of.

11.3 Reciprocal reflexives *p. 386*

► Reciprocal reflexives express a shared or reciprocal action between two or more people or things. Only the plural forms (**nos, os, se**) are used.

Cuando **nos vimos** en la calle, **nos abrazamos**.

► Common verbs that can express reciprocal actions:

abrazar(se), **ayudar(se)**, **besar(se)**, **conocer(se)**, **encontrar(se)**, **escribir(se)**, **escuchar(se)**, **hablar(se)**, **llamar(se)**, **mirar(se)**, **saludar(se)**, **ver(se)**

11.4 Stressed possessive adjectives and pronouns

pp. 388–389

Stressed possessive adjectives	
Masculine	**Feminine**
mío(s)	mía(s)
tuyo(s)	tuya(s)
suyo(s)	suya(s)
nuestro(s)	nuestra(s)
vuestro(s)	vuestra(s)
suyo(s)	suya(s)

la impresora **suya → la suya**

las llaves **mías → las mías**

4 **Ángel y diablito** A Juan le gusta pedir consejos a su ángel y a su diablito imaginarios. Completa las respuestas con mandatos familiares desde las dos perspectivas. 8 pts.

1. Estoy manejando. ¿Voy más rápido?
   Á No, no ________ más rápido.
   D Sí, ________ más rápido.
2. Es el reproductor de música de mi hermana. ¿Lo pongo en mi mochila?
   Á No, no ________ en tu mochila.
   D Sí, ________ en tu mochila.
3. Necesito estirar (*to stretch*) las piernas. ¿Doy un paseo?
   Á Sí, ________ un paseo.
   D No, no ________ un paseo.
4. Mi amigo necesita imprimir algo. ¿Apago la impresora?
   Á No, no ________ la impresora.
   D Sí, ________ la impresora.

5 **Oraciones** Forma oraciones para expresar acciones recíprocas con el tiempo indicado. 6 pts.

modelo

tú y yo / conocer / bien (presente) *Tú y yo nos conocemos bien.*

1. José y Paco / llamar / una vez por semana (imperfecto)
2. mi novia y yo / ver / todos los días (presente)
3. los compañeros de clase / ayudar / con la tarea (pretérito)
4. tú y tu mamá / escribir / por correo electrónico / cada semana (imperfecto)
5. mis hermanas y yo / entender / perfectamente (presente)
6. los profesores / saludar / con mucho respeto (pretérito)

6 **La tecnología** Escribe al menos seis oraciones diciéndole a un(a) amigo/a qué hacer para tener "una buena relación" con la tecnología. Usa mandatos familiares afirmativos y negativos. 12 pts.

7 **Saber compartir** Completa la expresión con los dos pronombres posesivos que faltan. ¡2 puntos EXTRA!

"Lo que° es ________ es ________."

Lo que *What*

Practice more at **vistas.vhlcentral.com.**

Lectura

Antes de leer

Estrategia

Recognizing borrowed words

One way languages grow is by borrowing words from each other. English words that relate to technology often are borrowed by Spanish and other languages throughout the world. Sometimes the words are modified slightly to fit the sounds of the languages that borrow them. When reading in Spanish, you can often increase your understanding by looking for words borrowed from English or other languages you know.

Examinar el texto

Observa la tira cómica°. ¿De qué trata°? ¿Cómo lo sabes?

Buscar

Esta lectura contiene una palabra tomada° del inglés. Trabaja con un(a) compañero/a para encontrarla.

____

Repasa° las palabras nuevas relacionadas con la tecnología que aprendiste en **Contextos** y expande la lista de palabras tomadas del inglés.

__________ __________
__________ __________
__________ __________

Sobre el autor

Juan Matías Loiseau (1974). Más conocido como Tute, este artista nació en Buenos Aires, Argentina. Estudió diseño gráfico, humorismo y cine. Sus tiras cómicas se publican en Estados Unidos, Francia y toda Latinoamérica.

tira cómica *comic strip* ¿De qué trata? *What is it about?* tomada *taken* Repasa *Review*

Después de leer

Comprensión

Indica si las oraciones son **ciertas** o **falsas**. Corrige las falsas.

Cierto	Falso	
_____	_____	1. Hay tres personajes en la tira cómica: un usuario de teléfono, un amigo y un empleado de la empresa (*company*) telefónica.
_____	_____	2. El nuevo servicio de teléfono incluye las llamadas telefónicas únicamente.
_____	_____	3. El empleado duerme en su casa.
_____	_____	4. El contrato de teléfono dura (*lasts*) un año.
_____	_____	5. El usuario y el amigo están trabajando (*working*).

Preguntas

Responde a estas preguntas con oraciones completas. Usa el pretérito y el imperfecto.

1. ¿Al usuario le gustaba usar el teléfono celular todo el tiempo?
____
2. ¿Por qué el usuario decidió tirar el teléfono al mar?
____
3. Según el amigo, ¿para qué tenía el usuario que tirar el teléfono celular al mar?
____
4. ¿Qué ocurrió cuando el usuario tiró el teléfono?
____
5. ¿Qué le dijo el empleado al usuario cuando salió del mar?
____

Conversar

En grupos pequeños, hablen de estos temas.

1. ¿Se sienten identificados/as con el usuario de teléfono de la tira cómica? ¿Por qué?
2. ¿Cuáles son los aspectos positivos y los negativos de tener teléfono celular?
3. ¿Cuál es para ustedes el límite que debe tener la tecnología en nuestras vidas?

te viene *comes with* **tipo** *guy, dude* **te avisa** *alerts you* **escuchás** *listen (Arg.)* **distraídos** *careless* **piso** *floor* **bolsa de dormir** *sleeping bag* **darle de baja** *to suspend* **harto** *fed up* **revolear** *throw it away with energy (S. America)* **bien hecho** *well done* **llamada perdida** *missed call*

Escritura

Estrategia
Listing key words

Once you have determined the purpose for a piece of writing and identified your audience, it is helpful to make a list of key words you can use while writing. If you were to write a description of your campus, for example, you would probably need a list of prepositions that describe location, such as **en frente de, al lado de,** and **detrás de.** Likewise, a list of descriptive adjectives would be useful to you if you were writing about the people and places of your childhood.

By preparing a list of potential words ahead of time, you will find it easier to avoid using the dictionary while writing your first draft. You will probably also learn a few new words in Spanish while preparing your list of key words.

Listing useful vocabulary is also a valuable organizational strategy, since the act of brainstorming key words will help you to form ideas about your topic. In addition, a list of key words can help you avoid redundancy when you write.

If you were going to help someone write a personal ad, what words would be most helpful to you? Jot a few of them down and compare your list with a partner's. Did you choose the same words? Would you choose any different or additional words, based on what your partner wrote?

1. ______________________________
2. ______________________________
3. ______________________________
4. ______________________________
5. ______________________________
6. ______________________________

Tema
Escribir instrucciones

Un(a) amigo/a tuyo/a quiere escribir un anuncio personal en un sitio web para citas románticas. Tú tienes experiencia con esto y vas a decirle qué debe y no debe decir en su perfil°.

Escríbele un correo en el que le explicas claramente° cómo hacerlo.

Cuando escribas tu correo, considera esta información:

- el nombre del sitio web
- mandatos afirmativos que describen en detalle lo que tu amigo/a debe escribir
- una descripción física, sus pasatiempos, sus actividades favoritas y otras cosas originales como el tipo de carro que tiene o su signo del zodiaco
- su dirección electrónica, su número de teléfono celular, etc.
- mandatos negativos sobre cosas que tu amigo/a no debe escribir en el anuncio

perfil *profile* **claramente** *clearly*

Escuchar

Audio: Activities

Estrategia

Recognizing the genre of spoken discourse

You will encounter many different genres of spoken discourse in Spanish. For example, you may hear a political speech, a radio interview, a commercial, a voicemail message, or a news broadcast. Try to identify the genre of what you hear so that you can activate your background knowledge about that type of discourse and identify the speakers' motives and intentions.

To practice this strategy, you will now listen to two short selections. Identify the genre of each one.

Preparación

Mira la foto de Ricardo Moreno. ¿Puedes imaginarte qué tipo de discurso vas a oír?

Ahora escucha

Mientras escuchas a Ricardo Moreno, responde a las preguntas.

1. ¿Qué tipo de discurso es?
   a. las noticias° por radio o televisión
   b. una conversación entre amigos
   c. un anuncio comercial
   d. una reseña° de una película
2. ¿De qué habla?
   a. del tiempo
   b. de su vida
   c. de un producto o servicio
   d. de algo que oyó o vio
3. ¿Cuál es el propósito°?
   a. informar
   b. vender
   c. relacionarse con alguien
   d. dar opiniones

noticias *news* **reseña** *review* **propósito** *purpose*

Practice more at **vistas.vhlcentral.com.**

Comprensión

Identificar

Indica si esta información está incluida en el discurso; si está incluida, escribe los detalles que escuchaste.

	Sí	No
1. El anuncio describe un servicio. ________	❍	❍
2. Explica cómo está de salud. ________	❍	❍
3. Informa sobre la variedad de productos. ________	❍	❍
4. Pide tu opinión. ________	❍	❍
5. Explica por qué es la mejor tienda. ________	❍	❍
6. Informa sobre el tiempo para mañana. ________	❍	❍
7. Informa dónde se puede conseguir el servicio. ________	❍	❍
8. Informa sobre las noticias del mundo. ________	❍	❍

Haz un anuncio

Con tres o cuatro compañeros, hagan un anuncio comercial de algún producto. No se olviden de dar toda la información necesaria. Después presenten su anuncio a la clase. Entre todos, decidan cuál es el mejor anuncio.

En pantalla

No sólo del fútbol y el béisbol viven los aficionados hispanos; también del automovilismo°. En Argentina es el segundo deporte más popular después del fútbol. En la Fórmula 1, la leyenda del argentino Juan Manuel Fangio aún sigue viva. España tiene circuitos importantes, como Jerez y Montmeló, y pilotos reconocidos como Fernando Alonso y Pedro de la Rosa. En México encontramos la tradicional Copa Turmex y las *NASCAR Corona Series*, y pilotos como Adrián Fernández y Esteban Gutiérrez. En NASCAR, el colombiano Juan Pablo Montoya y el cubano-americano Aric Almirola han hecho un buen papel°.

Vocabulario útil

¿Cómo quedó?	*How does it look?*
cuénteme	*tell me*
la llama	*flame; llama (the animal)*
malinterpretar	*misunderstand*
veamos	*let's see*

Preparación

¿Alguna vez le pediste a alguien que hiciera algo y te malinterpretó o se lo pediste a la persona equivocada?

Ordenar

Ordena cronológicamente estas oraciones.

a. El dueño del taller malinterpretó el pedido.
b. El cliente se sorprendió cuando lo vio y se le cayó el casco (*helmet*).
c. Pensó que el cliente no se refería a (*didn't refer to*) las llamas de fuego sino a los animales.
d. El cliente pidió que pintaran (*painted*) su carro con llamas.
e. El dueño estaba muy orgulloso (*proud*) cuando le mostró al cliente cómo quedó el carro.

¿Cómo terminó?

En parejas, imaginen el final de la historia. ¿Cómo se sentían el cliente y el dueño del taller? ¿Qué ocurrió después? ¿Encontraron una solución? Usen el pretérito y el imperfecto.

automovilismo *car racing* **han hecho un buen papel** *have done a good job*

Anuncio de Davivienda

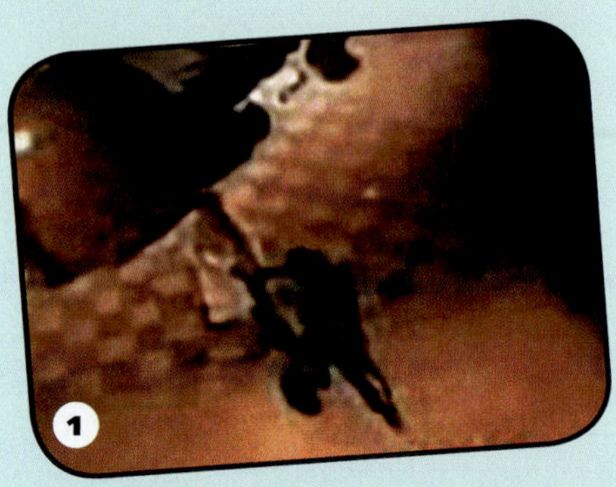

1 **Don Álex, lo estábamos esperando.**

2 **Cuénteme. ¿Cómo quedó mi carro?**

3 **Quedó espectacular [...] Llamas por arriba, por los lados...**

Video: TV Clip

Practice more at **vistas.vhlcentral.com.**

Flash CULTURA

Hoy día, en cualquier ciudad grande latinoamericana puedes encontrar **un cibercafé.** Allí uno puede disfrutar de° un refresco o un café mientras navega en Internet, escribe correo electrónico o chatea°. De hecho°, el negocio° del cibercafé está mucho más desarrollado° en Latinoamérica que en los Estados Unidos. En una ciudad hispana, es común ver varios en una misma cuadra°. Los cibercafés ofrecen servicios especializados que permiten su coexistencia. Por ejemplo, mientras que el cibercafé Videomax atrae° a los niños con videojuegos, el Conécta-T ofrece servicio de chat con cámara para jóvenes, y el Mundo° Ejecutivo atrae a profesionales, todos en la misma calle.

Vocabulario útil

chateando	*chatting*
comunidad indígena	*indigenous community*
localizados	*located*
usuarios	*users*

Preparación

¿Con qué frecuencia navegas en Internet? ¿Dónde lo haces, en tu casa o en un lugar público?

Elegir

Indica cuál de las dos opciones resume mejor este episodio.

a. En Cuzco, Internet es un elemento importante para las comunidades indígenas que quieren vender sus productos en otros países. Con Internet inalámbrica, estas comunidades chatean con clientes en otros países.

b. En Cuzco, la comunidad y los turistas usan la tecnología de los celulares e Internet para comunicarse con sus familias o vender productos. Para navegar en Internet, se pueden visitar las cabinas de Internet o ir a la Plaza de Armas con una computadora portátil.

disfrutar de *enjoy* chatea *chat (from the English verb* to chat*)* De hecho *In fact* negocio *business* desarrollado *developed* cuadra *(city) block* atrae *attracts* Mundo *World*

Maravillas de la tecnología

... los cibercafés se conocen comúnmente como "cabinas de Internet" y están localizados por todo el país.

... el primer *hotspot* de Cuzco [...] permite a los usuarios navegar de manera inalámbrica...

Puedo usar Internet en medio de la plaza y nadie me molesta.

Video: *Flash cultura*

Practice more at **vistas.vhlcentral.com.**

recursos	
VM pp. 311–312	vistas.vhlcentral.com Lección 11

Video: *Panorama cultural*
Interactive map

Argentina

El país en cifras

- **Área:** 2.780.400 km² (1.074.000 millas²)
  Argentina es el país de habla española más grande del mundo. Su territorio es dos veces el tamaño° de Alaska.
- **Población:** 42.548.000
- **Capital:** Buenos Aires (y su área metropolitana) —13.401.000
  En el gran Buenos Aires vive más del treinta por ciento de la población total del país. La ciudad es conocida° como el "París de Suramérica" por su estilo parisino°.

Buenos Aires

- **Ciudades principales:** Córdoba —1.552.000, Rosario —1.280.000, Mendoza —956.000

SOURCE: Population Division, UN Secretariat

- **Moneda:** peso argentino
- **Idiomas:** español (oficial), lenguas indígenas

Bandera de Argentina

Argentinos célebres

- **Jorge Luis Borges,** escritor (1899–1986)
- **María Eva Duarte de Perón ("Evita"),** primera dama° (1919–1952)
- **Mercedes Sosa,** cantante (1935–2009)
- **Leandro "Gato" Barbieri,** saxofonista (1932–)

Monte Fitz Roy (Chaltén)

Gaucho de las pampas

Vista de San Carlos de Bariloche

recursos		
WB pp. 133–134	VM pp. 269–270	vistas.vhlcentral.com Lección 11

tamaño *size* **conocida** *known* **parisino** *Parisian* **primera dama** *First Lady* **ancha** *wide* **mide** *it measures* **campo** *field*

¡Increíble pero cierto!

La Avenida 9 de Julio en Buenos Aires es la calle más ancha° del mundo. De lado a lado mide° cerca de 140 metros, lo que es equivalente a un campo° y medio de fútbol. Su nombre conmemora el Día de la Independencia de Argentina.

BRASIL

Historia • Inmigración europea

Se dice que Argentina es el país más "europeo" de toda Latinoamérica. Después del año 1880, inmigrantes italianos, alemanes, españoles e ingleses llegaron para establecerse en esta nación. Esta diversidad cultural ha dejado° una profunda huella° en la música, el cine y la arquitectura argentinos.

Artes • El tango

El tango es uno de los símbolos culturales más importantes de Argentina. Este género° musical es una mezcla de ritmos de origen africano, italiano y español, y se originó a finales del siglo XIX entre los porteños°. Poco después se hizo popular entre el resto de los argentinos y su fama llegó hasta París. Como baile, el tango en un principio° era provocativo y violento, pero se hizo más romántico durante los años 30. Hoy día, este estilo musical tiene adeptos° en muchas partes del mundo°.

Lugares • Las cataratas del Iguazú

Las famosas cataratas° del Iguazú se encuentran entre las fronteras de Argentina, Paraguay y Brasil, al norte de Buenos Aires. Cerca de ellas confluyen° los ríos Iguazú y Paraná. Estas extensas caídas de agua tienen hasta 80 metros (262 pies) de altura° y en época° de lluvias llegan a medir 4 kilómetros (2,5 millas) de ancho. Situadas en el Parque Nacional Iguazú, las cataratas son un destino° turístico muy visitado.

¿Qué aprendiste? Responde a cada pregunta con una oración completa.

1. ¿Qué porcentaje de la población de Argentina vive en el gran Buenos Aires?
2. ¿Quién era Mercedes Sosa?
3. Se dice que Argentina es el país más europeo de Latinoamérica. ¿Por qué?
4. ¿Qué tipo de baile es uno de los símbolos culturales más importantes de Argentina?
5. ¿Dónde y cuándo se originó el tango?
6. ¿Cómo era el baile del tango originalmente?
7. ¿En qué parque nacional están las cataratas del Iguazú?

Artesano en Buenos Aires

Conexión Internet Investiga estos temas en **vistas.vhlcentral.com.**

1. Busca información sobre el tango. ¿Te gustan los ritmos y sonidos del tango? ¿Por qué? ¿Se baila el tango en tu comunidad?
2. ¿Quiénes fueron Juan y Eva Perón y qué importancia tienen en la historia de Argentina?

Practice more at **vistas.vhlcentral.com.**

ha dejado *has left* **huella** *mark* **género** *genre* **porteños** *people of Buenos Aires* **en un principio** *at first* **adeptos** *followers* **mundo** *world* **cataratas** *waterfalls* **confluyen** *converge* **altura** *height* **época** *season* **destino** *destination*

La tecnología

la cámara digital/ de video	*digital/video camera*
el canal	*(TV) channel*
el cibercafé	*cybercafé*
el control remoto	*remote control*
el correo de voz	*voice mail*
el disco compacto	*CD*
el estéreo	*stereo*
el fax	*fax (machine)*
la pantalla táctil	*touch screen*
el radio	*radio (set)*
el reproductor de CD	*CD player*
el reproductor de MP3	*MP3 player*
el (teléfono) celular	*(cell) phone*
la televisión por cable	*cable television*
el televisor	*televison set*
el video	*video*
apagar	*to turn off*
funcionar	*to work*
llamar	*to call*
poner, prender	*to turn on*
sonar (o:ue)	*to ring*
descompuesto/a	*not working; out of order*
lento/a	*slow*
lleno/a	*full*

Verbos

abrazar(se)	*to hug; to embrace (each other)*
ayudar(se)	*to help (each other)*
besar(se)	*to kiss (each other)*
encontrar(se) (o:ue)	*to meet (each other); to run into (each other)*
saludar(se)	*to greet (each other)*

La computadora

el archivo	*file*
la arroba	*@ symbol*
el blog	*blog*
el cederrón	*CD-ROM*
la computadora (portátil)	*(portable) computer; (laptop)*
la conexión inalámbrica	*wireless (connection)*
la dirección electrónica	*e-mail address*
el disco compacto	*CD*
la impresora	*printer*
Internet	*Internet*
el mensaje de texto	*text message*
el monitor	*(computer) monitor*
la página principal	*home page*
la pantalla	*screen*
el programa de computación	*software*
el ratón	*mouse*
la red	*network; Web*
el reproductor de DVD	*DVD player*
el sitio web	*website*
el teclado	*keyboard*
borrar	*to erase*
descargar	*to download*
escanear	*to scan*
grabar	*to record*
guardar	*to save*
imprimir	*to print*
navegar (en Internet)	*to surf (the Internet)*

El carro

la autopista, la carretera	*highway*
el baúl	*trunk*
la calle	*street*
el capó, el cofre	*hood*
el carro, el coche	*car*
la circulación, el tráfico	*traffic*
el garaje, el taller (mecánico)	*garage; (mechanic's) repair shop*
la gasolina	*gasoline*
la gasolinera	*gas station*
la licencia de conducir	*driver's license*
la llanta	*tire*
el/la mecánico/a	*mechanic*
el navegador GPS	*GPS*
el parabrisas	*windshield*
la policía	*police (force)*
la velocidad máxima	*speed limit*
el volante	*steering wheel*
arrancar	*to start*
arreglar	*to fix; to arrange*
bajar(se) de	*to get off of/out of (a vehicle)*
conducir, manejar	*to drive*
estacionar	*to park*
llenar (el tanque)	*to fill (the tank)*
parar	*to stop*
revisar (el aceite)	*to check (the oil)*
subir(se) a	*to get on/into (a vehicle)*

Otras palabras y expresiones

por aquí	*around here*
por ejemplo	*for example*
por eso	*that's why; therefore*
por fin	*finally*

Por and **para**	*See pages 382–383.*
Stressed possessive adjectives and pronouns	*See pages 388–389.*
Expresiones útiles	*See page 373.*

recursos

LM p. 66	vistas.vhlcentral.com Lección 11

Audio: Vocabulary

La vivienda

12

Communicative Goals

You will learn how to:

- **Welcome people to your home**
- **Describe your house or apartment**
- **Talk about household chores**
- **Give instructions**

contextos

pages 404–407

- Parts of a house
- Household chores
- Table settings

fotonovela

pages 408–411

Felipe and Jimena have promised to clean the apartment in exchange for permission to take a trip to the Yucatan Peninsula. Can Marissa and Juan Carlos help them finish on time?

cultura

pages 412–413

- The central patio
- The floating islands of Lake Titicaca

estructura

pages 414–431

- Relative pronouns
- Formal (**usted/ustedes**) commands
- The present subjunctive
- Subjunctive with verbs of will and influence
- **Recapitulación**

adelante

pages 432–439

Lectura: **El Palacio de las Garzas**
Escritura: A rental agreement
Escuchar: A conversation about finding a home
En pantalla
Flash cultura
Panorama: Panamá

A PRIMERA VISTA

- **¿Están los chicos en casa?**
- **¿Viven en una casa o en un apartamento?**
- **¿Ya comieron o van a comer?**
- **¿Están de buen humor o de mal humor?**

Talking Picture, Tutorials & Games
Audio: Activities

La vivienda

Más vocabulario

las afueras	*suburbs; outskirts*
el alquiler	*rent (payment)*
el ama (*m., f.*) de casa	*housekeeper; caretaker*
el barrio	*neighborhood*
el edificio de apartamentos	*apartment building*
el/la vecino/a	*neighbor*
la vivienda	*housing*
el balcón	*balcony*
la entrada	*entrance*
la escalera	*stairs; stairway*
el garaje	*garage*
el jardín	*garden; yard*
el patio	*patio; yard*
el sótano	*basement; cellar*
la cafetera	*coffee maker*
el electrodoméstico	*electrical appliance*
el horno (de microondas)	*(microwave) oven*
la lavadora	*washing machine*
la luz	*light; electricity*
la secadora	*clothes dryer*
la tostadora	*toaster*
el cartel	*poster*
la mesita de noche	*night stand*
los muebles	*furniture*
alquilar	*to rent*
mudarse	*to move (from one house to another)*

Variación léxica

dormitorio ⟷ aposento (*Rep. Dom.*); recámara (*Méx.*)

apartamento ⟷ departamento (*Arg., Chile, Méx.*); piso (*Esp.*)

lavar los platos ⟷ lavar/fregar los trastes (*Amér. C., Rep. Dom.*)

recursos

WB pp. 135–136	LM p. 67	vistas.vhlcentral.com Lección 12

Los quehaceres domésticos

arreglar	*to neaten; to straighten up*
barrer el suelo	*to sweep the floor*
cocinar	*to cook*
ensuciar	*to get (something) dirty*
hacer quehaceres domésticos	*to do household chores*
lavar (el suelo, los platos)	*to wash (the floor, the dishes)*
limpiar la casa	*to clean the house*
planchar la ropa	*to iron the clothes*
quitar la mesa	*to clear the table*
quitar el polvo	*to dust*

Práctica

1 Escuchar Escucha la conversación y completa las oraciones.

1. Pedro va a limpiar primero ____________.
2. Paula va a comenzar en ____________.
3. Pedro va a ____________ en el sótano.
4. Pedro también va a limpiar ____________.
5. Ellos están limpiando la casa porque ______________________.

2 Respuestas Escucha las preguntas y selecciona la respuesta más adecuada. Una respuesta no se va a usar.

___ a. Sí, la alfombra estaba muy sucia.
___ b. No, porque todavía se están mudando.
___ c. Sí, sacudí la mesa y el estante.
___ d. Sí, puse el pollo en el horno.
___ e. Hice la cama, pero no limpié los muebles.
___ f. Sí, después de sacarla de la secadora.

3 Escoger Escoge la letra de la respuesta correcta.

1. Cuando quieres tener una lámpara y un despertador cerca de tu cama, puedes ponerlos en ______.
   a. el barrio   b. el cuadro   c. la mesita de noche
2. Si no quieres vivir en el centro de la ciudad, puedes mudarte ______.
   a. al alquiler   b. a las afueras   c. a la vivienda
3. Guardamos (*We keep*) los pantalones, las camisas y los zapatos en ______.
   a. la secadora   b. el armario   c. el patio
4. Para subir de la planta baja al primer piso, usas ______.
   a. la entrada   b. el cartel   c. la escalera
5. Ponemos cuadros y pinturas en ______.
   a. las paredes   b. los quehaceres   c. los jardines

4 Definiciones En parejas, identifiquen cada cosa que se describe. Luego inventen sus propias descripciones de algunas palabras y expresiones de **Contextos**.

modelo

Estudiante 1: *Es donde pones los libros.*
Estudiante 2: *el estante*

1. Es donde pones la cabeza cuando duermes.
2. Es el quehacer doméstico que haces después de comer.
3. Algunos de ellos son las cómodas y los sillones.
4. Son las personas que viven en tu barrio.
5. ______________________________
6. ______________________________

5 **Completar** Completa estas frases con las palabras más adecuadas.

1. Para tomar vino necesitas...
2. Para comer una ensalada necesitas...
3. Para tomar café necesitas...
4. Para poner la comida en la mesa necesitas...
5. Para limpiarte la boca después de comer necesitas...
6. Para cortar (*to cut*) un bistec necesitas...
7. Para tomar agua necesitas...
8. Para tomar sopa necesitas...

6 **Los quehaceres** Trabajen en grupos para indicar quién hace estos quehaceres domésticos en sus casas. Luego contesten las preguntas.

barrer el suelo	lavar los platos	planchar la ropa
cocinar	lavar la ropa	sacar la basura
hacer las camas	pasar la aspiradora	sacudir los muebles

modelo

Estudiante 1: ¿Quién pasa la aspiradora en tu casa?
Estudiante 2: Mi hermano y yo pasamos la aspiradora.

1. ¿Quién hace más quehaceres, tú o tus compañeros/as?
2. ¿Quiénes hacen la mayoría de los quehaceres, los hombres o las mujeres?
3. ¿Piensas que debes hacer más quehaceres? ¿Por qué?

Comunicación

7 **La vida doméstica** En parejas, describan las habitaciones que ven en estas fotos. Identifiquen y describan cinco muebles o adornos (*accessories*) de cada foto y digan dos quehaceres que se pueden hacer en cada habitación.

8 **Mi apartamento** Dibuja el plano (*floor plan*) de un apartamento amueblado (*furnished*) imaginario y escribe los nombres de las habitaciones y de los muebles. En parejas, siéntense espalda contra espalda (*sit back to back*). Uno/a de ustedes describe su apartamento mientras su compañero/a lo dibuja según la descripción. Cuando terminen, miren el segundo dibujo. ¿Es similar al dibujo original? Hablen de los cambios que se necesitan hacer para mejorar el dibujo. Repitan la actividad intercambiando papeles.

CONSULTA

To review bathroom-related vocabulary, see **Lección 7, Contextos,** p. 226.

9 **¡Corre, corre!** Tu profesor(a) va a darte una serie incompleta de dibujos que forman una historia. Tú y tu compañero/a tienen dos series diferentes. Descríbanse los dibujos para completar la historia.

modelo

Estudiante 1: Marta quita la mesa.
Estudiante 2: Francisco...

Los quehaceres

Jimena y Felipe deben limpiar el apartamento para poder ir de viaje con Marissa.

PERSONAJES

JIMENA

FELIPE

Video: ***Fotonovela***
Record and Compare

SR. DÍAZ Quieren ir a Yucatán con Marissa, ¿verdad?

SRA. DÍAZ Entonces, les sugiero que arreglen este apartamento. Regresamos más tarde.

SR. DÍAZ Les aconsejo que preparen la cena para las 8:30.

MARISSA ¿Qué pasa?

JIMENA Nuestros papás quieren que Felipe y yo arreglemos toda la casa.

FELIPE Y que, además, preparemos la cena.

MARISSA ¡Pues, yo les ayudo!

MARISSA Mis padres siempre quieren que mis hermanos y yo ayudemos con los quehaceres. No me molesta ayudar. Pero odio limpiar el baño.

JIMENA Lo que más odio yo es sacar la basura.

JUAN CARLOS Hola, Jimena. ¿Está Felipe? (*a Felipe*) Te olvidaste del partido de fútbol.

FELIPE Juan Carlos, ¿verdad que mi papá te considera como de la familia?

JUAN CARLOS Sí.

(Don Diego llega a ayudar a los chicos.)

FELIPE Tenemos que limpiar la casa hoy.

JIMENA ¿Nos ayuda, don Diego?

DON DIEGO Claro. Recomiendo que se organicen en equipos para limpiar.

MARISSA Yo lleno el lavaplatos... después de vaciarlo.

DON DIEGO Juan Carlos, ¿por qué no terminas de pasar la aspiradora? Y Felipe, tú limpia el polvo. ¡Ya casi acaban!

SRA. DÍAZ

SR. DÍAZ

MARISSA

JUAN CARLOS

DON DIEGO

7

(Los chicos preparan la cena y ponen la mesa.)

JUAN CARLOS ¿Dónde están los tenedores?

JIMENA Allá.

JUAN CARLOS ¿Y las servilletas?

MARISSA Aquí están.

8

FELIPE La sala está tan limpia. Le pasamos la aspiradora al sillón y a las cortinas. ¡Y también a las almohadas!

JIMENA Yucatán, ¡ya casi llegamos!

9

(Papá y mamá regresan a casa.)

SRA. DÍAZ ¡Qué bonita está la casa!

SR. DÍAZ Buen trabajo, muchachos. ¿Qué hay para cenar?

JIMENA Quesadillas. Vengan.

10

SRA. DÍAZ Don Diego, quédese a cenar con nosotros. Venga.

SR. DÍAZ Sí, don Diego. Pase.

DON DIEGO Gracias.

Expresiones útiles

Making recommendations

Le(s) sugiero que arregle(n) este apartamento.
I suggest you tidy up this apartment.
Le(s) aconsejo que prepare(n) la cena para las ocho y media.
I recommend that you have dinner ready for eight thirty.

Organizing work

Recomiendo que se organicen en equipos para limpiar.
I recommend that you divide yourselves into teams to clean.
Yo lleno el lavaplatos... después de vaciarlo.
I'll fill the dishwasher... after I empty it.
¿Por qué no terminas de pasar la aspiradora?
Why don't you finish vacuuming?
¡Ya casi acaban!
You're almost finished!
Felipe, tú quita el polvo.
Felipe, you dust.

Making polite requests

Don Diego, quédese a cenar con nosotros.
Don Diego, stay and have dinner with us.
Venga.
Come on.
Don Diego, pase.
Don Diego, come in.

Additional vocabulary

el plumero *duster*

recursos

VM	
VM pp. 235–236	vistas.vhlcentral.com Lección 12

¿Qué pasó?

1 **¿Cierto o falso?** Indica si lo que dicen estas oraciones es **cierto** o **falso**. Corrige las oraciones falsas.

	Cierto	Falso
1. Felipe y Jimena tienen que preparar el desayuno.	❍	❍
2. Don Diego ayuda a los chicos organizando los quehaceres domésticos.	❍	❍
3. Jimena le dice a Juan Carlos dónde están los tenedores.	❍	❍
4. A Marissa no le molesta limpiar el baño.	❍	❍
5. Juan Carlos termina de lavar los platos.	❍	❍

2 **Identificar** Identifica quién puede decir estas oraciones.

1. Yo les ayudo, no me molesta hacer quehaceres domésticos.
2. No me gusta sacar la basura, pero es necesario hacerlo.
3. Es importante que termines de pasar la aspiradora, Juan Carlos.
4. ¡La casa está muy limpia! ¡Qué bueno que pasamos la aspiradora!
5. ¡Buen trabajo, chicos! ¿Qué vamos a cenar?

3 **Completar** Los chicos y don Diego están haciendo los quehaceres. Adivina en qué cuarto está cada uno de ellos.

1. Jimena limpia el congelador. Jimena está en ________________.
2. Don Diego limpia el escritorio. Don Diego está en ________________.
3. Felipe pasa la aspiradora debajo de la mesa y las sillas. Felipe está en ________________.
4. Juan Carlos sacude el sillón. Juan Carlos está en ________________.
5. Marissa hace la cama. Marissa está en ________________.

4 **Mi casa** Dibuja el plano de una casa o de un apartamento. Puede ser el plano de la casa o del apartamento donde vives o de donde te gustaría (*you would like*) vivir. Después, trabajen en parejas y describan lo que se hace en cuatro de las habitaciones. Para terminar, pídanse (*ask for*) ayuda para hacer dos quehaceres domésticos. Pueden usar estas frases en su conversación.

Quiero mostrarte...	Al fondo hay...
Ésta es (la cocina).	Quiero que me ayudes a (sacar la basura).
Allí yo (preparo la comida).	Por favor, ayúdame con...

Practice more at **vistas.vhlcentral.com.**

Ortografía

Concepts

Mayúsculas y minúsculas

Here are some of the rules that govern the use of capital letters (**mayúsculas**) and lowercase letters (**minúsculas**) in Spanish.

Los estudiantes llegaron al aeropuerto a las dos.
Luego fueron al hotel.

In both Spanish and English, the first letter of every sentence is capitalized.

Rubén Blades **Panamá** **Colón** **los Andes**

The first letter of all proper nouns (names of people, countries, cities, geographical features, etc.) is capitalized.

Cien años de soledad ***Don Quijote de la Mancha***
El País ***Muy Interesante***

The first letter of the first word in titles of books, films, and works of art is generally capitalized, as well as the first letter of any proper names. In newspaper and magazine titles, as well as other short titles, the initial letter of each word is often capitalized.

la señora Ramos **don Francisco**
el presidente **Sra. Vives**

Titles associated with people are *not* capitalized unless they appear as the first word in a sentence. Note, however, that the first letter of an abbreviated title is capitalized.

Último **Álex** **MENÚ** **PERDÓN**

Accent marks should be retained on capital letters. In practice, however, this rule is often ignored.

lunes **viernes** **marzo** **primavera**

The first letter of days, months, and seasons is not capitalized.

español **estadounidense** **japonés** **panameños**

The first letter of nationalities and languages is not capitalized.

Práctica Corrige las mayúsculas y minúsculas incorrectas.

1. soy lourdes romero. Soy Colombiana.
2. éste Es mi Hermano álex.
3. somos De panamá.
4. ¿es ud. La sra. benavides?
5. ud. Llegó el Lunes, ¿no?

Palabras desordenadas Lee el diálogo de las serpientes. Ordena las letras para saber de qué palabras se trata. Después escribe las letras indicadas para descubrir por qué llora Pepito.

m n a a P á ___ ___ ___ ___ ___ ___
s t e m r a ___ ___ ___ ___ ___ ___
i g s l é n ___ ___ ___ ___ ___ ___
y a U r u g u ___ ___ ___ ___ ___ ___ ___
r o ñ e s a ___ ___ ___ ___ ___ ___

¡___orque ___e acabo de morder° la ___en___u___!

venenosas *venomous* morder *to bite*

Respuestas: Panamá, martes, inglés, Uruguay, señora.
¡Porque me acabo de morder la lengua!

recursos
LM p. 68
vistas.vhlcentral.com Lección 12

EN DETALLE

Additional Reading

El patio central

En las tardes cálidas° de Oaxaca, México; Córdoba, España, o Popayán, Colombia, es un placer sentarse en **el patio central** de una casa y tomar un refresco disfrutando de° una buena conversación. De influencia árabe, esta característica arquitectónica° fue traída° a las Américas por los españoles. En la época° colonial, se construyeron casas, palacios, monasterios, hospitales y escuelas con patio central. Éste es un espacio privado e íntimo en donde se puede disfrutar del sol y de la brisa° estando aislado° de la calle.

El centro del patio es un espacio abierto. Alrededor de° él, separado por columnas, hay un pasillo cubierto°. Así, en el patio hay zonas de sol y de sombra°. El patio es una parte importante de la vivienda familiar y su decoración se cuida° mucho. En el centro del patio muchas veces hay una fuente°, plantas e incluso árboles°. El agua es un elemento muy importante en la cultura islámica porque simboliza la purificación del cuerpo y del alma°. Por esta razón y para disminuir° la temperatura, el agua en estas construcciones es muy importante. El agua y la vegetación ayudan a mantener la temperatura fresca y el patio proporciona° luz y ventilación a todas las habitaciones.

La distribución

Las casas con patio central eran usualmente las viviendas de familias adineradas°. Son casas de dos o tres pisos. Los cuartos de la planta baja son las áreas comunes: cocina, comedor, sala, etc., y tienen puertas al patio. En los pisos superiores están las habitaciones privadas de la familia.

cálidas *hot* **disfrutando de** *enjoying* **arquitectónica** *architectural* **traída** *brought* **época** *era* **brisa** *breeze* **aislado** *isolated* **Alrededor de** *Surrounding* **cubierto** *covered* **sombra** *shade* **se cuida** *is looked after* **fuente** *fountain* **árboles** *trees* **alma** *soul* **disminuir** *lower* **proporciona** *provides* **adineradas** *wealthy*

ACTIVIDADES

1 **¿Cierto o falso?** Indica si lo que dicen las oraciones es **cierto** o **falso**. Corrige las falsas.

1. Los patios centrales de Latinoamérica tienen su origen en la tradición indígena.
2. Los españoles llevaron a América el concepto del patio.
3. En la época colonial las casas eran las únicas construcciones con patio central.
4. El patio es una parte importante en estas construcciones, y es por eso que se le presta atención a su decoración.
5. El patio central es un lugar de descanso que da luz y ventilación a las habitaciones.
6. Las fuentes en los patios tienen importancia por razones culturales y porque bajan la temperatura.
7. En la cultura española el agua simboliza salud y bienestar del cuerpo y del alma.
8. Las casas con patio central eran para personas adineradas.
9. Los cuartos de la planta baja son privados.
10. Las alcobas están en los pisos superiores.

ASÍ SE DICE

La vivienda

el ático, el desván	el altillo
la cobija (Col., Méx.), la frazada (Arg., Cuba, Ven.)	la manta
el escaparate (Cuba, Ven.), el ropero (Méx.)	el armario
el fregadero	*kitchen sink*
el frigidaire (Perú); el frigorífico (Esp.), la nevera	el refrigerador
el lavavajillas (Arg., Esp., Méx.)	el lavaplatos

EL MUNDO HISPANO

Los muebles

- **Mecedora°** La mecedora es un mueble típico de Latinoamérica, especialmente de la zona del Caribe. A las personas les gusta relajarse mientras se mecen° en el patio.
- **Mesa camilla** Era un mueble popular en España hasta hace algunos años. Es una mesa con un bastidor° en la parte inferior° para poner un brasero°. En invierno, las personas se sentaban alrededor de la mesa camilla para conversar, jugar a las cartas o tomar café.

- **Hamaca** Se cree que los taínos hicieron las primeras hamacas con fibras vegetales. Su uso es muy popular en toda Latinoamérica para dormir y descansar.

Mecedora *Rocking chair* se mecen *they rock themselves* bastidor *frame* inferior *bottom* brasero *container for hot coals*

PERFIL

Las islas flotantes del lago Titicaca

Bolivia y Perú comparten **el lago Titicaca**, donde viven **los uros**, uno de los pueblos indígenas más antiguos de América. Hace muchos años, los uros fueron a vivir al lago escapando de **los incas**. Hoy en día, siguen viviendo allí en cuarenta **islas flotantes** que ellos mismos hacen con unos juncos° llamados **totora**. Primero tejen° grandes plataformas. Luego, con el mismo material, construyen sus casas sobre las plataformas. La totora es resistente, pero con el tiempo el agua la pudre°. Los habitantes de las islas necesitan renovar continuamente las plataformas y las casas. Sus muebles y sus barcos también están hechos° de juncos. Los uros viven de la pesca y del turismo; en las islas hay unas tiendas donde venden artesanías° hechas con totora.

juncos *reeds* tejen *they weave* la pudre *rots it* hechos *made* artesanías *handcrafts*

Conexión Internet

¿Cómo son las casas modernas en los países hispanos?

Go to **vistas.vhlcentral.com** to find more cultural information related to this **Cultura** section.

ACTIVIDADES

2 Comprensión Responde a las preguntas.

1. Tu amigo mexicano te dice: "La **cobija** azul está en el **ropero**". ¿Qué quiere decir?
2. ¿Quiénes hicieron las primeras hamacas? ¿Qué material usaron?
3. ¿Qué grupo indígena vive en el lago Titicaca?
4. ¿Qué pueden comprar los turistas en las islas flotantes del lago Titicaca?

3 Viviendas tradicionales Escribe cuatro oraciones sobre una vivienda tradicional que conoces. Explica en qué lugar se encuentra, de qué materiales está hecha y cómo es.

Practice more at **vistas.vhlcentral.com.**

12.1 Relative pronouns

Tutorial

ANTE TODO In both English and Spanish, relative pronouns are used to combine two sentences or clauses that share a common element, such as a noun or pronoun. Study this diagram.

Mis padres me regalaron **la aspiradora**.
My parents gave me the vacuum cleaner.

La aspiradora funciona muy bien.
The vacuum cleaner works really well.

La aspiradora **que** me regalaron mis padres funciona muy bien.
The vacuum cleaner that my parents gave me works really well.

Lourdes es muy inteligente.
Lourdes is very intelligent.

Lourdes estudia español.
Lourdes is studying Spanish.

Lourdes, **quien** estudia español, es muy inteligente.
Lourdes, who studies Spanish, is very intelligent.

Nuestros papás quieren que arreglemos la casa.

Él es Juan Carlos, quien es como mi hermano.

- Spanish has three frequently-used relative pronouns. **¡Atención!** Even though interrogative words (**qué**, **quién**, etc.) always carry an accent, relative pronouns never carry a written accent.

que	*that; which; who*
quien(es)	*who; whom; that*
lo que	*that which; what*

- **Que** is the most frequently used relative pronoun. It can refer to things or to people. Unlike its English counterpart, *that,* **que** is never omitted.

¿Dónde está la cafetera **que** compré?
Where is the coffee maker (that) I bought?

El hombre **que** limpia es Pedro.
The man who is cleaning is Pedro.

- The relative pronoun **quien** refers only to people, and is often used after a preposition or the personal **a. Quien** has only two forms: **quien** (singular) and **quienes** (plural).

¿Son las chicas **de quienes** me hablaste la semana pasada?
Are they the girls (that) you told me about last week?

Eva, **a quien** conocí anoche, es mi nueva vecina.
Eva, whom I met last night, is my new neighbor.

¡LENGUA VIVA!

In English, it is generally recommended that *who(m)* be used to refer to people, and that *that* and *which* be used to refer to things. In Spanish, however, it is perfectly acceptable to use **que** when referring to people.

- **Quien(es)** is occasionally used instead of **que** in clauses set off by commas.

Lola, **quien** es cubana, es médica.
Lola, who is Cuban, is a doctor.

Su tía, **que** es alemana, ya llegó.
His aunt, who is German, already arrived.

- Unlike **que** and **quien(es), lo que** doesn't refer to a specific noun. It refers to an idea, a situation, or a past event and means *what, that which,* or *the thing that.*

Lo que me molesta es el calor.
What bothers me is the heat.

Lo que quiero es una casa.
What I want is a house.

Este supermercado tiene todo **lo que** necesito.

A Samuel no le gustó **lo que** le dijo Violeta.

¡INTÉNTALO! Completa estas oraciones con pronombres relativos.

1. Voy a utilizar los platos ___que___ me regaló mi abuela.
2. Ana comparte un apartamento con la chica a ________ conocimos en la fiesta de Jorge.
3. Esta oficina tiene todo ________ necesitamos.
4. Puedes estudiar en el dormitorio ________ está a la derecha de la cocina.
5. Los señores ________ viven en esa casa acaban de llegar de Centroamérica.
6. Los niños a ________ viste en nuestro jardín son mis sobrinos.
7. La piscina ________ ves desde la ventana es la piscina de mis vecinos.
8. Fue Úrsula ________ ayudó a mamá a limpiar el refrigerador.
9. Ya te dije que fue mi padre ________ alquiló el apartamento.
10. ________ te dijo Pablo no es cierto.
11. Tengo que sacudir los muebles ________ están en el altillo una vez al mes.
12. No entiendo por qué no lavaste los vasos ________ te dije.
13. La mujer a ________ saludaste vive en las afueras.
14. ¿Sabes ________ necesita este dormitorio? ¡Unas cortinas!
15. No quiero volver a hacer ________ hice ayer.
16. No me gusta vivir con personas a ________ no conozco.

recursos

WB pp. 137–138

LM p. 69

vistas.vhlcentral.com Lección 12

Práctica

1

Combinar Combina elementos de la columna A y la columna B para formar oraciones lógicas.

A

1. Ése es el hombre ____.
2. Rubén Blades, ____.
3. No traje ____.
4. ¿Te gusta la manta ____?
5. ¿Cómo se llama el programa ____?
6. La mujer ____.

B

a. con quien bailaba es mi vecina
b. que te compró Cecilia
c. quien es de Panamá, es un cantante muy bueno
d. que arregló mi lavadora
e. lo que necesito para la clase de matemáticas
f. que comiste en el restaurante
g. que escuchaste en la radio anoche

NOTA CULTURAL

Rubén Blades es un cantante, compositor y actor panameño muy famoso. Este versátil abogado fue también Ministro de Turismo en su país (2004-2009) y fue nombrado Embajador contra el racismo por las Naciones Unidas en el 2000.

2

Completar Completa la historia sobre la casa que Jaime y Tina quieren comprar, usando los pronombres relativos **que, quien, quienes** o **lo que**.

1. Jaime y Tina son los chicos a ________ conocí la semana pasada.
2. Quieren comprar una casa ________ está en las afueras de la ciudad.
3. Es una casa ________ era de una artista famosa.
4. La artista, a ________ yo conocía, murió el año pasado y no tenía hijos.
5. Ahora se vende la casa con todos los muebles ________ ella tenía.
6. La sala tiene una alfombra ________ ella trajo de Kuwait.
7. La casa tiene muchos estantes, ________ a Tina le encanta.

3

Oraciones Javier y Ana acaban de casarse y han comprado (*they have bought*) una casa y muchas otras cosas. Combina sus declaraciones para formar una sola oración con los pronombres relativos **que, quien(es)** y **lo que**.

modelo

Vamos a usar los vasos nuevos mañana. Los pusimos en el comedor.
Mañana vamos a usar los vasos nuevos que pusimos en el comedor.

1. Tenemos una cafetera nueva. Mi prima nos la regaló.
2. Tenemos una cómoda nueva. Es bueno porque no hay espacio en el armario.
3. Esos platos no nos costaron mucho. Están encima del horno.
4. Esas copas me las regaló mi amiga Amalia. Ella viene a visitarme mañana.
5. La lavadora está casi nueva. Nos la regalaron mis suegros.
6. La vecina nos dio una manta de lana. Ella la compró en México.

Practice more at **vistas.vhlcentral.com.**

Comunicación

4

Entrevista En parejas, túrnense para hacerse estas preguntas.

1. ¿Qué es lo que más te gusta de vivir en las afueras o en la ciudad?
2. ¿Cómo son las personas que viven en tu barrio?
3. ¿Cuál es el quehacer doméstico que pagarías (*you would pay*) por no hacer?
4. ¿Quién es la persona que hace los quehaceres domésticos en tu casa?
5. ¿Hay vecinos que te caen bien? ¿Quiénes?
6. ¿De qué vecino es el coche que más te gusta?
7. ¿Cuál es el barrio de tu ciudad que más te gusta y por qué?
8. ¿Quién es la persona a quien le pedirías (*you would ask*) que te ayude con los quehaceres?
9. ¿Cuál es el lugar de la casa donde te sientes más cómodo/a? ¿Por qué?
10. ¿Qué es lo que más te gusta de tu barrio?
11. ¿Qué hace el vecino que más llama la atención?
12. ¿Qué es lo que menos te gusta de tu barrio?

5

Adivinanza En grupos, túrnense para describir distintas partes de una vivienda usando pronombres relativos. Los demás compañeros tienen que hacer preguntas hasta que adivinen (*they guess*) la palabra.

modelo

Estudiante 1: Es lo que tenemos en el dormitorio.
Estudiante 2: ¿Es el mueble que usamos para dormir?
Estudiante 1: No. Es lo que usamos para guardar la ropa.
Estudiante 3: Lo sé. Es la cómoda.

Síntesis

6

Definir En parejas, definan las palabras. Usen los pronombres relativos **que, quien(es)** y **lo que.** Luego compartan sus definiciones con la clase.

alquiler	flan	patio	tenedor
amigos	guantes	postre	termómetro
aspiradora	jabón	sillón	vaso
enfermera	manta	sótano	vecino

modelo

lavadora Es lo que se usa para lavar la ropa.
pastel Es un postre que comes en tu cumpleaños.

AYUDA

Remember that **de,** followed by the name of a material, means *made of.*

Es de algodón.
It's made of cotton.

•••

Es un tipo de means *It's a kind/sort of...*

Es un tipo de flor.
It's a kind of flower.

12.2 Formal (usted/ustedes) commands

Tutorial

ANTE TODO As you learned in **Lección 11**, the command forms are used to give orders or advice. Formal commands are used with people you address as **usted** or **ustedes.** Observe these examples, then study the chart.

Hable con ellos, don Francisco.
Talk with them, Don Francisco.

Coma frutas y verduras.
Eat fruits and vegetables.

Laven los platos ahora mismo.
Wash the dishes right now.

Beban menos té y café.
Drink less tea and coffee.

AYUDA

By learning formal commands, it will be easier for you to learn the subjunctive forms that are presented in **Estructura 12.3**, p. 422.

Formal commands (Ud. and Uds.)

Infinitive	Present tense yo form	Ud. command	Uds. command
limpiar	limpi**o**	limpi**e**	limpi**en**
barrer	barr**o**	barr**a**	barr**an**
sacudir	sacud**o**	sacud**a**	sacud**an**
decir (e:i)	dig**o**	dig**a**	dig**an**
pensar (e:ie)	piens**o**	piens**e**	piens**en**
volver (o:ue)	vuelv**o**	vuelv**a**	vuelv**an**
servir (e:i)	sirv**o**	sirv**a**	sirv**an**

- The **usted** and **ustedes** commands, like the negative **tú** commands, are formed by dropping the final **-o** of the **yo** form of the present tense. For **-ar** verbs, add **-e** or **-en**. For **-er** and **-ir** verbs, add **-a** or **-an**.

- Verbs with irregular **yo** forms maintain the same irregularity in their formal commands. These verbs include **conducir, conocer, decir, hacer, ofrecer, oír, poner, salir, tener, traducir, traer, venir,** and **ver.**

Oiga, don Manolo...
Listen, Don Manolo...

¡Salga inmediatamente!
Leave immediately!

Ponga la mesa, por favor.
Set the table, please.

Hagan la cama antes de salir.
Make the bed before leaving.

- Note also that verbs maintain their stem changes in **usted** and **ustedes** commands.

e:ie

No **pierda** la llave.
Cierren la puerta.

o:ue

Vuelva temprano, joven.
Duerman bien, chicos.

e:i

Sirva la sopa, por favor.
Repitan las frases.

AYUDA

These spelling changes are necessary to ensure that the words are pronounced correctly. See **Lección 8, Pronunciación,** p. 271, and **Lección 9, Pronunciación,** p. 307.

•••

It may help you to study the following five series of syllables. Note that, within each series, the consonant sound doesn't change.

ca que qui co cu
za ce ci zo zu
ga gue gui go gu
ja ge gi jo ju

▶ Verbs ending in **-car, -gar,** and **-zar** have a spelling change in the command forms.

sa**car**	**c → qu**	sa**qu**e, sa**qu**en
ju**gar**	**g → gu**	jue**gu**e, jue**gu**en
almor**zar**	**z → c**	almuer**c**e, almuer**c**en

▶ These verbs have irregular formal commands.

Infinitive	Ud. command	Uds. command
dar	**dé**	**den**
estar	**esté**	**estén**
ir	**vaya**	**vayan**
saber	**sepa**	**sepan**
ser	**sea**	**sean**

▶ To make a formal command negative, simply place **no** before the verb.

No ponga las maletas en la cama.
Don't put the suitcases on the bed.

No ensucien los sillones.
Don't dirty the armchairs.

▶ In affirmative commands, reflexive, indirect and direct object pronouns are always attached to the end of the verb.

Siénten**se**, por favor.
Síga**me,** Laura.
Acuésten**se** ahora.
Póngan**las** en el suelo, por favor.

▶ **¡Atención!** When a pronoun is attached to an affirmative command that has two or more syllables, an accent mark is added to maintain the original stress.

limpie → **límpielo**
diga → **dígamelo**
lean → **léanlo**
sacudan → **sacúdanlos**

▶ In negative commands, these pronouns always precede the verb.

No **se** preocupe.
No **me lo** dé.
No **los** ensucien.
No **nos las** traigan.

▶ **Usted** and **ustedes** can be used with the command forms to strike a more formal tone. In such instances, they follow the command form.

Muéstrele usted la foto a su amigo.
Show the photo to your friend.

Tomen ustedes esta mesa.
Take this table.

recursos

WB pp. 139–140

LM p. 70

vistas.vhlcentral.com Lección 12

¡INTÉNTALO! Indica los mandatos (*commands*) afirmativos y negativos correspondientes.

1. escucharlo (Ud.) Escúchelo. No lo escuche.
2. decírmelo (Uds.) ________. ________.
3. salir (Ud.) ________. ________.
4. servírnoslo (Uds.) ________. ________.
5. barrerla (Ud.) ________. ________.
6. hacerlo (Ud.) ________. ________.

Práctica

1

Completar La señora González quiere mudarse de casa. Ayúdala a organizarse. Indica el mandato formal de cada verbo.

1. __________ los anuncios del periódico y __________. (Leer, guardarlos)
2. __________ personalmente y __________ las casas usted misma. (Ir, ver)
3. Decida qué casa quiere y __________ al agente. __________ un contrato de alquiler. (llamar, Pedirle)
4. __________ un camión *(truck)* para ese día y __________ la hora exacta de llegada. (Contratar, preguntarles)
5. El día de la mudanza *(On moving day)* __________ tranquila. __________ a revisar su lista para completar todo lo que tiene que hacer. (estar, Volver)
6. Primero, __________ a todos en casa que usted va a estar ocupada. No __________ que usted va a hacerlo todo. (decirles, decirles)
7. __________ tiempo para hacer las maletas tranquilamente. No __________ las maletas a los niños más grandes. (Sacar, hacerles)
8. No __________. __________ que todo va a salir bien. (preocuparse, Saber)

2

¿Qué dicen? Mira los dibujos y escribe un mandato lógico para cada uno. Usa palabras que aprendiste en **Contextos**.

1. ______________________________

2. ______________________________

3. ______________________________

4. ______________________________

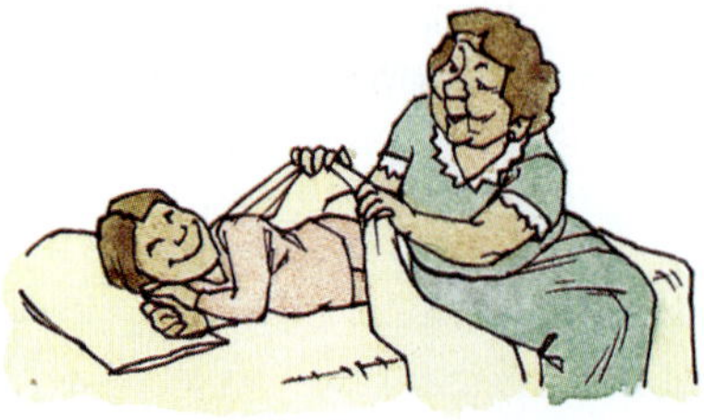

5. ______________________________

6. ______________________________

Practice more at **vistas.vhlcentral.com.**

Comunicación

3

Solucionar Trabajen en parejas. Un(a) estudiante presenta los problemas de la columna A y el/la otro/a los de la columna B. Usen mandatos formales y túrnense para ofrecer soluciones.

modelo

Estudiante 1: Vilma se torció un tobillo jugando al tenis. Es la tercera vez.
Estudiante 2: *No juegue más al tenis. / Vaya a ver a un especialista.*

A

1. Se me perdió el libro de español con todas mis notas.
2. A Vicente se le cayó la botella de vino para la cena.
3. ¿Cómo? ¿Se le olvidó traer el traje de baño a la playa?
4. Se nos quedaron los boletos en la casa. El avión sale en una hora.

B

1. Mis hijas no se levantan temprano. Siempre llegan tarde a la escuela.
2. A mi abuela le robaron (*stole*) las maletas. Era su primer día de vacaciones.
3. Nuestra casa es demasiado pequeña para nuestra familia.
4. Me preocupo constantemente por Roberto. Trabaja demasiado.

4

Conversaciones En parejas, escojan dos situaciones y preparen conversaciones para presentar a la clase. Usen mandatos formales.

modelo

Lupita: Señor Ramírez, siento mucho llegar tan tarde. Mi niño se enfermó. ¿Qué debo hacer?
Sr. Ramírez: *No se preocupe. Siéntese y descanse un poco.*

SITUACIÓN 1 Profesor Rosado, no vine la semana pasada porque el equipo jugaba en Boquete. ¿Qué debo hacer para ponerme al día *(catch up)*?

SITUACIÓN 2 Los invitados de la boda llegan a las cuatro de la tarde, las mesas están sin poner y el champán sin servir. Son las tres de la tarde y los camareros apenas están llegando. ¿Qué deben hacer los camareros?

SITUACIÓN 3 Mi novio es un poco aburrido. No le gustan ni el cine, ni los deportes, ni salir a comer. Tampoco habla mucho. ¿Qué puedo hacer?

▶ **SITUACIÓN 4** Tengo que preparar una presentación para mañana sobre el Canal de Panamá. ¿Por dónde comienzo?

NOTA CULTURAL

El 31 de diciembre de 1999, los Estados Unidos cedió el control del **Canal de Panamá** al gobierno de Panamá, terminando así con casi cien años de administración estadounidense.

Síntesis

5

Presentar En grupos, preparen un anuncio de televisión para presentar a la clase. El anuncio debe tratar de un detergente, un electrodoméstico o una agencia inmobiliaria (*real estate agency*). Usen mandatos, los pronombres relativos (**que, quien(es)** o **lo que**) y el **se** impersonal.

modelo

Compre el lavaplatos Destellos. Tiene todo lo que usted desea. Es el lavaplatos que mejor funciona. Venga a verlo ahora mismo... No pierda ni un minuto más. Se aceptan tarjetas de crédito.

12.3 The present subjunctive

Tutorial

ANTE TODO With the exception of commands, all the verb forms you have been using have been in the indicative mood. The indicative is used to state facts and to express actions or states that the speaker considers to be real and definite. In contrast, the subjunctive mood expresses the speaker's attitudes toward events, as well as actions or states the speaker views as uncertain or hypothetical.

- The present subjunctive is formed very much like **usted**, **ustedes** and *negative* **tú** commands. From the **yo** form of the present indicative, drop the **-o** ending, and replace it with the subjunctive endings.

INFINITIVE	PRESENT INDICATIVE	VERB STEM	PRESENT SUBJUNCTIVE
hablar	**hablo**	**habl-**	**hable**
comer	**como**	**com-**	**coma**
escribir	**escribo**	**escrib-**	**escriba**

- The present subjunctive endings are:

-ar verbs		-er and -ir verbs	
-e	**-emos**	**-a**	**-amos**
-es	**-éis**	**-as**	**-áis**
-e	**-en**	**-a**	**-an**

Present subjunctive of regular verbs

		hablar	comer	escribir
SINGULAR FORMS	yo	habl**e**	com**a**	escrib**a**
	tú	habl**es**	com**as**	escrib**as**
	Ud./él/ella	habl**e**	com**a**	escrib**a**
PLURAL FORMS	nosotros/as	habl**emos**	com**amos**	escrib**amos**
	vosotros/as	habl**éis**	com**áis**	escrib**áis**
	Uds./ellos/ellas	habl**en**	com**an**	escrib**an**

AYUDA

Note that, in the present subjunctive, **-ar** verbs use endings normally associated with present tense **-er** and **-ir** verbs. Likewise, **-er** and **-ir** verbs in the present subjunctive use endings normally associated with **-ar** verbs in the present tense. Note also that, in the present subjunctive, the **yo** form is the same as the **Ud./él/ella** form.

¡LENGUA VIVA!

You may think that English has no subjunctive, but it does! While once common, it now survives mostly in set expressions such as *If I were you...* and *Be that as it may...*

- Verbs with irregular **yo** forms show the same irregularity in all forms of the present subjunctive.

Infinitive	Present indicative	Verb stem	Present subjunctive
conducir	conduzco	**conduzc-**	**conduzca**
conocer	conozco	**conozc-**	**conozca**
decir	digo	**dig-**	**diga**
hacer	hago	**hag-**	**haga**
ofrecer	ofrezco	**ofrezc-**	**ofrezca**
oír	oigo	**oig-**	**oiga**
parecer	parezco	**parezc-**	**parezca**
poner	pongo	**pong-**	**ponga**
tener	tengo	**teng-**	**tenga**
traducir	traduzco	**traduzc-**	**traduzca**
traer	traigo	**traig-**	**traiga**
venir	vengo	**veng-**	**venga**
ver	veo	**ve-**	**vea**

- To maintain the **-c, -g,** and **-z** sounds, verbs ending in **-car, -gar,** and **-zar** have a spelling change in all forms of the present subjunctive.

sacar:	sa**qu**e, sa**qu**es, sa**qu**e, sa**qu**emos, sa**qu**éis, sa**qu**en
jugar:	jue**gu**e, jue**gu**es, jue**gu**e, ju**gu**emos, ju**gu**éis, jue**gu**en
almorzar:	almuer**c**e, almuer**c**es, almuer**c**e, almor**c**emos, almor**c**éis, almuer**c**en

Present subjunctive of stem-changing verbs

AYUDA

Note that stem-changing verbs and verbs that have a spelling change have the same ending as regular verbs in the present subjunctive.

- **-Ar** and **-er** stem-changing verbs have the same stem changes in the subjunctive as they do in the present indicative.

pensar (e:ie):	p**ie**nse, p**ie**nses, p**ie**nse, pensemos, penséis, p**ie**nsen
mostrar (o:ue):	m**ue**stre, m**ue**stres, m**ue**stre, mostremos, mostréis, m**ue**stren
entender (e:ie):	ent**ie**nda, ent**ie**ndas, ent**ie**nda, entendamos, entendáis, ent**ie**ndan
volver (o:ue):	v**ue**lva, v**ue**lvas, v**ue**lva, volvamos, volváis, v**ue**lvan

- **-Ir** stem-changing verbs have the same stem changes in the subjunctive as they do in the present indicative, but in addition, the **nosotros/as** and **vosotros/as** forms undergo a stem change. The unstressed **e** changes to **i,** while the unstressed **o** changes to **u.**

pedir (e:i):	p**i**da, p**i**das, p**i**da, p**i**damos, p**i**dáis, p**i**dan
sentir (e:ie):	s**ie**nta, s**ie**ntas, s**ie**nta, s**i**ntamos, s**i**ntáis, s**ie**ntan
dormir (o:ue):	d**ue**rma, d**ue**rmas, d**ue**rma, d**u**rmamos, d**u**rmáis, d**ue**rman

Irregular verbs in the present subjunctive

- These five verbs are irregular in the present subjunctive.

Irregular verbs in the present subjunctive

		dar	estar	ir	saber	ser
SINGULAR FORMS	yo	**dé**	**esté**	**vaya**	**sepa**	**sea**
	tú	**des**	**estés**	**vayas**	**sepas**	**seas**
	Ud./él/ella	**dé**	**esté**	**vaya**	**sepa**	**sea**
PLURAL FORMS	nosotros/as	**demos**	**estemos**	**vayamos**	**sepamos**	**seamos**
	vosotros/as	**deis**	**estéis**	**vayáis**	**sepáis**	**seáis**
	Uds./ellos/ellas	**den**	**estén**	**vayan**	**sepan**	**sean**

- **¡Atención!** The subjunctive form of **hay** (*there is, there are*) is also irregular: **haya**.

General uses of the subjunctive

- The subjunctive is mainly used to express: 1) will and influence, 2) emotion, 3) doubt, disbelief, and denial, and 4) indefiniteness and nonexistence.

- The subjunctive is most often used in sentences that consist of a main clause and a subordinate clause. The main clause contains a verb or expression that triggers the use of the subjunctive. The conjunction **que** connects the subordinate clause to the main clause.

Main clause	Connector	Subordinate clause
Es muy importante	que	**vayas** al hotel ahora mismo.

- These impersonal expressions are always followed by clauses in the subjunctive:

Es bueno que... *It's good that...*	**Es mejor que...** *It's better that...*	**Es malo que...** *It's bad that...*
Es importante que... *It's important that...*	**Es necesario que...** *It's necessary that...*	**Es urgente que...** *It's urgent that...*

¡INTÉNTALO! Indica el presente de subjuntivo de estos verbos.

1. (alquilar, beber, vivir) que yo alquile, beba, viva
2. (estudiar, aprender, asistir) que tú ______
3. (encontrar, poder, tener) que él ______
4. (hacer, pedir, dormir) que nosotras ______
5. (dar, hablar, escribir) que ellos ______
6. (pagar, empezar, buscar) que ustedes ______
7. (ser, ir, saber) que yo ______
8. (estar, dar, oír) que tú ______

recursos
WB pp. 141–142
LM p. 71
vistas.vhlcentral.com Lección 12

Práctica y Comunicación

1 **Completar** Completa las oraciones con el presente de subjuntivo de los verbos entre paréntesis. Luego empareja las oraciones del primer grupo con las del segundo grupo.

NOTA CULTURAL

Las casas colgadas (*hanging*) de Cuenca, España, son muy famosas. Situadas en un acantilado (*cliff*), forman parte del paisaje de la ciudad.

A

1. Es mejor que ________ en casa. (nosotros, cenar) ____
2. Es importante que ________ las casas colgadas de Cuenca. (tú, visitar) ____
3. Señora, es urgente que le ________ el diente. Tiene una infección. (yo, sacar) ____
4. Es malo que Ana les ________ tantos dulces a los niños. (dar) ____
5. Es necesario que ________ a la una de la tarde. (ustedes, llegar) ____
6. Es importante que ________ temprano. (nosotros, acostarse) ____

B

a. Es importante que ________ más verduras. (ellos, comer)
b. No, es mejor que ________ a comer. (nosotros, salir)
c. Y yo creo que es bueno que ________ a Madrid después. (yo, ir)
d. En mi opinión, no es necesario que ________ tanto. (nosotros, dormir)
e. ¿Ah, sí? ¿Es necesario que me ________ un antibiótico también? (yo, tomar)
f. Para llegar a tiempo, es necesario que ________ temprano. (nosotros, almorzar)

2 **Minidiálogos** En parejas, completen los minidiálogos con expresiones impersonales de una manera lógica.

modelo

Miguelito: Mamá, no quiero arreglar mi cuarto.
Sra. Casas: *Es necesario que lo arregles. Y es importante que sacudas los muebles también.*

1. **MIGUELITO** Mamá, no quiero estudiar. Quiero salir a jugar con mis amigos.
   SRA. CASAS ________________________________
2. **MIGUELITO** Mamá, es que no me gustan las verduras. Prefiero comer pasteles.
   SRA. CASAS ________________________________
3. **MIGUELITO** ¿Tengo que poner la mesa, mamá?
   SRA. CASAS ________________________________
4. **MIGUELITO** No me siento bien, mamá. Me duele todo el cuerpo y tengo fiebre.
   SRA. CASAS ________________________________

3 **Entrevista** Trabajen en parejas. Entrevístense usando estas preguntas. Expliquen sus respuestas.

1. ¿Es importante que las personas sepan una segunda lengua? ¿Por qué?
2. ¿Es urgente que los norteamericanos aprendan otras lenguas?
3. Si un(a) norteamericano/a quiere aprender francés, ¿es mejor que lo aprenda en Francia?
4. ¿Es necesario que una persona sepa decir "te amo" en la lengua nativa de su pareja?
5. ¿Es importante que un cantante de ópera entienda italiano?

Practice more at **vistas.vhlcentral.com.**

12.4 Subjunctive with verbs of will and influence

Tutorial

ANTE TODO You will now learn how to use the subjunctive with verbs and expressions of will and influence.

- Verbs of will and influence are often used when someone wants to affect the actions or behavior of other people.

  Enrique **quiere** que salgamos a cenar.
  Enrique wants us to go out to dinner.

  Paola **prefiere** que cenemos en casa.
  Paola prefers that we have dinner at home.

- Here is a list of widely used verbs of will and influence.

Verbs of will and influence

aconsejar	*to advise*	**pedir** (e:i)	*to ask (for)*
desear	*to wish; to desire*	**preferir** (e:ie)	*to prefer*
importar	*to be important; to matter*	**prohibir**	*to prohibit*
		querer (e:ie)	*to want*
insistir (en)	*to insist (on)*	**recomendar** (e:ie)	*to recommend*
mandar	*to order*	**rogar** (o:ue)	*to beg; to plead*
necesitar	*to need*	**sugerir** (e:ie)	*to suggest*

- Some impersonal expressions, such as **es necesario que, es importante que, es mejor que,** and **es urgente que,** are considered expressions of will or influence.

- When the main clause contains an expression of will or influence, the subjunctive is required in the subordinate clause, provided that the two clauses have different subjects.

Main clause — Connector — Subordinate clause

VERB OF WILL — SUBJUNCTIVE

Mi mamá **prefiere** que yo **saque** la basura.

¡ATENCIÓN!

In English, verbs or expressions of will and influence often use a construction with an infinitive, such as *I want you to go.* This is not the case in Spanish, where the subjunctive would be used in a subordinate clause.

- Indirect object pronouns are often used with the verbs **aconsejar, importar, mandar, pedir, prohibir, recomendar, rogar,** and **sugerir.**

Te aconsejo que estudies.
I advise you to study.

Le sugiero que vaya a casa.
I suggest that he go home.

Les recomiendo que barran el suelo.
I recommend that you sweep the floor.

Le ruego que no venga.
I'm begging you not to come.

- Note that all the forms of **prohibir** in the present tense carry a written accent, except for the **nosotros/as** form: **prohíbo, prohíbes, prohíbe, prohibimos, prohibís, prohíben.**

Ella les **prohíbe** que miren la televisión.
She prohibits them from watching TV.

Nos **prohíben** que nademos en la piscina.
They prohibit that we swim in the swimming pool.

- The infinitive is used with words or expressions of will and influence if there is no change of subject in the sentence.

No quiero **sacudir** los muebles.
I don't want to dust the furniture.

Paco prefiere **descansar.**
Paco prefers to rest.

Es importante **sacar** la basura.
It's important to take out the trash.

No es necesario **quitar** la mesa.
It's not necessary to clear the table.

¡INTÉNTALO! Completa cada oración con la forma correcta del verbo entre paréntesis.

1. Te sugiero que ___vayas___ (ir) con ella al supermercado.
2. Él necesita que yo le ________ (prestar) dinero.
3. No queremos que tú ________ (hacer) nada especial para nosotros.
4. Mis papás quieren que yo ________ (limpiar) mi cuarto.
5. Nos piden que la ________ (ayudar) a preparar la comida.
6. Quieren que tú ________ (sacar) la basura todos los días.
7. Quiero ________ (descansar) esta noche.
8. Es importante que ustedes ________ (limpiar) los estantes.
9. Su tía les manda que ________ (poner) la mesa.
10. Te aconsejo que no ________ (salir) con él.
11. Mi tío insiste en que mi prima ________ (hacer) la cama.
12. Prefiero ________ (ir) al cine.
13. Es necesario ________ (estudiar).
14. Recomiendo que ustedes ________ (pasar) la aspiradora.

recursos

WB pp. 143–144

LM p. 72

vistas.vhlcentral.com Lección 12

Práctica

1 **Completar** Completa el diálogo con verbos de la lista.

cocina	haga	quiere	sea
comas	ponga	saber	ser
diga	prohíbe	sé	vaya

IRENE Tengo problemas con Vilma. Sé que debo hablar con ella. ¿Qué me recomiendas que le (1)__________?

JULIA Pues, necesito (2)__________ más antes de darte consejos.

IRENE Bueno, para empezar me (3)__________ que traiga dulces a la casa.

JULIA Pero chica, tiene razón. Es mejor que tú no (4)__________ cosas dulces.

IRENE Sí, ya lo sé. Pero quiero que (5)__________ más flexible. Además, insiste en que yo (6)__________ todo en la casa.

JULIA Yo (7)__________ que Vilma (8)__________ y hace los quehaceres todos los días.

IRENE Sí, pero siempre que hay fiesta me pide que (9)__________ los cubiertos y las copas en la mesa y que (10)__________ al sótano por las servilletas y los platos. ¡Es lo que más odio: ir al sótano!

JULIA Mujer, ¡Vilma sólo (11)__________ que ayudes en la casa!

2 **Aconsejar** En parejas, lean lo que dice cada persona. Luego den consejos lógicos usando verbos como **aconsejar, recomendar** y **prohibir**. Sus consejos deben ser diferentes de lo que la persona quiere hacer.

modelo

Isabel: Quiero conseguir un comedor con los muebles más caros del mundo.

Consejo: *Te aconsejamos que consigas unos muebles menos caros.*

1. **DAVID** Pienso poner el cuadro del lago de Maracaibo en la cocina.
2. **SARA** Voy en bicicleta a comprar unas copas de cristal.
3. **SR. ALARCÓN** Insisto en comenzar a arreglar el jardín en marzo.
4. **SRA. VILLA** Quiero ver las tazas y los platos de la tienda El Ama de Casa Feliz.
5. **DOLORES** Voy a poner servilletas de tela (*cloth*) para los cuarenta invitados.
6. **SR. PARDO** Pienso poner todos mis muebles nuevos en el altillo.
7. **SRA. GONZÁLEZ** Hay una fiesta en casa esta noche, pero no quiero limpiarla.
8. **CARLITOS** Hoy no tengo ganas de hacer las camas ni de quitar la mesa.

NOTA CULTURAL

En el **lago de Maracaibo,** en Venezuela, hay casas suspendidas sobre el agua que se llaman **palafitos**. Este tipo de construcciones les recordó a los conquistadores la ciudad de Venecia, Italia, de donde viene el nombre "Venezuela", que significa "pequeña Venecia".

3 **Preguntas** En parejas, túrnense para contestar las preguntas. Usen el subjuntivo.

1. ¿Te dan consejos tus amigos/as? ¿Qué te aconsejan? ¿Aceptas sus consejos? ¿Por qué?
2. ¿Qué te sugieren tus profesores que hagas antes de terminar los cursos que tomas?
3. ¿Insisten tus amigos/as en que salgas mucho con ellos?
4. ¿Qué quieres que te regalen tu familia y tus amigos/as en tu cumpleaños?
5. ¿Qué le recomiendas tú a un(a) amigo/a que no quiere salir los sábados con su novio/a?
6. ¿Qué les aconsejas a los nuevos estudiantes de tu universidad?

Practice more at **vistas.vhlcentral.com.**

Comunicación

4 **Inventar** En parejas, preparen una lista de seis personas famosas. Un(a) estudiante da el nombre de una persona famosa y el/la otro/a le da un consejo.

modelo

Estudiante 1: Judge Judy.
Estudiante 2: Le recomiendo que sea más simpática con la gente.
Estudiante 2: Orlando Bloom.
Estudiante 1: Le aconsejo que haga más películas.

5 **Hablar** En parejas, miren la ilustración. Imaginen que Gerardo es su hermano y necesita ayuda para arreglar su casa y resolver sus problemas románticos y económicos. Usen expresiones impersonales y verbos como **aconsejar, sugerir** y **recomendar**.

modelo

Es mejor que arregles el apartamento más a menudo.
Te aconsejo que no dejes para mañana lo que puedes hacer hoy.

Síntesis

6 **La doctora Salvamórez** Hernán tiene problemas con su novia y le escribe a la doctora Salvamórez, columnista del periódico *Panamá y su gente*. Ella responde a las cartas de personas con problemas románticos. En parejas, lean el mensaje de Hernán y después usen el subjuntivo para escribir los consejos de la doctora.

Estimada doctora Salvamórez:
Mi novia nunca quiere que yo salga de casa. No le molesta que vengan mis amigos a visitarme. Pero insiste en que nosotros sólo miremos los programas de televisión que ella quiere. Necesita saber dónde estoy en cada momento, y yo necesito que ella me dé un poco de independencia. ¿Qué hago?

Hernán

Recapitulación

Concepts Diagnostics

Completa estas actividades para repasar los conceptos de gramática que aprendiste en esta lección.

1 **Completar** Completa el cuadro con la forma correspondiente del presente de subjuntivo. 12 pts.

yo/él/ella	tú	nosotros/as	Uds./ellos/ellas
limpie			
	vengas		
		queramos	
			ofrezcan

2 **El apartamento ideal** Completa este folleto (*brochure*) informativo con la forma correcta del presente de subjuntivo. 8 pts.

¿Eres joven y buscas tu primera vivienda? Te ofrezco estos consejos:

- Te sugiero que primero (tú) (1) __________ (escribir) una lista de las cosas que quieres en un apartamento.
- Quiero que después (2) __________ (pensar) muy bien cuáles son tus prioridades. Es necesario que cada persona (3) __________ (tener) sus prioridades claras, porque el hogar (*home*) perfecto no existe.
- Antes de decidir en qué área quieren vivir, les aconsejo a ti y a tu futuro/a compañero/a de apartamento que (4) __________ (salir) a ver la ciudad y que (5) __________ (conocer) los distintos barrios y las afueras.
- Pidan que el agente les (6) __________ (mostrar) todas las partes de cada casa.
- Finalmente, como consumidores, es importante que nosotros (7) __________ (saber) bien nuestros derechos (*rights*); por eso, deben insistir en que todos los puntos del contrato (8) __________ (estar) muy claros antes de firmarlo (*signing it*).

¡Buena suerte!

RESUMEN GRAMATICAL

12.1 Relative pronouns pp. 414–415

Relative pronouns	
que	*that; which; who*
quien(es)	*who; whom; that*
lo que	*that which; what*

12.2 Formal commands pp. 418–419

Formal commands (Ud. and Uds.)

Infinitive	Present tense yo form	Ud(s). command
limpiar	limpio	limpie(n)
barrer	barro	barra(n)
sacudir	sacudo	sacuda(n)

► Verbs with stem changes or irregular **yo** forms maintain the same irregularity in the formal commands:

hacer: yo **hago** → **Hagan** la cama.

Irregular formal commands	
dar	**dé (Ud.); den (Uds.)**
estar	**esté(n)**
ir	**vaya(n)**
saber	**sepa(n)**
ser	**sea(n)**

12.3 The present subjunctive pp. 422–424

Present subjunctive of regular verbs

hablar	comer	escribir
hable	coma	escriba
hables	comas	escribas
hable	coma	escriba
hablemos	comamos	escribamos
habléis	comáis	escribáis
hablen	coman	escriban

Irregular verbs in the present subjunctive		
dar		dé, des, dé, demos, deis, den
estar	est- +	-é, -és, -é, -emos, -éis, -én
ir	vay- +	-a, -as, -a, -amos, -áis, -an
saber	sep- +	
ser	se- +	

12.4 Subjunctive with verbs of will and influence

pp. 426–427

- Verbs of will and influence: **aconsejar, desear, importar, insistir (en), mandar, necesitar, pedir** (e:i), **preferir** (e:ie), **prohibir, querer** (e:ie), **recomendar** (e:ie), **rogar** (o:ue), **sugerir** (e:ie)

3 **Relativos** Completa las oraciones con **lo que**, **que** o **quien**. 8 pts.

1. Me encanta la alfombra ________ está en el comedor.
2. Mi amiga Tere, con ________ trabajo, me regaló ese cuadro.
3. Todas las cosas ________ tenemos vienen de la casa de mis abuelos.
4. Hija, no compres más cosas. ________ debes hacer ahora es organizarlo todo.
5. La agencia de decoración de ________ le hablé se llama Casabella.
6. Esas flores las dejaron en la puerta mis nuevos vecinos, a ________ aún (*yet*) no conozco.
7. Leonor no compró nada, porque ________ le gustaba era muy caro.
8. Mi amigo Aldo, a ________ visité ayer, es un cocinero excelente.

4 **Preparando la casa** Martín y Ángela van a hacer un curso de verano en Costa Rica y una vecina va a cuidarles (*take care of*) la casa mientras ellos no están. Completa las instrucciones de la vecina con mandatos formales. Usa cada verbo una sola vez y agrega pronombres de objeto directo o indirecto si es necesario. 10 pts.

arreglar	dejar	hacer	pedir	sacudir
barrer	ensuciar	limpiar	poner	tener

Primero, (1) ________ ustedes las maletas. Las cosas que no se llevan a Costa Rica, (2) ________ en el altillo. Ángela, (3) ________ las habitaciones y Martín, (4) ________ usted la cocina y el baño. Después, los dos (5) ________ el suelo y (6) ________ los muebles de toda la casa. Ángela, no (7) ________ sus joyas (*jewelry*) en el apartamento. (8) ________ cuidado ¡y no (9) ________ nada antes de irse! Por último, (10) ________ a alguien que recoja (*pick up*) su correo.

5 **Los quehaceres** A tu compañero/a de cuarto no le gusta ayudar con los quehaceres. Escribe al menos seis oraciones dándole consejos para hacer más divertidos los quehaceres. 12 pts.

modelo
Te sugiero que pongas música mientras lavas los platos...

6 **El circo** Completa esta famosa frase que tiene su origen en el circo (*circus*). ¡2 puntos EXTRA!

"¡________ (Pasar) ustedes y ________ (ver)! El espectáculo va a comenzar."

Practice more at **vistas.vhlcentral.com.**

Audio: Reading
Additional Reading

Lectura

Antes de leer

Estrategia

Locating the main parts of a sentence

Did you know that a text written in Spanish is an average of 15% longer than the same text written in English? Since the Spanish language tends to use more words to express ideas, you will often encounter long sentences when reading in Spanish. Of course, the length of sentences varies with genre and with authors' individual styles. To help you understand long sentences, identify the main parts of the sentence before trying to read it in its entirety. First locate the main verb of the sentence, along with its subject, ignoring any words or phrases set off by commas. Then reread the sentence, adding details like direct and indirect objects, transitional words, and prepositional phrases.

Examinar el texto

Mira el formato de la lectura. ¿Qué tipo de documento es? ¿Qué cognados encuentras en la lectura? ¿Qué te dicen sobre el tema de la selección?

¿Probable o improbable?

Mira brevemente el texto e indica si estas oraciones son probables o improbables.

1. Este folleto° es de interés turístico.
2. Describe un edificio moderno cubano.
3. Incluye algunas explicaciones de arquitectura.
4. Espera atraer° a visitantes al lugar.

Oraciones largas

Mira el texto y busca algunas oraciones largas. Con un(a) compañero/a, identifiquen las partes principales de la oración y después examinen las descripciones adicionales. ¿Qué significan las oraciones?

folleto *brochure* **atraer** *to attract* **épocas** *time periods*

Bienvenidos al Palacio de las Garzas

El palacio está abierto de martes a domingo.
Para más información,
llame al teléfono 507-226-7000.
También puede solicitar° un folleto
a la casilla° 3467,
Ciudad de Panamá, Panamá.

Después de leer

Ordenar

Pon estos eventos en el orden cronológico adecuado.

_____ El palacio se convirtió en residencia presidencial.
_____ Durante diferentes épocas°, maestros, médicos y banqueros ejercieron su profesión en el palacio.
_____ El Dr. Belisario Porras ocupó el palacio por primera vez.
_____ Los españoles construyeron el palacio.
_____ Se renovó el palacio.
_____ Los turistas pueden visitar el palacio de martes a domingo.

El Palacio de las Garzas° es la residencia oficial del Presidente de Panamá desde 1903. Fue construido en 1673 para ser la casa de un gobernador español. Con el paso de los años fue almacén, escuela, hospital, aduana, banco y por último, palacio presidencial.

En la actualidad el edificio tiene tres pisos, pero los planos originales muestran una construcción de un piso con un gran patio en el centro. La restauración del palacio comenzó en el año 1922 y los trabajos fueron realizados por el arquitecto Villanueva-Myers y el pintor Roberto Lewis. El palacio, un monumento al estilo colonial, todavía conserva su elegancia y buen gusto, y es una de las principales atracciones turísticas del barrio Casco Viejo°.

Planta baja

El Patio de las Garzas

Una antigua puerta de hierro° recibe a los visitantes. El patio interior todavía conserva los elementos originales de la construcción: piso de mármol°, columnas cubiertas° de nácar° y una magnífica fuente° de agua en el centro. Aquí están las nueve garzas que le dan el nombre al palacio y que representan las nueve provincias de Panamá.

Primer piso

El Salón Amarillo

Aquí el turista puede visitar una galería de cuarenta y un retratos° de gobernadores y personajes ilustres de Panamá. La principal atracción de este salón es el sillón presidencial, que se usa especialmente cuando hay cambio de presidente. Otros atractivos de esta área son el comedor Los Tamarindos, que se destaca° por la elegancia de sus muebles y sus lámparas de cristal, y el Patio Andaluz, con sus coloridos mosaicos que representan la unión de la cultura indígena y la española.

El Salón Dr. Belisario Porras

Este elegante y majestuoso salón es uno de los lugares más importantes del Palacio de las Garzas. Lleva su nombre en honor al Dr. Belisario Porras, quien fue tres veces presidente de Panamá (1912–1916, 1918–1920 y 1920–1924).

Segundo piso

Es el área residencial del palacio y el visitante no tiene acceso a ella. Los armarios, las cómodas y los espejos de la alcoba fueron comprados en Italia y Francia por el presidente Porras, mientras que las alfombras, cortinas y frazadas° son originarias de España.

solicitar *request* **casilla** *post office box* **Garzas** *Herons* **Casco Viejo** *Old Quarter* **hierro** *iron* **mármol** *marble* **cubiertas** *covered* **nácar** *mother-of-pearl* **fuente** *fountain* **retratos** *portraits* **se destaca** *stands out* **frazadas** *blankets*

Preguntas

Contesta las preguntas.

1. ¿Qué sala es notable por sus muebles elegantes y sus lámparas de cristal?
2. ¿En qué parte del palacio se encuentra la residencia del presidente?
3. ¿Dónde empiezan los turistas su visita al palacio?
4. ¿En qué lugar se representa artísticamente la rica herencia cultural de Panamá?
5. ¿Qué salón honra la memoria de un gran panameño?
6. ¿Qué partes del palacio te gustaría (*would you like*) visitar? ¿Por qué? Explica tu respuesta.

Conversación

En grupos de tres o cuatro estudiantes, hablen sobre lo siguiente:

1. ¿Qué tiene en común el Palacio de las Garzas con otras residencias presidenciales u otras casas muy grandes?
2. ¿Te gustaría vivir en el Palacio de las Garzas? ¿Por qué?
3. Imagina que puedes diseñar tu palacio ideal. Describe los planos para cada piso del palacio.

Escritura

Estrategia

Using linking words

You can make your writing sound more sophisticated by using linking words to connect simple sentences or ideas and create more complex sentences. Consider these passages, which illustrate this effect:

Without linking words

En la actualidad el edificio tiene tres pisos. Los planos originales muestran una construcción de un piso con un gran patio en el centro. La restauración del palacio comenzó en el año 1922. Los trabajos fueron realizados por el arquitecto Villanueva-Myers y el pintor Roberto Lewis.

With linking words

En la actualidad el edificio tiene tres pisos, pero los planos originales muestran una construcción de un piso con un gran patio en el centro. La restauración del palacio comenzó en el año 1922 y los trabajos fueron realizados por el arquitecto Villanueva-Myers y el pintor Roberto Lewis.

Linking words

cuando	*when*
mientras	*while*
o	*or*
pero	*but*
porque	*because*
pues	*since*
que	*that; who; which*
quien(es)	*who*
sino	*but (rather)*
y	*and*

Tema

Escribir un contrato de arrendamiento°

Eres el/la administrador(a)° de un edificio de apartamentos. Prepara un contrato de arrendamiento para los nuevos inquilinos°. El contrato debe incluir estos detalles:

- la dirección° del apartamento y del/de la administrador(a)
- las fechas del contrato
- el precio del alquiler y el día que se debe pagar
- el precio del depósito
- información y reglas° acerca de:
  - la basura
  - el correo
  - los animales domésticos
  - el ruido°
  - los servicios de electricidad y agua
  - el uso de electrodomésticos
- otros aspectos importantes de la vida comunitaria

contrato de arrendamiento *lease* **administrador(a)** *manager* **inquilinos** *tenants* **dirección** *address* **reglas** *rules* **ruido** *noise*

Escuchar

Audio: Activities

Estrategia

Using visual cues

Visual cues like illustrations and headings provide useful clues about what you will hear.

To practice this strategy, you will listen to a passage related to the following photo. Jot down the clues the photo gives you as you listen.

Preparación

Mira el dibujo. ¿Qué pistas te da para comprender la conversación que vas a escuchar? ¿Qué significa *bienes raíces*?

Ahora escucha

Mira los anuncios de esta página y escucha la conversación entre el señor Núñez, Adriana y Felipe. Luego indica si cada descripción se refiere a la casa ideal de Adriana y Felipe, a la casa del anuncio o al apartamento del anuncio.

Frases	La casa ideal	La casa del anuncio	El apartamento del anuncio
Es barato.	___	___	___
Tiene cuatro alcobas.	___	___	___
Tiene una oficina.	___	___	___
Tiene un balcón.	___	___	___
Tiene una cocina moderna.	___	___	___
Tiene un jardín muy grande.	___	___	___
Tiene un patio.	___	___	___

18G

Bienes raíces

Se vende.
4 alcobas, 3 baños, cocina moderna, jardín con árboles frutales.
B/. 225.000

Se alquila.
2 alcobas, 1 baño.
Balcón.
Urbanización Las Brisas. B/. 525

Comprensión

Preguntas

1. ¿Cuál es la relación entre el señor Núñez, Adriana y Felipe? ¿Cómo lo sabes?
2. ¿Qué diferencia de opinión hay entre Adriana y Felipe sobre dónde quieren vivir?
3. Usa la información de los dibujos y la conversación para entender lo que dice Adriana al final. ¿Qué significa "todo a su debido tiempo"?

Conversación

En parejas, túrnense para hacer y responder a las preguntas.

1. ¿Qué tienen en común el apartamento y la casa del anuncio con el lugar donde tú vives?
2. ¿Qué piensas de la recomendación del señor Núñez?
3. ¿Qué tipo de sugerencias te da tu familia sobre dónde vivir?
4. ¿Dónde prefieres vivir tú, en un apartamento o en una casa? Explica por qué.

Practice more at **vistas.vhlcentral.com.**

En pantalla

En los países hispanos el costo del servicio de electricidad y de los electrodomésticos es muy caro. Es por eso que no es muy común tener muchos electrodomésticos. Por ejemplo, en los lugares donde hace mucho calor, mucha gente no tiene aire acondicionado°; utiliza los ventiladores°, que usan menos electricidad. Muchas personas lavan la ropa a mano o barren el piso en vez de usar una lavadora o una aspiradora.

Vocabulario útil

mascota	*pet*
un poco asustado	*a bit scared*
suavizante	*(fabric) softener*
suavizar	*to soften*

Preparación

¿Lavas tu ropa, cocinas, barres? ¿Te piden que hagas algunos quehaceres domésticos en casa?

Preguntas

Contesta estas preguntas.

1. ¿Qué le encanta al osito (*little bear*)*Softy*?
2. ¿Por qué se lastimó cuando se cayó sobre las toallas?
3. Según el anuncio, ¿qué es lo que un suavizante barato no puede hacer?
4. ¿Cómo se siente *Softy* cuando llega el médico: tranquilo o asustado?
5. ¿Qué le recomienda el médico a la mujer?

Consejos

Cuando la mujer visita a *Softy* en el hospital, el médico le da consejos y órdenes sobre cómo tratar a su mascota. En parejas, preparen una lista de los consejos y órdenes que el médico le da. Usen el subjuntivo y el imperativo.

aire acondicionado *air conditioning* ventiladores *fans*

Anuncio de Comfort

1

¡Hola! Soy *Softy* y me encanta la ropa suave.

2

¡Ay, mi brazo!

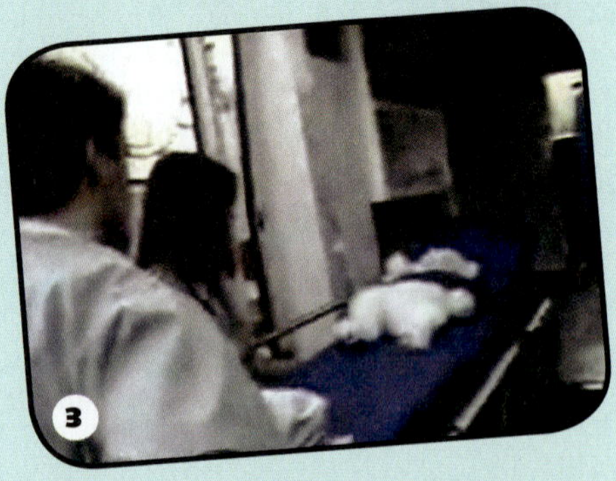

3

Si usted quiere a su mascota, tiene que usar siempre Comfort.

Video: TV Clip

Practice more at **vistas.vhlcentral.com.**

Flash CULTURA

En el sur de la Ciudad de México hay una construcción que fusiona° el funcionalismo con elementos de la cultura mexicana. Es la casa y estudio° en que el muralista Diego Rivera y su esposa, Frida Kahlo, vivieron hasta 1934. El creador fue el destacado° arquitecto y pintor mexicano Juan O'Gorman, amigo de la pareja. Como Frida y Diego necesitaban cada uno un lugar tranquilo para trabajar, O'Gorman hizo dos casas, cada una con un taller°, conectadas por un puente° en la parte superior°. En 1981, años después de la muerte de los artistas, se creó ahí el Museo Casa Estudio Diego Rivera y Frida Kahlo. Este museo busca conservar, investigar y difundir° la obra° de estos dos mexicanos, como lo hace el Museo Casa de Frida Kahlo, que vas a ver a continuación.

Vocabulario útil

jardinero	*gardener*
muros	*walls*
la silla de ruedas	*wheelchair*
las valiosas obras	*valuable works*

Preparación

Imagina que eres un(a) artista, ¿cómo sería (*would be*) tu casa? ¿Sería muy diferente de la casa en donde vives ahora?

¿Cierto o falso?

Indica si lo que dicen estas oraciones es **cierto** o **falso**.

1. La casa de Frida Kahlo está en el centro de México, D.F.
2. La casa de Frida se transformó en un museo en los años 50.
3. Frida Kahlo vivió sola en su casa.
4. Entre las obras que se exhiben está el cuadro (*painting*) *Las dos Fridas*.
5. El jardinero actual (*current*) jamás conoció ni a Frida ni a Diego.
6. En el museo se exhiben la silla de ruedas y los aparatos ortopédicos de Frida.

fusiona *fuse* **estudio** *studio* **destacado** *prominent* **taller** *art studio* **puente** *bridge* **parte superior** *top* **difundir** *to spread* **obra** *work*

La casa de Frida

El hogar en que nació la pintora Frida Kahlo en 1907 se caracteriza por su arquitectura típicamente mexicana...

Esta casa tiene varios detalles que revelan el amor de esta mexicana por la cultura de su país, por ejemplo, la cocina.

Uno de los espacios más atractivos de esta casa es este estudio que Diego instaló...

Video: *Flash cultura*

Practice more at **vistas.vhlcentral.com.**

recursos
VM pp. 313–314
vistas.vhlcentral.com Lección 12

Video: *Panorama cultural*
Interactive map

Panamá

El país en cifras

- **Área:** 78.200 km^2 (30.193 millas^2), *aproximadamente el área de Carolina del Sur*
- **Población:** 3.773.000
- **Capital:** La Ciudad de Panamá —1.527.000
- **Ciudades principales:** Colón, David

SOURCE: Population Division, UN Secretariat

- **Moneda:** balboa; es equivalente al dólar estadounidense.

En Panamá circulan los billetes de dólar estadounidense. El país centroamericano, sin embargo, acuña° su propia moneda. "El peso" es una moneda grande equivalente a cincuenta centavos°. La moneda de cinco centavos es llamada frecuentemente "real".

- **Idiomas:** español (oficial), lenguas indígenas, inglés

Muchos panameños son bilingües. La lengua materna del 14% de los panameños es el inglés.

Bandera de Panamá

Panameños célebres

- **Mariano Rivera,** beisbolista (1969–)
- **Mireya Moscoso,** política (1946–)
- **Rubén Blades,** músico y político (1948–)

acuña *mints* centavos *cents* peaje *toll* promedio *average*

Mujer kuna lavando una mola

Un turista disfruta del bosque tropical colgado de un cable.

Ruinas de un fuerte panameño

recursos

WB pp. 145–146	VM pp. 271–272	vistas.vhlcentral.com Lección 12

¡Increíble° pero cierto!

¿Conocías estos datos sobre el Canal de Panamá?

- Gracias al Canal de Panamá, el viaje en barco de Nueva York a Tokio es 3.000 millas más corto.
- Su construcción costó 639 millones de dólares.
- Hoy lo usan en promedio 39 barcos al día.
- El peaje° promedio° cuesta 54.000 dólares.

Lugares • El Canal de Panamá

El Canal de Panamá conecta el océano Pacífico con el océano Atlántico. La construcción de este cauce° artificial empezó en 1903 y concluyó diez años después. Es una de las principales fuentes° de ingresos° del país, gracias al dinero que aportan los más de 14.000 buques° que transitan anualmente por esta ruta y a las actividades comerciales que se han desarrollado° en torno a° ella.

Artes • La mola

La mola es una forma de arte textil de los kunas, una tribu indígena que vive principalmente en las islas San Blas. Esta pieza artesanal se confecciona con fragmentos de tela° de colores vivos. Algunos de sus diseños son abstractos, inspirados en las formas del coral, y otros son geométricos, como en las molas más tradicionales. Antiguamente, estos tejidos se usaban sólo como ropa, pero hoy día también sirven para decorar las casas.

Naturaleza • El mar

Panamá, cuyo° nombre significa "lugar de muchos peces°", es un país muy frecuentado por los aficionados del buceo y la pesca. El territorio panameño cuenta con una gran variedad de playas en los dos lados del istmo°, con el mar Caribe a un lado y el océano Pacífico al otro. Algunas zonas costeras están destinadas al turismo. Otras están protegidas por la diversidad de su fauna marina, en la que abundan los arrecifes° de coral, como el Parque Nacional Marino Isla Bastimentos.

COLOMBIA

Vista de la Ciudad de Panamá

¿Qué aprendiste? Responde a cada pregunta con una oración completa.

1. ¿Cuál es la lengua materna del catorce por ciento de los panameños?
2. ¿A qué unidad monetaria (*monetary unit*) es equivalente el balboa?
3. ¿Qué océanos une el Canal de Panamá?
4. ¿Quién es Mariano Rivera?
5. ¿Qué son las molas?
6. ¿Cómo son los diseños de las molas?
7. ¿Para qué se usan las molas?
8. ¿Cómo son las playas de Panamá?
9. ¿Qué significa "Panamá"?

Conexión Internet Investiga estos temas en **vistas.vhlcentral.com.**

1. Investiga la historia de las relaciones entre Panamá y los Estados Unidos y la decisión de devolver (*give back*) el Canal de Panamá. ¿Estás de acuerdo con la decisión? Explica tu opinión.
2. Investiga sobre los kunas u otro grupo indígena de Panamá. ¿En qué partes del país viven? ¿Qué lenguas hablan? ¿Cómo es su cultura?

Practice more at **vistas.vhlcentral.com.**

cauce *channel* fuentes *sources* ingresos *income* buques *ships* han desarrollado *have developed* en torno a *around* tela *fabric* cuyo *whose* peces *fish* istmo *isthmus* arrecifes *reefs*

Las viviendas

las afueras	*suburbs; outskirts*
el alquiler	*rent (payment)*
el ama (*m., f.*) de casa	*housekeeper; caretaker*
el barrio	*neighborhood*
el edificio de apartamentos	*apartment building*
el/la vecino/a	*neighbor*
la vivienda	*housing*
alquilar	*to rent*
mudarse	*to move (from one house to another)*

Los cuartos y otros lugares

el altillo	*attic*
el balcón	*balcony*
la cocina	*kitchen*
el comedor	*dining room*
el dormitorio	*bedroom*
la entrada	*entrance*
la escalera	*stairs; stairway*
el garaje	*garage*
el jardín	*garden; yard*
la oficina	*office*
el pasillo	*hallway*
el patio	*patio; yard*
la sala	*living room*
el sótano	*basement; cellar*

Los muebles y otras cosas

la alfombra	*carpet; rug*
la almohada	*pillow*
el armario	*closet*
el cartel	*poster*
la cómoda	*chest of drawers*
las cortinas	*curtains*
el cuadro	*picture*
el estante	*bookcase; bookshelves*
la lámpara	*lamp*
la luz	*light; electricity*
la manta	*blanket*
la mesita	*end table*
la mesita de noche	*night stand*
los muebles	*furniture*
la pared	*wall*
la pintura	*painting; picture*
el sillón	*armchair*
el sofá	*couch; sofa*

Los electrodomésticos

la cafetera	*coffee maker*
la cocina, la estufa	*stove*
el congelador	*freezer*
el electrodoméstico	*electric appliance*
el horno (de microondas)	*(microwave) oven*
la lavadora	*washing machine*
el lavaplatos	*dishwasher*
el refrigerador	*refrigerator*
la secadora	*clothes dryer*
la tostadora	*toaster*

La mesa

la copa	*wineglass; goblet*
la cuchara	*(table or large) spoon*
el cuchillo	*knife*
el plato	*plate*
la servilleta	*napkin*
la taza	*cup*
el tenedor	*fork*
el vaso	*glass*

Los quehaceres domésticos

arreglar	*to neaten; to straighten up*
barrer el suelo	*to sweep the floor*
cocinar	*to cook*
ensuciar	*to get (something) dirty*
hacer la cama	*to make the bed*
hacer quehaceres domésticos	*to do household chores*
lavar (el suelo, los platos)	*to wash (the floor, the dishes)*
limpiar la casa	*to clean the house*
pasar la aspiradora	*to vacuum*
planchar la ropa	*to iron the clothes*
poner la mesa	*to set the table*
quitar la mesa	*to clear the table*
quitar el polvo	*to dust*
sacar la basura	*to take out the trash*
sacudir los muebles	*to dust the furniture*

Verbos y expresiones verbales

aconsejar	*to advise*
insistir (en)	*to insist (on)*
mandar	*to order*
recomendar (e:ie)	*to recommend*
rogar (o:ue)	*to beg; to plead*
sugerir (e:ie)	*to suggest*
Es bueno que...	*It's good that...*
Es importante que...	*It's important that...*
Es malo que...	*It's bad that...*
Es mejor que...	*It's better that...*
Es necesario que...	*It's necessary that...*
Es urgente que...	*It's urgent that...*

Relative pronouns	*See page 414.*
Expresiones útiles	*See page 409.*

recursos

LM p. 72 | vistas.vhlcentral.com Lección 12

Audio: Vocabulary

Consulta

Plan de escritura

1 Ideas y organización

Begin by organizing your writing materials. If you prefer to write by hand, you may want to have a few spare pens and pencils on hand, as well as an eraser or correction fluid. If you prefer to use a word-processing program, make sure you know how to type Spanish accent marks, the **tilde**, and Spanish punctuation marks. Then make a list of the resources you can consult while writing. Finally, make a list of the basic ideas you want to cover. Beside each idea, jot down a few Spanish words and phrases you may want to use while writing.

2 Primer borrador

Write your first draft, using the resources and ideas you gathered in **Ideas y organización.**

3 Comentario

Exchange papers with a classmate and comment on each other's work, using these questions as a guide. Begin by mentioning what you like about your classmate's writing.

a. How can your classmate make his or her writing clearer, more logical, or more organized?

b. What suggestions do you have for making the writing more interesting or complete?

c. Do you see any spelling or grammatical errors?

4 Redacción

Revise your first draft, keeping in mind your classmate's comments. Also, incorporate any new information you may have. Before handing in the final version, review your work using these guidelines:

a. Make sure each verb agrees with its subject. Then check the gender and number of each article, noun, and adjective.

b. Check your spelling and punctuation.

c. Consult your **Anotaciones para mejorar la escritura** (see description below) to avoid repetition of previous errors.

5 Evaluación y progreso

You may want to share what you've written with a classmate, a small group, or the entire class. After your instructor has returned your paper, review the comments and corrections. On a separate sheet of paper, write the heading **Anotaciones para mejorar** (*Notes for improving*) **la escritura** and list your most common errors. Place this list and your corrected document in your writing portfolio (**Carpeta de trabajos**) and consult it from time to time to gauge your progress.

Spanish Terms for Direction Lines and Classroom Use

Below is a list of useful terms that you might hear your instructor say in class. It also includes Spanish terms that appear in the direction lines of your textbook.

En las instrucciones	*In direction lines*
Cambia/Cambien...	*Change...*
Camina/Caminen por la clase.	*Walk around the classroom.*
Ciertas o falsas	*True or false*
Cierto o falso	*True or false*
Circula/Circulen por la clase.	*Walk around the classroom.*
Completa las oraciones de una manera lógica.	*Complete the sentences logically.*
Con un(a) compañero/a...	*With a classmate...*
Contesta las preguntas.	*Answer the questions.*
Corrige las oraciones falsas.	*Correct the false statements.*
Cuenta/Cuenten...	*Tell...*
Di/Digan...	*Say...*
Discute/Discutan...	*Discuss...*
En grupos...	*In groups...*
En parejas...	*In pairs...*
Entrevista...	*Interview...*
Escúchala	*Listen to it*
Forma oraciones completas.	*Create/Make complete sentences.*
Háganse preguntas.	*Ask each other questions.*
Haz el papel de...	*Play the role of...*
Haz los cambios necesarios.	*Make the necessary changes.*
Indica/Indiquen si las oraciones...	*Indicate if the sentences...*
Intercambia/Intercambien...	*Exchange...*
Lee/Lean en voz alta.	*Read aloud.*
Pon/Pongan...	*Put...*
... que mejor completa...	*...that best completes...*
Reúnete...	*Get together...*
... se da/dan como ejemplo.	*...is/are given as a model.*
Toma nota...	*Take note...*
Tomen apuntes.	*Take notes.*
Túrnense...	*Take turns...*

Palabras útiles	*Useful words*
la adivinanza	*riddle*
el anuncio	*advertisement/ad*
los apuntes	*notes*
el borrador	*draft*
la canción	*song*
la concordancia	*agreement*
el contenido	*contents*
el cortometraje	*short film*
eficaz	*efficient*
la encuesta	*survey*
el equipo	*team*
el esquema	*outline*
el folleto	*brochure*
las frases	*statements*
la hoja de actividades	*activity sheet/handout*
la hoja de papel	*piece of paper*
la información errónea	*incorrect information*
el/la lector(a)	*reader*
la lectura	*reading*
las oraciones	*sentences*
la ortografía	*spelling*
el papel	*role*
el párrafo	*paragraph*
el paso	*step*
la(s) persona(s) descrita(s)	*the person (people) described*
la pista	*clue*
por ejemplo	*for example*
el propósito	*purpose*
los recursos	*resources*
el reportaje	*report*
los resultados	*results*
según	*according to*
siguiente	*following*
la sugerencia	*suggestion*
el sustantivo	*noun*
el tema	*topic*
último	*last*
el último recurso	*last resort*

Verbos útiles	*Useful verbs*
adivinar	*to guess*
anotar	*to jot down*
añadir	*to add*
apoyar	*to support*
averiguar	*to find out*
cambiar	*to change*
combinar	*to combine*
compartir	*to share*
comprobar (o:ue)	*to check*
corregir (e:i)	*to correct*
crear	*to create*
devolver (o:ue)	*to return*
doblar	*to fold*
dramatizar	*to act out*
elegir (e:i)	*to choose/select*
emparejar	*to match*
entrevistar	*to interview*
escoger	*to choose*
identificar	*to identify*
incluir	*to include*
informar	*to report*
intentar	*to try*
intercambiar	*to exchange*
investigar	*to research*
marcar	*to mark*
preguntar	*to ask*
recordar (o:ue)	*to remember*
responder	*to answer*
revisar	*to revise*
seguir (e:i)	*to follow*
seleccionar	*to select*
subrayar	*to underline*
traducir	*to translate*
tratar de	*to be about*

Expresiones útiles	*Useful expressions*
Ahora mismo.	*Right away.*
¿Cómo no?	*But of course.*
¿Cómo se dice ________ en español?	*How do you say ________ in Spanish?*
¿Cómo se escribe ________?	*How do you spell ________?*
¿Comprende(n)?	*Do you understand?*
Con gusto.	*With pleasure.*
Con permiso.	*Excuse me.*
De acuerdo.	*Okay.*
De nada.	*You're welcome.*
¿De veras?	*Really?*
¿En qué página estamos?	*What page are we on?*
¿En serio?	*Seriously?*
Enseguida.	*Right away.*
hoy día	*nowadays*
Más despacio, por favor.	*Slower, please.*
Muchas gracias.	*Thanks a lot.*
No entiendo.	*I don't understand.*
No hay de qué.	*Don't mention it.*
No importa.	*No problem./It doesn't matter.*
¡No me digas!	*You don't say!*
No sé.	*I don't know.*
¡Ojalá!	*Hopefully!*
Perdone.	*Pardon me.*
Por favor.	*Please.*
Por supuesto.	*Of course.*
¡Qué bien!	*Great!*
¡Qué gracioso!	*How funny!*
¡Qué pena!	*What a shame/pity!*
¿Qué significa ________?	*What does ________ mean?*
Repite, por favor.	*Please repeat.*
Tengo una pregunta.	*I have a question.*
¿Tiene(n) alguna pregunta?	*Do you have any questions?*
Vaya(n) a la página dos.	*Go to page 2.*

Glossary of Grammatical Terms

ADJECTIVE A word that modifies, or describes, a noun or pronoun.

muchos libros *many books*	un hombre **rico** *a rich man*
las mujeres **altas** *the tall women*	

Demonstrative adjective An adjective that specifies which noun a speaker is referring to.

esta fiesta *this party*	**ese** chico *that boy*
aquellas flores *those flowers*	

Possessive adjective An adjective that indicates ownership or possession.

mi mejor vestido *my best dress*	Éste es **mi** hermano. *This is my brother.*

Stressed possessive adjective A possessive adjective that emphasizes the owner or possessor.

Es un libro **mío**.
*It's **my** book./It's a book **of mine**.*

Es amiga **tuya**; yo no la conozco.
*She's a friend **of yours**; I don't know her.*

ADVERB A word that modifies, or describes, a verb, adjective, or other adverb.

Pancho escribe **rápidamente**.
*Pancho writes **quickly**.*

Este cuadro es **muy** bonito.
*This picture is **very** pretty.*

ARTICLE A word that points out a noun in either a specific or a non-specific way.

Definite article An article that points out a noun in a specific way.

el libro *the book*	**la** maleta *the suitcase*
los diccionarios *the dictionaries*	**las** palabras *the words*

Indefinite article An article that points out a noun in a general, non-specific way.

un lápiz *a pencil*	**una** computadora *a computer*
unos pájaros *some birds*	**unas** escuelas *some schools*

CLAUSE A group of words that contains both a conjugated verb and a subject, either expressed or implied.

Main (or Independent) clause A clause that can stand alone as a complete sentence.

Pienso ir a cenar pronto.
I plan to go to dinner soon.

Subordinate (or Dependent) clause A clause that does not express a complete thought and therefore cannot stand alone as a sentence.

Trabajo en la cafetería **porque necesito dinero para la escuela.**
*I work in the cafeteria **because I need money for school.***

COMPARATIVE A construction used with an adjective or adverb to express a comparison between two people, places, or things.

Este programa es **más interesante que** el otro.
*This program is **more interesting than** the other one.*

Tomás no es **tan alto como** Alberto.
*Tomás is not **as tall as** Alberto.*

CONJUGATION A set of the forms of a verb for a specific tense or mood or the process by which these verb forms are presented.

Preterite conjugation of **cantar:**

cant**é**	cant**amos**
cant**aste**	cant**asteis**
cant**ó**	cant**aron**

CONJUNCTION A word used to connect words, clauses, or phrases.

Susana es de Cuba **y** Pedro es de España.
*Susana is from Cuba **and** Pedro is from Spain.*

No quiero estudiar **pero** tengo que hacerlo.
*I don't want to study, **but** I have to.*

CONTRACTION The joining of two words into one. The only contractions in Spanish are **al** and **del**.

Mi hermano fue **al** concierto ayer.
*My brother went **to the** concert yesterday.*

Saqué dinero **del** banco.
*I took money **from the** bank.*

DIRECT OBJECT A noun or pronoun that directly receives the action of the verb.

Tomás lee **el libro.** — *Tomás reads **the book.***
La pagó ayer. — *She paid **it** yesterday.*

GENDER The grammatical categorizing of certain kinds of words, such as nouns and pronouns, as masculine, feminine, or neuter.

Masculine
articles **el, un**
pronouns **él, lo, mío, éste, ése, aquél**
adjective **simpático**

Feminine
articles **la, una**
pronouns **ella, la, mía, ésta, ésa, aquélla**
adjective **simpática**

IMPERSONAL EXPRESSION A third-person expression with no expressed or specific subject.

Es muy importante. — ***It's very important.***
Llueve mucho. — ***It's raining** hard.*

Aquí **se habla** español.
*Spanish **is spoken** here.*

INDIRECT OBJECT A noun or pronoun that receives the action of the verb indirectly; the object, often a living being, to or for whom an action is performed.

Eduardo **le** dio un libro **a Linda**.
*Eduardo gave a book **to Linda**.*

La profesora **me** puso una C en el examen.
*The professor gave **me** a C on the test.*

INFINITIVE The basic form of a verb. Infinitives in Spanish end in **-ar**, **-er**, or **-ir**.

hablar	**correr**	**abrir**
to speak	*to run*	*to open*

INTERROGATIVE An adjective or pronoun used to ask a question.

¿**Quién** habla? — ***Who** is speaking?*
¿**Cuántos** compraste? — ***How many** did you buy?*

¿**Qué** piensas hacer hoy?
***What** do you plan to do today?*

INVERSION Changing the word order of a sentence, often to form a question.

Statement: Elena pagó la cuenta del restaurante.

Inversion: ¿Pagó Elena la cuenta del restaurante?

MOOD A grammatical distinction of verbs that indicates whether the verb is intended to make a statement or command or to express a doubt, emotion, or condition contrary to fact.

Imperative mood Verb forms used to make commands.

Di la verdad. — ***Tell** the truth.*
Caminen ustedes conmigo. — ***Walk** with me.*

¡**Comamos** ahora!
***Let's eat** now!*

Indicative mood Verb forms used to state facts, actions, and states considered to be real.

Sé que **tienes** el dinero.
*I know that **you have** the money.*

Subjunctive mood Verb forms used principally in subordinate (dependent) clauses to express wishes, desires, emotions, doubts, and certain conditions, such as contrary-to-fact situations.

Prefieren que **hables** en español.
*They prefer that **you speak** in Spanish.*

Dudo que Luis **tenga** el dinero necesario.
*I doubt that Luis **has** the necessary money.*

NOUN A word that identifies people, animals, places, things, and ideas.

hombre / *man*	**gato** / *cat*
México / *Mexico*	**casa** / *house*
libertad / *freedom*	**libro** / *book*

NUMBER A grammatical term that refers to singular or plural. Nouns in Spanish and English have number. Other parts of a sentence, such as adjectives, articles, and verbs, can also have number.

Singular	Plural
una cosa *a thing*	**unas** cosas *some things*
el profesor ***the** professor*	**los** profesores ***the** professors*

NUMBERS Words that represent amounts.

Cardinal numbers Words that show specific amounts.

cinco minutos
***five** minutes*

el año **dos mil veintitrés**
*the year **2023***

Ordinal numbers Words that indicate the order of a noun in a series.

el **cuarto** jugador *the **fourth** player*	la **décima** hora *the **tenth** hour*

PAST PARTICIPLE A past form of the verb used in compound tenses. The past participle may also be used as an adjective, but it must then agree in number and gender with the word it modifies.

Han **buscado** por todas partes.
*They have **searched** everywhere.*

Yo no había **estudiado** para el examen.
*I hadn't **studied** for the exam.*

Hay una **ventana abierta** en la sala.
*There is an **open window** in the living room.*

PERSON The form of the verb or pronoun that indicates the speaker, the one spoken to, or the one spoken about. In Spanish, as in English, there are three persons: first, second, and third.

Person	Singular	Plural
1st	**yo** *I*	**nosotros/as** *we*
2nd	**tú, Ud.** *you*	**vosotros/as, Uds.** *you*
3rd	**él, ella** *he, she*	**ellos, ellas** *they*

PREPOSITION A word or words that describe(s) the relationship, most often in time or space, between two other words.

Anita es **de** California.
*Anita is **from** California.*

La chaqueta está **en** el carro.
*The jacket is **in** the car.*

Marta se peinó **antes de** salir.
*Marta combed her hair **before** going out.*

PRESENT PARTICIPLE In English, a verb form that ends in *-ing*. In Spanish, the present participle ends in **-ndo**, and is often used with **estar** to form a progressive tense.

Mi hermana está **hablando** por teléfono ahora mismo.
*My sister is **talking** on the phone right now.*

PRONOUN A word that takes the place of a noun or nouns.

Demonstrative pronoun A pronoun that takes the place of a specific noun.

Quiero **ésta**.
*I want **this one**.*

¿Vas a comprar **ése**?
*Are you going to buy **that one**?*

Juan prefirió **aquéllos**.
*Juan preferred **those** (over there).*

Object pronoun A pronoun that functions as a direct or indirect object of the verb.

Te digo la verdad.
*I'm telling **you** the truth.*

Me lo trajo Juan.
*Juan brought **it** to **me**.*

Reflexive pronoun A pronoun that indicates that the action of a verb is performed by the subject on itself. These pronouns are often expressed in English with *-self: myself, yourself*, etc.

Yo **me bañé** antes de salir.
***I bathed (myself)** before going out.*

Elena **se acostó** a las once y media.
*Elena **went to bed** at eleven-thirty.*

Relative pronoun A pronoun that connects a subordinate clause to a main clause.

El chico **que** nos escribió viene de visita mañana.
*The boy **who** wrote us is coming to visit tomorrow.*

Ya sé **lo que** tenemos que hacer.
*I already know **what** we have to do.*

Subject pronoun A pronoun that replaces the name or title of a person or thing, and acts as the subject of a verb.

Tú debes estudiar más.
***You** should study more.*

Él llegó primero.
***He** arrived first.*

SUBJECT A noun or pronoun that performs the action of a verb and is often implied by the verb.

María va al supermercado.
***María** goes to the supermarket.*

(**Ellos**) Trabajan mucho.
***They** work hard.*

Esos **libros** son muy caros.
*Those **books** are very expensive.*

SUPERLATIVE A word or construction used with an adjective or adverb to express the highest or lowest degree of a specific quality among three or more people, places, or things.

De todas mis clases, ésta es la **más interesante**.
*Of all my classes, this is the **most interesting**.*

Raúl es el **menos simpático** de los chicos.
*Raúl is the **least pleasant** of the boys.*

TENSE A set of verb forms that indicates the time of an action or state: past, present, or future.

Compound tense A two-word tense made up of an auxiliary verb and a present or past participle. In Spanish, there are two auxiliary verbs: **estar** and **haber**.

En este momento, **estoy estudiando**.
*At this time, **I am studying**.*

El paquete no **ha llegado** todavía.
*The package **has** not **arrived** yet.*

Simple tense A tense expressed by a single verb form.

María **estaba** enferma anoche.
*María **was** sick last night.*

Juana **hablará** con su mamá mañana.
*Juana **will speak** with her mom tomorrow.*

VERB A word that expresses actions or states-of-being.

Auxiliary verb A verb used with a present or past participle to form a compound tense. **Haber** is the most commonly used auxiliary verb in Spanish.

Los chicos **han** visto los elefantes.
*The children **have** seen the elephants.*

Espero que **hayas** comido.
*I hope you **have** eaten.*

Reflexive verb A verb that describes an action performed by the subject on itself and is always used with a reflexive pronoun.

Me compré un carro nuevo.
*I **bought myself** a new car.*

Pedro y Adela **se levantan** muy temprano.
*Pedro and Adela **get (themselves) up** very early.*

Spelling change verb A verb that undergoes a predictable change in spelling, in order to reflect its actual pronunciation in the various conjugations.

practicar	c→qu	practico	practi**qu**é
dirigir	g→j	dirigí	diri**j**o
almorzar	z→c	almorzó	almor**c**é

Stem-changing verb A verb whose stem vowel undergoes one or more predictable changes in the various conjugations.

entender (e:ie)	ent**ie**ndo
pedir (e:i)	p**i**den
dormir (o:ue, u)	d**ue**rmo, d**u**rmieron

Verb Conjugation Tables

The verb lists

The list of verbs below, and the model-verb tables that start on page A-11 show you how to conjugate every verb taught in **VISTAS**. Each verb in the list is followed by a model verb conjugated according to the same pattern. The number in parentheses indicates where in the verb tables you can find the conjugated forms of the model verb. If you want to find out how to conjugate **divertirse**, for example, look up number 33, **sentir**, the model for verbs that follow the **e:ie** stem-change pattern.

How to use the verb tables

In the tables you will find the infinitive, present and past participles, and all the simple forms of each model verb. The formation of the compound tenses of any verb can be inferred from the table of compound tenses, pages A-11–12, either by combining the past participle of the verb with a conjugated form of **haber** or by combining the present participle with a conjugated form of **estar**.

abrazar (z:c) like cruzar (37)
abrir like vivir (3) *except* past participle is **abierto**
aburrir(se) like vivir (3)
acabar de like hablar (1)
acampar like hablar (1)
acompañar like hablar (1)
aconsejar like hablar (1)
acordarse (o:ue) like contar (24)
acostarse (o:ue) like contar (24)
adelgazar (z:c) like cruzar (37)
afeitarse like hablar (1)
ahorrar like hablar (1)
alegrarse like hablar (1)
aliviar like hablar (1)
almorzar (o:ue) like contar (24) *except* (z:c)
alquilar like hablar (1)
andar like hablar (1) *except* preterite stem is **anduv-**
anunciar like hablar (1)
apagar (g:gu) like llegar (41)
aplaudir like vivir (3)
apreciar like hablar (1)
aprender like comer (2)
apurarse like hablar (1)
arrancar (c:qu) like tocar (43)
arreglar like hablar (1)
asistir like vivir (3)
aumentar like hablar (1)
ayudar(se) like hablar (1)
bailar like hablar (1)
bajar(se) like hablar (1)
bañarse like hablar (1)
barrer like comer (2)
beber like comer (2)
besar(se) like hablar (1)
borrar like hablar (1)
brindar like hablar (1)
bucear like hablar (1)
buscar (c:qu) like tocar (43)
caber (4)
caer(se) (5)
calentarse (e:ie) like pensar (30)
calzar (z:c) like cruzar (37)
cambiar like hablar (1)
caminar like hablar (1)
cantar like hablar (1)
casarse like hablar (1)
cazar (z:c) like cruzar (37)
celebrar like hablar (1)
cenar like hablar (1)
cepillarse like hablar (1)
cerrar (e:ie) like pensar (30)
cobrar like hablar (1)
cocinar like hablar (1)
comenzar (e:ie) (z:c) like empezar (26)
comer (2)
compartir like vivir (3)
comprar like hablar (1)
comprender like comer (2)
comprometerse like comer (2)
comunicarse (c:qu) like tocar (43)
conducir (c:zc) (6)
confirmar like hablar (1)
conocer (c:zc) (35)
conseguir (e:i) (g:gu) like seguir (32)
conservar like hablar (1)
consumir like vivir (3)
contaminar like hablar (1)
contar (o:ue) (24)
contratar like hablar (1)
contestar like hablar (1)
conversar like hablar (1)
controlar like hablar (1)
correr like comer (2)
costar (o:ue) like contar (24)
creer (y) (36)
cruzar (z:c) (37)
cuidar like hablar (1)
cumplir like vivir (3)
dañar like hablar (1)
dar (7)
deber like comer (2)
decidir like vivir (3)
decir (e:i) (8)
declarar like hablar (1)
dejar like hablar (1)
depositar like hablar (1)
desarrollar like hablar (1)
desayunar like hablar (1)
descansar like hablar (1)
descargar like llegar (41)
describir like vivir (3) *except* past participle is **descrito**
descubrir like vivir (3) *except* past participle is **descubierto**
desear like hablar (1)
despedirse (e:i) like pedir (29)
despertarse (e:ie) like pensar (30)
destruir (y) (38)
dibujar like hablar (1)
dirigir (g:j) like vivir (3) *except* (g:j)
disfrutar like hablar (1)
divertirse (e:ie) like sentir (33)
divorciarse like hablar (1)
doblar like hablar (1)
doler (o:ue) like volver (34) *except* past participle is regular
dormir(se) (o:ue, u) (25)
ducharse like hablar (1)
dudar like hablar (1)
durar like hablar (1)
echar like hablar (1)
elegir (e:i) like pedir (29) *except* (g:j)

emitir like vivir (3)
empezar (e:ie) (z:c) (26)
enamorarse like hablar (1)
encantar like hablar (1)
encontrar(se) (o:ue) like contar (24)
enfermarse like hablar (1)
engordar like hablar (1)
enojarse like hablar (1)
enseñar like hablar (1)
ensuciar like hablar (1)
entender (e:ie) (27)
entrenarse like hablar (1)
entrevistar like hablar (1)
enviar (envío) (39)
escalar like hablar (1)
escanear like hablar (1)
escoger (g:j) like proteger (42)
escribir like vivir (3) *except* past participle is escrito
escuchar like hablar (1)
esculpir like vivir (3)
esperar like hablar (1)
esquiar (esquío) like enviar (39)
establecer (c:zc) like conocer (35)
estacionar like hablar (1)
estar (9)
estornudar like hablar (1)
estudiar like hablar (1)
evitar like hablar (1)
explicar (c:qu) like tocar (43)
faltar like hablar (1)
fascinar like hablar (1)
firmar like hablar (1)
fumar like hablar (1)
funcionar like hablar (1)
ganar like hablar (1)
gastar like hablar (1)
grabar like hablar (1)
graduarse (gradúo) (40)
guardar like hablar (1)
gustar like hablar (1)
haber (hay) (10)
hablar (1)
hacer (11)
importar like hablar (1)
imprimir like vivir (3)
indicar (c:qu) like tocar (43)
informar like hablar (1)
insistir like vivir (3)
interesar like hablar (1)
invertir (e:ie) like sentir (33)
invitar like hablar (1)
ir(se) (12)
jubilarse like hablar (1)
jugar (u:ue) (g:gu) (28)
lastimarse like hablar (1)
lavar(se) like hablar (1)
leer (y) like creer (36)
levantar(se) like hablar (1)
limpiar like hablar (1)
llamar(se) like hablar (1)
llegar (g:gu) (41)
llenar like hablar (1)
llevar(se) like hablar (1)
llover (o:ue) like volver (34) *except* past participle is regular
luchar like hablar (1)
mandar like hablar (1)
manejar like hablar (1)
mantener(se) (e:ie) like tener (20)
maquillarse like hablar (1)
mejorar like hablar (1)
merendar (e:ie) like pensar (30)
mirar like hablar (1)
molestar like hablar (1)
montar like hablar (1)
morir (o:ue) like dormir (25) *except* past participle is muerto
mostrar (o:ue) like contar (24)
mudarse like hablar (1)
nacer (c:zc) like conocer (35)
nadar like hablar (1)
navegar (g:gu) like llegar (41)
necesitar like hablar (1)
negar (e:ie) like pensar (30) *except* (g:gu)
nevar (e:ie) like pensar (30)
obedecer (c:zc) like conocer (35)
obtener (e:ie) like tener (20)
ocurrir like vivir (3)
odiar like hablar (1)
ofrecer (c:zc) like conocer (35)
oír (13)
olvidar like hablar (1)
pagar (g:gu) like llegar (41)
parar like hablar (1)
parecer (c:zc) like conocer (35)
pasar like hablar (1)
pasear like hablar (1)
patinar like hablar (1)
pedir (e:i) (29)
peinarse like hablar (1)
pensar (e:ie) (30)
perder (e:ie) like entender (27)
pescar (c:qu) like tocar (43)
pintar like hablar (1)
planchar like hablar (1)
poder (o:ue) (14)
poner(se) (15)
practicar (c:qu) like tocar (43)
preferir (e:ie) like sentir (33)
preguntar like hablar (1)
prender like comer (2)
preocuparse like hablar (1)
preparar like hablar (1)
presentar like hablar (1)
prestar like hablar (1)
probar(se) (o:ue) like contar (24)
prohibir like vivir (3)
proteger (g:j) (42)
publicar (c:qu) like tocar (43)
quedar(se) like hablar (1)
querer (e:ie) (16)
quitar(se) like hablar (1)
recetar like hablar (1)
recibir like vivir (3)
reciclar like hablar (1)
recoger (g:j) like proteger (42)
recomendar (e:ie) like pensar (30)
recordar (o:ue) like contar (24)
reducir (c:zc) like conducir (6)
regalar like hablar (1)
regatear like hablar (1)
regresar like hablar (1)
reír(se) (e:i) (31)
relajarse like hablar (1)
renunciar like hablar (1)
repetir (e:i) like pedir (29)
resolver (o:ue) like volver (34)
respirar like hablar (1)
revisar like hablar (1)
rogar (o:ue) like contar (24) *except* (g:gu)
romper(se) like comer (2) *except* past participle is roto
saber (17)
sacar (c:qu) like tocar (43)
sacudir like vivir (3)
salir (18)
saludar(se) like hablar (1)
secar(se) (c:qu) like tocar (43)
seguir (e:i) (32)
sentarse (e:ie) like pensar (30)
sentir(se) (e:ie) (33)
separarse like hablar (1)
ser (19)
servir (e:i) like pedir (29)
solicitar like hablar (1)
sonar (o:ue) like contar (24)
sonreír (e:i) like reír(se) (31)
sorprender like comer (2)
subir like vivir (3)
sudar like hablar (1)
sufrir like vivir (3)
sugerir (e:ie) like sentir (33)
suponer like poner (15)
temer like comer (2)
tener (e:ie) (20)
terminar like hablar (1)
tocar (c:qu) (43)
tomar like hablar (1)
torcerse (o:ue) like volver (34) *except* (c:z) and past participle is regular; e.g., **yo tuerzo**
toser like comer (2)
trabajar like hablar (1)
traducir (c:zc) like conducir (6)
traer (21)
transmitir like vivir (3)
tratar like hablar (1)
usar like hablar (1)
vender like comer (2)
venir (e:ie, i) (22)
ver (23)
vestirse (e:i) like pedir (29)
viajar like hablar (1)
visitar like hablar (1)
vivir (3)
volver (o:ue) (34)
votar like hablar (1)

Regular verbs: simple tenses

Infinitive	INDICATIVE Present	Imperfect	Preterite	Future	Conditional	SUBJUNCTIVE Present	Past	IMPERATIVE
1 hablar	hablo	hablaba	hablé	hablaré	hablaría	hable	hablara	
	hablas	hablabas	hablaste	hablarás	hablarías	hables	hablaras	habla tú (no hables)
Participles:	habla	hablaba	habló	hablará	hablaría	hable	hablara	hable Ud.
hablando	hablamos	hablábamos	hablamos	hablaremos	hablaríamos	hablemos	habláramos	hablemos
hablado	habláis	hablabais	hablasteis	hablaréis	hablaríais	habléis	hablarais	hablad (no habléis)
	hablan	hablaban	hablaron	hablarán	hablarían	hablen	hablaran	hablen Uds.
2 comer	como	comía	comí	comeré	comería	coma	comiera	
	comes	comías	comiste	comerás	comerías	comas	comieras	come tú (no comas)
Participles:	come	comía	comió	comerá	comería	coma	comiera	coma Ud.
comiendo	comemos	comíamos	comimos	comeremos	comeríamos	comamos	comiéramos	comamos
comido	coméis	comíais	comisteis	comeréis	comeríais	comáis	comierais	comed (no comáis)
	comen	comían	comieron	comerán	comerían	coman	comieran	coman Uds.
3 vivir	vivo	vivía	viví	viviré	viviría	viva	viviera	
	vives	vivías	viviste	vivirás	vivirías	vivas	vivieras	vive tú (no vivas)
Participles:	vive	vivía	vivió	vivirá	viviría	viva	viviera	viva Ud.
viviendo	vivimos	vivíamos	vivimos	viviremos	viviríamos	vivamos	viviéramos	vivamos
vivido	vivís	vivíais	vivisteis	viviréis	viviríais	viváis	vivierais	vivid (no viváis)
	viven	vivían	vivieron	vivirán	vivirían	vivan	vivieran	vivan Uds.

All verbs: compound tenses

PERFECT TENSES											
INDICATIVE								SUBJUNCTIVE			
Present Perfect		Past Perfect		Future Perfect		Conditional Perfect		Present Perfect		Past Perfect	
he		había		habré		habría		haya		hubiera	
has	hablado	habías	hablado	habrás	hablado	habrías	hablado	hayas	hablado	hubieras	hablado
ha	comido	había	comido	habrá	comido	habría	comido	haya	comido	hubiera	comido
hemos	vivido	habíamos	vivido	habremos	vivido	habríamos	vivido	hayamos	vivido	hubiéramos	vivido
habéis		habíais		habréis		habríais		hayáis		hubierais	
han		habían		habrán		habrían		hayan		hubieran	

PROGRESSIVE TENSES											
INDICATIVE								SUBJUNCTIVE			
Present Progressive		Past Progressive		Future Progressive		Conditional Progressive		Present Progressive		Past Progressive	
estoy estás está estamos estáis están	hablando comiendo viviendo	estaba estabas estaba estábamos estabais estaban	hablando comiendo viviendo	estaré estarás estará estaremos estaréis estarán	hablando comiendo viviendo	estaría estarías estaría estaríamos estaríais estarían	hablando comiendo viviendo	esté estés esté estemos estéis estén	hablando comiendo viviendo	estuviera estuvieras estuviera estuviéramos estuvierais estuvieran	hablando comiendo viviendo

Irregular verbs

		INDICATIVE					SUBJUNCTIVE		IMPERATIVE
	Infinitive	Present	Imperfect	Preterite	Future	Conditional	Present	Past	
4	caber	**quepo**	cabía	**cupe**	**cabré**	**cabría**	**quepa**	**cupiera**	
		cabes	cabías	**cupiste**	**cabrás**	**cabrías**	**quepas**	**cupieras**	cabe tú (no **quepas**)
	Participles:	cabe	cabía	**cupo**	**cabrá**	**cabría**	**quepa**	**cupiera**	**quepa** Ud.
	cabiendo	cabemos	cabíamos	**cupimos**	**cabremos**	**cabríamos**	**quepamos**	**cupiéramos**	**quepamos**
	cabido	cabéis	cabíais	**cupisteis**	**cabréis**	**cabríais**	**quepáis**	**cupierais**	cabed (no **quepáis**)
		caben	cabían	**cupieron**	**cabrán**	**cabrían**	**quepan**	**cupieran**	**quepan** Uds.
5	caer(se)	**caigo**	caía	caí	caeré	caería	**caiga**	**cayera**	
		caes	caías	**caíste**	caerás	caerías	**caigas**	**cayeras**	cae tú (no **caigas**)
	Participles:	cae	caía	**cayó**	caerá	caería	**caiga**	**cayera**	**caiga** Ud.
	cayendo	caemos	caíamos	**caímos**	caeremos	caeríamos	**caigamos**	**cayéramos**	**caigamos**
	caído	caéis	caíais	**caísteis**	caeréis	caeríais	**caigáis**	**cayerais**	caed (no **caigáis**)
		caen	caían	**cayeron**	caerán	caerían	**caigan**	**cayeran**	**caigan** Uds.
6	conducir	**conduzco**	conducía	**conduje**	conduciré	conduciría	**conduzca**	**condujera**	
	(c:zc)	conduces	conducías	**condujiste**	conducirás	conducirías	**conduzcas**	**condujeras**	conduce tú (no **conduzcas**)
		conduce	conducía	**condujo**	conducirá	conduciría	**conduzca**	**condujera**	**conduzca** Ud.
	Participles:	conducimos	conducíamos	**condujimos**	conduciremos	conduciríamos	**conduzcamos**	**condujéramos**	**conduzcamos**
	conduciendo	conducís	conducíais	**condujisteis**	conduciréis	conduciríais	**conduzcáis**	**condujerais**	conducid (no **conduzcáis**)
	conducido	conducen	conducían	**condujeron**	conducirán	conducirían	**conduzcan**	**condujeran**	**conduzcan** Uds.

		INDICATIVE					SUBJUNCTIVE		IMPERATIVE
	Infinitive	Present	Imperfect	Preterite	Future	Conditional	Present	Past	
7	dar	**doy**	daba	**di**	daré	daría	**dé**	**diera**	
		das	dabas	**diste**	darás	darías	**des**	**dieras**	da tú (no des)
	Participles:	da	daba	**dio**	dará	daría	**dé**	**diera**	**dé** Ud.
	dando	damos	dábamos	**dimos**	daremos	daríamos	**demos**	**diéramos**	**demos**
	dado	dais	dabais	**disteis**	daréis	daríais	**deis**	**dierais**	dad (no **deis**)
		dan	daban	**dieron**	darán	darían	**den**	**dieran**	**den** Uds.
8	decir (e:i)	**digo**	decía	**dije**	**diré**	**diría**	**diga**	**dijera**	
		dices	decías	**dijiste**	**dirás**	**dirías**	**digas**	**dijeras**	**di** tú (no **digas**)
	Participles:	**dice**	decía	**dijo**	**dirá**	**diría**	**diga**	**dijera**	**diga** Ud.
	diciendo	decimos	decíamos	**dijimos**	**diremos**	**diríamos**	**digamos**	**dijéramos**	**digamos**
	dicho	decís	decíais	**dijisteis**	**diréis**	**diríais**	**digáis**	**dijerais**	decid (no **digáis**)
		dicen	decían	**dijeron**	**dirán**	**dirían**	**digan**	**dijeran**	**digan** Uds.
9	estar	**estoy**	estaba	**estuve**	estaré	estaría	esté	**estuviera**	
		estás	estabas	**estuviste**	estarás	estarías	estés	**estuvieras**	está tú (no estés)
	Participles:	está	estaba	**estuvo**	estará	estaría	esté	**estuviera**	esté Ud.
	estando	estamos	estábamos	**estuvimos**	estaremos	estaríamos	estemos	**estuviéramos**	estemos
	estado	estáis	estabais	**estuvisteis**	estaréis	estaríais	estéis	**estuvierais**	estad (no estéis)
		están	estaban	**estuvieron**	estarán	estarían	estén	**estuvieran**	estén Uds.
10	haber	**he**	había	**hube**	**habré**	**habría**	**haya**	**hubiera**	
		has	habías	**hubiste**	**habrás**	**habrías**	**hayas**	**hubieras**	
	Participles:	**ha**	había	**hubo**	**habrá**	**habría**	**haya**	**hubiera**	
	habiendo	**hemos**	habíamos	**hubimos**	**habremos**	**habríamos**	**hayamos**	**hubiéramos**	
	habido	**habéis**	habíais	**hubisteis**	**habréis**	**habríais**	**hayáis**	**hubierais**	
		han	habían	**hubieron**	**habrán**	**habrían**	**hayan**	**hubieran**	
11	hacer	**hago**	hacía	**hice**	**haré**	**haría**	**haga**	**hiciera**	
		haces	hacías	**hiciste**	**harás**	**harías**	**hagas**	**hicieras**	**haz** tú (no **hagas**)
	Participles:	hace	hacía	**hizo**	**hará**	**haría**	**haga**	**hiciera**	**haga** Ud.
	haciendo	hacemos	hacíamos	**hicimos**	**haremos**	**haríamos**	**hagamos**	**hiciéramos**	**hagamos**
	hecho	hacéis	hacíais	**hicisteis**	**haréis**	**haríais**	**hagáis**	**hicierais**	haced (no **hagáis**)
		hacen	hacían	**hicieron**	**harán**	**harían**	**hagan**	**hicieran**	**hagan** Uds.
12	ir	**voy**	**iba**	**fui**	iré	iría	**vaya**	**fuera**	
		vas	**ibas**	**fuiste**	irás	irías	**vayas**	**fueras**	**ve** tú (no **vayas**)
	Participles:	**va**	**iba**	**fue**	irá	iría	**vaya**	**fuera**	**vaya** Ud.
	yendo	**vamos**	**íbamos**	**fuimos**	iremos	iríamos	**vayamos**	**fuéramos**	**vamos**
	ido	**vais**	**ibais**	**fuisteis**	iréis	iríais	**vayáis**	**fuerais**	id (no **vayáis**)
		van	**iban**	**fueron**	irán	irían	**vayan**	**fueran**	**vayan** Uds.
13	oír (y)	**oigo**	oía	**oí**	oiré	oiría	**oiga**	**oyera**	
		oyes	oías	**oíste**	oirás	oirías	**oigas**	**oyeras**	**oye** tú (no **oigas**)
	Participles:	**oye**	oía	**oyó**	oirá	oiría	**oiga**	**oyera**	**oiga** Ud.
	oyendo	**oímos**	oíamos	**oímos**	oiremos	oiríamos	**oigamos**	**oyéramos**	**oigamos**
	oído	**oís**	oíais	**oísteis**	oiréis	oiríais	**oigáis**	**oyerais**	oíd (no **oigáis**)
		oyen	oían	**oyeron**	oirán	oirían	**oigan**	**oyeran**	**oigan** Uds.

	Infinitive	INDICATIVE					SUBJUNCTIVE		IMPERATIVE
		Present	Imperfect	Preterite	Future	Conditional	Present	Past	
14	poder (o:ue) **Participles:** **pudiendo** podido	**puedo** **puedes** **puede** podemos podéis **pueden**	podía podías podía podíamos podíais podían	**pude** **pudiste** **pudo** **pudimos** **pudisteis** **pudieron**	**podré** **podrás** **podrá** **podremos** **podréis** **podrán**	**podría** **podrías** **podría** **podríamos** **podríais** **podrían**	**pueda** **puedas** **pueda** podamos podáis **puedan**	**pudiera** **pudieras** **pudiera** **pudiéramos** **pudierais** **pudieran**	**puede** tú (no **puedas**) **pueda** Ud. podamos poded (no podáis) **puedan** Uds.
15	poner **Participles:** poniendo **puesto**	**pongo** pones pone ponemos ponéis ponen	ponía ponías ponía poníamos poníais ponían	**puse** **pusiste** **puso** **pusimos** **pusisteis** **pusieron**	**pondré** **pondrás** **pondrá** **pondremos** **pondréis** **pondrán**	**pondría** **pondrías** **pondría** **pondríamos** **pondríais** **pondrían**	**ponga** **pongas** **ponga** **pongamos** **pongáis** **pongan**	**pusiera** **pusieras** **pusiera** **pusiéramos** **pusierais** **pusieran**	**pon** tú (no **pongas**) **ponga** Ud. **pongamos** poned (no **pongáis**) **pongan** Uds.
16	querer (e:ie) **Participles:** queriendo querido	**quiero** **quieres** **quiere** queremos queréis **quieren**	quería querías quería queríamos queríais querían	**quise** **quisiste** **quiso** **quisimos** **quisisteis** **quisieron**	**querré** **querrás** **querrá** **querremos** **querréis** **querrán**	**querría** **querrías** **querría** **querríamos** **querríais** **querrían**	**quiera** **quieras** **quiera** queramos queráis **quieran**	**quisiera** **quisieras** **quisiera** **quisiéramos** **quisierais** **quisieran**	**quiere** tú (no **quieras**) **quiera** Ud. **queramos** quered (no queráis) **quieran** Uds.
17	saber **Participles:** sabiendo sabido	**sé** sabes sabe sabemos sabéis saben	sabía sabías sabía sabíamos sabíais sabían	**supe** **supiste** **supo** **supimos** **supisteis** **supieron**	**sabré** **sabrás** **sabrá** **sabremos** **sabréis** **sabrán**	**sabría** **sabrías** **sabría** **sabríamos** **sabríais** **sabrían**	**sepa** **sepas** **sepa** **sepamos** **sepáis** **sepan**	**supiera** **supieras** **supiera** **supiéramos** **supierais** **supieran**	sabe tú (no **sepas**) **sepa** Ud. **sepamos** sabed (no **sepáis**) **sepan** Uds.
18	salir **Participles:** saliendo salido	**salgo** sales sale salimos salís salen	salía salías salía salíamos salíais salían	salí saliste salió salimos salisteis salieron	**saldré** **saldrás** **saldrá** **saldremos** **saldréis** **saldrán**	**saldría** **saldrías** **saldría** **saldríamos** **saldríais** **saldrían**	**salga** **salgas** **salga** **salgamos** **salgáis** **salgan**	saliera salieras saliera saliéramos salierais salieran	**sal** tú (no **salgas**) **salga** Ud. **salgamos** salid (no **salgáis**) **salgan** Uds.
19	ser **Participles:** siendo sido	**soy** **eres** **es** **somos** **sois** **son**	**era** **eras** **era** **éramos** **erais** **eran**	**fui** **fuiste** **fue** **fuimos** **fuisteis** **fueron**	seré serás será seremos seréis serán	sería serías sería seríamos seríais serían	**sea** **seas** **sea** **seamos** **seáis** **sean**	**fuera** **fueras** **fuera** **fuéramos** **fuerais** **fueran**	**sé** tú (no **seas**) **sea** Ud. **seamos** sed (no **seáis**) **sean** Uds.
20	tener (e:ie) **Participles:** teniendo tenido	**tengo** **tienes** **tiene** tenemos tenéis **tienen**	**tenía** **tenías** **tenía** **teníamos** **teníais** **tenían**	**tuve** **tuviste** **tuvo** **tuvimos** **tuvisteis** **tuvieron**	**tendré** **tendrás** **tendrá** **tendremos** **tendréis** **tendrán**	**tendría** **tendrías** **tendría** **tendríamos** **tendríais** **tendrían**	**tenga** **tengas** **tenga** **tengamos** **tengáis** **tengan**	**tuviera** **tuvieras** **tuviera** **tuviéramos** **tuvierais** **tuvieran**	**ten** tú (no **tengas**) **tenga** Ud. **tengamos** tened (no **tengáis**) **tengan** Uds.

	Infinitive	INDICATIVE Present	Imperfect	Preterite	Future	Conditional	SUBJUNCTIVE Present	Past	IMPERATIVE
21	traer	**traigo**	traía	**traje**	traeré	traería	**traiga**	**trajera**	
		traes	traías	**trajiste**	traerás	traerías	**traigas**	**trajeras**	trae tú (no **traigas**)
	Participles:	trae	traía	**trajo**	traerá	traería	**traiga**	**trajera**	**traiga** Ud.
	trayendo	traemos	traíamos	**trajimos**	traeremos	traeríamos	**traigamos**	**trajéramos**	**traigamos**
	traído	traéis	traíais	**trajisteis**	traeréis	traeríais	**traigáis**	**trajerais**	traed (no **traigáis**)
		traen	traían	**trajeron**	traerán	traerían	**traigan**	**trajeran**	**traigan** Uds.
22	venir (e:ie)	**vengo**	venía	**vine**	**vendré**	**vendría**	**venga**	**viniera**	
		vienes	venías	**viniste**	**vendrás**	**vendrías**	**vengas**	**vinieras**	**ven** tú (no **vengas**)
	Participles:	**viene**	venía	**vino**	**vendrá**	**vendría**	**venga**	**viniera**	**venga** Ud.
	viniendo	venimos	veníamos	**vinimos**	**vendremos**	**vendríamos**	**vengamos**	**viniéramos**	**vengamos**
	venido	venís	veníais	**vinisteis**	**vendréis**	**vendríais**	**vengáis**	**vinierais**	venid (no **vengáis**)
		vienen	venían	**vinieron**	**vendrán**	**vendrían**	**vengan**	**vinieran**	**vengan** Uds.
23	ver	**veo**	**veía**	**vi**	veré	vería	**vea**	**viera**	
		ves	**veías**	**viste**	verás	verías	**veas**	**vieras**	**ve** tú (no **veas**)
	Participles:	ve	**veía**	**vio**	verá	vería	**vea**	**viera**	**vea** Ud.
	viendo	vemos	**veíamos**	**vimos**	veremos	veríamos	**veamos**	**viéramos**	**veamos**
	visto	veis	**veíais**	**visteis**	veréis	veríais	**veáis**	**vierais**	ved (no **veáis**)
		ven	**veían**	**vieron**	verán	verían	**vean**	**vieran**	**vean** Uds.

Stem-changing verbs

	Infinitive	INDICATIVE Present	Imperfect	Preterite	Future	Conditional	SUBJUNCTIVE Present	Past	IMPERATIVE
24	contar (o:ue)	**cuento**	contaba	conté	contaré	contaría	**cuente**	contara	
		cuentas	contabas	contaste	contarás	contarías	**cuentes**	contaras	**cuenta** tú (no **cuentes**)
	Participles:	**cuenta**	contaba	contó	contará	contaría	**cuente**	contara	**cuente** Ud.
	contando	contamos	contábamos	contamos	contaremos	contaríamos	contemos	contáramos	contemos
	contado	contáis	contabais	contasteis	contaréis	contaríais	contéis	contarais	contad (no contéis)
		cuentan	contaban	contaron	contarán	contarían	**cuenten**	contaran	**cuenten** Uds.
25	dormir (o:ue)	**duermo**	dormía	dormí	dormiré	dormiría	**duerma**	**durmiera**	
		duermes	dormías	dormiste	dormirás	dormirías	**duermas**	**durmieras**	**duerme** tú (no **duermas**)
	Participles:	**duerme**	dormía	**durmió**	dormirá	dormiría	**duerma**	**durmiera**	**duerma** Ud.
	durmiendo	dormimos	dormíamos	dormimos	dormiremos	dormiríamos	**durmamos**	**durmiéramos**	**durmamos**
	dormido	dormís	dormíais	dormisteis	dormiréis	dormiríais	**durmáis**	**durmierais**	dormid (no **durmáis**)
		duermen	dormían	**durmieron**	dormirán	dormirían	**duerman**	**durmieran**	**duerman** Uds.
26	empezar (e:ie) (z:c)	**empiezo**	empezaba	**empecé**	empezaré	empezaría	**empiece**	empezara	
		empiezas	empezabas	empezaste	empezarás	empezarías	**empieces**	empezaras	**empieza** tú (no **empieces**)
		empieza	empezaba	empezó	empezará	empezaría	**empiece**	empezara	**empiece** Ud.
	Participles:	empezamos	empezábamos	empezamos	empezaremos	empezaríamos	**empecemos**	empezáramos	**empecemos**
	empezando	empezáis	empezabais	empezasteis	empezaréis	empezaríais	**empecéis**	empezarais	empezad (no **empecéis**)
	empezado	**empiezan**	empezaban	empezaron	empezarán	empezarían	**empiecen**	empezaran	**empiecen** Uds.

	Infinitive	INDICATIVE					SUBJUNCTIVE		IMPERATIVE
		Present	Imperfect	Preterite	Future	Conditional	Present	Past	
27	entender (e:ie) **Participles:** entendiendo entendido	**entiendo** **entiendes** **entiende** entendemos entendéis **entienden**	entendía entendías entendía entendíamos entendíais entendían	entendí entendiste entendió entendimos entendisteis entendieron	entenderé entenderás entenderá entenderemos entenderéis entenderán	entendería entenderías entendería entenderíamos entenderíais entenderían	**entienda** **entiendas** **entienda** entendamos entendáis **entiendan**	entendiera entendieras entendiera entendiéramos entendierais entendieran	**entiende** tú (no **entiendas**) **entienda** Ud. entendamos entended (no entendáis) **entiendan** Uds.
28	jugar (u:ue) (g:gu) **Participles:** jugando jugado	**juego** **juegas** **juega** jugamos jugáis **juegan**	jugaba jugabas jugaba jugábamos jugabais jugaban	**jugué** jugaste jugó jugamos jugasteis jugaron	jugaré jugarás jugará jugaremos jugaréis jugarán	jugaría jugarías jugaría jugaríamos jugaríais jugarían	**juegue** **juegues** **juegue** juguemos juguéis **jueguen**	jugara jugaras jugara jugáramos jugarais jugaran	**juega** tú (no **juegues**) **juegue** Ud. juguemos jugad (no juguéis) **jueguen** Uds.
29	pedir (e:i) **Participles:** **pidiendo** pedido	**pido** **pides** **pide** pedimos pedís **piden**	pedía pedías pedía pedíamos pedíais pedían	pedí pediste **pidió** pedimos pedisteis **pidieron**	pediré pedirás pedirá pediremos pediréis pedirán	pediría pedirías pediría pediríamos pediríais pedirían	**pida** **pidas** **pida** **pidamos** **pidáis** **pidan**	**pidiera** **pidieras** **pidiera** **pidiéramos** **pidierais** **pidieran**	**pide** tú (no **pidas**) **pida** Ud. **pidamos** pedid (no **pidáis**) **pidan** Uds.
30	pensar (e:ie) **Participles:** pensando pensado	**pienso** **piensas** **piensa** pensamos pensáis **piensan**	pensaba pensabas pensaba pensábamos pensabais pensaban	pensé pensaste pensó pensamos pensasteis pensaron	pensaré pensarás pensará pensaremos pensaréis pensarán	pensaría pensarías pensaría pensaríamos pensaríais pensarían	**piense** **pienses** **piense** pensemos penséis **piensen**	pensara pensaras pensara pensáramos pensarais pensaran	**piensa** tú (no **pienses**) **piense** Ud. pensemos pensad (no penséis) **piensen** Uds.
31	reír(se) (e:i) **Participles:** **riendo** **reído**	**río** **ríes** **ríe** **reímos** **reís** **ríen**	reía reías reía reíamos reíais reían	**reí** **reíste** **rió** **reímos** **reísteis** **rieron**	reiré reirás reirá reiremos reiréis reirán	reiría reirías reiría reiríamos reiríais reirían	**ría** **rías** **ría** **riamos** **riáis** **rían**	**riera** **rieras** **riera** **riéramos** **rierais** **rieran**	**ríe** tú (no **rías**) **ría** Ud. **riamos** reíd (no **riáis**) **rían** Uds.
32	seguir (e:i) (gu:g) **Participles:** **siguiendo** seguido	**sigo** **sigues** **sigue** seguimos seguís **siguen**	seguía seguías seguía seguíamos seguíais seguían	seguí seguiste **siguió** seguimos seguisteis **siguieron**	seguiré seguirás seguirá seguiremos seguiréis seguirán	seguiría seguirías seguiría seguiríamos seguiríais seguirían	**siga** **sigas** **siga** **sigamos** **sigáis** **sigan**	**siguiera** **siguieras** **siguiera** **siguiéramos** **siguierais** **siguieran**	**sigue** tú (no **sigas**) **siga** Ud. **sigamos** seguid (no **sigáis**) **sigan** Uds.
33	sentir (e:ie) **Participles:** **sintiendo** sentido	**siento** **sientes** **siente** sentimos sentís **sienten**	sentía sentías sentía sentíamos sentíais sentían	sentí sentiste **sintió** sentimos sentisteis **sintieron**	sentiré sentirás sentirá sentiremos sentiréis sentirán	sentiría sentirías sentiría sentiríamos sentiríais sentirían	**sienta** **sientas** **sienta** **sintamos** **sintáis** **sientan**	**sintiera** **sintieras** **sintiera** **sintiéramos** **sintierais** **sintieran**	**siente** tú (no **sientas**) **sienta** Ud. **sintamos** sentid (no **sintáis**) **sientan** Uds.

	Infinitive	INDICATIVE Present	Imperfect	Preterite	Future	Conditional	SUBJUNCTIVE Present	Past	IMPERATIVE
34	volver (o:ue)	**vuelvo**	volvía	volví	volveré	volvería	**vuelva**	volviera	
		vuelves	volvías	volviste	volverás	volverías	**vuelvas**	volvieras	**vuelve** tú (no **vuelvas**)
	Participles:	**vuelve**	volvía	volvió	volverá	volvería	**vuelva**	volviera	**vuelva** Ud.
	volviendo	volvemos	volvíamos	volvimos	volveremos	volveríamos	volvamos	volviéramos	volvamos
	vuelto	volvéis	volvíais	volvisteis	volveréis	volveríais	volváis	volvierais	volved (no volváis)
		vuelven	volvían	volvieron	volverán	volverían	**vuelvan**	volvieran	**vuelvan** Uds.

Verbs with spelling changes only

	Infinitive	INDICATIVE Present	Imperfect	Preterite	Future	Conditional	SUBJUNCTIVE Present	Past	IMPERATIVE
35	conocer	**conozco**	conocía	conocí	conoceré	conocería	**conozca**	conociera	
	(c:zc)	conoces	conocías	conociste	conocerás	conocerías	**conozcas**	conocieras	conoce tú (no **conozcas**)
		conoce	conocía	conoció	conocerá	conocería	**conozca**	conociera	**conozca** Ud.
	Participles:	conocemos	conocíamos	conocimos	conoceremos	conoceríamos	**conozcamos**	conociéramos	**conozcamos**
	conociendo	conocéis	conocíais	conocisteis	conoceréis	conoceríais	**conozcáis**	conocierais	conoced (no **conozcáis**)
	conocido	conocen	conocían	conocieron	conocerán	conocerían	**conozcan**	conocieran	**conozcan** Uds.
36	creer (y)	creo	creía	**creí**	creeré	creería	crea	**creyera**	
		crees	creías	**creíste**	creerás	creerías	creas	**creyeras**	cree tú (no creas)
	Participles:	cree	creía	**creyó**	creerá	creería	crea	**creyera**	crea Ud.
	creyendo	creemos	creíamos	**creímos**	creeremos	creeríamos	creamos	**creyéramos**	creamos
	creído	creéis	creíais	**creísteis**	creeréis	creeríais	creáis	**creyerais**	creed (no creáis)
		creen	creían	**creyeron**	creerán	creerían	crean	**creyeran**	crean Uds.
37	cruzar (z:c)	cruzo	cruzaba	**crucé**	cruzaré	cruzaría	**cruce**	cruzara	
		cruzas	cruzabas	cruzaste	cruzarás	cruzarías	**cruces**	cruzaras	cruza tú (no **cruces**)
	Participles:	cruza	cruzaba	cruzó	cruzará	cruzaría	**cruce**	cruzara	**cruce** Ud.
	cruzando	cruzamos	cruzábamos	cruzamos	cruzaremos	cruzaríamos	**crucemos**	cruzáramos	**crucemos**
	cruzado	cruzáis	cruzabais	cruzasteis	cruzaréis	cruzaríais	**crucéis**	cruzarais	cruzad (no **crucéis**)
		cruzan	cruzaban	cruzaron	cruzarán	cruzarían	**crucen**	cruzaran	**crucen** Uds.
38	destruir (y)	**destruyo**	destruía	destruí	destruiré	destruiría	**destruya**	**destruyera**	
		destruyes	destruías	destruiste	destruirás	destruirías	**destruyas**	**destruyeras**	**destruye** tú (no **destruyas**)
	Participles:	**destruye**	destruía	**destruyó**	destruirá	destruiría	**destruya**	**destruyera**	**destruya** Ud.
	destruyendo	destruimos	destruíamos	destruimos	destruiremos	destruiríamos	**destruyamos**	**destruyéramos**	**destruyamos**
	destruido	destruís	destruíais	destruisteis	destruiréis	destruiríais	**destruyáis**	**destruyerais**	destruid (no **destruyáis**)
		destruyen	destruían	**destruyeron**	destruirán	destruirían	**destruyan**	**destruyeran**	**destruyan** Uds.
39	enviar	**envío**	enviaba	envié	enviaré	enviaría	**envíe**	enviara	
	(envío)	**envías**	enviabas	enviaste	enviarás	enviarías	**envíes**	enviaras	**envía** tú (no **envíes**)
		envía	enviaba	envió	enviará	enviaría	**envíe**	enviara	**envíe** Ud.
	Participles:	enviamos	enviábamos	enviamos	enviaremos	enviaríamos	**enviemos**	enviáramos	enviemos
	enviando	enviáis	enviabais	enviasteis	enviaréis	enviaríais	**enviéis**	enviarais	enviad (no **enviéis**)
	enviado	**envían**	enviaban	enviaron	enviarán	enviarían	**envíen**	enviaran	**envíen** Uds.

	Infinitive	INDICATIVE Present	Imperfect	Preterite	Future	Conditional	SUBJUNCTIVE Present	Past	IMPERATIVE
40	graduarse	**gradúo**	graduaba	gradué	graduaré	graduaría	**gradúe**	graduara	
	(gradúo)	**gradúas**	graduabas	graduaste	graduarás	graduarías	**gradúes**	graduaras	**gradúa** tú (no **gradúes**)
		gradúa	graduaba	graduó	graduará	graduaría	**gradúe**	graduara	**gradúe** Ud.
	Participles:	graduamos	graduábamos	graduamos	graduaremos	graduaríamos	graduemos	graduáramos	graduemos
	graduando	graduáis	graduabais	graduasteis	graduaréis	graduaríais	graduéis	graduarais	graduad (no graduéis)
	graduado	**gradúan**	graduaban	graduaron	graduarán	graduarían	**gradúen**	graduaran	**gradúen** Uds.
41	llegar (g:gu)	llego	llegaba	**llegué**	llegaré	llegaría	**llegue**	llegara	
		llegas	llegabas	llegaste	llegarás	llegarías	**llegues**	llegaras	llega tú (no **llegues**)
	Participles:	llega	llegaba	llegó	llegará	llegaría	**llegue**	llegara	**llegue** Ud.
	llegando	llegamos	llegábamos	llegamos	llegaremos	llegaríamos	**lleguemos**	llegáramos	**lleguemos**
	llegado	llegáis	llegabais	llegasteis	llegaréis	llegaríais	**lleguéis**	llegarais	llegad (no **lleguéis**)
		llegan	llegaban	llegaron	llegarán	llegarían	**lleguen**	llegaran	**lleguen** Uds.
42	proteger (g:j)	**protejo**	protegía	protegí	protegeré	protegería	**proteja**	protegiera	
		proteges	protegías	protegiste	protegerás	protegerías	**protejas**	protegieras	protege tú (no **protejas**)
	Participles:	protege	protegía	protegió	protegerá	protegería	**proteja**	protegiera	**proteja** Ud.
	protegiendo	protegemos	protegíamos	protegimos	protegeremos	protegeríamos	**protejamos**	protegiéramos	**protejamos**
	protegido	protegéis	protegíais	protegisteis	protegeréis	protegeríais	**protejáis**	protegierais	proteged (no **protejáis**)
		protegen	protegían	protegieron	protegerán	protegerían	**protejan**	protegieran	**protejan** Uds.
43	tocar (c:qu)	toco	tocaba	**toqué**	tocaré	tocaría	**toque**	tocara	
		tocas	tocabas	tocaste	tocarás	tocarías	**toques**	tocaras	toca tú (no **toques**)
	Participles:	toca	tocaba	tocó	tocará	tocaría	**toque**	tocara	**toque** Ud.
	tocando	tocamos	tocábamos	tocamos	tocaremos	tocaríamos	**toquemos**	tocáramos	**toquemos**
	tocado	tocáis	tocabais	tocasteis	tocaréis	tocaríais	**toquéis**	tocarais	tocad (no **toquéis**)
		tocan	tocaban	tocaron	tocarán	tocarían	**toquen**	tocaran	**toquen** Uds.

Guide to Vocabulary

Note on alphabetization

For purposes of alphabetization, **ch** and **ll** are not treated as separate letters, but **ñ** follows **n**. Therefore, in this glossary you will find that **año**, for example, appears after **anuncio**.

Abbreviations used in this glossary

adj.	adjective	*form.*	formal	*pl.*	plural
adv.	adverb	*indef.*	indefinite	*poss.*	possessive
art.	article	*interj.*	interjection	*prep.*	preposition
conj.	conjunction	*i.o.*	indirect object	*pron.*	pronoun
def.	definite	*m.*	masculine	*ref.*	reflexive
d.o.	direct object	*n.*	noun	*sing.*	singular
f.	feminine	*obj.*	object	*sub.*	subject
fam.	familiar	*p.p.*	past participle	*v.*	verb

Spanish-English

A

a *prep.* at; to 1
  ¿A qué hora...? At what time...? 1
  a bordo aboard 1
  a dieta on a diet 15
  a la derecha to the right 2
  a la izquierda to the left 2
  a la plancha grilled 8
  a la(s) + *time* at + *time* 1
  a menos que unless 13
  a menudo *adv.* often 10
  a nombre de in the name of 5
  a plazos in installments 14
  A sus órdenes. At your service. 11
  a tiempo *adv.* on time 10
  a veces *adv.* sometimes 10
  a ver let's see
¡Abajo! *adv.* Down! 15
abeja *f.* bee
abierto/a *adj.* open 5, 14
abogado/a *m., f.* lawyer 16
abrazar(se) *v.* to hug; to embrace (each other) 11
abrazo *m.* hug
abrigo *m.* coat 6
abril *m.* April 5
abrir *v.* to open 3
abuelo/a *m., f.* grandfather; grandmother 3
abuelos *pl.* grandparents 3
aburrido/a *adj.* bored; boring 5
aburrir *v.* to bore 7
aburrirse *v.* to get bored 17
acabar de (+ ***inf.*****)** *v.* to have just done something 6
acampar *v.* to camp 5
accidente *m.* accident 10
acción *f.* action 17
  de acción action (genre) 17
aceite *m.* oil 8
aceptar: ¡Acepto casarme contigo! I'll marry you! 17
ácido/a *adj.* acid 13
acompañar *v.* to accompany 14
aconsejar *v.* to advise 12
acontecimiento *m.* event 18
acordarse (de) (o:ue) *v.* to remember 7
acostarse (o:ue) *v.* to go to bed 7
activo/a *adj.* active 15
actor *m.* actor 16
actriz *f.* actor 16
actualidades *f., pl.* news; current events 18
acuático/a *adj.* aquatic 4
adelgazar *v.* to lose weight; to slim down 15
además (de) *adv.* furthermore; besides 10
adicional *adj.* additional
adiós *m.* good-bye 1
adjetivo *m.* adjective
administración de empresas *f.* business administration 2
adolescencia *f.* adolescence 9
¿adónde? *adv.* where (to)? (destination) 2
aduana *f.* customs 5
aeróbico/a *adj.* aerobic 15
aeropuerto *m.* airport 5
afectado/a *adj.* affected 13
afeitarse *v.* to shave 7
aficionado/a *adj.* fan 4
afirmativo/a *adj.* affirmative
afuera *adv.* outside 5
afueras *f., pl.* suburbs; outskirts 12
agencia de viajes *f.* travel agency 5
agente de viajes *m., f.* travel agent 5
agosto *m.* August 5
agradable *adj.* pleasant 5
agua *f.* water 8
  agua mineral mineral water 8
aguantar *v.* to endure, to hold up 14
ahora *adv.* now 2
  ahora mismo right now 5
ahorrar *v.* to save (money) 14
ahorros *m.* savings 14
aire *m.* air 5
ajo *m.* garlic 8
al (*contraction of* **a + el)** 2
  al aire libre open-air 6
  al contado in cash 14
  (al) este (to the) east 14
  al fondo (de) at the end (of) 12
  al lado de beside 2
  (al) norte (to the) north 14
  (al) oeste (to the) west 14
  (al) sur (to the) south 14
alcoba *f.* bedroom 12
alcohol *m.* alcohol 15
alcohólico/a *adj.* alcoholic 15
alegrarse (de) *v.* to be happy 13
alegre *adj.* happy; joyful 5
alegría *f.* happiness 9
alemán, alemana *adj.* German 3
alérgico/a *adj.* allergic 10
alfombra *f.* carpet; rug 12
algo *pron.* something; anything 7
algodón *m.* cotton 6
alguien *pron.* someone; somebody; anyone 7
algún, alguno/a(s) *adj.* any; some 7
alimento *m.* food
  alimentación *f.* diet
aliviar *v.* to reduce 15
  aliviar el estrés/la tensión to reduce stress/tension 15
allá *adv.* over there 2
allí *adv.* there 2
  allí mismo right there 14
alma *f.* soul 9
almacén *m.* department store 6

almohada *f.* pillow 12
almorzar (o:ue) *v.* to have lunch 4
almuerzo *m.* lunch 4, 8
aló *interj.* hello (*on the telephone*) 11
alquilar *v.* to rent 12
alquiler *m.* rent (payment) 12
altar *m.* altar 9
altillo *m.* attic 12
alto/a *adj.* tall 3
aluminio *m.* aluminum 13
ama de casa *m., f.* housekeeper; caretaker 12
amable *adj.* nice; friendly 5
amarillo/a *adj.* yellow 6
amigo/a *m., f.* friend 3
amistad *f.* friendship 9
amor *m.* love 9
  amor a primera vista love at first sight 9
anaranjado/a *adj.* orange 6
ándale *interj.* come on 14
andar *v.* **en patineta** to skateboard 4
ángel *m.* angel 9
anillo *m.* ring 17
animal *m.* animal 13
aniversario (de bodas) *m.* (wedding) anniversary 9
anoche *adv.* last night 6
anteayer *adv.* the day before yesterday 6
antes *adv.* before 7
  antes (de) que *conj.* before 13
  antes de *prep.* before 7
antibiótico *m.* antibiotic 10
antipático/a *adj.* unpleasant 3
anunciar *v.* to announce; to advertise 18
anuncio *m.* advertisement 16
año *m.* year 5
  año pasado last year 6
apagar *v.* to turn off 11
aparato *m.* appliance
apartamento *m.* apartment 12
apellido *m.* last name 3
apenas *adv.* hardly; scarcely 10
aplaudir *v.* to applaud 17
apreciar *v.* to appreciate 17
aprender (a + *inf.*) *v.* to learn 3
apurarse *v.* to hurry; to rush 15
aquel, aquella *adj.* that; those (over there) 6
aquél, aquélla *pron.* that; those (over there) 6
aquello *neuter, pron.* that; that thing; that fact 6
aquellos/as *pl. adj.* those (over there) 6
aquéllos/as *pl. pron.* those (ones) (over there) 6
aquí *adv.* here 1
  Aquí está(n)... Here is/are... 5
  aquí mismo right here 11
árbol *m.* tree 13
archivo *m.* file 11
arete *m.* earing 6
Argentina *f.* Argentina 1
argentino/a *adj.* Argentine 3
armario *m.* closet 12
arqueología *f.* archaeology 2
arqueólogo/a *m., f.* archaeologist 16
arquitecto/a *m., f.* architect 16
arrancar *v.* to start (*a car*) 11
arreglar *v.* to fix; to arrange 11; to neaten; to straighten up 12
arreglarse *v.* to get ready 7; to fix oneself (*clothes, hair, etc. to go out*) 7
arriba: hasta arriba to the top 15
arroba *f.* @ symbol 11
arroz *m.* rice 8
arte *m.* art 2
artes *f., pl.* arts 17
artesanía *f.* craftsmanship; crafts 17
artículo *m.* article 18
artista *m., f.* artist 3
artístico/a *adj.* artistic 17
arveja *m.* pea 8
asado/a *adj.* roast 8
ascenso *m.* promotion 16
ascensor *m.* elevator 5
así *adv.* like this; so (*in such a way*) 10
asistir (a) *v.* to attend 3
aspiradora *f.* vacuum cleaner 12
aspirante *m., f.* candidate; applicant 16
aspirina *f.* aspirin 10
atún *m.* tuna 8
aumentar *v.* to grow; to get bigger 13
aumentar *v.* **de peso** to gain weight 15
aumento *m.* increase 16
  aumento de sueldo pay raise 16
aunque although
autobús *m.* bus 1
automático/a *adj.* automatic
auto(móvil) *m.* auto(mobile) 5
autopista *f.* highway 11
ave *f.* bird 13
avenida *f.* avenue
aventura *f.* adventure 17
  de aventura adventure (genre) 17
avergonzado/a *adj.* embarrassed 5
avión *m.* airplane 5
¡Ay! *interj.* Oh!
  ¡Ay, qué dolor! Oh, what pain!
ayer *adv.* yesterday 6
ayudar(se) *v.* to help (each other) 11, 12
azúcar *m.* sugar 8
azul *adj. m., f.* blue 6

B

bailar *v.* to dance 2
bailarín/bailarina *m., f.* dancer 17
baile *m.* dance 17
bajar(se) de *v.* to get off of/out of (a vehicle) 11
bajo/a *adj.* short (*in height*) 3
bajo control under control 7
balcón *m.* balcony 12
balde *m.* bucket 5
ballena *f.* whale 13
baloncesto *m.* basketball 4
banana *f.* banana 8
banco *m.* bank 14
banda *f.* band 17
bandera *f.* flag
bañarse *v.* to bathe; to take a bath 7
baño *m.* bathroom 7
barato/a *adj.* cheap 6
barco *m.* boat 5
barrer *v.* to sweep 12
  barrer el suelo *v.* to sweep the floor 12
barrio *m.* neighborhood 12
bastante *adv.* enough; rather 10; pretty 13
basura *f.* trash 12
baúl *m.* trunk 11
beber *v.* to drink 3
bebida *f.* drink 8
  bebida alcohólica *f.* alcoholic beverage 15
béisbol *m.* baseball 4
bellas artes *f., pl.* fine arts 17
belleza *f.* beauty 14
beneficio *m.* benefit 16
besar(se) *v.* to kiss (each other) 11
beso *m.* kiss 9
biblioteca *f.* library 2
bicicleta *f.* bicycle 4
bien *adj.* well 1
bienestar *m.* well-being 15
bienvenido(s)/a(s) *adj.* welcome 12
billete *m.* paper money; ticket
billón *m.* trillion
biología *f.* biology 2
bisabuelo/a *m., f.* great-grandfather/great-grandmother 3
bistec *m.* steak 8
bizcocho *m.* biscuit
blanco/a *adj.* white 6
blog *m.* blog 11
(blue)jeans *m., pl.* jeans 6
blusa *f.* blouse 6
boca *f.* mouth 10
boda *f.* wedding 9
boleto *m.* ticket 2, 17
bolsa *f.* purse, bag 6
bombero/a *m., f.* firefighter 16
bonito/a *adj.* pretty 3
borrador *m.* eraser 2
borrar *v.* to erase 11

bosque *m.* forest 13
bosque tropical tropical forest; rainforest 13
bota *f.* boot 6
botella *f.* bottle 9
botella de vino bottle of wine 9
botones *m., f. sing.* bellhop 5
brazo *m.* arm 10
brindar *v.* to toast (*drink*) 9
bucear *v.* to scuba dive 4
bueno *adv.* well
buen, bueno/a *adj.* good 3, 6
buena forma good shape (*physical*) 15
Buena idea. Good idea.
Buenas noches. Good evening; Good night. 1
Buenas tardes. Good afternoon. 1
buenísimo/a extremely good
Bueno. Hello. (*on telephone*) 11
Buenos días. Good morning. 1
bulevar *m.* boulevard
buscar *v.* to look for 2
buzón *m.* mailbox 14

C

caballero *m.* gentleman, sir 8
caballo *m.* horse 5
cabe: no cabe duda de there's no doubt 13
cabeza *f.* head 10
cada *adj. m., f.* each 6
caerse *v.* to fall (down) 10
café *m.* café 4; *adj. m., f.* brown 6; *m.* coffee 8
cafeína *f.* caffeine 14
cafetera *f.* coffee maker 12
cafetería *f.* cafeteria 2
caído/a *p.p.* fallen 14
caja *f.* cash register 6
cajero/a *m., f.* cashier 14
cajero automático *m.* ATM 14
calavera de azúcar *f.* skull made out of sugar 9
calcetín (calcetines) *m.* sock(s) 6
calculadora *f.* calculator 2
caldo *m.* soup
calentamiento global *m.* global warming 13
calentarse (e:ie) *v.* to warm up 15
calidad *f.* quality 6
calle *f.* street 11
calor *m.* heat 4
caloría *f.* calorie 15
calzar *v.* to take size... shoes 6
cama *f.* bed 5
cámara digital *f.* digital camera 11
cámara de video *f.* video camera 11
camarero/a *m., f.* waiter/ waitress 8
camarón *m.* shrimp 8
cambiar (de) *v.* to change 9
cambio: de cambio in change 2
cambio *m.* **climático** climate change 13
cambio *m.* **de moneda** currency exchange
caminar *v.* to walk 2
camino *m.* road
camión *m.* truck; bus
camisa *f.* shirt 6
camiseta *f.* t-shirt 6
campo *m.* countryside 5
canadiense *adj.* Canadian 3
canal *m.* (TV) channel 11; 17
canción *f.* song 17
candidato/a *m., f.* candidate 18
canela *f.* cinnamon 10
cansado/a *adj.* tired 5
cantante *m., f.* singer 17
cantar *v.* to sing 2
capital *f.* capital city 1
capó *m.* hood 11
cara *f.* face 7
caramelo *m.* caramel 9
carne *f.* meat 8
carne de res *f.* beef 8
carnicería *f.* butcher shop 14
caro/a *adj.* expensive 6
carpintero/a *m., f.* carpenter 16
carrera *f.* career 16
carretera *f.* highway 11
carro *m.* car; automobile 11
carta *f.* letter 4; (*playing*) card 5
cartel *m.* poster 12
cartera *f.* wallet 4, 6
cartero *m.* mail carrier 14
casa *f.* house; home 2
casado/a *adj.* married 9
casarse (con) *v.* to get married (to) 9
casi *adv.* almost 10
catorce *adj.* fourteen 1
cazar *v.* to hunt 13
cebolla *f.* onion 8
cederrón *m.* CD-ROM 11
celebrar *v.* to celebrate 9
cementerio *m.* cemetery 9
cena *f.* dinner 8
cenar *v.* to have dinner 2
centro *m.* downtown 4
centro comercial shopping mall 6
cepillarse los dientes/el pelo *v.* to brush one's teeth/one's hair 7
cerámica *f.* pottery 17
cerca de *prep.* near 2
cerdo *m.* pork 8
cereales *m., pl.* cereal; grains 8
cero *m.* zero 1
cerrado/a *adj.* closed 5, 14
cerrar (e:ie) *v.* to close 4
cerveza *f.* beer 8
césped *m.* grass
ceviche *m.* marinated fish dish 8
ceviche de camarón *m.* lemon-marinated shrimp 8
chaleco *m.* vest
champán *m.* champagne 9
champiñón *m.* mushroom 8
champú *m.* shampoo 7
chaqueta *f.* jacket 6
chau *fam. interj.* bye 1
cheque *m.* (bank) check 14
cheque (de viajero) *m.* (traveler's) check 14
chévere *adj., fam.* terrific
chico/a *m., f.* boy/girl 1
chino/a *adj.* Chinese 3
chocar (con) *v.* to run into
chocolate *m.* chocolate 9
choque *m.* collision 18
chuleta *f.* chop (*food*) 8
chuleta de cerdo *f.* pork chop 8
cibercafé *m.* cybercafé
ciclismo *m.* cycling 4
cielo *m.* sky 13
cien(to) one hundred 2
ciencia *f.* science 2
ciencias ambientales environmental sciences 2
de ciencia ficción *f.* science fiction (genre) 17
científico/a *m., f.* scientist 16
cierto *m.* certain 13
es cierto it's certain 13
no es cierto it's not certain 13
cima *f.* top, peak 15
cinco five 1
cincuenta fifty 2
cine *m.* movie theater 4
cinta *f.* (audio)tape
cinta caminadora *f.* treadmill 15
cinturón *m.* belt 6
circulación *f.* traffic 11
cita *f.* date; appointment 9
ciudad *f.* city 4
ciudadano/a *m., f.* citizen 18
Claro (que sí). *fam.* Of course.
clase *f.* class 2
clase de ejercicios aeróbicos *f.* aerobics class 15
clásico/a *adj.* classical 17
cliente/a *m., f.* customer 6
clínica *f.* clinic 10
cobrar *v.* to cash (a check) 14
coche *m.* car; automobile 11
cocina *f.* kitchen; stove 9, 12
cocinar *v.* to cook 12
cocinero/a *m., f.* cook, chef 16
cofre *m.* hood 14
cola *f.* line 14
colesterol *m.* cholesterol 15
color *m.* color 6
comedia *f.* comedy; play 17
comedor *m.* dining room 12
comenzar (e:ie) *v.* to begin 4
comer *v.* to eat 3
comercial *adj.* commercial; business-related 16
comida *f.* food; meal 4, 8
como like; as 8
¿cómo? what?; how? 1

¿Cómo es...? What's... like? 3
¿Cómo está usted? *form.* How are you? 1
¿Cómo estás? *fam.* How are you? 1
¿Cómo les fue...? *pl.* How did ... go for you? 15
¿Cómo se llama usted? *(form.)* What's your name? 1
¿Cómo te llamas? *fam.* What's your name? 1
cómoda *f.* chest of drawers 12
cómodo/a *adj.* comfortable 5
compañero/a de clase *m., f.* classmate 2
compañero/a de cuarto *m., f.* roommate 2
compañía *f.* company; firm 16
compartir *v.* to share 3
completamente *adv.* completely 5, 16
compositor(a) *m., f.* composer 17
comprar *v.* to buy 2
compras *f., pl.* purchases 5
ir de compras go shopping 5
comprender *v.* to understand 3
comprobar *v.* to check
comprometerse (con) *v.* to get engaged (to) 9
computación *f.* computer science 2
computadora *f.* computer 1
computadora portátil *f.* portable computer; laptop 11
comunicación *f.* communication 18
comunicarse (con) *v.* to communicate (with) 18
comunidad *f.* community 1
con *prep.* with 2
Con él/ella habla. Speaking./ This is he/she. (*on telephone*) 11
con frecuencia *adv.* frequently 10
Con permiso. Pardon me; Excuse me. 1
con tal (de) que provided (that) 13
concierto *m.* concert 17
concordar *v.* to agree
concurso *m.* game show; contest 17
conducir *v.* to drive 6, 11
conductor(a) *m., f.* driver 1
conexión *f.* **inalámbrica** wireless (connection) 11
confirmar *v.* to confirm 5
confirmar *v.* **una reservación** *f.* to confirm a reservation 5
confundido/a *adj.* confused 5
congelador *m.* freezer 12
congestionado/a *adj.* congested; stuffed-up 10
conmigo *pron.* with me 4, 9
conocer *v.* to know; to be acquainted with 6
conocido *adj.; p.p.* known
conseguir (e:i) *v.* to get; to obtain 4
consejero/a *m., f.* counselor; advisor 16
consejo *m.* advice
conservación *f.* conservation 13
conservar *v.* to conserve 13
construir *v.* to build
consultorio *m.* doctor's office 10
consumir *v.* to consume 15
contabilidad *f.* accounting 2
contador(a) *m., f.* accountant 16
contaminación *f.* pollution 13
contaminación del aire/del agua air/water pollution 13
contaminado/a *adj.* polluted 13
contaminar *v.* to pollute 13
contar (o:ue) *v.* to count; to tell 4
contar (con) *v.* to count (on) 12
contento/a *adj.* happy; content 5
contestadora *f.* answering machine 11
contestar *v.* to answer 2
contigo *fam. pron.* with you 5, 9
contratar *v.* to hire 16
control *m.* control 7
control remoto remote control 11
controlar *v.* to control 13
conversación *f.* conversation 1
conversar *v.* to converse, to chat 2
copa *f.* wineglass; goblet 12
corazón *m.* heart 10
corbata *f.* tie 6
corredor(a) *m., f.* **de bolsa** stockbroker 16
correo *m.* mail; post office 14
correo electrónico *m.* e-mail 4
correo de voz *m.* voice mail 11
correr *v.* to run 3
cortesía *f.* courtesy
cortinas *f., pl.* curtains 12
corto/a *adj.* short (*in length*) 6
cosa *f.* thing 1
Costa Rica *f.* Costa Rica 1
costar (o:ue) *f.* to cost 6
costarricense *adj.* Costa Rican 3
cráter *m.* crater 13
creer *v.* to believe 13
creer (en) *v.* to believe (in) 3
no creer (en) *v.* not to believe (in) 13
creído/a *adj., p.p.* believed 14
crema de afeitar *f.* shaving cream 5, 7
crimen *m.* crime; murder 18
cruzar *v.* to cross 14
cuaderno *m.* notebook 1
cuadra *f.* (city) block 14
¿cuál(es)? which?; which one(s)? 2
¿Cuál es la fecha de hoy? What is today's date? 5
cuadro *m.* picture 12
cuadros *m., pl.* plaid 6
cuando when 7; 13
¿cuándo? when? 2
¿cuánto(s)/a(s)? how much/how many? 1
¿Cuánto cuesta...? How much does... cost? 6
¿Cuántos años tienes? How old are you? 3
cuarenta forty 2
cuarto de baño *m.* bathroom 7
cuarto *m.* room 2; 7
cuarto/a *adj.* fourth 5
menos cuarto quarter to (time)
y cuarto quarter after (time) 1
cuatro four 1
cuatrocientos/as four hundred 2
Cuba *f.* Cuba 1
cubano/a *adj.* Cuban 3
cubiertos *m., pl.* silverware
cubierto/a *p.p.* covered
cubrir *v.* to cover
cuchara *f.* (table or large) spoon 12
cuchillo *m.* knife 12
cuello *m.* neck 10
cuenta *f.* bill 8; account 14
cuenta corriente *f.* checking account 14
cuenta de ahorros *f.* savings account 14
cuento *m.* short story 17
cuerpo *m.* body 10
cuidado *m.* care 3
cuidar *v.* to take care of 13
¡Cuídense! Take care! 14
cultura *f.* culture 2, 17
cumpleaños *m., sing.* birthday 9
cumplir años *v.* to have a birthday 9
cuñado/a *m., f.* brother-in-law; sister-in-law 3
currículum *m.* résumé 16
curso *m.* course 2

D

danza *f.* dance 17
dañar *v.* to damage; to break down 10
dar *v.* to give 6, 9
dar un consejo *v.* to give advice
darse con *v.* to bump into; to run into (something) 10
darse prisa *v.* to hurry; to rush 15
de *prep.* of; from 1
¿De dónde eres? *fam.* Where are you from? 1
¿De dónde es usted? *form.* Where are you from? 1
¿De parte de quién? Who is speaking/calling? (*on telephone*) 11
¿de quién...? whose...? (*sing.*) 1
¿de quiénes...? whose...? (*pl.*) 1
de algodón (made) of cotton 6
de aluminio (made) of aluminum 13
de buen humor in a good mood 5
de compras shopping 5
de cuadros plaid 6

de excursión hiking 4
de hecho in fact
de ida y vuelta roundtrip 5
de la mañana in the morning; A.M. 1
de la noche in the evening; at night; P.M. 1
de la tarde in the afternoon; in the early evening; P.M. 1
de lana (made) of wool 6
de lunares polka-dotted 6
de mal humor in a bad mood 5
de mi vida of my life 15
de moda in fashion 6
De nada. You're welcome. 1
de niño/a as a child 10
de parte de on behalf of 11
de plástico (made) of plastic 13
de rayas striped 6
de repente suddenly 6
de seda (made) of silk 6
de vaqueros western (genre) 17
de vez en cuando from time to time 10
de vidrio (made) of glass 13
debajo de *prep.* below; under 2
deber (+ *inf.*) *v.* should; must; ought to 3
Debe ser... It must be... 6
deber *m.* responsibility; obligation 18
debido a due to (the fact that)
débil *adj.* weak 15
decidido/a *adj.* decided 14
decidir (+ *inf.*) *v.* to decide 3
décimo/a *adj.* tenth 5
decir (e:i) *v.* **(que)** to say (that); to tell (that) 4, 9
decir la respuesta to say the answer 4
decir la verdad to tell the truth 4
decir mentiras to tell lies 4
declarar *v.* to declare; to say 18
dedo *m.* finger 10
dedo del pie *m.* toe 10
deforestación *f.* deforestation 13
dejar *v.* to let 12; to quit; to leave behind 16
dejar de (+ *inf.*) *v.* to stop (*doing something*) 13
dejar una propina *v.* to leave a tip 9
del (*contraction of* de + el) of the; from the
delante de *prep.* in front of 2
delgado/a *adj.* thin; slender 3
delicioso/a *adj.* delicious 8
demás *adj.* the rest
demasiado *adj., adv.* too much 6
dentista *m., f.* dentist 10
dentro de (diez años) within (ten years) 16; inside
dependiente/a *m., f.* clerk 6
deporte *m.* sport 4
deportista *m.* sports person
deportivo/a *adj.* sports-related 4
depositar *v.* to deposit 14
derecha *f.* right 2
derecho *adj.* straight (ahead) 14
a la derecha de to the right of 2
derechos *m., pl.* rights 18
desarrollar *v.* to develop 13
desastre (natural) *m.* (natural) disaster 18
desayunar *v.* to have breakfast 2
desayuno *m.* breakfast 8
descafeinado/a *adj.* decaffeinated 15
descansar *v.* to rest 2
descargar *v.* to download 11
descompuesto/a *adj.* not working; out of order 11
describir *v.* to describe 3
descrito/a *p.p.* described 14
descubierto/a *p.p.* discovered 14
descubrir *v.* to discover 13
desde *prep.* from 6
desear *v.* to wish; to desire 2
desempleo *m.* unemployment 18
desierto *m.* desert 13
desigualdad *f.* inequality 18
desordenado/a *adj.* disorderly 5
despacio *adv.* slowly 10
despedida *f.* farewell; good-bye
despedir (e:i) *v.* to fire 16
despedirse (de) (e:i) *v.* to say goodbye (to) 7
despejado/a *adj.* clear (*weather*)
despertador *m.* alarm clock 7
despertarse (e:ie) *v.* to wake up 7
después *adv.* afterwards; then 7
después de after 7
después de que *conj.* after 13
destruir *v.* to destroy 13
detrás de *prep.* behind 2
día *m.* day 1
día de fiesta holiday 9
diario *m.* diary 1; newspaper 18
diario/a *adj.* daily 7
dibujar *v.* to draw 2
dibujo *m.* drawing 17
dibujos animados *m., pl.* cartoons 17
diccionario *m.* dictionary 1
dicho/a *p.p.* said 14
diciembre *m.* December 5
dictadura *f.* dictatorship 18
diecinueve nineteen 1
dieciocho eighteen 1
dieciséis sixteen 1
diecisiete seventeen 1
diente *m.* tooth 7
dieta *f.* diet 15
comer una dieta equilibrada to eat a balanced diet 15
diez ten 1
difícil *adj.* difficult; hard 3
Diga. Hello. (*on telephone*) 11
diligencia *f.* errand 14
dinero *m.* money 6
dirección *f.* address 14
dirección electrónica *f.* e-mail address 11
director(a) *m., f.* director; (*musical*) conductor 17
dirigir *v.* to direct 17
disco compacto compact disc (CD) 11
discriminación *f.* discrimination 18
discurso *m.* speech 18
diseñador(a) *m., f.* designer 16
diseño *m.* design
disfraz *m.* costume
disfrutar (de) *v.* to enjoy; to reap the benefits (of) 15
disminuir *v.* to reduce 16
diversión *f.* fun activity; entertainment; recreation 4
divertido/a *adj.* fun 7
divertirse (e:ie) *v.* to have fun 9
divorciado/a *adj.* divorced 9
divorciarse (de) *v.* to get divorced (from) 9
divorcio *m.* divorce 9
doblar *v.* to turn 14
doble *adj.* double
doce twelve 1
doctor(a) *m., f.* doctor 3; 10
documental *m.* documentary 17
documentos de viaje *m., pl.* travel documents
doler (o:ue) *v.* to hurt 10
dolor *m.* ache; pain 10
dolor de cabeza *m.* head ache 10
doméstico/a *adj.* domestic 12
domingo *m.* Sunday 2
don *m.* Mr.; sir 1
doña *f.* Mrs.; ma'am 1
donde *prep.* where
¿Dónde está...? Where is...? 2
¿dónde? where? 1
dormir (o:ue) *v.* to sleep 4
dormirse (o:ue) *v.* to go to sleep; to fall asleep 7
dormitorio *m.* bedroom 12
dos two 1
dos veces *f.* twice; two times 6
doscientos/as two hundred 2
drama *m.* drama; play 17
dramático/a *adj.* dramatic 17
dramaturgo/a *m., f.* playwright 17
droga *f.* drug 15
drogadicto/a *adj.* drug addict 15
ducha *f.* shower 7
ducharse *v.* to shower; to take a shower 7
duda *f.* doubt 13
dudar *v.* to doubt 13
no dudar *v.* not to doubt 13
dueño/a *m., f.* owner; landlord 8
dulces *m., pl.* sweets; candy 9
durante *prep.* during 7
durar *v.* to last 18

E

e *conj. (used instead of* **y** *before words beginning with* **i** *and* **hi***)* and 4
echar *v.* to throw
echar (una carta) al buzón *v.* to put (a letter) in the mailbox 14; to mail 14
ecología *f.* ecology 13
ecologista *m., f.* ecologist 13; *adj.* ecological 13
economía *f.* economics 2
ecoturismo *m.* ecotourism 13
Ecuador *m.* Ecuador 1
ecuatoriano/a *adj.* Ecuadorian 3
edad *f.* age 9
edificio *m.* building 12
edificio de apartamentos apartment building 12
(en) efectivo *m.* cash 6
ejercer *v.* to practice/exercise (a degree/profession) 16
ejercicio *m.* exercise 15
ejercicios aeróbicos aerobic exercises 15
ejercicios de estiramiento stretching exercises 15
ejército *m.* army 18
el *m., sing., def. art.* the 1
él *sub. pron.* he 1; *adj. pron.* him
elecciones *f., pl.* election 18
electricista *m., f.* electrician 16
electrodoméstico *m.* electric appliance 12
elegante *adj. m., f.* elegant 6
elegir (e:i) *v.* to elect 18
ella *sub. pron.* she 1; *obj. pron.* her
ellos/as *sub. pron.* they 1; them 1
embarazada *adj.* pregnant 10
emergencia *f.* emergency 10
emitir *v.* to broadcast 18
emocionante *adj. m., f.* exciting
empezar (e:ie) *v.* to begin 4
empleado/a *m., f.* employee 5
empleo *m.* job; employment 16
empresa *f.* company; firm 16
en *prep.* in; on; at 2
en casa at home 7
en caso (de) que in case (that) 13
en cuanto as soon as 13
en efectivo in cash 14
en exceso in excess; too much 15
en línea in-line 4
¡En marcha! Let's get going! 15
en mi nombre in my name
en punto on the dot; exactly; sharp (*time*) 1
en qué in what; how 2
¿En qué puedo servirles? How can I help you? 5
en vivo live 7
enamorado/a (de) *adj.* in love (with) 5
enamorarse (de) *v.* to fall in love (with) 9
encantado/a *adj.* delighted; pleased to meet you 1
encantar *v.* to like very much; to love (*inanimate objects*) 7
¡Me encantó! I loved it! 15
encima de *prep.* on top of 2
encontrar (o:ue) *v.* to find 4
encontrar(se) (o:ue) *v.* to meet (each other); to run into (each other) 11
encontrarse con to meet up with 7
encuesta *f.* poll; survey 18
energía *f.* energy 13
energía nuclear nuclear energy 13
energía solar solar energy 13
enero *m.* January 5
enfermarse *v.* to get sick 10
enfermedad *f.* illness 10
enfermero/a *m., f.* nurse 10
enfermo/a *adj.* sick 10
enfrente de *adv.* opposite; facing 14
engordar *v.* to gain weight 15
enojado/a *adj.* mad; angry 5
enojarse (con) *v.* to get angry (with) 7
ensalada *f.* salad 8
ensayo *m.* essay 3
enseguida *adv.* right away
enseñar *v.* to teach 2
ensuciar *v.* to get (something) dirty 12
entender (e:ie) *v.* to understand 4
enterarse *v.* to find out 16
entonces *adv.* so, then 5, 7
entrada *f.* entrance 12; ticket 17
entre *prep.* between; among 2
entregar *v.* to hand in 11
entremeses *m., pl.* hors d'oeuvres; appetizers 8
entrenador(a) *m., f.* trainer 15
entrenarse *v.* to practice; to train 15
entrevista *f.* interview 16
entrevistador(a) *m., f.* interviewer 16
entrevistar *v.* to interview 16
envase *m.* container 13
enviar *v.* to send; to mail 14
equilibrado/a *adj.* balanced 15
equipado/a *adj.* equipped 15
equipaje *m.* luggage 5
equipo *m.* team 4
equivocado/a *adj.* wrong 5
eres *fam.* you are 1
es he/she/it is 1
Es bueno que... It's good that... 12
Es de... He/She is from... 1
es extraño it's strange 13
es igual it's the same 5
Es importante que... It's important that... 12
es imposible it's impossible 13
es improbable it's improbable 13
Es malo que... It's bad that... 12
Es mejor que... It's better that... 12
Es necesario que... It's necessary that... 12
es obvio it's obvious 13
es ridículo it's ridiculous 13
es seguro it's sure 13
es terrible it's terrible 13
es triste it's sad 13
Es urgente que... It's urgent that... 12
Es la una. It's one o'clock. 1
es una lástima it's a shame 13
es verdad it's true 13
esa(s) *f., adj.* that; those 6
ésa(s) *f., pron.* that (one); those (ones) 6
escalar *v.* to climb 4
escalar montañas *v.* to climb mountains 4
escalera *f.* stairs; stairway 12
escalón *m.* step 15
escanear *v.* to scan 11
escoger *v.* to choose 8
escribir *v.* to write 3
escribir un mensaje electrónico to write an e-mail message 4
escribir una postal to write a postcard 4
escribir una carta to write a letter 4
escrito/a *p.p.* written 14
escritor(a) *m., f.* writer 17
escritorio *m.* desk 2
escuchar *v.* to listen to
escuchar la radio to listen (to) the radio 2
escuchar música to listen (to) music 2
escuela *f.* school 1
esculpir *v.* to sculpt 17
escultor(a) *m., f.* sculptor 17
escultura *f.* sculpture 17
ese *m., sing., adj.* that 6
ése *m., sing., pron.* that one 6
eso *neuter, pron.* that; that thing 6
esos *m., pl., adj.* those 6
ésos *m., pl., pron.* those (ones) 6
España *f.* Spain 1
español *m.* Spanish (*language*) 2
español(a) *adj. m., f.* Spanish 3
espárragos *m., pl.* asparagus 8
especialidad: las especialidades del día today's specials 8
especialización *f.* major 2
espectacular *adj.* spectacular 15
espectáculo *m.* show 17
espejo *m.* mirror 7
esperar *v.* to hope; to wish 13
esperar (+ *infin.*) *v.* to wait (for); to hope 2
esposo/a *m., f.* husband/wife; spouse 3
esquí (acuático) *m.* (water) skiing 4

esquiar *v.* to ski 4
esquina *m.* corner 14
está he/she/it is, you are
Está (muy) despejado. It's (very) clear. (*weather*)
Está lloviendo. It's raining. 5
Está nevando. It's snowing. 5
Está (muy) nublado. It's (very) cloudy. (*weather*) 5
Está bien. That's fine. 11
esta(s) *f., adj.* this; these 6
esta noche tonight 4
ésta(s) *f., pron.* this (one); these (ones) 6
Ésta es... *f.* This is... (*introducing someone*) 1
establecer *v.* to establish 16
estación *f.* station; season 5
estación de autobuses bus station 5
estación del metro subway station 5
estación de tren train station 5
estacionamiento *m.* parking lot 14
estacionar *v.* to park 11
estadio *m.* stadium 2
estado civil *m.* marital status 9
Estados Unidos *m., pl.* (EE.UU.; E.U.) United States 1
estadounidense *adj. m., f.* from the United States 3
estampado/a *adj.* print
estampilla *f.* stamp 14
estante *m.* bookcase; bookshelves 12
estar *v.* to be 2
estar a (veinte kilómetros) de aquí to be (20 kilometers) from here 11
estar a dieta to be on a diet 15
estar aburrido/a to be bored 5
estar afectado/a (por) to be affected (by) 13
estar bajo control to be under control 7
estar cansado/a to be tired 5
estar contaminado/a to be polluted 13
estar de acuerdo to agree 17
Estoy de acuerdo. I agree. 17
No estoy de acuerdo. I don't agree. 17
estar de moda to be in fashion 6
estar de vacaciones *f., pl.* to be on vacation 5
estar en buena forma to be in good shape 15
estar enfermo/a to be sick 10
estar harto/a de... to be sick of... 18
estar listo/a to be ready 15
estar perdido/a to be lost 14
estar roto/a to be broken 10
estar seguro/a to be sure 5
estar torcido/a to be twisted; to be sprained 10
No está nada mal. It's not bad at all. 5
estatua *f.* statue 17
este *m.* east 14
este *m., sing., adj.* this 6
éste *m., sing., pron.* this (one) 6
Éste es... *m.* This is... (*introducing someone*) 1
estéreo *m.* stereo 11
estilo *m.* style
estiramiento *m.* stretching 15
esto *neuter pron.* this; this thing 6
estómago *m.* stomach 10
estornudar *v.* to sneeze 10
estos *m., pl., adj.* these 6
éstos *m., pl., pron.* these (ones) 6
estrella *f.* star 13
estrella de cine *m., f.* movie star 17
estrés *m.* stress 15
estudiante *m., f.* student **1, 2**
estudiantil *adj. m., f.* student 2
estudiar *v.* to study 2
estufa *f.* stove 12
estupendo/a *adj.* stupendous 5
etapa *f.* stage 9
evitar *v.* to avoid 13
examen *m.* test; exam 2
examen médico physical exam 10
excelente *adj. m., f.* excellent 5
exceso *m.* excess; too much 15
excursión *f.* hike; tour; excursion 4
excursionista *m., f.* hiker
éxito *m.* success 16
experiencia *f.* experience 18
explicar *v.* to explain 2
explorar *v.* to explore
expresión *f.* expression
extinción *f.* extinction 13
extranjero/a *adj.* foreign 17
extrañar *v.* to miss 16
extraño/a *adj.* strange 13

F

fábrica *f.* factory 13
fabuloso/a *adj* fabulous 5
fácil *adj.* easy 3
falda *f.* skirt 6
faltar *v.* to lack; to need 7
familia *f.* family 3
famoso/a *adj.* famous 16
farmacia *f.* pharmacy 10
fascinar *v.* to fascinate 7
favorito/a *adj.* favorite 4
fax *m.* fax (machine) 11
febrero *m.* February 5
fecha *f.* date 5
feliz *adj.* happy 5
¡Felicidades! Congratulations! 9
¡Felicitaciones! Congratulations! 9
¡Feliz cumpleaños! Happy birthday! 9
fenomenal *adj.* great, phenomenal 5
feo/a *adj.* ugly 3
festival *m.* festival 17
fiebre *f.* fever 10
fiesta *f.* party 9
fijo/a *adj.* fixed, set 6
fin *m.* end 4
fin de semana weekend 4
finalmente *adv.* finally 15
firmar *v.* to sign (*a document*) 14
física *f.* physics 2
flan (de caramelo) *m.* baked (caramel) custard 9
flexible *adj.* flexible 15
flor *f.* flower 13
folclórico/a *adj.* folk; folkloric 17
folleto *m.* brochure
fondo *m.* end 12
forma *f.* shape 15
formulario *m.* form 14
foto(grafía) *f.* photograph 1
francés, francesa *adj. m., f.* French 3
frecuentemente *adv.* frequently 10
frenos *m., pl.* brakes
frente (frío) *m.* (cold) front 5
fresco/a *adj.* cool 5
frijoles *m., pl.* beans 8
frío/a *adj.* cold 5
frito/a *adj.* fried 8
fruta *f.* fruit 8
frutería *f.* fruit store 14
frutilla *f.* strawberry 8
fuera *adv.* outside
fuerte *adj. m., f.* strong 15
fumar *v.* to smoke 15
(no) fumar *v.* (not) to smoke 15
funcionar *v.* to work 11; to function
fútbol *m.* soccer 4
fútbol americano *m.* football 4
futuro/a *adj.* future 16
en el futuro in the future 16

G

gafas (de sol) *f., pl.* (sun)glasses 6
gafas (oscuras) *f., pl.* (sun)glasses
galleta *f.* cookie 9
ganar *v.* to win 4; to earn (money) 16
ganga *f.* bargain 6
garaje *m.* garage; (mechanic's) repair shop 11; garage (*in a house*) 12
garganta *f.* throat 10
gasolina *f.* gasoline 11
gasolinera *f.* gas station 11
gastar *v.* to spend (*money*) 6

gato *m.* cat 13
gemelo/a *m., f.* twin 3
genial *adj.* great 16
gente *f.* people 3
geografía *f.* geography 2
gerente *m., f.* manager 8, 16
gimnasio *m.* gymnasium 4
gobierno *m.* government 13
golf *m.* golf 4
gordo/a *adj.* fat 3
grabar *v.* to record 11
gracias *f., pl.* thank you; thanks 1
Gracias por invitarme. Thanks for having me. 9
graduarse (de/en) *v.* to graduate (from/in) 9
gran, grande *adj.* big; large 3
grasa *f.* fat 15
gratis *adj. m., f.* free of charge 14
grave *adj.* grave; serious 10
gravísimo/a *adj.* extremely serious 13
grillo *m.* cricket
gripe *f.* flu 10
gris *adj. m., f.* gray 6
gritar *v.* to scream, to shout 7
grito *m.* scream 5
guantes *m., pl.* gloves 6
guapo/a *adj.* handsome; good-looking 3
guardar *v.* to save (on a computer) 11
guerra *f.* war 18
guía *m., f.* guide
gustar *v.* to be pleasing to; to like 2
Me gustaría... I would like...
gusto *m.* pleasure 1
El gusto es mío. The pleasure is mine. 1
Gusto de verlo/la. *(form.)* It's nice to see you.
Gusto de verte. *(fam.)* It's nice to see you.
Mucho gusto. Pleased to meet you. 1
¡Qué gusto verlo/la! *(form.) How nice to see you!* 18
¡Qué gusto verte! *(fam.) How nice to see you!* 18

H

haber *(auxiliar) v.* to have (done something) 15
Ha sido un placer. It's been a pleasure. 15
habitación *f.* room 5
habitación doble double room 5
habitación individual single room 5
hablar *v.* to talk; to speak 2
hacer *v.* to do; to make 4
Hace buen tiempo. The weather is good. 5
Hace (mucho) calor. It's (very) hot. *(weather)* 5
Hace fresco. It's cool. *(weather)* 5
Hace (mucho) frío. It's (very) cold. *(weather)* 5
Hace mal tiempo. The weather is bad. 5
Hace (mucho) sol. It's (very) sunny. *(weather)* 5
Hace (mucho) viento. It's (very) windy. *(weather)* 5
hacer cola to stand in line 14
hacer diligencias to run errands 14
hacer ejercicio to exercise 15
hacer ejercicios aeróbicos to do aerobics 15
hacer ejercicios de estiramiento to do stretching exercises 15
hacer el papel (de) to play the role (of) 17
hacer gimnasia to work out 15
hacer juego (con) to match (with) 6
hacer la cama to make the bed 12
hacer las maletas to pack (one's) suitcases 5
hacer quehaceres domésticos to do household chores 12
hacer (wind)surf to (wind)surf 5
hacer turismo to go sightseeing
hacer un viaje to take a trip 5
¿Me harías el honor de casarte conmigo? Would you do me the honor of marrying me? 17
hacia *prep.* toward 14
hambre *f.* hunger 3
hamburguesa *f.* hamburger 8
hasta *prep.* until 6; toward
Hasta la vista. See you later. 1
Hasta luego. See you later. 1
Hasta mañana. See you tomorrow. 1
hasta que until 13
Hasta pronto. See you soon. 1
hay there is; there are 1
Hay (mucha) contaminación. It's (very) smoggy.
Hay (mucha) niebla. It's (very) foggy.
Hay que It is necessary that 14
No hay duda de There's no doubt 13
No hay de qué. You're welcome. 1
hecho/a *p.p.* done 14
heladería *f.* ice cream shop 14
helado/a *adj.* iced 8
helado *m.* ice cream 9
hermanastro/a *m., f.* stepbrother/stepsister 3
hermano/a *m., f.* brother/sister 3
hermano/a mayor/menor *m., f.* older/younger brother/sister 3
hermanos *m., pl.* siblings (brothers and sisters) 3
hermoso/a *adj.* beautiful 6
hierba *f.* grass 13
hijastro/a *m., f.* stepson/stepdaughter 3
hijo/a *m., f.* son/daughter 3
hijo/a único/a *m., f.* only child 3
hijos *m., pl.* children 3
híjole *interj.* wow 6
historia *f.* history 2; story 17
hockey *m.* hockey 4
hola *interj.* hello; hi 1
hombre *m.* man 1
hombre de negocios *m.* businessman 16
hora *f.* hour 1; the time
horario *m.* schedule 2
horno *m.* oven 12
horno de microondas *m.* microwave oven 12
horror *m.* horror 17
de horror horror (genre) 17
hospital *m.* hospital 10
hotel *m.* hotel 5
hoy *adv.* today 2
hoy día *adv.* nowadays
Hoy es... Today is... 2
hueco *m.* hole 4
huelga *f.* strike *(labor)* 18
hueso *m.* bone 10
huésped *m., f.* guest 5
huevo *m.* egg 8
humanidades *f., pl.* humanities 2
huracán *m.* hurricane 18

I

ida *f.* one way *(travel)*
idea *f.* idea 4
iglesia *f.* church 4
igualdad *f.* equality 18
igualmente *adv.* likewise 1
impermeable *m.* raincoat 6
importante *adj. m., f.* important 3
importar *v.* to be important to; to matter 7
imposible *adj. m., f.* impossible 13
impresora *f.* printer 11
imprimir *v.* to print 11
improbable *adj. m., f.* improbable 13
impuesto *m.* tax 18
incendio *m.* fire 18
increíble *adj. m., f.* incredible 5
indicar cómo llegar *v.* to give directions 14
individual *adj.* private *(room)* 5
infección *f.* infection 10
informar *v.* to inform 18
informe *m.* report; paper *(written work)* 18
ingeniero/a *m., f.* engineer 3

inglés *m.* English (*language*) 2
inglés, inglesa *adj.* English 3
inodoro *m.* toilet 7
insistir (en) *v.* to insist (on) 12
inspector(a) de aduanas *m., f.* customs inspector 5
inteligente *adj. m., f.* intelligent 3
intento *m.* attempt 11
intercambiar *v.* to exchange
interesante *adj. m., f.* interesting 3
interesar *v.* to be interesting to; to interest 7
internacional *adj. m., f.* international 18
Internet Internet 11
inundación *f.* flood 18
invertir (e:ie) *v.* to invest 16
invierno *m.* winter 5
invitado/a *m., f.* guest 9
invitar *v.* to invite 9
inyección *f.* injection 10
ir *v.* to go 4
ir a (+ *inf.*) to be going to do something 4
ir de compras to go shopping 5
ir de excursión (a las montañas) to go on a hike (in the mountains) 4
ir de pesca to go fishing
ir de vacaciones to go on vacation 5
ir en autobús to go by bus 5
ir en auto(móvil) to go by auto(mobile); to go by car 5
ir en avión to go by plane 5
ir en barco to go by boat 5
ir en metro to go by subway
ir en motocicleta to go by motorcycle 5
ir en taxi to go by taxi 5
ir en tren to go by train
irse *v.* to go away; to leave 7
italiano/a *adj.* Italian 3
izquierdo/a *adj.* left 2
a la izquierda de to the left of 2

J

jabón *m.* soap 7
jamás *adv.* never; not ever 7
jamón *m.* ham 8
japonés, japonesa *adj.* Japanese 3
jardín *m.* garden; yard 12
jefe, jefa *m., f.* boss 16
jengibre *m.* ginger 10
joven *adj. m., f., sing.* (**jóvenes** *pl.*) young 3
joven *m., f., sing.* (**jóvenes** *pl.*) youth; young person 1
joyería *f.* jewelry store 14
jubilarse *v.* to retire (*from work*) 9
juego *m.* game
jueves *m., sing.* Thursday 2
jugador(a) *m., f.* player 4
jugar (u:ue) *v.* to play 4
jugar a las cartas *f., pl.* to play cards 5
jugo *m.* juice 8
jugo de fruta *m.* fruit juice 8
julio *m.* July 5
jungla *f.* jungle 13
junio *m.* June 5
juntos/as *adj.* together 9
juventud *f.* youth 9

K

kilómetro *m.* kilometer 1

L

la *f., sing., def. art.* the 1
la *f., sing., d.o. pron.* her, it, *form.* you 5
laboratorio *m.* laboratory 2
lago *m.* lake 13
lámpara *f.* lamp 12
lana *f.* wool 6
langosta *f.* lobster 8
lápiz *m.* pencil 1
largo/a *adj.* long 6
las *f., pl., def. art.* the 1
las *f., pl., d.o. pron.* them; *form.* you 5
lástima *f.* shame 13
lastimarse *v.* to injure oneself 10
lastimarse el pie to injure one's foot 10
lata *f.* (*tin*) can 13
lavabo *m.* sink 7
lavadora *f.* washing machine 12
lavandería *f.* laundromat 14
lavaplatos *m., sing.* dishwasher 12
lavar *v.* to wash 12
lavar (el suelo, los platos) to wash (the floor, the dishes) 12
lavarse *v.* to wash oneself 7
lavarse la cara to wash one's face 7
lavarse las manos to wash one's hands 7
le *sing., i.o. pron.* to/for him, her, *form.* you 6
Le presento a... *form.* I would like to introduce you to (name). 1
lección *f.* lesson 1
leche *f.* milk 8
lechuga *f.* lettuce 8
leer *v.* to read 3
leer correo electrónico to read e-mail 4
leer un periódico to read a newspaper 4
leer una revista to read a magazine 4
leído/a *p.p.* read 14
lejos de *prep.* far from 2
lengua *f.* language 2
lenguas extranjeras *f., pl.* foreign languages 2
lentes de contacto *m., pl.* contact lenses
lentes (de sol) (sun)glasses
lento/a *adj.* slow 11
les *pl., i.o. pron.* to/for them, *form.* you 6
letrero *m.* sign 14
levantar *v.* to lift 15
levantar pesas to lift weights 15
levantarse *v.* to get up 7
ley *f.* law 13
libertad *f.* liberty; freedom 18
libre *adj. m., f.* free 4
librería *f.* bookstore 2
libro *m.* book 2
licencia de conducir *f.* driver's license 11
limón *m.* lemon 8
limpiar *v.* to clean 12
limpiar la casa *v.* to clean the house 12
limpio/a *adj.* clean 5
línea *f.* line 4
listo/a *adj.* ready; smart 5
literatura *f.* literature 2
llamar *v.* to call 11
llamar por teléfono to call on the phone
llamarse *v.* to be called; to be named 7
llanta *f.* tire 11
llave *f.* key 5; wrench 11
llegada *f.* arrival 5
llegar *v.* to arrive 2
llenar *v.* to fill 11, 14
llenar el tanque to fill the tank 11
llenar (un formulario) to fill out (a form) 14
lleno/a *adj.* full 11
llevar *v.* to carry 2; *v.* to wear; to take 6
llevar una vida sana to lead a healthy lifestyle 15
llevarse bien/mal (con) to get along well/badly (with) 9
llorar *v.* to cry 15
llover (o:ue) *v.* to rain 5
Llueve. It's raining. 5
lluvia *f.* rain
lo *m., sing. d.o. pron.* him, it, *form.* you 5
¡Lo he pasado de película! I've had a fantastic time! 18
lo mejor the best (thing) 18
lo que that which; what 12
Lo siento. I'm sorry. 1
loco/a *adj.* crazy 6
locutor(a) *m., f.* (TV or radio) announcer 18
lodo *m.* mud
los *m., pl., def. art.* the 1

los *m. pl., d.o. pron.* them, *form.* you 5
luchar (contra/por) *v.* to fight; to struggle (against/for) 18
luego *adv.* then 7; *adv.* later 1
lugar *m.* place 2, 4
luna *f.* moon 13
lunares *m.* polka dots 6
lunes *m., sing.* Monday 2
luz *f.* light; electricity 12

M

madrastra *f.* stepmother 3
madre *f.* mother 3
madurez *f.* maturity; middle age 9
maestro/a *m., f.* teacher 16
magnífico/a *adj.* magnificent 5
maíz *m.* corn 8
mal, malo/a *adj.* bad 3
maleta *f.* suitcase 1
mamá *f.* mom 3
mandar *v.* to order 12; to send; to mail 14
manejar *v.* to drive 11
manera *f.* way 16
mano *f.* hand 1
manta *f.* blanket 12
mantener (e:ie) *v.* to maintain 15
  mantenerse en forma to stay in shape 15
mantequilla *f.* butter 8
manzana *f.* apple 8
mañana *f.* morning, a.m. 1; tomorrow 1
mapa *m.* map 2
maquillaje *m.* makeup 7
maquillarse *v.* to put on makeup 7
mar *m.* sea 5
maravilloso/a *adj.* marvelous 5
mareado/a *adj.* dizzy; nauseated 10
margarina *f.* margarine 8
mariscos *m., pl.* shellfish 8
marrón *adj. m., f.* brown 6
martes *m., sing.* Tuesday 2
marzo *m.* March 5
más *pron.* more 2
  más de (+ *number*) more than 8
  más tarde later (on) 7
  más... que more... than 8
masaje *m.* massage 15
matemáticas *f., pl.* mathematics 2
materia *f.* course 2
matrimonio *m.* marriage 9
máximo/a *adj.* maximum 11
mayo *m.* May 5
mayonesa *f.* mayonnaise 8
mayor *adj.* older 3
  el/la mayor *adj.* eldest 8; oldest
me *sing., d.o. pron.* me 5; *sing. i.o. pron.* to/for me 6
  Me duele mucho. It hurts me a lot. 10
  Me gusta... I like... 2
  No me gustan nada. I don't like them at all. 2
  Me gustaría(n)... I would like... 17
  Me llamo... My name is... 1
  Me muero por... I'm dying to (for)...
mecánico/a *m., f.* mechanic 11
mediano/a *adj.* medium
medianoche *f.* midnight 1
medias *f., pl.* pantyhose, stockings 6
medicamento *m.* medication 10
medicina *f.* medicine 10
médico/a *m., f.* doctor 3; *adj.* medical 10
medio/a *adj.* half 3
  medio ambiente *m.* environment 13
  medio/a hermano/a *m., f.* half-brother/half-sister 3
  mediodía *m.* noon 1
  medios de comunicación *m., pl.* means of communication; media 18
  y media thirty minutes past the hour (time) 1
mejor *adj.* better 8
  el/la mejor *m., f.* the best 8
mejorar *v.* to improve 13
melocotón *m.* peach 8
menor *adj.* younger 3
  el/la menor *m., f.* youngest 8
menos *adv.* less 10
  menos cuarto..., menos quince... quarter to... (*time*) 1
  menos de (+ *number*) fewer than 8
  menos... que less... than 8
mensaje *m.* **de texto** text message 11
mensaje electrónico *m.* e-mail message 4
mentira *f.* lie 4
menú *m.* menu 8
mercado *m.* market 6
  mercado al aire libre open-air market 6
merendar (e:ie) *v.* to snack 8; to have an afternoon snack
merienda *f.* afternoon snack 15
mes *m.* month 5
mesa *f.* table 2
mesita *f.* end table 12
  mesita de noche night stand 12
meterse en problemas *v.* to get into trouble 13
metro *m.* subway 5
mexicano/a *adj.* Mexican 3
México *m.* Mexico 1
mí *pron., obj. of prep.* me 8
mi(s) *poss. adj.* my 3
microonda *f.* microwave 12
  horno de microondas *m.* microwave oven 12
miedo *m.* fear 3
miel *f.* honey 10
mientras *adv.* while 10
miércoles *m., sing.* Wednesday 2
mil *m.* one thousand 2
  mil millones billion
milla *f.* mile 11
millón *m.* million 2
millones (de) *m.* millions (of)
mineral *m.* mineral 15
minuto *m.* minute 1
mío(s)/a(s) *poss.* my; (of) mine 11
mirar *v.* to look (at); to watch 2
  mirar (la) televisión to watch television 2
mismo/a *adj.* same 3
mochila *f.* backpack 2
moda *f.* fashion 6
módem *m.* modem
moderno/a *adj.* modern 17
molestar *v.* to bother; to annoy 7
monitor *m.* (computer) monitor 11
  monitor(a) *m., f.* trainer
mono *m.* monkey 13
montaña *f.* mountain 4
montar *v.* **a caballo** to ride a horse 5
montón: un montón de a lot of 4
monumento *m.* monument 4
morado/a *adj.* purple 6
moreno/a *adj.* brunet(te) 3
morir (o:ue) *v.* to die 8
mostrar (o:ue) *v.* to show 4
motocicleta *f.* motorcycle 5
motor *m.* motor
muchacho/a *m., f.* boy; girl 3
mucho/a *adj., adv.* a lot of; much 2; many 3
  (Muchas) gracias. Thank you (very much); Thanks (a lot). 1
  muchas veces *adv.* a lot; many times 10
  Muchísimas gracias. Thank you very, very much. 9
  Mucho gusto. Pleased to meet you. 1
muchísimo very much 2
mudarse *v.* to move (from one house to another) 12
muebles *m., pl.* furniture 12
muela *f.* tooth
muerte *f.* death 9
muerto/a *p.p.* died 14
mujer *f.* woman 1
  mujer de negocios *f.* business woman 16
  mujer policía *f.* female police officer
multa *f.* fine
mundial *adj. m., f.* worldwide
mundo *m.* world 8, 13
muro *m.* wall 15
músculo *m.* muscle 15
museo *m.* museum 4
música *f.* music 2, 17
musical *adj. m., f.* musical 17

músico/a *m., f.* musician 17
muy *adv.* very 1
Muy amable. That's very kind of you. 5
(Muy) bien, gracias. (Very) well, thanks. 1

N

nacer *v.* to be born 9
nacimiento *m.* birth 9
nacional *adj. m., f.* national 18
nacionalidad *f.* nationality 1
nada nothing 1; not anything 7
nada mal not bad at all 5
nadar *v.* to swim 4
nadie *pron.* no one, nobody, not anyone 7
naranja *f.* orange 8
nariz *f.* nose 10
natación *f.* swimming 4
natural *adj. m., f.* natural 13
naturaleza *f.* nature 13
navegador *m.* **GPS** GPS 11
navegar (en Internet) *v.* to surf (the Internet) 11
Navidad *f.* Christmas 9
necesario/a *adj.* necessary 12
necesitar (+ *inf.*) *v.* to need 2
negar (e:ie) *v.* to deny 13
no negar (e:ie) *v.* not to deny 13
negocios *m., pl.* business; commerce 16
negro/a *adj.* black 6
nervioso/a *adj.* nervous 5
nevar (e:ie) *v.* to snow 5
Nieva. It's snowing. 5
ni...ni neither... nor 7
niebla *f.* fog
nieto/a *m., f.* grandson/ granddaughter 3
nieve *f.* snow
ningún, ninguno/a(s) *adj.* no; none; not any 7
niñez *f.* childhood 9
niño/a *m., f.* child 3
no no; not 1
¿no? right? 1
No cabe duda de... There is no doubt... 13
No es para tanto. It's not a big deal. 12
no es seguro it's not sure 13
no es verdad it's not true 13
No está nada mal. It's not bad at all. 5
no estar de acuerdo to disagree
No estoy seguro. I'm not sure.
no hay there is not; there are not 1
No hay de qué. You're welcome. 1
No hay duda de... There is no doubt... 13
No hay problema. No problem. 7
¡No me diga(s)! You don't say!
No me gustan nada. I don't like them at all. 2
no muy bien not very well 1
No quiero. I don't want to. 4
No sé. I don't know.
No se preocupe. (*form.*) Don't worry. 7
No te preocupes. (*fam.*) Don't worry. 7
no tener razón to be wrong 3
noche *f.* night 1
nombre *m.* name 1
norte *m.* north 14
norteamericano/a *adj.* (North) American 3
nos *pl., d.o. pron.* us 5; *pl., i.o. pron.* to/for us 6
Nos vemos. See you. 1
nosotros/as *sub. pron.* we 1; *ob. pron.* us
noticia *f.* news 11
noticias *f., pl.* news 18
noticiero *m.* newscast 18
novecientos/as nine hundred 2
noveno/a *adj.* ninth 5
noventa ninety 2
noviembre *m.* November 5
novio/a *m., f.* boyfriend/ girlfriend 3
nube *f.* cloud 13
nublado/a *adj.* cloudy 5
Está (muy) nublado. It's very cloudy. 5
nuclear *adj. m. f.* nuclear 13
nuera *f.* daughter-in-law 3
nuestro(s)/a(s) *poss. adj.* our 3; (of ours) 11
nueve nine 1
nuevo/a *adj.* new 6
número *m.* number 1; (shoe) size 6
nunca *adj.* never; not ever 7
nutrición *f.* nutrition 15
nutricionista *m., f.* nutritionist 15

O

o or 7
o... o; either... or 7
obedecer *v.* to obey 18
obra *f.* work (*of art, literature, music, etc.*) 17
obra maestra *f.* masterpiece 17
obtener *v.* to obtain; to get 16
obvio/a *adj.* obvious 13
océano *m.* ocean
ochenta eighty 2
ocho eight 1
ochocientos/as eight hundred 2
octavo/a *adj.* eighth 5
octubre *m.* October 5
ocupación *f.* occupation 16
ocupado/a *adj.* busy 5
ocurrir *v.* to occur; to happen 18
odiar *v.* to hate 9
oeste *m.* west 14
oferta *f.* offer 12
oficina *f.* office 12
oficio *m.* trade 16
ofrecer *v.* to offer 6
oído *m.* (sense of) hearing; inner ear 10
oído/a *p.p.* heard 14
oír *v.* to hear 4
Oiga/Oigan. *form., sing./pl.* Listen. (*in conversation*) 1
Oye. *fam., sing.* Listen. (*in conversation*) 1
ojalá (que) *interj.* I hope (that); I wish (that) 13
ojo *m.* eye 10
olvidar *v.* to forget 10
once eleven 1
ópera *f.* opera 17
operación *f.* operation 10
ordenado/a *adj.* orderly 5
ordinal *adj.* ordinal (*number*)
oreja *f.* (outer) ear 10
organizarse *v.* to organize oneself 12
orquesta *f.* orchestra 17
ortografía *f.* spelling
ortográfico/a *adj.* spelling
os *fam., pl. d.o. pron.* you 5; *fam., pl. i.o. pron.* to/for you 6
otoño *m.* autumn 5
otro/a *adj.* other; another 6
otra vez again

P

paciente *m., f.* patient 10
padrastro *m.* stepfather 3
padre *m.* father 3
padres *m., pl.* parents 3
pagar *v.* to pay 6, 9
pagar a plazos to pay in installments 14
pagar al contado to pay in cash 14
pagar en efectivo to pay in cash 14
pagar la cuenta to pay the bill 9
página *f.* page 11
página principal *f.* home page 11
país *m.* country 1
paisaje *m.* landscape 5
pájaro *m.* bird 13
palabra *f.* word 1
paleta helada *f.* popsicle 4
pálido/a *adj.* pale 14
pan *m.* bread 8
pan tostado *m.* toasted bread 8
panadería *f.* bakery 14

pantalla *f.* screen 11
pantalla táctil *f.* touch screen 11
pantalones *m., pl.* pants 6
pantalones cortos *m., pl.* shorts 6
pantuflas *f.* slippers 7
papa *f.* potato 8
papas fritas *f., pl.* fried potatoes; French fries 8
papá *m.* dad 3
papás *m., pl.* parents 3
papel *m.* paper 2; role 17
papelera *f.* wastebasket 2
paquete *m.* package 14
par *m.* pair 6
par de zapatos pair of shoes 6
para *prep.* for; in order to; by; used for; considering 11
para que so that 13
parabrisas *m., sing.* windshield 11
parar *v.* to stop 11
parecer *v.* to seem 6
pared *f.* wall 12
pareja *f.* (married) couple; partner 9
parientes *m., pl.* relatives 3
parque *m.* park 4
párrafo *m.* paragraph
parte: de parte de on behalf of 11
partido *m.* game; match (*sports*) 4
pasado/a *adj.* last; past 6
pasado *p.p.* passed
pasaje *m.* ticket 5
pasaje de ida y vuelta *m.* roundtrip ticket 5
pasajero/a *m., f.* passenger 1
pasaporte *m.* passport 5
pasar *v.* to go through 5
pasar la aspiradora to vacuum 12
pasar por el banco to go by the bank 14
pasar por la aduana to go through customs
pasar tiempo to spend time
pasarlo bien/mal to have a good/bad time 9
pasatiempo *m.* pastime; hobby 4
pasear *v.* to take a walk; to stroll 4
pasear en bicicleta to ride a bicycle 4
pasear por to walk around 4
pasillo *m.* hallway 12
pasta *f.* **de dientes** toothpaste 7
pastel *m.* cake; pie 9
pastel de chocolate *m.* chocolate cake 9
pastel de cumpleaños *m.* birthday cake
pastelería *f.* pastry shop 14
pastilla *f.* pill; tablet 10
patata *f.* potato; 8
patatas fritas *f., pl.* fried potatoes; French fries 8
patinar (en línea) *v.* to (inline) skate 4
patineta *f.* skateboard 4
patio *m.* patio; yard 12
pavo *m.* turkey 8
paz *f.* peace 18
pedir (e:i) *v.* to ask for; to request 4; to order (*food*) 8
pedir prestado *v.* to borrow 14
pedir un préstamo *v.* to apply for a loan 14
Todos me dijeron que te pidiera disculpas de su parte. They all told me to ask you to excuse them/forgive them. 18
peinarse *v.* to comb one's hair 7
película *f.* movie 4
peligro *m.* danger 13
peligroso/a *adj.* dangerous 18
pelirrojo/a *adj.* red-haired 3
pelo *m.* hair 7
pelota *f.* ball 4
peluquería *f.* beauty salon 14
peluquero/a *m., f.* hairdresser 16
penicilina *f.* penicillin 10
pensar (e:ie) *v.* to think 4
pensar (+ *inf.*) *v.* to intend to; to plan to (*do something*) 4
pensar en *v.* to think about 4
pensión *f.* boardinghouse
peor *adj.* worse 8
el/la peor *adj.* the worst 8
pequeño/a *adj.* small 3
pera *f.* pear 8
perder (e:ie) *v.* to lose; to miss 4
perdido/a *adj.* lost 13, 14
Perdón. Pardon me.; Excuse me. 1
perezoso/a *adj.* lazy
perfecto/a *adj.* perfect 5
periódico *m.* newspaper 4
periodismo *m.* journalism 2
periodista *m., f.* journalist 3
permiso *m.* permission
pero *conj.* but 2
perro *m.* dog 13
persona *f.* person 3
personaje *m.* character 17
personaje principal *m.* main character 17
pesas *f. pl.* weights 15
pesca *f.* fishing
pescadería *f.* fish market 14
pescado *m.* fish (*cooked*) 8
pescar *v.* to fish 5
peso *m.* weight 15
pez *m., sing.* (**peces** *pl.*) fish (*live*) 13
pie *m.* foot 10
piedra *f.* stone 13
pierna *f.* leg 10
pimienta *f.* black pepper 8
pintar *v.* to paint 17
pintor(a) *m., f.* painter 16
pintura *f.* painting; picture 12, 17
piña *f.* pineapple 8
piscina *f.* swimming pool 4
piso *m.* floor (*of a building*) 5
pizarra *f.* blackboard 2
placer *m.* pleasure 15
Ha sido un placer. It's been a pleasure. 15
planchar la ropa *v.* to iron the clothes 12
planes *m., pl.* plans 4
planta *f.* plant 13
planta baja *f.* ground floor 5
plástico *m.* plastic 13
plato *m.* dish (*in a meal*) 8; *m.* plate 12
plato principal *m.* main dish 8
playa *f.* beach 5
plaza *f.* city or town square 4
plazos *m., pl.* periods; time 14
pluma *f.* pen 2
plumero *m.* duster 12
población *f.* population 13
pobre *adj. m., f.* poor 6
pobrecito/a *adj.* poor thing 3
pobreza *f.* poverty
poco/a *adj.* little; few 5; 10
poder (o:ue) *v.* to be able to; can 4
¿Podría pedirte algo? Could I ask you something? 17
¿Puedo dejar un recado? May I leave a message? 11
poema *m.* poem 17
poesía *f.* poetry 17
poeta *m., f.* poet 17
policía *f.* police (force) 11
política *f.* politics 18
político/a *m., f.* politician 16; *adj.* political 18
pollo *m.* chicken 8
pollo asado *m.* roast chicken 8
ponchar *v.* to go flat
poner *v.* to put; to place 4; *v.* to turn on (*electrical appliances*) 11
poner la mesa *v.* to set the table 12
poner una inyección *v.* to give an injection 10
ponerse (+ *adj.*) *v.* to become (+ *adj.*) 7; to put on 7
ponerle el nombre to name someone/something 9
por *prep.* in exchange for; for; by; in; through; around; along; during; because of; on account of; on behalf of; in search of; by way of; by means of 11
por aquí around here 11
por avión by plane
por ejemplo for example 11
por eso that's why; therefore 11
por favor please 1
por fin finally 11
por la mañana in the morning 7
por la noche at night 7
por la tarde in the afternoon 7
por lo menos *adv.* at least 10
¿por qué? why? 2
Por supuesto. Of course.
por teléfono by phone; on the phone

por último finally 7
porque *conj.* because 2
portátil *m.* portable 11
portero/a *m., f.* doorman/doorwoman 1
porvenir *m.* future 16
¡Por el porvenir! Here's to the future! 16
posesivo/a *adj.* possessive 3
posible *adj.* possible 13
es posible it's possible 13
no es posible it's not possible 13
postal *f.* postcard 4
postre *m.* dessert 9
practicar *v.* to practice 2
practicar deportes *m., pl.* to play sports 4
precio (fijo) *m.* (fixed; set) price 6
preferir (e:ie) *v.* to prefer 4
pregunta *f.* question
preguntar *v.* to ask (*a question*) 2
premio *m.* prize; award 17
prender *v.* to turn on 11
prensa *f.* press 18
preocupado/a (por) *adj.* worried (about) 5
preocuparse (por) *v.* to worry (about) 7
preparar *v.* to prepare 2
preposición *f.* preposition
presentación *f.* introduction
presentar *v.* to introduce; to present 17; to put on (*a performance*) 17
Le presento a... I would like to introduce you to (name). (*form.*) 1
Te presento a... I would like to introduce you to (name). (*fam.*) 1
presiones *f., pl.* pressures 15
prestado/a *adj.* borrowed
préstamo *m.* loan 14
prestar *v.* to lend; to loan 6
primavera *f.* spring 5
primer, primero/a *adj.* first 2, 5
primo/a *m., f.* cousin 3
principal *adj. m., f.* main 8
prisa *f.* haste 3
darse prisa *v.* to hurry; to rush 15
probable *adj. m., f.* probable 13
es probable it's probable 13
no es probable it's not probable 13
probar (o:ue) *v.* to taste; to try 8
probarse (o:ue) *v.* to try on 7
problema *m.* problem 1
profesión *f.* profession 3; 16
profesor(a) *m., f.* teacher 1, 2
programa *m.* 1
programa de computación *m.* software 11
programa de entrevistas *m.* talk show 17
programa de realidad *m.* reality show 17
programador(a) *m., f.* computer programmer 3
prohibir *v.* to prohibit 10; to forbid
pronombre *m.* pronoun
pronto *adv.* soon 10
propina *f.* tip 8
propio/a *adj.* own 16
proteger *v.* to protect 13
proteína *f.* protein 15
próximo/a *adj.* next 3, 16
proyecto *m.* project 11
prueba *f.* test; quiz 2
psicología *f.* psychology 2
psicólogo/a *m., f.* psychologist 16
publicar *v.* to publish 17
público *m.* audience 17
pueblo *m.* town 4
puerta *f.* door 2
Puerto Rico *m.* Puerto Rico 1
puertorriqueño/a *adj.* Puerto Rican 3
pues *conj.* well
puesto *m.* position; job 16
puesto/a *p.p.* put 14
puro/a *adj.* pure 13

Q

que *pron.* that; which; who 12
¿En qué...? In which...? 2
¡Qué...! How...!
¡Qué dolor! What pain!
¡Qué ropa más bonita! What pretty clothes! 6
¡Qué sorpresa! What a surprise!
¿qué? what? 1
¿Qué día es hoy? What day is it? 2
¿Qué hay de nuevo? What's new? 1
¿Qué hora es? What time is it? 1
¿Qué les parece? What do you (*pl.*) think?
Qué onda? What's up? 14
¿Qué pasa? What's happening? What's going on? 1
¿Qué pasó? What happened? 11
¿Qué precio tiene? What is the price?
¿Qué tal...? How are you?; How is it going? 1; How is/are...? 2
¿Qué talla lleva/usa? What size do you wear? 6
¿Qué tiempo hace? How's the weather? 5
quedar *v.* to be left over; to fit (*clothing*) 7; to be left behind; to be located 14
quedarse *v.* to stay; to remain 7
quehaceres domésticos *m., pl.* household chores 12
quemado/a *adj.* burned (out) 11
quemar (un CD/DVD) *v.* to burn (a CD/DVD)
querer (e:ie) *v.* to want; to love 4
queso *m.* cheese 8
quien(es) *pron.* who; whom; that 12
¿quién(es)? who?; whom? 1
¿Quién es...? Who is...? 1
¿Quién habla? Who is speaking/calling? (*telephone*) 11
química *f.* chemistry 2
quince fifteen 1
menos quince quarter to (time) 1
y quince quarter after (time) 1
quinceañera *f.* young woman celebrating her fifteenth birthday 9
quinientos/as *adj.* five hundred 2
quinto/a *adj.* fifth 5
quisiera *v.* I would like 17
quitar el polvo *v.* to dust 12
quitar la mesa *v.* to clear the table 12
quitarse *v.* to take off 7
quizás *adv.* maybe 5

R

racismo *m.* racism 18
radio *f.* radio (*medium*) 2; *m.* radio (set) 2
radiografía *f.* X-ray 10
rápido/a *adv.* quickly 10
ratón *m.* mouse 11
ratos libres *m., pl.* spare (free) time 4
raya *f.* stripe 6
razón *f.* reason 3
rebaja *f.* sale 6
receta *f.* prescription 10
recetar *v.* to prescribe 10
recibir *v.* to receive 3
reciclaje *m.* recycling 13
reciclar *v.* to recycle 13
recién casado/a *m., f.* newlywed 9
recoger *v.* to pick up 13
recomendar (e:ie) *v.* to recommend 8, 12
recordar (o:ue) *v.* to remember 4
recorrer *v.* to tour an area
recorrido *m.* tour 13
recuperar *v.* to recover 11
recurso *m.* resource 13
recurso natural *m.* natural resource 13
red *f.* network; Web 11
reducir *v.* to reduce 13
refresco *m.* soft drink 8
refrigerador *m.* refrigerator 12
regalar *v.* to give (a gift) 9
regalo *m.* gift 6
regatear *v.* to bargain 6
región *f.* region; area 13
regresar *v.* to return 2
regular *adv.* so-so.; OK 1

reído *p.p.* laughed 14
reírse (e:i) *v.* to laugh 9
relaciones *f., pl.* relationships
relajarse *v.* to relax 9
reloj *m.* clock; watch 2
renovable *adj.* renewable 13
renunciar (a) *v.* to resign (from) 16
repetir (e:i) *v.* to repeat 4
reportaje *m.* report 18
reportero/a *m., f.* reporter; journalist 16
representante *m., f.* representative 18
reproductor de CD *m.* CD player 11
reproductor de DVD *m.* DVD player 11
reproductor de MP3 *m.* MP3 player 11
resfriado *m.* cold (*illness*) 10
residencia estudiantil *f.* dormitory 2
resolver (o:ue) *v.* to resolve; to solve 13
respirar *v.* to breathe 13
responsable *adj.* responsible 8
respuesta *f.* answer
restaurante *m.* restaurant 4
resuelto/a *p.p.* resolved 14
reunión *f.* meeting 16
revisar *v.* to check 11
revisar el aceite *v.* to check the oil 11
revista *f.* magazine 4
rico/a *adj.* rich 6; *adj.* tasty; delicious 8
ridículo/a *adj.* ridiculous 13
río *m.* river 13
riquísimo/a *adj.* extremely delicious 8
rodilla *f.* knee 10
rogar (o:ue) *v.* to beg; to plead 12
rojo/a *adj.* red 6
romántico/a *adj.* romantic 17
romper *v.* to break 10
romperse la pierna *v.* to break one's leg 10
romper (con) *v.* to break up (with) 9
ropa *f.* clothing; clothes 6
ropa interior *f.* underwear 6
rosado/a *adj.* pink 6
roto/a *adj.* broken 10, 14
rubio/a *adj.* blond(e) 3
ruso/a *adj.* Russian 3
rutina *f.* routine 7
rutina diaria *f.* daily routine 7

S

sábado *m.* Saturday 2
saber *v.* to know; to know how 6; to taste 8
saber a to taste like 8
sabrosísimo/a *adj.* extremely delicious 8
sabroso/a *adj.* tasty; delicious 8
sacar *v.* to take out
sacar buenas notas to get good grades 2
sacar fotos to take photos 5
sacar la basura to take out the trash 12
sacar(se) un diente to have a tooth removed 10
sacudir *v.* to dust 12
sacudir los muebles to dust the furniture 12
sal *f.* salt 8
sala *f.* living room 12; room
sala de emergencia(s) emergency room 10
salario *m.* salary 16
salchicha *f.* sausage 8
salida *f.* departure; exit 5
salir *v.* to leave 4; to go out
salir (con) to go out (with); to date 9
salir de to leave from
salir para to leave for (*a place*)
salmón *m.* salmon 8
salón de belleza *m.* beauty salon 14
salud *f.* health 10
saludable *adj.* healthy 10
saludar(se) *v.* to greet (each other) 11
saludo *m.* greeting 1
saludos a... greetings to... 1
sandalia *f.* sandal 6
sandía *f.* watermelon
sándwich *m.* sandwich 8
sano/a *adj.* healthy 10
se *ref. pron.* himself, herself, itself, *form.* yourself, themselves, yourselves 7
se *impersonal* one 10
Se nos dañó... The... broke down. 11
Se hizo... He/she/it became...
Se nos pinchó una llanta. We had a flat tire. 11
secadora *f.* clothes dryer 12
secarse *v.* to dry oneself 7
sección de (no) fumar *f.* (non) smoking section 8
secretario/a *m., f.* secretary 16
secuencia *f.* sequence
sed *f.* thirst 3
seda *f.* silk 6
sedentario/a *adj.* sedentary; related to sitting 15
seguir (e:i) *v.* to follow; to continue 4
según according to
segundo/a *adj.* second 5
seguro/a *adj.* sure; safe 5
seis six 1
seiscientos/as six hundred 2
sello *m.* stamp 14
selva *f.* jungle 13
semáforo *m.* traffic light 14
semana *f.* week 2
fin *m.* **de semana** weekend 4
semana *f.* **pasada** last week 6
semestre *m.* semester 2
sendero *m.* trail; trailhead 13
sentarse (e:ie) *v.* to sit down 7
sentir(se) (e:ie) *v.* to feel 7; to be sorry; to regret 13
señor (Sr.); don *m.* Mr.; sir 1
señora (Sra.); doña *f.* Mrs.; ma'am 1
señorita (Srta.) *f.* Miss 1
separado/a *adj.* separated 9
separarse (de) *v.* to separate (from) 9
septiembre *m.* September 5
séptimo/a *adj.* seventh 5
ser *v.* to be 1
ser aficionado/a (a) to be a fan (of) 4
ser alérgico/a (a) to be allergic (to) 10
ser gratis to be free of charge 14
serio/a *adj.* serious
servicio *m.* service 15
servilleta *f.* napkin 12
servir (e:i) *v.* to serve 8; to help 5
sesenta sixty 2
setecientos/as *adj.* seven hundred 2
setenta seventy 2
sexismo *m.* sexism 18
sexto/a *adj.* sixth 5
sí *adv.* yes 1
si *conj.* if 4
SIDA *m.* AIDS 18
sido *p.p.* been 15
siempre *adv.* always 7
siete seven 1
silla *f.* seat 2
sillón *m.* armchair 12
similar *adj. m., f.* similar
simpático/a *adj.* nice; likeable 3
sin *prep.* without 2, 13
sin duda without a doubt
sin embargo however
sin que *conj.* without 13
sino but (rather) 7
síntoma *m.* symptom 10
sitio *m.* place 3
sitio *m.* **web**; website 11
situado/a *p.p.* located
sobre *m.* envelope 14; *prep.* on; over 2
sobre todo above all 13
(sobre)población *f.* (over)population 13
sobrino/a *m., f.* nephew; niece 3
sociología *f.* sociology 2
sofá *m.* couch; sofa 12
sol *m.* sun 4; 5; 13
solar *adj. m., f.* solar 13
soldado *m., f.* soldier 18
soleado/a *adj.* sunny
solicitar *v.* to apply (*for a job*) 16
solicitud (de trabajo) *f.* (job) application 16
sólo *adv.* only 3
solo/a *adj.* alone
soltero/a *adj.* single 9
solución *f.* solution 13

sombrero *m.* hat 6
Son las dos. It's two o'clock. 1
sonar (o:ue) *v.* to ring 11
sonreído *p.p.* smiled 14
sonreír (e:i) *v.* to smile 9
sopa *f.* soup 8
sorprender *v.* to surprise 9
sorpresa *f.* surprise 9
sótano *m.* basement; cellar 12
soy I am 1
  Soy de... I'm from... 1
  Soy yo. That's me.
su(s) *poss. adj.* his; her; its; *form.* your; their 3
subir(se) a *v.* to get on/into (*a vehicle*) 11
sucio/a *adj.* dirty 5
sudar *v.* to sweat 15
suegro/a *m., f.* father-in-law; mother-in-law 3
sueldo *m.* salary 16
suelo *m.* floor 12
sueño *m.* sleep 3
suerte *f.* luck 3
suéter *m.* sweater 6
sufrir *v.* to suffer 10
  sufrir muchas presiones to be under a lot of pressure 15
  sufrir una enfermedad to suffer an illness 10
sugerir (e:ie) *v.* to suggest 12
supermercado *m.* supermarket 14
suponer *v.* to suppose 4
sur *m.* south 14
sustantivo *m.* noun
suyo(s)/a(s) *poss.* (of) his/her; (of) hers; (of) its; (of) *form.* your, (of) yours, (of) their 11

T

tabla de (wind)surf *f.* surf board/sailboard 3
tal vez *adv.* maybe 5
talentoso/a *adj.* talented 17
talla *f.* size 6
  talla grande *f.* large
taller *m.* **mecánico** garage; mechanic's repairshop 11
también *adv.* also; too 2; 7
tampoco *adv.* neither; not either 7
tan *adv.* so 5
  tan... como as... as 8
  tan pronto como *conj.* as soon as 13
tanque *m.* tank 11
tanto *adv.* so much
  tanto... como as much... as 8
  tantos/as... como as many... as 8
tarde *adv.* late 7; *f.* afternoon; evening; P.M. 1
tarea *f.* homework 2
tarjeta *f.* (post) card
tarjeta de crédito *f.* credit card 6
tarjeta postal *f.* postcard 4
taxi *m.* taxi 5
taza *f.* cup 12
te *sing., fam., d.o. pron.* you 5; *sing., fam., i.o. pron.* to/for you 6
  Te presento a... *fam.* I would like to introduce you to (name). 1
  ¿Te gustaría? Would you like to? 17
  ¿Te gusta(n)...? Do you like...? 2
té *m.* tea 8
  té helado *m.* iced tea 8
teatro *m.* theater 17
teclado *m.* keyboard 11
técnico/a *m., f.* technician 16
tejido *m.* weaving 17
teleadicto/a *m., f.* couch potato 15
(teléfono) celular *m.* (cell) phone 11
telenovela *f.* soap opera 17
teletrabajo *m.* telecommuting 16
televisión *f.* television 2; 11
televisión por cable *f.* cable television 11
televisor *m.* television set 11
temer *v.* to fear 13
temperatura *f.* temperature 10
temporada *f.* period of time 5
temprano *adv.* early 7
tenedor *m.* fork 12
tener *v.* to have 3
  tener... años to be... years old 3
  Tengo... años. I'm... years old. 3
  tener (mucho) calor to be (very) hot 3
  tener (mucho) cuidado to be (very) careful 3
  tener dolor to have a pain 10
  tener éxito to be successful 16
  tener fiebre to have a fever 10
  tener (mucho) frío to be (very) cold 3
  tener ganas de (+ *inf.*) to feel like (*doing something*) 3
  tener (mucha) hambre *f.* to be (very) hungry 3
  tener (mucho) miedo (de) to be (very) afraid (of); to be (very) scared (of) 3
  tener miedo (de) que to be afraid that
  tener planes *m., pl.* to have plans 4
  tener (mucha) prisa to be in a (big) hurry 3
  tener que (+ *inf.*) *v.* to have to (*do something*) 3
  tener razón *f.* to be right 3
  tener (mucha) sed *f.* to be (very) thirsty 3
  tener (mucho) sueño to be (very) sleepy 3
  tener (mucha) suerte to be (very) lucky 3
  tener tiempo to have time 4
  tener una cita to have a date; to have an appointment 9
tenis *m.* tennis 4
tensión *f.* tension 15
tercer, tercero/a *adj.* third 5
terco/a *adj.* stubborn 10
terminar *v.* to end; to finish 2
  terminar de (+ *inf.*) *v.* to finish (*doing something*) 4
terremoto *m.* earthquake 18
terrible *adj. m., f.* terrible 13
ti *prep., obj. of prep., fam.* you
tiempo *m.* time 4; weather 5
  tiempo libre free time
tienda *f.* shop; store 6
tierra *f.* land; soil 13
tinto/a *adj.* red (wine) 8
tío/a *m., f.* uncle; aunt 3
tíos *m., pl.* aunts and uncles 3
título *m.* title 16
tiza *f.* chalk 2
toalla *f.* towel 7
tobillo *m.* ankle 10
tocar *v.* to play (*a musical instrument*) 17; to touch 13
todavía *adv.* yet; still 3, 5
todo *m.* everything 5
  en todo el mundo throughout the world 13
  Todo está bajo control. Everything is under control. 7
  todo derecho straight (ahead) 14
todo(s)/a(s) *adj.* all 4; whole
todos *m., pl.* all of us; *m., pl.* everybody; everyone
todos los días *adv.* every day 10
tomar *v.* to take; to drink 2
  tomar clases *f., pl.* to take classes 2
  tomar el sol to sunbathe 4
  tomar en cuenta to take into account
  tomar fotos *f., pl.* to take photos 5
  tomar la temperatura to take someone's temperature 10
  tomar una decisión to make a decision 15
tomate *m.* tomato 8
tonto/a *adj.* silly; foolish 3
torcerse (o:ue) (el tobillo) *v.* to sprain (one's ankle) 10
torcido/a *adj.* twisted; sprained 10
tormenta *f.* storm 18
tornado *m.* tornado 18
tortilla *f.* tortilla 8
  tortilla de maíz corn tortilla 8
tortuga (marina) *f.* (sea) turtle 13
tos *f., sing.* cough 10
toser *v.* to cough 10
tostado/a *adj.* toasted 8
tostadora *f.* toaster 12
trabajador(a) *adj.* hard-working 3
trabajar *v.* to work 2
trabajo *m.* job; work 16

traducir *v.* to translate 6
traer *v.* to bring 4
tráfico *m.* traffic 11
tragedia *f.* tragedy 17
traído/a *p.p.* brought 14
traje *m.* suit 6
traje (de baño) *m.* (bathing) suit 6
trajinera *f.* type of barge 3
tranquilo/a *adj.* calm; quiet 15
Tranquilo. Don't worry.; Be cool. 7
Tranquilo/a, cariño. Relax, sweetie. 11
transmitir *v.* to broadcast 18
tratar de (+ *inf.*) *v.* to try (*to do something*) 15
trece thirteen 1
treinta thirty 1, 2
y treinta thirty minutes past the hour (time) 1
tren *m.* train 5
tres three 1
trescientos/as *adj.* three hundred 2
trimestre *m.* trimester; quarter 2
triste *adj.* sad 5
tú *fam. sub. pron.* you 1
Tú eres... You are... 1
tu(s) *fam. poss. adj.* your 3
turismo *m.* tourism 5
turista *m., f.* tourist 1
turístico/a *adj.* touristic
tuyo(s)/a(s) *fam. poss. pron.* your; (of) yours 11

U

Ud. *form. sing.* you 1
Uds. *form., pl.* you 1
último/a *adj.* last 7
la última vez the last time 7
un, uno/a *indef. art.* a; one 1
uno/a *m., f., sing. pron.* one 1
a la una at one o'clock 1
una vez once; one time 6
una vez más one more time 9
único/a *adj.* only 3; unique 9
universidad *f.* university; college 2
unos/as *m., f., pl. indef. art.* some 1
los unos a los otros each other 11
unos/as *pron.* some 1
urgente *adj.* urgent 12
usar *v.* to wear; to use 6
usted (Ud.) *form. sing.* you 1
ustedes (Uds.) *form., pl.* you 1
útil *adj.* useful
uva *f.* grape 8

V

vaca *f.* cow 13
vacaciones *f. pl.* vacation 5
valle *m.* valley 13
vamos let's go 4
vaquero *m.* cowboy 17
de vaqueros *m., pl.* western (genre) 17
varios/as *adj. m. f., pl.* various; several 8
vaso *m.* glass 12
veces *f., pl.* times 6
vecino/a *m., f.* neighbor 12
veinte twenty 1
veinticinco twenty-five 1
veinticuatro twenty-four 1
veintidós twenty-two 1
veintinueve twenty-nine 1
veintiocho twenty-eight 1
veintiséis twenty-six 1
veintisiete twenty-seven 1
veintitrés twenty-three 1
veintiún, veintiuno/a twenty-one 1
vejez *f.* old age 9
velocidad *f.* speed 11
velocidad máxima *f.* speed limit 11
vencer *v.* to expire 14
vendedor(a) *m., f.* salesperson 6
vender *v.* to sell 6
venir *v.* to come 3
ventana *f.* window 2
ver *v.* to see 4
a ver *v.* let's see 2
ver películas *f., pl.* to see movies 4
verano *m.* summer 5
verbo *m.* verb
verdad *f.* truth
¿verdad? right? 1
verde *adj., m. f.* green 6
verduras *pl., f.* vegetables 8
vestido *m.* dress 6
vestirse (e:i) *v.* to get dressed 7
vez *f.* time 6
viajar *v.* to travel 2
viaje *m.* trip 5
viajero/a *m., f.* traveler 5
vida *f.* life 9
video *m.* video 1, 11
videoconferencia *f.* videoconference 16
videojuego *m.* video game 4
vidrio *m.* glass 13
viejo/a *adj.* old 3
viento *m.* wind 5
viernes *m., sing.* Friday 2
vinagre *m.* vinegar 8
vino *m.* wine 8
vino blanco *m.* white wine 8
vino tinto *m.* red wine 8
violencia *f.* violence 18
visitar *v.* to visit 4
visitar monumentos *m., pl.* to visit monuments 4
visto/a *p.p.* seen 14
vitamina *f.* vitamin 15
viudo/a *adj.* widower/widow 9
vivienda *f.* housing 12
vivir *v.* to live 3
vivo/a *adj.* bright; lively; living
volante *m.* steering wheel 11
volcán *m.* volcano 13
vóleibol *m.* volleyball 4
volver (o:ue) *v.* to return 4
volver a ver(te, lo, la) *v.* to see (you, him, her) again 18
vos *pron.* you
vosotros/as *form., pl.* you 1
votar *v.* to vote 18
vuelta *f.* return trip
vuelto/a *p.p.* returned 14
vuestro(s)/a(s) *poss. adj.* your 3; (of) yours *fam.* 11

W

walkman *m.* walkman

Y

y *conj.* and 1
y cuarto quarter after (time) 1
y media half-past (time) 1
y quince quarter after (time) 1
y treinta thirty (minutes past the hour) 1
¿Y tú? *fam.* And you? 1
¿Y usted? *form.* And you? 1
ya *adv.* already 6
yerno *m.* son-in-law 3
yo *sub. pron.* I 1
Yo soy... I'm... 1
yogur *m.* yogurt 8

Z

zanahoria *f.* carrot 8
zapatería *f.* shoe store 14
zapatos de tenis *m., pl.* tennis shoes, sneakers 6

English-Spanish

A

a **un/a** *m., f., sing.; indef. art.* 1
@ *(symbol)* **arroba** *f.* 11
A.M. **mañana** *f.* 1
able: be able to **poder (o:ue)** *v.* 4
aboard **a bordo** 1
above all **sobre todo** 13
accident **accidente** *m.* 10
accompany **acompañar** *v.* 14
account **cuenta** *f.* 14
  on account of **por** *prep.* 11
accountant **contador(a)** *m., f.* 16
accounting **contabilidad** *f.* 2
ache **dolor** *m.* 10
acquainted: be acquainted with **conocer** *v.* 6
action (genre) **de acción** *f.* 17
active **activo/a** *adj.* 15
actor **actor** *m.*, **actriz** *f.* 16
addict *(drug)* **drogadicto/a** *adj.* 15
additional **adicional** *adj.*
address **dirección** *f.* 14
adjective **adjetivo** *m.*
adolescence **adolescencia** *f.* 9
adventure (genre) **de aventura** *f.* 17
advertise **anunciar** *v.* 18
advertisement **anuncio** *m.* 16
advice **consejo** *m.* 6
  give advice **dar consejos** 6
advise **aconsejar** *v.* 12
advisor **consejero/a** *m., f.* 16
aerobic **aeróbico/a** *adj.* 15
  aerobics class **clase de ejercicios aeróbicos** 15
  to do aerobics **hacer ejercicios aeróbicos** 15
affected **afectado/a** *adj.* 13
  be affected (by) **estar** *v.* **afectado/a (por)** 13
affirmative **afirmativo/a** *adj.*
afraid: be (very) afraid (of) **tener (mucho) miedo (de)** 3
  be afraid that **tener miedo (de) que**
after **después de** *prep.* 7; **después de que** *conj.* 13
afternoon **tarde** *f.* 1
afterward **después** *adv.* 7
again **otra vez**
age **edad** *f.* 9
agree **concordar** *v.*
agree **estar** *v.* **de acuerdo** 17
  I agree. **Estoy de acuerdo.** 17
  I don't agree. **No estoy de acuerdo.** 17
agreement **acuerdo** *m.* 16
AIDS **SIDA** *m.* 18
air **aire** *m.* 13
  air pollution **contaminación del aire** 13
airplane **avión** *m.* 5
airport **aeropuerto** *m.* 5
alarm clock **despertador** *m.* 7
alcohol **alcohol** *m.* 15
  to consume alcohol **consumir alcohol** 15
alcoholic **alcohólico/a** *adj.* 15
all **todo(s)/a(s)** *adj.* 4
  all of us **todos** 1
  all over the world **en todo el mundo**
allergic **alérgico/a** *adj.* 10
  be allergic (to) **ser alérgico/a (a)** 10
alleviate **aliviar** *v.*
almost **casi** *adv.* 10
alone **solo/a** *adj.*
along **por** *prep.* 11
already **ya** *adv.* 6
also **también** *adv.* 2; 7
altar **altar** *m.* 9
aluminum **aluminio** *m.* 13
  (made) of aluminum **de aluminio** 13
always **siempre** *adv.* 7
American *(North)* **norteamericano/a** *adj.* 3
among **entre** *prep.* 2
amusement **diversión** *f.*
and **y** 1, **e** *(before words beginning with i or hi)* 4
  And you? **¿Y tú?** *fam.* 1; **¿Y usted?** *form.* 1
angel **ángel** *m.* 9
angry **enojado/a** *adj.* 5
  get angry (with) **enojarse** *v.* **(con)** 7
animal **animal** *m.* 13
ankle **tobillo** *m.* 10
anniversary **aniversario** *m.* 9
  (wedding) anniversary **aniversario** *m.* **(de bodas)** 9
announce **anunciar** *v.* 18
announcer *(TV/radio)* **locutor(a)** *m., f.* 18
annoy **molestar** *v.* 7
another **otro/a** *adj.* 6
answer **contestar** *v.* 2; **respuesta** *f.*
answering machine **contestadora** *f.*
antibiotic **antibiótico** *m.* 10
any **algún, alguno/a(s)** *adj.* 7
anyone **alguien** *pron.* 7
anything **algo** *pron.* 7
apartment **apartamento** *m.* 12
apartment building **edificio de apartamentos** 12
appear **parecer** *v.*
appetizers **entremeses** *m., pl.* 8
applaud **aplaudir** *v.* 17
apple **manzana** *f.* 8
appliance (electric) **electrodoméstico** *m.* 12
applicant **aspirante** *m., f.* 16
application **solicitud** *f.* 16
  job application **solicitud de trabajo** 16
apply *(for a job)* **solicitar** *v.* 16
  apply for a loan **pedir (e:ie)** *v.* **un préstamo** 14
appointment **cita** *f.* 9
  have an appointment **tener** *v.* **una cita** 9
appreciate **apreciar** *v.* 17
April **abril** *m.* 5
aquatic **acuático/a** *adj.*
archaeologist **arqueólogo/a** *m., f.* 16
archaeology **arqueología** *f.* 2
architect **arquitecto/a** *m., f.* 16
area **región** *f.* 13
Argentina **Argentina** *f.* 1
Argentine **argentino/a** *adj.* 3
arm **brazo** *m.* 10
armchair **sillón** *m.* 12
army **ejército** *m.* 18
around **por** *prep.* 11
  around here **por aquí** 11
arrange **arreglar** *v.* 11
arrival **llegada** *f.* 5
arrive **llegar** *v.* 2
art **arte** *m.* 2
  (fine) arts **bellas artes** *f., pl.* 17
article *m.* **artículo** 18
artist **artista** *m., f.* 3
artistic **artístico/a** *adj.* 17
arts **artes** *f., pl.* 17
as **como** 8
  as a child **de niño/a** 10
  as... as **tan... como** 8
  as many... as **tantos/as... como** 8
  as much... as **tanto... como** 8
  as soon as **en cuanto** *conj.* 13; **tan pronto como** *conj.* 13
ask *(a question)* **preguntar** *v.* 2
  ask for **pedir (e:i)** *v.* 4
asparagus **espárragos** *m., pl.* 8
aspirin **aspirina** *f.* 10
at **a** *prep.* 1; **en** *prep.* 2
  at + *time* **a la(s)** + *time* 1
  at home **en casa** 7
  at least **por lo menos** 10
  at night **por la noche** 7
  at the end (of) **al fondo (de)** 12
  At what time...? **¿A qué hora...?** 1
  At your service. **A sus órdenes.** 11
ATM **cajero automático** *m.* 14
attempt **intento** *m.* **11**
attend **asistir (a)** *v.* 3
attic **altillo** *m.* 12
attract **atraer** *v.* 4
audience **público** *m.* 17
August **agosto** *m.* 5
aunt **tía** *f.* 3
  aunts and uncles **tíos** *m., pl.* 3
automobile **automóvil** *m.* 5; **carro** *m.*; **coche** *m.* 11
autumn **otoño** *m.* 5
avenue **avenida** *f.*
avoid **evitar** *v.* 13
award **premio** *m.* 17

B

backpack **mochila** *f.* 2
bad **mal, malo/a** *adj.* 3
  It's bad that... **Es malo que...** 12

It's not at all bad. **No está nada mal.** 5
bag **bolsa** *f.* 6
bakery **panadería** *f.* 14
balanced **equilibrado/a** *adj.* 15
to eat a balanced diet **comer una dieta equilibrada** 15
balcony **balcón** *m.* 12
ball **pelota** *f.* 4
banana **banana** *f.* 8
band **banda** *f.* 17
bank **banco** *m.* 14
bargain **ganga** *f.* 6; **regatear** *v.* 6
baseball (*game*) **béisbol** *m.* 4
basement **sótano** *m.* 12
basketball (*game*) **baloncesto** *m.* 4
bathe **bañarse** *v.* 7
bathing suit **traje** *m.* **de baño** 6
bathroom **baño** *m.* 7; **cuarto de baño** *m.* 7
be **ser** *v.* 1; **estar** *v.* 2
be... years old **tener... años** 3
be sick of... **estar harto/a de...** 18
beach **playa** *f.* 5
beans **frijoles** *m., pl.* 8
beautiful **hermoso/a** *adj.* 6
beauty **belleza** *f.* 14
beauty salon **peluquería** *f.* 14; **salón** *m.* **de belleza** 14
because **porque** *conj.* 2
because of **por** *prep.* 11
become (+ *adj.*) **ponerse (+ *adj.*)** 7; **convertirse** *v.*
bed **cama** *f.* 5
go to bed **acostarse (o:ue)** *v.* 7
bedroom **alcoba** *f.*; **dormitorio** *m.* 12; **recámara** *f.*
beef **carne de res** *f.* 8
been **sido** *p.p.* 15
beer **cerveza** *f.* 8
before **antes** *adv.* 7; **antes de** *prep.* 7; **antes (de) que** *conj.* 13
beg **rogar (o:ue)** *v.* 12
begin **comenzar (e:ie)** *v.* 4; **empezar (e:ie)** *v.* 4
behalf: on behalf of **de parte de** 11
behind **detrás de** *prep.* 2
believe (in) **creer** *v.* **(en)** 3; **creer** *v.* 13
not to believe **no creer** 13
believed **creído/a** *p.p.* 14
bellhop **botones** *m., f. sing.* 5
below **debajo de** *prep.* 2
belt **cinturón** *m.* 6
benefit **beneficio** *m.* 16
beside **al lado de** *prep.* 2
besides **además (de)** *adv.* 10
best **mejor** *adj.*
the best **el/la mejor** *m., f.* 8; **lo mejor** *neuter* 18
better **mejor** *adj.* 8
It's better that... **Es mejor que...** 12
between **entre** *prep.* 2
beverage **bebida** *f.*
alcoholic beverage **bebida alcohólica** *f.* 15
bicycle **bicicleta** *f.* 4
big **gran, grande** *adj.* 3
bill **cuenta** *f.* 9
billion **mil millones**
biology **biología** *f.* 2
bird **ave** *f.* 13; **pájaro** *m.* 13
birth **nacimiento** *m.* 9
birthday **cumpleaños** *m., sing.* 9
have a birthday **cumplir** *v.* **años** 9
black **negro/a** *adj.* 6
blackboard **pizarra** *f.* 2
blanket **manta** *f.* 12
block (city) **cuadra** *f.* 14
blog **blog** *m.* 11
blond(e) **rubio/a** *adj.* 3
blouse **blusa** *f.* 6
blue **azul** *adj. m., f.* 6
boarding house **pensión** *f.*
boat **barco** *m.* 5
body **cuerpo** *m.* 10
bone **hueso** *m.* 10
book **libro** *m.* 2
bookcase **estante** *m.* 12
bookshelves **estante** *m.* 12
bookstore **librería** *f.* 2
boot **bota** *f.* 6
bore **aburrir** *v.* 7
bored **aburrido/a** *adj.* 5
be bored **estar** *v.* **aburrido/a** 5
get bored **aburrirse** *v.* 17
boring **aburrido/a** *adj.* 5
born: be born **nacer** *v.* 9
borrow **pedir (e:ie)** *v.* **prestado** 14
borrowed **prestado/a** *adj.*
boss **jefe** *m.*, **jefa** *f.* 16
bother **molestar** *v.* 7
bottle **botella** *f.* 9
bottle of wine **botella de vino** 9
bottom **fondo** *m.*
boulevard **bulevar** *m.*
boy **chico** *m.* 1; **muchacho** *m.* 3
boyfriend **novio** *m.* 3
brakes **frenos** *m., pl.*
bread **pan** *m.* 8
break **romper** *v.* 10
break (one's leg) **romperse (la pierna)** 10
break down **dañar** *v.* 10
The... broke down. **Se nos dañó el/la...** 11
break up (with) **romper** *v.* **(con)** 9
breakfast **desayuno** *m.* 2, 8
have breakfast **desayunar** *v.* 2
breathe **respirar** *v.* 13
bring **traer** *v.* 4
broadcast **transmitir** *v.* 18; **emitir** *v.* 18
brochure **folleto** *m.*
broken **roto/a** *adj.* 10, 14
be broken **estar roto/a** 10
brother **hermano** *m.* 3
brother-in-law **cuñado** *m., f.* 3
brothers and sisters **hermanos** *m., pl.* 3
brought **traído/a** *p.p.* 14
brown **café** *adj.* 6; **marrón** *adj.* 6
brunet(te) **moreno/a** *adj.* 3
brush **cepillar** *v.* 7
brush one's hair **cepillarse el pelo** 7
brush one's teeth **cepillarse los dientes** 7
bucket **balde** *m.* 5
build **construir** *v.* 4
building **edificio** *m.* 12
bump into (*something accidentally*) **darse con** 10; (*someone*) **encontrarse** *v.* 11
burn (a CD/DVD) **quemar** *v.* **(un CD/DVD)**
burned (out) **quemado/a** *adj.* 11
bus **autobús** *m.* 1
bus station **estación** *f.* **de autobuses** 5
business **negocios** *m. pl.* 16
business administration **administración** *f.* **de empresas** 2
business-related **comercial** *adj.* 16
businessperson **hombre** *m.* **/ mujer** *f.* **de negocios** 16
busy **ocupado/a** *adj.* 5
but **pero** *conj.* 2; (rather) **sino** *conj.* (*in negative sentences*) 7
butcher shop **carnicería** *f.* 14
butter **mantequilla** *f.* 8
buy **comprar** *v.* 2
by **por** *prep.* 11; **para** *prep.* 11
by means of **por** *prep.* 11
by phone **por teléfono** 11
by plane **en avión** 5
by way of **por** *prep.* 11
bye **chau** *interj. fam.* 1

C

cable television **televisión** *f.* **por cable** *m.* 11
café **café** *m.* 4
cafeteria **cafetería** *f.* 2
caffeine **cafeína** *f.* 15
cake **pastel** *m.* 9
chocolate cake **pastel de chocolate** *m.* 9
calculator **calculadora** *f.* 2
call **llamar** *v.* 11
be called **llamarse** *v.* 7
call on the phone **llamar por teléfono**
calm **tranquilo/a** *adj.* 15
calorie **caloría** *f.* 15
camera **cámara** *f.* 11
camp **acampar** *v.* 5
can (*tin*) **lata** *f.* 13
can **poder (o:ue)** *v.* 4

Could I ask you something? **¿Podría pedirte algo?** 17
Canadian **canadiense** *adj.* 3
candidate **aspirante** *m., f.* 16; candidate **candidato/a** *m., f.* 18
candy **dulces** *m., pl.* 9
capital city **capital** *f.* 1
car **coche** *m.* 11; **carro** *m.* 11; **auto(móvil)** *m.* 5
caramel **caramelo** *m.* 9
card **tarjeta** *f.*; (*playing*) **carta** *f.* 5
care **cuidado** *m.* 3
Take care! **¡Cuídense!** *v.* 15
take care of **cuidar** *v.* 13
career **carrera** *f.* 16
careful: be (very) careful **tener** *v.* **(mucho) cuidado** 3
caretaker **ama** *m., f.* **de casa** 12
carpenter **carpintero/a** *m., f.* 16
carpet **alfombra** *f.* 12
carrot **zanahoria** *f.* 8
carry **llevar** *v.* 2
cartoons **dibujos** *m, pl.* **animados** 17
case: in case (that) **en caso (de) que** 13
cash (a check) **cobrar** *v.* 14; cash **(en) efectivo** 6
cash register **caja** *f.* 6
pay in cash **pagar** *v.* **al contado** 14; **pagar en efectivo** 14
cashier **cajero/a** *m., f.*
cat **gato** *m.* 13
CD **disco compacto** *m.* 11
CD player **reproductor de CD** *m.* 11
CD-ROM **cederrón** *m.* 11
celebrate **celebrar** *v.* 9
celebration **celebración** *f.*
young woman's fifteenth birthday celebration **quinceañera** *f.* 9
cellar **sótano** *m.* 12
(cell) phone **(teléfono) celular** *m.* 11
cemetery **cementerio** *m.* 9
cereal **cereales** *m., pl.* 8
certain **cierto** *m.*; **seguro** *m.* 13
it's (not) certain **(no) es cierto/seguro** 13
chalk **tiza** *f.* 2
champagne **champán** *m.* 9
change: in change **de cambio** 2
change **cambiar** *v.* **(de)** 9
channel (*TV*) **canal** *m.* 11; 17
character (*fictional*) **personaje** *m.* 11, 17
(main) character *m.* **personaje (principal)** 17
chat **conversar** *v.* 2
chauffeur **conductor(a)** *m., f.* 1
cheap **barato/a** *adj.* 6
check **comprobar (o:ue)** *v.*; **revisar** *v.* 11; (*bank*) **cheque** *m.* 14
check the oil **revisar el aceite** 11
checking account **cuenta** *f.* **corriente** 14
cheese **queso** *m.* 8
chef **cocinero/a** *m., f.* 16
chemistry **química** *f.* 2
chest of drawers **cómoda** *f.* 12
chicken **pollo** *m.* 8
child **niño/a** *m., f.* 3
childhood **niñez** *f.* 9
children **hijos** *m., pl.* 3
Chinese **chino/a** *adj.* 3
chocolate **chocolate** *m.* 9
chocolate cake **pastel** *m.* **de chocolate** 9
cholesterol **colesterol** *m.* 15
choose **escoger** *v.* 8
chop (*food*) **chuleta** *f.* 8
Christmas **Navidad** *f.* 9
church **iglesia** *f.* 4
cinnamon **canela** *f.* 10
citizen **ciudadano/a** *adj.* 18
city **ciudad** *f.* 4
class **clase** *f.* 2
take classes **tomar clases** 2
classical **clásico/a** *adj.* 17
classmate **compañero/a** *m., f.* **de clase** 2
clean **limpio/a** *adj.* 5; **limpiar** *v.* 12
clean the house *v.* **limpiar la casa** 12
clear (*weather*) **despejado/a** *adj.*
clear the table **quitar la mesa** 12
It's (very) clear. (*weather*) **Está (muy) despejado.**
clerk **dependiente/a** *m., f.* 6
climate change **cambio climático** *m.* 13
climb **escalar** *v.* 4
climb mountains **escalar montañas** 4
clinic **clínica** *f.* 10
clock **reloj** *m.* 2
close **cerrar (e:ie)** *v.* 4
closed **cerrado/a** *adj.* 5
closet **armario** *m.* 12
clothes **ropa** *f.* 6
clothes dryer **secadora** *f.* 12
clothing **ropa** *f.* 6
cloud **nube** *f.* 13
cloudy **nublado/a** *adj.* 5
It's (very) cloudy. **Está (muy) nublado.** 5
coat **abrigo** *m.* 6
coffee **café** *m.* 8
coffee maker **cafetera** *f.* 12
cold **frío** *m.* 5; (*illness*) **resfriado** *m.* 10
be (*feel*) (very) cold **tener (mucho) frío** 3
It's (very) cold. (*weather*) **Hace (mucho) frío.** 5
college **universidad** *f.* 2
collision **choque** *m.* 18
color **color** *m.* 6
comb one's hair **peinarse** *v.* 7
come **venir** *v.* 3
come on **ándale** *interj.* 14
comedy **comedia** *f.* 17
comfortable **cómodo/a** *adj.* 5
commerce **negocios** *m., pl.* 16
commercial **comercial** *adj.* 16
communicate (with) **comunicarse** *v.* **(con)** 18
communication **comunicación** *f.* 18
means of communication **medios** *m. pl.* **de comunicación** 18
community **comunidad** *f.* 1
company **compañía** *f.* 16; **empresa** *f.* 16
comparison **comparación** *f.*
completely **completamente** *adv.* 16
composer **compositor(a)** *m., f.* 17
computer **computadora** *f.* 1
computer disc **disco** *m.*
computer monitor **monitor** *m.* 11
computer programmer **programador(a)** *m., f.* 3
computer science **computación** *f.* 2
concert **concierto** *m.* 17
conductor (*musical*) **director(a)** *m., f.* 17
confirm **confirmar** *v.* 5
confirm a reservation **confirmar una reservación** 5
confused **confundido/a** *adj.* 5
congested **congestionado/a** *adj.* 10
Congratulations! **¡Felicidades!**; **¡Felicitaciones!** *f., pl.* 9
conservation **conservación** *f.* 13
conserve **conservar** *v.* 13
considering **para** *prep.* 11
consume **consumir** *v.* 15
container **envase** *m.* 13
contamination **contaminación** *f.*
content **contento/a** *adj.* 5
contest **concurso** *m.* 17
continue **seguir (e:i)** *v.* 4
control **control** *m.*; **controlar** *v.* 13
be under control **estar bajo control** 7
conversation **conversación** *f.* 1
converse **conversar** *v.* 2
cook **cocinar** *v.* 12; **cocinero/a** *m., f.* 16
cookie **galleta** *f.* 9
cool **fresco/a** *adj.* 5
Be cool. **Tranquilo.** 7
It's cool. (*weather*) **Hace fresco.** 5
corn **maíz** *m.* 8
corner **esquina** *f.* 14
cost **costar (o:ue)** *v.* 6
Costa Rica **Costa Rica** *f.* 1
Costa Rican **costarricense** *adj.* 3
costume **disfraz** *m.*
cotton **algodón** *f.* 6
(made of) cotton **de algodón** 6
couch **sofá** *m.* 12
couch potato **teleadicto/a** *m., f.* 15
cough **tos** *f.* 10; **toser** *v.* 10
counselor **consejero/a** *m., f.* 16

count (on) **contar (o:ue)** *v.* **(con)** 4, 12
country (*nation*) **país** *m.* 1
countryside **campo** *m.* 5
(married) couple **pareja** *f.* 9
course **curso** *m.* 2; **materia** *f.* 2
courtesy **cortesía** *f.*
cousin **primo/a** *m., f.* 3
cover **cubrir** *v.*
covered **cubierto/a** *p.p.*
cow **vaca** *f.* 13
crafts **artesanía** *f.* 17
craftsmanship **artesanía** *f.* 17
crater **cráter** *m.* 13
crazy **loco/a** *adj.* 6
create **crear** *v.*
credit **crédito** *m.* 6
  credit card **tarjeta** *f.* **de crédito** 6
crime **crimen** *m.* 18
cross **cruzar** *v.* 14
cry **llorar** *v.* 15
Cuba **Cuba** *f.* 1
Cuban **cubano/a** *adj.* 3
culture **cultura** *f.* 2, 17
cup **taza** *f.* 12
currency exchange **cambio** *m.* **de moneda**
current events **actualidades** *f., pl.* 18
curtains **cortinas** *f., pl.* 12
custard (*baked*) **flan** *m.* 9
custom **costumbre** *f.* 1
customer **cliente/a** *m., f.* 6
customs **aduana** *f.* 5
  customs inspector **inspector(a)** *m., f.* **de aduanas** 5
cybercafé **cibercafé** *m.* 11
cycling **ciclismo** *m.* 4

D

dad **papá** *m.* 3
daily **diario/a** *adj.* 7
  daily routine **rutina** *f.* **diaria** 7
damage **dañar** *v.* 10
dance **bailar** *v.* 2; **danza** *f.* 17; **baile** *m.* 17
dancer **bailarín/bailarina** *m., f.* 17
danger **peligro** *m.* 13
dangerous **peligroso/a** *adj.* 18
date (*appointment*) **cita** *f.* 9; (*calendar*) **fecha** *f.* 5; (*someone*) **salir** *v.* **con (alguien)** 9
  have a date **tener una cita** 9
daughter **hija** *f.* 3
daughter-in-law **nuera** *f.* 3
day **día** *m.* 1
  day before yesterday **anteayer** *adv.* 6
deal: It's not a big deal. **No es para tanto.** 12
death **muerte** *f.* 9
decaffeinated **descafeinado/a** *adj.* 15
December **diciembre** *m.* 5
decide **decidir** *v.* **(+ *inf.*)** 3
decided **decidido/a** *adj. p.p.* 14
declare **declarar** *v.* 18
deforestation **deforestación** *f.* 13
delicious **delicioso/a** *adj.* 8; **rico/a** *adj.* 8; **sabroso/a** *adj.* 8
delighted **encantado/a** *adj.* 1
dentist **dentista** *m., f.* 10
deny **negar (e:ie)** *v.* 13
  not to deny **no dudar** 13
department store **almacén** *m.* 6
departure **salida** *f.* 5
deposit **depositar** *v.* 14
describe **describir** *v.* 3
described **descrito/a** *p.p.* 14
desert **desierto** *m.* 13
design **diseño** *m.*
designer **diseñador(a)** *m., f.* 16
desire **desear** *v.* 2
desk **escritorio** *m.* 2
dessert **postre** *m.* 9
destroy **destruir** *v.* 13
develop **desarrollar** *v.* 13
diary **diario** *m.* 1
dictatorship **dictadura** *f.* 18
dictionary **diccionario** *m.* 1
die **morir (o:ue)** *v.* 8
died **muerto/a** *p.p.* 14
diet **dieta** *f.* 15; **alimentación**
  balanced diet **dieta equilibrada** 15
  be on a diet **estar a dieta** 15
difficult **difícil** *adj. m., f.* 3
digital camera **cámara** *f.* **digital** 11
dining room **comedor** *m.* 12
dinner **cena** *f.* 2, 8
  have dinner **cenar** *v.* 2
direct **dirigir** *v.* 17
director **director(a)** *m., f.* 17
dirty **ensuciar** *v.*; **sucio/a** *adj.* 5
  get (something) dirty **ensuciar** *v.* 12
disagree **no estar de acuerdo**
disaster **desastre** *m.* 18
discover **descubrir** *v.* 13
discovered **descubierto/a** *p.p.* 14
discrimination **discriminación** *f.* 18
dish **plato** *m.* 8, 12
  main dish *m.* **plato principal** 8
dishwasher **lavaplatos** *m., sing.* 12
disk **disco** *m.*
disorderly **desordenado/a** *adj.* 5
dive **bucear** *v.* 4
divorce **divorcio** *m.* 9
divorced **divorciado/a** *adj.* 9
  get divorced (from) **divorciarse** *v.* **(de)** 9
dizzy **mareado/a** *adj.* 10
do **hacer** *v.* 4
  do aerobics **hacer ejercicios aeróbicos** 15
  do household chores **hacer quehaceres domésticos** 12
  do stretching exercises **hacer ejercicios de estiramiento** 15
(I) don't want to. **No quiero.** 4
doctor **doctor(a)** *m., f.* 3; 10; **médico/a** *m., f.* 3
documentary (*film*) **documental** *m.* 17
dog **perro** *m.* 13
domestic **doméstico/a** *adj.*
  domestic appliance **electrodoméstico** *m.*
done **hecho/a** *p.p.* 14
door **puerta** *f.* 2
doorman/doorwoman **portero/a** *m., f.* 1
dormitory **residencia** *f.* **estudiantil** 2
double **doble** *adj.* 5
  double room **habitación** *f.* **doble** 5
doubt **duda** *f.* 13; **dudar** *v.* 13
  not to doubt 13
  There is no doubt that... **No cabe duda de** 13; **No hay duda de** 13
Down with…! **¡Abajo el/la…!**
download **descargar** *v.* 11
downtown **centro** *m.* 4
drama **drama** *m.* 17
dramatic **dramático/a** *adj.* 17
draw **dibujar** *v.* 2
drawing **dibujo** *m.* 17
dress **vestido** *m.* 6
  get dressed **vestirse (e:i)** *v.* 7
drink **beber** *v.* 3; **bebida** *f.* 8; **tomar** *v.* 2
drive **conducir** *v.* 6; **manejar** *v.* 11
driver **conductor(a)** *m., f.* 1
drug **droga** *f.* 15
  drug addict **drogadicto/a** *adj.* 15
dry oneself **secarse** *v.* 7
during **durante** *prep.* 7; **por** *prep.* 11
dust **sacudir** *v.* 12; **quitar** *v.* **el polvo** 12
dust the furniture **sacudir los muebles** 12
duster **plumero** *m.* 12
DVD player **reproductor** *m.* **de DVD** 11

E

each **cada** *adj.* 6
each other **los unos a los otros** 11
eagle **águila** *f.*
ear (outer) **oreja** *f.* 10
earing **arete** *m.* 6
early **temprano** *adv.* 7
earn **ganar** *v.* 16
earthquake **terremoto** *m.* 18
ease **aliviar** *v.*
east **este** *m.* 14
  to the east **al este** 14
easy **fácil** *adj. m., f.* 3
eat **comer** *v.* 3
ecological **ecologista** *adj. m., f.* 13
ecologist **ecologista** *m., f.* 13

ecology **ecología** *f.* 13
economics **economía** *f.* 2
ecotourism **ecoturismo** *m.* 13
Ecuador **Ecuador** *m.* 1
Ecuadorian **ecuatoriano/a** *adj.* 3
effective **eficaz** *adj. m., f.*
egg **huevo** *m.* 8
eight **ocho** 1
eight hundred **ochocientos/as** 2
eighteen **dieciocho** 1
eighth **octavo/a** 5
eighty **ochenta** 2
either... or **o... o** *conj.* 7
eldest **el/la mayor** 8
elect **elegir** *v.* 18
election **elecciones** *f. pl.* 18
electric appliance **electrodoméstico** *m.* 12
electrician **electricista** *m., f.* 16
electricity **luz** *f.* 12
elegant **elegante** *adj. m., f.* 6
elevator **ascensor** *m.* 5
eleven **once** 1
e-mail **correo** *m.* **electrónico** 4
e-mail address **dirrección** *f.* **electrónica** 11
  e-mail message **mensaje** *m.* **electrónico** 4
  read e-mail **leer** *v.* **el correo electrónico** 4
embarrassed **avergonzado/a** *adj.* 5 embrace (each other) **abrazar(se)** *v.* 11
emergency **emergencia** *f.* 10
  emergency room **sala** *f.* **de emergencia** 10
employee **empleado/a** *m., f.* 5
employment **empleo** *m.* 16
end **fin** *m.* 4; **terminar** *v.* 2
  end table **mesita** *f.* 12
endure **aguantar** *v.* 14
energy **energía** *f.* 13
engaged: get engaged (to) **comprometerse** *v.* **(con)** 9
engineer **ingeniero/a** *m., f.* 3
English (*language*) **inglés** *m.* 2; **inglés, inglesa** *adj.* 3
enjoy **disfrutar** *v.* **(de)** 15
enough **bastante** *adv.* 10
entertainment **diversión** *f.* 4
entrance **entrada** *f.* 12
envelope **sobre** *m.* 14
environment **medio ambiente** *m.* 13
environmental sciences **ciencias ambientales** 2
equality **igualdad** *f.* 18
equipped **equipado/a** *adj.* 15
erase **borrar** *v.* 11
eraser **borrador** *m.* 2
errand **diligencia** *f.* 14
essay **ensayo** *m.* 3
evening **tarde** *f.* 1
event **acontecimiento** *m.* 18
every day **todos los días** 10
everything **todo** *m.* 5
  Everything is under control. **Todo está bajo control.** 7
exactly **en punto** 1
exam **examen** *m.* 2
excellent **excelente** *adj.* 5
excess **exceso** *m.* 15
  in excess **en exceso** 15
exchange **intercambiar** *v.*
  in exchange for **por** 11
exciting **emocionante** *adj. m., f.*
excursion **excursión** *f.*
excuse **disculpar** *v.*
Excuse me. (*May I?*) **Con permiso.** 1; (*I beg your pardon.*) **Perdón.** 1
exercise **ejercicio** *m.* 15; **hacer** *v.* **ejercicio** 15; (a degree/profession) **ejercer** *v.* 16
exit **salida** *f.* 5
expensive **caro/a** *adj.* 6
experience **experiencia** *f.* 18
expire **vencer** *v.* 14
explain **explicar** *v.* 2
explore **explorar** *v.*
expression **expresión** *f.*
extinction **extinción** *f.* 13
extremely delicious **riquísimo/a** *adj.* 8
extremely serious **gravísimo** *adj.* 13
eye **ojo** *m.* 10

F

fabulous **fabuloso/a** *adj.* 5
face **cara** *f.* 7
facing **enfrente de** *prep.* 14
fact: in fact **de hecho**
factory **fábrica** *f.* 13
fall (down) **caerse** *v.* 10
  fall asleep **dormirse (o:ue)** *v.* 7
  fall in love (with) **enamorarse** *v.* **(de)** 9
fall (season) **otoño** *m.* 5
fallen **caído/a** *p.p.* 14
family **familia** *f.* 3
famous **famoso/a** *adj.* 16
fan **aficionado/a** *adj.* 4
  be a fan (of) **ser aficionado/a (a)** 4
far from **lejos de** *prep.* 2
farewell **despedida** *f.*
fascinate **fascinar** *v.* 7
fashion **moda** *f.* 6
  be in fashion **estar de moda** 6
fast **rápido/a** *adj.*
fat **gordo/a** *adj.* 3; **grasa** *f.* 15
father **padre** *m.* 3
father-in-law **suegro** *m.* 3
favorite **favorito/a** *adj.* 4
fax (machine) ***fax*** *m.* 11
fear **miedo** *m.* 3; **temer** *v.* 13
February **febrero** *m.* 5
feel **sentir(se) (e:ie)** *v.* 7
  feel like (*doing something*) **tener ganas de (+ *inf.*)** 3
festival **festival** *m.* 17
fever **fiebre** *f.* 10
  have a fever **tener** *v.* **fiebre** 10
few **pocos/as** *adj. pl.*
  fewer than **menos de** (+ *number*) 8
field: major field of study **especialización** *f.*
fifteen **quince** 1
  fifteen-year-old girl **quinceañera** *f.*
  young woman celebrating her fifteenth birthday **quinceañera** *f.* 9
fifth **quinto/a** 5
fifty **cincuenta** 2
fight (for/against) **luchar** *v.* **(por/contra)** 18
figure (*number*) **cifra** *f.*
file **archivo** *m.* 11
fill **llenar** *v.* 11
  fill out (a form) **llenar (un formulario)** 14
  fill the tank **llenar el tanque** 11
finally **finalmente** *adv.* 15; **por último** 7; **por fin** 11
find **encontrar (o:ue)** *v.* 4
  find (each other) **encontrar(se)**
  find out **enterarse** *v.* 16
fine **multa** *f.*
  That's fine. **Está bien.** 11
(fine) arts **bellas artes** *f., pl.* 17
finger **dedo** *m.* 10
finish **terminar** *v.* 2
  finish (*doing something*) **terminar** *v.* **de (+ *inf.*)** 4
fire **incendio** *m.* 18; **despedir (e:i)** *v.* 16
firefighter **bombero/a** *m., f.* 16
firm **compañía** *f.* 16; **empresa** *f.* 16
first **primer, primero/a** 2, 5
fish (*food*) **pescado** *m.* 8; **pescar** *v.* 5; (*live*) **pez** *m., sing.* (**peces** *pl.*) 13
  fish market **pescadería** *f.* 14
fishing **pesca** *f.* 5
fit (*clothing*) **quedar** *v.* 7
five **cinco** 1
five hundred **quinientos/as** 2
fix (*put in working order*) **arreglar** *v.* 11; (*clothes, hair, etc. to go out*) **arreglarse** 7
fixed **fijo/a** *adj.* 6
flag **bandera** *f.*
flank steak **lomo** *m.* 8
flat tire: We had a flat tire. **Se nos pinchó una llanta.** 11
flexible **flexible** *adj.* 15
flood **inundación** *f.* 18
floor (*of a building*) **piso** *m.* 5; **suelo** *m.* 12
  ground floor **planta baja** *f.* 5
  top floor **planta** *f.* **alta**
flower **flor** *f.* 13
flu **gripe** *f.* 10
fog **niebla** *f.*
folk **folclórico/a** *adj.* 17

follow **seguir (e:i)** *v.* 4
food **comida** *f.* 4, 8
foolish **tonto/a** *adj.* 3
foot **pie** *m.* 10
football **fútbol** *m.* **americano** 4
for **para** *prep.* 11; **por** *prep.* 11
for example **por ejemplo** 11
for me **para mí** 8
forbid **prohibir** *v.*
foreign **extranjero/a** *adj.* 17
foreign languages **lenguas** *f., pl.* **extranjeras** 2
forest **bosque** *m.* 13
forget **olvidar** *v.* 10
fork **tenedor** *m.* 12
form **formulario** *m.* 14
forty **cuarenta** *m.* 2
four **cuatro** 1
four hundred **cuatrocientos/as** 2
fourteen **catorce** 1
fourth **cuarto/a** *m., f.* 5
free **libre** *adj. m., f.* 4
be free (of charge) **ser gratis** 14
free time **tiempo libre**; spare (free) time **ratos libres** 4
freedom **libertad** *f.* 18
freezer **congelador** *m.* 12
French **francés, francesa** *adj.* 3
French fries **papas** *f., pl.* **fritas** 8; **patatas** *f., pl.* **fritas** 8
frequently **frecuentemente** *adv.* 10; **con frecuencia** *adv.* 10
Friday **viernes** *m., sing.* 2
fried **frito/a** *adj.* 8
fried potatoes **papas** *f., pl.* **fritas** 8; **patatas** *f., pl.* **fritas** 8
friend **amigo/a** *m., f.* 3
friendly **amable** *adj. m., f.* 5
friendship **amistad** *f.* 9
from **de** *prep.* 1; **desde** *prep.* 6
from the United States **estadounidense** *m., f. adj.* 3
from time to time **de vez en cuando** 10
He/She/It is from... **Es de...**; I'm from... **Soy de...** 1
front: (cold) front **frente (frío)** *m.* 5
fruit **fruta** *f.* 8
fruit juice **jugo** *m.* **de fruta** 8
fruit store **frutería** *f.* 14
full **lleno/a** *adj.* 11
fun **divertido/a** *adj.* 7
fun activity **diversión** *f.* 4
have fun **divertirse (e:ie)** *v.* 9
function **funcionar** *v.*
furniture **muebles** *m., pl.* 12
furthermore **además (de)** *adv.* 10
future **futuro** *adj.* 16; **porvenir** *m.* 16
Here's to the future! **¡Por el porvenir!** 16
in the future **en el futuro** 16

G

gain weight **aumentar** *v.* **de peso** 15; **engordar** *v.* 15
game **juego** *m.*; (*match*) **partido** *m.* 4
game show **concurso** *m.* 17
garage (*in a house*) **garaje** *m.* 12; **garaje** *m.* 11; **taller (mecánico)** 11
garden **jardín** *m.* 12
garlic **ajo** *m.* 8
gas station **gasolinera** *f.* 11
gasoline **gasolina** *f.* 11
gentleman **caballero** *m.* 8
geography **geografía** *f.* 2
German **alemán, alemana** *adj.* 3
get **conseguir (e:i)** *v.* 4; **obtener** *v.* 16
get along well/badly (with) **llevarse bien/mal (con)** 9
get bigger **aumentar** *v.* 13
get bored **aburrirse** *v.* 17
get good grades **sacar buenas notas** 2
get into trouble **meterse en problemas** *v.* 13
get off of (a vehicle) **bajar(se)** *v.* **de** 11
get on/into (a vehicle) **subir(se)** *v.* **a** 11
get out of (a vehicle) **bajar(se)** *v.* **de** 11
get ready **arreglarse** *v.* 7
get up **levantarse** *v.* 7
gift **regalo** *m.* 6
ginger **jengibre** *m.* 10
girl **chica** *f.* 1; **muchacha** *f.* 3
girlfriend **novia** *f.* 3
give **dar** *v.* 6, 9; (*as a gift*) **regalar** 9
give directions **indicar cómo llegar** 14
glass (*drinking*) **vaso** *m.* 12; **vidrio** *m.* 13
(made) of glass **de vidrio** 13
glasses **gafas** *f., pl.* 6
sunglasses **gafas** *f., pl.* **de sol** 6
global warming **calentamiento global** *m.* 13
gloves **guantes** *m., pl.* 6
go **ir** *v.* 4
go away **irse** 7
go by boat **ir en barco** 5
go by bus **ir en autobús** 5
go by car **ir en auto(móvil)** 5
go by motorcycle **ir en motocicleta** 5
go by taxi **ir en taxi** 5
go by the bank **pasar por el banco** 14
go down **bajar(se)** *v.*
go on a hike (in the mountains) **ir de excursión (a las montañas)** 4
go out **salir** *v.* 9
go out (with) **salir** *v.* **(con)** 9
go up **subir** *v.*
Let's go. **Vamos.** 4
goblet **copa** *f.* 12
going to: be going to (*do something*) **ir a (+ *inf.*)** 4
golf **golf** *m.* 4
good **buen, bueno/a** *adj.* 3, 6
Good afternoon. **Buenas tardes.** 1
Good evening. **Buenas noches.** 1
Good idea. **Buena idea.** 4
Good morning. **Buenos días.** 1
Good night. **Buenas noches.** 1
It's good that... **Es bueno que...** 12
goodbye **adiós** *m.* 1
say goodbye (to) **despedirse** *v.* **(de) (e:i)** 7
good-looking **guapo/a** *adj.* 3
government **gobierno** *m.* 13
GPS **navegador GPS** *m.* 11
graduate (from/in) **graduarse** *v.* **(de/en)** 9
grains **cereales** *m., pl.* 8
granddaughter **nieta** *f.* 3
grandfather **abuelo** *m.* 3
grandmother **abuela** *f.* 3
grandparents **abuelos** *m., pl.* 3
grandson **nieto** *m.* 3
grape **uva** *f.* 8
grass **hierba** *f.* 13
grave **grave** *adj.* 10
gray **gris** *adj. m., f.* 6
great **fenomenal** *adj. m., f.* 5; **genial** *adj.* 16
great-grandfather **bisabuelo** *m.* 3
great-grandmother **bisabuela** *f.* 3
green **verde** *adj. m., f.* 6
greet (each other) **saludar(se)** *v.* 11
greeting **saludo** *m.* 1
Greetings to... **Saludos a...** 1
grilled **a la plancha** 8
ground floor **planta baja** *f.* 5
grow **aumentar** *v.* 13
guest (*at a house/hotel*) **huésped** *m., f.* 5 (*invited to a function*) **invitado/a** *m., f.* 9
guide **guía** *m., f.* 13
gymnasium **gimnasio** *m.* 4

H

hair **pelo** *m.* 7
hairdresser **peluquero/a** *m., f.* 16
half **medio/a** *adj.* 3
half-brother **medio hermano** 3
half-sister **media hermana** 3
half-past... (*time*) **...y media** 1
hallway **pasillo** *m.* 12
ham **jamón** *m.* 8
hamburger **hamburguesa** *f.* 8

hand **mano** *f.* 1
hand in **entregar** *v.* 11
handsome **guapo/a** *adj.* 3
happen **ocurrir** *v.* 18
happiness **alegría** *v.* 9
Happy birthday! **¡Feliz cumpleaños!** 9
happy **alegre** *adj.* 5; **contento/a** *adj.* 5; **feliz** *adj. m., f.* 5
be happy **alegrarse** *v.* **(de)** 13
hard **difícil** *adj. m., f.* 3
hard-working **trabajador(a)** *adj.* 3
hardly **apenas** *adv.* 10
haste **prisa** *f.* 3
hat **sombrero** *m.* 6
hate **odiar** *v.* 9
have **tener** *v.* 3
have time **tener tiempo** 4
have to (*do something*) **tener que (+ *inf.*)** 3; **deber (+ *inf.*)**
have a tooth removed **sacar(se) un diente** 10
he **él** 1
head **cabeza** *f.* 10
headache **dolor** *m.* **de cabeza** 10
health **salud** *f.* 10
healthy **saludable** *adj. m., f.* 10; **sano/a** *adj.* 10
lead a healthy lifestyle **llevar** *v.* **una vida sana** 15
hear **oír** *v.* 4
heard **oído/a** *p.p.* 14
hearing: sense of hearing **oído** *m.* 10
heart **corazón** *m.* 10
heat **calor** *m.* 5
Hello. **Hola.** 1; (*on the telephone*) **Aló.** 11; **Bueno.** 11; **Diga.** 11
help **ayudar** *v.* 12; **servir (e:i)** *v.* 5
help each other **ayudarse** *v.* 11
her **su(s)** *poss. adj.* 3; (of) hers **suyo(s)/a(s)** *poss.* 11
her **la** *f., sing., d.o. pron.* 5
to/for her **le** *f., sing., i.o. pron.* 6
here **aquí** *adv.* 1
Here is/are... **Aquí está(n)...** 5
Hi. **Hola.** 1
highway **autopista** *f.* 11; **carretera** *f.* 11
hike **excursión** *f.* 4
go on a hike **hacer una excursión** 5; **ir de excursión** 4
hiker **excursionista** *m., f.*
hiking **de excursión** 4
him: to/for him **le** *m., sing., i.o. pron.* 6
hire **contratar** *v.* 16
his **su(s)** *poss. adj.* 3; (of) his **suyo(s)/a(s)** *poss. pron.* 11
his **lo** *m., sing., d.o. pron.* 5
history **historia** *f.* 2; 17
hobby **pasatiempo** *m.* 4
hockey **hockey** *m.* 4
hold up **aguantar** *v.* 14
hole **hueco** *m.* 4
holiday **día** *m.* **de fiesta** 9
home **casa** *f.* 2
home page **página** *f.* **principal** 11
homework **tarea** *f.* 2
honey **miel** *f.* 10
hood **capó** *m.* 11; **cofre** *m.* 11
hope **esperar** *v.* **(+ *inf.*)** 2; **esperar** *v.* 13
I hope (that) **ojalá (que)** 13
horror (genre) **de horror** *m.* 17
hors d'oeuvres **entremeses** *m., pl.* 8
horse **caballo** *m.* 5
hospital **hospital** *m.* 10
hot: be (*feel*) (very) hot **tener (mucho) calor** 3
It's (very) hot. **Hace (mucho) calor.** 5
hotel **hotel** *m.* 5
hour **hora** *f.* 1
house **casa** *f.* 2
household chores **quehaceres** *m. pl.* **domésticos** 12
housekeeper **ama** *m., f.* **de casa** 12
housing **vivienda** *f.* 12
How...! **¡Qué...!**
how **¿cómo?** *adv.* 1
How are you? **¿Qué tal?** 1
How are you?**¿Cómo estás?** *fam.* 1
How are you?**¿Cómo está usted?** *form.* 1
How can I help you? **¿En qué puedo servirles?** 5
How did it go for you...? **¿Cómo le/les fue...?** 15
How is it going? **¿Qué tal?** 1
How is/are...? **¿Qué tal...?** 2
How is the weather? **¿Qué tiempo hace?** 15
How much/many? **¿Cuánto(s)/a(s)?** 1
How much does... cost? **¿Cuánto cuesta...?** 6
How old are you? **¿Cuántos años tienes?** *fam.* 3
however **sin embargo**
hug (each other) **abrazar(se)** *v.* 11
humanities **humanidades** *f., pl.* 2
hundred **cien, ciento** 2
hunger **hambre** *f.* 3
hungry: be (very) hungry **tener** *v.* **(mucha) hambre** 3
hunt **cazar** *v.* 13
hurricane **huracán** *m.* 18
hurry **apurarse** *v.* 15; **darse prisa** *v.* 15
be in a (big) hurry **tener** *v.* **(mucha) prisa** 3
hurt **doler (o:ue)** *v.* 10
It hurts me a lot... **Me duele mucho...** 10
husband **esposo** *m.* 3

I

I **yo** 1
I am... **Yo soy...** 1
I hope (that) **Ojalá (que)** *interj.* 13
I wish (that) **Ojalá (que)** *interj.* 13
ice cream **helado** *m.* 9
ice cream shop **heladería** *f.* 14
iced **helado/a** *adj.* 8
iced tea **té** *m.* **helado** 8
idea **idea** *f.* 4
if **si** *conj.* 4
illness **enfermedad** *f.* 10
important **importante** *adj.* 3
be important to **importar** *v.* 7
It's important that... **Es importante que...** 12
impossible **imposible** *adj.* 13
it's impossible **es imposible** 13
improbable **improbable** *adj.* 13
it's improbable **es improbable** 13
improve **mejorar** *v.* 13
in **en** *prep.* 2; **por** *prep.* 11
in the afternoon **de la tarde** 1; **por la tarde** 7
in a bad mood **de mal humor** 5
in the direction of **para** *prep.* 1;
in the early evening **de la tarde** 1
in the evening **de la noche** 1; **por la tarde** 7
in a good mood **de buen humor** 5
in the morning **de la mañana** 1; **por la mañana** 7
in love (with) **enamorado/a (de)** 5
in search of **por** *prep.* 11
in front of **delante de** *prep.* 2
increase **aumento** *m.* 16
incredible **increíble** *adj.* 5
inequality **desigualdad** *f.* 18
infection **infección** *f.* 10
inform **informar** *v.* 18
injection **inyección** *f.* 10
give an injection *v.* **poner una inyección** 10
injure (oneself) **lastimarse** 10
injure (one's foot) **lastimarse** *v.* **(el pie)** 10
inner ear **oído** *m.* 10
inside **dentro** *adv.*
insist (on) **insistir** *v.* **(en)** 12
installments: pay in installments **pagar** *v.* **a plazos** 14
intelligent **inteligente** *adj.* 3
intend to **pensar** *v.* **(+ *inf.*)** 4
interest **interesar** *v.* 7
interesting **interesante** *adj.* 3
be interesting to **interesar** *v.* 7
international **internacional** *adj. m., f.* 18
Internet **Internet** 11

interview **entrevista** *f.* 16;
 interview **entrevistar** *v.* 16
interviewer **entrevistador(a)** *m., f.* 16
introduction **presentación** *f.*
 I would like to introduce you to (name). **Le presento a...** *form.* 1; **Te presento a...** *fam.* 1
invest **invertir (e:ie)** *v.* 16
invite **invitar** *v.* 9
iron (clothes) **planchar** *v.* **la ropa** 12
it **lo/la** *sing., d.o., pron.* 5
Italian **italiano/a** *adj.* 3
its **su(s)** *poss. adj.* 3; **suyo(s)/a(s)** *poss. pron.* 11
It's me. **Soy yo.**
it's the same **es igual** 5

J

jacket **chaqueta** *f.* 6
January **enero** *m.* 5
Japanese **japonés, japonesa** *adj.* 3
jeans **(blue)jeans** *m., pl.* 6
jewelry store **joyería** *f.* 14
job **empleo** *m.* 16; **puesto** *m.* 16; **trabajo** *m.* 16
 job application **solicitud** *f.* **de trabajo** 16
jog **correr** *v.*
journalism **periodismo** *m.* 2
journalist **periodista** *m., f.* 3; **reportero/a** *m., f.* 16
joy **alegría** *f.* 9
 give joy **dar** *v.* **alegría** 9
joyful **alegre** *adj.* 5
juice **jugo** *m.* 8
July **julio** *m.* 5
June **junio** *m.* 5
jungle **selva, jungla** *f.* 13
just **apenas** *adv.*
 have just done something **acabar de (+ *inf.*)** 6

K

key **llave** *f.* 5
keyboard **teclado** *m.* 11
kilometer **kilómetro** *m.* 11
kind: That's very kind of you. **Muy amable.** 5
kiss **beso** *m.* 9
 kiss each other **besarse** *v.* 11
kitchen **cocina** *f.* 9, 12
knee **rodilla** *f.* 10
knife **cuchillo** *m.* 12
know **saber** *v.* 6; **conocer** *v.* 6
know how **saber** *v.* 6

L

laboratory **laboratorio** *m.* 2
lack **faltar** *v.* 7
lake **lago** *m.* 13
lamp **lámpara** *f.* 12
land **tierra** *f.* 13
landlord **dueño/a** *m., f.* 8
landscape **paisaje** *m.* 5
language **lengua** *f.* 2
laptop (computer) **computadora** *f.* **portátil** 11
large **grande** *adj.* 3
large (*clothing size*) **talla grande**
last **durar** *v.* 18; **pasado/a** *adj.* 6; **último/a** *adj.* 7
 last name **apellido** *m.* 3
 last night **anoche** *adv.* 6
 last week **semana** *f.* **pasada** 6
 last year **año** *m.* **pasado** 6
 the last time **la última vez** 7
late **tarde** *adv.* 7
later (on) **más tarde** 7
 See you later. **Hasta la vista.** 1; **Hasta luego.** 1
laugh **reírse (e:i)** *v.* 9
laughed **reído** *p.p.* 14
laundromat **lavandería** *f.* 14
law **ley** *f.* 13
lawyer **abogado/a** *m., f.* 16
lazy **perezoso/a** *adj.*
learn **aprender** *v.* **(a + *inf.*)** 3
least, at **por lo menos** *adv.* 10
leave **salir** *v.* 4; **irse** *v.* 7
 leave a tip **dejar una propina** 9
 leave behind **dejar** *v.* 16
 leave for (*a place*) **salir para**
 leave from **salir de**
left **izquierdo/a** *adj.* 2
 be left over **quedar** *v.* 7
 to the left of **a la izquierda de** 2
leg **pierna** *f.* 10
lemon **limón** *m.* 8
lend **prestar** *v.* 6
less **menos** *adv.* 10
 less... than **menos... que** 8
 less than **menos de (+ *number*)**
lesson **lección** *f.* 1
let **dejar** *v.* 12
let's see **a ver** 2
letter **carta** *f.* 4, 14
lettuce **lechuga** *f.* 8
liberty **libertad** *f.* 18
library **biblioteca** *f.* 2
license (*driver's*) **licencia** *f.* **de conducir** 11
lie **mentira** *f.* 4
life **vida** *f.* 9
 of my life **de mi vida** 15
lifestyle: lead a healthy lifestyle **llevar una vida sana** 15
lift **levantar** *v.* 15
 lift weights **levantar pesas** 15
light **luz** *f.* 12
like **como** *prep.* 8; **gustar** *v.* 2
 I don't like them at all. **No me gustan nada.** 2
 I like... **Me gusta(n)...** 2
 like this **así** *adv.* 10
 like very much **encantar** *v.*; **fascinar** *v.* 7
 Do you like...? **¿Te gusta(n)...?** 2
likeable **simpático/a** *adj.* 3
likewise **igualmente** *adv.* 1
line **línea** *f.* 4; **cola** (*queue*) *f.* 14
listen (to) **escuchar** *v.* 2
 Listen! (*command*) **¡Oye!** *fam., sing.* 1; **¡Oiga/Oigan!** *form., sing./pl.* 1
 listen to music **escuchar música** 2
 listen (to) the radio **escuchar la radio** 2
literature **literatura** *f.* 2
little (*quantity*) **poco/a** *adj.* 5; **poco** *adv.* 10
live **vivir** *v.* 3; **en vivo** *adj.* 7
living room **sala** *f.* 12
loan **préstamo** *m.* 14; **prestar** *v.* 6, 14
lobster **langosta** *f.* 8
located **situado/a** *adj.*
 be located **quedar** *v.* 14
long **largo/a** *adj.* 6
look (at) **mirar** *v.* 2
look for **buscar** *v.* 2
lose **perder (e:ie)** *v.* 4
 lose weight **adelgazar** *v.* 15
lost **perdido/a** *adj.* 13, 14
 be lost **estar perdido/a** 14
lot, a **muchas veces** *adv.* 10
lot of, a **mucho/a** *adj.* 2, 3; **un montón de** 4
love (*another person*) **querer (e:ie)** *v.* 4; (*inanimate objects*) **encantar** *v.* 7; **amor** *m.* 9
 in love **enamorado/a** *adj.* 5
 I loved it! **¡Me encantó!** 15
 love at first sight **amor a primera vista** 9
luck **suerte** *f.* 3
lucky: be (very) lucky **tener (mucha) suerte** 3
luggage **equipaje** *m.* 5
lunch **almuerzo** *m.* 4, 8
 have lunch **almorzar (o:ue)** *v.* 4

M

ma'am **señora (Sra.); doña** *f.* 1
mad **enojado/a** *adj.* 5
magazine **revista** *f.* 4
magnificent **magnífico/a** *adj.* 5
mail **correo** *m.* 14; **enviar** *v.*, **mandar** *v.* 14; **echar (una carta) al buzón** 14
 mail **correo** *m.* 14; **enviar** *v.*, **mandar** *v.* 14
 mail carrier **cartero** *m.* 14
mailbox **buzón** *m.* 14
main **principal** *adj. m., f.* 8
maintain **mantener** *v.* 15
major **especialización** *f.* 2

make **hacer** *v.* 4
make a decision **tomar una decisión** 15
make the bed **hacer la cama** 12
makeup **maquillaje** *m.* 7
put on makeup **maquillarse** *v.* 7
man **hombre** *m.* 1
manager **gerente** *m., f.* 8, 16
many **mucho/a** *adj.* 3
many times **muchas veces** 10
map **mapa** *m.* 2
March **marzo** *m.* 5
margarine **margarina** *f.* 8
marinated fish **ceviche** *m.* 8
lemon-marinated shrimp **ceviche** *m.* **de camarón** 8
marital status **estado** *m.* **civil** 9
market **mercado** *m.* 6
open-air market **mercado al aire libre** 6
marriage **matrimonio** *m.* 9
married **casado/a** *adj.* 9
get married (to) **casarse** *v.* **(con)** 9
I'll marry you! **¡Acepto casarme contigo!** 17
marvelous **maravilloso/a** *adj.* 5
massage **masaje** *m.* 15
masterpiece **obra maestra** *f.* 17
match (*sports*) **partido** *m.* 4
match (with) **hacer** *v.* **juego (con)** 6
mathematics **matemáticas** *f., pl.* 2
matter **importar** *v.* 7
maturity **madurez** *f.* 9
maximum **máximo/a** *adj.* 11
May **mayo** *m.* 5
May I leave a message? **¿Puedo dejar un recado?** 11
maybe **tal vez** 5; **quizás** 5
mayonnaise **mayonesa** *f.* 8
me **me** *sing., d.o. pron.* 5
to/for me **me** *sing., i.o. pron.* 6
meal **comida** *f.* 4, 8
means of communication **medios** *m., pl.* **de comunicación** 18
meat **carne** *f.* 8
mechanic **mecánico/a** *m., f.* 11
mechanic's repair shop **taller mecánico** 11
media **medios** *m., pl.* **de comunicación** 18
medical **médico/a** *adj.* 10
medication **medicamento** *m.* 10
medicine **medicina** *f.* 10
medium **mediano/a** *adj.*
meet (each other) **encontrar(se)** *v.* 11; **conocerse(se)** *v.* 8
meet up with **encontrarse con** 7
meeting **reunión** *f.* 16
menu **menú** *m.* 8
message **mensaje** *m.*
Mexican **mexicano/a** *adj.* 3
Mexico **México** *m.* 1
microwave **microonda** *f.* 12
microwave oven **horno** *m.***de microondas** 12
middle age **madurez** *f.* 9
midnight **medianoche** *f.* 1
mile **milla** *f.* 11
milk **leche** *f.* 8
million **millón** *m.* 2
million of **millón de** 2
mine **mío(s)/a(s)** *poss.* 11
mineral **mineral** *m.* 15
mineral water **agua** *f.* **mineral** 8
minute **minuto** *m.* 1
mirror **espejo** *m.* 7
Miss **señorita (Srta.)** *f.* 1
miss **perder (e:ie)** *v.* 4; **extrañar** *v.* 16
mistaken **equivocado/a** *adj.*
modem **módem** *m.*
modern **moderno/a** *adj.* 17
mom **mamá** *f.* 3
Monday **lunes** *m., sing.* 2
money **dinero** *m.* 6
monitor **monitor** *m.* 11
monkey **mono** *m.* 13
month **mes** *m.* 5
monument **monumento** *m.* 4
moon **luna** *f.* 13
more **más** 2
more... than **más... que** 8
more than **más de (+ *number*)** 8
morning **mañana** *f.* 1
mother **madre** *f.* 3
mother-in-law **suegra** *f.* 3
motor **motor** *m.*
motorcycle **motocicleta** *f.* 5
mountain **montaña** *f.* 4
mouse **ratón** *m.* 11
mouth **boca** *f.* 10
move (*from one house to another*) **mudarse** *v.* 12
movie **película** *f.* 4
movie star **estrella** *f.* **de cine** 17
movie theater **cine** *m.* 4
MP3 player **reproductor** *m.* **de MP3** 11
Mr. **señor (Sr.); don** *m.* 1
Mrs. **señora (Sra.); doña** *f.* 1
much **mucho/a** *adj.* 2, 3
very much **muchísimo/a** *adj.* 2
mud **lodo** *m.*
murder **crimen** *m.* 18
muscle **músculo** *m.* 15
museum **museo** *m.* 4
mushroom **champiñón** *m.* 8
music **música** *f.* 2, 17
musical **musical** *adj., m., f.* 17
musician **músico/a** *m., f.* 17
must **deber** *v.* **(+ *inf.*)** 3
It must be... **Debe ser...** 6
my **mi(s)** *poss. adj.* 3; **mío(s)/a(s)** *poss. pron.* 11

N

name **nombre** *m.* 1
be named **llamarse** *v.* 7
in the name of **a nombre de** 5
last name **apellido** *m.*
My name is... **Me llamo...** 1
name someone/something **ponerle el nombre** 9
napkin **servilleta** *f.* 12
national **nacional** *adj. m., f.* 18
nationality **nacionalidad** *f.* 1
natural **natural** *adj. m., f.* 13
natural disaster **desastre** *m.* **natural** 18
natural resource **recurso** *m.* **natural** 13
nature **naturaleza** *f.* 13
nauseated **mareado/a** *adj.* 10
near **cerca de** *prep.* 2
neaten **arreglar** *v.* 12
necessary **necesario/a** *adj.* 12
It is necessary that... **Hay que...** 12, 14
neck **cuello** *m.* 10
need **faltar** *v.* 7; **necesitar** *v.* **(+ *inf.*)** 2
neighbor **vecino/a** *m., f.* 12
neighborhood **barrio** *m.* 12
neither **tampoco** *adv.* 7
neither... nor **ni... ni** *conj.* 7
nephew **sobrino** *m.* 3
nervous **nervioso/a** *adj.* 5
network **red** *f.* 11
never **nunca** *adj.* 7; **jamás** 7
new **nuevo/a** *adj.* 6
newlywed **recién casado/a** *m., f.* 9
news **noticias** *f., pl.* 18; **actualidades** *f., pl.* 18; **noticia** *f.* 11
newscast **noticiero** *m.* 18
newspaper **periódico** 4; **diario** *m.* 18
next **próximo/a** *adj.* 3, 16
next to **al lado de** *prep.* 2
nice **simpático/a** *adj.* 3; **amable** *adj. m., f.* 5
niece **sobrina** *f.* 3
night **noche** *f.* 1
night stand **mesita** *f.* **de noche** 12
nine **nueve** 1
nine hundred **novecientos/as** 2
nineteen **diecinueve** 1
ninety **noventa** 2
ninth **noveno/a** 5
no **no** 1; **ningún, ninguno/a(s)** *adj.* 7
no one **nadie** *pron.* 7
No problem. **No hay problema.**
nobody **nadie** 7
none **ningún, ninguno/a(s)** *adj.* 7

noon **mediodía** *m.* 1
nor **ni** *conj.* 7
north **norte** *m.* 14
to the north **al norte** 14
nose **nariz** *f.* 10
not **no** 1
not any **ningún, ninguno/a(s)** *adj.* 7
not anyone **nadie** *pron.* 7
not anything **nada** *pron.* 7
not bad at all **nada mal** 5
not either **tampoco** *adv.* 7
not ever **nunca** *adv.* 7; **jamás** *adv.* 7
not very well **no muy bien** 1
not working **descompuesto/a** *adj.* 11
outside **afuera** *adv.* 5
notebook **cuaderno** *m.* 1
nothing **nada** 1; 7
noun **sustantivo** *m.*
November **noviembre** *m.* 5
now **ahora** *adv.* 2
nowadays **hoy día** *adv.*
nuclear **nuclear** *adj. m., f.* 13
nuclear energy **energía nuclear** 13
number **número** *m.* 1
nurse **enfermero/a** *m., f.* 10
nutrition **nutrición** *f.* 15
nutritionist **nutricionista** *m., f.* 15

O

o'clock: It's... o'clock **Son las...** 1
It's one o'clock. **Es la una.** 1
obey **obedecer** *v.* 18
obligation **deber** *m.* 18
obtain **conseguir (e:i)** *v.* 4; **obtener** *v.* 16
obvious **obvio/a** *adj.* 13
it's obvious **es obvio** 13
occupation **ocupación** *f.* 16
occur **ocurrir** *v.* 18
October **octubre** *m.* 5
of **de** *prep.* 1
Of course. **Claro que sí.; Por supuesto.**
offer **oferta** *f.* 12; **ofrecer (c:zc)** *v.* 6
office **oficina** *f.* 12
doctor's office **consultorio** *m.* 10
often **a menudo** *adv.* 10
Oh! **¡Ay!**
oil **aceite** *m.* 8
OK **regular** *adj.* 1
It's okay. **Está bien.**
old **viejo/a** *adj.* 3
old age **vejez** *f.* 9
older **mayor** *adj. m., f.* 3
older brother, sister **hermano/a mayor** *m., f.* 3
oldest **el/la mayor** 8
on **en** *prep.* 2; **sobre** *prep.* 2
on behalf of **por** *prep.* 11
on the dot **en punto** 1
on time **a tiempo** 10
on top of **encima de** 2
once **una vez** 6
one **un, uno/a** *m., f., sing. pron.* 1
one hundred **cien(to)** 2
one million **un millón** *m.* 2
one more time **una vez más** 9
one thousand **mil** 2
one time **una vez** 6
onion **cebolla** *f.* 8
only **sólo** *adv.* 3; **único/a** *adj.* 3
only child **hijo/a único/a** *m., f.* 3
open **abierto/a** *adj.* 5, 14; **abrir** *v.* 3
open-air **al aire libre** 6
opera **ópera** *f.* 17
operation **operación** *f.* 10
opposite **enfrente de** *prep.* 14
or **o** *conj.* 7
orange **anaranjado/a** *adj.* 6; **naranja** *f.* 8
orchestra **orquesta** *f.* 17
order **mandar** 12; (*food*) **pedir (e:i)** *v.* 8
in order to **para** *prep.* 11
orderly **ordenado/a** *adj.* 5
ordinal (*numbers*) **ordinal** *adj.*
organize oneself **organizarse** *v.* 12
other **otro/a** *adj.* 6
ought to **deber** *v.* **(+ *inf.*)** *adj.* 3
our **nuestro(s)/a(s)** *poss. adj.* 3; *poss. pron.* 11
out of order **descompuesto/a** *adj.* 11
outside **afuera** *adv.* 5
outskirts **afueras** *f., pl.* 12
oven **horno** *m.* 12
over **sobre** *prep.* 2
(over)population **(sobre)población** *f.* 13
over there **allá** *adv.* 2
own **propio/a** *adj.* 16
owner **dueño/a** *m., f.* 8

P

p.m. **tarde** *f.* 1

pack (one's suitcases) **hacer** *v.* **las maletas** 5
package **paquete** *m.* 14
page **página** *f.* 11
pain **dolor** *m.* 10
have a pain **tener** *v.* **dolor** 10
paint **pintar** *v.* 17
painter **pintor(a)** *m., f.* 16
painting **pintura** *f.* 12, 17
pair **par** *m.* 6
pair of shoes **par** *m.* **de zapatos** 6
pale **pálido/a** *adj.* 14
pants **pantalones** *m., pl.* 6
pantyhose **medias** *f., pl.* 6
paper **papel** *m.* 2; (*report*) **informe** *m.* 18
Pardon me. (*May I?*) **Con permiso.** 1; (*Excuse me.*) Pardon me. **Perdón.** 1
parents **padres** *m., pl.* 3; **papás** *m., pl.* 3
park **estacionar** *v.* 11; **parque** *m.* 4
parking lot **estacionamiento** *m.* 14
partner (*one of a married couple*) **pareja** *f.* 9
party **fiesta** *f.* 9
passed **pasado/a** *p.p.*
passenger **pasajero/a** *m., f.* 1
passport **pasaporte** *m.* 5
past **pasado/a** *adj.* 6
pastime **pasatiempo** *m.* 4
pastry shop **pastelería** *f.* 14
patient **paciente** *m., f.* 10
patio **patio** *m.* 12
pay **pagar** *v.* 6
pay in cash **pagar** *v.* **al contado; pagar en efectivo** 14
pay in installments **pagar** *v.* **a plazos** 14
pay the bill **pagar la cuenta** 9
pea **arveja** *m.* 8
peace **paz** *f.* 18
peach **melocotón** *m.* 8
peak **cima** *f.* 15
pear **pera** *f.* 8
pen **pluma** *f.* 2
pencil **lápiz** *m.* 1
penicillin **penicilina** *f.* 10
people **gente** *f.* 3
pepper (*black*) **pimienta** *f.* 8
per **por** *prep.* 11
perfect **perfecto/a** *adj.* 5
period of time **temporada** *f.* 5
person **persona** *f.* 3
pharmacy **farmacia** *f.* 10
phenomenal **fenomenal** *adj.* 5
photograph **foto(grafía)** *f.* 1
physical (exam) **examen** *m.* **médico** 10
physician **doctor(a), médico/a** *m., f.* 3
physics **física** *f. sing.* 2
pick up **recoger** *v.* 13
picture **cuadro** *m.* 12; **pintura** *f.* 12
pie **pastel** *m.* 9
pill (tablet) **pastilla** *f.* 10
pillow **almohada** *f.* 12
pineapple **piña** *f.* 8
pink **rosado/a** *adj.* 6
place **lugar** *m.* 2, 4; **sitio** *m.* 3; **poner** *v.* 4
plaid **de cuadros** 6
plans **planes** *m., pl.* 4
have plans **tener planes** 4
plant **planta** *f.* 13
plastic **plástico** *m.* 13
(made) of plastic **de plástico** 13

plate **plato** *m.* 12
play **drama** *m.* 17; **comedia** *f.* 17
  jugar (u:ue) *v.* 4; (*a musical instrument*) **tocar** *v.* 17; (*a role*) **hacer el papel de** 17; (*cards*) **jugar a (las cartas)** 5; (*sports*) **practicar deportes** 4
player **jugador(a)** *m., f.* 4
playwright **dramaturgo/a** *m., f.* 17
plead **rogar (o:ue)** *v.* 12
pleasant **agradable** *adj.* 5
please **por favor** 1
Pleased to meet you. **Mucho gusto.** 1; **Encantado/a.** *adj.* 1
pleasing: be pleasing to **gustar** *v.* 7
pleasure **gusto** *m.* 1; **placer** *m.* 15
  It's a pleasure to... **Gusto de** (*+ inf.*) 18
  It's been a pleasure. **Ha sido un placer.** 15
  The pleasure is mine. **El gusto es mío.** 1
poem **poema** *m.* 17
poet **poeta** *m., f.* 17
poetry **poesía** *f.* 17
police (force) **policía** *f.* 11
political **político/a** *adj.* 18
politician **político/a** *m., f.* 16
politics **política** *f.* 18
polka-dotted **de lunares** 6
poll **encuesta** *f.* 18
pollute **contaminar** *v.* 13
polluted **contaminado/a** *m., f.* 13
  be polluted **estar contaminado/a** 13
pollution **contaminación** *f.* 13
pool **piscina** *f.* 4
poor **pobre** *adj., m., f.* 6
  poor thing **pobrecito/a** *adj.* 3
popsicle **paleta helada** *f.* 4
population **población** *f.* 13
pork **cerdo** *m.* 8
  pork chop **chuleta** *f.* **de cerdo** 8
portable **portátil** *adj.* 11
  portable computer **computadora** *f.* **portátil** 11
position **puesto** *m.* 16
possessive **posesivo/a** *adj.* 3
possible **posible** *adj.* 13
  it's (not) possible **(no) es posible** 13
post office **correo** *m.* 14
postcard **postal** *f.* 4
poster **cartel** *m.* 12
potato **papa** *f.* 8; **patata** *f.* 8
pottery **cerámica** *f.* 17
practice **entrenarse** *v.* 15; **practicar** *v.* 2; (a degree/ profession) **ejercer** *v.* 16
prefer **preferir (e:ie)** *v.* 4
pregnant **embarazada** *adj. f.* 10
prepare **preparar** *v.* 2
preposition **preposición** *f.*
prescribe (*medicine*) **recetar** *v.* 10
prescription **receta** *f.* 10
present **regalo** *m.*; **presentar** *v.* 17
press **prensa** *f.* 18
pressure **presión** *f.*
  be under a lot of pressure **sufrir muchas presiones** 15
pretty **bonito/a** *adj.* 3; **bastante** *adv.* 13
price **precio** *m.* 6
  (fixed, set) price **precio** *m.* **fijo** 6
print **estampado/a** *adj.*; **imprimir** *v.* 11
printer **impresora** *f.* 11
private (*room*) **individual** *adj.*
prize **premio** *m.* 17
probable **probable** *adj.* 13
  it's (not) probable **(no) es probable** 13
problem **problema** *m.* 1
profession **profesión** *f.* 3; 16
professor **profesor(a)** *m., f.*
program **programa** *m.* 1
programmer **programador(a)** *m., f.* 3
prohibit **prohibir** *v.* 10
project **proyecto** *m.* 11
promotion (*career*) **ascenso** *m.* 16
pronoun **pronombre** *m.*
protect **proteger** *v.* 13
protein **proteína** *f.* 15
provided (that) **con tal (de) que** *conj.* 13
psychologist **psicólogo/a** *m., f.* 16
psychology **psicología** *f.* 2
publish **publicar** *v.* 17
Puerto Rican **puertorriqueño/a** *adj.* 3
Puerto Rico **Puerto Rico** *m.* 1
pull a tooth **sacar una muela**
purchases **compras** *f., pl.* 5
pure **puro/a** *adj.* 13
purple **morado/a** *adj.* 6
purse **bolsa** *f.* 6
put **poner** *v.* 4; **puesto/a** *p.p.* 14
  put (a letter) in the mailbox **echar (una carta) al buzón** 14
  put on (*a performance*) **presentar** *v.* 17
  put on (*clothing*) **ponerse** *v.* 7
  put on makeup **maquillarse** *v.* 7

Q

quality **calidad** *f.* 6
quarter (*academic*) **trimestre** *m.* 2
  quarter after (*time*) **y cuarto** 1; **y quince** 1
  quarter to (*time*) **menos cuarto** 1; **menos quince** 1
question **pregunta** *f.* 2
quickly **rápido** *adv.* 10
quiet **tranquilo/a** *adj.* 15
quit **dejar** *v.* 16
quiz **prueba** *f.* 2

R

racism **racismo** *m.* 18
radio (*medium*) **radio** *f.* 2
  radio (set) **radio** *m.* 11
rain **llover (o:ue)** *v.* 5; **lluvia** *f.* 13
  It's raining. **Llueve.** 5; **Está lloviendo.** 5
raincoat **impermeable** *m.* 6
rainforest **bosque** *m.* **tropical** 13
raise (*salary*) **aumento de sueldo** 16
rather **bastante** *adv.* 10
reality show **programa de realidad** *m.* 17
read **leer** *v.* 3; **leído/a** *p.p.* 14
  read e-mail **leer correo electrónico** 4
  read a magazine **leer una revista** 4
  read a newspaper **leer un periódico** 4
ready **listo/a** *adj.* 5
  (Are you) ready? **¿(Están) listos?** 15
reap the benefits (of) *v.* **disfrutar** *v.* **(de)** 15
receive **recibir** *v.* 3
recommend **recomendar (e:ie)** *v.* 8; 12
record **grabar** *v.* 11
recover **recuperar** *v.* 11
recreation **diversión** *f.* 4
recycle **reciclar** *v.* 13
recycling **reciclaje** *m.* 13
red **rojo/a** *adj.* 6
red-haired **pelirrojo/a** *adj.* 3
reduce **reducir** *v.* 13; **disminuir** *v.* 16
  reduce stress/tension **aliviar el estrés/la tensión** 15
refrigerator **refrigerador** *m.* 12
region **región** *f.* 13
regret **sentir (e:ie)** *v.* 13
related to sitting **sedentario/a** *adj.* 15
relatives **parientes** *m., pl.* 3
relax **relajarse** *v.* 9
  Relax, sweetie. **Tranquilo/a, cariño.** 11
remain **quedarse** *v.* 7
remember **acordarse (o:ue)** *v.* **(de)** 7; **recordar (o:ue)** *v.* 4
remote control **control remoto** *m.* 11
renewable **renovable** *adj.* 13
rent **alquilar** *v.* 12; (payment) **alquiler** *m.* 12
repeat **repetir (e:i)** *v.* 4
report **informe** *m.* 18; **reportaje** *m.* 18
reporter **reportero/a** *m., f.* 16
representative **representante** *m., f.* 18
request **pedir (e:i)** *v.* 4
reservation **reservación** *f.* 5

S

sir **señor (Sr.), don** *m.* 1; **caballero** *m.* 8
sister **hermana** *f.* 3
sister-in-law **cuñada** *f.* 3
sit down **sentarse (e:ie)** *v.* 7
six **seis** 1
six hundred **seiscientos/as** 2
sixteen **dieciséis** 1
sixth **sexto/a** 5
sixty **sesenta** 2
size **talla** *f.* 6
shoe size *m.* **número** 6
(in-line) skate **patinar (en línea)** 4
skateboard **andar en patineta** *v.* 4
ski **esquiar** *v.* 4
skiing **esquí** *m.* 4
water-skiing **esquí** *m.* **acuático** 4
skirt **falda** *f.* 6
skull made out of sugar **calavera de azúcar** *f.* 9
sky **cielo** *m.* 13
sleep **dormir (o:ue)** *v.* 4; **sueño** *m.* 3
go to sleep **dormirse (o:ue)** *v.* 7
sleepy: be (very) sleepy **tener (mucho) sueño** 3
slender **delgado/a** *adj.* 3
slim down **adelgazar** *v.* 15
slippers **pantuflas** *f.* 7
slow **lento/a** *adj.* 11
slowly **despacio** *adv.* 10
small **pequeño/a** *adj.* 3
smart **listo/a** *adj.* 5
smile **sonreír (e:i)** *v.* 9
smiled **sonreído** *p.p.* 14
smoggy: It's (very) smoggy. **Hay (mucha) contaminación.** 4
smoke **fumar** *v.* 8; 15
(not) to smoke **(no) fumar** 15
smoking section **sección** *f.* **de fumar** 8
(non) smoking section *f.* **sección de (no) fumar** 8
snack **merendar** *v.* 8; 15;
afternoon snack **merienda** *f.* 15
have a snack **merendar** *v.*
sneakers **los zapatos de tenis** 6
sneeze **estornudar** *v.* 10
snow **nevar (e:ie)** *v.* 5; **nieve** *f.*
snowing: It's snowing. **Nieva.** 5; **Está nevando.** 5
so (*in such a way*) **así** *adv.* 10; **tan** *adv.* 5; **tan** *adv.* 5, 7
so much **tanto** *adv.*
so-so **regular** 1
so that **para que** *conj.* 13
soap **jabón** *m.* 7
soap opera **telenovela** *f.* 17
soccer **fútbol** *m.* 4
sociology **sociología** *f.* 2
sock(s) **calcetín (calcetines)** *m.* 6
sofa **sofá** *m.* 12
soft drink **refresco** *m.* 8
software **programa** *m.* **de computación** 11
soil **tierra** *f.* 13
solar **solar** *adj., m., f.* 13
solar energy **energía solar** 13
soldier **soldado** *m., f.* 18
solution **solución** *f.* 13
solve **resolver (o:ue)** *v.* 13
some **algún, alguno/a(s)** *adj.* 7; **unos/as** *pron./ m., f., pl; indef. art.* 1
somebody **alguien** *pron.* 7
someone **alguien** *pron.* 7
something **algo** *pron.* 7
sometimes **a veces** *adv.* 10
son **hijo** *m.* 3
song **canción** *f.* 17
son-in-law **yerno** *m.* 3
soon **pronto** *adv.* 10
See you soon. **Hasta pronto.** 1
sorry: be sorry **sentir (e:ie)** *v.* 13
I'm sorry. **Lo siento.** 1
soul **alma** *f.* 9
soup **caldo** *m.* **sopa** *f.*
south **sur** *m.* 14
to the south **al sur** 14
Spain **España** *f.* 1
Spanish (*language*) **español** *m.* 2; **español(a)** *adj.* 3
spare (free) time **ratos libres** 4
speak **hablar** *v.* 2
Speaking. (*on the telephone*) **Con él/ella habla.** 11
special: today's specials **las especialidades del día** 8
spectacular **espectacular** *adj. m., f.* 15
speech **discurso** *m.* 18
speed **velocidad** *f.* 11
speed limit **velocidad** *f.* **máxima** 11
spelling **ortografía** *f.*, **ortográfico/a** *adj.*
spend (*money*) **gastar** *v.* 6
spoon (*table or large*) **cuchara** *f.* 12
sport **deporte** *m.* 4
sports-related **deportivo/a** *adj.* 4
spouse **esposo/a** *m., f.* 3
sprain (one's ankle) **torcerse (o:ue)** *v.* **(el tobillo)** 10
sprained **torcido/a** *adj.* 10
be sprained **estar torcido/a** 10
spring **primavera** *f.* 5
(city or town) square **plaza** *f.* 4
stadium **estadio** *m.* 2
stage **etapa** *f.* 9
stairs **escalera** *f.* 12
stairway **escalera** *f.* 12
stamp **estampilla** *f.* 14; **sello** *m.* 14
stand in line **hacer** *v.* **cola** 14
star **estrella** *f.* 13
start (*a vehicle*) **arrancar** *v.* 11
station **estación** *f.* 5
statue **estatua** *f.* 17
status: marital status **estado** *m.* **civil** 9
stay **quedarse** *v.* 7
stay in shape **mantenerse en forma** 15
steak **bistec** *m.* 8
steering wheel **volante** *m.* 11
step **escalón** *m.* 15
stepbrother **hermanastro** *m.* 3
stepdaughter **hijastra** *f.* 3
stepfather **padrastro** *m.* 3
stepmother **madrastra** *f.* 3
stepsister **hermanastra** *f.* 3
stepson **hijastro** *m.* 3
stereo **estéreo** *m.* 11
still **todavía** *adv.* 5
stockbroker **corredor(a)** *m., f.* **de bolsa** 16
stockings **medias** *f., pl.* 6
stomach **estómago** *m.* 10
stone **piedra** *f.* 13
stop **parar** *v.* 11
stop (*doing something*) **dejar de (+ *inf.*)** 13
store **tienda** *f.* 6
storm **tormenta** *f.* 18
story **cuento** *m.* 17; **historia** *f.* 17
stove **cocina, estufa** *f.* 9, 12
straight **derecho** *adj.* 14
straight (ahead) **derecho** 14
straighten up **arreglar** *v.* 12
strange **extraño/a** *adj.* 13
it's strange **es extraño** 13
strawberry **frutilla** *f.* 8, **fresa**
street **calle** *f.* 11
stress **estrés** *m.* 15
stretching **estiramiento** *m.* 15
do stretching exercises **hacer ejercicios**; *m. pl.* **de estiramiento** 15
strike (*labor*) **huelga** *f.* 18
stripe **raya** *f.* 6
striped **de rayas** 6
stroll **pasear** *v.* 4
strong **fuerte** *adj. m. f.* 15
struggle (for/against) **luchar** *v.* **(por/contra)** 18
student **estudiante** *m., f.* 1; 2; **estudiantil** *adj.* 2
study **estudiar** *v.* 2
stuffed-up (*sinuses*) **congestionado/a** *adj.* 10
stupendous **estupendo/a** *adj.* 5
style **estilo** *m.*
suburbs **afueras** *f., pl.* 12
subway **metro** *m.* 5
subway station **estación** *f.* **del metro** 5
success **éxito** *m.* 16
successful: be successful **tener éxito** 16
such as **tales como**
suddenly **de repente** *adv.* 6
suffer **sufrir** *v.* 10
suffer an illness **sufrir una enfermedad** 10
sugar **azúcar** *m.* 8
suggest **sugerir (e:ie)** *v.* 12
suit **traje** *m.* 6
suitcase **maleta** *f.* 1
summer **verano** *m.* 5
sun **sol** *m.* 5; 13

sunbathe **tomar** *v.* **el sol** 4
Sunday **domingo** *m.* 2
(sun)glasses **gafas** *f., pl.* **(oscuras/de sol)** 6; **lentes** *m. pl.* **(de sol)** 6
sunny: It's (very) sunny. **Hace (mucho) sol.** 5
supermarket **supermercado** *m.* 14
suppose **suponer** *v.* 4
sure **seguro/a** *adj.* 5
  be sure **estar seguro/a** 5
surf (*the Internet*) **navegar** *v.* **(en Internet)** 11
surfboard **tabla de surf** *f.* 5
surprise **sorprender** *v.* 9; **sorpresa** *f.* 9
survey **encuesta** *f.* 18
sweat **sudar** *v.* 15
sweater **suéter** *m.* 6
sweep the floor **barrer el suelo** 12
sweets **dulces** *m., pl.* 9
swim **nadar** *v.* 4
swimming **natación** *f.* 4
  swimming pool **piscina** *f.* 4
symptom **síntoma** *m.* 10

T

table **mesa** *f.* 2
tablespoon **cuchara** *f.* 12
tablet (*pill*) **pastilla** *f.* 10
take **tomar** *v.* 2; **llevar** *v.* 6;
  take care of **cuidar** *v.* 13
  take someone's temperature **tomar** *v.* **la temperatura** 10
  take (*wear*) a shoe size **calzar** *v.* 6
  take a bath **bañarse** *v.* 7
  take a shower **ducharse** *v.* 7
  take off **quitarse** *v.* 7
  take out the trash *v.* **sacar la basura** 12
  take photos **tomar** *v.* **fotos** 5; **sacar** *v.* **fotos** 5
talented **talentoso/a** *adj.* 17
talk **hablar** *v.* 2
  talk show **programa** *m.* **de entrevistas** 17
tall **alto/a** *adj.* 3
tank **tanque** *m.* 11
taste **probar (o:ue)** *v.* 8; **saber** *v.* 8
  taste like **saber a** 8
tasty **rico/a** *adj.* 8; **sabroso/a** *adj.* 8
tax **impuesto** *m.* 18
taxi **taxi** *m.* 5
tea **té** *m.* 8
teach **enseñar** *v.* 2
teacher **profesor(a)** *m., f.* 1, 2; **maestro/a** *m., f.* 16
team **equipo** *m.* 4
technician **técnico/a** *m., f.* 16
telecommuting **teletrabajo** *m.* 16
telephone **teléfono** 11
  (cell) phone **(teléfono)** *m.* **celular** 11
television **televisión** *f.* 2; 11
  television set **televisor** *m.* 11
tell **contar** *v.* 4; **decir** *v.* 4
tell (that) **decir** *v.* **(que)** 4, 9
  tell lies **decir mentiras** 4
  tell the truth **decir la verdad** 4
temperature **temperatura** *f.* 10
ten **diez** 1
tennis **tenis** *m.* 4
  tennis shoes **zapatos** *m., pl.* **de tenis** 6
tension **tensión** *f.* 15
tent **tienda** *f.* **de campaña**
tenth **décimo/a** 5
terrible **terrible** *adj. m., f.* 13
  it's terrible **es terrible** 13
terrific **chévere** *adj.*
test **prueba** *f.* 2; **examen** *m.* 2
text message **mensaje** *m.* **de texto** 11
Thank you. **Gracias.** *f., pl.* 1
  Thank you (very much). **(Muchas) gracias.** 1
  Thank you very, very much. **Muchísimas gracias.** 9
  Thanks (a lot). **(Muchas) gracias.** 1
  Thanks for having me. **Gracias por invitarme.** 9
that **que, quien(es), lo que** *pron.* 12
  that (one) **ése, ésa, eso** *pron.* 6; **ese, esa,** *adj.* 6
  that (*over there*) **aquél, aquélla, aquello** *pron.* 6; **aquel, aquella** *adj.* 6
  that which **lo que** *conj.* 12
  that's me **soy yo**
  that's why **por eso** 11
the **el** *m.*, **la** *f. sing.*, **los** *m.*, **las** *f., pl.* 1
theater **teatro** *m.* 17
their **su(s)** *poss. adj.* 3; **suyo(s)/a(s)** *poss. pron.* 11
them **los/las** *pl., d.o. pron.* 5
  to/for them **les** *pl., i.o. pron.* 6
then (*afterward*) **después** *adv.* 7; (*as a result*) **entonces** *adv.* 5, 7; (*next*) **luego** *adv.* 7; **pues** *adv.* 15
there **allí** *adv.* 2
  There is/are... **Hay...** 1;
  There is/are not... **No hay...** 1
therefore **por eso** 11
these **éstos, éstas** *pron.* 6; **estos, estas** *adj.* 6
they **ellos** *m.*, **ellas** *f. pron.*
  They all told me to ask you to excuse them/forgive them. **Todos me dijeron que te pidiera disculpas de su parte.** 18
thin **delgado/a** *adj.* 3
thing **cosa** *f.* 1
think **pensar (e:ie)** *v.* 4; (believe) **creer** *v.*
  think about **pensar en** *v.* 4
third **tercero/a** 5
thirst **sed** *f.* 3
thirsty: be (very) thirsty **tener (mucha) sed** 3
thirteen **trece** 1
thirty **treinta** 1, 2; thirty (*minutes past the hour*) **y treinta; y media** 1
this **este, esta** *adj.*; **éste, ésta, esto** *pron.* 6
  This is... (*introduction*) **Éste/a es...** 1
  This is he/she. (*on telephone*) **Con él/ella habla.** 11
those **ésos, ésas** *pron.* 6; **esos, esas** *adj.* 6
those (over there) **aquéllos, aquéllas** *pron.* 6; **aquellos, aquellas** *adj.* 6
thousand **mil** *m.* 6
three **tres** 1
three hundred **trescientos/as** 2
throat **garganta** *f.* 10
through **por** *prep.* 11
throughout: throughout the world **en todo el mundo** 13
Thursday **jueves** *m., sing.* 2
thus (*in such a way*) **así** *adj.*
ticket **boleto** *m.* 2, 17; **pasaje** *m.* 5
tie **corbata** *f.* 6
time **vez** *f.* 6; **tiempo** *m.* 4
  have a good/bad time **pasarlo bien/mal** 9
  I've had a fantastic time. **Lo he pasado de película.** 18
  What time is it? **¿Qué hora es?** 1
  (At) What time...? **¿A qué hora...?** 1
times **veces** *f., pl.* 6
  many times **muchas veces** 10
  two times **dos veces** 6
tip **propina** *f.* 9
tire **llanta** *f.* 11
tired **cansado/a** *adj.* 5
  be tired **estar cansado/a** 5
to **a** *prep.* 1
toast (*drink*) **brindar** *v.* 9
  toast **pan** *m.* **tostado**
toasted **tostado/a** *adj.* 8
  toasted bread **pan tostado** *m.* 8
toaster **tostadora** *f.* 12
today **hoy** *adv.* 2
  Today is... **Hoy es...** 2
toe **dedo** *m.* **del pie** 10
together **juntos/as** *adj.* 9
toilet **inodoro** *m.* 7
tomato **tomate** *m.* 8
tomorrow **mañana** *f.* 1
  See you tomorrow. **Hasta mañana.** 1
tonight **esta noche** *adv.* 4
too **también** *adv.* 2; 7
  too much **demasiado** *adv.* 6; **en exceso** 15
tooth **diente** *m.* 7
toothpaste **pasta** *f.* **de dientes** 7
top **cima** *f.* 15
  to the top **hasta arriba** 15
tornado **tornado** *m.* 18
tortilla **tortilla** *f.* 8
touch **tocar** *v.* 13; 17
touch screen **pantalla táctil** *f.* 11
tour **excursión** *f.* 4; **recorrido** *m.* 13
tour an area **recorrer** *v.*
tourism **turismo** *m.* 5

tourist **turista** *m., f.* 1; **turístico/a** *adj.*
toward **hacia** *prep.* 14; **para** *prep.* 11
towel **toalla** *f.* 7
town **pueblo** *m.* 4
trade **oficio** *m.* 16
traffic **circulación** *f.* 11; **tráfico** *m.* 11
  traffic light **semáforo** *m.* 14
tragedy **tragedia** *f.* 17
trail **sendero** *m.* 13
  trailhead **sendero** *m.* 13
train **entrenarse** *v.* 15; **tren** *m.* 5
  train station **estación** *f.* **(de) tren** *m.* 5
trainer **entrenador(a)** *m., f.* 15
translate **traducir** *v.* 6
trash **basura** *f.* 12
travel **viajar** *v.* 2
  travel agent **agente** *m., f.* **de viajes** 5
traveler **viajero/a** *m., f.* 5
  (traveler's) check **cheque (de viajero)** 14
treadmill **cinta caminadora** *f.* 15
tree **árbol** *m.* 13
trillion **billón** *m.*
trimester **trimestre** *m.* 2
trip **viaje** *m.* 5
  take a trip **hacer un viaje** 5
tropical forest **bosque** *m.* **tropical** 13
true **verdad** *adj.* 13
  it's (not) true **(no) es verdad** 13
trunk **baúl** *m.* 11
truth **verdad** *f.*
try **intentar** *v.*; **probar (o:ue)** *v.* 8
  try (*to do something*) **tratar de (+ *inf.*)** 15
  try on **probarse (o:ue)** *v.* 7
t-shirt **camiseta** *f.* 6
Tuesday **martes** *m., sing.* 2
tuna **atún** *m.* 8
turkey **pavo** *m.* 8
turn **doblar** *v.* 14
  turn off (*electricity/appliance*) **apagar** *v.* 11
  turn on (*electricity/appliance*) **poner** *v.* 11; **prender** *v.* 11
twelve **doce** 1
twenty **veinte** 1
twenty-eight **veintiocho** 1
twenty-five **veinticinco** 1
twenty-four **veinticuatro** 1
twenty-nine **veintinueve** 1
twenty-one **veintiún, veintiuno/a** 1
twenty-seven **veintisiete** 1
twenty-six **veintiséis** 1
twenty-three **veintitrés** 1
twenty-two **veintidós** 1
twice **dos veces** 6
twin **gemelo/a** *m., f.* 3
twisted **torcido/a** *adj.* 10
  be twisted **estar torcido/a** 10
two **dos** 1
  two hundred **doscientos/as** 2
  two times **dos veces** 6

U

ugly **feo/a** *adj.* 3
uncle **tío** *m.* 3
under **bajo** *adv.* 7; **debajo de** *prep.* 2
understand **comprender** *v.* 3; **entender (e:ie)** *v.* 4
underwear **ropa interior** 6
unemployment **desempleo** *m.* 18
unique **único/a** *adj.* 9
United States **Estados Unidos (EE.UU.)** *m. pl.* 1
university **universidad** *f.* 2
unless **a menos que** *adv.* 13
unmarried **soltero/a** *adj.*
unpleasant **antipático/a** *adj.* 3
until **hasta** *prep.* 6; **hasta que** *conj.* 13
up **arriba** *adv.* 15
urgent **urgente** *adj.* 12
  It's urgent that… **Es urgente que…** 12
us **nos** *pl., d.o. pron.* 5
  to/for us **nos** *pl., i.o. pron.* 6
use **usar** *v.* 6
used for **para** *prep.* 11
useful **útil** *adj. m., f.*

V

vacation **vacaciones** *f., pl.* 5
  be on vacation **estar de vacaciones** 5
  go on vacation **ir de vacaciones** 5
vacuum **pasar** *v.* **la aspiradora** 12
  vacuum cleaner **aspiradora** *f.* 12
valley **valle** *m.* 13
various **varios/as** *adj. m., f. pl.* 8
vegetables **verduras** *pl., f.* 8
verb **verbo** *m.*
very **muy** *adv.* 1
  very much **muchísimo** *adv.* 2
  (Very) well, thank you. **(Muy) bien, gracias.** 1
video **video** *m.* 1, 11
  video camera **cámara** *f.* **de video** 11
videoconference **videoconferencia** *f.* 16
  video game **videojuego** *m.* 4
vinegar **vinagre** *m.* 8
violence **violencia** *f.* 18
visit **visitar** *v.* 4
  visit monuments **visitar monumentos** 4
vitamin **vitamina** *f.* 15
voice mail **correo de voz** *m.* 11
volcano **volcán** *m.* 13
volleyball **vóleibol** *m.* 4
vote **votar** *v.* 18

W

wait (for) **esperar** *v.* **(+ *inf.*)** 2
waiter/waitress **camarero/a** *m., f.* 8
wake up **despertarse (e:ie)** *v.* 7
walk **caminar** *v.* 2
  take a walk **pasear** *v.* 4;
  walk around **pasear por** 4
walkman ***walkman*** *m.*
wall **pared** *f.* 12; **muro** *m.* 15
wallet **cartera** *f.* 4, 6
want **querer (e:ie)** *v.* 4
war **guerra** *f.* 18
warm (oneself) up **calentarse (e:ie)** *v.* 15
wash **lavar** *v.* 12
  wash one's face/hands **lavarse la cara/las manos** 7
  wash (the floor, the dishes) **lavar (el suelo, los platos)** 12
  wash oneself **lavarse** *v.* 7
washing machine **lavadora** *f.* 12
wastebasket **papelera** *f.* 2
watch **mirar** *v.* 2; **reloj** *m.* 2
  watch television **mirar (la) televisión** 2
water **agua** *f.* 8
  water pollution **contaminación del agua** 13
  water-skiing **esquí** *m.* **acuático** 4
way **manera** *f.* 16
we **nosotros(as)** *m., f.* 1
weak **débil** *adj. m., f.* 15
wear **llevar** *v.* 6; **usar** *v.* 6
weather **tiempo** *m.*
  The weather is bad. **Hace mal tiempo.** 5
  The weather is good. **Hace buen tiempo.** 5
weaving **tejido** *m.* 17
Web **red** *f.* 11
website **sitio** *m.* **web** 11
wedding **boda** *f.* 9
Wednesday **miércoles** *m., sing.* 2
week **semana** *f.* 2
weekend **fin** *m.* **de semana** 4
weight **peso** *m.* 15
  lift weights **levantar** *v.* **pesas** *f., pl.* 15
welcome **bienvenido(s)/a(s)** *adj.* 12
well: (Very) well, thanks. **(Muy) bien, gracias.** 1
well-being **bienestar** *m.* 15
well organized **ordenado/a** *adj.*
west **oeste** *m.* 14
  to the west **al oeste** 14
western (*genre*) **de vaqueros** 17
whale **ballena** *f.* 13
what **lo que** *pron.* 12
what? **¿qué?** 1
  At what time…? **¿A qué hora…?** 1

What a pleasure to...! **¡Qué gusto (+ *inf.*)...!** 18
What day is it? **¿Qué día es hoy?** 2
What do you guys think? **¿Qué les parece?** 9
What happened? **¿Qué pasó?** 11
What is today's date? **¿Cuál es la fecha de hoy?** 5
What nice clothes! **¡Qué ropa más bonita!** 6
What size do you take? **¿Qué talla lleva (usa)?** 6
What time is it? **¿Qué hora es?** 1
What's going on? **¿Qué pasa?** 1
What's happening? **¿Qué pasa?** 1
What's... like? **¿Cómo es...?** 3
What's new? **¿Qué hay de nuevo?** 1
What's the weather like? **¿Qué tiempo hace?** 5
What's up? **¿Qué onda?** 14
What's wrong? **¿Qué pasó?** 11
What's your name? **¿Cómo se llama usted?** *form.* 1
What's your name? **¿Cómo te llamas (tú)?** *fam.* 1
when **cuando** *conj.* 7; 13
When? **¿Cuándo?** 2
where **donde**
where (to)? (*destination*) **¿adónde?** 2; (*location*) **¿dónde?** 1
Where are you from? **¿De dónde eres (tú)?** (*fam.*) 1; **¿De dónde es (usted)?** (*form.*) 1
Where is...? **¿Dónde está...?** 2
(to) where? **¿adónde?** 2
which **que** *pron.*, **lo que** *pron.* 12
which? **¿cuál?** 2; **¿qué?** 2
In which...? **¿En qué...?** 2
which one(s)? **¿cuál(es)?** 2
while **mientras** *adv.* 10
white **blanco/a** *adj.* 6
white wine **vino blanco** 8
who **que** *pron.* 12; **quien(es)** *pron.* 12
who? **¿quién(es)?** 1
Who is...? **¿Quién es...?** 1
Who is speaking/calling? (*on telephone*) **¿De parte de quién?** 11
Who is speaking? (*on telephone*) **¿Quién habla?** 11
whole **todo/a** *adj.*
whom **quien(es)** *pron.* 12
whose? **¿de quién(es)?** 1
why? **¿por qué?** 2
widower/widow **viudo/a** *adj.* 9
wife **esposa** *f.* 3
win **ganar** *v.* 4
wind **viento** *m.* 5
window **ventana** *f.* 2
windshield **parabrisas** *m., sing.* 11
windy: It's (very) windy. **Hace (mucho) viento.** 5
wine **vino** *m.* 8
red wine **vino tinto** 8
white wine **vino blanco** 8
wineglass **copa** *f.* 12
winter **invierno** *m.* 5
wireless (connection) **conexión inalámbrica** *f.* 11
wish **desear** *v.* 2; **esperar** *v.* 13
I wish (that) **ojalá (que)** 13
with **con** *prep.* 2
with me **conmigo** 4; 9
with you **contigo** *fam.* 5, 9
within (ten years) **dentro de (diez años)** *prep.* 16
without **sin** *prep.* 2; 13; 15; **sin que** *conj.* 13
woman **mujer** *f.* 1
wool **lana** *f.* 6
(made of) wool **de lana** 6
word **palabra** *f.* 1
work **trabajar** *v.* 2; **funcionar** *v.* 11; **trabajo** *m.* 16
work (*of art, literature, music, etc.*) **obra** *f.* 17
work out **hacer gimnasia** 15
world **mundo** *m.* 8, 13
worldwide **mundial** *adj. m., f.*
worried (about) **preocupado/a (por)** *adj.* 5
worry (about) **preocuparse** *v.* **(por)** 7
Don't worry. **No se preocupe.** *form.* 7; **Tranquilo.; No te preocupes.** *fam.* 7
worse **peor** *adj. m., f.* 8
worst **el/la peor** 8
Would you like to...? **¿Te gustaría...?** *fam.* 4
Would you do me the honor of marrying me? **¿Me harías el honor de casarte conmigo?** 17
wow **híjole** *interj.* 6
wrench **llave** *f.* 11
write **escribir** *v.* 3
write a letter/post card/e-mail message **escribir una carta/postal/mensaje electrónico** 4
writer **escritor(a)** *m., f* 17
written **escrito/a** *p.p.* 14
wrong **equivocado/a** *adj.* 5
be wrong **no tener razón** 3

X

X-ray **radiografía** *f.* 10

Y

yard **jardín** *m.* 12; **patio** *m.* 12
year **año** *m.* 5
be... years old **tener... años** 3
yellow **amarillo/a** *adj.* 6
yes **sí** *interj.* 1
yesterday **ayer** *adv.* 6
yet **todavía** *adv.* 5
yogurt **yogur** *m.* 8
You **tú** *fam.* **usted (Ud.)** *form. sing.* **vosotros/as** *m., f. fam.* **ustedes (Uds.)** *form.* 1; (to, for) you *fam. sing.* **te** *pl.* **os** 6; *form. sing.* **le** *pl.* **les** 6
you **te** *fam., sing.,* **lo/la** *form., sing.,* **os** *fam., pl.,* **los/las** *form., pl, d.o. pron.* 5
You don't say! **¡No me digas!** *fam.;* **¡No me diga!** *form.* 11
You are... **Tú eres...** 1
You're welcome. **De nada.** 1; **No hay de qué.** 1
young **joven** *adj., sing.* (**jóvenes** *pl.*) 3
young person **joven** *m., f., sing.* (**jóvenes** *pl.*) 1
young woman **señorita (Srta.)** *f.*
younger **menor** *adj. m., f.* 3
younger: younger brother, sister *m., f.* **hermano/a menor** 3
youngest **el/la menor** *m., f.* 8
your **su(s)** *poss. adj. form.* 3
your **tu(s)** *poss. adj. fam. sing.* 3
your **vuestro/a(s)** *poss. adj. form. pl.* 3
your(s) *form.* **suyo(s)/a(s)** *poss. pron. form.* 11
your(s) **tuyo(s)/a(s)** *poss. fam. sing.* 11
your(s) **vuestro(s)/a(s)** *poss. fam.* 11
youth *f.* **juventud** 9

Z

zero **cero** *m.* 1

M

N

Ñ

O

P

V

W

Y

Z

Text Credits

31 © Joaquín Salvador Lavado (QUINO). *Toda Mafalda* – Ediciones de La Flor, 1993.
394–395 © Juan Matías Loiseau "Tute", *El celular*, reprinted by permission of the author.
498–499 © Denevi, Marco, *Cartas peligrosas y otros cuentos. Obras completas, Tomo 5*, Buenos Aires, Corregidor, 1999, págs. 192–193.
530–531 © Gabriel García Márquez, *Un día de éstos*, reprinted by permission of Carmen Balcells.
564–565 © Julia de Burgos, "A Julia de Burgos" from *Song of the Simple Truth: The Complete Poems of Julia de Burgos*, 1996. Published by Curbstone Press. Distributed by Consortium.
600–601 © Federico García Lorca, *Danza, Las seis cuerdas, La guitarra.* Reprinted by permission of Herederos de Federico García Lorca.

Photography Credits

All images © Vista Higher Learning unless otherwise noted.

Cover: © Jean-Dominique Dallet/Getty Images

Frontmatter: iii (l) © Andresr/Shutterstock; **xxviii** (tl, tml, ml, tr, tmr, mr, ml, bl) Carolina Zapata; **xxix** (tl, tr, b) Carolina Zapata.

All Fotonovela photos taken by Carolina Zapata.

Lesson One: 1 (full pg) Paula Díez; **2** © John Henley/Corbis; **3** Martín Bernetti; **4** Martín Bernetti; **10** (l) Rachel Distler; (r) Ali Burafi; **11** (l) © Mark Mainz/Getty Images; (m) Paola Rios-Schaaf; (r) © Hans Georg Roth/Corbis; **12** (l) Janet Dracksdorf; (r) © Tom Grill/Corbis; **16** (l) © José Girarte/iStockphoto; (r) © Blend Images/Alamy; **19** (m) Anne Loubet; (r) © Getty Images/Digital Vision; **31** (ml) Ana Cabezas Martín; (mml) Martín Bernetti; (mmr) © Serban Enache/Dreamstime; (mr) Vanessa Bertozzi; (bl) © Corey Hochachka/Design Pics/Corbis; (br) Ramiro Isaza © Fotocolombia.com; **32** Carolina Zapata; **33** Paula Diez; **36** (t) © Robert Holmes/Corbis; (m) © Jon Arnold Images Ltd./Alamy; (b) © Andresr/Shutterstock; **37** (tl) © PhotoDisc; (tr) © Tony Arruza/Corbis; (ml) © Schwarz Shaul/Corbis SYGMA; (br) Marta Mesa.

Lesson Two: 39 (full pg) Paula Diez; **42** Martín Bernetti; **48** (r) © Pablo Corral V/Corbis; **49** (t) © Murle/Dreamstime; (b) © Paul Almasy/Corbis; **57** © Stephen Coburn/Shutterstock; **59** (l) Paola Rios-Schaaf; (r) © Image Source/Corbis; **67** (l) © Rick Gomez/Corbis; (r) © Hola Images/Workbook.com; **68** José Blanco; **69** (r) Pascal Pernix; **70** (b) Martín Bernetti; **71** Nora y Susana © Fotocolombia.com; **74** (tl) Sarah Kenney; (tr) José Blanco; (m) © Elke Stolzenberg/Corbis; (b) © Reuters/Corbis; **75** (tl) © Washington Post/Getty Images; (tmr) José Blanco; (ml) Diego Velázquez. *Las meninas*. 1656. Derechos reservados © Museo Nacional del Prado, Madrid. © Erich Lessing/Art Resource; (bl) © Iconotec/Fotosearch; (mbr) © Owen Franken/Corbis.

Lesson Three: 77 (full pg) © Ronnie Kaufman/Corbis; **79** Martín Bernetti; **80** (tl) Anne Loubet; (tr) © Blend Images/Alamy; (tml) Ana Cabezas Martín; (bml, br) Martín Bernetti; (bl) © Ariel Skelley/Corbis; **86** (tl) © David Cantor/AP Wide World Photos; (tr) © Rafael Perez/Reuters/Corbis; (b) © Martial Trezzini/epa./Corbis; **87** (t) © Dani Cardona/Reuters/Corbis; (b) © Ballesteros/epa/Corbis; **90** (l, r) Martín Bernetti; **92** © Andres Rodriguez/Alamy; **97** (l) © Warren Morgan/Corbis; (r) Martín Bernetti; **98** Martín Bernetti; **106** (t, m, b) Martín Bernetti; **107** (t) Nora y Susana © Fotocolombia.com; (m) © Chuck Savage/Corbis; (b) Martín Bernetti; **108** © Tom & Dee Ann McCarthy/Corbis; **109** Martín Bernetti; **112** (tr, tl, ml, b) Martín Bernetti; (mr) Lauren Krolick; **113** (tl, ml, bl) Martín Bernetti; (tr) Oswaldo Guayasamín. *Madre y niño en azul*. 1986. Cortesía Fundación Guayasamín. Quito, Ecuador.; (br) © Gerardo Mora.

Lesson Four: 115 (full pg) © Digital Vision/Getty Images; **117** © George Shelley/Corbis; **119** © Nora y Susana/fotocolombia.com; **124** (l) © Javier Soriano/AFP/Getty Images; (r) © Alberto Estévez/EFE/Corbis; **125** (t) © sportgraphic/Shutterstock; (b) © Aurora Photos/Alamy; **135** © Twentieth Century-Fox Film Corporation/The Kobal Collection/The Picture-desk; **139** Anne Loubet; **141** © Images.com/Corbis; **142** Martín Bernetti; **143** © Fernando Llano/AP Wide World Photos; **144** Martín Bernetti; **145** © Rick Gomez/Corbis; **148** (tl) © Randy Miramontez/Shutterstock; (tr) Frida Kahlo. *Autorretrato con mono*. 1938. Oil on masonite, overall 16 x 12" (40.64 x 30.48 cms.). Albright-Knox Art Gallery, Buffalo, New York. Bequest of A Conger Goodyear, 1966. © Albright-Knox Art Gallery/Corbis; (ml) Ruben Varela; (mr) Isabelle Alouane; (b) © Henry Romero/Reuters/Corbis; **149** (tl) © Radius Images/Alamy; (tr) © Bettmann/Corbis; (b) © David R. Frazier Photolibrary, Inc./Alamy.

Lesson Five: 151 (full pg) © Gavin Hellier/Getty Images; **162** © Gary Cook/Alamy; **163** (t) © AFP/Getty Images; (b) © Mark A. Johnson/Corbis; **180** Carlos Gaudier; **181** (tr, m, b) Carlos Gaudier; **182** Carolina Zapata; **186** (tl) © Nanniqui/Dreamstime; (tr) José Blanco; (ml) Carlos Gaudier; (mr) © Capricornis Photographic Inc./Shutterstock; (b) © Dave G. Houser/Corbis; **187** (tl, bl) Carlos Gaudier; (tr) © Lawrence Manning/Corbis; (br) © StockTrek/Getty Images.

Lesson Six: 189 (full pg) © Asiapix Royalty-Free/Inmagine; **198** (l) © Robert Frerck/Odyssey; (b) Janet Dracksdorf; **199** (t) © Carlos Alvarez/Getty Images; (bl) © Guiseppe Carace/Getty Images; (br) © Mark Mainz/Getty Images; **204** (tl, tm, tr, bl, bm, br) Pascal Pernix; **209** (tl, tr, ml, mr) Martín Bernetti; **210** (t, b) Paula Díez; **211** Paula Díez; **216** Paula Díez; **217** Paula Díez; **218** © Noam/fotolia; **222** (t, mtl, mtr, mb) Pascal Pernix; (b) © PhotoDisk/Getty Images; **223** (tl) © Don Emmert/AFP/Getty Images; (tr, bl) Pascal Pernix; (br) © Road Movie Prods/The Kobal Collection/The Picture-desk.

Lesson Seven: 225 (full pg) © Flying Colours Ltd/Getty Images; **234** © Stewart Cohen/Blend Images/Corbis; **235** (t) Ali Burafi; (b) Janet Dracksdorf; **237** (l, r) Martín Bernetti; **239** (l) Martín Bernetti; (r) © Ariel Skelley/Corbis; **242** José Blanco; **243** (b) Martín Bernetti; **252-253** © DIDEM HIZAR/fotolia; **254** © i love images/Alamy; **255** Martín Bernetti; **256** © Kevin Dodge/Masterfile; **258** (t, mtr) Martín Bernetti; (mbl) © RICHARD SMITH/CORBIS SYGMA; (mbr) © Charles & Josette Lenars/Corbis; (b) © Yan Arthus-Peleaz Inc./Corbis; **259** (tr) © Mick Roessler/Corbis; (bl) © Jeremy Horner/Corbis; (br) © Marshall Bruce/iStockphoto.

Lesson Eight: 261 (full pg) © Mark Leibowitz/Masterfile; **267** (r) Anne Loubet; **272** (t) Rachel Distler; (b) © Greg Elms/Lonely Planet Images; **273** (t, m) © Carlos Cazalis/Corbis; (b) © Studio Bonisolli/Stockfood; **276** Paula Díez; **278** (l) © Pixtal/Age Fotostock; (r) José Blanco; **282** (r) José Blanco; **283** (l) José Blanco; **292** Vanessa Bertozzi; **293** © Jack Hollingsworth/Getty Images; **296** (t) © Henryk Sadura/Shutterstock; (ml, b) © Dave G. Houser/Corbis; (mr) © Henryk Sadura/Shutterstock; **297** (tl) © Jenkedco/Shutterstock; (tr) © Michael & Patricia Fogden/Corbis; (bl) © Vladimir Korostyshevskiy/Shutterstock; (br) © Paul W. Liebhardt/Corbis.

Lesson Nine: 299 (full pg) © Susana/Fotocolombia.com; **308** (l) © Sylwia Blaszczyszyn/Dreamstime; (r) © PictureNet/Corbis; **309** (t) © Simon Cruz/AP Wide World Photos; (b) © Rune Hellestad/Corbis; **322** (t) © Katrina Brown/123RF; (b) Esteban Corbo; **323** Armando Brito; **324** © Blend Images/Alamy; **328** (tl, tr, mtr) Lauren Krolick; (mtl) Kathryn Alena Korf; (mbl) © Bettmann/Corbis; (mbr) © MACARENA MINGUELL/AFP/Getty Images; (b) Bruce R. Korf; **329** (tl) Lars Rosen Gunnilstam; (tr, br) Lauren Krolick; (bl) © Nikolay Starchenko/Shutterstock.

Lesson Ten: 331 (full pg) © Steve Cole/iStockphoto; **340** (t) Ali Burafi; (b) © Ricardo Figueroa/AP Wide World Photos; **341** (t) © The Art Archive/Templo Mayor Library Mexico/Dagli Orti/The Picture-desk; (m) © face to face Bildagentur GmbH/Alamy; (b) © AFP/Getty Images; **345** © ISO K° - photography/fotolia; **349** Oscar Artavia Solano; **350** (l) © LisaInGlasses/iStockphoto; (r) © Krek/Dreamstime; **359** © mlstock@mountainlight.com; **360** © Anthony Redpath/Masterfile; **361** Paula Díez; **365** (tl, tr, mm, mr) Oscar Artavia Solano; (ml) © Bill Gentile/Corbis; (b) © Bob Winsett/Corbis; **366** (tl) © Frank Burek/Corbis; (mr) © Martin Rogers/Corbis; (ml) © Jacques M. Chenet/Corbis; (b) Oscar Artavia Solano.

Lesson Eleven: 367 (full pg) Paula Díez; **376** (l) © Ariel Skelley/Getty Images; (r) Paula Díez; **377** (t) © Zsolt Nyulaszi/Shutterstock; (b) © Gabrielle Wallace; **381** © LdF/iStockphoto; **385** Katie Wade; **386** (l, r) Paula Díez; **390** (t) © gmnicholas/iStockphoto; (ml, bm) Martín Bernetti; (mm) © Auris/iStockphoto; (tr[1]) © NickyBlade/iStockphoto; (tr[2], tm) © LdF/iStockphoto; (br) © Art Directors & TRIP/Alamy; **396** © Chad Johnston/Masterfile; **397** © morchella/fotolia; **400** (t, b) Ali Burafi; (ml) María Eugenia Corbo; (mm) © Galen Rowell/Corbis; (mr) Lauren Krolick; **401** (tl) María Eugenia Corbo; (tr, b) Ali Burafi; (m) © Michael Hieber/Shutterstock.

Lesson Twelve: 403 (full pg) © Rolf Bruderer/Corbis; **407** (t) © TerryJ/iStockphoto; (b) © Harry Neave/fotolia; **412** (l) © Dusko Despotovic/Corbis; (r) Martín Bernetti; **413** (l) Maribel Garcia; (r) © Michele Falzone/Alamy; **415** (l) © Monkeybusinessimages/Dreamstime; (r) Anne Loubet; **416** © Blend Images/Alamy; **432** © Danny Lehman/Corbis; **434** Martín Bernetti; **438** (tl) © Kevin Schafer/Corbis; (tr) © Danny Lehman/Corbis; (m) © Hernan H. Hernandez A./Shutterstock; **439** (tl, tr) © Danny Lehman/Corbis; (b) © Claudio Lovo/Shutterstock.

Lesson Thirteen: 441 (full pg) © Gabriela Medina/Getty Images; **443** (tl) © gaccworship/Big Stock Photo; (bl) © National Geographic Singles 65/Inmagine; (br) © Les Cunliffe/123RF; **450** (t) Lauren Krolick; (b) © Digital Vision/Fotosearch; **451** (t) © Cédric Hunt; (bl) Doug Myerscough; (br) © David South/Alamy; **459** (t, b) Mary Axtmann; **468** © Ric Ergenbright/Corbis; **472** (tr) © Cédric Hunt; (b) © Adam Woolfitt/Corbis; **473** (tl) Mónica María González; (tr) © Reuters/Corbis; (br) © Jeremy Horner/Corbis.

Lesson Fourteen: 475 (full pg) © David R. Frazier/Danita Delimont; **484** (l) www.metro.df.gob.mx; (r) Ali Burafi; **485** (t, b) © Barragan Foundation, Switzerland/ProLitteris, Zürich, Switzerland; **491** Paula Díez; **499** © Radius Images/Alamy; **501** Paula Díez; **504** (t) © Janne Hämäläinen/Shutterstock; (mt) © Alexander Chaikin/Shutterstock; (mb) © Buddy Mays/Corbis; (b) © Vladimir Melnik/Shutterstock; **505** (tl) © Reuters/Corbis; (tr) © Royalty Free/Corbis; (bl) © Pablo Corral V./Corbis; (br) © Mireille Vautier/Alamy.

Lesson Fifteen: 507 (full pg) © Thinkstock/Getty Images; **511** © Javier Larrea/Age Fotostock; **516** (l) © Krysztof Dydynski/Getty Images; (r) Oscar Artavia Solano; **517** (t, b) Oscar Artavia Solano; **524** © diego_cervo/iStockphoto; **530–531** © Tom Grill/Corbis; **532** Martín Bernetti; **533** © Javier Larrea/Age Fotostock; **538** (tr) © SIME/eStock Photo; (m) © INTERFOTO/Alamy; **539** (t) © Daniel Wiedemann/Shutterstock; (m) © Anders Ryman/Alamy; (b) Martín Bernetti.

Lesson Sixteen: 541 (full pg) © Peter Beck/Corbis; **545** (t) © Orange Line Media/Shutterstock; (b) Paula Díez; **550** (l) © PhotoAlto/Alamy; **551** (t) © 2002 USPS; (b) © Galen Rowell/Corbis; **560** © pezography/Big Stock Photo; **561** © rj lerich/Big Stock Photo; **564** (b) Frida Kahlo. *Las dos Fridas.* 1939. Oil on Canvas. 5'8.5" x 5'8.5" © Banco de México Trust. © Schalkwijk/Art Resource; **566** Martín Bernetti; **567** Paula Díez; **572** (tl) © Holger Mette/Shutterstock; (tr) © rj lerich/Shutterstock; (mt) © tobe_dw/Shutterstock; (mb) © Bill Gentile/Corbis; (b) © Scott B. Rosen/Alamy; **573** (t) © Grigory Kubatyan/Shutterstock; (m) © Claudia Daut/Reuters/Corbis; (b) © holdeneye/Shutterstock; **574** (tr) © Reinhard Eisele/Corbis; (m) © Richard Bickel/Corbis; (b) Columbus, Christopher (Italian Cristoforo Colombo). Navigator, discoverer of America. Genoa 1451-Valladolid 20.5.1506. Portrait. Painting by Ridolfo Ghirlandaio (1483–1561). © akg-images/The Image Works; **575** (t) © Jeremy Horner/Corbis; (m) © Reuters/Corbis; (b) © Lawrence Manning/Corbis.

Lesson Seventeen: 577 (full pg) © Index Stock Imagery Inc.; **586** (l) © Exposicion Cuerpo Plural, Museo de Arte Contemporaneo, Caracas, Venezuala, octubre 2005 (Sala 1). Fotografia Morella Munoz-Tebar. Archivo MAC.; (r) Joan Miró. *La lección de esquí.* © Art Resource, NY; **587** (t) © Raul Benegas; (b) Fernando Botero. *El alguacil.* 20th Century © Fernando Botero © Christie's Images/Corbis; **591** © Marvel Productions/The Kobal Collection/The Picture-desk; **602** Martín Bernetti; **606** (tl) © José F. Poblete/Corbis; (tr) © L. Kragt Bakker/Shutterstock; (ml) © Leif Skoogfors/Corbis; (mr) © Andre Nantel/Shutterstock; (b) © Royalty Free/Corbis; **607** (t) © Guy Motil/Corbis; (m) © Royalty Free/Corbis; (b) © Romeo A. Escobar, *La Sala de La Miniatura*, San Salvador. www.ilobasco.net.; **608** (tl) © Stuart Westmorland/Corbis; (tr) © ImageState/Alamy; (ml) © Sandra A. Dunlap/Shutterstock; (mr) © ImageState/Alamy; **609** (t) © Holger Mette/Shutterstock; (m) © Elmer Martinez/AFP/Getty Images; (b) José Antonio Velásquez. *San Antonio de Oriente.* 1957. Colección: Art Museum of the Americas, Organization of American States, Washington, D.C. © Coleccion: Art of the Americas, Organization of American States. Washington D.C.

Lesson Eighteen: 611 (full pg) © Douglas Kirkland/Corbis; **615** (t) © robert paul van beets/Shutterstock; (b) Janet Dracksdorf; **620** (l) José Blancoe; (r) © Homer Sykes/Alamy; **621** © Alex Ibanez, HO/AP Wide World Photos; **624** Anne Loubet; **629** (l) © Dave G. Houser/Corbis; **634** © Joel Nito/AFP/Getty Images; **635** © John Lund/Corbis; **638** (t) © Peter Guttman/Corbis; (ml) © Paul Almasy/Corbis; (b) © Carlos Carrion/Corbis; **639** (t) © Chris R. Sharp/DDB Stock; (m) © Joel Creed; Ecoscene/Corbis; (b) © Francis E. Caldwell/DDB Stock; **640** (tl) © Bettmann/Corbis; (tr) © Reuters/Corbis; (m, b) María Eugenia Corbo; **641** (tl) Janet Dracksdorf; (tr) © Simon Bruty/SI; (m) © Andres Stapff/Reuters/Corbis; (b) © Wolfgang Kaehler/Corbis.

About the Authors

José A. Blanco founded Vista Higher Learning in 1998. A native of Barranquilla, Colombia, Mr. Blanco holds a B.A. in Literature from the University of California, Santa Cruz, and a M.A. in Hispanic Studies from Brown University. He has worked as a writer, editor, and translator for Houghton Mifflin and D.C. Heath and Company and has taught Spanish at the secondary and university levels. Mr. Blanco is also the co-author of several other Vista Higher Learning programs: **Panorama, Aventuras,** and **¡Viva!** at the introductory level, **Ventanas, Facetas, Enfoques, Imagina,** and **Sueña** at the intermediate level, and **Revista** at the advanced conversation level.

Philip Redwine Donley received his M.A. in Hispanic Literature from the University of Texas at Austin in 1986 and his Ph.D. in Foreign Language Education from the University of Texas at Austin in 1997. Dr. Donley taught Spanish at Austin Community College, Southwestern University, and the University of Texas at Austin. He published articles and conducted workshops about language anxiety management, and the development of critical thinking skills, and was involved in research about teaching languages to the visually impaired. Dr. Donley was also the co-author of **Aventuras** and **Panorama,** two other introductory college Spanish textbook programs published by Vista Higher Learning.

About the Illustrators

Yayo, an internationally acclaimed illustrator, was born in Colombia. He has illustrated children's books, newspapers, and magazines, and has been exhibited around the world. He currently lives in Montreal, Canada.

Pere Virgili lives and works in Barcelona, Spain. His illustrations have appeared in textbooks, newspapers, and magazines throughout Spain and Europe.

Born in Caracas, Venezuela, **Hermann Mejía** studied illustration at the *Instituto de Diseño de Caracas*. Hermann currently lives and works in the United States.

Estados Unidos
Golfo de México
Bahía de Campeche
Océano Pacífico
Golfo de California
BAJA CALIFORNIA
México
YUCATÁN
ISTMO DE TEHUANTEPEC
Belice
Guatemala
Honduras
El Salvador
R. Colorado
Río Grande
Río Bravo del Norte
R. Conchos
R. Balsas
Sierra Madre Oriental
Sierra Madre Occidental
Tijuana
Mexicali
Nogales
Hermosillo
Ciudad Juárez
Chihuahua
La Paz
Mazatlán
Nuevo Laredo
Reynosa
Matamoros
Monterrey
Saltillo
Ciudad Victoria
Tampico
Zacatecas
San Luis Potosí
Aguascalientes
León
Guanajuato
Guadalajara
Puerto Vallarta
Morelia
Uruapan
México, D.F.
Cuernavaca
Puebla
Jalapa
Veracruz
Acapulco
Oaxaca
Villahermosa
Campeche
Mérida
Cancún
N
S
E
O

México

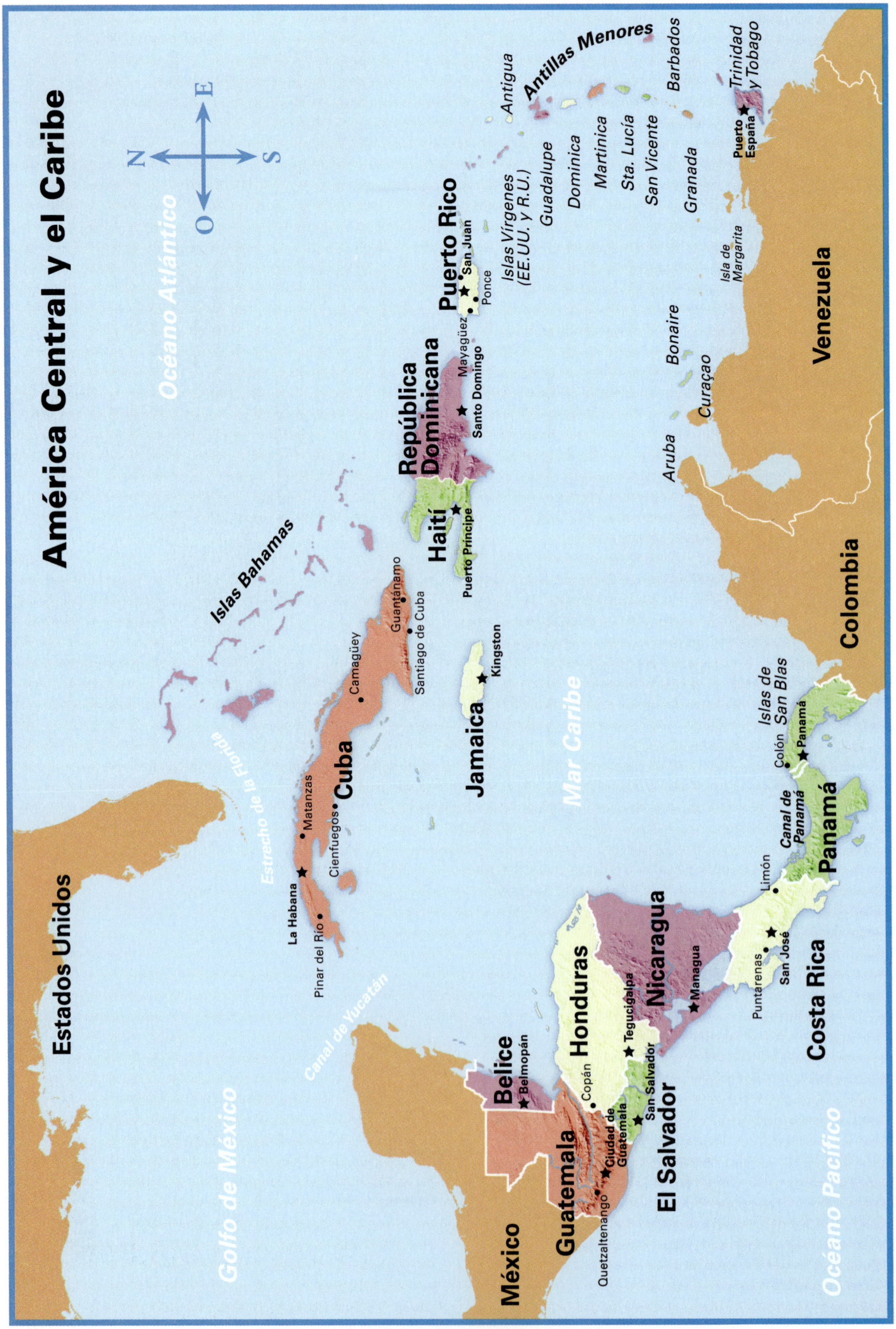
América Central y el Caribe
N
S
E
O
Océano Atlántico
Golfo de México
Océano Pacífico
Mar Caribe
Estados Unidos
México
Guatemala
Belice
Belmopán
Honduras
El Salvador
Nicaragua
Costa Rica
Panamá
Colombia
Venezuela
Cuba
Jamaica
Haití
República Dominicana
Puerto Rico
Islas Bahamas
Antillas Menores
Estrecho de la Florida
Canal de Yucatán
Canal de Panamá
Islas de San Blas
Quetzaltenango
Ciudad de Guatemala
Copán
San Salvador
Tegucigalpa
Managua
Puntarenas
San José
Limón
Colón
Panamá
La Habana
Pinar del Río
Matanzas
Cienfuegos
Camagüey
Guantánamo
Santiago de Cuba
Kingston
Puerto Príncipe
Santo Domingo
Mayagüez
Ponce
San Juan
Islas Vírgenes (EE.UU. y R.U.)
Antigua
Guadalupe
Dominica
Martinica
Sta. Lucía
San Vicente
Barbados
Granada
Trinidad y Tobago
Puerto España
Isla de Margarita
Bonaire
Curaçao
Aruba

América del Sur
Mar Caribe
Océano Pacífico
Océano Atlántico
Venezuela
Colombia
Ecuador
Perú
Bolivia
Brasil
Chile
Argentina
Paraguay
Uruguay
Guyana
Surinam
Guayana Francesa
Trinidad y Tobago
Barranquilla
Maracaibo
Caracas
Puerto España
Georgetown
Paramaribo
Cayena
Medellín
Bogotá
Cali
Pasto
Quito
Guayaquil
Iquitos
Manaus
Belém
Recife
Salvador
Lima
Cuzco
Lago Titicaca
Arequipa
La Paz
Sucre
Arica
Iquique
Antofagasta
Salta
Asunción
Brasília
Belo Horizonte
Río de Janeiro
São Paulo
Santos
Porto Alegre
Córdoba
Rosario
Mendoza
Valparaíso
Santiago
Buenos Aires
Montevideo
Concepción
Bahía Blanca
Puerto Montt
Punta Arenas
Estrecho de Magallanes
Islas Malvinas
Tierra del Fuego
R. Orinoco
R. Negro
R. Amazonas
R. Madeira
R. Paraguay
R. Paraná
R. Uruguay
Cordillera de los Andes
N
S
E
O
Islas Galápagos
Océano Pacífico
Isla Pinta
Isla Marchena
Isla Genovesa
Isla Isabela
Línea Ecuatorial
ECUADOR
Volcán Darwin
Isla Santiago (San Salvador)
Isla Fernandina
Puerto Ayora
Isla Santa Cruz
Isla San Cristóbal
Santo Tomás
Puerto Baquerizo Moreno
Isla Santa María
Isla Española

España
Portugal
Andorra
Marruecos
Océano Atlántico
Mar Cantábrico
Mar Mediterráneo
Estrecho de Gibraltar
Pirineos
Islas Baleares
Menorca
Mallorca
Palma
Ibiza
Formentera
GALICIA
ASTURIAS
CANTABRIA
PAÍS VASCO
NAVARRA
LA RIOJA
CATALUÑA
ARAGÓN
CASTILLA-LEÓN
CASTILLA-LA MANCHA
COMUNIDAD VALENCIANA
EXTREMADURA
ANDALUCÍA
Sierra Morena
Sierra Nevada
Serra da Estrela
Madrid
Lisboa
La Coruña
Pontevedra
Vigo
Avilés
Gijón
Oviedo
Santander
Bilbao
San Sebastián
Pamplona
Burgos
Palencia
Valladolid
Zamora
Salamanca
Ávila
Segovia
Toledo
Cáceres
Mérida
Badajoz
Córdoba
Jaén
Granada
Sevilla
Huelva
Cádiz
Algeciras
Gibraltar (R.U.)
Ceuta (Esp.)
Málaga
Almería
Melilla (Esp.)
Murcia
Cartagena
Albacete
Alicante
Valencia
Zaragoza
Lérida
Barcelona
Tarragona
Gerona
Braga
Oporto
Coimbra
Setúbal
Islas Canarias
La Palma
Santa Cruz de la Palma
Tenerife
Santa Cruz de Tenerife
Gomera
Hierro
Gran Canaria
Las Palmas
Lanzarote
Arrecife
Fuerteventura
Puerto del Rosario
N
S
E
O